Also by Nelson D. Lankford

AN IRISHMAN IN DIXIE
Thomas Conolly's Diary of the Fall of the Confederacy

OSS AGAINST THE REICH
The World War II Diaries of Colonel David K. E. Bruce

The Last
American Aristocrat

The Last American Aristocrat

The Biography of David K. E. Bruce,
1898–1977

by

Nelson D. Lankford

LITTLE, BROWN AND COMPANY

BOSTON   NEW YORK   TORONTO   LONDON

For Judy

Copyright © 1996 by Nelson D. Lankford

First Edition

The author is grateful for permission to include the following previously copyrighted material:

Excerpts from the letters of David K. E. Bruce and photographs
by permission of Evangeline B. Bruce and David S. Bruce.

Excerpts from the letters of David K. E. Bruce and Ailsa Mellon Bruce
from the Paul Mellon Papers by permission of Paul Mellon.

Excerpts from the papers of David K. E. Bruce and family
from the Virginia Historical Society by permission of the Virginia Historical Society.

Library of Congress Cataloging-in-Publication Data

Lankford, Nelson D.
    The last aristocrat: the biography of David K. E. Bruce, 1898–1977 / by
Nelson D. Lankford. — 1st ed.
        p.   cm.
    Includes bibliographical references and index.
    ISBN 0-316-51501-9 (HC : alk. paper)
    1. Bruce, David Kirkpatrick Este.   2. Ambassadors — United States —
Biography. I. Title.
E748.B853L36 1996
327.2'092 — dc20   95-38094

10 9 8 7 6 5 4 3 2 1

MV-NY

*Published simultaneously in Canada
by Little, Brown & Company (Canada) Limited*

Printed in the United States of America

Contents

Acknowledgments

$\mathcal{G}$ROWING UP after World War II, a child of the suburbs, I discovered at an early age that miraculous institution, the local public library. I cannot recall precisely the first time I set foot in ours, but I still have hazy, golden memories of being taken there. The children's section of the library in Newport News, Virginia, as I recall, was then on the floor below the main library. That was an appropriate spot, for it was an Aladdin's cave filled with wonderful things. Though no child would be silly enough to analyze the experience in analytical, adult terms, it was in fact my introduction to the imagination. It must have been much the same, I suspect, when David Bruce encountered the great world through his own books half a century before. And so my first acknowledgment, after thanking my parents for introducing me to the wonder of books, is to the librarians who made this discovery possible and continue to do so for succeeding generations.

I wish to thank the staffs of the following institutions, who assisted my research, firsthand, by mail, by phone, or by fax: the Dwight D. Eisenhower Presidential Library, Abilene, Kansas; the Gerald R. Ford Presidential Library, Ann Arbor, Michigan; the Lyndon Baines Johnson Presidential Library, Austin, Texas; the John F. Kennedy Presidential Library, Boston, Massachusetts; the Maryland Hall of Records, Annapolis, Maryland; the University of Maryland Library, College Park, Maryland; the Fondation Jean Monnet Pour l'Europe, Lausanne, Switzerland; the Library of Congress, Washington, D.C.; the National Archives, Washington, D.C.; the archives of the National Gallery of Art, Washington, D.C.; the New-York Historical Society; the New York Public Library; the Public Record Office, Kew, England; the Richmond Public

Library, Richmond, Virginia; the Franklin D. Roosevelt Presidential Library, Hyde Park, New York; the Boatwright Memorial Library, University of Richmond, Virginia; the Ransom Humanities Center, University of Texas, Austin; the Harry S. Truman Presidential Library, Independence, Missouri; the James Branch Cabell Library, Virginia Commonwealth University; and the Alderman Library, University of Virginia, Charlottesville.

A small grant from the Travel to Collections program of the National Endowment for the Humanities funded part of a research trip to London. Kent State University Press kindly granted permission to adapt portions of my 1991 edition of Bruce's wartime diaries, *OSS Against the Reich*.

The Virginia Historical Society is the main repository of David Bruce's papers, and I thank the director, Charles F. Bryan, Jr., for permission to use them. Though this was a project I undertook beyond "office hours," Charlie never failed to encourage my research for this effort, now of some seven years' duration. Among my colleagues on the staff of the VHS, I would especially like to express my appreciation as well to Sara B. Bearss, Howson Cole, Frances S. Pollard, AnnMarie Price, Janet Schwarz, E. Lee Shepard, and Paulette Ubben.

Many friends read part or all of the manuscript or in other ways helped me piece together the puzzle. I am especially indebted to Betsy Fahlman, John Flanigan, John Melville Jennings, Herbert H. Kaplan, Robert L. Musick, Jr., Reginald Pettus, Virgil Randolph III, James L. Srodes, William H. Sydnor, Jesse E. Todd, Jr., and Stephen H. Watts II.

David S. Bruce has given helpful advice since I began editing his father's wartime diaries before I began work on the biography. He and his wife, Janet Parker Bruce, graciously opened their home, Staunton Hill, to me and my wife on numerous occasions. From the beginning, Evangeline Bell Bruce opened doors for me in my research, and I shall always be grateful to her for so many kindnesses. Through her, my knowledge of her husband's vast circle of acquaintances was greatly expanded. Her critique of a draft of the manuscript caught numerous errors. She never insisted on her interpretation of events when she and I differed. That this is not an official or authorized biography did not limit her encouragement or enthusiasm for my work. I deeply regret that she did not live to share in the satisfaction of publication, for she died suddenly in the Georgetown house over which she had presided with such grace for many years.

This would have been a far different and lesser book were it not for my editor at Little, Brown and Company. Roger Donald gave me such a wealth of excellent criticism from the earliest drafts I sent him that my concept of writing is forever changed. As an editor by profession, used to dishing it out rather than taking criticism, I nevertheless gladly submitted to his editorial strictures. Also at Little Brown my book has benefited from the close attention of Geoff Kloske, Amanda Murray, Mike Mattil, Peggy Freudenthal, and Faith Hanson.

Throughout it all, Judy gave me counsel and advice, sometimes stern but always perceptive. I could not have written the book without her. Though many have contributed to this book, any errors are of course my own.

Nelson D. Lankford
Richmond, Virginia
December 18, 1995

The Last American Aristocrat

Prologue

ON THE AFTERNOON of August 25, 1944, a jeep raced down the sunlit boulevards of Paris. The two American passengers held tight as their driver alternately accelerated and downshifted to avoid retreating German tanks and mobs of joyful Parisians. The jeep led others filled with French partisans, and after a few unplanned detours, they all screeched to a halt at the Ritz. The hotel manager, accustomed to receiving the cream of European society, looked up with alarm as these disheveled, heavily armed men burst through the door. He relaxed when he recognized the two leaders as former guests Ernest Hemingway and Col. David K. E. Bruce of the Office of Strategic Services (OSS). With the unctuous hauteur of his profession, he asked if there was anything he could give them. Bruce looked at him and drily replied, "Fifty martini cocktails."

Bruce and Hemingway had met by chance five days earlier outside the city at Rambouillet, then in a swath of territory occupied by neither army. Bruce was there to rendezvous with his boss, Gen. William "Wild Bill" Donovan, head of the OSS. He found Hemingway instead. The writer was busily asserting his machismo by taking command of a French Resistance group and in the process violating his status as a war correspondent. Both Americans were itching to reach Paris. When Donovan failed to show up, Bruce decided to ride with Hemingway's mongrel outfit toward the City of Light.

They joined Gen. Jacques LeClerc's 2d French Armored Division, the first Allied unit to enter Paris. Along the way, they gave LeClerc the intelligence he needed to avoid remaining German strongpoints. The advance momentarily faltered in the outskirts, retarded by snipers and crowds of euphoric civilians oblivious to all but the heaviest firing. "We yelled ourselves hoarse, shouting 'Vive la France,'" Bruce said, "as we passed through the crowds. Everyone thrust drinks at us that they had been hoarding for this occasion. It was impossible to refuse them, but the combination was enough to wreck one's constitution. In the course of the afternoon, we had beer, cider, white and red Bordeaux, white and red Burgundy, champagne, rum, whiskey, cognac, armagnac, and Calvados."[1]

Bruce was one of the few Americans to witness the glorious twenty-fifth of August in the heart of Paris. Surging throngs surrounded his jeep. "It was a wonderful sunny day and a wonderful scene," he said. "The women were dressed in their best clothes, and all wore somewhere the tricolor — on their blouses, in their hair, and even as earrings."[2] (He apparently missed the Parisienne who showed her patriotic ardor by removing her skirt to display her pubic hair — dyed red, white, and blue.[3])

All the Germans had not left, and intense bursts of gunfire continued throughout the day. When Bruce spotted three enemy tanks ahead, he ducked into the side streets to reach the Arc de Triomphe. From the top of the monument, he looked out at an unforgettable panorama. In the distance he saw a truck ablaze in the Place de la Concorde. In the Tuileries Gardens beyond, a disabled tank smoldered. Smoke rose from the Crillon Hotel and from the Chamber of Deputies across the river too. "The view was breathtaking," he said. "One saw the golden dome of the Invalides, the green roof of the Madeleine, Sacre-Coeur, and other familiar landmarks. Tanks were firing in various streets. Part of the Arc was under fire from snipers. A shell from a German 88 nicked one of its sides."[4] As the afternoon sun flashed against the rooftops, it seemed like the bells of every church in Paris were pealing, while snatches of the "Marseillaise" floated up from ecstatic crowds.[5]

The OSS colonel then drove to the Travellers Club and found it empty except for a few old-timers in the bar, uncorking magnums of champagne. "We next collected our gang," Bruce wrote, "and, not knowing what was ahead except for the usual indiscriminate popping of small arms, dashed to the Café de la Paix. The Place de l'Opéra was a solid mass of cheering people, and, after kissing several thousand men, women, and babies . . . we escaped to the Ritz." The food at the hotel was better than the martinis, and the eight officers who dined there with Bruce that evening were momentarily the only Americans officially authorized to be in the city. "That knowledge," one of them recalled, "made us more giddy" than the champagne.[6]

When he left the city four days later, Bruce mused over the wild scenes he had witnessed. "Already, the so-called Liberation of Paris seems almost like a dream. I have never imagined a scene that was, all in all, so dramatic, so moving, and so beautiful and picturesque. The day of the German surrender, the weather was incomparable, the sky cloudless, the sun bright and hot. The frenzied joy of the crowds is impossible to describe." He was convinced that "whatever other part OSS may have or may play during this war, its participation in the French Resistance movement represents a proud achievement."[7]

He had reason to be proud. There was more to his achievement than those dramatic moments with Hemingway. As one of Donovan's original partners in the Office of Strategic Services — before it had that name, even before Pearl Harbor — he helped create this precursor of the CIA and the mystique that still surrounds it half a century later. In 1943 "Wild Bill" sent him to London to run the largest OSS center outside Washington. Under Bruce it grew from a handful to more than three thousand men and women who pored over intelligence reports, analyzed decrypted German radio transmissions, and parachuted agents and supplies to the Resistance in Nazi-occupied Europe. He and Donovan witnessed the Normandy invasion from shipboard and were on Utah Beach, under fire and against orders, within twenty-four hours of D-Day. After the invasion Bruce shuttled back and forth between London and France to inspect his units in the field. Thanks to him, OSS/London contributed more than its share to Allied victory. He had a very good war.

He was no career army officer, though. Indeed, he hardly had a profession. He did not need one after 1926, when at age twenty-eight he married Ailsa Mellon, joint heir to the third largest fortune in America. He then tasted luxury that most people could only imagine by reading the books of his friend F. Scott Fitzgerald. No one loved the good life more than David Bruce. Stylish sophisticate, avid world traveler, and lotus eater extraordinaire, he passed his fortieth birthday in gilded satiety. In the end, however, Hitler's war gave him a chance to do something of real value, at great personal risk.

A romantic figure, immensely charming and widely read, he parlayed his OSS experience into a leading role in postwar international affairs. As head of the Marshall Plan in France, and then as ambassador there, he was an active participant in steeling Western Europe against the Soviet threat. Inspired by the vision of his friend Jean Monnet, the author of every major plan for postwar European integration, Bruce became a very early and influential American godparent of today's European Union.

"For its new diplomatic role," John Taft has written, "the United States apparently needed a very old diplomatic model."[8] He meant Bruce. The tall, reserved southerner was an unapologetic elitist to the core who styled himself in the eighteenth-century English manner, ill at ease in the rough and tumble of democratic politics. "Perhaps what [Secretary of State Dean] Acheson and others saw in Bruce," Taft surmised, "was a Platonic archetype of themselves, the sort of person that they at their best wanted to be." At the same time, Bruce valued talent whatever its source. A subordinate once said, "He liked bright people, and he didn't care whether they came from the New York ghetto or the southern aristocracy."[9]

For three decades Bruce held an unprecedented string of appointments. No one will ever match it. In promoting American engagement in Europe and planning European unity he served his country well. The same was true of his years as ambassador in Bonn and London, senior delegate to the caustic Vietnam peace negotiations, America's first emissary to the People's Republic of China, and ambassador to NATO.

Yet, despite his accomplishments, Bruce was the most overlooked diplomat of substance that America produced after World War II. Some people took him for granted or underrated his contribution. Because he was such a keen bon vivant, others dismissed him as merely a social ambassador. They could not have been more wrong. Money and an inclination to live well abroad cannot alone explain why six presidents repeatedly sought Bruce's advice.

For a generation, against extremes of left and right, he helped ensure that the center held at crucial turning points in American foreign relations. Every occupant of the White House from Truman to Ford knew he would represent the republic with self-assurance under trying circumstances. They saw the toughness of mind and the vision for

America's world role that lay behind the courtly demeanor, a blending of traits that endeared Bruce to foreign policy professionals. The combination of immense personal appeal, stamina, style, and probity, of being steadfast no matter how unpalatable his assignment, made Bruce the indispensable diplomat. He became the model for a generation of foreign service officers, the essential man. Not surprisingly, many career diplomats, schooled in contempt for presidential appointees, have said simply, "He was one of us."

Besides the glittering successes, however, his career was tinged with setback, even failure. There were personal troubles too. Behind the gracious facade that captivated his diplomatic colleagues, Bruce silently bore private tragedy of almost classical proportions. Because he carried personal loss with equanimity, his public accomplishments seemed all the more heroic to his friends. British publisher Hamish Hamilton captured only the diplomat's outward essence when he said, "David epitomised Charles II's definition of a gentleman: 'One who is easy in himself and makes others easy.'"[10] Bruce only made it seem so. The weight of his private sadnesses would have crushed most men, much less allowed them to make others feel easy in their company.

For someone whose work placed him constantly in the public eye, Bruce revealed little of the private man. To those who knew him well, though, there was another aspect than the polished and diplomatic persona.

Lady Antonia Fraser called him "a true Prince among men"; Hemingway admitted telling himself repeatedly he should "emulate Dave Bruce"; Jacqueline Onassis said he had "grace and imagination and the virtues of another time"; Susan Mary Alsop, the doyenne of Georgetown, said that no man ever concealed a keener intellect under an easy, engaging manner; and Sir Isaiah Berlin, the premier intellectual of postwar Britain, recalled that everyone "behaved better and thought better of themselves in his presence."[11]

To understand how he gained this reputation requires going back to the nineteenth century, into which he was born, if not all the way back to the eighteenth, where he found the model for his style and deportment, his sense of civic virtue, and his particular blend of world-weary, Continental pessimism and irrepressible American optimism.

CHAPTER 1

Under the Shadow of Washington's Hand

The past is never dead. It's not even past.

— William Faulkner

THE STORY OF HIS FAMILY, and of the perspective on life that David Bruce inherited, begins with the ancestral mansion that overlooks wooded hills and red clay tobacco fields in Charlotte County, Virginia. In 1847 his grandfather began planning a grand estate to signify the heights his family had scaled in that part of the state called Southside. Like the broad-acred English gentry he emulated, Charles Bruce built for the generations to come in serene confidence that his family's social standing, and the economic system that undergirded it, would endure. In one sense he succeeded, for the house he built continued to provide a reference point, an abiding sense of place, for his grandson long after the plantation economy vanished.

Like many sons of the planter elite, Charles Bruce went north for schooling, in his case to Harvard. In a painting of the young Virginian, the artist Thomas Sully captured Charles's outlook, giving his unlined face the look of smooth, vacuous elegance radiating optimism born of self-assurance. His half brother once admonished him for being a "sybarite" with "rather an expensive taste."[1] With the easy confidence of his class, after returning from college, Charles planned his grand house, was betrothed to Sarah Seddon of Fredericksburg, and sailed off to Europe to complete the cultural education of a rich young southern gentleman.

Before he left, he chose as his architect a man ominously described as having "more taste than prudence."[2] When it came to spending other people's money, John Evans Johnson lacked none of his profession's talent for guiltless extravagance. When Charles returned from his extended Grand Tour, he found that Johnson had spent double the specified sum, and the house was still unfinished. He did not protest, however, because Johnson had fashioned on a remote bluff high above the Staunton River a dramatic creation that fulfilled his dream.

With its crenellated facade, corner turrets, and mullioned windows, Staunton Hill flaunted the current vogue for Gothic Revival. Its striking feature was an octagonal vestibule opening onto a sinuous, double flying staircase rising to the upper floors. Johnson spared nothing on the details: he ordered ten slender, fluted columns of soft gray Italian marble, and the portico they supported, at a cost nearly equal to that of all the masonry in the rest of the house combined.

The means that enabled Charles to build Staunton Hill, and to accept calmly his builder's excesses, came to him through inheritance. Charles's father, James, had bought tobacco at depressed prices during the War of 1812 and sold high, hardly the labor of a virtuous Jeffersonian farmer. James married well — the widow of Patrick Henry's son — and increased the value of his estate many times over. He made his fortune as a commodities speculator, but like other men of substance in Virginia, he invested in agriculture, which is to say, in tobacco, which is to say, in slaves.

On reaching his majority in 1847, Charles became by some accounts the richest grandee of the state. His northern education and affinity for the trappings of European culture reinforced his self-confidence as a leader of his region. And he betrayed no regret that his fortune, and the future prospects of his family, rested on the backs of three hundred slaves who sweltered in the brutal, shimmering heat of Charlotte County's tobacco fields.

When the crisis triggered by secessionist fire-eaters in Charleston overtook Charles's way of life, white Virginians agonized over what to do. Unlike South Carolina — dismissed by a unionist as "too small to be a republic and too large to be an insane asylum" — Virginia voted first to oppose secession and then, after Fort Sumter, to embrace it. Charles outfitted a battery at his own expense and called it the Staunton

Hill Artillery. His wife Sarah's brother, James A. Seddon, became the Confederate secretary of war.

After years of struggle, the Bruces took no comfort from the injunction of Charles's half brother to "put your wife and children on the smallest amount of food, kill dogs, and old negroes if necessary to keep our army alive."[3] In April 1865 the Bruce children looked up from their games on the sloping lawn at Staunton Hill to listen to gunfire from the last skirmishes in the neighboring county — Appomattox.[4]

Like planters across the South, Bruce saw his wealth consumed by Confederate bonds and freedom for the long-suffering slaves. "De white folks was all sad en er cryin'," recalled one of them, Levi Pollard, as he contrasted the jubilation in the slave quarters with sentiment in the big house on the day Bruce told them they were free at last.[5]

Charles retained his cheerful outlook even as he saw his world order swept away. Sarah was differently disposed. She complained bitterly that their architect had not been even more extravagant, because Staunton Hill at least survived the war intact. "She had little humor," her son discreetly recalled.[6] Unlike her sanguine husband, who personified the convivial, horse-racing, Episcopalian gentry, she was a dour Presbyterian overflowing with the unforgiving Calvinist piety of that other overworked southern stereotype.

In its fall from antebellum splendor, the family was in good company and even kept 5,000 acres besides the house. If the Bruces had little ready cash, they did maintain better than most of their class the veneer of the past. Surrounded by deferential servants and sustained by an undiminished sense of noblesse oblige, they lived to instill in their children the highborn pride of Virginia Bruces. This, at any rate, was the recollection of their devoted son William Cabell Bruce, sixth of eight surviving children. In recalling his youth, Cabell cited his parents' preoccupation with debt as a testimony to their character. Their privation cannot have been onerous, though: his mother haughtily swore that "good servants are three-fourths of the happiness of life."[7]

After the biblical span of three score and ten years, Charles Bruce died in the mansion he had built as a youth. His death in 1896 prompted reverent comments about the passing of the last *grand seigneur* of the county. His simple funeral was a sublime tableau to votaries of Old Virginia. His body was carried in its coffin from the master's bedroom to the library, where the service was held, and then borne high on the shoulders of eight former slaves to the private graveyard on the grounds nearby.[8] Sad though this interment was, it would not be the most tragic witnessed at the Bruce family plot.

Encumbered by debt, the estate nearly slipped out of the family's hands. Proud Sarah Bruce spurned the charity of her husband's college classmates, who did not allow civil war and the passage of time to dim their happy memories of Harvard's Porcellian Club. Undaunted, these aging Yankees made their way to Staunton Hill and satisfied the widow's sense of honor by purchasing at inflated prices enough ancient, vinegary Madeira from Charles's cellar to keep the creditors at bay.

William Cabell Bruce knew there was no future in Southside for him. When he left home for college, though, he took with him an unreconstructed, moonlight-and-magnolias image of antebellum Virginia that he would cherish over the years. At the University of Virginia what engaged him most were the debating societies, where he matched wits with Woodrow Wilson. A long-standing feud between them climaxed when Cabell won an award the future president coveted. Irritated when reminded of the incident after Wilson entered the White House, Bruce feigned chagrin and compared himself to another Virginian "whose only claim to fame was knocking down young George Washington in a scuffle."[9] Wilson did not forget either, and their undergraduate clash poisoned their later relations.

Cabell moved to Baltimore in 1880 to study law and lived at a boardinghouse with an older brother, Philip. Philip Alexander Bruce's own law practice soured, but he did make astute social contacts that his younger brother employed to make his way in a strange place. Thanks to Philip's connections and his own diligence, within five years of passing the bar Cabell became a partner in the leading firm of William A. Fisher. Cabell's engagement to his boss's daughter showed anyone paying attention how quickly the talented young Virginian was establishing himself in his adopted city.

Cabell was not content merely to marry well and make money at the bar. Like professional men and women throughout urban America at the turn of the century, he embraced the Progressive goals of civil service reform and efficient government. He joined the Baltimore Reform League. He won a seat in the state senate. Two years later he captured Maryland's attention when, as a reform Democrat in a legislature divided by one vote, he threatened to support the Republicans unless the unreformed Democrats elected him senate president. They did.[10] He had modest success improving local government but felt that corruption blocked his advancement. This sounded like sour grapes, but Maryland politics, then and long after, stank worse than the fetid mounds of blue crab and oyster shells that piled up beside the canneries of Baltimore harbor.

Although a reformer, William Cabell Bruce was nobody's radical. His stolid personality, social aspirations, and pride in his Virginia gentry roots unsuited him to the role of zealot. Progressivism for him meant clean, honest government by the better sort of people in place of the squalid machine politics that catered to the lower classes. As a successful lawyer who knew how to conceal ambition beneath a genteel mien, he was also an ideal son-in-law to a family highly placed in Baltimore society.

Louise Este Fisher — Loulie to her friends — did not know the sense of loss that Cabell's family felt when they contemplated the past glory of Staunton Hill. It is true that bitterness lingered in Baltimore from the divided sentiments of the war years, but the city had not known the devastation of the Bruces' world. Her father, Judge William A. Fisher, married to wealthy Louise Este, came from a prosperous banking and legal family and retired from the bench to take up private practice. He was a modern man of the law, less given to the florid oratory of the preceding generation and more concerned with "sober reasoning," his son-in-law said, than emotional appeals to the jury.[11] In short, he was a hopelessly dull speaker.

Louise's parents had promised to send her to boarding school in Farmington, Connecticut, but when the time came were reluctant to lose her. So they offered her a choice of Farmington or a horse, and she cheerfully took the bribe. The judge's daughter crackled with an extraordinary level of energy that everyone remarked upon, energy she applied to those good works deemed suitable for genteel women. Short in stature like all the Fishers, she compensated for her size with vigor.

Louise Fisher and William Cabell Bruce were engaged in 1886 and married the next year. Their first child died in infancy from scarlet fever. Two years later a second son was born, and they named him James, for Cabell's grandfather with the Midas touch. The third son carried his father's name. The fourth and youngest was freighted with three Christian names in honor of Louise's brother, who was Cabell's junior law partner.

David Kirkpatrick Este Bruce was born at a quarter to five in the morning on Lincoln's birthday, Saturday, February 12, 1898. He was baptized at Emmanuel Episcopal Church.[12] In Washington, William McKinley sat in the White House. Abroad, Queen Victoria reigned over the quarter of the globe shaded in British imperial red. The status derived from such colonies began to tempt America's leaders who hankered for an invitation to the high table of the great powers. Opportunity knocked three days after David's birth when the battleship *Maine* blew up in Havana harbor, and the nation plunged headlong into Secretary of State John Hay's "splendid little war" with Spain.

David did not arrive to a settled household. About this time Judge Fisher asked his daughter to move into his new house and help care for her rich grandmother Este, who lived with the judge and his wife and in fact had purchased the house herself. Louise Bruce received the summons from the parental bench with dismay and confessed later that she resented it. Because she dutifully complied, however, the William Cabell Bruces moved to 8 West Mount Vernon Place with its four generations, numerous servants, and three libraries — one for the judge, one for the Bruces, and one for the boys. "Nothing in that house was in the singular," James would recall, remembering the multiple parlors and dining rooms.[13]

Without question the most fashionable address in Baltimore — critic Brendan Gill has called it "the finest city square in the country" — Mount Vernon Place at the turn of the century exuded a dignified air of repose, indeed, of arrival. The classical proportions of the houses lining the square imparted a Parisian accent, or so said an enthusiastic partisan. In the damp evenings of summer, platoons of gas street lamps cast their diffused light, like a Stieglitz photogravure print, over the tree-lined green filled with manicured flower beds. The focal point of the square was the monument, a tall stone column topped by a statue of George Washington, hand outstretched. Like Cockneys born within earshot of the bells of Bow Church, Baltimore natives are said to be born "under the shadow of Washington's hand."[14] For the Bruce boys the metaphor had daily resonance.

Baltimore at the turn of the century was a thrusting, growing place, a town on the make with all of the excitement and prejudices suggested by its brash civic boosterism. Its distinguishing trait was its location at the head of that "immense protein factory," the Chesapeake Bay, which provided an endless wealth of shellfish and seafood.[15] Cities were arguably noisier then because of the clatter of iron-shod hoofs and wagon wheels on cobbled streets. They were certainly more redolent from relying on literal horse power. And Baltimore's sewers all flowed into Back Basin, with its weak tidal current rarely dispelling the aroma in high summer. "Baltimoreans of those days," sneered native son H. L. Mencken, "were complacent beyond the ordinary, and agreed with their envious visitors that life in their town was swell," even in the face of annual typhoid epidemics and the occasional outbreak of malaria and smallpox.[16]

Louise Bruce applied her energy to the efficient running of the household and the family's social relations. This suited Cabell, who busied himself with law and politics. A benign patriarch who deferred to his wife's zeal, he once confessed stuffily that he had "no more to do with the government of my house than with the Government of Great Britain."[17]

Like Sarah Seddon Bruce, Louise took seriously the role of transmitting religious values. For many southern families of that era, the day began with prayers. In the Bruce household they were held in Louise's bedroom, with readings from the Book of Common Prayer and homilies by Cabell recounting for the boys those things they ought to have done and those they ought not to have done. The Sunday drill included hymn singing at home in the evening to supplement morning church service. In due course, at sixteen David was confirmed at the family's parish church.

For the boys, a house full of servants and older relatives — in David's words, "a perfect horde of family" — offered an ideal perch for observing the petty dramas of human society in microcosm, at least what could be gleaned of it in a wealthy household.[18] The butler, to whom Cabell attributed the manners of a grand duke, and Gus, the head coachman who presided over the stables behind the house, were most popular with the children. The stables offered them a private version of the neighborhood livery, fondly recalled by Mencken as "the favorite bivouac and chapel-of-ease of all healthy males of tender years."[19]

David's earliest memory was of being taken on his fourth birthday by his great-grandmother to see George M. Cohan's vaudeville act — and of being given his first taste of alcohol. Louise Este was the basis of his most vivid childhood recollections in part because of her great age, then nearly a hundred, but even more because of her unconventional manner. Cabell recalled all of the women in his wife's family with polite *Gone With the Wind* gallantry but of Louise Este could bring himself only to say cryptically that she was "a most interesting woman."[20]

In her day, Louise Miller Este had been a great hostess, schooled in European culture. "She cared nothing about money but took her pleasures seriously."[21] Even as a centenarian she was "rather given to drink," David recalled, "and had the habit, which she said was excellent for her health . . . of imbibing a good deal of champagne both at lunch and at dinner."[22] New Orleans was the city she really loved, and she detested Baltimore from the day she moved there after her husband died. She did not think much of her Baltimore relations either and often addressed them in French, knowing they did not understand a word of it. When she discovered that one of David's Este cousins in Cincinnati, Natalie Barney, could speak flawless French, she said to the girl, "You are someone after my own heart."[23] To young people who knew her, especially Natalie and David, the old lady radiated a romantic love of everything French.

She took a shine to her great-grandson and left a lasting impression on him. During the great fire of 1904 she took David up on the roof, in the smoke and falling ashes, to sit in deck chairs and watch the business district burn. Sensible Louise Bruce sent the children to the country when flames threatened their house but not before her youngest enjoyed another memorable day with his great-grandmother.

Louise thought Virginia was too hot in the summers for small children, so she took the boys instead to Lake George, the Adirondacks, and Atlantic City while Cabell visited his mother at Staunton Hill. The oppressive heat of high summer in Charlotte County, where only the drone of cicadas broke the isolated quiet, was certainly off-putting. Strong-willed Louise more likely stayed away out of dread at being in the country under the same roof with her equally strong-willed mother-in-law. In any event, she did not take the boys for summer visits to Staunton Hill until after the senior Mrs. Bruce died in 1907.

By then, rapacious plowing had eroded the land. Chemical fertilizer, in Cabell's opinion, only kept the soil going "like a feeble heart reenforced by doses of digitalis."[24] But David did not see the marginal fields reclaimed by broomstraw and scrub pine. He did not notice the dilapidated farms, or the poverty, or the ignorance. Rather, he was just old enough to begin imbibing the Old South mystique that the family's plantation evoked. The affectation was especially acute in the Old Dominion, for Virginians were steeped in an obsessive worship of their ancestors with a piety that would put a devout Shintoist to shame.[25] It was also the era when white southerners fervently nurtured the myths of the Lost Cause. David and every other white southern boy constantly relived the Civil War. For them, William Faulkner said, it was always still not yet two o'clock on that afternoon in July 1863 when Pickett fidgeted awaiting Longstreet's order, and maybe this time his charge would succeed.

For the Bruces, family circumstance powerfully reinforced nostalgia. The servants faithfully tending Staunton Hill gave credence to the picture that Cabell painted of gracious antebellum times. Within, in parlors choked with bric-a-brac, Gothic gilt-framed mirrors, high-backed Victorian rosewood sofas, and thick Brussels carpets, the hush itself exuded an aura of faded gentility. A marble bust of Sarah Bruce presided over the house as it had done since before the war. All these things created in David's imagination a sense of place, in location and in rank, of what it meant to be a Bruce of Virginia.

Among other things, it meant being related to the "best" families, whose genealogies, Cabell said, were "a tangle of fishhooks, so closely interlocked that it is impossible to pick up one without drawing three or four after it."[26] He probably did not dwell on the strain of insanity that ran through his numerous clan when he told David about his Virginia relations. According to malicious family tradition, more Bruces lived inside the lunatic asylum at Western State Hospital than outside it. Though David grew up in Baltimore in the house of his mother's family, it was the Virginia plantation that gave him a sense of identity with his forebears through his father's line rather than the Fishers. The only exception was an important one: it was great-grandmother Este who stimulated that sybaritic streak he shared with her as well as with his paternal grandfather.

Charlotte County was a remote, romantic place for a boy raised in town. Lighted only by candles and kerosene lamps, deep in the stillness of the countryside, Staunton Hill wove its distinctive spell on David. Besides summer visits there were shorter ones at Christmas, which the smell of wood smoke and country cooking and the rustle of leaves underfoot imprinted on his mind. Other visits at Easter etched in memory the intoxicating scents of woodland springtime and the blossoms of his grandfather's ornamental trees.

At Staunton Hill he learned to shoot. The guest book recorded a tally of quail, dove, and pheasant in the game bag as faithfully as it preserved the names of visiting friends. Tramping over the stubble of cornfields with his gun on crisp autumn mornings, he developed so finely both appetite and skill for the ritual slaughter of feathered innocents that it became his favorite sport.

The tobacco culture of Southside Virginia framed his earliest memories of Staunton Hill. He liked to recall how he watched with schoolboy amazement at a local inn as men expertly spat tobacco juice across the room into stained brass spittoons. He and his brothers pilfered leaves from tobacco curing barns for their corncob pipes. His mother caught and scolded him, to no effect, after he graduated to rolling his own cigarettes from hidden caches of Duke's Mixture and Bull Durham. From that point on, the air around his head was thick with smoke, the reflex of flicking tobacco ash as involuntary as breathing. He tried many times to quit but could not break his addiction to the noxious weed that had made his family's fortune.[27]

David saw an uglier side of the South when he visited Charlotte County. Ambiguities in race relations gave way by the twentieth century to a rigid system defined by Jim Crow segregation laws. Staunton Hill's rural setting (Cabell called it ethnically "English with a deep Negro pigmentation") was far from the legal apartheid of town.[28] Still, habit and prejudice placed barriers between blacks and whites and governed all contact between the races.

At Staunton Hill David learned instinctively where his family fit into the social hierarchy. The natives liked to say that three kinds of people inhabited Charlotte County — white folks, black folks, and Bruces. For David the unpremeditated arrogance that belonged by right to the owners of Staunton Hill came naturally. When young Master Bruce, all of fourteen years old, wrote his mother about going to the estate for Thanksgiving in 1912, his demands were not all tongue in

cheek: "I will arrive Wednesday night, and I want the following preparations made for me. I want Mammy to bring all of my shooting clothes
and a perfectly good pair of leggings to the house. . . . I want you to
prepare dinner for Uncle Willie and myself to take with us Thursday
shooting. Please have all these things in readiness under pain of my
great displeasure! . . . Be sure to have that dinner ready. I am sorry to
write such a sloppy letter, but my time is taken up with important
business."[29]

A contemporary described the best English public schools as "feed-
ing sham pearls to real swine."[30] Louise Bruce was determined that her
sons' education not merit a similar indictment. At Staunton Hill and
at home in Baltimore, she set a routine for her boys that stigmatized
idleness. She filled their days with lessons — dancing, tennis, language,
and, in David's case, violin lessons. David ignored the *fräulein* who
brought German grammar to Mount Vernon Place but did retain some
scraps from his French tutorials. Louise engaged a clergyman to come
to their house and keep the boys' noses to the grindstone. Some of
what they learned stuck, and they absorbed the value of discipline. The
saving grace of her approach was in bombarding them with opportunities and then encouraging each boy to apply himself to whatever
especially appealed to him.

When the time came, David went to Gilman, the local private
academy that his mother had helped found. From an early age he loved
to read. Louise often caught him with a book propped up on the
bathroom shelf while he brushed his teeth or on the floor beside his
foot as he laced his shoes. She said he read the *Iliad* when he was seven,
though how much he comprehended is open to question. In one of his
earliest letters, dated February 1906, he wrote when she was in Boston,
"I wish I was there, I think I just would love it there. Look around and
see if you can see any good books, so, when I have finished all the books
I have now, I can send for them."[31] This childish missive revealed more
than love of reading. Here was evidence that at the tender age of eight
he had taken to heart that ineffable assumption of the privileged that,
whatever one wishes, one of course may have: "I can send for them."

With an overabundance of literary relatives, it is easy to see why
David took naturally to reading and writing. After quitting law, his
Uncle Philip made a name for himself as the premier historian of

colonial Virginia. Another uncle taught university classes on Arthurian legends. His uncle by marriage, Thomas Nelson Page, was a best-selling author, whose ghost, another writer complained, haunted southern literature, "keening in Negro dialect over the Confederacy's fallen glory."[32] His father too set an example. Although Cabell wrote more after David left home, his research for a life of Benjamin Franklin that won a Pulitzer showed his son the pleasures of writing books as well as reading them. None of this would have mattered if David had not shown a natural affinity. The "scholar" of the family was how his brother James remembered him as a boy. Without question he inherited the family gene to become, in his own phrase, "another scribbling Bruce."[33]

In a slim red volume that he received one Christmas, he began to record on the gilt-edged pages the titles of the books he added to his personal library. They were largely but not entirely American, English, and Continental classics. For Shakespeare, Dickens, Cervantes, and Dante rubbed shoulders with assorted guides on hunting and fishing among the more than three hundred titles he collected by the time he went to college. It is doubtful he read them all — many were gifts that reflected the taste of the giver. By the time he finished Gilman, though, the largest number were of his own choosing. The habit of buying them for himself and of reading widely was already deeply ingrained.

In adding books to his library, David discovered the joys of collecting. He set himself the goal of buying first editions of modern authors. He amassed other objects too, from baseball cards, then sold in cigarette packs, to Indian artifacts gleaned from the fields of rural Virginia, to cigar-store figures and other bits of folk art. (His favorite, a picture of a nude Indian girl riding a white horse, displeased his mother, and she threw it out as soon as he left home.[34]) In collecting, as in hunting and smoking, the child was father of the man. From these modest collections grew an appetite, almost an obsession, that would fill his adult leisure in pursuit of much grander things than his schoolboy trinkets.

Sheltered from the rougher side of life outside his home, he enjoyed blissful early years. During the same months that Kenneth Grahame wrote about the adventures of Badger and Mole, David enjoyed a real-life *Wind in the Willows* childhood. To be sure, he suffered the normal bumps and shocks of boyhood. There were bouts with measles and chicken pox. When he was seven, his brother William Cabell Jr. gave the family a fright when a rabid dog bit him. There were also the deaths, not unexpected, of aged grandparents. In his twelfth year, however, a much sharper tragedy jolted his cozy universe. William Cabell Jr., the most athletic of the three boys and only a year older than David, sickened and died.

It was not a quick death. The family suffered through four months of alternating hope and despair. Specialists could do nothing about the streptococcal infection that gradually weakened his heart, and the boy died in June 1910. The family was devastated. For them, the portents of calamity that accompanied Halley's Comet that spring came true. Neither the return of her remarkable energy nor the success of her surviving sons could fill the void for Louise. She never spoke of William Cabell Jr. again without tears.

With a poignancy that broke his mother's heart, just before he died, William Cabell Jr. made plans to dispose of his personal effects. "He asked to have his baseball glove, his bat and his ball brought to him, he regarded these as his most precious possessions," Louise wrote. "Then he asked to see David, whom he loved dearly, and when David came to his bed side, he handed to him the things I have just mentioned, with perfect composure, told him that he wanted him to have them; telling him that *he* would never be able to use them again. That touching scene was almost more than my bleeding heart could stand."[35] And so, at his family's parish church, David faced the coffin containing his brother's remains while he heard the minister intone the words from the Episcopal burial service, "in the midst of life we are in death; of whom may we seek for succor, but of thee, O Lord?"

After the funeral Louise and Cabell took David for a holiday in Maine. He was their youngest child, already his mother's favorite even before William Cabell Jr. died, and that tragedy intensified the attachment. "Added to our great grief," she said, "was our feeling of deep sympathy for James and David in their loss, especially for David, as he and William Cabell were always together." "If anything could have added to my own suffering, in the loss of my precious William Cabell, it was the loneliness, without him, that David especially suffered."[36] Because abdominal surgery posed such a risk then, when David's appendix ruptured in 1912, the threat of losing another son became real again for Louise and Cabell. Fortunately for them all, he recovered rapidly.

With the resilience of youth, David filled his adolescent years with activity fed by his energy and appetite for novelty. He went to Woodrow Wilson's inauguration in 1913 and to New England for summer fishing trips. He began to manifest the winning personality that would charm so many people. But William Cabell Jr.'s death affected him more than he realized. The sense of melancholy that friends later detected on those rare occasions when he let down his guard may very well have had its origins in the traumatic summer of 1910. Years later, a perceptive observer noticed that the photograph in a little silver frame that he always kept on his desk was of the brother closest to him, with whom he shared his boyhood adventures.

To fill the void left by his brother's death, David escaped into his books. More than ever, he imbued the past with a romanticism that made it come alive for him and colored his view of the world. The captains and the kings, the trumpets of battle on a hundred fields, and the mysteries of faraway places filled his daydreams with a heroic, idealized notion of history. He could hear the longbows sing at Agincourt and Sir Francis Drake taunt the Spaniards. For him the rococo gaiety of Versailles came alive and also the clatter of the tumbrils bearing proud aristocrats to their rendezvous with the people's razor.

He spent most of his time at summer camp in the Poconos translating French classics. "I would have read even more since I have been here," he wrote home, "had it not been for the long time it took me to translate Hernani, which is a play of 150 pages. I enjoyed it immensely, in spite of my difficulty in translating it, and I think, with the exception of some of Shakespeare's it is the most powerful play which I have ever read." David must have overdone it. One of the counselors, he wrote, "expects me to do more petty jobs around the camp than anyone else because . . . when I want to study and read most of the day, he thinks I am loafing."[37]

G. M. Trevelyan once said that the appeal of history "lies in the quasi-miraculous fact that once, on this earth, on this familiar spot of ground walked other men and women as actual as we are today, thinking their own thoughts, swayed by their own passions but now all gone, vanished after another, gone as utterly as we ourselves shall be gone like ghosts at cockcrow."[38] Something of that romantic, poetic sense informed David's view of the past.

After William Cabell Jr.'s death, Louise and Cabell invested their hopes more intensely than ever in their remaining sons. Because they were more than five years apart, James was the revered elder brother whose footsteps were meant to be followed. For the time being, the relationship was a simple one of admiration by younger brother for older. Only later — as David began to eclipse James in the wider world — would the relationship become edged and complex.

Distance and friction clouded the relationship of Cabell Bruce and his younger son. With his walrus mustache, wing collars, and bushy brows, Cabell looked every inch the United States Senator that he later became. Despite his public career, though, the elder Bruce was a private man, formal, courtly, and shy, never fully at ease with other men, and slow to show feelings. He was more comfortable as private man than as public figure. As James wryly put it, he was "a warm and wonderful man who did not show his warmth to everybody." An "introspective writer" rather than a politician, despite his lifelong public prominence, Cabell was "a big-hearted, bashful man, much more interested in ideas and the people close to him."[39]

As a young man, David thought his father stuffy and pompous. There was cause. According to family tradition, essential equipment for listening to one of Cabell's speeches included a pillow and a dictionary. In turn, the father lamented the son's restlessness in choosing a career. Cabell, who had overcome the reduced circumstances of a once-prosperous family, found David's unwillingness to settle down utterly maddening. In the years before David left home, however, these reciprocal irritations were only beginning to manifest themselves.

Though he considered Cabell unloving, his relationship with Loulie was warmer. He was her favorite. She indulged him more, and it was his father rather than she who badgered him about choosing a career. Plucky and worldly wise, she radiated a forceful social presence and possessed a great gift for making friends. "A Rock of Gibraltar" was how he described her. "She had more generosity and unselfishness about those she loved than any one I have ever known."[40] From her he inherited enormous stamina, and from her too came his easy grasp of social skills and sense of style.

Another member of the household was as close as either parent. Born two years before the Supreme Court ruled that Dred Scott was human chattel, Evelyn Mackall spent her adult life in service to the Bruces. Like many white southern children, David formed a strong bond with the black woman his parents chose, in effect, to raise him. "Deputy-mother" was Cabell's term for the servant entrusted with his own upbringing.[41] The same relationship applied to David and Mackall. As a university student he wrote to her that "although you have no children of your own, remember that there is one who respects and loves you as a mother, and though he is a grown man now, to you he will always be your devoted boy."[42] Of all the letters he later received from home while abroad, one of the few that he saved came from Mackall.

In 1915 David spent most of a rainy August at Staunton Hill, his last vacation before college. Photographs from the period show that he had grown tall like his father, slim and lanky. Unlike Cabell he had a ready, mischievous smile and a love of mimickry that instantly dispelled the awkwardness his tall adolescent frame suggested. With his intense blue eyes, high forehead, and long chestnut hair, he made a strong presence even as a teenager.

That visit to Charlotte County was the first time they took their car. On the way home they had to drive the long Packard in low gear through rutted tracks of thick red mud, stopping every ten minutes or so to fill a hissing radiator. Toward nightfall they lost their way and had to spend the night in the car. Family and servants huddled uneasily in the darkness. The sinister screeching of night insects mirrored Louise's discomfort over the strain on the social hierarchy, and both kept her awake. David slept soundly through it all.[43]

In September 1915 the animated chatter of students filled the platform at Princeton Junction, halfway along the rail line between Philadelphia and New York. As trains pulled into the station, Princeton prepared once more to receive a new cohort of favored young men and speed them toward their appointed destinies in America's ruling elite. By later standards, fifteen hundred students seems a small community, but for the 385 freshmen who made up the incoming class of '19, it provided a vast universe of potential new friends. Thanks to an ambitious building program, when David arrived Princeton had grown beyond the few ancient buildings clustered around Old Nassau Hall, the pre-Revolutionary campus center that was covered with the ivy ritually planted by each graduating class. Ivy also gave an aura of instant antiquity to those modern faux Gothic buildings that were the university's latest source of pride.

The air of contemplative repose that those vine-covered, dreaming spires evoke belies the truth that for entering students a campus is not a quiet haven but a vibrant new world full of possibility. It was certainly so for David. His grades were respectable but not so good anyone mistook him for a grind. And his omnivorous reading, rather than turning him into a full-time bookworm, enabled him to finesse examinations more easily than his peers and devote time to less bookish pursuits. A high-spirited young man, he nevertheless managed to keep his name off the records of the Princeton town police, unlike some of his friends.[44]

A constant flurry of lectures — along the lines of "Christianity Today" and "Literature and the Well-Rounded Man," not to mention earnest discussions about woman's suffrage — gave the campus a veneer of erudition. It was only a gloss, for an obsession with class spirit and team sports suffused the undergraduates' existence. The life of the mind may have been there, somewhere among Princeton's groves of academe, but freshmen experienced less a cultural awakening than a drumbeat of vicious hazing, frenetic athleticism, and extracurricular froth that one critic in 1915 called a "vortex of excited and unproductive achievement."[45]

David decided to try out for the *Daily Princetonian* because, he said with too much confidence, "the Board of Editors are the fellows who really amount to something in College."[46] They did not choose him. He did make the debate team, though, and on trips to other colleges he discovered that only an hour and a half separated Princeton from Pennsylvania Station and the bright lights of Broadway.

One of his best friends was Richard Cleveland, son of the former president. The bond deepened, ironically, after he defeated David for freshman class president. Another friend was F. Scott Fitzgerald. Of the writer who became the emblem of his self-indulgent generation, David later said with the benefit of brutal hindsight, "He could do everything well except order his own life. He was strikingly handsome, almost hysterically gay, a brilliant conversationalist, unsure of himself, and as a result always trying to attract attention by some reverberating demonstration."[47]

In his second year David embraced a reverberating demonstration of his own. He found it by leading a movement to overthrow the system that dominated undergraduate culture. Every year upperclassmen's eating clubs elected some rising sophomores to membership, but not all. The distinctions among the clubs, as well as the lowered status of those social lepers not inducted at all, were hurtful in the best tradition of adolescent snobbery. When the most exclusive club, Ivy, took only eleven students one year, a disappointed sophomore lamented, "Even Jesus Christ took twelve."[48]

A dim view of brainless college traditions fostered David's attitude toward the clubs. He once scolded the school newspaper for championing petty rules that demeaned freshmen. "Is it in keeping with the principles of democracy," he demanded to know, "that one set of men should take upon themselves . . . the right to dictate the daily dress and habits of a large number of their fellow students?" He admitted that the freshman might be "quiet and well-mannered" after the indignities heaped on him, "but is it not equally true that much of his spontaneity and individuality has been crushed out in the process?"[49] He became popular enough that the sophomore class elected him vice-president, but increasingly it was "spontaneity and individuality" — and independence from the control of others — that became his lodestars, not college tradition.

With these opinions, it is no surprise that he became a ringleader of the group opposed to the clubs. In the name of democracy, he and four friends urged their classmates to eat at the new commons building and make the clubs superfluous. The clubs, they said, compelled each member to "repress his individuality" in favor of group standards. The system raised artificial barriers between members and those who hoped to join. "'Bootlicking' and the fear of being suspected of 'bootlicking' prevent friendships" across the divide, David and his friends argued. "Internal reform of the clubs would be unsatisfactory," they concluded, "as a social system with all of its accompanying false standards would still exist."[50]

In a letter to Louise Bruce, a friend of the family unwittingly alluded to the contrary tendencies that had begun to war for David's allegiance: noblesse oblige superiority versus egalitarianism. Only "real aristocrats" like her son, the friend said, could "challenge traditions and lead crowds."[51] Like Fitzgerald's Gatsby, David was busy creating himself in his own image, but he had not yet hit upon the right model.

When Woodrow Wilson had been president of Princeton, his attempt to end the clubs from above had failed. In 1917 the revolt came from below, and it rent the college from top to bottom. An alumnus who had been there in Wilson's day wrote David to encourage him, saying "beautiful buildings, landscape gardening, and luxurious living do not make a university."[52] Minor tempest that it was, the rebellion burned itself deeply into the institutional memory of Princeton. Some upperclassmen denounced David and his allies as "revolutionists" who did not understand that "even if our clubs were abolished and the entire College dined in an atmosphere of Utopian socialistic love, men would still continue to form cliques of congeniality." Others rallied to the insurgents, saying the clubs did little but "encourage luxury, idleness, and snobbery."[53]

For David, the revolt quickened a spirit of rebellion against his father's plans for him. The egalitarian rhetoric of the rebels gave him a frisson of rejecting his family's patrician status. It was a rebellion, however, whose water he could dip his toes into knowing it was not deep enough to drown in.

Even before the revolt against the clubs climaxed, the struggle lost its hold on him, and he toyed with the improbable notion of going to England to study for the mission field. Given the cosmopolitan tenor of his mature years, this idea seems wildly out of character. If told about this scheme to devote himself to the glory of God, the sophisticated friends of his adult years would have denied it could ever have been true of the man of the world they knew. Their skepticism would have been justified. On the road he was traveling, David was about to be struck by a different blinding flash than Saul, and his destination would not be Damascus but another city of light.

This latest of his schemes, though, did fit the larger pattern unfolding in his life: an incandescent impatience with the expectations of his parents. Cabell inflamed matters when he chastised his son to stop "hatching plans for breaking away." He should "ruthlessly repress all your migratory impulses."[54] In the spring of 1917, it was an open question whether David would stay the course and take his degree.

CHAPTER 2

The Discovery of Europe

In Europe they knew what gas smelt like and the sweet sick stench of bodies buried too shallow and the grey look of the skin of starved children. . . .

Today is Paris pink sunlight hazy on the clouds against patches of robins-egg. . . . Today is the sunny morning of the first day of spring . . . the first morning of the first day of the first year.

— John Dos Passos, *Nineteen Nineteen*

WHEN DAVID MATRICULATED at Princeton, his peers in Europe had been engaged for a year in a grimmer tuition. In August 1914, while he was enjoying another golden, schoolboy summer holiday, on the broad plains of East Prussia and in the tidy fields of Belgium young men learned to kill one another with sickening efficiency. During his last autumn at prep school, the first campaigns of maneuver in the West gave way to a stalemated line of trenches zigzagging from the Swiss border to the English Channel. By the time he reached Princeton, the war had begun to sweep away the old order in ways the antagonists could not begin to fathom.

At first Americans overwhelmingly favored neutrality. Woodrow Wilson, with the earnest rectitude of an academic moralist, embodied the national will to stay out of the fight. "In 1917," wrote one witness, "it seemed to Americans of many opinions, pacifistic or patriotic, that the war in Europe was becoming an enormous carnival of death. Nothing else in the history of the continent, not even the Black Death, had produced such an extravagance of corpses."[1] Americans became more confused as the carnage continued. The quirky industrialist Henry Ford, who called the war a contrivance of bankers and Jews, chartered a "peace ship" and sailed to Europe with other pacifists in a much-derided attempt to end the conflict. Others favored intervening on the side of the Allies. Some, not ready to take that step, nevertheless believed America should rely on real military preparedness, not three thousand miles of open water or utopian hopes for peace.

In the White House, Cabell Bruce's college adversary reluctantly agreed to enlarge the army and navy. Teddy Roosevelt grumbled that it amounted only to "half-preparedness." Horrified by Wilson's change of heart, many Progressives opposed preparedness as surrender to militarism and betrayal of the struggle for social reform.

More pragmatic politicians, like Cabell Bruce, cared less for social reform and leaped to the challenge of defense. He sent David off for military training in July 1915 and 1916 to a camp at Plattsburg, New York, which owed its existence to patriotic fervor triggered by the sinking of the *Lusitania*. Along the shore of Lake Champlain, David and eventually thousands of other students trained during the summer months. Heavy rains turned the camp to mud, badly cooked food bred mutinous thoughts, and the latrines overflowed. With the bone-tiring physical exercise, it all had the desired effect of instilling solidarity in these pampered sons of the East Coast elite. Bird hunting at Staunton Hill earned David awards for marksmanship, and his little red index to his library began to include books on parade ground drill as well as literary classics and field sports.

Because the students paid their own way, the camp hardly attracted a cross section of American youth. "It seemed to me that all the right people went," one of them recalled.[2] David cheerily wrote home, "I am enjoying myself immensely. There are about 700 fellows here and they are a fine crowd."[3] All the same, Cabell reminded his son of the family honor and admonished him to "shun as you would pestilence the slightest contact with abandoned women." For good measure he added tales of "debased morals" and "loathsome and incurable forms of disease" in case the warning seemed inadvertently tempting.[4]

However David regarded the advice, Plattsburg profoundly influenced him. At camp these privileged youths "learned the smell and feel of the ground and the rain." The day began with cold showers at 5:15.

In the evening, lectures were held out in the open in a spectacular setting where the land sloped down toward the deep blue of the lake, with a hazy view of Vermont's Green Mountains in the distance. "Sitting and lying in a huge semicircle, resting their tired muscles, and with pipes glowing in the darkening twilight," these would-be soldiers imbibed a spirit of national service that few of them had given much thought to before.[5] David returned from camp singing its praises and, to use his own phrase, the good work done by his fellow "missionaries in the cause of national defense."[6]

Because it attracted mainly Ivy League students, the camp introduced him to other sons of the ruling elite — "the better educated classes" he called them — including Hamilton Fish Jr., Elihu Root Jr., and Teddy Roosevelt's sons.[7] Some would become part of the Eastern establishment that dominated American foreign policy. John J. McCloy, later the unofficial chairman of that club, was there with David. He recalled that as the colors were lowered at the end of the day, with the students standing at salute, silent, no matter how tired they were, none of them ever witnessed that patriotic observance "without having a tiny thrill run up his spine."[8] The shared experience of Plattsburg became their playing fields of Eton.

By 1917, pressure from both Allied and Central powers drove Wilson's strategy for keeping out of war to the brink of failure. While David and his classmates fought over the eating clubs, Germany renounced the rules limiting submarine engagement and began sinking ships indiscriminately, finally forcing Wilson's hand. The president whose reelection had rested squarely on peace and Progressivism reluctantly chose to take up the sword.

An extraordinary session of Congress convened on April 2 to hear Wilson address a packed chamber. The skills he had honed in debate in Charlottesville were put to the test as he sought to justify taking his nation into a war he knew would not give the catharsis many of his unthinking countrymen expected. They, like the zealots of 1914 in London, Paris, Berlin, Vienna, and St. Petersburg, would be disabused the hard way. When he reached the point at which he asked Congress to declare war, the audience rose to cheer, but only briefly. Wilson continued with his sober invocation of idealism tempered by intimations of tragedy. Although he feared the "spirit of ruthless brutality" that war would inject into American life, he asked Congress to enter the struggle to "make the world itself at last free."[9]

After the Senate and House passed the declaration, it came to Wilson's desk on Good Friday, April 6, 1917. The next day David abandoned his studies, the revolt against the eating clubs, and fleeting visions of mission work to join the Maryland National Guard.

The enthusiasm of American undergraduates that spring was captured, like that of their European peers three years before, in Rupert Brooke's war sonnets — "Now, God be thanked Who has matched us with His hour, / And caught our youth, and wakened us from sleeping" — a prayer that the suffering and privation of war would in the end purify and cleanse. As naive as Brooke's idealized sentiments were, even they were too exalted to describe David's reaction. Like many his age, he simply viewed it all as a great adventure.

In the year America went to war, Europe had been bleeding for nearly three, a generation of youth devoured in the meat grinder of the trenches. On a single day in 1916 a hundred thousand British Tommies began the battle of the Somme by walking calmly into no-man's-land, where perhaps as few as a hundred German machine-gun teams killed or maimed sixty thousand by nightfall.[10] The butcher's bill for Verdun reached nearly a third of a million for both sides. Behind the lines hardship and hunger grew as each side tried to starve the other into submission. Under the strain, the social structure of nations began to crack. Revolution threw out the tsar in 1917, and the spiral down into the abyss began. The day after David enlisted, Lenin left Zurich for Petrograd, courtesy of the German General Staff, on the infamous sealed train carrying the bacillus of revolution to infect Russia. Upheaval was not confined to the East. Widespread disaffection undermined even France, where, its armies bled white, the common soldiers rebelled in outright mutiny.

While terrible events convulsed Europe, David found himself no nearer the action. When the regular army absorbed the Maryland National Guard, he went to a training camp in the South. Despite Plattsburg, he was not commissioned but instead worked his way up from private to sergeant in Battery F of the 110th Field Artillery, 29th Division, the Blue and Gray of Maryland and Virginia. Camp McClellan, near the ugly rail town of Anniston, Alabama, in the foothills of the Appalachians, was a long way from the Western Front. For three months Louise Bruce played the well-intentioned, suffocating role Douglas MacArthur's mother had performed earlier at West Point and rented a house in the town to be near her soldier son. David resented the attention, and when she finally went home he warned her, "Do not come [back] to Anniston. I have no time to see anyone."[11]

The longer he remained there, in a tent city with forty thousand others, the more restless he became. "I am tired of staying here instead of going abroad. I joined the army to fight & not to spend a year in a God forsaken camp," he angrily told his mother.[12] He asked her to arrange a transfer, but a month later he petulantly denounced both parents for pulling strings on his behalf, concluding, with convenient amnesia about his earlier requests, "If there is anything I have come to detest in the Army it is the use or attempted use of influence."[13]

After a year of training, his unit sailed for Europe on June 28, 1918. As soon as he left sight of land, he was caught up in the war he thought he would never see. "There are 90 men in our crew, of all nationalities," he wrote about the *Keemun*, a small British freighter making its first trip as a troop transport. "There are Americans, English, Chinese, Japanese, French-speaking negroes, & one old boy of undetermined parentage who looks more like a walrus than a man."[14] On their crossing from England, a U-boat had fired its deck gun at them, so they were edgy about sailing unescorted up the coast to Nova Scotia, their nerves chafed raw by the threat from below. Two ships were sunk nearby the day before David's reached Halifax. In dense fog the *Keemun* narrowly escaped a collision, and its officers thought it a miracle they reached port without incident. Luckily for the men crowded in the stale air below deck, calm winds and a rising barometer kept the stench of seasickness to a minimum, for the moment.

Halifax appeared peaceful to David's untrained eye, "looking in the mist like an etching by Whistler."[15] It was, in fact, a principal rendezvous for convoys, with the harbor protected by minefields and antisubmarine nets. The *Keemun* joined twelve other transports guarded by eleven warships. The convoy headed out into the gray North Atlantic to face the kaiser's U-boats on the Fourth of July, the first such national holiday, David wistfully noted, forgetting Plattsburg, that he had spent away from home.

One night while he stood guard duty on deck, other vessels in the convoy suddenly turned on their lights, "like lanterns at a lawn fête," as sirens wailed and ships loomed up dangerously close. "One minute utter darkness," he wrote, "another minute we were the center of a city of weird lights, strange noises, mysterious blinking messages." A homeward-bound convoy had barreled through their midst, almost colliding with the three parallel lines of overcrowded troop transports.

The first death impressed him less as a reminder of mortality than for the haunting, elegiac quality of burial at sea. "There was a funeral on the next ship this morning," he wrote. "The flag was lowered to half mast & a weighted body was slowly lowered into the deep to the playing of 'Taps,' the most melancholy & beautiful of all bugle calls."

Two days before landfall a violent explosion rocked his ship. A destroyer came steaming through the fog, pouring smoke from every funnel and dropping depth charges in a circle. As the *Keemun* shook from the concussions, an oil slick frothed to the surface to mark the grave of another U-boat and its entombed crew. After the incident David chattered just a little too animatedly with a crew member about other gruesome submarine deaths, perhaps in a nervous attempt to sublimate his fears.

The convoy finally reached grimy, welcoming Liverpool. Louise Bruce learned that her son had survived the crossing when she received a Red Cross postcard bearing his signature below the impersonal, if reassuring, preprinted message: "The ship on which I sailed has arrived safely overseas."[16]

Europe in 1918 was sick from four years of bloodletting, but no end was in sight. The Berlin high command rushed troops from east to west after imposing a draconian peace on Russia's new Communist masters. The bacillus had done its work. The Allies barely contained the powerful German offensive that followed and desperately needed fresh troops to withstand the next hammer blows. In June, Wilson heeded their pleas and rushed thousands of young Americans across the ocean, David among them. Like other green soldiers, he fancied himself a hard-headed realist. "'To make the world safe for Democracy' seems an abstract principle to a soldier," he wrote. "Civilians idealize the war," unlike soldiers, who "regard it as a disagreeable experience which ought to be ended as quickly as possible."[17] He had forgotten his own excitement in April 1917.

A visiting British officer had told soldiers at Camp McClellan that he joined up not to fight for king and country but because he thought the war would be "jolly good sport." In that expectation, he warned his eager listeners, he was very much mistaken. David did not buy that cautionary tale. If he did not believe the war was a crusade for Wilson's Fourteen Points, he did think it a grand adventure. Churchill famously wrote of the conflict that "war, which used to be cruel and magnificent, has now become cruel and squalid. . . . It is all the fault of Democracy and Science."[18] For David it had lost none of its terrible splendor. It surprised him that convalescing British soldiers, like veterans of all wars, rarely spoke of combat: "They do not discuss it unless you ask about it," he said, and then, "they relate tales of the bravest deeds as if bravery and danger were too commonplace to be exciting."[19] No amount of propaganda or debased awards could cure the weariness that oppressed all the armies. On the other side of the wire, an Austrian cynically remarked that the only sure way to avoid the Iron Cross, Second Class, was suicide.[20]

At each camp his battery occupied, David conjured up those romanticized, martial stories that had filled his adolescent reading. At every chance, he delved into local bookshops to read about whatever province his unit happened to be in. The trumpet calls of medieval battles that had stirred his schoolboy fancy still appealed to him. In Poitiers he recounted the town's associations with Richard the Lionhearted and Joan of Arc. He learned that the province had been fought over by "Gaul & Roman, Paganism and Christianity, Visigoths & Franks, Capetians & Plantagenets, Rome & Geneva, Revolution & 'Ancien Regime.'"[21] In another village he discovered that Clovis had battled the Visigoths, the English and French had quarreled in the time of the Black Prince, and Arab troops had camped during the Franco-Prussian War. He saw himself as the latest in a long line of soldiers about, he hoped, to atone for America's passivity. "For three years," he said, "France fought her battles alone while we looked on, and I am heartily ashamed that we did nothing more."[22]

He was not oblivious to the destruction, just untouched personally by its tragedies and inspired by his mission, like so many unbloodied

American soldiers rushed abroad in 1918, whose most popular poem was "I Have a Rendezvous with Death."[23] Though he retained his naive enthusiasm for combat, he did see what years of conflict had done to the French. "The children are prematurely aged, and the old people are burned out," he said with a flash of insight. "There is no sparkle of life over here. Everything is as gray and sombre as dead tobacco ashes. The plain people, the backbone of the country, are sick, beyond the consolation of their ancient religion, from seeing their sons and friends killed. I have not seen a *happy* face in France. The French smile, they play, but one is always aware that all mirth is for outward show, and that their holiday faces, like the painted visages at a mummer's ball, conceal their real passions."[24]

Reaching France did not mean going to the front immediately. By letter, his parents begged him to take a commission, but he would not be pushed and reacted with the indignation of self-righteous youth. If he left "on the eve of going to the Front, in order to immolate myself in the security of an officer's school with the possibility of never seeing active service I should forfeit my self-respect."[25] He wanted a commission but looked for promotion from the ranks. Failing that, he refused to take an officer training course until he had faced the enemy.

As if the scourge of combat were not enough, influenza killed millions, ultimately as many as the war itself. David caught it too and, writing home, made light of the illness. Louise and Cabell took little pleasure from his account of the first flu death in the regiment, a stone-cutter: "it was the irony of fate that the only one of our number who could have properly marked the graves of his comrades should be the first to go."[26]

For a time the battery's frantic drilling absorbed him. Moving guns, caissons, horses, and men in complicated maneuvers appealed to his sense of accomplishment. He came to appreciate the sinister beauty of artillery fire. "Our battery has just returned from a night on the range," he wrote. "We fired last night shells with tracers attached which enable one to observe the entire path of the projectile. It was a beautiful sight, the trajectory looking like a bow of fire, the vivid flash of the guns, and, at the end, the red burst."[27]

As the weeks passed, he grew restless. "The whole land is being pelted by torrential rains," he groused, "we drag ourselves thru a sea of viscous, slimy, bottomless mud, which rivals the red clay of Charlotte County."[28] Convinced by mid-October that the war would soon end, on the advice of his captain he enrolled in an officer training class. He clung to the hope that by some slim chance the fighting would continue and allow him to reach the front as an officer in the final push, or, as he put it, to "be in at the death."[29] He had not lost his romanticized notion of combat — or his ability to distress his parents. And he also made it absolutely clear that only fading prospects of action and the urging of his captain — certainly not parental pleading — persuaded him to seek a commission.

The massive German offensives of 1918 nearly succeeded. With the collapse of Russia, Berlin achieved its goal of creating a Teutonic *Mitteleuropa* stretching from the Baltic to the Black Sea, from Belgium to the Ukrainian steppes, an economic sphere that would not be achieved again until Hitler in the 1940s and Helmut Kohl in the 1990s. Only the arrival of American troops thwarted the kaiser's bid to dictate terms in the West as he had done in the East. But those Americans were enough to do the job. Unable to stem the autumn Allied counteroffensive, the Germans quit. Their grasp for world power, undertaken so audaciously four years before and pressed to within an ace of winning, had failed.

Because the German army was intact and still on foreign soil at the armistice, however, seeds were planted that would blossom later into a charge of betrayal. In a military hospital, recovering from a gas attack on his regiment, Adolf Hitler learned of the capitulation. He resolved to avenge Germany's humiliation at the hands of the "miserable and degenerate criminals" who had sold out the Reich.[30] For the moment, though, the armistice whistles that blew over the trenches on November 11, 1918, signaled unqualified Allied victory. Because his unit never made it up to the line, David would have to wait for another war to be shot at.

Unlike Corporal Hitler and millions of others on both sides, Sergeant Bruce never knew firsthand the horrors of the Western Front, the barbed wire and the mustard gas hell of the trenches. His brother, an artillery captain, did see heavy fighting at St. Mihiel, the Marne, and the Argonne and counted many friends among the 148 Princeton men who died. David, whose idealistic visions of glory were never disabused in combat, felt cheated and repeatedly spoke of his "great disappointment." Never forced to see his friends ripped apart before his eyes or reduced to gibbering victims of shell shock, he carried home a far different memory of the Great War than those who did.

Armistice Day found him at the officer school at Saumur, a somnolent town of blue-slate-roofed houses in the Loire Valley, whose vineyards and limestone hills seemed to him "the most beautiful country I have ever seen."[31] He would have a chance to use the same expression many times over as he began to discover Europe. To his delight the end to war did not mean instant demobilization. With two million American soldiers abroad and no quick way to ship them all home, the more enterprising ones found ways to prolong their time in Europe.

He was still ambivalent about a commission. "An enlisted man receives few comforts, few rewards, and little appreciation," he mused. "On the other hand, his life is freer and more democratic than that of an officer, and often happier. I am aware that the man who is utterly devoid of ambition is indeed a poor creature. Yet I have a greater contempt for one whose every thought is devoted to the pursuit of a Sam Browne belt. . . . I have known many men commissioned, but I have not noticed any corresponding moral or physical metamorphosis. The character of some enlisted men is as fine and their abilities as great as those of the officers from whom they receive their orders, a condition which is the happy result of a republican form of government. . . . I shall never regret my enlistment. The happiest days of my life were spent in the ranks of Battery F, with the finest set of men I have ever known."[32]

It did not bother him much, then, when the course ended without commissions being given. "In view of my experiences in this war I cannot be termed *Fortunio*, can I?" he concluded. "However, that is how things happen in the Army, and I am a wiser and a poorer man, with nothing except some of the accoutrements of an officer, for which about 1000 francs have flowed from my pockets into those of French & English tradesmen."[33]

Other opportunities beckoned. Allied intervention in the Russian civil war caught the eye of many would-be adventurers at Saumur, and when his father learned of David's wish to fight the Red Army, he exploded. If he went, Cabell thundered, "you are at dagger's draw with your daddy."[34] In the end David skipped the anti-Bolshevik expedition, but only because the army forbade a transfer.

In the new year he left Saumur and returned to his old unit at Bourbonne-les-Bains. Billeted with a French couple, he slept in their kitchen doubled up in an old Breton cupboard bed too short for his tall frame. As he began to study the language, he learned to speak most fluently about food and acquired a premature reputation as a gourmet.

Denied the great adventure of war, as he saw it, he searched for stimulation in less heroic quarters. He longed for "the simple luxuries which mean so little when one has them — a bathtub, an open fire, honey, rolls, butter, sugar, the noise of street-cars, the bustle of a real city. Music and lights, theatres & pageants, & all the other non-essentials of life."[35] With little to do in his battery, he finagled every chance to get away from camp. "The tragedy of travel," he said in lamenting the cancellation of a trip to Algiers, is that "every new scene inspires one with a passion to go further and to pile novelty upon novelty, world without end."[36]

He rarely admitted to homesickness, but it was obvious at a party eight of his buddies gave him on his twenty-first birthday. Thick and maudlin from dubious champagne, they sat up late in the flickering light of their poky hut singing Stephen Foster tunes and toasting David on his majority. "Your cablegram congratulating me upon my assumption of the *toga virilis* arrived this morning," he wrote his parents with a hint of self-mockery. "Whatever of happiness I have enjoyed in these first twenty-one years of my life has been largely due to your love and kindness, . . . your never-failing generosity and ready sympathy. Such things as these are so often taken for granted that you may sometimes believe them unappreciated, but, believe me, I am deeply conscious of them."[37]

After the party he applied for a study furlough at an approved French university. (He did not tell his parents that enrolling meant giving up priority for a quick return home.) When he rejoined his battery after a short leave that introduced him to wicked Marseilles and Avignon by moonlight, he was jubilant to find orders directing him to Bordeaux University.[38] His claim years later that he arrived there not knowing a word of French exaggerated his ignorance. Those early lessons at home — not to mention translating Victor Hugo at summer camp — were not entirely forgotten and, combined with conversation by the fireside at Bourbonne-les-Bains, gave him a passable comprehension by the time he reached Bordeaux. There he was "transported to a land of poetry by the eloquence & magnetism of the Professor."[39] The fluency he eventually achieved served him well, despite, or perhaps because, he always pronounced French with a distinctive Tidewater accent that rarely failed to enchant native speakers.

Having a room of his own after two years of communal army quarters made Bordeaux all the more appealing. He luxuriated in a daily routine, "where you may imagine me at 8 o'clock of a morning, sitting up in bed, nattily attired in a suit of Red Cross pajamas, sipping my chocolate" and reading eighteenth-century French essayists.[40] He conceived the idea of amassing a library of French literature and made a start by collecting the works of Racine, Molière, Montesquieu, Pascal, Hugo, Lamartine, and La Fontaine. Although pleased with Bordeaux, he transferred to the Sorbonne to take a course in international law — and be where the action was. With the luck that followed him through life, he arrived in Paris for the first time in April 1919.

The capital began to return to normal as the first peacetime spring in five years enticed home the million residents who had fled German shelling. By then the invasion of Paris by David's countrymen had reached floodtide. The previous autumn Wilson had sailed for Europe with a full retinue of expert advisers. In the snide words of British diplomat Harold Nicolson, his ship, appropriately the *George Washington,* had "creaked and groaned across the Atlantic under the weight of their erudition."[41]

Wilson's high-mindedness mesmerized Europe at first. On the train to Saumur, David had seen a bizarre example of that special American genius for fusing idealism and practicality, which the president personified. "As we passed thru Nantes," he wrote, "the streets were crowded with people, gazing at a U.S. airship, sailing serenely like a huge bubble in the sky, from which were being thrown copies of President Wilson's latest note to Germany."[42] The appeal of Wilsonian idealism soon faded, as jockeying for territory came to the fore. French negotiators openly hammered the proposed League of Nations into a blunt instrument to punish Germany in perpetuity. At the signing even

Marshal Foch would say, "This is not a peace treaty, it is an armistice for twenty years."[43]

That spring the hotels of Paris burst at their seams. Every nationality in Europe and beyond was represented by a contingent, including all of the newly liberated peoples of Central Europe. Serbs and Koreans, Poles and Bessarabians, Ho Chi Minh from far-off Indochina, and fierce desert Arabs championed by the visionary Colonel T. E. Lawrence thronged the sidewalk cafés. One American recalled that "around the edges of the recognized delegations hovered all sorts of adventurers peddling oil concessions or manganese mines, pretenders to dukedoms and thrones, cranks with shortcuts to Utopia in their briefcases, secret agents, art dealers, rug salesmen, procurers and pimps. *Petites femmes* solicited strangers on the boulevards with scraps of all the languages of Europe."[44]

When he reached Paris, David found lodgings on the rue Dulac near the Montparnasse station. He was lucky: Eleanor Roosevelt was there with Franklin on Navy Department business and said "people wander the streets unable to find a bed."[45] When the owner of the house in the rue Dulac, a poor but haughty widow of a Louvre curator, demanded references, David flippantly gave the president's name. For meals he relied on the ubiquitous Red Cross canteens, "the most perfect piece of social machinery, in my opinion, the world has ever known."[46] He discovered only after settling in that the Sorbonne's professor of international law was too busy advising the diplomats to hold class as scheduled.

Worse, in his own exaggerated words, David almost "died of loneliness" in the City of Light, an improbable fate for one already steeped in French history and literature. He disliked solitude and never more than as a forlorn young American in Paris. "Wretched" was how he described himself. In his battery he had had the company of many Marylanders, a few of them Baltimore friends, including one of his cousins. But on his own, loneliness threatened to spoil everything. His spirits soared when three American soldiers invited him to share their flat on the rue St. Jacques opposite the Sorbonne. The kindness of his brother officers made all the difference to his enjoyment of the capital. They were his brother officers because right after arriving in Paris he learned that he would be commissioned a second lieutenant after all.[47]

"To an aesthete," he exulted, "there can be nothing more delightful than the thousand and one graces that [Paris] reveals to him in a thousand and one distinct and unexpected places. . . . I have drunk deep of the solid, external beauty of this enchanting place."[48] He wrote these words after he had been in the capital for a week. He dismissed tourists as neck-craning geese with lorgnettes, clutching their Baedeker guidebooks and returning home thinking they had seen the real Paris, but he did all the touristy things too. His schoolboy reading about the France of Dumas and Hugo, of Richelieu and Marie Antoinette, primed him for the experience, and his generous streak of romanticism blossomed into vigorous, luxuriant growth. "Oh! these days in Paris," he exclaimed, "where instead of smoke and superheated air, one breathes a waft of history and art at every corner and the very breezes whisper a story."[49]

He took in the expected sights: Notre-Dame, the Luxembourg gardens, St. Germain des Prés, and all the other architectural gems he had read about. To brighten his apartment he brought back roses and honeysuckle from the garden of Malmaison, home of Josephine Bonaparte. He laid flowers on Lafayette's grave. The stained-glass splendor of Sainte Chapelle predictably dazzled him.[50] Like Henry James's protagonist in *The Americans*, that genteel connoisseur who acquired "an aesthetic headache" from viewing canvases in the Louvre, David said he felt "almost satiated with beauty" after pacing the long corridors of pictures.[51]

Excursions to St. Cloud and Fontainebleau quickened his fascination for the finery of high French material culture.[52] It was, as yet, an eclectic, undigested jumble of interests that would take time to sort out. For the moment he could be as captivated by the medieval as the baroque. Near his apartment was the Hôtel de Cluny, where the abbots "spent their days in prayer and service and their nights in genuflection and flagellation." Inside, he said, "like a magnificent pageant unroll the stories of the Flemish tapestries, the wood carving, the suits of armor." Just as easily he could jump the centuries in either direction. Outside his flat "sometimes at night there is a tramping of horses' feet in the Rue St. Jacques and one waits to see the Imperial Arms go by or Marshal Ney's squadrons crash along, but instead it is a troop of those no less devoted and splendid soldiers — the dragoons of France."[53]

In the Bastille district, an old house caught his eye. "It requires only a bit of imagination," he said, "to people it with silk stockinged, knee-ribboned seigneurs and lace-flounting grandes dames. . . . A useless, proud, selfish race, no doubt, but an aristocracy which served its turn and played its part, whether in drawing-room or on battlefield." On second thought, he went back and crossed out the word "useless."[54]

While he was superficially soaking up culture, tensions that had festered during the war erupted in civil unrest. He showed little interest, save a passing mention. "I have been told, confidentially," he wrote, "that there have been several socialist outbreaks here recently which have been settled after much bloodshed but of which no news has appeared in the papers. The French understand thoroughly how to suppress Bolshevism."[55] It was a time when, the radical writer John Dos Passos said, "some people caught socialism the way others caught the flu."[56] But not David.

On the other hand, the army gave him an unexpected lesson about race. As a boy he had been taught a patronizing sense of noblesse oblige. When he learned from home of an incident at Staunton Hill, he instinctively denounced Klansmen who had threatened a Bruce servant. "No body of people except a set of churlish cowards," he wrote with patrician disdain, "would threaten a helpless and defenseless old colored man."[57] But in Paris he learned that blacks were not simply passive objects of charity. He asked his mother to "tell Mammy. . . . There are several colored soldiers at the Sorbonne."[58] "The African troops," he wrote of the French army, "have won a tremendous reputation. The same is true, in a lesser degree as yet, of the American Negroes. It seems to me that when they return home after their struggles to make the world safe for democracy, they might rightly require greater democracy & justice to themselves in their own country."[59]

David's uncle by marriage, the writer Thomas Nelson Page, was then ambassador to Italy. His second marriage into the Field family of Chicago enabled him to afford the appointment's expense. He came to Paris briefly that spring and treated his nephew to breakfast at the Crillon Hotel overlooking the symbolic heart of France, the Place de la Concorde. The Crillon basked in the world's attention, as diplomats disposed of the future of Europe in the lounges and corridors as much as at the formal talks at the foreign ministry. The experience gave David a glimpse of a far different world from Red Cross canteens and the artillery mess.

The United States delegation in Paris included every young diplomat who could concoct an excuse to be present at what has been called "America's geopolitical coming-out party."[60] These included the future leaders of the foreign policy establishment for the next generation, among them William Bullitt, Adolf Berle, Christian Herter, and the Dulles brothers.

To be in Paris then, however, was more than the chance to witness diplomats dismantle empires and ratify a flawed peace. It was to breathe the same air as writers and artists at the giddy beginning of *les années folles*, the start of the Lost Generation. Walter Lippmann, Dorothy Thompson, and John Dos Passos were there as journalists. Gertrude Stein, Ernest Hemingway, and Ezra Pound were already busily and more or less consciously creating their literary legends. Other Americans too, like the Ohio heiress whose salon became a focus of Left Bank lesbian and poetic circles, added to the intrigue of expatriate Paris. Sylvia Beach's bookstore Shakespeare & Company was one center of the literary scene. David would recall, "She was a picturesque figure when I first went to Paris, passionately interested in literature and people. . . . I admired her and her glamorous Bohemian friends at a distance but was not admitted to their circle."[61]

John Dos Passos has left us the best image of that spring in his kaleidoscopic novel *Nineteen Nineteen*. A part-time Virginian, Dos Passos was enrolled with David in the army-sponsored study program at the Sorbonne. Was it entirely coincidence, then, that in his novel he has a character go for a drink in the Brasserie Weber and afterward prowl through second-hand bookstores with "an artillery 2nd lieutenant named Staunton Wills who was studying at the Sorbonne"?[62]

David was not part of the intellectual community of Montparnasse, nor did he get beyond the periphery of the diplomatic delegation. But he shared with both groups the fantastic, unforgettable sensations of Paris that spring, an encounter that gave him a special comradeship with anyone else who was there, an example and a portent of his knack for being present at moments of high drama in Europe.

More than the monuments and the buildings, the Parisians themselves enthralled him, especially habitués of the Left Bank. "Last night, I dined in the basement of a café in the Latin quarter," he noted shortly after arriving, "where long-haired artists and short-skirted models were much in evidence. They were all insouciant and refreshing."[63]

Cabell Bruce's abandoned women of Plattsburgh could not compete with the temptations of Paris. James Thurber, like David a wide-eyed soldier turned loose in paradise that spring, wrote that "girls snatched overseas caps and tunic buttons from American soldiers, paying for them in hugs and kisses, and even warmer coin."[64] David replied with irritation to his parents' constant fretting over just such prospects. "If you would stop warning me against 'entangling foreign alliances,'" he retorted, "I should be ever so much obliged."[65]

Sitting at the little round marble-topped café tables along the avenues, whether at fashionable Fouquet's on the Champs Elysées or outside humbler bistros along the Boulevard St. Germain, sipping wine and watching the *beau monde* pass by, David imagined himself a sophisticated *boulevardier*. "The French café system should also be adopted by us," he enthused. "It is the most delightful, interesting and innocent method for passing the time which man has ever devised."[66] A first sampling of European pleasures did nothing to diminish this precocious young American's self-esteem. One of the things he learned about himself that year was that he was no ascetic. Ambrose Bierce, who described an abstainer as "a weak person who yields to the temptations of denying himself a pleasure," would have counted him among the strong. Grandfather Charles's sybaritic genes had skipped a generation, but they resurfaced in David with a vengeance.

In these pleasant reveries began his love affair with Europe. "I am inordinately proud of being an American," he said, "but one cannot be a good American unless he is conscious of his own shortcomings. . . . Europe has much to learn of the United States. On the other hand, the United States has much, very much, to learn from Europe. The nearer one approaches the heart of France, the more one loves that heart, and I have no doubt the same is true of other countries, a little decadent, a little mossy perhaps to a cursory glance, yet veined with a vast store of riches."[67] The romanticized view of France, its people, and its history that he acquired that summer would powerfully inform his reaction to future threats to peace in Europe and, indeed, would stay with him as long as he lived.

Neither the academic climate of the Sorbonne nor the hedonistic pleasures of the Rive Gauche were enough to satisfy his appetite for adventure and novelty very long. He toyed with the idea of going to newly independent Poland, then locked in combat with the Red Army. "I feel so impotent," he said, "sitting still and doing nothing. Look at Poland! In the midst of their own troubles, her patriots found the time and inclination to help us in our war of independence, but now that she is warring successfully for her own independence she has found few volunteers from the republic across the seas."[68] He realized the idea was impractical as long as he wore a uniform. In mid-June, though, another opportunity arose that promised almost as much excitement.

Before World War I, American diplomats relied on informal, haphazard expedients to send dispatches. In 1918, the Army Courier Service was created using junior officers to carry documents between the Paris conference and embassies and legations across the Continent. Thanks to the lucky timing of his commission and to fellow Princetonian and future spymaster Allen Dulles, already dabbling in international intrigue, David joined this service in June. He acquired a *passeport diplomatique* that opened all of Europe to him and gave him his first taste of diplomatic life. He did not think it would last long because everyone expected the peace conference to end soon. The treaty with Germany was indeed signed with Gallic theatricality in the Hall of Mirrors at Versailles on June 28, five years to the day after the assassinations at Sarajevo. But because no settlement had yet been reached with Austria-Hungary, the need for the fledgling courier service continued through the summer and gave David three more sublime months of discovery on Uncle Sam's expense account.

The Great War destroyed the ancient empires of Central Europe and created in their place a host of new nations supposedly based on ethnic lines. Even before Versailles a series of vicious conflicts among these successor states vindicated cynics in their belief that fine Wilsonian notions of self-determination were no vaccine against war. On the night of the armistice, Churchill had said to Lloyd George, "The War of the Giants has ended; the quarrels of the pygmies have begun."[69] In the new age of democracy, irredentist claims of neighbor against neighbor embroiled nations in war as easily as the entangling alliances of the old order. David's orders took him into this turbulence at a time when Slovenes and Austrians were fighting over their common border and Rumanians and others were attacking the Communist regime of Béla Kun in Hungary. Borders drawn on a map by diplomats could not resolve age-old ethnic antagonisms: for every district added to one state, so much was taken from its neighbor. David would have a chance to see the consequences up close. "In drawing boundary lines," he said even before he knew he would be going to the Balkans, "one should consult not only the geological conformation of a country but the passions of the peoples."[70]

He found to his delight that his diplomatic papers conferred first-class, deferential treatment from fawning bureaucrats wherever he went: "Soldiers of every army gladly assist you, consuls, ministers and ambassadors consult your comfort, and *surtout,* mirabile dictu, train officials and porters bow before your passport. I never had such a gorgeous time in my life." And again: "I love this life. It seems as if my dreams were coming true."[71] He left Paris four days after transferring to the courier service, not on the cattle cars or clapped-out passenger coaches reserved for the field artillery, but aboard the fabled Simplon Orient Express. Linen tablecloths in the dining car and a menu that brought to mind the opulence of the Crillon now replaced the Red Cross canteen.

The line of travel carried him through the Swiss mountains and down to the Adriatic, before going on to Bucharest and other points east. The cosmopolitan mix of his fellow passengers set the tone: an Italian businessman, a Serbian officer, a Rumanian courier, an American stationed in Montenegro, and an Armenian bound for Istanbul. He learned about the instability of Central Europe as he listened with rapt concentration to two Hungarians explain why they were on their way to fight the Bolsheviks in Budapest.

Another mission took him to Istanbul — he insisted on calling it Constantinople — where the allure of the East seduced yet another impressionable Westerner. The din of the bazaar, a babble of tongues hawking fragrant and exotic wares, captivated him: "The red fez with the black tassel," he rhapsodized, "turbans of all descriptions, soldiers of all races, bearded Persians with heaps of rugs thrown over their shoulders . . . cafés where there is card playing, drinking and water pipe smoking, men sleeping in gutters or on arches, women peeping through grates . . . stores loaded with the riches of the Orient, domes of mosques, blue of the sky rivalling blue of the water, the flag of the crescent and the star, moneychangers, matchsellers, frail barks, men o' war, dirt and filth undescribable."[72]

Social faux pas — boarding a streetcar reserved for women and failing to remove his shoes at a mosque — taught him to be sensitive to cultural differences. One of the developing benchmarks in his notion of right conduct was having a sense of style and knowing how to comport himself. His self-deprecating letters home recounting these gaffes belie the value he increasingly placed on knowing the proper form. Earlier, at a dance for servicemen hosted by a Paris women's group, he looked with distaste on the boorishness of his peers. "The mothers seem to regard us as strange, amusing, harmless animals. And, I must confess, it must have seemed strange to them to see our soldiers sauntering around the ball room with their hands in their pockets and cigarettes in their mouths. Some of our university graduates do not hesitate to chew tobacco under the very eyes of their professors, and, add to similar habits, a love of noise and a readiness for any lark, together with the fact that America is still regarded as only half-civilized by the Continentals, and one could see why Europeans thought as they did."[73] David was determined that no one would ever regard *him* as half-civilized.

The frequent letters he sent to Baltimore revealed his growing fascination with Europe and his parents' unhappiness that he continued to find ways to delay coming home. He knew he was being given something that money could not buy. "I wonder if you know what this experience means to me," he wrote. "Every minute of it is precious. If there is any good in me, this education will heighten it." He sensed that "the weapons to power lie in an intelligent taking advantage of such an experience as I am now having."[74]

He still spoke naively of missing combat, but he knew the value of the courier service. On the train from Bucharest "there was also a charming Roumanian courier aboard, only twenty-three, decorated several times for bravery. I feel like a fool when I see so many men of my age or only a little older who have seen so much of war and life while I have seen so little . . . [but] I never had so much fun and education in all the rest of my life together."[75] Europe was an epiphany and a narcotic. David shared the sense of being at a critical divide. "We are about to pledge ourselves to look beyond the confines of our own wide borders and to contribute to the guidance and police of the whole world," he wrote. "National distinctions, prejudices & jealousies have always existed and, no doubt, always will exist. They are inherent and natural, but they should not prove an insurmountable barrier to an universal entente cordiale. We are indeed living in a most interesting and epoch-making time, and, at present, Paris is the centre of history."[76] And the transcendent, vertiginous experience of being there that spring and summer would stay with him always.

He had an unrivaled vantage point for observing the birth of the world order that would govern his early adult life and for reflecting too on the defects of Versailles that led to later grief. For him and for others of his class — the East Coast elite — familiarity with Europe bred not contempt but abiding affection. For them Europe was not a foreign place. That simple fact put him and them at odds with the majority of Americans. In spring 1919 it was an unimportant distinction but would not always be so.

Two and a half years in uniform only increased the restlessness that possessed him at Princeton. The twin elements of his letters — his deepening, romanticized love of Europe and disputes with his parents over his future — defined the themes of his life for the next years. The omens were not good for family harmony. He once told his mother sardonically, "I am glad that Father is mapping out my future. I hope that his plans coincide with mine."[77] When he blithely dismissed his father's demanding cables — "I insist that you come home with your division," Cabell Bruce bellowed in one of them — all the parties knew the stage was set for family discord.[78] His mother's main worry, he knew, was for his safe return. His father's concern, however, posed a greater threat: Cabell wanted his son to follow his footsteps into the law and, indeed, into his own firm. David knew that as soon as he returned home his room for maneuver would be severely constricted.

CHAPTER 3

On a Holiday Excursion

Young David has dallied a while along the primrose path, tasting the rarer
sweets of life, deftly foiling the attempts of his guardian angel to hurry him
to righteousness, peace and an ordered life.

— A Baltimore journalist's assessment of David Bruce
made in 1924

AMERICA SOBERED UP QUICKLY from the euphoria of
Armistice Day. Recession in 1919 marred the first, stumbling efforts to
retool for peacetime. The Red Scare, sparked by overreaction to anar-
chist bombings, culminated in the mass deportation of radicals. The
young J. Edgar Hoover headed up a new unit in the Justice Department
to monitor subversives. In July a bloody race riot in Chicago inaugu-
rated a summer of lynchings. Disillusionment with foreign affairs
peaked that fall when David Bruce returned home. In September a
haggard President Wilson crossed the country to promote the League
of Nations. A stroke cut short his whistle-stop tour, and the Senate
killed the League treaty in November.

When David reached America, he still wore his second lieutenant's
bars. Orders sent him to San Francisco for demobilization, with a
stopover in Chicago. Cocksure from his first exposure to Europe, he
dismissed Midwesterners for their obsession with work: "Everyone . . .
seemed to be living at high tension. They were rushing to their offices,
rushing to their meals, to their homes, and even to their entertainments." "The contrast between American and European business con-

ditions which is most obnoxious to me," he declared, "is that of our mania for hurry with their mañana attitude."[1]

The desert Southwest did not impress him, but California, still a generation before it became America's future, did. When he received his honorable discharge at the Presidio, he looked out beyond the Golden Gate toward the dun-purple hills of Marin County and toyed with the idea of living there. It was a fleeting notion, on a par with his undergraduate fancy for the mission fields and his desire to fight Bolsheviks in Siberia. In three weeks he was at the University of Virginia to study law, a provisional capitulation to his father, one in a series of tactical retreats in a personal war he intended to win.

Earlier that year at Bordeaux University, he stopped devouring French literature long enough to send his parents a letter that revealed his thoughts about returning home. There was, he said, one thing that money could not buy, "an old family place that is certain to influence for the best any one who lives on it."[2] He was thinking about Staunton Hill, of course, and his goal of setting up there as a country gentleman, surrounded by his library of European classics, his escritoire, and his inherited sense of place. His little red volume recorded more than 400 titles added since Christmas 1911, but on returning from the army, he gave up keeping track with a terse final entry confirming that "French books 125 Vols" shipped from Bordeaux had arrived. The prospect of a cultivated lifestyle, mixed with a generous dose of gentry field sports, and no need to work for a living, fit his developing self-image as a gentleman of civilized tastes. It was a daydream. The Bruces were prosperous but not that well off.

Before he was forced to face this hard fact, the dream vanished abruptly when he learned that his father intended to sell Staunton Hill. In Cabell's mind, financial drain finally outweighed sentiment. David unhappily rationalized the loss and declared that "the old Southern life is almost dead, because people no longer care anything for a cultured existence but prefer to concentrate themselves in large cities for the unhealthy excitement of moneymaking." Better to forget it, then, and look to the future. "Let us bury Staunton Hill with the past," he wrote, shifting gears with the supple ease of youth. "Sell the place by all means, but sell it as a whole. Do not lop off the trees and divide the plantation into lots. Staunton Hill is an ideal rich man's fancy. *Cherchez* the rich man."[3]

His future course was still a muddle. He needed to square the conflicting impulses that filled his head — egalitarian ideas left over from the Princeton revolt and army service in the ranks, the allure of European high culture, unease over a career at law, and the continuing tug of identity with the Virginia gentry ideal that did not die with the sale of Staunton Hill.

At his father's alma mater, David took up residence at 18 East Lawn, a favored room in the colonnaded, Palladian "academical village" designed by Thomas Jefferson. His roommate was Braxton Cameron, a cousin of John Dos Passos. David declined to return to Princeton and never completed his undergraduate degree. Whether he went to Charlottesville to please his father or because it offered the appeal of genteel Virginia is unclear. In any event, for a time he became a familiar figure striding across the Lawn, as the campus is called, wearing his favorite outfit, golfing plus fours.[4]

Like returning servicemen everywhere, he found it a hard routine. After enduring army discipline for two years and then roving across Europe, he knew the scholar's cloister was not for him — not even at Virginia, still, as in Poe's day, "the most idealistic and most dissolute college in America."[5] His irritation showed in a sarcastic closing to a letter home: "Best love to all, Your devoted 22yr. old son, David. Big Boy Now."[6] Cabell only inflamed matters when he scolded David that he was not "on a holiday excursion, or simply to work off the restlessness with which you have been more or less possessed ever since you came back from Europe."[7]

That restlessness was aggravated by David's fondness for tobacco. "Every smoker knows," he said in a fanciful essay, "that the brain is whetted, the tongue loosened, and the invention rendered fantastic by the stimulus of tobacco. As one exhales a cloud of smoke and watches its currents and eddies, the imagination goes a-journeying to far countries, and the work-a-day world fades to a distant shore."[8] But forty cigarettes a day did more than tickle his imagination. "Your health will infallibly suffer," Cabell cautioned him. "I am very nervously constituted. So is your mother. So is James. So are you. . . . tobacco used at all to excess is simply a poison."[9] But David was having none of it, not Cabell's advice on smoking and not the straitjacket of Charlottesville.

Five months of torts and contracts were all he could bear. He withdrew from school in April 1920 without completing any credits and dashed back to Europe. His pretext — assignment as a special reporter for the Baltimore *Sun*. Cheap fares and a robust dollar put the Continent at his feet. He sailed on the mail steamer *New York* and joined his oldest friend, army buddy Macgill James, who was already abroad, for an idiosyncratic Grand Tour. After a month in Britain, they flitted through Paris, Berlin, Prague, Vienna, Venice, Florence, Rome, Madrid, and North Africa too.

The *Sun* published a conventional, upbeat account David wrote about democracy in Czechoslovakia. The new hybrid nation, he said, possessed "the soundest economic and political future of any country in Central Europe, provided, of course, that it is unmolested by any rapacious power." A more original piece came from a visit to Ireland in the midst of the Troubles.

Britain still nominally ruled, but Sinn Fein, the republican insurgency, held sway most places outside Dublin and Ulster. Aware of the danger, David and Macgill armed themselves in London beforehand. It was a silly gesture. The hard men on either side would have made mincemeat of these two American dandies brandishing their puny, silver-topped malacca swordsticks from Wilkinson's. As it was, they nonchalantly sauntered down the twisting rural lanes, between high hedges covered in wild fuchsias ideal for concealing gunmen in ambush. In Limerick, where their hotel room exuded the "air of past gentility" and reeked of cabbage, they watched a British patrol in action out in the streets where rebels had just killed three soldiers.[10]

David talked to partisans on all sides of the "sacral nationalism," as Conor Cruise O'Brien has described the passions that ate at Ireland, and he condemned terrorist violence, interference by America, and feeble attempts at Westminster to legislate a solution. With the insurgency triumphant nearly everywhere, he wrote, "the British Parliament is debating a bill which meets the satisfaction of no party, and whose application to this country has been aptly compared to that of a poultice to a volcano."[11] He recommended Dominion status, something pristine nationalists rejected the next year but that saner Irish patriots accepted — minus Ulster. His essay took a measured, undogmatic approach, sensitive to the aspirations of the factions, and aware of the ancient prejudices that hemmed in all parties on every side.

Here was an early precursor of the reflective cables that would become the stuff of State Department legend, eloquent, a bit old-fashioned in style, but distinctive and clear in analysis. It also showed his care for precision in language and dislike of editorial tinkering. When he sent the essay home, he said, "I do not want it published if it is altered in any material way."[12] When his uncle, Philip Bruce, peering through his professorial pince-nez, read his nephew's article, he exclaimed, "Every hope that I have of family distinction, in the next generation, is embarked upon David."[13]

Even more revealing than its inspiration for his writing, the trip confirmed David's willing surrender to the seductions of haute cuisine, wine, architecture, theater, and literature that first enticed him the year before. Free of army constraints, he indulged himself unstintingly. Back in Paris, he exulted, "I felt I had entered Heaven."

He and Macgill dined at the Escargot d'Or, "an excellent and euphonious name, fragrant of promise. As soon as we sat down, we began to cherish an affection for the place. It is a den, a lair of gourmets. . . . one loses all sense of time and place. The appetite . . . forbids application or thought to any other subject than anxiety over the appearance of the next dish." Finishing with a bottle of Chambertin and *fraises des bois* — wild strawberries smothered in cream — he agreed contentedly that "those old philosophers who placed the seat of the affections in the stomach had strong provocation."[14]

Mornings were less energetic, given over to recuperating from the previous night's excesses. Usually, he said, we "take our chocolate in the morning at the Hub of the Universe — the Café de la Paix. Like a cinema which never ends and never repeats."[15] This was a part of the Parisian day that captivated him, too, like the expatriate who extolled "an awakening Paris . . . the rumble of carts and hoofs over the cobbles, the imperialism of small shopkeepers annexing the sidewalk for their displays, the little tobacco shops where one may purchase a single cigarette, the *bistros,* the chauffeurs and *ouvriers* stopping in for a morning drink on their way to work, the flower vendors, the kiosks with the world news flaming at one in headlines, the rapidly filling cafés and café terraces, the ubiquitous *pissoirs.*"[16]

No other city could match Paris in David's esteem, but he happily sampled what others had to offer. He liked Berlin despite its austerity and thought Vienna gracious, the Czech capital beautiful, but Rome sadly disappointing. The decayed glory of Venice enchanted him. "The sky was blue — ultramarine as only the sky can be above the ocean. A half-moon was hung in it, as if suspended from heaven by a careful hand. St. Mark's gleamed softly in the silver sheen, an unbelievable structure, dreamed of opium and created by swift magic of genii and fairies. The four bronze horses, returned from their exile in Rome, stretch out toward the piazza, each with eager foreleg upraised." He fancied himself more sophisticated than other travelers: "Met two American girls last night [at the Uffizi museum in Florence]. They spoke no language except English. Consequently, their method of paying a taxi driver was to hand him money until he smiled. . . . They acquired three cheap madonnas yesterday, and expect to purchase the remainder of the Holy Family today."[17]

The former doughboys made their way down the Italian coast and crossed the sea to Tunis, which to David's eye had a magical quality. A "city white and dazzling," he called it, "with mystery in the air at night. As soon as one sets foot on African soil, the so-called real ceases to exist — anything seems possible."[18] They mused about ancient history at Carthage, took a train to Algiers and its teeming kasbah, and then, deciding by the flip of a coin, sailed on a tramp steamer to Tangier instead of Port Said.

Morocco offered more of the mysterious, slightly sinister intrigue that David expected to find in North Africa. It would be a few more years before Tangier took on the identity that writer William Burroughs gave it of a "fevered, fictional, drug-inspired evocation of the boom town year of Sodom-on-Sea." But even before the Great War, the city had a reputation for raffish decadence and for that reason was already a familiar stopping place on the tourist route. "Almost any thirst could be assuaged," wrote a journalist, "boys or pubescent girls of half-a-dozen races were two-a-penny."[19]

After a cryptic reference of his own to dancing girls in the town and avaricious merchants in the bazaar, David said he and Macgill retreated to a garden overlooking the sea. After mint tea, their guide suggested that they smoke hashish, with the promise that "one pipe make you hungry, two make you laugh, three make you drunk." David suspected that whatever the Moroccan gave him was adulterated because "although we smoked six or seven pipes apiece, its only effect was to make us hungry."[20] On the day he left North Africa, he pronounced Tangier, with the exception of Paris, "the most interesting city we have yet visited."[21]

A long, slow trek through Spain — the Alhambra, Toledo's cathedral, Goya's ogre paintings at the Prado, and a grisly bullfight that Hemingway would have adored — brought them by roundabout paths to Paris again. Entering the city, David rejoiced, "Paris at last — same queer feeling — my heart in my throat." At the Folies Bergère, he exclaimed, "some of the actresses appeared absolutely nude from the waist up. . . . Montmartre at night — great champagne revels — the gayest spot in the world." Nightclubs, the Comédie Française, the Opéra, and tiny, avant-garde Left Bank theaters all vied for his attention.

He scrimped on expenses during the day in order to dine repeatedly at La Tour d'Argent, where, he believed, "cooking is carried to perfection." In that setting, with its spectacular view of the flying buttresses of Notre-Dame, he gave himself up to the pleasures of food and, especially, of wine brought up lovingly by the sommelier from deep, vaulted cellars. (Expansive and generous, he even made a small loan to the wine steward to help him set up in business for himself.) From the cheap champagne and *vins ordinaires* he and his army pals had quaffed the year before, David graduated to an appreciation of some extraordinary wines indeed — his favorite Burgundy (Chambertin), the *grands crus* of Bordeaux, champagne from Pol Roger, and finally, the rich, luscious, intense sauterne of Château d'Yquem from the great vintages of the turn of the century.

He and Macgill walked through the Loire Valley, dazzled by its châteaux — Blois, Chaumont, Amboise, Azay-le-Rideau, Chinon, Loches. Chenonceaux, he thought, looked "from a distance like [a] palace reared by Merlin's enchantments." He approved of the owner's care of the estate. "I would not begrudge him ten times his fortune. That is the true way to administer vast wealth, to expend it on the giving of happiness. Lovely paintings, tapestries, cabinets, chests."[22] Most tourists would have been satiated after viewing a fraction of the

French renaissance that David eagerly did that summer. But for this precocious twenty-two-year-old, there would never be enough.

Sailing home aboard the *Lorraine,* while below in steerage emigrant families dreamed of a new life in America, in first class David gaily diverted his dinner companions — a pianist, a Fifth Avenue dressmaker, and a dancer at the Paris Opéra — with tales of his travels. He arrived in New York with twelve cents in his pocket.

In the autumn he submitted to another restless year of study, this time at the University of Maryland law school, where he earned satisfactory grades with the ironic exception of a failure in international law. In spring 1921 he escaped once more to Europe, once more with a journalistic pretext. Before he imbibed the pleasures of Paris again, he toured northern Europe, where upheavals to the east sent tremors rippling through Scandinavia. Intrigued by the turmoil in Russia, he visited bits of the tsarist empire that had broken free during the civil war and wrote more articles for the Baltimore newspaper. Cabell Bruce worried that his son was burdening the paper with too much copy, but the editor found it compelling and said he would print as much as David sent him. Cabell beamed.

On the Soviet Union, David remained true to his class. Revolt against Princeton tradition was one thing, red revolution quite another. The tsar, as his cousin the kaiser once remarked, may have been fit only to live in the country and grow turnips,[23] but he did not deserve to be shot to death with his whole family in a cellar in Ekaterinburg. David interviewed refugees in newly independent Finland, people whose plights impressed on him the terror that communism had brought to Russia, which that summer suffered from famine induced by the poisonous mix of civil war and Leninism. He concluded that "men and women by the thousands, of all ranks and classes, with the faces of ghosts and the eyes of those who have looked on things which ought never to have been seen and can never be forgotten, do not flee with execration, with loathing and with horror from a country in which a humane government exists."[24]

In 1919 the chief gullible of the decade, Lincoln Steffens, set the tone for fellow travelers when he returned from the Soviet Union, winking at oppression, and cheerily declared that he had seen the future and it worked. David was never tempted by that dark utopia, which enthralled many of his self-styled enlightened peers. He ended his analysis with a warning that people should not delude themselves into thinking the Soviets were better than their enemies alleged. He questioned the value of foreign intervention, however, and the wisdom of subsidizing counterrevolution by émigré cliques endlessly plotting in the cafés of Paris. These efforts, he observed, only united the country against external threats: "Any change in Russia will come from within," from "one of the numerous 'little Napoleons' who are secretly building up their own political and military organizations."[25] At the time he wrote these words, Stalin quietly maneuvered in the shadows.

When David first arrived in Norway, he luxuriated in the knowledge that Europe once again lay at his feet, and he would be gloriously out of touch with home all summer. "A meteorite has no post office," a relative said of him. In Christiania, Copenhagen, Stockholm, Helsingfors, and Viborg he sought out refugees from the turmoil farther east as well as the natives and every minor American diplomat who would break bread with him. The former head of the tsar's palace guard, the Wallenberg banking family of Stockholm, foreign journalists, and members of "a Russian-Hungarian-German Monarchistic meeting which most European correspondents would have relished getting hold of" — all had a chance to be captivated by the inquisitive young American.[26]

In 1919 his uniform barred him from helping the Poles. By 1921 the Polish-Soviet War was over, and when he reached Warsaw, the Kosciusko Squadron, a group of American flyers who helped repel the Bolsheviks, had demobilized. Many of the pilots remained, though, and he struck up friendships with four of them. One was Merian Cooper, full of tall tales and authentic adventures after just escaping from a Soviet jail. He was later better known for producing the film *King Kong*, but in 1921 he and his fellow aviators personified the swashbuckling soldiers of fortune that David admired.

He returned home in the fall. He had felt the hot breath of adult responsibility on his neck before but had avoided the monster ever since his army discharge. He could avoid it no longer. He pleased his parents when he placed first in the bar examination in November 1921. After he was admitted to practice, the Baltimore city directory listed his father's law office with the title David had dreaded: "Wm. C. Bruce

& Son." The next year he escaped — marginally — to the city's leading firm, Semmes, Bowen & Semmes. To him the law was Dickensian drudgery, a life sentence in the copperplate prison of Jarndyce and Jarndyce. To his father's dismay, he did not settle down. His firm sent him on two business trips abroad, one to Ecuador, another, blessedly, to Paris. That was all the good, in his eyes, that came of his legal career.

At the University of Virginia he had devoted more energy to writing dramas and screenplays than cracking the law books. Now he began to dabble in writing essays and found an outlet for them in an obscure magazine published in the Virginia capital. Though venerating the mummified Lost Cause of the Confederacy was the chief pursuit of Richmond's inbred leading citizens — people who "embraced the dead thing with a passion they had never felt while it lived"[27] — the city also harbored unconventional literary talent. Emily Clark's journal *The Reviewer* published a wide range of writers, including the now-forgotten literati of New York. Clark's irreverence appealed to David, and he called her periodical "the most chic and charming and airy magazine in America."[28]

H. L. Mencken had inspired Clark to spark a literary renaissance that scorned the traditional sentimentality of southern letters. "The South produced nothing and reads nothing," Mencken sneered. "It is, culturally, about as dead as Yucatan."[29] Despite an idealized view of southern history, which Mencken also shared, David found Clark's iconoclasm appealing. He was still tugged in contradictory directions — Europhile aestheticism and devotion to a dead South on the one hand, literary irreverence and the rough democracy of the NCOs' mess on the other.

His tours of the manors of prerevolutionary nobles forced him to confront his ambivalence, if only briefly: "What a Paradise France must have been to an aristocrat in those days. With no business except that of being charming, it is no wonder they were a fascinating race. But one cannot talk even now with a French peasant without knowing that their ascendancy could never have endured. . . . The right of the individual to life, liberty and the pursuit of happiness is as deep rooted a conviction in the bosom of a Frenchman, as indestructible an essence of his life, as it is to every true American."[30] For a while he jettisoned his British-sounding middle initials. "David is going in very heavily now for democracy," Clark said in 1923, "he won't be called David K.

Este Bruce anymore, but just David Bruce."[31] At the same time, though, he could say disdainfully that Zelda Fitzgerald could "drink more than any woman he has ever seen, and is a trifle ordinary and Alabamian, but has brains."[32]

His essays imitated the hedonism of sophisticated writers and fantasized about the pleasures that wealth made possible. "I listen unmoved to a recital of the business exploits of the Rothschilds," he wrote, "but let mention be made of their cultivation of the Chateau Lafite vineyards, and a delicious languor, induced by past delights and future joys, to be derived from that source, bids me cry Hosannah on their name."[33] Clark told a friend he had chucked blue-blooded pretense and was going all out for democracy. It was egalitarianism of a decidedly pale, aristocratic hue, an option he examined, only to discard later for a perspective that suited him better.

Unlike his analyses of the foreign scene, David's essays were stilted. "I don't believe Mencken likes David's writing," Clark concluded. She rejected the first one he sent her: "it was horrid."[34] She eventually published five of them, though, in part because there was a chance he might provide financial backing for the magazine but even more because she was enchanted by the author himself.

His efforts produced only a mannered, belletristic froth. On champagne, for example, he wrote, "its effects incline one to be inconsequential, to indulge in badinage, to spin gossamer fancies, to engage in facetious sallies. Solitary topers disdain it, nor does it appeal to those of morose tempers. It has never been a monastic drink, it has never had a place at serious boards. But in the boudoirs and in the coulisses, in the monde and demi-monde, and in all places with intriguing and naughty French names it has no peer."[35] Still, his choice of subjects identified the things he valued most: three of his titles were "Tobacco," "Et Cetera and Wine Glasses," and "Random Reflections of a Gourmet." In the last of these, he argued that "food is, with the exception of sleep, perhaps the greatest necessity and pleasure of human existence."[36]

It was not all dead loss, though. Through Clark, he gained entrée to artistic New York at the dawn of its heyday. Manhattan had first intrigued him during trips from Princeton. Now he met the literary giants, members of the Algonquin Round Table before it acquired the name. Clark introduced him to Carl Van Vechten, novelist, aesthete, critic, and catalyst. One of *The Reviewer*'s most faithful contributors, the gaudy, shambling Van Vechten was described as "the dowager Chinese empress gone berserk" in his flowing silk robes. He championed the work of Gertrude Stein, experimental composers and artists, and the Harlem Renaissance.[37] His novels presented "a perverse and exotic comedy of manners in which restless sophisticates seek sensation and run from boredom."[38] No wonder that he and David got along so well, and no wonder that his parties on West 55th Street — in a house filled with antiques, Oriental carpets, malachite statues, and the owner's art photography — enthralled the younger man with their alcohol-soaked brilliance.[39] They sparkled with the unorthodox and the successful, the self-important and the genuinely talented. On the same evening David could find Gershwin playing the piano there, Paul Robeson singing, James Weldon Johnson reciting, and through it all, Theodore Dreiser brooding in a corner.[40]

At the same time he was nibbling around the edges of the flamboyant, sexually ambiguous literary avant-garde, David also gave a bow to more conventional pursuits: he entered the Democratic primary for the Maryland House of Delegates. With Cabell Bruce just elected to the United States Senate and with Cousin Howard Bruce managing the Democratic gubernatorial campaign, David enjoyed powerful advantages. He won the primary as one of six Democrats representing Baltimore's second district. In January 1924 he took his oath of office.

Annapolis was a Lilliputian village, with a skyline dominated by the wooden dome of the colonial statehouse and a nautical flavor conveyed by the United States Naval Academy on the edge of town. In this quaint setting David's youth did not set him apart — men under thirty held most of the urban districts — but his refusal to follow the path of deference expected in freshman delegates did. An internationalist in foreign affairs, he supported the League of Nations despite qualms about what his father called the "pale moonbeams" of "wobbly idealism" preached by his old nemesis Wilson.[41] When the former president died, David made a generous memorial speech in the General Assembly.

His primary interests lay in opposing the twin scourges of Prohibition and the Ku Klux Klan. A 1921 newspaper article he wrote in

Norway on Prohibition there showed his grasp of ridicule. "Deaths by poisoning among those who drink not wisely but too well are by no means unknown here. Some drinkers have discovered delicate sub-flavors in hair tonics, other connoisseurs are said to go into ecstasies, suggestive of delirium tremens, over cans of shoe polish, while a concoction known as 'sky jumper,' compounded of beer, naphtha, tooth powder and other ingredients is universally recommended."[42] Later he said that "nothing is more indicative of the modern revolt against elegance than the prohibition of alcoholic beverages."[43]

Early in the session he proposed a resolution calling on Congress to repeal the Volstead Act. He appealed to the state's origins as a Catholic colony in an age of religious bigotry, a heritage that should have disinclined Marylanders from curtailing personal liberties. On another occasion he chose less elevated words — "we've had too much in the way of moral uplift" — to express his distaste for Prohibition. When both houses passed his resolution, he earned a reputation as an "aggressive wet." Reporters for the Baltimore papers took note, and one spread the story that David's colleagues might back him for a seat in Congress.[44]

David also favored women's rights and introduced a bill "designed to remove certain unjust . . . antiquated, legal disabilities or discriminations to which the women of Maryland have long been subjected." Like law, however, politics failed to engage him for long. "The fact is, I don't know so much about politics," he blithely admitted. "Perhaps I will decide to learn. One can never tell."[45] But the give and take, the dispensing of patronage, the petty corruption, and the backstairs dealing that oiled state government and were the bread and butter of legislative careers bored him. Capable of making an eloquent argument against Prohibition and clever enough to see his measure pass both chambers, he also stepped over the line and was chastised for kidding the speaker of the house. One term in the legislature was enough for him.

A sympathetic observer pegged him as a bright but frivolous youth who took "politics and life more or less as a joke."[46] He admitted as much when he said that a term in the legislature would be "a sort of mid-winter frolic." His uncle, Philip Bruce, recognized David's restlessness and his talent. "Heaven did not endow you," he told his nephew, "with powers of expression and the quality of thought and fancy, simply that you might allow it all to ooze itself away into the dry sands of business or professional life." With that opinion David was entirely in agreement.[47]

Though bored by law and politics and drawn instead to literature and art, David was no alienated intellectual. Much as he liked to associate himself in later years with the literary expatriates, he was never consumed by rage against conventionality, never drawn to Dadaism or Surrealism or any other modish "ism." The difference was neatly captured in an account of one celebrated drunken revel of expatriate writers in Paris. At the symbolic height of their party, "they too had their moment of slaying the past by urinating on the collected works of Racine" — the very same plays and essays that David was avidly collecting.[48]

It did not occur to him even in his egalitarian phase to feel the slightest guilt because his hands were uncallused. Indifferent to proletarian culture, and drawn instead to the opulence of aristocratic France, he easily fit the definition of a frivolous reactionary in the eyes of the decade's earnest intellectuals, who were themselves besotted by the Soviet and Fascist experiments.

He revolted against his father's plans for him and against puritanism, not against capitalism or the good life that it made possible. A whimsical, stylish romanticism was the prime element of his rebellion. In collecting books he took a fancy to Henry James, who captured the essence of upper-class manners and the American abroad. David was even then nurturing a reputation for courteous demeanor — recall his praise for French aristocrats who had "no business except that of being charming" — that would prompt a friend later to say he had "better manners than anybody in Henry James even."[49]

He was enchanted by the exaggerated, mannered, and, even then, outdated society novels of Ouida (Marie Louise de la Ramée). Even before he returned home from the courier service, the strain of whimsy was well developed. "Athens is dazzling white," he said in 1919, "and one needs smoked glasses because of the glare. . . . The Acropolis is, of course, wonderful. I should like to live on the porch of the Parthenon."[50]

The sort of people he admired suggest the nature of his romanticism. A fleeting, platonic infatuation with a much older woman he had not even met provides the first exhibit. Amélie Troubetskoi, novelist and daughter of a Virginia diplomat, had been feted in London society.

Oscar Wilde introduced her to her future husband, a Russian painter, because, Wilde said, he was compelled to bring two such beautiful people together. "Passion is perfume and flame," the novelist wrote, "and is its own excuse and raison d'être. But half the married people one knows live in tepid mud."[51]

David also admired novelist Joseph Hergesheimer, not for his writing but for once having ostentatiously spent his last dollar in the world just to be in Venice. With equal extravagance David said, "That is the most perfect thing a man ever did, and if he had done it he would have shot himself when it was over."[52] He meant it only as an outrageous expression, but it eerily anticipated the suicide a few years later of Harry Crosby, the most flamboyant expatriate-hedonist of David's generation, who tasted all the sensualities of Europe and decided there was nothing more to live for.[53]

David's friends constituted a more varied palette than might be expected. Most of them were from his own class, of course, the narrow circle of upper-crust WASP Baltimore and other Eastern cities. Some had far more money than he — for example, Ronald Tree, a nephew of his Uncle Tom Page through the writer's second wife. As such, Ronnie was a beneficiary of the Chicago Field family's vast wealth, far beyond anything the Bruces commanded. But David was not a class snob as much as an aesthetic and intellectual one. His literary friends, Emily Clark and her book reviewer Hunter Stagg, have been described as "social misfits." Clark hobnobbed with the "best people" of Richmond but was excluded from their inner circle. She got her revenge by writing a series of wicked vignettes on the "stuffed peacocks" of Virginia society, a perspective that David said he "loved." Hunter Stagg, an alcoholic homosexual book critic subject to epileptic seizures, further defied convention. David thought him the cleverest of the *Reviewer* set and showed him around Baltimore even though Stagg turned up blind drunk at the christening of Macgill James's son.[54]

More unusual still were David's associations made through Carl Van Vechten. For all his decadent whimsicality, Van Vechten took a serious interest in the black intelligentsia of Harlem, and through him David did as well for a time. Slumming in Harlem may have been de rigueur for New York sophisticates, but it was unusual for a white southerner. Among his acquaintances was Langston Hughes, then at the beginning of his literary career. David was wildly enthusiastic about black musicians Taylor Gordon and Rosamond Johnson. At one of the interracial literary parties in Manhattan, where the guests included black poet and civil rights leader James Weldon Johnson, Van Vechten said, "David admitted frankly that he could not tell the blacks from the whites."[55]

A caricature drawn by a friend around 1921 captured David's state of mind.[56] Three figures are linked together in a procession marching to the left. The central one is David, head bowed. He is led by a ring through his nose attached to a leash held high by a flashily dressed debutante called "Society." His hands are shackled behind him to the third figure, representing grim sobriety and labeled "Law." A fourth figure in the background, walking in the opposite direction, is dressed like a Renaissance condottiere, sword at the ready, and labeled "Romance."

In 1920 David's Princeton friend F. Scott Fitzgerald burst upon the literary scene. With *This Side of Paradise* he became the premier interpreter of their generation and the unfolding decade. The novel was partly autobiographical, but David would tell people long after that the main character was a composite based on himself and another Princeton friend.[57] In his languid arrogance, Amory Blaine was indeed a fictional David Bruce bearing a striking resemblance to the original item. As much was apparent from Fitzgerald's description of Blaine as a "Romantic Egotist," oscillating between aristocratic vanity and scorn for artificial social barriers and conventions.[58]

Another writer saw in David "an abounding self-esteem, a consciousness of superiority, which brings in its train a certainty and an aloofness."[59] But David's was an unpremeditated arrogance, a superiority he bore with the confidence of his class at a time when young men of his background took it for granted that they were the elite.

It was an arrogance lightly borne. His ability to convey his intense, romantic enthusiasms to those around him and draw them to him made him an increasingly appealing figure. His Uncle Philip described his own wife as a "pleased victim" of David's winning ways and spoke of a fellow professor at the University of Virginia as a man "who suffers from one of the best cases of Daviditis of anyone I know."[60] David learned to focus intently on everyone he talked to, giving them undivided attention, making them feel they were the center of his interests.

It was rare in a person of his enthusiasms and energy, especially one so young, but he was beginning to develop the great gift of listening to others.

The Baltimore columnist who observed his superior attitude also used the same word as Emily Clark to describe David — "dilettante." He "poses fearfully," Clark observed. To Van Vechten, he seemed "an eighteenth century Virginia remnant that got mislaid."[61] For all that incipient charm, he was still too full of himself, a carefree, overeager, and self-absorbed young man. "Those who were lucky enough to be born a little before the end of the last century," said one of the expatriates, "went through much of their lives with a feeling that the new century was about to be placed in their charge."[62] In that expectation, David represented his peers precisely.

In May 1919, just as he was becoming intoxicated by Paris, he wrote his mother that Macgill James's parents should send him to France: "The most important thing is that he would be thrown for the first time in his life on his own resources. . . . he would, I feel sure, do something with his talents. Do not tell anyone I told you this. He will never work as long as he is in a place where he can speak English and has enough money to eat and play all day long. He does not know the value of money, and he is never going to work for it until he is forced to."[63] He might have been describing someone else. Youthful experimentation was well and good for a time but could not go on indefinitely.

CHAPTER 4

Ailsa

"Her voice is full of money," he said suddenly. That was it. I'd never understood before. It was full of money — that was the inexhaustible charm that rose and fell in it.

— F. Scott Fitzgerald, *The Great Gatsby*

$\mathcal{A}$S THE SURGING PROSPERITY of the twenties gathered steam, David's father joined the best club in Washington. Just before Cabell was elected to the Senate, former president Wilson warned that he was "incapable of loyalty" and "by nature envious and intensely jealous."[1] An increasingly conservative Democrat, Cabell felt right at home in the arcane customs of the Senate cloakroom during a Republican era. The Bruces sold 8 West Mount Vernon Place and began to divide their time between Washington and Louise's family estate at Ruxton, just north of Baltimore.

Still at loose ends, David gravitated to Washington. Neither his exiguous legal practice at Semmes, Bowen & Semmes nor his duties at the Maryland statehouse would demand much of his time. Washington, he thought, might offer more attractions than Annapolis or Baltimore.

The seat of government it may have been, but Washington was a modest capital, a middling southern town with a few grand buildings plopped down on the village green. But only a few. The ranks of museums that today march up the Mall were then unthought of. Before air conditioning, in the long, notoriously muggy summers that settle over the Potomac basin, the town's somnolent, southern quality was most tangible. The pace of life and of government slowed. People instinctively adjusted their motions to the increased languor, women in cotton dresses of bright floral prints, men in Panama hats and cream-colored linen suits.

In this modest setting, though, the diplomatic corps and a sprinkling of rich Washingtonians — who mainly had made their fortunes elsewhere but chose to display them in the capital — began to fill their embassies and houses with a social whirl of some international gloss. Publishers Ned and Evalyn McLean were wealthy parvenus in the sight of old Washington families, the "Cave Dwellers," but their New Year's Eve party became a lavish new tradition.[2] Charity balls proliferated. Polo matches gave military attachés a chance to shine. "Lent apparently holds no terrors for Washington's social organizations," one observer noted archly, "and though a few dances have been eliminated, dinners and informal dances continue with a vim."[3] The most fashionable precincts lay in the cluster of mansions that had sprung up along Connecticut, Massachusetts, and Wisconsin avenues. The Bruces' new house at 1640 Connecticut placed them in the center of things.

David fell in with a smart set, the "gilded throng" of Embassy Row, and the gossip columnists took note of him. He was, they agreed, one of the handsomest bachelors about town. Exactly six feet tall, he carried himself with an erect, confident stride that made him seem taller. He kept his chesnut-colored hair trimmed rather long on the top but always perfectly groomed, parted fashionably high, almost in the middle, and swept back to accentuate his strong, high forehead. "The love of self-adornment is a vanity peculiar to man," he wrote in 1924. It was a diversion he happily indulged in.[4] Even before his first trip abroad, he acquired a taste for the leading London shirtmakers. He often wore a gold collar bar that held his tie knot firmly at his throat and gave an air of control to his well-tailored attire. The picture of sleek, stylish, self-assured youth, he looked like he just stepped out of one of the soigné advertisements for Arrow shirts that defined twenties elegance. But the feature that people noticed most was those intense blue eyes, like the blue of a Maxfield Parrish illustration, radiating David's restless energy and increasingly winning charm.

Swanning about town, he turned heads just as he had begun to do before the war. One of his friends from Baltimore had been that vivacious opportunist Wallis Warfield, future Duchess of Windsor. He later recalled her as a "high-spirited girl, great to have around — in fact, the best company I knew."[5] At the University of Virginia, Philip and Betty Bruce noted the talent of their nephew, "that charmer David," to leave "piles of devastated hearts in his track."[6]

Emily Clark called him "the best looking man in the twenties, I think, that I have seen." Later she wrote mysteriously about ending "my wild experiment with him." Even so, she admitted that he seemed to her "really beautiful and thoroughbred to look at," forever trailing a string of debutantes chasing after him.[7] When his name was linked romantically with a divorced woman in Baltimore, the social elite arched its collective eyebrows. His parents breathed easier when his attention turned elsewhere.

On January 16, 1925, an entry in the marriage license column of the Baltimore *Sun* named David Bruce and a certain Regina Mellon. This tiny, two-line announcement might easily have passed unnoticed. Unfortunately for Louise and Cabell Bruce, it did not. The next day they faced the distasteful task of fending off reporters who camped out on their doorstep for some answers.

At first David's father blustered that it was all a mistake: "I don't know anything about it and I'm inclined to think my son doesn't either. . . . It's a private matter, anyway, and not a public one." Louise Bruce admitted it was a joke perpetrated by her son for reasons she would not explain.[8] The press confirmed that David had personally obtained the document from the Baltimore Marriage License Bureau, an early clue to the prankster's romantic aspirations. Despite the Bruces' reluctance to comment, Washington cognoscenti knew exactly who the woman in question was.

By the time of his little joke, at the dinner dances and embassy parties he attended, David had met the woman who became the object of his attentions and would for better and for worse change his life. Ailsa Mellon — not the fictitious Regina — came from a background of dazzling wealth that would soon come under intense scrutiny by the press. Anyone bold enough to contemplate marrying into such a family as the Mellons would find himself constrained by far more than the prying of journalists.

When the Republicans reclaimed the White House in 1920, Warren G. Harding offered the post of treasury secretary to Andrew W. Mellon of Pittsburgh. The sixty-six-year-old Mellon guarded his privacy so jealously that few people knew who he was. A thin, frail, desiccated man, with a mournful expression etched into his face, Mellon rarely smiled. When he did, it was a gesture without joy, "like a tired double-entry bookkeeper afraid of losing his job." Above all, he was possessed of a "measureless shyness."[9] In his subdued, elegant suits, the slight, reticent Mellon belied the stereotype of the loud, red-faced, corpulent archcapitalist. Yet through his control of aluminum, oil, copper, and banking, he was — after only Ford and Rockefeller — the richest man in America. Whether Mellon looked the part or not, the dark satanic mills and furnaces of Pittsburgh bore witness to the handiwork of this unknown financier.

In his early years his only interest had been the family bank. The richer he became, the more withdrawn. On a trip to Britain when he was forty-five, against all expectations he was smitten by love. Nora McMullen, the fiery daughter of an English brewing family, could not have been more unlike him. But it was just that vivacious difference that drew Andrew to her.

A year after they married in England in 1900, a daughter was born. Nora gave her the obscure Scottish name of Ailsa. Six years later the Mellons named a son Paul. By then Nora had sickened of Pittsburgh. She described Andrew's empire in the words of an incendiary Socialist. The workers, she said, were "all toilers in my husband's vineyard . . . working on the estate and adding to its wealth, but not recognized as part of it. The whole community spirit was as cold and hard as the steel it made, and chilled my heart to the core."[10] Her son later found it easy to empathize: "The belching flames of the steel mills and the coke ovens glowing in the deep Pittsburgh dusk," he wrote, "must certainly have seemed a prelude to hell."[11]

Adultery, not Pittsburgh grime, undid the marriage. Nora's indiscretions with an English bounder who enjoyed taking a rich cuckold's money led to an agreement to separate, then a generous divorce settlement and shared custody of the children. The problem did not end, however, in the civilized, well-funded parting that became the lucrative idiosyncrasy of so many later Mellon divorces.

Nora wanted sole custody of the children. When Andrew resisted, she said she would make Pittsburgh "ring with scandal" to get her way. Her lawyer threatened disclosures that would suggest Andrew had venereal disease and had procured an abortion for a unnamed young woman. "If the children suffered," Nora warned, then "they would have to suffer."[12] And so they did. Andrew was not the only one with a hard heart.

A vicious dispute led to charge and countercharge of kidnapping, wiretapping, and harassment. It was not just the obsession with balance sheets that led Paul to liken his father to John Galsworthy's tormented Soames Forsythe. The family that he described could not have been more wretched: "Poor Ailsa, then aged eight, needed someone to whom she could show her affections. There was I, aged two, who worshiped Ailsa, and there was Father, aged fifty-five, whose affections were much more difficult to predict. I do not know . . . why Father was so seemingly devoid of feeling and so tightly contained in his lifeless, hard shell. One always had the impression that deep in his psyche there was an unbounded sadness, a deep despair that it would have been death for him to realize or reveal."[13]

Before the courts decided their fate, Ailsa and Paul lived in a rented house with Nora. The pain inflicted on them when Andrew visited must have been intense. "Mother," Paul remembered, "had nearly always been in the room when Father was there with us and invariably made belittling remarks about him."[14] Andrew's friends sneaked a revision of the divorce law through the legislature to eliminate the jury trial that Nora wanted. She countered with hypocritical press releases. "Even in faraway England, someone managed to ask a question in the House of Commons about this reported ill-treatment of an Englishwoman abroad."[15] The court ruled that Nora had a right to her trial, but when Andrew agreed to alter the grounds from adultery to desertion, she waived that right, and a divorce was quietly granted in 1912.

"It was not much fun to be . . . the offspring of divorced parents in Pittsburgh," Paul remembered.[16] The process emotionally battered Ailsa. Once during the custody fight she had been "torn screaming hysterically from her mother's arms."[17] Her brother called the divorce "an ugly climax that cast a blight over Ailsa's life and mine."[18] They lived at first in a gloomy mansion in the suburb of East Liberty. Even when they moved to a more cheerful house, their uncommunicative father was still incapable of showing emotion toward the children he had fought so hard to keep. All they got from him was a dry, censorious remoteness.

They did see parental emotion when they lived with Nora, but it was not love or warmth or joy. She tried to poison their minds with a malicious torrent of ridicule directed against their father. Her efforts bore unintended fruit: both children eventually realized that the bitterness she attributed to her former husband consumed her as well.

Growing up, Ailsa enjoyed holidays abroad and a close circle of carefully selected friends. Her "deliberate, self-conscious diction," influenced by summers at a castle that her McMullen grandparents rented from the marquess of Salisbury, prompted American friends to call her prissy. Fastidious habits reinforced the image. Paul remembered her as being happy at times, though what that meant for a Mellon requires some interpolation. In retrospect, he noticed signs of melancholy after she went away to boarding school. The resilience of youth masked these problems, however, and Ailsa, like her father too, could be animated in small groups of people.[19]

Despite Mellon's dread of the duties of government service — the principal horror to him being public speaking — he accepted Harding's offer. He began to think Pittsburgh lacked scope for Ailsa and told her he agreed to move to Washington just for her sake. If that was not the whole truth, his decision did heighten her anticipation of the nation's capital, just as Cabell Bruce's election to the Senate did for David.

The cabinet secretary from Pittsburgh became a familiar figure walking in his chinchilla coat to his office at the Treasury, always smoking a cheap little cigar. He indulged a fondness for poker evenings at the White House, a conspicuously elegant player among Harding's crass Ohio cronies. The taciturn financier usually won.[20]

He was one of the strongest cabinet members of the decade. At the Republican convention of 1924, the only spontaneity came with an incongruous ovation for this "frail, gray-haired wisp of a man."[21] In his fifteen-room penthouse at the McCormick Apartments at 1785 Massachusetts Avenue, a block east of Dupont Circle, his Old Masters found a new home. For if Mellon read little, did not listen to music, and was indifferent to the theater, he had developed one interest outside work, and that was collecting art.[22] In a city that lacked a first-rank art museum, his paintings were the finest in town.

Surprising himself, Mellon discovered that he liked Washington social life. He especially enjoyed the dinner parties for a dozen or so that he and Ailsa planned with the help of Anna Randolph, one of the city's legendary social secretaries whose sister gave the same advice at the White House. If the appeal of an invitation to Mellon's table was the chance to see his pictures, even these fabulous Corots and Rembrandts could not overcome the host's shortcoming as a conversationalist. The flaw became more apparent after Calvin Coolidge succeeded Harding, and when Silent Cal dined with his treasury secretary, the two men "conversed almost entirely in pauses."[23] They were ideally suited. Franklin Roosevelt quipped that Coolidge "would like to have God on his side, but he must have Andrew Mellon."[24]

Ailsa performed competently as her father's hostess but never mastered the art of small talk, much less the sparkle of good conversation. People cruelly contrasted her with Theodore Roosevelt's daughter, Alice Roosevelt Longworth. Few could compete with vibrant, acidulous Alice, one of David Bruce's best friends in Washington, whom he admired for her "wickedly indiscreet" wit.[25] Ailsa's reticence invited speculation over how, as hostess sitting at Coolidge's left, she managed to get through those dinners. It did not occur to the speculators that the laconic president and the shy young woman may both have been relieved to have at one elbow a dinner partner who did not expect endless bright chatter.

The McCormick provided Ailsa every comfort. There was only one luxurious, 11,000-square-foot apartment on each of the five floors; the Mellons occupied the top one. Magnificent reception rooms, spacious servants' quarters, and a kitchen complete with walk-in refrigerator and, in the butler's pantry, walk-in silver vault, offered tenants a chance to entertain on a grand scale.

Ailsa's sanctuary was her corner bedroom, where she hung her favorite painting, Sir Joshua Reynolds's portrait of Lady Caroline Howard. This pensive little girl, wearing a bombazine cape over a white silk dress, sitting on the ground and touching a rose bush, could stand as a painterly surrogate for the person whose room she adorned.[26]

"Neither Ailsa nor Paul seems to fit into the state of affairs in Washington especially well," opined a society columnist, "nor do they relish the prominence given them when they would prefer to come and go unheralded." Gradually she opened up. "Quite astonished are Washingtonians at Ailsa Mellon's newly found verve and animation," gushed one gossip, "after the air of indifference to which the Capital has become accustomed."

She lacked for nothing. The papers tried to make her sound frugal by noting that she wore the same dress twice. In fact, she spent vast sums on clothes, thousands every month according to one report. About the time he met her, David wrote an essay that could easily have referred to Ailsa. "The toilette of a wealthy lady," he noted with mock sarcasm, "is compounded of refined delights. . . . The wonders of Cathay are woven for her whim, the European midinette is the hand-maiden of her caprice. . . . tradesmen of remote countries haggle in outlandish jargons over precious stones which will coruscate upon her breast."[27]

When she ventured out of the McCormick, her father's one-of-a-kind limousine, fabricated entirely of aluminum, was at her disposal. "It was not a particularly beautiful car," an admirer said, "being some-what angular, but obviously it was Mr. Mellon's car and traffic parted before it as the Red Sea parted for the children of Israel."[28]

When neighbors moved out, the word went round that Mellon would rent their apartment just for Ailsa: "She wants to entertain some friends from Pittsburgh and naturally she needs eighteen rooms and five baths for the purpose." "Now that she can stage her own affairs and can entertain at will," wrote a society reporter, "Ailsa's frown and anxious look have vanished." She and her cousin Olyve Graef indulged in amateur theatricals, but the obligations of her father's office limited her private parties. As an observer of the Christmas season of 1923 noted, "Ailsa Mellon has been, one might say, almost jerked out of her beloved environment and has taken the place of second lady in the Cabinet circle."[29]

The daughter of any cabinet officer would attract attention in the hothouse of Washington. When she was also joint heir to a fortune almost beyond calculation, her dance card was sure to be full. Ailsa was tall, slim, and darkly attractive. Her expression was more often one of earnestness than of frivolity, a demeanor that accentuated her aloof bearing. "Although she is very quiet herself," said a sympathetic ob-server, "she admires vivacity in others." She did not find it among Mellon's guests — Supreme Court justices, cabinet members, senators, and their wives, all of a much older generation. "Looking bored to extinction" was how one reporter described Ailsa.[30]

Her mother's nationality set tongues to wagging about a transatlantic match. Suitors included a British cabinet minister, a White House aide, a brace of military attachés at the British embassy, and Parker Gilbert, one of Mellon's men at the Treasury. When Gilbert denied rumors that he was about to become his boss's son-in-law, Mellon allegedly replied, "I don't know but I'd just as soon have you for one."[31] David Bruce called another suitor, Otto von Bismarck, grandson of the Iron Chancellor and future Nazi diplomat, a touchy young man, "highly educated, intense, with an unfortunate habit of focussing his conversation on you and then bedewing you through his somewhat separated front teeth."[32]

Another European briefly had better luck. Prince Gelasio Caetani, the new Italian ambassador, set social-climbing families to scheming for a title for one of their daughters. Although the prince was nearly fifty, "Washington chuckles quietly at his attentions to Ailsa Mellon." The Italians feted her at their embassy so often that people called it a crude attempt to ingratiate themselves with her father, who would have something to say about Italy's failure to pay its war debt. "If Miss Mellon suspects any other reason than her own personal charms," however, "she never betrays such knowledge."[33]

Her first impression of the prince stuck. At a dinner dance Mellon gave in honor of his new Italian neighbor, she complained that Caetani seemed indifferent to women and preferred instead to talk with men. "I was convinced," a reporter wrote, "that on this occasion the rather over-petted daughter of the Mellons nourished a genuine grievance."[34] And so Ailsa did not marry the handsome aristocrat and move to Fascist Rome.

She kept most of her suitors at a distance, in fact. "Ailsa is rather practical," said one observer, "and suspects all swains of fortune-hunting propensities." Her aloof bearing was on display at a 1925 New Year's Eve diplomatic party: "Ailsa seems to frown upon the foreign hand-kissing custom, and . . . few succeeded in her case. Miss Mellon's black velvet gown had sleeves almost to her fingers and were fur-trimmed, and she kept her hands firmly clutched around her corsage bouquet."[35]

She may have met David at a diplomatic reception. Another account says it was at a tea given by one of Ailsa's friends, another at a dance hosted by Senator and Mrs. Bruce. Whatever the occasion, a plausible family tradition says Louise Bruce encouraged the match with the acquiescence of Andrew Mellon. Certainly the Bruces and Mellon were well acquainted. As an independent-minded Democrat who felt at ease with Republicans, reserved Cabell Bruce found taciturn Andrew Mellon entirely agreeable company.

David's own recollections, made years later, reveal little. "I fell in love with Ailsa," he said. "In the latter part of 1925 I began to call on her frequently, especially after I had moved to Washington. . . . I [periodically] returned to my law office in Baltimore, but saw Ailsa as often as I could."[36]

His chronology was off a bit, for the relationship likely began earlier in 1925. At the start of the year she had signaled her disdain of pursuers: "The Mellon heiress does not permit herself to be exploited," oozed a society watcher, "and has firmly squelched the efforts of a group of aspiring young diplomats to give her a costume ball at one of the modish clubs."[37] Her rebuff did not discourage David: two weeks later he placed his joke marriage notice in the Baltimore paper. Gossips said he worked hard to woo her, taking her out to modest cafés away from the glitter of Embassy Row, a slice of ordinary life that was pure novelty to someone as cosseted as she had been.

Bored by routine, she was drawn to David and his contagious enthusiasms. During their long rambles in the parks, listening to his stories of Europe after the war, a Europe in his telling more romantic than she had known, she was captivated in a way no other suitor had managed. She had never before met a young man of her generation — he was three years older — who had read so much, who had seen so much, and who conveyed his enjoyment of life with such conviction.

The announcement of their engagement came fifteen months after David's hoax. On May 3, 1926, Mellon told the press his daughter would marry Senator Bruce's younger son at the end of the month. The announcement surprised those betting on flashier contenders. "Among countless Washington cavaliers who have paid court to Ailsa Mellon," opined one, "young Dave Bruce . . . seemed to the untrained eye the least conspicuous and the most resigned to his fate if the winsome heiress proved chilly. Yet he quietly slipped into high gear and carried off the prize."[38]

In Ailsa, David saw the same slim society beauty that everyone else did. He appreciated a fey sense of humor that occasionally peeked out from behind her Mellon reticence. And the aloofness that came with knowing who she was appealed to his equally lofty sense of himself. He accepted her boredom and haughtiness as challenges. Behind the appeals of physical attraction, of endearing quirks of character, and of shared interests in the fine arts, however, lay something else. As his college friend F. Scott Fitzgerald had just written in another context, "Her voice . . . was full of money — that was the inexhaustible charm that rose and fell in it, the jingle of it, the cymbals' song of it. . . . High in a white palace the king's daughter, the golden girl."[39] He had changed since the day, as an artillery sergeant in France, when he wrote to Ellen Keyser on the eve of her marriage to his brother, "I believe, with many other soldiers, that money and material success can be wholly forfeited without occasioning a single regret."[40]

The nuptials took place on May 29, 1926, a perfect day of blue skies and acclaim by the arbiters of high society for the most brilliant wedding Washington had seen in years. The second most common thread of conversation compared it with the weddings of the daughters of presidents Roosevelt and Wilson. The ceremony took place at the National Cathedral of Sts. Peter and Paul, in the small Bethlehem Chapel, the only part then complete. The chapel's size limited the guest list to family and close friends. And, of course, President Coolidge and his cabinet. A full choir of men and boys sang the music that Ailsa had selected.

Strict cathedral rules limited floral display; the only decoration besides the tall candles and American flag were six goblets filled with lilies. Outside, the bridal party — four bridesmaids in gowns of orchid chiffon, the maid of honor in a slightly darker shade, and lastly Ailsa — approached the chapel through the gardens of the bishop's house. The bride wore a gown of lace, *pointe d'angleterre*, with a court train of the same and a veil of yards of tulle held to her hair by a coronet of pearls. Ailsa had sketched the design herself.

It was a proud moment for Louise and Cabell Bruce as they watched

David, standing there expectantly, waiting for the ceremony to begin. They had lost one son as an infant and another as a boy of thirteen. James was married and set on a promising career in business. Now their youngest, who for all his intellect and energy had resisted settling down, was about to marry into one of the richest, most influential families in the nation. David never did things by halves. What accomplishments might the Mellon fortune now make possible for his native talents? Their pride was obvious. "Even though the Bruce clan carefully conceal any signs of jubilation over the excellent match which Dave made," said one paper, "you couldn't blame them for rejoicing a bit after the butler has cleared the last crumbs from the [wedding] table."[41]

After President and Mrs. Coolidge entered the chapel, the familiar strains of Wagner's *Lohengrin* gave the bridal party the signal to begin. First came David's ushers — no fewer than twenty young men. Then the four bridesmaids and maid of honor, and finally Ailsa, on the arm of her father, to meet the groom at the altar before the officiating bishop, resplendent in scarlet and black robes. Outside, a line of policemen held back throngs of curious onlookers.

Two thousand guests received invitations to the reception at the Pan American Building. Though few of Cabell Bruce's colleagues attended because the Senate was in session, the Supreme Court, led by the ample figure of Chief Justice William Howard Taft, came as a group. Thirteen ambassadors, the Swedish crown prince and princess, and Gen. John "Black Jack" Pershing lent a cosmopolitan aura. Everyone received a slice of cake in a box with the bride's and groom's monograms embossed in silver. Besides the luminaries who attended, the presidents of the twenty-one nations of the Pan American Union sent Ailsa congratulatory telegrams.

Few newlyweds could boast that the Marine Corps band played "Hail to the Chief" as the president arrived to greet them. But the day celebrated more than the union of David and Ailsa. Through this marriage of two of its favored children, the ruling elite of the era celebrated its own ascendancy, confident of its right to rule.

The most common topic of discussion, of course, was money. Not David's. He, the newspapers sniffed, was more noted for "the blueness of his blood" than for his family's fortune. Great-grandfather James Bruce may have been the third richest American in the antebellum era, if family stories were true, but that wealth was long gone. Rather than at the time of Andrew and Nora's divorce, this was when the public first learned about Mellon's millions. There was the $100,000 pearl necklace he gave Ailsa and the improbable rumor that he spent the same on the reception. He did rent an apartment to display the gifts for an admiring public to view, under the protection of Secret Service agents.

Books were prominent — a set of English poetry, a rare edition of *Don Quixote* from the British ambassador. The cabinet gave an enormous, engraved silver tray. The Pennsylvania congressional delegation also gave a gift of silver, and there was a profusion of silver picture frames, silver candlesticks, and silver serving pieces. But the most precious present came from the Bruce family — prized silver heirlooms that Charles Bruce had buried at Staunton Hill at the end of the Civil War to hide from marauding bands of deserters.

Some speculated that Mellon gave $10 million to his daughter as a wedding present, a rumor that his genial secretary with the Dickensian name of Arthur Sixsmith firmly denied.[42] Such speculation was beside the point. During the next few years Mellon would siphon off much of his wealth to Paul and Ailsa. A gift of $10 million would have been a poor bauble indeed when set beside these princely amounts.

People wondered too about Mellon's financial relationship with David. Some said that Mellon, so old-fashioned he could not bear to think of his son-in-law depending on Ailsa's money, solved his discomfort by settling a fine grant of capital directly on David.[43] The amount mentioned varied from a paltry million to ten times that. The Mellon family's financial records are so closely held that the answer may never be known. In a sense, the speculation is irrelevant, for David did very well from his Mellon connections. (If, as was rumored, the engagement ring he gave Ailsa cost $15,000, the money likely did not come from his own pocket or his father's.) Whether his good fortune came directly from his father-in-law or indirectly from the dozens of corporate boards he sat on by virtue of being a Mellon in-law is beside the point. Louise Bruce hinted at the magnitude when she wrote Andrew later to express her joy that David was "so very fond of you as he most certainly should be as you have been nobly generous and kind to him."[44]

How he would handle the temptations of riches was no mean challenge, for he faced a life beyond the wildest daydreams of avarice. Louise Bruce began to worry. Could her son deal with the money and the chief hobgoblins of her fears, those "many designing people," smooth, fawning sycophants who would try to wheedle and toady their way into his favor?[45] She need not have worried on his account.

A year before the wedding, David had decided to join the foreign service, an apt choice given his cosmopolitan interests and itch for travel. After four months in the Army Courier Service, he thought the life of a diplomat less exotic than before. "Diplomacy is no longer as picturesque or as mysterious as it once was," he wrote in 1921. "Together with the outward symbols of splendor and courtesy, the intrigues of statecraft appear to have vanished. We no longer hear of messengers kidnapped and tortured in remote fastnesses, of secret conferences in hunting lodges, of petticoat government, of the policies of nations being dictated from tea tables."[46]

Enough of the romance remained, though, to appeal to him. For others there would have been the drawback of the less-than-desirable postings handed out to junior diplomats. Because connection still counted for everything, however, the son of a United States senator could expect special consideration. When he was also the son-in-law of the treasury secretary, he did not need to worry about being sent to the lazy heat of a Central American backwater. As much was plain to the reporter who, in speculating about Bruce's prospects, referred to Mellon as a man with "considerable drag in quarters where ministers and ambassadors are picked out."[47]

The service that David entered had just been restructured to give at least lip service to making it more professional. The Rogers Act of 1924 merged the consular and diplomatic services and established modest salaries and a course of instruction for prospective officers. To hidebound senior diplomats, the absence of salaries had kept out the riffraff: only men with independent incomes need apply. Opening the ranks to a few nonwealthy applicants made little difference. Far from rejecting the style of the traditional, moneyed foreign policy elite, they were, in the words of Felix Frankfurter, "more Grotty than the men who actually went to Groton."[48] The service remained male and Anglo-Saxon, of course, but also Eastern, Ivy League, and usually affluent — just the sort of exclusive club that young Bruce would find congenial even if he had not scored first among the 147 men taking the entrance examination.[49] After he finished the course of instruction and married, he was ready for his first posting: vice-consul in Rome.

Only minor disputes ruffled Italian-American relations. The Italians resented a tougher American immigration law; Mussolini's erosion of democracy began to worry some. In general, though, American commentators on both left and right professed admiration for the regime's alleged efficiency and pragmatism. The liberal historian Charles A. Beard likened Mussolini to Teddy Roosevelt and the "American gospel of action, action, action."[50] Solicitous of Italian feelings, Washington shut down an anti-Fascist exile newspaper in New York that had offended Ambassador Caetani. The hapless editor had to choose deportation or jail.[51] The two countries reached a settlement of war debts on generous terms for the Italians. Mellon defended these conditions before Congress. (He could not escape all requirements to speak in public.) The Italian press praised him for defending Il Duce against critics in American papers.[52] Bruce could expect a warm reception in Rome.

Four days after their wedding, Mr. and Mrs. David Bruce boarded the SS *President Harding* in New York harbor, in a shower of confetti and rice tossed by friends. A newspaper photograph captured their attitudes — David all smiles and optimism, striking a jaunty pose against the ship's railing, Ailsa demurely pretty but a bit drawn and tentative. "Mrs. Bruce and I have both been to Rome before," he told a reporter, suggesting more intimacy with the Eternal City than his brief visit in 1920 warranted. "We both have many friends there whom we look forward to seeing again."[53] That this was no ordinary junior vice-consul already occurred to one functionary, the State Department's shipping agent who had to make special provision for sending four heavy cases of the Bruces' best silverware.[54]

The newlyweds were in no hurry. After their liner docked in Cherbourg, the smart two-seater car they had brought with them was winched out of the hold and eased down onto the quay. As David grasped the wheel, Ailsa, dressed in a gray fur coat and silver fox scarf, took her seat beside him, and they motored off to tour Normandy.

David also wanted to show Ailsa the Paris that had inspired him, a side of the city she had never seen. But in the main he now enjoyed a far different Paris. Before, he had sampled the Paris of the literary expatriates when he rented a room in Montparnasse and shared a student flat near the Sorbonne. That community of artists and writers could not have been psychologically farther away from the Paris he now inhabited. Now, to use the phrase of expatriate Malcolm Cowley, he moved into that other America-in-Paris, that of the rich on the other side of the Seine. Its landmarks stretched from the posh neighborhood of the Arc de Triomphe to the nightclubs and chic dressmakers' shops close to the rue de la Paix, to the grand hotels, especially the Ritz, and the American banks across the Place Vendôme from it. The only point where the two universes coincided, it was said, was over a bowl of onion soup that society party-goers shared with humbler folk just before dawn at Les Halles.[55] David could revisit his old haunts on the Left Bank, but Paris for him had become something altogether different.

He reported for duty in Rome in July. In 1920 he had said that the people looked as though they had not bathed since the destruction of the Baths of Caracalla: "Sole occupation, reproduction of species — result, thousands of half-naked, wholly filthy children with beautiful eyes. . . . Beggars, beggars, beggars — favorite outdoor sport in Italy."[56] Six years later it would be prudent to avoid such talk in public. When he met Mussolini, he complained that customs was holding up his luggage. The trunks were delivered within hours, or so he said much later. Perhaps. But all such tales told by the older David Bruce deserve a skeptical hearing because he loved to embellish stories from his youth. This one has an authentic ring, for it illustrates his attitude in those flush, early days of great wealth, before experience gave him a reflective maturity that he lacked that summer.

When the couple set up house in a palatial apartment, they gave the lie to reports that she swore to forsake money for love and live on his salary. The question was not whether they would live on his $2,500 a year — she spent that much visiting a single Paris couturier — but whether she would find the lot of a junior diplomat's wife to her liking. Equally important, would David find consular work to his taste and temperament?

Two weeks after Vice-Consul Bruce reported for duty, his father-in-law crossed the Atlantic. When Mellon reached Rome, he mixed museum going and cozy chats with Il Duce. He denied the talks with Mussolini had anything to do with rescheduling war debts. They were merely courtesy calls. "I repeat," he told the skeptics, "I am in Europe solely on a vacation and to visit my daughter."[57]

When he was reunited with her and his new son-in-law, he learned that from her first day in Rome Ailsa had been sick. A strange malady, marked by listlessness and a low-level, intermittent fever, sapped her energy. The Italian doctors called it "sandfly fever." As it showed no signs of abating, David's concern grew.

A decision was reached in family conclave. On August 9, David asked for a leave of absence to take his wife to a healthier climate. She had, he said, been "ailing constantly since her arrival in Rome." His boss, Consul Leon Dominian, cabled the request to Washington.[58] With a perfunctory nod to timing, Mellon waited a few hours and then sent his own telegram to Secretary of State Frank Kellogg, asking him to look kindly on his son-in-law's request.[59] Two days later he took Ailsa to a fashionable French spa until David could join them.

Kellogg, of course, agreed without delay. This decision, made so easily and generously in the unhurried Victorian headquarters of the old State Department building, spelled trouble in Rome. Consular work was routine, but summer was the busy season. Dominian transferred another vice-consul from Genoa as Bruce left to join his wife.[60]

Evian-les-Bains, on the shore of Lake Geneva, throbbed with its mid-season peak of excitement. "Every day one sees socially, financially and politically prominent people from three continents at the baths," the press gushed, "while at night the Casino provides a colorful spectacle around the gaming tables and at the theatre."[61] The treasury secretary held court as financiers, including Sir Robert Horne, former British chancellor of the exchequer and one of Ailsa's unsuccessful suitors, came to his suite in the opulent Hotel Royal. Rumors that Mellon would talk with Premier Raymond Poincaré irrationally boosted the franc on the Paris bourse. Europe's newspapers would not be outdone by American dailies in truckling before the purported wizardry of the great financial alchemist. Mellon repeated that he was on a private holiday and developed a fondness for rowing out on the lake.

Just before David arrived, a reporter wrote, "the climate has agreed with Mrs. Bruce and she is rapidly regaining her health, which was affected by the hot summer in Rome."[62] A few days later Mellon left

Evian for the voyage home, but not before being feted in Paris and then again in London by Winston Churchill at the chancellor's residence at 11 Downing Street.

The improvement in Ailsa's condition was only temporary. From the start of her illness, David's paramount concern was her recovery. Now, suddenly, unexpectedly, he might have to relinquish his post, but that was a small thing to sacrifice to restore his wife's health.

Although he went back to his office briefly at the end of the year, early in 1927 he told Kellogg that Ailsa's doctors forbade her from returning to Rome and requested an indefinite leave without pay.[63] When her illness worsened, he took her to a fashionable clinic that tried one diagnosis after another. "As her condition persisted," he would recount years later, "yielding to no applied treatments, she lost weight, could take no exercise, and was advised to go to the Doctor Kocher clinique in Berne, Switzerland, for further diagnosis. This famous doctor at first thought she might be tubercular, but after many examinations that speculation was dropped. By then it was evident that she was dangerously ill, and no diagnosis either then or in her later life ever revealed the true cause of the almost incessant temperature that made her health subnormal."[64]

David next took her to Paris, where she entered the hospital at Neuilly for an appendectomy. Despite a successful operation, her ailment continued, and he extended his unpaid leave again. (While she was convalescing, he was one of the lucky few to dine at the American ambassador's house with Charles Lindbergh on the night of his electrifying flight across the ocean.[65]) He gradually learned that Ailsa's illness was both more and less than it seemed. Less because the best diagnostic minds in Europe never found evidence of organic illness. More because the sickness reflected the beginning of permanent emotional maladies.

Looking back, Paul Mellon traced the roots of her problem. After her parents' divorce, "she seemed somehow to withdraw from all social contact and become more and more obsessed with her health. . . . past experience and the onset of adolescence seem to have conspired together to defeat Ailsa. She was gradually becoming more and more introspective and hypochondriacal. I often reminded her that she was always complaining about her health, saying that there was something wrong with her glands, something wrong with this, or something wrong with that."[66] Her friends whispered behind her back that her name was really "What Ails Her." There were other factors — including the sudden death of two friends, one of them a suicide — that compounded her introspection. But the trauma of the divorce was paramount.

David had thought Ailsa was desperately ill when he bade farewell at the Rome station as she, reduced to a helpless invalid, left with her father for the bracing air of Lake Geneva. He should have wondered when he arrived there two weeks later. For the debilitating condition that had prostrated her in Rome had miraculously relented, and she eagerly took every chance to go with her father for lengthy motorboat cruises around the lake.[67]

For the time being, David assumed the cause was a mysterious, recurring organic illness, as did the many physicians who treated her. When he gradually began to see that her problem was largely emotional, he was no less solicitous than when he thought she had tuberculosis. The tender letters filled with endearments that he sent her when they were apart suggest that he was intensely supportive, whether the source of her troubles was emotional or organic.

The press knew nothing about any emotional problems and indulged in wild guessing. "Naturally Baltimore society is speculating on the arrival of the stork in the David Bruce ménage," the gossip sheet *Town Topics* ventured in spring 1927 when it learned that David and Ailsa were returning home, only to write two months later that "unfortunately the cogent reason which existed in April no longer influences" the couple's schedule.[68] Was Ailsa pregnant, and did she have a miscarriage? Probably not. *Town Topics*, like all that high-powered medical consultation in Europe, was thoroughly stumped by Ailsa's illness.

There was the matter too of her haughty attitude. "Even though the State Department has its finger at its lips concerning all questions about the resignation of David Bruce," a reporter said, "it is freely asserted among Dave's friends that he faced losing Ailsa unless he forswore his yearning to reach the top rung in his diplomatic career." According to the same source, "If ever Ailsa sees Europe again, especially Italy, I understand, it will be because she has been sand-bagged or chloroformed and dragged thither without her knowledge."[69]

Her own friends said her malady was not as drastic as David would later make it out to be — certainly not life-threatening — and was largely a pretext to reinforce her demand that he give up the appointment in Rome.

The State Department suggested that he return to Washington to work on a conference scheduled for September 1927. Then, if his wife were still unable to go abroad with him, the department would accept his resignation. In the meantime, for two months the Bruces languidly sailed the Mediterranean with Mellon on a rented yacht, the summer heat not bothering Ailsa then. David gratefully accepted the department's suggestion, but it merely delayed the inevitable. By autumn he was once more a private citizen.

His diplomatic gambit thus effectively ended after little more than a month. It was not the outcome he had expected, but Ailsa's health was more important. Back home, Mellon's reluctance to be apart from his daughter grew. Friends told the press they were "convinced that he is eager to have Mr. and Mrs. Bruce return to the United States to be near him, for he has made no secret of his loneliness in Washington since his daughter's marriage."[70] This comment, divulged by friends to the *Washington Post*, might have been embarrassing to David, but he was willing to explore alternatives that did not put Ailsa's health at risk.

Even if Ailsa had found Rome agreeable, it is doubtful that the consular service would have suited her husband. While he worried about getting those four cases of silverware shipped out from America, his colleagues in Rome struggled with the city's high cost of living. For those who lacked private means, their modest salaries were not up to the challenge. The man who replaced Bruce had to dip into savings to make ends meet. Another had to borrow from his parents, and a third could barely provide food and shelter on his salary, to say nothing of a wardrobe appropriate to his station.[71]

In a few weeks the fairy-tale romance that filled the front pages of America's newspapers and produced the society wedding of the decade turned into something quite unexpected. David had won Fitzgerald's golden girl. More than any other young American of his day, he incarnated the successful pursuit of riches, which the spirit of the decade unashamedly worshiped. Was he now to endure the pathology of wealth that infected Jay Gatsby's world? Up to this point in his life, David, like Ailsa, had pretty much had what he wanted. He had danced through youth free of the workaday need to earn his daily bread and free to indulge his extravagant tastes. After Rome, and futile consultations with doctors across Europe, he was beginning to see that Ailsa's problems were more complicated than a simple fever. She had been terribly spoiled and then emotionally traumatized by the divorce. David was spoiled by privilege too, but his childhood had been golden. Even the tragic death of William Cabell Jr. could not compare to the psychological damage that Ailsa suffered and suppressed until it reemerged after her marriage.

By the end of 1927 Bruce was officially out of the foreign service. That December Mellon bought a house for his daughter as a Christmas present, an estate of a hundred acres on Long Island at Syosset. It became the Bruces' principal country home.[72] If he let it, this $1.5 million, stuccoed Italianate villa of thirty-six rooms, set among sunken gardens tended by a platoon of groundsmen, could have reminded Bruce of the disappointment of Rome.

CHAPTER 5

The Mellon Embrace

With no money left for rent, unemployed men and their entire families began
to build shacks where they could find unoccupied land. Along the railroad
embankment, beside the garbage incinerator, in the city dumps, there appeared
towns of tarpaper and tin, old packing boxes and old car bodies.

— Arthur M. Schlesinger Jr., *The Crisis of the Old Order*

I was drowning in honey, stingless.

— Evelyn Waugh, *Brideshead Revisited*

*A*FTER THE FALSE START in diplomacy, David Bruce turned
to investment banking. No son-in-law of Andrew Mellon would find
many doors closed to him in the paneled citadels of high finance.
Through Mellon, he not only learned about business but also cultivated
the love of art that first stirred him as a young soldier gaping in wonder
at the canvases in the Louvre. Now good fortune allowed him to indulge
those tastes on a scale given to few Americans.

At first he worked at Banker's Trust but by early 1929 moved to W. A.
Harriman & Co., an investment firm with offices at 38 Broadway. Seven
years older than Bruce, W. Averell Harriman had inherited a vast
fortune from the railroad magnate who had provoked Teddy Roosevelt's
famous blast against "malefactors of great wealth." The younger Harriman displayed "that curious contempt for elegance that only the
wealthy can afford" and was known for a peculiar blend of arrogance,

generosity, vanity, and rudeness. For the first but not the last time this self-promoting "Philistine prince" did Bruce a favor.[1]

With an insider's view of Wall Street at its dizziest, Bruce took advantage for his personal account and made very good money. He was lucky. Despite his gold-plated credit, the frenzy of the biggest bull market ever was as good a time to lose a fortune as make one for investors just a little too greedy. He told a skeptical reporter that he really was keen to learn the business from the bottom up and concluded, "I am sure that I shall prefer banking to a diplomatic career."[2]

Harriman ought to have paid more attention to his advice, especially about AVCO, his Aviation Corporation of America, but he was drawn more to the adrenaline surge of making deals than the tedium of company governance. Bruce, an AVCO board member, warned him against the firm's loose management and its habit of paying exorbitant prices to grow by acquisition. When the market fell, AVCO stock did too, and just as spectacularly.[3]

The novelty of investing wore off, especially after the good times ended. There had always been a bit of playacting about the work anyway, decisions made by proper young Ivy League gentlemen in plush offices carried out by their minions on the trading floors. In 1932 some of his brokers hounded him for collateral. "I went to Rolling Rock for ten days," he said, referring to the Mellons' private country club near Pittsburgh, "and played some golf until the storm blew over. They never got me."[4] He exaggerated. Bruce showed sound judgment in his investments, a friend recalled, and was never in danger of losing big. For the next several years he kept a private office at 230 Park Avenue. Behind a door that listed no business titles, only his name, he kept track of the less onerous duties of a director on more than two dozen corporate boards.

The economy began to slow after the Crash, though people like the Bruces noticed no decline in the quality of life. In the Indian summer of the great Atlantic luxury liners, the wealthy could follow the seasons at a stately pace, and David and Ailsa did. In 1931, next to the duke of Connaught's place on Cap Ferrat, they rented a villa with rooms for thirty guests. "I was as out of touch with business," Bruce wrote, "as if I had been at the North Pole."[5] The heat of the Mediterranean in that exclusive niche of the Riviera did not seem to bother Ailsa. There were also western holidays at Harriman's ranch, where the low humidity, they hoped, might strengthen her. And shooting trips to Scotland, too, where the grouse learned to fear David's finely tooled Purdey shotguns. All the while, the *Totentanz* of the old order in America spiraled to its end as the Great Depression deepened.

Andrew Mellon's political fortunes took a turn for the worse. He had been the most powerful figure of the Harding and Coolidge era. People joked that he was the only cabinet officer to have three presidents serve under him. But Herbert Hoover, who inherited Mellon from Coolidge, did not see eye to eye with the man acclaimed as the greatest secretary of the treasury since Alexander Hamilton. After the stock market nose-dived, people gave the epithet a sarcastic twist.

Mellon's policies during the boom years — efficiency in government and lower taxes — had helped the economy flourish. But when the soup kitchen replaced the ticker tape as the symbol of the age, he became even more than ever the hate icon of the left and the butt of popular humor. According to the story retold more than any other, he once asked Hoover for a nickel to telephone a friend. "Here," the president said, "take a dime, call all your friends."[6]

In February 1932 Mellon agreed to become ambassador to Britain, a step down from the Treasury but quite appealing to an Ulster immigrant's son self-taught in the genteel pleasures of Anglophilia. Ailsa went along to be her father's hostess just as in the old days. Though still subject to the same vague maladies, she could handle the undemanding social duties that Mellon required. David went too as his father-in-law's unofficial aide. The ambassador's residence that was home to Mellon and the Bruces for a year consisted of two row houses in Princes Gate, Knightsbridge, just south of Hyde Park.

Few troubles clouded Anglo-American relations. True, the week Mellon arrived, former prime minister David Lloyd George published a book denouncing him as a ruthless "weasel." In general, though, the London press fawned over him in the hope that he brought some magic solution to the conundrum of war debts and reparations. Even the vacuous Prince of Wales spoke of "the advice which the great financier can give Europe."[7] Mellon contented himself with making hazy pronouncements about international finance and slipping away to admire pictures at the National Gallery.

The British upper classes were having a last fling. Much less rich than before, but not yet aware that their day had passed, the upper-crust youth escaped into frivolous pursuits like their American counterparts. Bruce made a few lasting friendships among these sons and daughters of the establishment, denizens of clubland and charity balls, country house weekends and grouse moors. Most of the Bright Young Things were of no consequence, but "some of those languid lounge-lizards who adorned London," he said years later, perhaps with his own pampered youth in mind, "became the toughest, most ruthless commandos of World War II."[8]

Two *salonnières* dominated the scene. A modest, warm-hearted person, Sybil Colefax gathered an eclectic mix of people for her luncheons and dinners. "The need to collect celebrities," someone cattily recalled, "was for her an addiction as strong as alcohol or drugs."[9] She liked American art collectors, the most remarkable in her opinion being the quiet little man who had just become the new ambassador in London.[10] The other preeminent hostess was Emerald Cunard, a tiny expatriate American with an "electric personality blazing away at her guests."[11] Aside from her soirees, she was known for her durable affair with conductor Sir Thomas Beecham and for her estranged daughter, Nancy, an alcoholic enfant terrible of expatriate literary Paris. In the contest to be first to entertain the new ambassador and his entourage, Cunard edged out Colefax. Her luncheon for the Americans was attended by assorted peers, politicians, and Evelyn Waugh, then completing *Black Mischief* and indulging in smart Mayfair parties to forget his first wife's betrayal.[12] Such were the urbane personalities that defined the social world David and Ailsa glided through.

The great event of the summer season for Ailsa Bruce was being presented at court. To satisfy protocol, Madame de Fleuriau, the French ambassador's wife, agreed to present her. Four days before the ceremony, an assassin inconveniently shot dead the president of France. George V and Mary declared the court in mourning. The de Fleuriaus left for the state funeral. To Ailsa's relief, Buckingham Palace did not cancel her big event, and Madame Oilveira de Regis, wife of the Brazilian ambassador, stepped into the breach as her sponsor.

Ailsa's husband whiled away his time in pursuits of equal weight. His army chum Macgill James twitted him for a routine of playing squash in the morning, sipping sherry before lunch, and dabbling at writing in the afternoon. James was not far off the mark. Bruce admitted the most strenuous activity he faced was "fierce bouts of tennis" at the estate of Esmond Harmsworth, heir of the Rothermere publishing empire. At a levee given by George V at St. James's Palace, the marshal of the diplomatic corps introduced David and others from the embassy. In the antique idiom of the court, they were "named to the King by the Lord Chamberlain."[13]

"There is nothing of interest to tell you about here," Bruce wrote Harriman. "Life in London has thus far been most pleasant."[14] Ailsa was content to be her father's chatelaine and moved at an unhurried pace through a light, untaxing schedule of embassy receptions. Mellon lunched at Windsor with the king. Most pleasant, indeed.

In America banks failed by the hundreds. Hoover and Mellon were damned on all sides. "The fog of despair hung over the land," wrote one historian. "One out of every four American workers lacked a job. Factories that had once darkened the skies with smoke stood ghostly and silent, like extinct volcanoes. Families slept in tarpaper shacks and tin-lined caves and scavenged like dogs for food in the city dump."[15] In October 1931, after David and Ailsa returned from their summer at Cap Ferrat, Hoover had tried to bolster confidence by talking to thirty top financiers. To avoid panic in the press, he convened them secretly, not at the White House but at Mellon's apartment. Seated below the treasury secretary's rows of Old Masters, these titans of finance listened as the president implored them to cease foreclosures and find more money to invest. Instead, they called in more loans.[16]

To no one's surprise, the Democrats recaptured the White House in 1932. It did not matter that Franklin Roosevelt campaigned on a platform as orthodox as his opponent's: the great slump began on Hoover and Mellon's watch, and the voters punished them for it.

In this climate, the son-in-law of the most vilified treasury secretary since Alexander Hamilton expected appointment to high office, having kept his Democratic loyalties despite being a Mellon in-law. He even returned briefly from England to work in FDR's campaign. "Everything here will work out in time," he said right after the inauguration, "but I believe we are in for a period of drastic readjustment. On the whole, however, I think we are nearer the light than we have been for several years."[17]

It took a heroic dose of wishful thinking to believe Roosevelt would appoint someone tainted by association — if only by marriage — with the discredited Republican era. Cabell Bruce shared his son's delusions and pulled what strings remained at a former senator's command, including persistent letters to Jim Farley, FDR's chief spoilsman. Cabell had the delicacy to say that, though his son would like an assistant secretaryship in any department, the Treasury might not be the best choice. "Every one seems to think," David wrote his wife, "that there is no chance of my getting into the Treasury, and the politicians frankly say that it is out of the question since it might be construed as an indication that your father was still exercising influence there." Quite. "On the whole," he concluded, "I should prefer to be in the State Department."[18] Louise Bruce campaigned too by badgering her friend Admiral Cary Grayson, an affable Virginian and White House physician since Wilson's day. Her son's lack of credentials was apparent in the résumé she sent Grayson: it boasted mostly of his feats at Princeton and law school.[19]

David returned to America to manage his campaign. "Father and Mother have been working manfully (and womanfully if you please) in the good cause," he wrote his wife in London. "Father has . . . written floods of letters as has Mother, and I have added my mite to their efforts." "Washington," he told Ailsa, "is going to be the most interesting place in the world in the next few months," whereas "New York is really depressing, & every one [is] in a state of profound gloom." He tried to keep up his hopes but admitted, "I am really most anxious to get a position in Washington, & shall be frightfully disappointed if I do not." He suspected he could wangle a minor diplomatic post, but that did not interest him. "I have tried to arrange to meet Roosevelt personally," he revealed, "but have not been able to do so." As he began to see that his expectations were naive, his self-deprecating humor returned. "A week has gone by since the inauguration," he told Ailsa, "& still the President seems able to run the government without calling on my services."[20]

The New Deal had other plans in store for the Mellon family than rewarding its in-laws. Because Mellon antagonized powerful enemies during his decade of influence, there were scores to be settled. H. L. Mencken had said, "I know of no other country in which . . . so preposterous a vacuum as Andy Mellon would be venerated as a great statesman."[21] John Nance "Cactus Jack" Garner, immortalized for comparing the vice-presidency to "a pitcher of warm piss," threatened to "look into Uncle Andy's books."[22] Wright Patman, another contentious Texan, called Mellon the greediest of the money changers cast out of the temple. Expulsion was not enough: Patman wanted him harried and humiliated. Mellon's favorite phrase was "no good deed goes unpunished." He was about to learn how true it was.

No incident did more to enrage the Roosevelt-hating rich than the accusation that Mellon had cheated on his income tax. Treasury Secretary Henry Morgenthau Jr. said, "I consider that Mr. Mellon is not on trial but democracy and the privileged rich and I want to see who will win." "Mr. Mellon had made out his tax return in one economic era," *Fortune* magazine concluded, "and was being prosecuted for it in another."[23]

When a grand jury, mainly of workingmen, refused to indict Mellon on criminal charges, FDR insisted that the government proceed with a civil case. In this highly charged atmosphere, Mellon retained Frank J. Hogan, a flamboyant lawyer best known for his maxim that "an ideal client is a very rich man, thoroughly scared."[24] In Mellon he found his man, with the New Deal in full cry for the blood of this discredited Republican malefactor of great wealth.

Ailsa and David moved to Pittsburgh to give him moral support during his interrogation before the Board of Tax Appeals. The hearings began in February 1935 as another depression winter settled in the valleys of Allegheny County. There, where Mellon first became a name to conjure with, David Bruce's father-in-law confronted his accusers. As the wind whipped down the steep hillsides, past idled steel mills unhappily no longer spewing out pollution, Bruce learned a lesson about reversal of fortune and about fidelity. Walking faithfully beside his dour father-in-law each day to the hearings, bundled up against the cold in black homburgs and overcoats, the dress uniform of sober businessmen, he also conceived a lifelong dislike for the president of his own party.

The effusive publicity about the family vanished with the Great Depression. Journalist Walter Lippmann said Mellon had been "surrounded by an adulation which would sicken a man of finer sensibilities."[25] Once people believed his economic wizardry was a failure and his personal finances a scandal, the publicity turned nasty. His son recalled a ditty scrawled on a public urinal: "Hoover blew the whistle./

Mellon rang the bell./ Wall Street gave the signal/ And the country went to hell."[26]

The press characterized Bruce as an inconsequential Mellon hanger-on, "a gay, rollicking young blade" with far more money than was good for his immortal soul.[27] Even before FDR's election, two debunking journalists dredged up David's vice-consular record to show that the State Department was shot through with favoritism. They held up David as an example and deplored a system that allowed him "nine months' leave of absence out of the first twelve months of his service."[28] In Pittsburgh the workers who formerly spoke of Mellon in hushed, forelock-tugging tones now vied with one another to tell tales of his perfidy and the inanity of his indolent, parasitic offspring. A visitor to the steel city concluded, "The awe is gone; the worship has ended; the glamour has utterly disappeared."[29]

The most intriguing aspect of the tax case focused on deductions for giving paintings to the A. W. Mellon Educational and Charitable Trust. Mellon meant them to be the nucleus of the art museum he intended to give to the nation. One inconvenient fact made the deductions so provocative: the canvases still hung on his and the Bruces' walls. In laborious detail, the government presented the convoluted transactions that enabled Mellon to reduce his tax liability. As an in-law, a director of the trust, and an admirer of those paintings, Bruce was by implication a beneficiary of Mellon's alleged deceit. He was not indicted himself, but the sense of personal affront made him feel like he was.

As the case dragged on, he wrote a parody for the family's private enjoyment. In it he referred to FDR as "the Dictator," who in pursuit of Mellon was "as spritely as a stump-tailed bull in fly-time." Treasury Secretary Morgenthau was a "chicken farmer," the administration, "the New Zeal for Character Assassination." No member of the First Family escaped ridicule for their "pet propaganda project," as he called the vendetta against Mellon. He feigned indignation at the government's men being thwarted. "Can you," his narrator breathlessly asked, "without a shudder, foresee the fate of the New Deal if, when the Administration attacks an innocent man, he is allowed by the Courts to defend himself? Such a precedent might shake the whole fabric of patronage, and might . . . result in the failure of the President to be reelected."[30]

Despite his sardonic view, the case was deadly serious. It made him a bitter foe of Roosevelt, not just another disaffected conservative

Democrat. Long afterward he could hardly speak FDR's name without anger. The attack on his father-in-law was an offense Bruce never forgave. Without a qualm, he voted for Roosevelt's opponent in 1936. He never repented and paid a price for it not long after.

Even before the tax case drew them together in adversity, Bruce and his father-in-law were growing closer. Mellon relied increasingly on his son-in-law, and Bruce respected the old man. David Finley, his soft-spoken assistant, said that Mr. Mellon — he was always called Mr. Mellon — "had a way of making you feel badly if you failed him." Bruce agreed. He recalled that Mellon "was famous for his judgment about men and affairs. His often dreamy look cloaked a will of steel." For good reasons, few people liked Mellon, and there were fewer still who personally knew the cold-blooded financier and could still say, as Bruce did, that he was "remarkable, distinguished, admirable."[31]

In 1935 he accompanied his father-in-law to Europe in the hope that London and especially a Rembrandt exhibition in Amsterdam would revive him after the stress of the tax hearings. They spent their days on the *Berengaria* on Mellon's private verandah and ate in his sitting room. "Tonight," David wrote Ailsa at the end of the voyage, "for the first time we expect to put on dinner coats and go to the dining-room. It sounds very dull but it is really most pleasant. He is a sweet old gentleman." Some of David's friends mockingly said the Mellon he was in love with was not Ailsa but her father.[32]

As Mellon relied more on him, Bruce took a hand in buying paintings and planning for the as-yet-unbuilt gallery. Mellon had begun collecting before Bruce was born. As in his investments — never a pioneer, always a buyer of proven successes — he purchased art with an excruciatingly conservative eye. He was positively "inarticulate on the subject of art," and yet it became his chief preoccupation.[33]

Only authentic Old Masters validated by the leading experts would do. He possessed works by all of the greats: Gainsborough, Hals, El Greco, Turner, Vermeer, Titian, Van Eyck, Botticelli, Raphael, Rembrandt. It never occurred to him to collect the works of an unknown artist, either because they might grow in value or because he simply liked them. Recent art had not been judged over time. He could not enjoy what his millions brought within his grasp, beyond the tepid, vicarious satisfaction that came from knowing that others — art experts — pronounced his canvases great.

Mellon and his fellow tycoons served as a way station in the transfer of Old Masters from strapped European aristocrats to American museums. His greatest acquisition, though, came in 1930–31 when he indirectly helped Stalin build the Soviet state. The deal made by the archcapitalist and the Communist tyrant traded twenty-one superb canvases from Leningrad's Hermitage for less than $7 million. (Stalin liquidated one of the curators afterward, not for selling a national treasure, but for letting it go too cheaply.) While the American Left pilloried Mellon for tax fraud and praised Soviet economics, the financier was secretly exploiting Stalin's need for cash to build the core of what became America's National Gallery of Art.[34]

Mellon relied on the most orthodox art dealers. His favorite was the flashy Briton Joseph Duveen. (At one point during the tax hearings, the imperious Duveen told the prosecutor, in his plummiest, most disdainful manner, "Really my dear fellow, art works do not rise and fall in value like pig iron."[35]) He based his career on the observation that there was plenty of art in Europe and plenty of money in America. Mellon became his most important client.[36]

Through his father-in-law's hobby, Bruce advanced his own cultural education. During the year in London, he learned that a canvas of extraordinary historical, if not aesthetic, value was coming on the market and persuaded Mellon to buy it. This early painting of Pocahontas shows the Virginia Indian in Jacobean costume when she was presented at court.[37]

Bruce's knowledge of the fine arts soon outstripped his father-in-law's. Unlike Mellon, he loved art for its own sake. He valued the opinion of experts but did not depend on them in the sad way Mellon did. He would have cringed to read the wartime letters he had sent home from France indiscriminately praising art of all periods. Medievalism no longer attracted him. On the other hand, he cared little for contemporary art. Neither the sinuous lines of the Beaux Arts style, new during his childhood, nor the confident angularity of Art Deco appealed to him. He settled, instead, on an older style, the rococo flamboyance of the French *ancien régime*, to his mind the highest expression of beauty. Collecting the fine arts in general, not just paintings and certainly not just those certified as Old Masters, became a lifelong avocation.

Mellon may have sensed that his son-in-law enjoyed art more than he ever could and, knowing he himself lacked that sensitivity, depended on Bruce's advice all the more. Certainly David had a greater knack for dealing with people than Mellon's closest adviser, the abrasive lawyer Donald Shepard. "David had law training," a friend said, "and he had a wonderful personality, which Mr. Shepard did not have. So A. W. [Mellon] depended on him, David could do all sorts of things for A. W. He was interested in history, he had a wonderful eye for furniture, English silver, pictures. So knowledgeable."[38]

It pained Mellon that his tax troubles convinced people his long-planned National Gallery was a tax dodge. It could hardly have been just that because of the value of the paintings alone. Yet the suspicion remained. His notion of creating the museum, modeled on the National Gallery in London, had first occurred more than a decade before. It was his misfortune that he did not advance the idea — beyond adding to the collection and setting up a trust — before Roosevelt's partisans made an example of him. He formally offered to create the gallery at a personal meeting with FDR in 1936 while a decision in the tax case was still pending. That alone was enough to raise eyebrows. The president agreed, and plans for the museum moved ahead. A skeptical public looked on it as the payoff for resolving the charges against Mellon in his favor. They were settled, but not until after he died.

Mellon had always looked frail, even emaciated, "like a dried up dollar bill that any wind might whisk away."[39] In 1937 he abandoned his daily walks, lost his appetite, and gave up his evil little Grand Central Cheroots. Ailsa and David convinced him to leave Washington before the summer humidity set in. He refused medical care but tolerated Bruce's charade that the doctor who also moved into the mansion at Syosset was just a house guest. Bronchitis led to pneumonia and then to uremic poisoning. Mellon died there, age eighty-two. Appropriately, it was the son-in-law who gave the family's terse and unrevealing statement to the press: "The end was perfectly peaceful," Bruce said, "he was very weak."[40]

Before he died, Mellon saw construction begin on the vast neoclassical domed hall on Constitution Avenue that John Russell Pope had designed to house his paintings. After Mellon's death, Bruce, as chairman of the trust, saw to it that the philanthropist's wishes were followed. This was not a matter of rubber-stamping routine, for Bruce locked horns with the architect's successors. (Pope died the day after Mellon.) Like simple-minded disciples, they tried to make the building a purer example of Pope's style than he would have insisted on. Bruce retained a friend, architect William A. Delano, as a consultant on masses of interior details, down to handrails and radiator grills, that still remained to be ironed out. In concert with his brother-in-law, Bruce squelched the attempt of Pope's colleagues to add inappropriate decorations to the exterior of the building. He also hired Macgill James. It was not simple favoritism because, thanks to Bruce's generosity in underwriting his graduate education, James was the only original top administrator with formal museum training.[41]

Bruce also courted other potential donors Mellon had hoped would contribute to the gallery. A notable early success was acquisition of the Joseph Widener collection. The most important additional donors were Paul and Ailsa, but their greatest gifts would come much later. For the moment, Ailsa was unhappy her father did not consult her about the gallery. She was especially upset when she learned that her favorite painting, Reynolds's *Lady Caroline Howard*, would not be hers but would go to the nation.

Her brother was also upset. An unhappy, insecure young man, Paul wrote a memo to himself to sort out his rage against his father: "He has never . . . given me a word of advice or encouragement about business or my life. . . . The Gallery to him is just one more investment, one more tremendous Mellon Interest . . . one more prop for the scaffolding which holds up his gigantic, intensive, mysterious ego." It was a comfort to Mellon to have David to rely on if his own children were not emotionally capable of dealing with decisions about the gallery. "My father always thought very highly of David," Paul admitted.[42]

During the crucial years just before and after Mellon's death, Bruce was the key family member in the affairs of the gallery. He was, according to its long-time director John Walker, "the one who made the *ultimate* decisions, of course."[43] Thanks largely to Bruce, the completed museum precisely expressed the wishes of its ultraconservative patron. It was a building that was "instantly old," a critic said, yet it worked. Its severe, cool grandeur and classic proportions resonated serenity and calm, and unlike the inhospitable spaces designed by other museum architects, the National Gallery deferred to the treasures it displayed.[44]

On the exterior, faced with Tennessee marble that turns pink in the rain, Mellon insisted that there be no plaque listing his name as benefactor. Bruce made sure the wish was honored. "The giver of this building," FDR said at the 1941 dedication, without a hint of hypocrisy in his voice, "has matched the richness of his gift with the modesty of his spirit, stipulating that the Gallery shall be known not by his name but by the Nation's."[45]

Mellon's arrangement for its governance, however, ensured that the museum and his name would always be linked. The trustees included the chief justice of the Supreme Court and the secretaries of the Treasury, State, and Smithsonian. These in practice deferred to five private members — the "general trustees" — originally Mellon himself, his lawyer Donald Shepard, his former Treasury subordinate Parker Gilbert, collector Duncan Phillips, and David Bruce. Because Mellon and Gilbert died during the first year, the remaining general trustees tested their authority as a self-perpetuating clique. The government did not contest their action in filling the vacancies, and its repetition down the years continues the Mellon family's influence to the present day. The board elected Bruce vice-president and then president (following Paul Mellon's tenure in that office) in recognition of his leadership.[46]

By the time the gallery engaged Bruce, his marriage had soured. From the first mysterious illness in Rome, Ailsa Bruce became an increasingly withdrawn and melancholy woman, her unhappiness apparent in the pinched expression always on her face in newspaper photographs. Despite her father's inability to show emotion and despite the vicious tales her mother told her about him, she loathed long separations from him. In a twisted way, Andrew Mellon exerted a powerful influence over his indecisive daughter.

David tried to accommodate Ailsa's moodiness, and for the first years of their marriage, he sympathized with her hypochondria and emotional problems. The birth of their daughter Audrey in 1933 might have drawn the couple together, had they had different temperaments. Unfortunately for their marriage and their daughter, they did not. The blame was equal. David had no interest in children. Ailsa was no one's model of parenthood either, and so Audrey passed through a succession of nannies and governesses, the sad fate of so many children of great wealth. By the end of the decade, David and Ailsa tacitly agreed to keep up the public pretense, though friends knew their marriage had failed.

By then too the flamboyant style of David's youth had faded, and a more reserved persona developed. He had learned to master his impulsiveness and to internalize his nervous energy. Gradually he came to be seen not only as an appealing man but also as an immensely self-controlled one. Few people, even his friends, would know or suspect that inwardly this paragon of reserve and self-assurance always believed he was a nervous person.

The contrast between David and Ailsa in the capacity to make friends could not have been greater. He kept up with those Kosciusko Squadron pilots he had met in Warsaw and had business dealings with each of them. He helped Macgill James and others who had fallen on hard times. During the depression his actions endeared and indebted many people to him. His generosity long predated his wealth. Reveling in his enjoyment of Paris right after the war, he made a tiny loan to an acquaintance just mustered out of the French army, Raoul Boyer, sommelier at the Tour d'Argent. Boyer leveraged these few dollars into a successful wine shop that had, Bruce was delighted to learn later, near-monopoly distribution of Haut-Brion.

In London in 1932, Bruce began writing historical essays about seven American presidents. His historian uncle, Philip Bruce, had once told him that he had the ability to "write a book that will make you famous" and "keep your memory green for many generations."[47] Uncle Philip was a better historian than prophet.

Privately printed in 1936 and dedicated to his father, the book had no introduction or conclusion, no explanation for why it was written. He gave it the title *Seven Pillars of the Republic*, an obvious imitation of T. E. Lawrence's influential *Seven Pillars of Wisdom*, published a year before. In 1939 Bruce published an expanded version covering all the presidents from Washington to Lincoln. He later called the book "a shallow work and [I] am sorry that in my callow middle age I even published it."[48] Its style resembled his father's, littered with semicolons and round, mellifluous passages. One reviewer said he was too polite to his subjects. Another dismissed the book as elitist "sugar-coated history."[49]

He avoided any reference to present-day politics with one revealing exception in his assessment of Martin Van Buren and the panic of 1837. Writing when his own dislike of FDR had reached boiling point, he said approvingly of Van Buren, "He did not equivocate, he did not curry favor with a disturbed, embittered and apprehensive populace, as he might easily have done, by a distribution of public largesse, but he chose the hard course, that ultimately proved to be the wise one, of letting the wounds of the depression be healed by natural processes, without attempting to hasten the cure by the application of quack political medicaments."[50]

For all its limitations, the book offers insight into Bruce's mind. George Washington, the virtuous republican leader, was in Bruce's words the epitome of the selfless eighteenth-century gentleman, the sort of Virginia patriot role he fancied for himself. He quoted with approval the acerbic description of Washington attributed to John Randolph of Roanoke: "I am an aristocrat, I love liberty, I hate equality." He was thinking of himself as well. The reserved balance that Bruce saw in Washington's manner toward others reflected his own finely calibrated notion of proper conduct: "At his receptions and levees, he was urbane and gracious; courteous, without humility, to foreigners; cordial, without familiarity, to strangers; hospitable to acquaintances; and friendly to intimates."[51]

Bruce, however, did not show the same tenacity as Washington to make something of himself. Washington may have married well, but the similarity ended there. Bruce looked back on the 1930s as a lost time in his life. Certainly the dissonance between his experience of the depression and that of nearly all other Americans was overwhelming. Most of his contemporaries could not have imagined a lifestyle more remote from theirs than his.

Early in the New Deal, Irving Wexler learned that, like Andrew Mellon, his tax returns for 1931 had come to the attention of the Internal Revenue Service. Wexler, alias Waxey Gordon, was a beer racketeer with a penchant for gray suits and pearl-colored fedoras.[52] With Dutch Schultz he dominated organized crime in New York. To Bruce's horror, in 1935 the *New York Times* linked his name with this unsavory underworld figure in its investigation of the National Grain Yeast Corporation of Belleville, New Jersey. The paper alleged that, although

FDR's son James was president of the company, the real owner was Wexler, by then in prison for income tax evasion. The *Times* named Bruce as a principal stockholder.

Luckily, he was able to explain that he had sold his interest in the firm before Jimmie Roosevelt became president and knew nothing of Wexler's involvement.[53] He avoided scandal because of a decision he had made the previous year. Early in 1934 he decided to resign from most of his corporate boards. "I do not like the idea of continuing as an idle director," he said. "I have moved my residence to Virginia, and with the exception of a couple of small companies in which I have a substantial stock interest wish to get out of business in New York entirely."[54]

He turned from corporate obligations to the emblem of his family's earlier prominence. After Cabell sold it, the grand symbol of Bruce ascendancy had come to a sad pass. During the 1920s Staunton Hill was a hunt club owned by a syndicate composed of James and David Bruce and their friends. One spiteful neighbor expressed her glee at the "desecration" of this seat of the mighty.[55] The muddy boots of hunters did nothing for the house's state of preservation, nor did David's decision to keep a pack of foxhounds there that belonged to a local bootlegger languishing in jail.

When he learned in 1919 that his father intended to sell Staunton Hill, he had urged him not to break up the estate. It was, he said, "an ideal rich man's fancy."[56] Now he could have that fancy himself, and in 1933 he repurchased the house. "Everything is becoming somewhat dilapidated," he told a friend, "which I suppose is inevitable in a house that is seldom used. The moths are here in myriads, the roof has leaked, the ceilings are cracked, the paint hangs in damp festoons, but it all seems relatively unimportant." The decay only heightened the romantic appeal: "Bright crisp nights — with fox-hounds running all last night and their cry echoing from the river valley against the hills, frost on the ground in the morning making you think it is time for hog-killing and sausage and buck-wheat cakes. Today is real Indian summer."[57] New York seemed far away. "In the solitude of Virginia[,] parties seem not only distant but rather undesirable compared with the really important things of life such as planting tobacco and beating rugs."[58]

The remodeling energized him. "Kiss the little one for me," he wrote Ailsa during his first foray to assess the restoration, "I am crazy to have her come here. She would simply love it."[59] After entertaining three bids, he chose the one submitted by a friend. William Delano respected the original Gothic Revival exterior and did not propose, as did the other bidders, to cover it with another derivative Colonial Revival design like those in vogue among the latter-day Virginia gentry. Ailsa had pushed for the colonial look, but Delano said, "Anybody can have a Georgian house but few have as ugly a house as yours."[60]

Bruce decorated it with his European antiques and hunting prints, and he tricked up the bathrooms to imitate those at the Paris Ritz. The house for him, as for his father in his day, became the embodiment of the family's roots, its honor, its position in society — an antiquated, even feudal notion, to be sure, but one that motivated him and that his wealth allowed him to indulge.

As a man of property he surpassed even his grandfather. He acquired more than ten thousand acres. He made the usual local philanthropic gestures but beginning in 1937 began a series of far greater benefactions by building and endowing public libraries in Charlotte and eleven surrounding counties. In some sense this area had not progressed much since a colonial governor had prayed, "Thank God we have no free schools nor printing in Virginia." Bruce's gift, made with an anonymity that could not long be maintained, endeared him to rural Virginians. Locals affectionately called the original librarians "David's Children." Long afterward he said, "All libraries are good. They're one of the few institutions that never did anybody any harm."[61]

He also showed a solicitude for the county's poor, acts of noblesse oblige, but real cash donations all the same that kept families together in hard times. The poverty he had ignored as a boy now was all too visible. "You see the same little unpainted cabins surrounded by thickets and forests," he wrote a friend, "the same pathetic and unenterprising attempts to scratch a lodging in the soil for a few potatoes or yams that must have been characteristic two centuries ago. Space, time, and the outside world do not exist very vividly in the imagination of our locals."[62] He asked a local boy to drive him around the unpaved back roads and show him where the neediest residents lived. He took a special interest in the education of blacks. If most rural whites were impoverished, their black neighbors were more destitute. During the depths of depression and segregation, their separate and unequal schoolhouses were scandalously inadequate. Bruce's gifts made a real difference.[63] As if, however, to prove his father-in-law's favorite maxim about the fate of good deeds, others would soon find reason to doubt his motives.

Like his father and grandfather, Bruce sought to present himself to the voters as a candidate for office. The notion of public service flowed naturally from his image of himself as a man of property, a latter-day *grand seigneur* of the tobacco belt. The problem was how to find a seat in the rigidly controlled state legislature. As it happened, the vagaries of politics offered up just the opportunity he sought.

The oligarchic machine of U.S. Senator Harry F. Byrd Sr. so dominated Virginia that the classic account of southern politics called the state "a political museum piece."[64] Like the rest of the Solid South, one-party Virginia voted Democratic, but opponents of Byrd, called the Antis, were beginning to stir within the party. The Democratic primary in August 1939 shaped up as a contest between the factions. When Charlotte County's long-serving member of the House of Delegates sided with the Antis, the machine looked for someone to oppose him. In the wealthy scion of the county's most illustrious family, newly ensconced at Staunton Hill and hankering for political purpose, Byrd found his man.

Everything seemed set, but just as Bruce announced his candidacy, he was stunned by a bolt from the blue. He had voted against FDR in 1936, and the Virginia Democratic party forbade anyone who voted against the party in the last general election from running on its slate. With a hint of self-pity, Bruce admitted in an open letter to the press that he had violated the rule and painfully abandoned his goal of representing "this County to which I am attached by the strongest ties of personal affection and of family sentiment."[65]

It paid to have powerful friends. Just as suddenly as his candidacy seemed doomed, his political patron rescued him. A ruling by Byrd's attorney general four days before the filing deadline announced brazenly that the regulation did not apply in Bruce's case. The Antis were livid. They called Bruce a carpetbagger. His money corrupted all it touched. He had bought off Charlotte County with his gift of a library, they cried, and now he was flouting the rules of the game. They ridiculed his admission that he had voted for Alf Landon "to retain my self-respect." Was this not a gross insult to the honest burghers of

Charlotte County who had overwhelmingly supported FDR?[66] He had, in fact, given the county library two years before. Further, his generosity to blacks could hardly have been a bribe: they could not vote. But he would have been naive to think his opponents would fail to suggest a sordid link between his philanthropy and his political aspirations.

On a blistering August polling day, with the dust from the unpaved road billowing up every time a pickup truck pulled into the voting station, Bruce mingled with the voters. He was hardly a man of the people, but he dressed in an open-collared shirt and Panama hat like the tobacco farmers he greeted and showed the deference candidates must give to their electors. His efforts paid off; he garnered 2,078 votes to only 519 for his opponent.

Unlike his earlier stint in the Maryland legislature, he was determined to be a serious presence in the Virginia House of Delegates. He rented a house on the most fashionable street in Richmond and began through the adroit use of parties to play the political host. It was equally clear that his aloof wife would do little to advance her husband's prospects.[67] With a wink and a nod from Harry Byrd, he received appointments to the finance and courts of justice committees. Even before the primary the senator had written Louise Bruce a soppy note saying, "I love David very dearly."[68] In Bruce's first session, the winter term of 1940, a bill came forward that gave him a chance to show his mettle.

Senate bill 25 would bar the use of public buildings to anyone who advocated overthrowing the government. No senators objected to the bill, but when it came before the House, Bruce's fellow freshman Francis Pickens Miller reminded his colleagues anachronistically that the bill would ban Robert E. Lee from every courthouse. Bruce objected to the bill as a threat to free speech with an address of his own that, in a quiet way, riveted the attention of everyone who heard him. He was ill at ease in public speaking — perhaps from too much close company with reticent Mellons and too many years out of practice since he blithely spoke his mind in Annapolis. His discomfort showed as he stood pale-faced before the committee assigned to take evidence, a volume of Jefferson's letters he held in his hands shaking ever so slightly as he spoke.[69]

The delegate from Charlotte County argued that the bill would "make Virginia ridiculous" by proclaiming its "fear of talkative minorities." Britain, in the midst of the war that just began in September, still permitted speakers at Hyde Park Corner to denounce the empire. Why, then, should Virginians fear free speech? In its effort to throttle Communists, the bill violated the Bill of Rights. By its passage, he argued, "you would dignify them, you would make them seem powerful where they are weak."[70]

His speech draw widespread praise. Even Harry Byrd cautiously and diplomatically admitted that Bruce made a "wonderful impression" on his colleagues. Despite Bruce's eloquence, the bill passed, but that was not the end of the story. When oratory failed, Bruce and Miller went to the governor and convinced him to pocket veto the bill.

Membership in the legislature gave an imprimatur to his goal of setting himself up as a worthy descendant of the antebellum Bruces, but he had still not given up the life of a lotus-eater. He never intended to rusticate himself completely at Staunton Hill or to devote more than a few weeks a year to politics. New York and Washington still occupied more of his time, and Europe always beckoned. After shedding all those company directorships earlier, he was back on the boards of the biggest firms in America by the end of the decade and was investing as a venture capitalist in a variety of small start-up companies.

On summer nights at Jay Gatsby's Long Island estate, wrote Fitzgerald, the party-goers "came and went like moths among the whispering and the champagne and the stars."[71] The depression strangled that Fitzgeraldian extravagance, but in the Bruces' case it was Ailsa's problems and not lack of money that banished the mammoth lawn fetes of Gold Coast legend from their Long Island routine. Their parties were progressively smaller affairs that the recluse of Syosset could handle. Small, but not always sedate. A British acquaintance said that David "confirmed with some reservations Nelson Doubleday's story about his taking Sinclair Lewis to dine and play bridge at the Bruces' house and Lewis being drunk and being found in the bed of the German ambassador."[72] It is unclear when this event happened and what diplomat was involved.

At the same time, Ailsa's husband made a comfortable niche for himself in the New York smart set. His best friend was fast-living Tommy Hitchcock, also a Mellon in-law and the greatest polo player of the decade. Indeed, he had been the model for Fitzgerald's rival to

Jay Gatsby, Tom Buchanan.[73] A few perceptive friends reproached Bruce for frittering away his talents. The criticism stung, because he knew it was true.[74] He was becoming uncomfortable in the gilded Mellon cage but not enough to escape.

In 1939 David and Nelson Slater, a brash, roistering friend from New York, went on a safari in Tanganyika. For a month they lived under canvas and ate tinned food while blasting away at every species they could find on the Serengeti Plain. "My feet are a mass of blisters," he wrote when they returned to Nairobi, "while our bodies, from insect bites and thorn tears, look like Saint Sebastian's." After a month in the bush and enough animal heads to employ a squad of taxidermists, he had had enough.

When he returned home, he campaigned for the legislature. After winning the primary he planned another hunting trip, this time using the yacht of former King Michael of Rumania as a base for shooting wildfowl in the Danube delta. It was just as well he canceled the trip: September 1939 did not turn out to be the best of times for a holiday in Central Europe.

Despite his accomplishments he was still a dabbler, a dilettante on a larger, grander stage but still a dilettante, unhappily married to a troubled Medici princess and unable, or unwilling, to set himself free.

CHAPTER 6

The Heat of Burning London

The one thing everyone in Europe could agree on was the weather: it was the most hauntingly beautiful springtime in memory — soft, radiant, dazzling days stretching on one after another as if to blind people of what was to come.

— Richard M. Ketchum, *The Borrowed Years*

*I*N THE SAME MONTH of 1939 that Bruce won his Virginia primary election, those seeds that he saw the diplomats plant at Versailles twenty years before and that isolationists and appeasers had nurtured in the meantime produced a terrible crop ripening in the August sun. Stalin gave his blessing to Hitler's war in return for a share of the spoils, and the Western democracies at last saw the folly of their ways.

No one could accuse Hitler of failing to give warning — first the Rhineland, then Austria, then Czechoslovakia. When he attacked Poland on September 1, 1939, Britain and France finally came in. But once the Wehrmacht crushed the Poles, the combatants settled into a twilight war of small-scale air raids and isolated clashes at sea. Neville Chamberlain lingered on at 10 Downing Street; the French huddled behind their Maginot Line.

Americans took seriously George Washington's warning against entangling alliances and again put too much stock in the power of the ocean to protect them. The war confirmed ancient prejudices against the Old World. If many Britons believed with George V that "abroad is awful," most of America — the nation of immigrants — harbored even greater antipathy for foreigners.

Congress reflected popular sentiment with the neutrality laws of the 1930s. In the hinterlands, the powerful Midwestern wing of the Republican party cherished its ideal of an isolated America, no longer a City upon a Hill, no longer a beacon to foreigners, but an indifferent Fortress America stone-deaf to their quarrels. The left scorned military preparedness as immoral. People hid behind pious talk about the merchants of death in the arms trade to excuse their indifference to aggression. Across the political spectrum there was plenty of blame to go around. It was a time, as Churchill later wrote, when "the English-speaking peoples through their unwisdom, carelessness, and good nature allowed the wicked to rearm."[1]

Bruce's background, experience, and worldview put him at odds with most of his countrymen. His cosmopolitan circumstances made it inconceivable for him to sympathize with their distrust of things foreign. Indeed, to the "America First" crowd he personified the worldly elites of the Eastern seaboard whose Anglo- and Francophilia struck ordinary people as corrupt, effete, and subversive of good, honest, home-grown patriotism.

In the collective American memory, World War II shines as a time of national unity. The strength of the opposing sentiments that rent public opinion before Pearl Harbor is long forgotten. Charles Lindbergh, the emblematic hero of the interwar era, represented a far broader sentiment than Bruce and his friends did. Lindbergh stupidly allowed himself to be feted by the grandees of the Luftwaffe and accepted a medal expressly struck for him by Hitler. He preached frequently to large, appreciative audiences against those who would drag the nation into war. His naive sympathy for Germany and criticism of Britain struck responsive chords and showed the depth of feeling against intervention.

Bruce, by contrast, was in a minority within a minority. More than the memory of idyllic summers in Paris shaped his view. He was a director of firms with international markets. He belonged to a small club of prominent New Yorkers known simply as "The Room," possibly because of the plain apartment with an unlisted telephone number on East 62nd Street where they met once a month. The two dozen or so members, among them Nelson Doubleday, Teddy Roosevelt Jr., and

Vincent Astor, promoted Anglo-American ties. At a time when most people were indifferent to foreign affairs, they kept in close touch with like-minded men in London and probably, though the evidence is sketchy, with the British Secret Intelligence Service.[2] Their concerns were originally about communism, but they began to fear its siblings, fascism and national socialism.

Spring 1940 upset all calculations. After smashing Denmark and Norway, Hitler turned west on the tenth of May. In five days his panzers shattered the opposing defenses. In five more the lead tanks rumbled into Abbeville, near the point where the Somme flows into the English Channel, dividing the Allied armies and forcing them to face total ruin and defeat. Churchill, prime minister at last, gasped when he learned that after less than a fortnight's campaigning the French were ready to surrender their country and their honor. After abandoning their gear in a swath of mechanical litter across northern France, the British were plucked from the beaches at Dunkirk. By the end of June, England faced a hostile Continent. Stalin had befriended Hitler. America nervously reaffirmed neutrality.

Few people thought British phlegm and Churchill's rhetoric would be enough to repel the Nazis. Some expected the swastika to replace the Union Jack over Whitehall before the year was out. For a few Americans the war began that summer rather than with the thunder-clap of Pearl Harbor a year and a half later. These were people, like Bruce, disposed toward the Allies by kinship, commerce, sentiment, or experience and whose vision of world affairs came to be called inter-nationalist. Because their view triumphed, a sense of inevitability colors many accounts of their role, and a self-serving mythology has grown up that overstates their prescience. But they did exert a crucial influence on the course of world affairs, then and long after. Isolationist suspicions about them were paranoid but true: internationalists thought American national security began on the far shore of the Atlantic and not at the low tide line on Cape Cod. What united this group in 1940 — both Republicans and Democrats, conservatives and liberals — was the conviction that Britain was fighting for them.

After Dunkirk, Bruce urged Senator Harry Byrd to support a stronger defense. Some of his ideas — cuts in domestic spending and congressional oversight of presidential warmaking power — mirrored Bruce's orthodox anti–New Deal views, but others — a draft, a separate air force, more military observers sent abroad — reveal his belief that America must prepare for the war that was coming. Writing letters to senators hardly satisfied his desire to help Britain, but he did not have long to wait for something that did.

Two weeks after Hitler's troops occupied Paris in June, the luxury liner *Washington* slipped its moorings in New York harbor and sailed eastward into the war zone carrying a lone passenger. The ship's mission: to head for Galway, Ireland, and pick up American refugees fleeing the Nazi blitzkrieg. As he stood on deck and leaned against the taffrail, watching the foaming wake recede into the distance, David Bruce knew that at any moment a torpedo might send the unarmed vessel to the bottom.

The crew had reason to be on edge. They remembered all too vividly the last crossing when a German submarine stopped their ship and warned them not to return across the ocean. With that bizarre incident they had used up all their luck and dared not assume the same forbearance from the next U-boat commander. Some of them jumped ship in New York, and it took a last-minute scramble before sailing time for the *Washington*'s captain to sign on replacements.

Now, without escort, the liner steamed back through calm seas. Bruce paced the vacant decks, breathing the sea air in "solitary grandeur," as he described it.[3] On the same day of June twenty-two summers before, he had sailed in the cramped discomfort of a troopship smelling of stale sweat and vomit, not on an empty luxury liner. Yet in 1940 he reacted with the same impetuosity he displayed as a rash youth who joined the colors on the day America declared war on the kaiser.

The ship reached Galway unmolested and began to take on the anxious refugees crowding the quay — at the time the largest embarkation ever attempted from an Irish port.[4] At the dock was an American who had married into an old and titled Irish family. Nancy Adare decided to send her children to the United States out of fear that her adopted country would soon be invaded. Though the usual entertainments of Irish summers — society weddings, horticultural shows, and gossip about the turf — were about to resume, an undercurrent of barely suppressed panic gave these innocent pastimes a surreal air. Even as the busy season began for Irish holiday resorts, the Dublin city government took air raid precautions and urged parents with rural relations to send their children to the countryside. Despite her resolve to send her own progeny to more distant safety, Nancy Adare was distraught at the prospect of their leaving. Heightening her anguish, on the day the *Washington* hove into Galway, the *Irish Times* reported the sinking off the Scottish coast of a British passenger liner filled with prisoners of war.

Lady Adare wished she had worn her pearls to the dock that day so that she could have pressed them into the steward's hand as she begged him to watch over her children.[5] Tense, fearful, and confused, she was startled to learn that the *Washington's* solitary passenger was no stranger but a friend from more peaceful times, indeed, the godfather of her infant son. From her, Bruce heard firsthand of the fear of Nazi invasion that gripped even neutral Ireland. Listening to her story and seeing the apprehensive faces of the refugees, he could be forgiven for wondering if he had made the right decision to leave the safety of home.

He had done so because of the American Red Cross (ARC). While columns of refugees still clogged the roads of France, the ARC began plans to aid Britain. In June it appointed a committee of expatriates to supervise the work in London and provide a liaison with British relief agencies. The committee made a hash of things at first, and when the ARC decided to send a special delegate to sort them out, it turned to Bruce.

His reaction to the world crisis endeared him to chroniclers of the "Special Relationship" that England and America forged in adversity. At first, things almost turned out differently. When ARC chief Norman Davis asked him to be the special delegate to London, Bruce hesitated, thinking he lacked experience. Wanting to serve in some fashion, he approached Marshall Field III and suggested that Field take the post and he, Bruce, sign on as his deputy. He did not realize that Field had become a pathetic recluse absorbed with underwriting leftist causes. The erratic millionaire, in fact, had fallen under the baleful influence of Gregory Zilboorg, previously a minor official in the doomed provisional Russian government of 1917 but more recently recycled as an analyst to the neurotic rich. Field refused the Red Cross post because Zilboorg would not allow him to leave the country.[6]

Bruce then accepted Davis's original offer. As a soldier-student at the

Sorbonne in 1919 who ate most of his meals at Red Cross canteens, he had flippantly called them "the most perfect piece of social machinery." How he oiled that machinery in 1940 would challenge him far more than ironing out design details of the National Gallery or quashing repugnant bills in the Virginia legislature.

He could have lobbied for aid and written fat checks to Bundles for Britain from the safety of home. But the desire to throw himself into the thick of things ensured that, through his own doing, he would not pass World War II out of harm's way.

He reached London in early July in the pause after Dunkirk as both sides caught their breath. Just as the perennial borders of the parks and gardens reached their midseason peak of color, the Luftwaffe and the Royal Air Force began to duel for mastery of the skies over southern England. The capital seemed unexpectedly calm to him. The West End theaters flourished, and the *Times* matter-of-factly reported school cricket matches all over England. The sale of the Aga Khan's Irish yearlings for 4,400 guineas apiece still merited space in the newspapers.

But portents of war abounded. Though no bombs had yet fallen on London, sand-bagged buildings, silver flocks of barrage balloons, and the probing fingers of searchlights in the night sky warned of approaching danger. In the railway stations one could see children, clutching their toys and gas masks, being tearfully sent by their parents to safety in the countryside. In the papers Bruce could read between the lines and sense the unease thinly masked by bluff accounts of small victories at sea and on other fronts that would have no bearing on the outcome at home that summer.

After a few nights at Claridges, he accepted the hospitality of two of his oldest friends, Ronald and Nancy Tree. Born in America but raised in England, Ronnie was a Tory member of Parliament. He and David shared an uncle — through the two marriages of writer Thomas Nelson Page — and membership in the same wealthy Anglo-American circles. Ronnie's Virginia-born wife, Nancy, was like her aunt Nancy Astor, a witty, vivacious Virginian-in-exile.

To serve as a London pied-à-terre, the Trees had rented an eighteenth-century town house tucked away on a quiet street in Westminster, 26 Queen Anne's Gate, SW1. There, just off Birdcage Walk along the edge of St. James's Park, Bruce took up residence a stone's throw from Parliament Square. Nancy Tree frequently went to her Oxford-shire country home to operate a canteen service for refugees. Ronnie meanwhile kept the town house open to transient friends, among them out-of-town Britons, American journalists, and David Niven, just back from Hollywood to take the king's shilling.[7]

It was at that same town house that a small parliamentary group opposed to appeasement had met the previous September to hear their warnings confirmed in Chamberlain's sorrowful broadcast announcing that Britain was at war.[8] By June 1940, Tree was parliamentary private secretary to a member of that small circle, Alfred Duff Cooper. Bon vivant and frequently unfaithful husband of the society beauty Lady Diana Cooper, he was back in the cabinet as minister of information under Churchill supervising intelligence affairs. As Cooper's assistant, Tree was privy to information that his American houseguest would find useful in the coming months.

In July the air battle heated up over the south coast, the Wehrmacht planned Operation Sealion to cross the Channel, and Hitler grandilo-quently conferred a dozen field marshals' batons on his generals in a glittering ceremony at Berlin's Kroll Opera House. In London, as the Red Cross special delegate, Bruce faced a mountain of logistical tangles. The main task was to integrate the swelling flow of supplies from America with British requests for aid. By summer the Red Cross was sending shiploads of provisions as well as cash grants to create field kitchens, hospitals, and day nurseries for young evacuees. In July it set up shop at Thames House, on the river just upstream from Parliament, and then, to add to the confusion, in August it moved to Brettenham House on the Strand.

Norman Davis was perturbed by the amateurish start made by the committeemen and keen to see his special delegate sort them out. A quiet, deliberate, former diplomat, Davis had headed the American Red Cross since 1938.[9] It was the nation's most venerable volunteer service organization and suffered from the dilettantish ministrations of the Lady and Gentleman Bountiful types who ran its local chapters. This was no time for amateurs: Davis was taking a gamble in relying on the untested Mr. Bruce.

Davis summed up Bruce's task with the prophetic admonition "You are the real boss there but you must do it diplomatically."[10] They kept in touch by letter or cable sent through State Department channels.

When there was an emergency, they arranged for a telephone hookup, with Davis at the White House and Bruce at the American embassy. Over the crackle of transatlantic static, Bruce learned a useful lesson about keeping a finger on the pulse of his superiors.

His main task was to perform triage on the avalanche of requests from British agencies and to disabuse them of their belief that the Red Cross was "a sort of Santa Claus" that could fill every wish.[11] Though he was the special envoy of the national ARC with a personal brief from Davis, he knew he would have to tread gingerly with the proud egos of the London committeemen, all independent-minded business-men. There were also journalists to set right about their reporting on the Red Cross and the equally large egos in charge of British relief agencies that needed stroking or deflating as circumstances dictated.

Some of the principals of British war relief were new faces, but for Bruce many more were old friends whose names filled the pages of *Debrett's* and the rolls of the poshest clubs in St. James's. Two of the most important people in British relief work were women who, in Bruce's understated opinion, "do not suffer from mutual admiration of each other."[12] When he discovered that Lady Ward had "no business sense," he devised a way to disengage gracefully from her committee without ruffling highborn feathers.[13] He was especially impressed with Stella, dowager marchioness of Reading, the widow of a viceroy of India and founder of the Women's Voluntary Service for Civil Defense (WVS). It became clear to him that Lady Reading, a large woman whose deep voice and no-nonsense attitude commanded instant respect, ran the most efficient relief agency in the country. He called her "the most extraordinary woman in England today" and saw to it that the WVS received generous Red Cross aid.

His contacts that summer illustrate the ties between the upper reaches of British and American society. He saw Nancy Tree's acid-tongued aunt, Nancy Astor, for example, who had been the first woman to sit in the House of Commons and was the most famous American expatriate in Britain. By summer 1940 Lady Astor's solidarity with her bomb-scarred constituents in Plymouth had removed a bit of the tarnish of her links with prewar appeasement. Bruce did not hold her earlier opinions against this fellow Virginian. He even had kind words for Joseph P. Kennedy Sr., America's ambassador to the Court of St. James's, nominal head of the Red Cross London committee, and prophet of British defeat. (Perhaps these two Democrats discovered in their dislike of FDR something to agree on despite their radically different views on the war.)

Bruce expected to see more of the war than relief work and was not disappointed. In August the Germans began *Adlerangriff* ("Eagle Attack"), a major assault on fighter bases, radar networks, and command centers. By the end of the month the Luftwaffe pushed the RAF to the brink of statistical defeat. At the rate of losses then being suffered, Fighter Command would cease to exist as a coordinated force in a matter of days. Reprieve came only when the attackers switched to terror bombing of London.

Before that providential shift in tactics, Bruce often went with journalists to see the combat raging above the south coast. Shakespeare Cliff, towering over the Channel near Dover and described by Gloucester in *King Lear* as "the dread summit of this chaulky bourn," provided a favorite vantage point. "The cliff was almost a stage-setting," one reporter wrote, "so perfect was it as an observation point, and as a result the press of the whole democratic world gathered on it."[14] Disregarding their own safety, the journalists watched the closely matched Me-109s and Spitfires duel overhead.[15]

In this surreal setting, the battle ebbed and flowed above the watchers on the cliff. One minute the lazy peace of summertime, the next the crash and alarm of war. "We lay in the grass among the red currants and the butterflies," one of Bruce's companions wrote, "while the fate of the world was being decided for us." As they watched one day, a flight of Messerschmitts attacked targets nearby, shooting down barrage balloons in crimson flames. One of the planes peeled away from the rest and strafed the Americans on the cliff.

Many of the journalists were his closest friends that summer. Virginia Cowles wrote for the *New York Herald Tribune*. After the war she married a member of parliament, Aidan Crawley, and they both remained Bruce's lifelong friends. Helen Kirkpatrick sent a stream of front-line stories to the *Chicago Daily News* throughout the war. A tall woman of striking features, she was another of the talented transients, like Bruce, who took advantage of the Trees' hospitality at 26 Queen Anne's Gate.

Another journalist who shared the camaraderie was Ben Robertson, an exuberant South Carolinian who recklessly sought out danger and paid for it later with his life. He and Bruce liked to muse about the future. "David and I would talk about the South, about its problems and its progress and about our duty to it," Robertson wrote, "about settling there as soon as the chance offered and working for it. . . . I remember one afternoon when the sea was a lovely crystal glittering blue and the sky was blue with banks of enormous cumulus clouds, David and I sat on the cliff between two battles and talked through an afternoon about Lee and Jeb Stuart and Jackson, about the War between the States."[16] And about improving race relations. For Robertson and Bruce had that easy way of open-minded white southerners, inexplicable to outsiders, of talking unselfconsciously in the same breath about Confederate generals and the need to improve race relations.

In those brief, concentrated moments overlooking the Channel, Bruce was present for one of the most dramatic scenes of the war. With Robertson, Cowles, Kirkpatrick, and also with correspondents Edward R. Murrow, Vincent Sheean, and H. R. Knickerbocker, he shared the danger more than a year before their nation was at war.

The defiance of the British infected Bruce too. Before the real test came in the Blitz, he wrote home, "Personally, I believe that England is impregnable against a German invasion."[17] Street traffic, he said, made New York more dangerous than London — true enough for the moment, not counting forays to Shakespeare Cliff. Working alongside the British emboldened him to predict on August 22 that "London has not been bombed at all nor is it likely to be."[18] Two days later the first bombs exploded in the city center and demolished his prediction. Two weeks later the Blitz began.

When Hitler ordered the terror bombing of the capital, Bruce no longer needed to go to the south coast to see action. At Brettenham House, a modern office block at the north end of Waterloo Bridge, itself a favorite German target halfway between Westminster and the dome of St. Paul's, he looked out every morning and saw the Luftwaffe's handiwork.

At night when the sirens sounded he joined the procession of Londoners underground and waited as tension mounted until sometimes his air raid shelter shook from the explosions and dust settled on his fine Savile Row suit. Before long, this helpless confinement irritated him, and he began to take his chances in his own bed.

The convenient location of the Trees' house put it midway between two magnets for German bombers — Buckingham Palace and the Houses of Parliament. On the same night that two high-explosive bombs fell in a palace courtyard, scores of incendiaries rained phosphorescent fire down on Queen Anne's Gate. The next day an unexploded bomb blocked the street until an army disposal unit removed it. These men exhibited extraordinary heroism, Bruce thought. Whenever a delayed-action bomb fell, "they would rush to the scene and calmly proceed to pull the fuse out, in the full knowledge that the thing might go off in their faces at any instant. Indeed, many of them were killed at it."[19] When a similar device inconvenienced a meeting called by one of his friends, she calmly sent her guests the message "Lady Reading is very sorry, but she has to call her luncheon off — there's a time bomb in the garden."[20]

Bruce lived on adrenaline and three or four hours of sleep a night. After long days at the office, he often joined the more adventuresome souls who gathered at the Savoy and other watering spots for the well-to-do to dine and dance in defiance of the bombs.[21]

In the mornings paperwork and unloading supplies occupied the staff, but the sound of antiaircraft fire and exploding bombs replaced the normal background noises. He told a reporter that he feared fragments from antiaircraft shells as much as bombs: "There's absolutely no protection against them. You can't tell where they are going to fall."[22] While he was there, the bombs spared Red Cross headquarters, though not the grand pile of Somerset House across the street. He tried to open the office at 9 A.M., but the staff often straggled in throughout the morning, depending on how badly rubble from the night's bombing diverted traffic. When daylight attacks increased to the point of disrupting normal routine, the office posted its own lookout rather than heed the general air raid sirens as the signal to head for the shelters.

With journalistic exaggeration, *PM* magazine, a new periodical funded by Marshall Field, praised Bruce's contribution as the cavalier adventures of a suave American hero defying Nazi bombs to aid the plucky British. That a left-wing journal would glamorize such a beneficiary of monopoly capital as Bruce was an irony that should not have escaped him — not least because *PM*'s intellectual godparents included those chic Stalinists of American letters Lillian Hellman and Dashiell Hammett, who had little sympathy for Britain before Hitler attacked Stalin. At the same time an actress friend thoughtfully gave Bruce an identification bracelet: if he died in an air raid, the rescue crew that dragged his body from the rubble would at least know his name.[23] "The sky of south and east London was glowing with flames," a journalist friend wrote about a typical night, "guns were firing over the entire city, and bombs were falling in the southwest part. Antiaircraft shells were bursting in the clear yellow starry sky. . . . that night I spent on a couch in David Bruce's room."[24]

In years to come Bruce could share, as few other Americans could, the British national memory of that summer. After an overcast July and uncertain weather in August came a progression of days of cloudless, china-blue skies streaked with the contrails of hundreds of airplanes. By September 15 — the climax of the daylight clashes and celebrated ever since as Battle of Britain Day — Londoners could see swarms of Messerschmitts, Hurricanes, and Spitfires jinking and wheeling high overhead.

Bruce did not just share the memory of that experience but helped in a small way to create the mental picture Americans formed of it. Like his friend Edward R. Murrow, whose somber, no-nonsense voice Americans associated with the Blitz even more than Churchill's, Bruce made effective use of the radio. In a broadcast to America, he spoke of the insistent drone of bombers overhead and of fires bright enough for one to read a newspaper at midnight. His words helped his audience imagine the charred ruins that greeted Red Cross workers picking their way through the rubble to Brettenham House every morning. When he told his listeners that thousands of Britons thanked the relief agency for "the very clothes on their backs," he spoke with the quiet assurance of one who had personally felt the heat of burning London.[25]

He returned home in October, a month later than planned, leaving his tin helmet with Vincent Sheean, another of his extravagant, hard-living journalist friends, and his heart with the embattled city. After surviving the hottest month of the Blitz, he had no doubt whether his country should stand aside from the fight. By the time he left London, he won enthusiastic acclaim from all sides. His chief assistant wrote headquarters that he had "never met anybody so universally well liked as David Bruce." Here was a hint of the Bruce appeal that would become a legend among Europe's diplomats. Lady Reading put her finger on a particular Bruce trademark — his knack for resolving immediate conflicts and at the same time taking what she called "a long view."[26]

Three months later he returned to England for the Red Cross aboard a Pan American Clipper, one of the giant new seaplanes that had begun transatlantic service just before the war. On his flight eight other passengers, a crew of eleven, and three tons of mail crowded into the big flying boat. To extend their range, the planes were stripped of seats to make room for spare gasoline tanks, food, water, and emergency rafts. The route took him to Bermuda and then neutral Portugal. At Lisbon the flight crew weighed the passengers and fortified them with ham rolls, tea, and blankets before sending them off before dawn on a white-knuckled flight to England.

Though the Germans had abandoned major daylight raids, the nights still belonged to them, and they spared London on few evenings that winter. Again Bruce enjoyed the hospitality of Ronnie and Nancy Tree, including weekends at their country place. Just before the war they had bought an eighteenth-century Oxfordshire estate, Ditchley Park, and its contents — lock, stock, and ancestral portraits. Nancy, better known by her later name, Nancy Lancaster, redecorated Ditchley in the style that after the war she would use to transform the firm of Colefax and Fowler, premier interior designers to the gentry. Her warm, sun-faded chintzes, borrowed from memories of the shabby-genteel Virginia houses of her youth, became the trademark look of the English country house, a style that was then ironically reexported for American consumption.[27]

In mid-February two days before he left for home, Bruce shared Ditchley with a more famous guest. Out of fear that the prime minister's official country house, Chequers, would attract German bombers on nights when the moon was bright, Churchill secretly began to spend weekends at Ditchley.[28] The house party that weekend built up gradually, with Bruce among the earliest to arrive on Friday as the weak winter light began to fail in midafternoon. The handsome Red Cross envoy had the women to himself at tea — Nancy Tree, the prime minister's daughter Mary, and Lady Diana Cooper ("Divine Diana, most perfect of women," Bruce later described her[29]). By the time Churchill arrived, others had gathered, including prime ministerial intimates Brendan Bracken and Professor F. A. Lindemann, as well as the head of British military intelligence.

With his usual bad manners, the prime minister kept the others up well past midnight. The next day in characteristic form he summoned a senior army officer to his room for a briefing. Sitting up in bed in his dressing gown, cigar clenched in teeth and papers strewn all over the covers, he held court. The officer came away recalling vividly one phrase that suggests Bruce, or at least what he represented, was on Churchill's mind. The prime minister held up his fingers and said, "Do you play poker? Here is the hand that is going to win the war: a Royal Flush — Great Britain, the Sea, the Air, the Middle East, American Aid."[30]

On the trip home, Bruce again faced Luftwaffe fighter planes based in Brittany within striking range of the vulnerable civilian flights connecting England to Portugal. To avoid German hunters, pilots took their blacked-out aircraft in a wide arc out over the Bay of Biscay. Bruce's favorite pilot was a tall Dutchman who died the following year when the Germans, tipped off to the presence of a celebrity passenger on a certain flight, shot down the plane carrying actor Leslie Howard (Scarlett O'Hara's Ashley Wilkes) thinking he was Churchill. After flying in pitch dark through the night of February 17–18, praying his plane would not attract unfriendly attention, Bruce welcomed the lights of neutral, spy-ridden Lisbon and a hot bath in one of the deep marble tubs of the Hotel Aviz.[31]

After these dangerous, energizing trips, it was impossible to return to routine. There was no way the Virginia legislature could compete with aiding embattled Britain. (After being an absentee delegate for a second term, he did not run for reelection.) Neither could completing the National Gallery. For all its grandeur, this largest private gift to the nation seemed out of joint with the times. Even before his second trip to London, he made plans to move to Washington in the belief that American neutrality was about to end.[32]

For a time he continued Red Cross work at home and exhorted the ARC national convention to continue aiding "that extraordinarily brave and gallant race" of Britons.[33] After being on the receiving end of Hitler's bombs, he was even more convinced of his views than when he had sailed for London the previous summer. In April he joined the Fight For Freedom committee composed of prominent internationalists struggling against isolationist opinion. No one involved was surprised when one of the largest contributions the committee ever received — more than $10,000 — arrived from Mrs. David Bruce.[34]

The FFF committee was one of the most extreme internationalist organs. His support of the committee's strident position shows how strongly the normally circumspect, reserved Bruce felt about the war. According to the FFF, not even massive military aid to Britain was enough. Bruce now called for an outright declaration of war on Germany. "The present hazardous situation of Great Britain has partially awakened us from a state of lotus-eating torpor," he argued, perhaps with his own indolence in mind. "The shadows have lengthened, and one by one the lights of Europe have been extinguished. . . . We should amend our national thinking so as to realize that there are things worse than war. There are ideals worth fighting for. There are causes worth dying for. The maintenance of human freedom is such a cause."[35] The chances he took with his own safety validate these words as more than the pious opinions of an armchair patriot. He belonged to a small band of American heroes at a time, as Churchill later wrote, when "the British people held the fort ALONE till those who hitherto had been half blind were half ready."[36]

In the first year of Hitler's war, another American who shared Bruce's internationalist sentiments was President Roosevelt. For all his preoccupation with domestic ills, he had always taken a global view. Once Germany defeated France, he saw the folly of thinking America could stand aloof much longer. He could go only so fast in his effort to aid Britain, however, or he would outpace the public and risk losing reelection in November 1940. Although FDR instinctively sympathized with the British, he needed to know if they were likely to hold out.

He did know he could no longer trust his ambassador in London. A shrewd, corrupt power in the Massachusetts Democratic party who had made his fortune in bootlegging, Joseph P. Kennedy thought the British were finished. He said so openly, sent home defeatist cables, and suggested that Americans begin to think about living with a Europe dominated by Hitler. Perhaps the Nazi New Order would not be so bad after all. Though he supported Bruce's Red Cross committee as its honorary chairman, Joe Kennedy was no friend of England. No one was fooled by public gestures, like his purchase for 300 pounds of a silver-gilt tea service donated by the queen for a war relief benefit sale at Christie's.[37] Roosevelt needed more reliable sources of information about conditions there, and the foremost observer he sent in summer 1940 was William Joseph Donovan.

America's most decorated hero of World War I, successful Wall Street lawyer, and fervent Republican, "Wild Bill" Donovan seemed an unlikely confidant for the architect of the New Deal. Despite their differences, FDR sensed that Donovan shared his view of foreign events and would provide him an unvarnished assessment. "If Bill Donovan had been a Democrat," FDR once generously said, "he'd be in my place today."[38] It was not true of course. Not even "Wild Bill" could match the famous FDR instinct for political intrigue. Donovan spent three pivotal weeks in London during the Battle of Britain at the president's request. The American ambassador writhed in silent fury as the British rolled out the red carpet for Donovan. "Wild Bill" told FDR that Kennedy was wrong: England would hold out. But it could not win without American aid.

While Bruce, Donovan, and others did their part to support the British and keep Washington informed, opinion began to shift. After France fell, most Americans acknowledged the need to spend more on defense but still recoiled from the thought of war. The 1941 bill to extend conscription, originally approved during the Battle of Britain the previous year, dramatized the national mood when it passed the House of Representatives by a single vote. The president himself, far from plotting deviously for war as conspiracy folklore has it, still doubted the wisdom of entering the conflict. While America hesitated, a greater, if less visible, peril than the Blitz threatened: Britain was losing the war at sea. By May 1941 U-boats were sinking merchantmen twice as fast as shipyards could replace them. Lose the Battle of the Atlantic, and all the aid would be in vain. Despite the efforts of David Bruce's Red Cross, Churchill's island nation would starve.

As Britain's requirements for the matériel of war grew desperate, so did the parallel need for intelligence. In the aftermath of Dunkirk, Canadian industrialist William Stephenson, better known by his code name "Intrepid," had arrived in New York to direct British intelligence activities in the Americas. One of the first men he approached was Donovan, whose trip to Britain later that summer may have resulted from the prompting of "Intrepid." The origins of British-American cooperation in intelligence are obscured by the heroic mythology surrounding these founding fathers of modern espionage. Even so, through Stephenson's reports and Donovan's visits, the British came to believe that "Wild Bill" had Roosevelt's ear. They also believed he was the one to create an American covert intelligence organization to work in tandem with their own hard-pressed services. They revealed their secret operations to him with remarkable openness, at least in the early days before he became competition.

In early 1941 Donovan lobbied hard to persuade FDR to create a civilian agency for gathering strategic intelligence. Powerful opponents, including J. Edgar Hoover, schemed against him. After months of intrigue, on July 11, 1941, Roosevelt created the agency Donovan desired and called it the Office of the Coordinator of Information, COI. The appropriately cryptic, 252-word executive order marked an event of unheralded political significance: it demonstrated American rejection of isolationism, and it provided a milestone in the expansion of presidential power. COI was not the only intelligence service — the army, navy, and FBI had theirs — and it was not the centralized, strategic operation of Donovan's dreams. But it gave "Wild Bill" all the authorization he needed to build his empire, with millions from FDR's secret, unvouchered funds hidden from congressional scrutiny.[39]

COI began with only two components, a foreign information service and, more important, a research and analysis division. The former dealt in propaganda, while the latter gathered and collated information on any subject that might be useful in wartime. Fortunately, espionage was not the first priority. Coordinating even nonsecret data into usable form was difficult enough. Both the agency's creative energy and its troubles flowed from Donovan's personality. Like other men of action, Donovan neglected good habits of administration and fostered the systemic chaos that always surrounded COI. His World War I friend G. Edward "Ned" Buxton joined as his unofficial deputy and often said his job was to clean up after "Wild Bill."[40]

If Donovan offended powerful men in Washington, he made sure to cultivate friends in the White House. The Donovan force of will that brought the agency into being in the first place also attracted a gifted staff and infused them with enthusiasm. Without regard to political philosophy, in a few months he hired a glittering pool of talent — academics, entrepreneurs, Ivy League Republican bankers, left-wing labor attorneys, anyone with a particular aptitude that he thought could contribute. That is the story COI veterans like to tell, and there is truth in it. Alumni included four future CIA directors (Allen Dulles, Richard Helms, William Colby, and William Casey) and Americans who went on to excel in many fields. Smithsonian director S. Dillon Ripley, *cuisinière* Julia Child, reporter Joseph Alsop, Supreme Court Justice Arthur Goldberg, historian Arthur M. Schlesinger Jr., and film director John Ford. Once FDR signed the authorizing order, Donovan ran roughshod over the civil service, flouted regulations, and spent vastly beyond his budget.

One of those he tapped for leadership was David Bruce. Well before the war Donovan knew of his British sympathies — like Bruce he was a member of "The Room." When Donovan reached England on his fact-finding trip in 1940, he saw firsthand Bruce's skill in solving Red Cross problems. Indeed, they shared the same address. Perhaps it was no coincidence that Ronnie Tree's town house stood only a few feet from the headquarters of MI-6, the British Secret Intelligence Service. It was certainly no coincidence that Donovan relied on Tree in his role as parliamentary private secretary to Duff Cooper, whose portfolio as minister of information included the secret services. Tree helped Donovan prepare his report to FDR on British capabilities. Bruce recalled long afterward that during that summer he observed some of the British clandestine operations "at a distance," perhaps a reference to what he gleaned from talking with Tree and Donovan when they unwound over drinks in the evenings back at Queen Anne's Gate.[41] In any event, Bruce and Donovan kept in close touch from that point on.

As a committed internationalist who had seen the Battle of Britain and the Blitz firsthand, who enjoyed important contacts in England and America, and who had the requisite motivation and worldview, Bruce was a promising choice for Donovan. He lacked the managerial experience of the executives Donovan also hired, but "Wild Bill" suspected that the tall, articulate southerner would rise to the occasion.

Bruce sensed that Donovan was onto something important. There would be other instances of his instinct for hitching his wagon to a cause on the rise but none more dramatic than when he joined the nascent intelligence agency on the eve of war. The Red Cross enabled him to escape from the routine of museum and corporate board meetings and from his failed marriage. The COI offered an uncharted sea full of danger and opportunity. The exhilaration of a cause gave him a sense of resolve.

That feeling recalled the intoxicating days at the end of the Great War. Then adventure drew him abroad. Twenty years on, he could more maturely articulate the cause that deserved defending. The COI, like the Red Cross, offered him a chance to achieve something in his own right, not because of Mellon connections. For Bruce, FDR's reliance on Donovan was crucial. It altered the course of his life. He could not deny it, but once again the decisions of "that man" in the White House, whom Bruce loathed for his persecution of Andrew Mellon, directly affected his own course.

In August 1941 Bruce went back to London, ostensibly for the Red Cross but more likely using that agency as a cover.[42] On October 10 he officially began work for the COI as a special assistant to Donovan at one dollar a year. Learning its espionage tradecraft from the British, the COI gave each employee a numerical code. Bruce's was "107," one digit removed from the more famous number given by his friend in British intelligence Ian Fleming to his fictional protagonist.[43] It was really the first full-time job Bruce held since the Army Courier Service, if one discounts the ill-fated consular post and the part-time work on Wall Street. As head of COI's newly created Secret Intelligence branch, he supervised the information-gathering component, known in the early days as "Special Activities — Bruce." His colleague, publisher M. Preston Goodfellow, oversaw the embryonic Special Operations branch, or "Special Activities — Goodfellow." In the corridors of Q building, one of many temporary wooden structures that sprang up on the Mall, some COI staffers called Goodfellow "irresponsible as a blue-bottle fly."[44] Bruce's social prominence tempted them to whisper the same about him, but they would have been mistaken to do so.

In the fall of 1941 the COI was still a frail creature, vulnerable to many enemies. But it energized Bruce to feel he was at the sharp edge of the internationalists' effort to wake America from its lethargy and prepare for the war he believed was coming. Years later, he reflected with nostalgia on the time he decided "to follow the Pied Piper" into COI.[45] In October 1941, though, America was still at peace. For all their sympathy for the British and other victims of Nazi aggression, most Americans even then still hoped the angel of death would pass over their doorway and leave them in peace. "Wild Bill" may have fancied himself a magus of the black arts of espionage, but that was wishful thinking at the time. What did he and Bruce hope to achieve — despite their can-do American bravado, mere babes in the intelligence woods compared to the German Abwehr and Britain's MI-6?

CHAPTER 7

OSS at War

Wherever the United States needed to lose any kind of virginity in global affairs, the British were on hand with unguents and aphrodisiacs of all kinds.

— Christopher Hitchens, *Blood, Class, and Nostalgia*

By MID-1941 the draft, the defense buildup, and Lend-Lease aid to Britain moved America closer to war. Tension increased when FDR froze Japanese assets by executive order. In the western Atlantic, U.S. Navy protection for convoys sailing to England invited U-boat attack. But for all their efforts to convince America to oppose Hitler, internationalists like Bruce could not drag the nation into war. Where they failed, carrier-based planes of the Imperial Japanese Fleet succeeded. Pearl Harbor brought home to all Americans the war that Bruce had seen up close for more than a year. Later, but well before victory was assured, he admitted that "the Jap attack was a blessing — even though well disguised at the time." It forced the United States "out of our lethargy in a manner that a less disastrous incident would not have accomplished."[1]

Now he could throw away the resolution he was preparing for the Virginia legislature just before Pearl Harbor. That document ended with a plea to abandon neutrality and declare war against Hitler. "The American people is witnessing a world revolution," he argued. "Two irreconcilable philosophies are contending for the mastery of the human soul. One must conquer and the other must die."

The few months of peace that COI enjoyed came to an end with

Pearl Harbor. Its growing pains did not. In early 1942 bureaucratic opponents nearly succeeded in garroting COI and cannibalizing the choicest bits. The head of army intelligence, designated G-2, Maj. Gen. George V. ("George the Fifth") Strong, despised Donovan and tried to kill his agency outright, calling it a "hydra-headed organization." J. Edgar Hoover loathed COI too. A man of long memory and little forgiveness, he had not forgotten that in 1924 Donovan, as assistant attorney general, opposed his appointment to the FBI. Hoover showed his hand when he learned that COI planned to burgle the Spanish embassy in Washington to photograph documents. He sent FBI cars racing up to the building with sirens wailing and forced the spies to flee. He acted not out of respect for the niceties of diplomatic immunity for the pro-Nazi Spanish but to embarrass COI.[2]

Bruce said these enemies "forgot their internecine animosities and joined in an attempt to strangle this unwanted newcomer at birth." He expressed unmitigated contempt for army intelligence. "Lights burned late in the Munitions Building," he said, "where a succession of chiefs observed, with jaundiced eye, the attempts of more progressive subordinates to inject some flavor of the twentieth century into the dank atmosphere of G-2."[3]

The British became so alarmed that early in 1942 they sent emissaries to Washington to assess COI's chances, an ironic mirror image of Donovan's earlier trip to size up Britain's prospects. One delegation, composed of journalist Ritchie Calder and David Bowes-Lyon, brother-in-law of the king, described COI aptly as "an amorphous group of activities which has developed out of the personality of Colonel Donovan."[4] They decided it would survive, and it did, but only by a whisker.[5]

Roosevelt gave American secret intelligence a second birth, on June 13, 1942, by reincarnating COI as the Office of Strategic Services directly under the joint chiefs of staff. Although it lost the "white," or overt, propaganda function to another agency, OSS grew into five major branches — Secret Intelligence (SI), Research and Analysis (R&A), Counterespionage (X-2), Special Operations (SO), and Morale Operations (MO) — and at its peak would employ more than 13,000 men and women around the world.

That growth lay in the future. While COI fought turf wars in Washington, in early 1942 America, Britain, and also Soviet Russia — betrayed by its German ally the previous summer — staggered from battlefield catastrophes. In numbing succession after Pearl Harbor came the fall of Hong Kong, Manila, and Singapore. Rommel approached his zenith in the desert. The battle of the Atlantic increased in ferocity, threatening to undo all the schemes and plans — they were still no more than that — for Allied victory.

In that first spring of America's war, the new agency could offer only the promise of intelligence coups and clandestine operations to come. British intelligence, with years of experience and no lack of lessons learned the hard way, opened its doors to the newcomers. The Americans had a lot to learn, even if they never subscribed to the remark, possibly apocryphal, of Secretary of War Henry Stimson: "Gentlemen do not read each other's mail." As one of Donovan's key deputies, forty-four-year-old David Bruce faced his most important challenge yet.

The agency consisted largely of civilians at first, though the top people emulated Donovan and took commissions. Not that it mattered much. Rank meant little in COI/OSS, military tradition less. In March Bruce became a major in the Army Air Corps attached informally to Colonel Donovan. A studio photograph shows how well his Brooks Brothers uniform suited the handsome major. A background check listed three United States senators as character references and cheerfully declared him to be without "suspicion or evidence of any Pro-Nazi or Fascist activities or connections."[6] His Georgetown residence did not fare so well. The technicians who swept the house on 34th Street for electronic bugs found nothing suspicious but pronounced it a first-class security risk and advised changes in the telephone service and wiring.[7]

In that spring the disorderly growth of Bruce's command accelerated as his growing team interviewed applicants and ordered the file cabinets, typewriters, government-issue gray metal desks, and other weapons of the bureaucrat-warrior. These were the woolly-headed academics, would-be spies, and "staff of Jewish scribblers" denounced in Berlin by Joseph Goebbels himself.[8] By March "Special Activities — Bruce," under the new title of Secret Intelligence branch (SI), began to issue concrete analyses and to spin out its first webs of agent networks. In the early days it concentrated on sub-Saharan Africa, along the supply routes to Britain's hard-pressed forces in Egypt. The State Department provided SI with VICTOR, a special communications channel that funneled oveseas messages to Bruce. Compared with the meager fruits of other branches in the early months, SI produced more of value than most of the agency, excepting only the academic sleuths in the Research and Analysis branch.[9]

From an early date the schizoid nature of OSS was apparent to Bruce. On the one hand, it was designed to collect information. This could be data sifted from published sources in the Library of Congress or gleaned from German newspapers bought in neutral countries. Or it could come from clandestine sources — spies, stolen papers, tapped phones, and the like. On the other hand, the agency also intended to mount secret, unconventional military operations. This combination gave OSS its unique character. The British, by contrast, kept those functions separate.

Increasingly, Donovan was drawn to the dramatic promise of unorthodox military action. He never saw a hare-brained scheme he did not like, and the penchant for promoting them grew with each passing month. War was his element. He was "constantly trying to get closer to the smell of cordite, rushing around the world setting up intelligence stations and approving covert operations. He was a romantic, and the glamour of uniforms and bravery strongly appealed to him."[10]

"Woe to the officer," Bruce said, "who turned down a project because, on its face, it seemed ridiculous, or at least unusual."[11] In October 1942 he proposed one of his own. He suggested to Donovan that they pressure the army to increase parachute training. With a million parachutists, he argued, "instead of talking about a bridgehead in France . . . we could perhaps talk with some optimism of establishing a bridgehead at Berlin or at Munich."[12] The agency's inclination for the bizarre gave OSS's detractors plenty of ammunition. "Full of politics, ballyhoo, and controversy" was Charles Lindbergh's opinion. The regular army looked askance at this "fly-by-night civilian outfit headed up by a wild man who was trying to horn in on the war."[13]

In June the head of SI went to England to negotiate an operational protocol with the British Secret Intelligence Service (MI-6). Plans for the trip took shape before Roosevelt decided to reconstitute COI as OSS. When Bruce left the country, he did not even know whether the agency would still exist when he returned.

By that summer a rudimentary system of transatlantic flights linked Britain and America using a northerly, three-legged route. Bruce took a Pan American Clipper stripped of all peacetime amenities from La Guardia to Newfoundland and then across to Ireland. Like him, most passengers were Army Air Corps officers bound for liaison missions in England. A last-minute snag arose when the Irish, jealous of their neutrality and keen to avoid any appearance of aiding Britain, forbade military uniforms on flights to their country. Scrambling to comply, he and his brother officers bought out a second-hand clothing merchant right before departure, and Irish honor was satisfied.

When the Clipper broke through the clouds over the green checkerboard of western Ireland and set down at Foynes, on the south side of the Shannon estuary, Major Bruce met some old friends. Among them were Helen Kirkpatrick, the journalist who had stood beside him on Shakespeare Cliff during the Battle of Britain, and Nancy Adare, his expatriate friend married to the heir of the earl of Dunraven. Before taking a plane to England, he drove with them to lunch at a nearby inn opposite the gates of the Dunraven estate.

At the Dunraven Arms he also met by prearrangement Capt. Charles "Dick" Ellis, deputy chief of Sir William Stephenson's British intelligence operation in New York. Bruce credited Ellis with helping him set up COI's Secret Intelligence branch. What he and his colleagues did not know was that before the war Ellis may have given MI-6's order of battle to the Germans and shared other British secrets with them and also with the Soviets via his wife's Russian émigré connections. According to the source of this information, Ellis later privately confessed to giving the Germans material for money before the war but denied any wartime transgressions or any Soviet connection.[14] It would still have been treason.

In London the breadth of Bruce's contacts was again apparent, as was British attentiveness to an important emissary of their American allies. On the first day he conferred with Brig. Gen. Stewart Menzies, code-named "C," the head of the Secret Intelligence Service. Whether Bruce had been inside MI-6 headquarters before is unclear. Certainly the building's facade was familiar to him: the address was 24 Queen Anne's Gate. He dined that evening at the Dorchester, where the party included Lady Colefax, Lord Louis Mountbatten, just appointed chief of combined operations in England, a couple of cabinet ministers, a famous jockey, and Freda Casa Maury (formerly Freda Dudley Ward), a former mistress of the Duke of Windsor. The next day he touched base with more secret agencies, including long talks at the Political Warfare Executive (PWE) and in the "veritable rabbit-warren of offices" belonging to the Special Operations Executive (SOE). After conferring with American ambassador John Winant, Averell Harriman (then FDR's special envoy to Britain), and the COI station chief, he dined with Audrey Bouverie, once described by Evelyn Waugh as a "strained, nervous, cross-patch of a woman," and yet another of the Duke of Windsor's former mistresses.[15]

The same pattern of day-long meetings and late-night dining with the top espionage figures and the social elite filled the month he spent in London. In conversations with these and other sympathetic Britons, he impressed them with his penchant for taking the long view, talking not of the current struggle but about postwar reconstruction. He was eager to look beyond the grim present — even as the Wehrmacht continued its advance in North Africa and across southern Russia — to plan for what he believed would be America's role as the greatest world power. Anglophile that he was, he twitted the British for sizing up Americans according to the simplistic yardstick of whether they were pro- or anti-British. "There are many Isolationists who are pro-British," he corrected London gossip and political cognoscente Robert Bruce Lockhart, and "quite a lot of Americans who wanted this war or, at least, felt it was necessary, who loathe the English!"[16]

Donovan arrived at the end of Bruce's visit, and they both learned a few days later that FDR had signed the order creating OSS. They left London in high spirits. The news about OSS justified Bruce's month of consultations and gave the two intelligence chiefs great expectations about working with their British allies.

At the end of the summer Bruce went into the field again, this time to inspect his SI networks strung out across central Africa on the air supply route to British forces in Egypt. He had taken a mysterious trip to South America the previous autumn just before Pearl Harbor, probably to check on his first agents there. He began the 1942 trip as one of twenty passengers on a C-47, the transport workhorse of the war. Island hopping through the Caribbean, he reached Brazil and then changed to a Clipper, spending the night sprawled on the floor of the plane as it crossed to Nigeria. Some of his agents were Pan American employees stationed there, and he praised them as making "better representatives of our country than do many of our diplomatic, consular, army and navy officers."[17]

As the plane flew from one remote, dusty airstrip to another across the waist of Africa, the number of passengers dwindled. Stopping overnight in the Sudan, retracing part of his 1939 safari route, he fought mud and flies, "like a Biblical plague." The plane took off the next morning just after dawn: "We were all glad to leave this place, which is simply a desert station, and this morning was totally without water. We are now down to nine passengers and a good deal of freight. Arrived at Khartoum on 10:20, left at 11:40 and reached Luxor, which abounds with American beer and cigarettes, at 3:55 P.M., we went to see the magnificent ruins of Karnak."

After the London Blitz and East Coast blackouts, he was surprised by the insouciance of the Cairenes, separated by a short drive across the sands from the lead panzers of the Afrika Korps. "Cairo is something of a shock in that life seems completely normal. One can buy anything in the shops," he marveled, "in fact in some respects goods seem more plentiful than at home," thanks to the robust black markets that feasted on the infusion of wartime supplies.[18]

One of the Americans he saw there was Theodore Morde, an espionage buccaneer and assistant to the OSS station chief. Morde later launched a scheme that may have been known to OSS, though it could have been a bit of "private enterprise." He tried to persuade the German ambassador to Turkey, former chancellor Franz von Papen, to lead a coup against Hitler. In return, Morde offered American assent to German hegemony in Central Europe, an offer that would have led to acute diplomatic embarrassment if his report to FDR had been leaked.[19] Whether Bruce knew of this scheme in Cairo is unclear; an inconclusive clue is the fact that, in addition to Egypt, his passport cleared him for travel to Turkey.

Bruce's talks with his British counterparts were neither perfunctory nor entirely cordial. "Nobody who did not experience it," a British officer wrote, "can possibly imagine the atmosphere of jealousy, suspicion, and intrigue which embittered the relations of the various secret and semi-secret departments in Cairo."[20] And he was talking just about British agencies. When it came to the Americans, in this remnant of empire the British meant to limit OSS as much as possible. They were not the only problem. The eccentric chief American diplomat, Alex Kirk, was equally unreceptive. "Have finished my business with Kirk," Bruce noted. "He is a queer fellow, uncooperative and seemingly uninterested in intelligence matters. His mind is quick, his wit mordant, but he is ill attuned to the times, particularly to matters pertaining to war."[21]

After a busy slate of consultations, he dined at Kirk's house at Mena. "We were served on the immense roof which gives a gorgeous view of the Pyramids under a full moon," he wrote of that surreal scene. "[Kirk] had a lot of high British officers there, and we heard the thunder of the guns in the distance."[22] Those sinister flashes on the night horizon, like summertime heat lightning, signaled the preamble to Rommel's last offensive a week later.

On the return flight across Africa, Bruce blocked out the drone of the engines by reading murder mysteries, Shakespeare, and in desperation, the army officer's manual. Flying across the South Atlantic on a B-24 bomber, "there was only one other passenger and a large cargo of mica. I slept somehow with my head on a machine gun and my feet on a box ominously labelled 'explosives.'" Near Puerto Rico the plane sighted a Nazi submarine and radioed its position. The pilot told Bruce, by then the only passenger, that he could choose the route back to Washington. Whimsically, he suggested a course that took them over Staunton Hill and thought "it looked tiny and odd, nestling in the trees."[23]

In 1943 Donovan gave the head of SI a new job. Bruce had been effective in Washington, but OSS needed him more abroad. By then the buildup of American forces in the United Kingdom moved into high gear to prepare for a return to the Continent that year or the next. Donovan could see where the center of the action would be and intended to make London his principal overseas post.

OSS began badly there. Until Pearl Harbor, COI in London consisted of two officials and equal numbers of secretaries and chauffeurs, hardly a staff conducive to independent action. The first head, William Dwight Whitney, Roosevelt's special representative, resigned after falling out with Donovan. Content to rely on MI-6, Whitney incompetently saw no reason for contacts with the refugee intelligence services of the European governments-in-exile.

After the compliant Whitney, the British allowed Donovan to keep his office in London but severely restricted it.[24] When Whitney's slightly more effective successor left in autumn 1942, Donovan sent Bruce. He knew from firsthand observation that the elegant southerner could put British officials at ease. His assured, patrician appeal and understated, self-deprecating air of competence provided just the tone needed to dispel their apprehension about ham-fisted American upstarts flailing about in clandestine operations. And his urbane style would also assuage the mandarins of Whitehall, with their classical educations and penchant for fine claret.

After more than a year in Washington, Bruce had seen the worst of bureaucratic infighting. His SI branch, a jury-rigged, protean organization, produced more results than most of COI/OSS. Donovan believed he was the right man to expand OSS in London and put it in the forefront of the Allied effort to reclaim Europe. He lacked extensive administrative experience, but then OSS was a completely new, amateur organization (amateurish, some said) that learned as it went. Bruce had, as one of his subordinates recalled later, "a gift for moving people in the direction he wanted them to go, and [was] rather a skeptic about established institutions. He liked bright people, and he didn't care whether they came from the New York ghetto or the southern aristocracy."[25] Another wrote to him on the eve of his departure, "you have worked harder than any of us — but even when the going was roughest your interest in and sympathy for our endless problems never flagged."[26]

It was symptomatic of his problems with the military that Donovan had to plead repeatedly to expedite orders sending Bruce to London. This minor irritant presaged his difficulties serving two masters, the theater commander in London and Donovan in Washington. Major Bruce's rank was another problem. It stemmed from the anomalous position of most officers in OSS and from Donovan's attempt to jump Bruce more than one grade at a time. Because Bruce would be dealing in London with foreign officials on a higher level than as head of SI branch in Washington, Donovan wanted him promoted. He was, but he did not learn that he was a lieutenant colonel until just before leaving for England.

As hostile as the American military bureaucrats were, even less friendly eyes were watching. The *Frankfurter Zeitung* reported with elliptical malevolence on Bruce's arrival. OSS was, it said, "close to

Roosevelt's confidence and is rarely in the public eye. All reports of the American espionage services are gathered and evaluated in the main office. Besides keeping the President directly informed, it is their task to combine as many international threads as possible in their web. . . . The new director [in London] David K. Bruce has recently been especially active in the 'Red Cross.' This organization . . . is used to scheme and make the most of its international connections."[27]

Bruce's command center started out at 70 Grosvenor Street, a five-story brick office block near the embassy. It soon expanded to cover a maze of offices around Grosvenor Square, itself destined by 1944 to be called "Eisenhower Platz."[28] From the handful of staff he inherited, his dominion mushroomed to more than three thousand. The weekly letters that he began to send Donovan, and that the CIA did not declassify until four decades later, catalog the frenzied, frustrating, and deadly earnest efforts of OSS during the year and a half run-up to the invasion of Hitler's Europe.

Bruce was formally head of OSS in the European Theater of Operations with the title of Strategic Services Officer. Although others did the dangerous work, the prospect of more inspection trips into the field, like the flight to Egypt, convinced him that he would be at the sharp end again before it was all over. He had able people to manage the various branches, which replicated the OSS structure in Washington. His own personal mission was to provide liaison — with the alternately helpful and hostile British intelligence organizations, with a confusing panoply of representatives of the European governments-in-exile and their espionage wings, and with the profoundly skeptical American military command. None of these objectives proved easy. It often seemed that these groups were his main enemies, not the Germans.

Bruce had to deal with three British agencies in particular. The most important was MI-6, also known as Broadway. The service began in World War I, though it liked to trace its antecedents back to the spies of Sir Francis Walsingham under Queen Elizabeth. British counterintelligence, the ferreting out of foreign spies in the United Kingdom, came under MI-5, known as Baker Street. Clandestine subversion came under the aegis of the Special Operations Executive (SOE), set up in 1940, in Churchill's phrase, to "set Europe ablaze."

The head of MI-6, Sir Stewart Menzies, liked Bruce for all the reasons Donovan had expected. But Menzies was no more willing to allow Bruce what he had denied his predecessors just because he knew the proper form on a grouse moor or in a Mayfair drawing room. Donovan and Bruce wanted OSS operations in Occupied Europe independent of British control, and that was precisely what Menzies resisted.[29] The British believed they had helped make it possible for Donovan's outfit to exist in the first place, and they wanted OSS to remain a grateful junior partner. Bruce privately admitted to Donovan, "The [OSS] men who are here [in London] are conscientious and hard working, but I must say quite frankly are, either through inexperience or youth, not competent to deal as equals with a dozen of the higher leaders in British S.O.E."[30] In a year's time OSS's staff would have experience enough, but their lack of it in 1943 gave credence to their British detractors. Soviet mole H. A. R. "Kim" Philby, whom Bruce had met in 1942, was not alone in scorning the fledgling OSS as a "notably bewildered group. . . . a service once described . . . as 'a bunch of amateur bums.'"[31]

Claude Dansey, a crusty professional soldier, had served in British intelligence since the Great War. As a boy, he had set his eye on a career in the Life Guards. At boarding school his seduction by an older man — who claimed to have been Oscar Wilde's first lover — dashed his hopes for the Guards when the scandal became public. Instead, his family sent him out to Africa to work for an American firm, and there, in exile and disgrace, Dansey conceived his hatred of Americans. As deputy to "C," he made it his personal mission to ensure that OSS received only processed intelligence reports and not raw data. OSS's cozy ties with the French intelligence service made him "absolutely livid," Bruce said, and Dansey did everything in his power to sabotage Franco-American relations and plans for sending OSS teams into occupied France.[32]

The often-quoted, condescending recollection of Malcolm Muggeridge, then an intelligence operative, captures the attitude held by many in the British secret services: "Ah, those first O.S.S. arrivals in London! How well I remember them — arriving like *jeunes filles en fleur* straight from a finishing school, all fresh and innocent, to start work in our frowsty old intelligence brothel! All too soon they were ravished and corrupted, becoming indistinguishable from seasoned pros who had been in the game for a quarter of a century and more."[33]

Americans answered in kind. Some of them suspected Britain's war aims as an attempt to shore up a tottering empire, especially in India, and often referred to the Allies' South East Asia Command (SEAC) as an acronym for "Save England's Asiatic Colonies." Even Bruce, perhaps spotting his ally's weakness, once ruefully noted the success of his people in "infiltrating almost every British department or agency of any consequence."[34]

Before he reached London, Bruce knew that he should develop good relations with the numerous governments-in-exile and their intelligence services. He saw a natural entree for OSS. "The suspicion," he observed, "with which the Fighting French and the British mutually regard each other makes it possible for the Americans to entertain a closer relationship than can the British with the various French elements, de Gaullist or otherwise." He proceeded to do just that. Similarly, his people established good relations with the Belgians in London, "superior to any which they have with the British." He also maintained close contact with the intelligence services of the Polish, Czechoslovak, Dutch, and Norwegian governments.[35]

Waging coalition warfare meant America needed to juggle the sensitivities of many allies, large and small. As a player in the intelligence game, Bruce spent many evenings dining with members of the European governments-in-exile. The Yugoslavs provided a tangled relationship, as Allied support shifted among the various anti-Nazi factions. Bruce occasionally saw the teenaged king of that unfortunate country, whom he said later "had been useful to us in OSS during the war, but is rather a dope."[36]

He vigorously defended the Free French against State Department criticism. When the American ambassador in London, John Winant, asked for his personal opinion, Bruce replied in June 1944, "I considered de Gaulle was truly the symbol of French resistance in metropolitan France, that I believed American prestige had gravely suffered from our refusal to accord a more complete measure of recognition to the French Provisional Government, that I had great confidence in the ability of the Resistance groups (which had in some degree already been justified), to assist our invading forces by harassing the enemy's communications lines, by sabotage, by physical subversion of all kinds, and to some extent, by guerilla warfare. . . . I stated in addition that, having dealt at one time or another with the leaders of practically every Resistance group in France, I felt none of them had an attitude of personal subserviency to General de Gaulle, and in my opinion the supposed State Department fear that he, if accorded full recognition, would, with the assistance of the Resistance groups, set himself up as a dictator, was without adequate foundation."[37]

Whatever problems he experienced with the British, Bruce attracted even more hostility from the American military. The first lesson came as soon as he reached London. He hoped to procure airplanes for clandestine activities by the Special Operations branch, either parachute drops or landings in occupied France. He had his eye on the B-24 Liberator, a twin-engined bomber that could be modified to suit OSS needs. Even though he knew there was a shortage of Liberators in Britain, he still held out hope. "The permanent assignment of perhaps three long range bombers," he wrote, "to operate from the existing [secret] British field, and manned by American crews would be most advantageous."[38] He soon learned that the army air force was not about to assign a single plane to OSS unless forced to do so by Washington.

When he arrived in London, he knew that if the agency were to win over the American brass, it had to overcome its image as an undisciplined civilian rabble without a proper military function. It was, he said, "an almost endless task" explaining to American staff officers exactly what OSS was meant to do.[39] G-2 at the American theater headquarters tried to circumscribe as narrowly as possible the intelligence-gathering activities of OSS. At first a legal technicality enabled it to restrict OSS to collecting only information for psychological warfare because OSS was not authorized to collect purely military intelligence. Bruce never recanted the low opinion he had of the men who ran army intelligence. He viewed G-2 as "deficient both in ability and personnel" and later wrote in exasperation that "we have obtained our strongest support, not from any American authority, but from our English competitors."[40]

On the eve of taking over his command, Bruce wrote a memorandum to his boss. In it, he enumerated the chief contacts with whom he would be dealing on a regular basis, from the American ambassador, to the prime ministers of the refugee governments, to the heads of the British secret services and those of the governments-in-exile based in London.

"In case the head of the OSS Office in London does not possess the rank of full Colonel," Bruce concluded, "it would be infinitely preferable that he be a civilian."[41] In this assessment, he proved to be more prescient than he would have liked.

The cumulative frustrations of his first three months erased his initial optimism, and in May he made an extraordinary suggestion to Donovan. "We should have here as Director of OSS a professional soldier of as high rank as possible, and preferably one who has been to West Point. . . . It is quite impossible for me," he wrote in his weekly summary, "aside from any of my natural shortcomings, to deal on the proper professional basis with the men in charge of this Theater. My personal contact with them has been pleasant and agreeable, but I cannot too strongly point out the advantages to be derived by OSS in having someone of the type of General Magruder or General Smith, who could handle matters of policy on the highest echelon." In urging Donovan to follow his advice, he concluded that if a professional general officer were in charge, "we could play an important part in connection with any projected continental invasion."[42]

He wanted to remain in some capacity in London, but his unsatisfactory dealings with the army compelled him to make this striking suggestion. Perhaps he began to doubt his own abilities. Fortunately, Donovan disagreed and kept him on as London chief. "Wild Bill" realized that anyone in charge of OSS there, West Point graduate or not, would face the problems Bruce confronted. With more perspective than Bruce had, he could already see that his man in London was succeeding more than he realized.

Bruce and his deputies struggled to maintain productive relations with their English colleagues, fought the American brass tooth and claw, and labored to keep control of their burgeoning staff. On top of these headaches they also had to contend with visits from Donovan. The general — he now had a star — was notorious for dropping in unannounced. During one such visit in June 1943, Bruce described Donovan's "inimitable circus-master" performance that kept them all on their toes. When "Wild Bill" blew into town he immediately began to chat up his British counterparts, entertain the American military, quiz the foreign intelligence chiefs. Bruce concluded drily, "I think a great deal was accomplished for the future glory and prosperity of OSS." He commented with bemused detachment about Donovan's antics but preferred his boss to remain in Washington.[43]

Donovan also interfered by ordering Bruce away from his office. In July 1943 a cable summoned him to Algiers and then Sicily. His improvised trip underscored the disarray of OSS in North Africa, which was not under Bruce's command. When Bruce arrived in Algiers, he could not find the local OSS chief or any trace of his organization. He finally tracked down Charlie Vanderblue, a West Point graduate who worked for OSS, and together they foraged for food and lodging, having no way to communicate with Donovan.

They were even more frustrated in finding a military sponsor to sign their papers for Sicily. After bumping over primitive roads in their jeep, past the burned-out carcasses of Afrika Korps tanks, in Bizerta they finally found Bill Eddy, head of OSS in Algiers. With a string of scholarly books to his name and a wooden leg from World War I, Eddy personified the buccaneering personality drawn to OSS. But this former college president was not much help. He refused to approve Bruce and Vanderblue for Sicily because, Eddy feared, if Gen. George Patton found out, he might expel OSS from his theater entirely. No better evidence of OSS's marginal status there could be given.

Dejected, they gave up the next day when they could not wangle permission from Eisenhower's headquarters. The flight back to Algiers would have provided a fitting end to the mission — when no one wanted to be bumped from the grossly overloaded transport, Bruce noted the pilot's reassuring words to his prospective passengers: "O.K., boys, hold everything. In five minutes you will all be safely in the air or you will all be dead."[44]

At the last minute before returning to England, Bruce convinced the Army Air Corps to send him to Sicily as an observer. Once there, he was on his own. Improvising as he went, he accepted a ride with a flamboyant journalist he knew from the Blitz, H. J. Knickerbocker, immortalized in Evelyn Waugh's *Scoop* after punching out the novelist in Ethiopia before the war.[45] When Bruce found OSS men with the proper credentials in Sicily, he learned that Donovan had left the island just hours before. Making the best of his situation, he toured newly captured towns where OSS was running the local printing presses overtime churning out propaganda leaflets to be dropped behind enemy lines. It was not entirely a waste, he learned in Enna, a town the

Germans had just abandoned. "From the hotel we went to the Governor's palace, a large and fine example of Mussolini architecture, which was completely undamaged. In its garage, where we were ferreting about for spare parts for our car, we found, in a tool chest, an up-to-date and detailed plan of all Italian and German defenses in Sicily."[46]

Although the trip gave Bruce a firsthand view of North Africa and the front in Sicily and was a diverting change from office routine, it was also another example of Donovan's irresponsibility. OSS contributed little to Allied success in Sicily, and Donovan's presence gave the generals more reason not to take him seriously. As head of OSS in London, Bruce could ill afford the luxury of rattling around the Mediterranean for two weeks or of antagonizing the top brass for no good reason.

Back in London his military superiors showed their low opinion of his organization by asking the British what its functions should be. "To those in OSS, Washington," Bruce wrote angrily to headquarters, "who seem to have a feeling that the OSS Mission in London is somewhat prone to allow its independence to be fettered by SIS and SOE, this communication . . . should afford interesting food for reflection." The action of the American top brass meant that it was necessary "for us to go hat-in-hand to Broadway and Baker Street and ask them to be as kind as possible to us. . . . On top of a performance such as this it seems to me sometimes remarkable that we enjoy any independence whatever."[47]

In addition to Bruce's frustrations about the situation in London, the Americans of OSS had to live with the fact that they did not engineer the greatest intelligence coup of the war in Europe — the breaking of German codes. At Bletchley Park, an ugly Victorian estate north of London, British cryptanalysts and mathematicians handed the Allies their greatest secret advantage by cracking the codes generated by the German Enigma machines. This "Ultra" secret, named for the decrypted messages that poured from Bletchley twenty-four hours a day, may not have won the war, but its absence would have made a close-run thing even tighter. The Nazis never guessed that their codes had been penetrated, and the secret did not even come to light until nearly three decades later.

Even when OSS, fueled by seemingly limitless American dollars, began to catch up with its British cousins in some areas of intelligence, it had to remain subordinate when it came to Ultra. Nevertheless, Bruce's OSS counterintelligence unit (X-2) was brought into the Ultra secret as a consumer of its findings. The head of London X-2, Hubert Will, later a federal judge, appreciated Bruce's light touch in letting him run his own show. Will was cleared to see more categories of Ultra decrypt than his boss, but Bruce of course knew all about the secret. He sometimes had to go to bat for X-2 when it had problems with its British counterparts, but that happened only rarely. When he did, Will recalled, Bruce was effective in a quiet, calm, decisive way.[48]

While spats with the American military and British secret services vexed their commander, Bruce's staff concentrated on plans for the invasion. The British continued to block OSS operations on the Continent independent of their own. Although Bruce's people submitted to this inferior status at first, in late 1943 they began to lay the groundwork for independent operations. Their contacts with the refugee intelligence services were excellent. Through these sources, OSS gathered the information it needed if the agents it planned to send to the Continent were to have a prayer of succeeding. Bruce's people made especially sure to keep on good terms with BCRA, the Free French intelligence service.

With these contacts and a large battery of language experts, the Morale Operations branch (MO) produced a flood of black propaganda designed to deceive the enemy. Bruce's people perfected the art of disinformation through fake newspapers and radio broadcasts, passports of surrender, and a variety of ingenious vehicles for sowing rumor, doubt, and worry among the Germans and their friends. Sometimes the efforts were too successful, and Allied intelligence on occasion was tricked into reporting MO-inspired propaganda at face value. One clever piece of anxiety-inducing deception described a fictitious organization of lonely German women recklessly offering sexual favors to any soldiers home on furlough, not just to their husbands and sweethearts. The effect on the Wehrmacht is not recorded, but the *Washington Post* got wind of the pamphlet and presented it as an authentic insight into the German home front. Other efforts produced print pieces that, appearing to be genuine German publications, sowed doubts about Hitler's health. The most successful deception, largely the work of the British but also involving OSS, convinced the German high command that the Normandy landings were a feint to mask the real invasion elsewhere.[49]

In the end, the British could not keep OSS completely isolated. Menzies and Bruce reached an agreement for an equal partnership in clandestine operations supporting the Allied invasion. The main collaboration was a project code-named Sussex, designed to parachute teams of two agents each into northern France to coordinate with the resistance forces. Even after agreeing to this venture, the British dragged their feet, and the American army brass in Britain seemed no more enthusiastic than MI-6.[50]

In charge of planning Sussex was Bruce's old friend from the Virginia legislature Francis Pickens Miller, an active prewar internationalist and by 1943 also a colonel in OSS. Miller fought constantly with the British. Because the Sussex teams were to be composed entirely of French agents, recruitment was a problem. He could not find an adequate supply from refugees in America. Too long absent from their country, they had no direct knowledge of French life under occupation. "I am dubious," Bruce wrote Donovan, "from an SI standpoint, of the feasibility of placing from this Theater more than a few agents on the Continent, because of the fact that those available locally for such tasks are so carefully picked over by the British and other foreign agencies."[51] That was not what Donovan wanted to hear, no matter how accurate. Eventually OSS turned to the Free French intelligence network to assist in recruiting agents from French North Africa. By late 1943 Miller was getting better cooperation from the British, and early in the new year a tripartite committee of British SOE, American OSS, and French BCRA officers took over Sussex plans.

The French worried about parachuting Sussex teams without notifying local Resistance committees. The British insisted on this precaution, fearing that the Germans had infiltrated much of the Resistance. This, the French sneered, was a Suicidex plan. As a compromise, the Allies agreed to drop Pathfinder agents into the target areas just ahead of the Sussex teams. The Pathfinders would be French citizens and former residents of the target area but not part of the Resistance network and thus not susceptible to being compromised, at least not for that reason.

In the months leading up to D-Day, OSS London focused on training the agents it planned to send behind the lines. The Sussex operation developed an intensive program for training agents in tradecraft and furnishing them with false identities and documentation. They had to know how to fieldstrip a Sten gun blindfolded, how to garrote an enemy, how to describe from the ground what a camouflaged munition dump would look like to Allied bombers overhead, and how to send a coded radio transmission in less than ideal conditions. They went armed with automatic weapons, concealed hacksaws for making emergency escapes in the event of capture, and in extremis, suicide pills. Above all, they had to develop a knack for staying alive in a hostile environment.

Another project similar to Sussex was code-named Jedburgh. The Jed teams, equal in number to Sussex, consisted of joint U.S.-British pairs of agents that would be parachuted in uniform throughout France to help the Resistance harass the Wehrmacht when the invasion came. Bruce had targeted this program as deserving the strongest support. He sent Donovan a prescient cable in March 1943 "suggesting our getting in on the ground floor, so to speak, with the British on their Jedburgh plan, which they now consider their most useful potential operation. . . . Personally, I think that such a combination offers great advantages from our standpoint, because of the shortness of time in which we must make progress."[52]

A year later, in April 1944, the first of nearly one hundred of Bruce's Sussex operatives began to jump out of transport aircraft into the night sky over northern France. These brave agents, floating down to unknown dangers in Hitler's Europe, carried with them the hopes of thousands of OSS workers in London. Together with the Jedburgh agents, the Sussex teams represented a large portion of the preparations made by Bruce's London branch for the past year. They were as prepared as months of rigorous training could make them. Even so, luck played an unsettling role in determining whether they would survive the next few days.

CHAPTER 8

The Liberation of Europe

He that outlives this day, and comes safe home,
Will stand a-tiptoe when this day is named.

— Shakespeare, *Henry V*

The frenzied joy of the crowds is impossible to describe.

— From Bruce's diary during the liberation of Paris

*A*T SOUTHWICK HOUSE, a mansion near Portsmouth where the Allied commander moved his headquarters in June 1944, Dwight Eisenhower began a twice-daily consultation with his dour Scottish meteorologist, Group Captain James Stagg. The invasion of Normandy was originally set for June 5, but despite clear skies over Portsmouth, on the 3rd Stagg forecast lowering clouds, high winds, and a driving rain for the appointed day. He convinced Eisenhower to put off D-Day for twenty-four hours. The danger of sending soldiers against Hitler's Atlantic Wall was great enough without having to contend with foul weather.[1]

Eisenhower knew, however, that postponement for even a day greatly reduced the window of opportunity for the right confluence of tide, moon, and all the other circumstances needed to give the landing a chance of succeeding. Worse, delay threatened his greatest advantage — surprise.

The winds and low clouds that arrived on cue vindicated Stagg. On the 4th, though, he gave a rosy forecast, and Eisenhower said simply, "O.K. Let's go." In France, members of the Resistance hunching over their clandestine radios heard through the crackle of static a "personal message" broadcast after the BBC news bulletin, a passage from Paul Verlaine's poem "Chanson d'Automne," the signal that invasion was imminent. The armada, already at sea for days, turned in intricately choreographed patterns and set a course for France.

When the invasion came, Bruce was not in London monitoring the Jedburgh and Sussex teams.[2] The two OSS chieftains had left London a week before with the cover story of visiting friends billeted outside the city. Donovan talked his way onto the heavy cruiser *Augusta* and then the cruiser *Tuscaloosa*. He ignored explicit orders from Washington denying him access to any navy ship.

With the fleet at sea awaiting Eisenhower's decision, Bruce worried about gaps and last-minute changes in plans. It appalled him to learn that destroyers just arriving from convoy duty had not been briefed in their invasion assignments. He expressed special contempt for the order not to fire on any plane beyond 1,000 yards to avoid hitting waves of C-47s carrying airborne troops over the fleet, a decision that would "afford German bombers an excellent opportunity to slip in."

The prospect of keeping such an immense undertaking secret, especially if Ike postponed it another day, troubled him as well. Reduced to the status of observer, with more time on his hands than he had known in months, he recited in his diary the catalog of factors that had to be right for the invasion to succeed and the ways in which it could go badly wrong. (He had begun the diary at Donovan's express request, contrary to general orders.) It was inconceivable to him that the Germans did not know a vast fleet deployed against a ninety-mile front was approaching their Atlantic Wall: "The success of this assault would appear to hinge largely on a series of optimistic assumptions. For example, the efficacy of the fire from the larger naval guns against the principal enemy batteries will depend primarily on the Air Force spotters detailed to this work. They will be flying far from their bases, and can remain for only a limited period of time over their targets. . . . And so one could go on almost ad infinitum. Perhaps too much hope has been founded on the element of surprise. We have selected for the attack the most obviously favorable points of attack. In spite of the projected diversions, it might be assumed that the enemy, seldom notorious for deficiency in staff work, has reached a generally correct estimate as to its direction." He concluded that all the planning would not have the last say: "The fickle British climate is the true mistress of these seas."

At 1:00 A.M. on June 6 he watched waves of C-47s return after dropping the 82nd Airborne Division behind the landing zones of Utah Beach. He guessed correctly that high winds had scattered the paratroops widely. Turning from the skies, he looked through the gloom and could just make out a mass of little boats: "On our port side is a seemingly endless row of landing craft. Some of them are tiny, and the troops, doubtless miserably cold and uncomfortable, have been on them for more than 24 hours."

In the waning hours of darkness, he watched bombing raids along the coast. "It is still cold and windy, and the overcast is heavy so that our men are bombing through cloud. Minesweepers, one of which was torpedoed and sunk on the way over, reported no mines encountered in the American area. When daylight came, the activity was intense. As bomb loads were discharged, great flashes of fire shot toward the sky, followed by columns of dust and smoke, whilst, overhead, tracers from Ack Ack made golden sparkling showers amid the dark or silver planes."

By 5:30 A.M. the awesome spectacle of artillery duels between the big ships and shore batteries transfixed Bruce and thousands of others watching from shipboard. Explosions painted the sky lurid colors. Now and then a stricken plane plummeted in flames from the dense formations of aircraft. It seemed impossible anyone on the shore could remain alive under such punishment. Repeated concussions from the *Tuscaloosa*'s eight-inch guns methodically pounding the coast numbed his head despite the cotton wool he stuffed in his ears. The air filled with the acrid smell of cordite, and the fine dust of disintegrated shell wadding settled on everything like lava ash. As shore batteries fired back, geysers of water erupted among the ships. "The Black Prince is bracketed and hit, and calls for a smoke screen. 2 planes skim the water and interpose a billowing blanket of cloud between it and the shore. One of the planes, however, is hit and seems to skid along the water's surface until it bursts into a glowing ball and then disappears."

By nightfall firing slackened. Exhausted sailors slept at their action stations, "collapsed over their guns, doubled up in corners." The weather changed for the better, and the sky turned completely blue. Despite fear of attack by torpedo boats and submarines after dark, Bruce was surprised how quietly the night passed. Before lying down at midnight he ate another meal of "eggs, orange juice and gunfire." By then enough reports had reached the ship for him to discard his earlier pessimism. He wanted to know what had become of the vaunted coastal defenses. Did the Allies' deceptions convince the Germans the invasion would come at the Pas de Calais and not Normandy? "Was complete surprise attained," he wondered, "in spite of our gloomy forebodings, or, knowing that they could not adequately defend the whole coast, are the Germans counting on sucking us inland, where they hope to destroy us with powerful counter-attacks?" Even when the news turned favorable, the tension of being cooped up and unable to affect the outcome, more than noises in the night, made for a restless sleep.

On June 7 Donovan and Bruce cadged rides from vessel to vessel, until they reached Utah Beach on board an amphibious vehicle and were at once attacked by German fighter planes — among the pathetic few the Luftwaffe managed to sortie that day. "As we reached the middle of the beach there was the drone of airplane motors and almost immediately afterwards machine gun fire as they swept immediately over us down the beach. The General, accustomed to such emergencies, rolled nimbly off the hood where we were sitting, onto the sand. I, with slower reflexes, followed, and fell squarely on General D., gashing his chin with my helmet. As the machinegun bullets spattered the . . . hood, the General grinned happily and said, 'Now it will be like this all the time.'"

Because Donovan wanted to interrogate civilians beyond the fluid front lines, in short order the two Americans were crouching behind a hedgerow with hostile machinegun fire chattering away not far off. Suddenly, unexpectedly, they faced being captured. Donovan thoughtfully offered Bruce one of his L pills of potassium cyanide when he discovered that his associate had not brought his along. Rummaging through his kit, the general then found that he did not have any suicide pills either, having left them on the dresser in his room at Claridges. After retreating they had the bad luck to run into Gen. Omar Bradley, who knew of the strict orders against Donovan being at the front. Donovan had the gall to tell him he and Bruce had just proved how easy it would be for OSS agents to slip between the lines. When he

Sporting his trademark mustache, wing collar, and bushy brows, David's father, William Cabell Bruce, was, despite his public career, a private man: formal, courtly, and shy, never fully at ease with other men, and slow to show feelings. *(David S. and Janet Parker Bruce)*

David inherited from his short, vigorous, worldly-wise mother, Louise Este Fisher Bruce, enormous stamina and a gift for making friends. *(Virginia Historical Society)*

Charles Bruce's antebellum Gothic mansion, Staunton Hill, in southern Virginia provided a reference point and a sense of place for his grandson long after the plantation economy had vanished. *(Virginia Division of Historic Landmarks)*

David's older brother, James, remembered him even as a child as "the scholar." In this photograph David is about eleven, with a book naturally. *(Virginia Historical Society)*

William Cabell Bruce, Jr., only a year older than David and his best childhood friend, died in 1910 when David was twelve. *(David S. and Janet Parker Bruce)*

David (second from left), still gangly but displaying that winning smile, fumed about the lengthy training at the army camp at Anniston, Alabama, during 1917–1918. He missed the horror of the trenches and discovered instead the cultural glories of Europe during his time with the Field Artillery and Army Courier Service. "If there is any thing good in me," he said at the time, "this education will heighten it." *(Virginia Historical Society)*

A studio photograph of Ailsa Mellon, about the time of her wedding. *(David S. and Janet Parker Bruce)*

During his two years in uniform with the American Expeditionary Force to France and the Army Courier Service, David Bruce began his lifelong love affair with Europe. *(Virginia Historical Society)*

On a perfect day of blue skies and universal acclaim by the arbiters of high society, David Bruce and Ailsa Mellon were married at the National Cathedral in the most brilliant wedding Washington had seen in years. *(David S. and Janet Parker Bruce)*

After her marriage, Ailsa Mellon Bruce remained close to her father even as she became increasingly reclusive and debilitated by hypochondria. She appears here with Andrew Mellon in the mid-1930s, probably at the Bruces' Long Island estate at Syosset. *(Gallery Archives, National Gallery of Art, Washington, D.C.)*

Below, left: Nominally in the United States Army Air Corps—uniform by Brooks Brothers—David Bruce helped create the Office of Strategic Services. *(Evangeline Bruce)*

Below: This prewar photograph of Evangeline Bell suggests what her college friend Arthur M. Schlesinger, Jr., had in mind when he recalled, "I can still conjure up the young girl's wry grace, effortless style, shy and subtle intelligence, and indestructible beauty." *(David S. and Janet Parker Bruce)*

During the last frantic days before the Liberation of Paris, Bruce (on the left) found himself the senior American officer at Rambouillet, in no-man's-land a short distance from the capital. He also found Ernest Hemingway, never too rushed to strike a romantic pose. *(John F. Kennedy Presidential Library)*

A little grayer around the temples and a lot more experienced than at the beginning of the war, Colonel Bruce receives the Distinguished Service medal from a grateful Bill Donovan in 1945. *(Virginia Historical Society)*

The head of the Marshall Plan in France test-drives a tractor from America.
(Evangeline Bruce)

In 1949 Bruce presented his credentials as ambassador to the president of the Fourth
Republic of France, Vincent Auriol. (*Evangeline Bruce*)

Behind the glamour and the fashions, Evangeline Bruce contributed full-time to the all-important social side of her husband's tour as ambassador to France. *(Evangeline Bruce)*

The Bruces' rented weekend house, La Lanterne, at Versailles. *(Evangeline Bruce)*

In Bonn, Bruce earned his keep working for a rigid boss, John Foster Dulles (left), and assuaging a rigid foreign leader, Konrad Adenauer (right). Churchill said that Dulles was the only bull who carried a china shop with him. *(Evangeline Bruce)*

Though he did not much care for Germans, Bruce, shown here guiding President Eisenhower down a receiving line during his 1959 visit to West Germany, served the nation well as ambassador to Bonn. *(Evangeline Bruce)*

brazenly offered to attach Bruce to Bradley's headquarters, Bradley gritted his teeth and snarled, "Suppose you now go back to wherever you came from."[3]

Another night aboard ship, lying just off the beaches, gave Bruce more opportunity to observe the mammoth sweep of the operation. "Up on deck again," he wrote after midnight, "'5' guns manned — E boats and aircraft reported near. From that time on there was plenty of action. Heavy bombing made furnace-like glows on the shore, while AA fire cascaded into the air, sometimes criss-crossing and intertwining beautiful yellow and red colors. We saw at least 3 airplanes shot down. A searchlight on land, supposedly German, made milky pathways fitfully through the sky, miles away. Star shells searched out an area of the sea. Constant reports rolled in, submarines and E boats were suspected of being near, the Radar was probably jammed, and rumors of every description were rampant. Meanwhile, bombing went on all about us and planes, friendly and unfriendly, were constantly overhead. Fires shot up on or near the beaches. We feared that Utah and Omaha were having a bad night of it."

While Donovan and Bruce risked their lives on Utah Beach, their teams of Sussex and Jedburgh agents were carrying out their orders with tremendous success. They reported an impressive volume of military intelligence. Francis Miller knew he had succeeded when the army air force praised the data his people provided. The air force told him it liked to bomb munition dumps identified by Sussex agents: unlike those located by other sources, they always produced huge secondary explosions.

Bruce's Jedburgh teams linked up with underground forces all over France and dramatically harassed German units moving toward the beachhead. The underground, with OSS help, successfully attacked nearly all of the 1,050 railroad targets assigned for the night of June 5–6. Through the bravery of OSS and the underground, German units throughout France experienced the same frustration and damage that afflicted the 2nd SS Panzer Division. Rommel persuaded Hitler to release this unit from reserve and expected it in the line of battle at Normandy on D plus three days. Because the Germans carried their own bridging equipment, the bridges blown by the Resistance did not slow the division much. But constant harassment along their line of march did; then the Jedburghs called in the air force to maul them further. The 2nd SS Panzers did not reach Normandy until D plus seventeen.[4]

The invasion of Normandy, like so many other pivotal moments of the war, could have gone either way. If a few more German divisions had reached the beach in the crucial early hours, they might have thrown the Allies back. Through the Sussex and Jedburgh agents, and other help to the French underground, OSS could rightly claim to have added to the vital margin of victory.

After returning to London and the first hot bath in a week, Bruce attended a meeting at Claridges where Donovan assembled the OSS branch heads. They expected praise but instead received a harangue about what to do next. The Jedburgh and Sussex operations were already history. What OSS should do now, he insisted, was to contribute to the campaign for France and then for Germany. He chided them for failing to place small OSS teams with army units in the field. With a dismissive wave of the hand, he brushed aside their excuses that army G-2, especially Col. "Monk" Dickson of First Army, resisted their overtures. For Donovan, failure was not an option.

In this latest off-the-cuff scheme, he hit upon the role that would make OSS's greatest contribution to the rest of the war. Popular uprisings at the time of the invasion forced the Allied high command to take seriously both the Resistance and the OSS-Resistance link. In particular, the Allies saw the benefit of OSS-gathered tactical intelligence and OSS-sponsored sabotage. Bruce was proud of OSS's aid to the Resistance and, despite initial doubts about focusing too much on tactics rather than strategic intelligence, embraced this innovation. He discovered too that the new arrangement enabled him to escape the constraints of London. With the need to be at forward headquarters in France to monitor units in the field, he no longer had to worry about his superiors constantly looking over his shoulder.

On June 13, 1944, as early morning darkness faded, a small aircraft with stubby wings and no propeller crossed the Channel to England, making a puttering noise and emitting a bright glow behind in the predawn sky. A spotter saw the craft over Kent shortly after it crossed the chalk cliffs where Bruce had watched the RAF and Luftwaffe duel four years before. Minutes later, its engine cut out, and it dove into the ground and exploded at Swanscombe, twenty miles east of London. The often-promised German secret weapon, the V-1 buzz bomb, had arrived. No one died at Swanscombe, but the thousands of V-1s to follow in the next ten months were not so benign.[5]

Bruce had expected the V-1s for more than a year and served as the conduit for information about Hitler's secret weapons that led to Allied countermeasures. According to one source, Allen Dulles, from his OSS outpost in Switzerland, obtained plans of the German rocket base at Peenemünde. He sent the data to Bruce, who passed it along to Churchill. In another version, an OSS scientist first made the link between reports from Dulles about heavy-water production in German-occupied Norway and work on a Nazi atomic bomb (an accurate connection) and then made the link between those activities and the base at Peenemünde (an erroneous connection). In this interpretation too the information made its way to Bruce, who passed it along to the British.

As a result, on the night of August 17–18, 1943, the RAF sent 597 heavy bombers, using untried new guidance techniques for precision bombing, to devastate the Baltic facility. About 700 people died, including key German scientists and many conscripted foreign workers. Forty of the planes did not return to base.

Though the first V-1s did not fly against Britain until the following year, it was clear in retrospect that the raid negligibly affected production and only slightly retarded development of the more terrifying V-2 rocket. Perversely, the raid may even have done the Germans a favor. The production program that they abandoned because of the Baltic raid was defective. When they resumed work at an underground factory in the Hartz Mountains, they made the necessary changes, perhaps sooner than if they had remained at Peenemünde, unmolested.[6]

The V-1s reminded Bruce of four summers before. Once more the sounds of explosions and sirens filled the air. London, which had endured the threat of invasion and the Blitz, faced another terror from the air. It was almost too much, and civilian morale nearly cracked. A million residents fled London voluntarily. A quarter of a million children were sent to the countryside.

"The robot bombs have now descended on London every day and night for over two weeks," Bruce noted on July 2 after returning from Normandy. "Although the weight of bombs dropped is comparatively small, they have induced considerable fear in the population. Each day, forty to one hundred and fifty persons are killed by them, and a considerably greater number gravely injured. These people are tired, and the mechanical, uncanny nature of this device seems to have affected the nerves of many of them. Countermeasures are relatively ineffective, so it is to be presumed that the nuisance will continue until the sites in the Dieppe and Pas de Calais area, from which they are chiefly propelled, are overrun by our troops." Though OSS casualties were light overall, one of Bruce's top officers, Col. Gus Guenther, died when a V-1 hit the Guards' Chapel at Wellington Barracks and killed nearly two hundred people during a memorial service for the fallen.

As the V-1 attacks mounted, Bruce received frantic cables from parents of two OSS women demanding transfers for their daughters. "I consider the request disgraceful," he said and left it to the employees to decide. By the end of summer he was deluged with marriage applications. Then there was the flap about the documentation of civilian employees in France. With their ID papers stamped "OSS," someone pointed out, they would be executed as spies if caught by the Germans. The cards were recalled.

Improvised organizations, especially those cobbled together during wartime by talented people, cannot avoid frequent personality clashes. The most serious ones invariably reached Bruce's desk for a Solomonic decision. When a rare day passed without dispute, he noted it: "The quietest day I have spent in the office for a long time. Not a single conversation on a controversial topic! So far as I can remember, this is unprecedented."[7]

As the beachhead slowly expanded, he began regular inspections of his units there. One visit began with a rough ride by PT boat. When the boat slammed into a large wave, he was momentarily paralyzed, though an X-ray revealed nothing worse than some cracked ribs. More typically, he flew to France. "After innumerable last-moment conferences at the office," he wrote eighteen days after D-Day, "I motored out beyond Reading to the 9th Air Force field at Grove, near Wantage, and boarded a C-47. It was filled with mail and cargo, and the only other passengers were a supply sergeant and a not over-feminine Army nurse. We lay on the sacks, and an hour and a quarter after leaving the airport landed in France on a metal runway near Omaha Beach. It was a beautiful flight. We were unescorted by fighters but saw no enemy planes."[8]

For the moment, OSS put its headquarters in a stone farmhouse whose courtyard was promiscuously filled with chickens, ducks, turkeys, and piles of field telephones, camouflaged tents, and other equipment. One of his inspection trips took him to Cherbourg on the day the last German holdouts, about four thousand men in the arsenal, surrendered to Pat Dolan, a flamboyant OSS officer. Bruce compared the scene with his prewar visits. "As one approached the docks . . . one had a conception of how complete skillfully managed demolition can be. All cranes were destroyed and great temple-like masses of concrete had been tossed about as if a giant had thrown them petulantly away. The Quais, alongside which trans-Atlantic liners had once discharged so many carefree passengers, looked as if a tornado had struck them."[9]

Tours close to the front accustomed him to being under fire. "Quitting Isigny, we went through Carentan," he wrote about one foray, "where our trip might well have come to an untimely end. Just as we were about to pass a shattered building, a German shell descended in the middle of the debris about twenty-five yards away, but, aside from throwing up a shower of dust and rubble, did no harm. It was followed by two others, uncomfortably close, as we sped by." He criticized commanders for wanting to possess every hamlet rather than bypass it. The result was slow going and the destruction of villages already deserted by the Germans, who in any case preferred to put their main defenses in the surrounding countryside, not in town. He was keen to see some prisoners to assess their morale. He noted approvingly the story of a POW who told a visiting Russian general he had heard that after the war "the Soviets would carve Germany into little bits. The General answered: 'Not Germany but Germans. Ha! Ha! Ha!'"[10]

Bruce did not let his inspection tours stand in the way of good eating. Like many Americans that summer, he became an expert at scrounging meals he would remember for the rest of his life, whether a farmhouse omelette washed down with *vin ordinaire* or an elegant meal at a restaurant within earshot of the front. And he participated in the widespread "liberation" of food and drink that was endemic to all wars.

On one return flight to London he and his officers piled aboard cheeses, wine, and brandy taken from the German commanding general's stores at Cherbourg.

Once, during a frontline tour, he took three of his officers and their soldier-drivers to a hostelry noted for its cuisine. It had not suffered under the occupation. "We had soup, grilled plaice, filet mignon, peas, carrots and potatoes, brown bread and butter, salad and cheese, and stewed cherries with the thickest of cream. No less important, we had a noteworthy bottle of 1937 Mersault, a bottle of red Mersault, and a fine champagne of the highest merit," and all to the accompaniment of distant artillery shelling.[11]

In the weeks following D-Day, the Allies landed staggering quantities of troops, vehicles, and supplies. Their air forces ruled the skies. Their predominance would tell in the end. And yet, they had fallen far behind schedule. After two months, they had taken little more than the Carentan peninsula. Bad weather, stubborn defenses, and overly cautious commanders slowed the advance. But by mid-August they finally broke out of the hedgerow country, the *bocage*, and sprinted toward Paris.

To be near his field units, by now the most productive part of his sprawling command, Bruce moved his office to a battered casino at St. Pair-sur-Mer near Granville. The constant cheering by civilians whenever a jeep drove past was a morale boost, but after a time Bruce complained of "a sort of finger palsy" that came from returning the V sign. The weather finally caught up with the season, and the profusion of hydrangeas, rambler roses, and dahlias that lined the roads during his inspection tours was gloriously incongruous with the evidence of war.

After driving through choking dust on roads filled with convoys of American supply trucks, he reached Le Mans, where he learned that OSS had found alive and well one of the Sussex agents parachuted behind enemy lines. Her companion was not so lucky but had been, in Bruce's words, "tortured in the most horrible manner before he died."[12]

The OSS commander learned at the same time the fate of three other Sussex teams that had landed nearby. When these young French people, five men and one woman, decided there was nothing to do in their drop zone, they radioed London for permission to go to Paris. Disguised as construction workers on Hitler's Atlantic Wall, they stole a German truck, put their bicycles in the back, and headed toward the capital. They were stopped at a roadblock. As they stepped out of the vehicle, a suitcase fell open, and their radio gear spilled out on the ground. The soldiers forced them back into the truck and drove at high speed to the local Wehrmacht headquarters. One agent, André Rigot, jumped from the moving vehicle and escaped as the soldiers clinging to the running boards fired at him wildly. A few days later a somber Colonel Bruce identified the remains of Rigot's colleagues, summarily executed, their corpses left unburied as a warning to others.[13]

Earlier Bruce had received more horrifying reports. A friend told him of seeing the bodies of three French boys capriciously shot by Germans a few hours before. Worse, he said, he had just been to a village morgue and seen the bodies of twelve more adolescents killed by the 17th SS Panzer Division. "The Germans," Bruce wrote, "had torn out their testicles, gouged out their eyes, and pulled their teeth" before killing them.[14] After the Great War, 2nd Lieutenant Bruce had returned home without hating the Germans; Colonel Bruce of the OSS was not so charitable.

As the campaign became confused — When would the Allies take Paris? Would the Germans counterattack? — Bruce toured the territory between the armies. With no set lines or large-scale forces from either side, Resistance bands roamed and clashed with German rear-guard units. At Chartres Cathedral his jeep came under heavy attack from snipers. After spending days organizing OSS contacts with the Resistance and with American forces, Bruce arranged to link up with Donovan at Rambouillet, just outside Paris. His boss never got there, but he found another American with a self-made, larger-than-life presence to match Donovan's.

Ernest Hemingway — complex, fascinating, and insufferable — shared Bruce's memories of France in happier times. Bruce later described him as "patriarchal, with his gray beard, red face, imposing physique, much like God, as painted by Michaelangelo."[15] In August 1944 Hemingway was in search of adventure. He had insinuated himself into command of an irregular Resistance band, an act that later embroiled him in controversy for violating his status as a war correspondent. "Papa" Hemingway made the Hôtel du Grand Veneur in Rambouillet his headquarters. Bruce, the senior officer in town, said the place was "like Bedlam." In the midst of rumors of a German counterattack, Hemingway's people liberated the wine cellar. Another band of partisans arrived at the hotel in a circus truck, prompting more celebrations. After a jumpy night no Germans attacked, although one of their patrols mined the road to Paris nearby. A delegation from the town presented the OSS colonel with a hand-lettered document expressing the gratitude of the citizenry.

That morning the chief of the local Resistance asked a favor of Bruce and Hemingway. "Mouthard has just made a report to Ernest and myself," Bruce wrote, "and has asked and been granted permission to go away for fifteen minutes to kill a civilian traitor. We lent him a .32 automatic." With that act, they became part of the controversial settling of accounts throughout France that summer and beyond. The summary punishment of collaborators went on for months, was badly carried out, and was guilty of many abuses. Though more than 10,000 died as a result, contrary to popular legend this was in proportion to population less severe than in Holland, Belgium, and Denmark.[16] If this rough justice seems unduly harsh, it should be set against the crimes that had gone before. The Vichy regime had sent thousands of French citizens to Germany in pressed labor levies. Many did not return. Thousands of French Jews went to a grimmer fate farther east. Vichy's enthusiasm for exceeding Nazi orders did not earn it much sympathy.

Of course, the great lie of that summer, perpetuated to this day, was the myth of "self-liberation." For most French citizens had acquiesced in the occupation, if not eagerly collaborated. Few joined the Resistance until very late. And with scant exception it was not French soldiers who chased the Germans out of France.

Bruce knew from his scouts that there were few German forces between Rambouillet and the capital and that part of Patton's army was in position to move on Paris. He worried that the Germans would make good use of the delay to disengage from the city. On August 23 he learned that General Jacques LeClerc, head of the only French division with the Allies, had been given permission to take Paris. That morning LeClerc arrived in Rambouillet and interrogated Bruce and Hemingway. When he had learned what he wanted, he dismissed them curtly, saying in French something Hemingway delicately translated in print as "Buzz off, you unspeakables!"

The events at Rambouillet, through the embellished recounting of

Hemingway and Bruce, became one of many celebrated vignettes of the Liberation. Both men would dine out often on the tale. In a rambling, self-justifying postwar letter to Bruce, Hemingway objected to an unflattering version of the story told by other journalists. "Actually, remember," he said, "we did absolutely solid recon, sent over complete enemy dispositions" that materially helped the French general's advance on the capital. But then "that prick of a LeClerc had told us to eff off when we had been asked to go to him to be thanked."[17] Bruce did not dissent from Hemingway's version and always believed he had given good advice to LeClerc.

The next morning they mounted their jeep and joined LeClerc's column. Relying on intelligence from Bruce and others, LeClerc bypassed German strongpoints and sped toward Paris. Five miles out the pace slowed. They had to clear roadblocks and then pass uncomfortably close to a burning munitions dump spewing small-arms ammunition, tracer rounds, and artillery shells in all directions. By afternoon, as they drove toward the Seine, joyful Parisians oblivious to all but the heaviest firing lined the streets. When the Germans held up the column, Bruce's contingent decided to find a house to spend the night and enter the city the next morning.

At the same time Albert Camus sat down to write his famous editorial for the Resistance newspaper *Combat*, beginning with the words "the greatness of man lies in his decision to be stronger than his condition."[18]

On the next day, the 25th of August, just after noon Bruce reached the Bois de Boulogne, where a firefight erupted between snipers in an apartment building and Allied troops in the streets. From that point forward, surging crowds of ecstatic Parisians surrounded the jeep. "It was a wonderful sunny day and a wonderful scene," Bruce said.[19] The Germans had not all quitted the city, however, and firing continued throughout the day. Once when Bruce spotted enemy tanks ahead of them, a guide led him to the Arc de Triomphe.

From the top of the monument the head of OSS in the European Theater took in a spectacular sight. With the afternoon sun flashing against the rooftops, he saw crowds cheering in the boulevards as tanks duelled in the side streets. Smoke rose from the Crillon Hotel, where he had breakfasted with his Uncle Tom Page in the long-ago spring of the Versailles treaty.

When he reached his jeep again, he found the bodies of half a dozen Germans killed just minutes before. Later, while sheltering under a tank to escape a firefight, Bruce and his party were startled when a man darted out to ask them to join him at his house for champagne. They agreed, happy to escape the gunfire. To Bruce it seemed that every civilian had a weapon and wanted to shoot it. Down on the street again, other Parisians plied soldiers with wine, a retired colonel directing his servant to bring bottles down from his apartment by the hamper-full.

When Bruce and Hemingway found the Champs-Elysées suddenly deserted, they roared down it at high speed to the Travellers Club. It was empty except for a few old-timers in the bar uncorking the cele-bratory champagne. "We next collected our gang," Bruce said, "and, not knowing what was ahead except for the usual indiscriminate pop-ping of small arms, dashed to the Café de la Paix. The Place de l'Opéra was a solid mass of cheering people." His jeep then rushed to its famous rendezvous with the Ritz. From this *opéra bouffe* performance was born one of the great tales of Liberation Day, a story fated to be embellished and expanded from the first time it was told.

"During the night," Bruce said, "there was almost incessant shoot-ing. The French Forces of the Interior are well out of hand, and draw on anybody whom they consider suspicious."[20] "There was no coffee," he said the next morning, "but we had an omelette and a bottle of Chablis."[21] He visited old Parisian friends that day, including wine merchant Raoul Boyer, and so missed the great event of liberation, the procession led by Charles de Gaulle down the Champs-Elysées and then to Notre-Dame. At the cathedral shots rang out. A gun battle between Free French soldiers and snipers ensued, but the service of thanksgiving continued.

Gradually the confusion subsided but not before embroiling the OSS colonel in more contretemps. Besides organizing the rudiments of an OSS office in Paris, Bruce went to the Chase Bank and stopped Free French soldiers from beating up the concierge to get at an alleged German radio operating from the bank. Later he rescued a French general from prison and the Morgan Bank from being shelled by one of LeClerc's tanks.

Familiar problems confronted him on his return to London. He faced them with equanimity, because in the matters that counted, OSS had contributed its part to the liberation of France. He dealt with requests for transfer to Paris; concerns about the black market; problems setting up a propaganda radio station; inquiries from the British about lost secret papers; the 8th Air Force hopping mad about Donovan "misplacing" one of their planes. In this confused jumble of activity two themes emerged. The American military had finally accepted OSS for its tactical value in the field, and OSS began to address the next objective — sending agents into the Reich itself.

By the end of the month many American commanders began to reassess their opinion of OSS field detachments. Irascible "Monk" Dickson, the head of G-2 in First Army, had scorned the offer of OSS aid: "I don't want a man from OSS, not a dwarf, not a pigmy, not a Goddamned soul."[22] But Eisenhower requested more of Bruce's units, and many of his commanders did too. The interservice squabbling that hampered OSS up until that point diminished, though it never disappeared. The army even approached Bruce about using OSS combat teams to capture Hitler's retreat at Berchtesgaden, a request unthinkable earlier in the war.

After chafing for so long as the junior partner of MI-6, OSS accepted the new task before it and moved rapidly ahead of the British in placing agents in Germany. To oversee this assignment, Bruce selected the newly arrived replacement as head of SI/London, a young New York attorney named Bill Casey, future director of the CIA and as fanatical in his own way as Donovan. OSS had gained invaluable experience with the Jedburgh and Sussex teams, but Germany was a different matter. Agents could not expect Resistance welcoming parties. It was a relief to Bruce and Casey to have their gloomy expectations about casualty rates proven wrong. On the other hand, few of the agents that made it into Germany transmitted much information despite OSS's ingenious advances in radio technology.

Bruce returned to the field to visit his teams attached to American army units. He accepted with gratitude, and a sense of vindication, the favorable comments army officers increasingly made about his people. With the Allies on the borders of the Reich, he visited Luxembourg, Belgium, and Holland as well as France. In October his command reached its peak level of 3,410 men and women.

In November he drove by car from France to Berne, Switzerland, to see his old friend Allen Dulles. Dulles, who had introduced Bruce to the Army Courier Service in 1919, accomplished more than any other OSS agent. He made first-rate contacts with disgruntled German officials and would soon negotiate the surrender of all Nazi forces in northern Italy. He had once coveted Bruce's post but decided after being in Switzerland that he was better off not being under the thumbs of the American brass in London.

Bruce began planning for his own replacement and his return to Washington but had to cheat death a few more times before his service overseas ended. In London he was subject to the newest German terror weapon, the V-2 rocket. Because of its great speed, it gave no warning before raining death from the stratosphere. On an inspection tour, flying from England to Belgium, his aircraft lost its way and came under German antiaircraft fire. On his way back to France from Berne, as his driver raced down an icy road, "the Packard skidded, got completely out of control, and careened into a ravine, where it toppled over on one side with a crash. We were lucky in coming to rest where we did, as the ravine was narrow enough in that place to hold us, wedged between two trees — twenty yards further on would have been a disastrous ending for us."[23] Shortly afterward, he was caught in the Battle of the Bulge and then narrowly escaped a plane crash in a snowstorm when he returned to Washington on Christmas Day.

Early in the new year at a small ceremony at OSS Washington headquarters, Donovan pinned the Distinguished Service medal on Bruce. The official photograph of the occasion shows an older man, grayer about the temples than when he went to London for the Red Cross. He was thinner despite eating and drinking well throughout. The photograph could not reveal how much he had changed, though. After all the dramatic events he had witnessed, he was a more reflective and sober person than the eager friend of Britain searching for a way to do his part in 1940.

For a few months in Washington he headed the OSS policy planning committee and returned for an inspection tour of Germany in summer 1945. By then the guns had fallen silent for the first time in almost six years. In London the "sinister, droning noise" of the buzz bombs had finally stopped. When he took off his Army Air Corps uniform for the last time, in November 1945, he had completed forty-nine months of service with COI and OSS.

The British were parsimonious in the honors they bestowed on their OSS allies — only ten were given in all — but they made sure to make a Commander of the British Empire of the man who effectively created OSS/London and guided it through its toughest challenges.

OSS did not survive the war for long. Donovan succeeded with FDR, as much as anyone did with that master of intrigue, but Harry Truman proved more resistant to "Wild Bill"'s blustery charms. Despite Donovan's public pronouncements that the new president would find OSS as useful as the late one had, it was not to be. In a dispatch to London shortly after Roosevelt died, the British embassy dryly observed that "there is some nervousness within the Office of Strategic Services as to the future of that vast and omnivorous organization under the new regime."[24] Enemies in Washington, always vigilant for a chance to discomfit its abrasive founder, finally gutted OSS, and the deadly struggle between J. Edgar Hoover and Donovan came to an end. The Office of Strategic Services expired in October 1945 on Truman's orders, its component branches disbanded or cannibalized by other federal agencies.

As much as any individual besides Donovan, Bruce helped create and perpetuate the swashbuckling myths of OSS. The agency may have been "the last refuge of the well-connected," as some critics have alleged, but it was not all fiction.[25] He had risked his life repeatedly, sometimes for good reason, sometimes not. OSS gave him a priceless opportunity to prove himself in a position of trust and to bring himself to the attention of some very influential people in ways that Mellon riches could not buy. He had seen firsthand the most dramatic points of the war in Western Europe — from the Blitz, to D-Day, to the buzz bomb attacks on London, to the liberation of Paris. The experience vindicated his internationalist sentiments. As early as 1942 he was already thinking about postwar reconstruction. He feared a resurgence of isolationism at home if the more idealistic internationalists alienated their countrymen and thereby undercut the pragmatic supporters of an American presence in Europe.

Through his commitment to Britain, Bruce became one of the leading American exemplars of the wartime Anglo-American Special Relationship, an example of the New World, as Churchill wrote, coming to redress the balance of the Old. The lessons he believed America should learn from the war cemented Bruce's prewar internationalist attitudes. How he could use the OSS experience to advance into the broad sunlit uplands of postwar American foreign affairs, however, was not at all apparent to him in 1945. His four years with Donovan had taught him there was more to life than the leisured ease of the Mellons. Though it was good to get away from the demands of OSS for a while, he soon became restless once more for something as meaningful to do. OSS gave him contacts and reputation that would serve him well later, but in 1945 that future was hidden from him.

CHAPTER 9

A Few Changes

It was as though a wicked fairy had appeared at her christening, waved a
wand, and blighted all future enjoyment of her wealth and beauty.

— Said of Ailsa Mellon Bruce

$\mathcal{A}$S SPRING RETURNED to Europe in 1945, Allied armies
closed in on the dying Third Reich from east and west. Even when the
thunder of Soviet artillery began to rumble over Berlin, Hitler took
heart. The tide was about to turn, he told his doubting entourage in
the Führerbunker. A miraculous reversal of fortune would rescue Germany, and its first fruit was word that the Reich's archenemy had died
at Warm Springs, Georgia. That news stunned Americans at home and
abroad; the average GI could not even remember another president.
With the nation's attention riveted on the sad, slow train that carried
Roosevelt's remains northward to Washington, David Bruce was absorbed by a more personal drama. On the same day that the funeral
coach reached the capital and a simple service was held in the White
House, divorce proceedings began in West Palm Beach for Mr. and Mrs.
David K. E. Bruce of Manhattan, Long Island, Washington, D.C., and
Charlotte County, Virginia.

Not the least of the ways the war changed America was its influence,
for good and ill, on the love life of a whole generation. Uncle Sam as
well as Glenn Miller put many of them "In the Mood." For some the
separation of military duty put intolerable strains on fragile marriages.
For some it made new liaisons possible. For others it brought the

bittersweet taste of both. The only hint in Bruce's diaries was a wistful comment about the increase in requests of him, as commanding officer, to approve marriages between his people and foreign nationals. "Cupid is doing a thriving business," he mused in July 1944. "It was the same during the Blitz of 1940 — people under such conditions seem to form more rapid attachments."[1] He knew very well about such attachments, for when he wrote those words he was already smitten himself and was desperately trying to undo the bonds solemnified before God and Calvin Coolidge in the National Cathedral eighteen years before.

It is doubtful that on that sunny morning in 1926 David realized what it meant to marry into a family of such staggering wealth, and of psychological problems to match. Apparently he had no inkling before the wedding of Ailsa's emotional fragility. Her hypochondria was muted then, and her shyness may have seemed to him merely an endearing, conventionally feminine trait rather than a premonition of the affliction that turned her into a knotted, brooding recluse. Her stubborn streak, though, was more than just an aloofness that was part of her attraction to David. If the society writers commenting on the wedding detected a haughtiness that her timidity did not entirely mask, the bridegroom should have noticed too. Ailsa's friends even said they were surprised the wedding was happening at all. They had doubted she would ever marry because she was so used to getting her own way all the time.[2]

As an adolescent she had been an eager horsewoman and was often seen cantering in the parks. "She was a beautiful young woman," David recalled about first meeting her, "full of spirit, with a model's figure, and seemingly in perfect health."[3] In short order all three qualities vanished. None of the few people who were ever close to her would disagree with Paul Mellon's lament about his sister. "After her disturbed childhood," he said, "she had gone on to lead a rather sad life."[4]

Whatever Bruce was thinking on his wedding day, he did not have long to wait before the storybook romance mutated in a disturbing way. The photograph in the *New York Times* showing the nation's most glamorous newlyweds sail off to Europe on their honeymoon captured it all on film. There was David — open, smiling, and carefree. Ailsa, in contrast, appeared pinched and drawn, apprehensive about the future when she had every reason to be expectant. David had made the world his oyster long before; now there would be oysters and Dom Perignon every day. It was his easy enjoyment of life and his contagious enthusiasms that appealed to his bride, just as Nora McMullen's ebullience had fatefully attracted Ailsa's father. For Ailsa the world would become a fearful place that would take all of the Mellon millions to keep at bay.

Within days of arriving in Rome, she took to her bed and figuratively never left it. Thus began a lifelong train of mysterious, debilitating maladies that relented from time to time but never went away entirely. Most of her problems — later characterized bluntly by her brother as "hypochondria" — had deep emotional roots. He attributed it, with good reason, to the horrible fight between their parents: "I am sure the dark and frightening days of the divorce and the evil rumors about Mother were more disturbing to her than anyone at the time imagined."[5]

With that background and her extremely sheltered adolescence, one might doubt that Ailsa brought to her marriage an especially enlightened attitude toward sexual relations. Though she had entertained a highly publicized string of suitors, she had lived a supremely closeted youth. "Ailsa discovered that she didn't like marriage. I suppose that meant sex," a Bruce family friend said.[6] The mysterious illness that began in Rome might have provided an escape from more than the city's heat.

During the first years after the wedding, Bruce tried his best to accommodate her. In the tender letters he sent her in 1933, when he returned to America while she remained in London, he called her "My darling sweet one," "Dearest Poodlemuff," and "Sweet Hobo." He complained of loneliness and chided her for not writing more. "Do not forget that you are to write to me at least twice a week, otherwise I shall devise some very annoying punishment for you. I miss you terribly. . . . All my love as always my own sweetheart. I had such a very very happy time in London with you."[7]

Despite his entreaty, she rarely wrote. "I am very depressed," he said. "Please write to me & cheer me up with something nice. I have stopped smoking so as to have roses in my cheeks when you come home! I miss you terribly as always. And don't sign your letters 'Affectionately.' All my love, David." Even the expression of endearments in private letters was beyond her. Again, "I wish to Heaven you would come home," he implored, "& if you don't do it soon you will find that I have become one of the lower forms of vegetable life. [Without my writing] . . . I think I should go quite mad."[8]

Clearly, he suffered more from their separation. Disappointed in his quest for office in 1933, he felt bad about letting Ailsa down. "I had hoped," he told her, "to have such a nice position in Washington for you to grace, so you would not feel that life would be too humdrum after London, but I am afraid that you will be disappointed. However, at least there will be a few flowers at Syosset, a few remaining bottles of wine, and a great deal of love to welcome you."[9]

As a youth, David romanticized history and gave an exaggerated gloss to the larger-than-life figures he read about. The same tendency spilled over in his attitude toward his friends. He often viewed them through rose-tinted glasses, attributing qualities to them far in excess of reality. He not surprisingly had a highly romantic notion of marital love, but as these plaintive letters hint, Ailsa did not reciprocate.

By the end of the decade, the tone of tenderness had disappeared from his letters, replaced by sentiments of stiff, conventional affection. Ominously, he took to calling her "The Princess." That hoax marriage license in 1925 with the name "Regina Mellon" was more accurate than he realized. Paul Mellon discreetly assessed their relationship. "As far as I could see they were reasonably happy. On the other hand, he was a very active and outgoing person. I would imagine it was depressing for him," he concluded with staggering understatement. "They were on different wavelengths."[10]

There is no evidence that Bruce was to blame for his wife's problems. Certainly none survives suggesting that he treated her with anything but affection in the early years before their marriage permanently soured. "Perhaps they began badly," said a close friend, "she got so ill in Rome when they were first married. . . . It was a difficult period. . . . If you've heard other people describe her she wasn't exactly Little Miss Fixit. She wasn't going to concern herself with her husband's running of his office. Besides that, you know, here you had David . . . always a brilliant student, the highest averages everywhere. And Ailsa? That school in Farmington. She wasn't sufficiently prepared to be the wife of somebody like that."[11] Audrey offered neither a solution to her mother's problems nor the means of drawing her parents together.

Much later Bruce would say that he did not want to distress his wife with talk of a divorce because of her emotional state. Perhaps, but as soon as he really wanted one, this gallant resolve, a self-denying ordinance with no sanction to it, went out the window. It is hard to imagine his seeking a divorce as long as Andrew Mellon lived. But the old man, who had been the central figure in his daughter's life in a twisted sort of way and whom David admired, left the scene in 1937. In the meantime, David and Ailsa followed their partly separate lives in the way wealthy couples do when a marriage fails but neither party sees the need for a formal break.

It was no secret in New York that ten years or so after their storybook wedding, David and Ailsa had problems. Because they spent so much time apart, he at Staunton Hill, Washington, or abroad, she in Manhattan or Syosset, the gossip columnists got wind of it and dropped hints. Both were rumored to have had affairs. They moved in rarified circles far removed from the constraints of conventional, middle-class morality. Bruce once approvingly quoted his friend Lady Diana Cooper, airily dismissing her husband's latest inamorata with the words "It's not the adultery I'd mind but I'm so afraid she'd let him catch cold."[12]

David was a handsome man, whose appeal increased as the years passed. He liked to be surrounded by beautiful women — and always was. This was not a matter of treating women as just one more kind of beautiful ornament to be collected. Although he was a product of his time and class, and very traditional in his views about the relations between men and women, such a judgment would be wide of the mark. He was genuinely more comfortable in the company of women than of men and counted more of them as friends.

By the end of the 1930s, neurotic, withdrawn Ailsa had close companionship in Lauder Greenway. A former president of the Metropolitan Opera and a pleasant fellow according to Bruce, Greenway was hardly a forceful personality. He could usually be found idling around the pool at Syosset, mixing drinks for guests. He loved a fey sense of humor that could now and then still be coaxed from Ailsa — especially when she had had a few of those drinks. "I never saw anybody improve with a martini the way Ailsa did," said her closest friend, cousin Peggy Hitchcock.[13]

While Ailsa slipped increasingly into a lonely existence, jollied up by Lauder and martinis, her husband followed a different course. By all accounts there were plenty of wild oats sowed as Bruce charmed his way through New York café society. Various names were mentioned, including "fabulous," wealthy Cordelia Duke Robertson, to use his own description of her. Unlike the flamboyant youth of Emily Clark's description in the early 1920s, Bruce in his early middle age had learned the virtues of discretion. As his Baltimore friend the duchess of Windsor said, "One must keep love affairs quiet."[14] About some things Bruce too had learned to be very quiet indeed.

When he went to London for the Red Cross, he cut a swath in Mayfair society during the Battle of Britain summer. A frenetic, living-for-the-moment atmosphere replaced the languor of debutante parties and charity balls. Dining and dancing at the Savoy in spite of the bombs added to his reputation for insouciant charm.

For a time actress Leonora Corbett, who drove a mobile Red Cross canteen, caught his eye.[15] In fact, she was more in love with him than he with her. When her friends teased her about spending unaccustomed time out of London, she brushed off their taunts by saying she had become so much a country girl that she sewed leather buttons on her negligee. When a friend questioned her about a new fur coat, she shocked her by saying she never had to buy her own. An admiring journalist called her "one of the most engaging persons in England."

What engaged Bruce was not just her glamorous good looks but her sparkling wit. Responding one evening to Churchill's dismissive comments on her long fingernails, she flourished them like an Oriental fan and retorted, "You have a bodyguard, Mr. Prime Minister, but these are all that I have." Though she visited Staunton Hill in 1941 when she came to play on Broadway in Noel Coward's *Blithe Spirit*, the liaison with Bruce was a transitory one.[16]

When Bruce returned to London for OSS, he roomed with Tommy Hitchcock, his best friend from New York, an adventurous, playboy polo champion, and, like him, a Mellon in-law wearing the Army Air Corps uniform. Before Hitchcock died test flying a new fighter plane, he and Bruce hosted occasional dinner parties. Some of these evenings included mostly the top air force brass. The best ones were more egalitarian, mixing senior officers and enlisted personnel promiscuously. Entertaining in wartime London had its problems. One cook turned out to be a drug addict whose last act in their employ was to indulge her habit with disastrous consequences in the middle of an important meal. Later they unluckily hired a vegetarian spiritualist maid who quarreled with the addict's successor in the kitchen.[17]

In affairs of the heart, though, if his flirtations with Corbett and others were more akin to the ephemeral socializing of those frantic months, the same was not true of another relationship that began in London in 1943.

If it was a man's war, many women realized its potential for them too. One was Evangeline Bell, a slim, shy Radcliffe graduate of twenty-five. As the daughter of an American diplomat and an English mother, she, like David Bruce, was desperate to go to London in summer 1940 and do her part. "I felt so guilty not being there," she remembered long after.[18] She had landed a good job in Washington as assistant to Francis Biddle, head of the Justice Department. Her big chance came when, at a dinner party at the Danish embassy in 1942, she sat next to Bill Donovan. Manic as ever, he insisted that she work for him, and she grasped the opportunity. Of all the possible government jobs, OSS was most likely to punch her ticket for England. She candidly told her OSS interviewers that that was why she was talking to them.

She guessed right. In 1942 she became assistant to William Phillips when he went to take command of the embryonic OSS post in London. A Boston Brahmin diplomat, Phillips was a friend of the Bell family, affectionately called "Uncle William." In mid-July they boarded a Pan American Clipper for the flight to England. The skeleton OSS staff met them at Paddington Station and took them to their two cramped offices at the embassy while workmen outfitted expanded quarters in Grosvenor Street. When Roosevelt sent Phillips as his special envoy to India in the fall, Bell chose to remain at her post.[19]

She was no stranger to London. She had been born there, and her mother, Etelka Surtees, came from a family prominent in County Durham, in the north of England, for centuries. Evangeline's grandfather, Brig. Gen. Sir Herbert Conyers Surtees, had been colonel of the Coldstream Guards and a Tory member of Parliament. She had less conventional antecedents too. Robert S. Surtees made his mark in Victorian fiction with a popular humorous character of the turf, John Jorrocks ("more people are flattered into virtue than bullied out of vice" was one of his tags). Then there was Evangeline's great-grandmother, the actress Ruth Herbert, mistress and favorite model of Dante Gabriel Rossetti. Herbert was, in the phrase of her great-granddaughter, *une grande horizontale.* She most definitely passed on to that great-granddaughter some of the ethereal beauty that had captivated the Pre-Raphaelite artist and poet.[20]

The winter before the Great War began, Etelka Surtees married a diplomat from an old New York family, Edward "Ned" Bell, then second secretary at the London embassy. The Bells were so Old New York that even before the war some of them were complaining about the nouveau riche invading Manhattan, not a surprising reaction for people who not so long before had kept those *arriviste* Astors off the Social Register. Ned Bell and his first wife had divorced, and then she married an obscure European aristocrat and later yet joined a famous group of Paris literary lesbians. It all sounded "like something out of Edith Wharton," Evangeline wrote in bemusement, long after.[21]

Ned Bell was a Harvard classmate of Franklin Roosevelt. They toured Britain during their junior year and celebrated Bell's twenty-first birthday at London's Café Royal. Between Harvard and his second marriage, Bell served in Egypt, Persia, Cuba, and Paris. He remained in London during World War I, where FDR visited him again as assistant secretary of the navy.[22] One of Bell's jobs was to supervise a rudimentary intelligence network at the embassy, and indeed one of his friends from that era was Allen Dulles. After the war he held posts in Japan and then China, where as a child Evangeline rode her Mongolian pony in the park of Peking's Temple of Heaven with a marine guard as a companion.

Her father died suddenly in China, and her mother then married British diplomat Sir James Dodds. By then Evangeline and her sister Virginia had begun shuttling among boarding schools across Europe. (Their mother insisted on sending them to French-speaking schools.) They attended the school of St. Catherine of Alexandria in Rome about the time David and Ailsa occupied their ill-starred luxury flat there. The Roman school was not so bad, unlike the terrible time they had at another one in Sweden. It was an exotic, but not idyllic childhood. She recalled the loneliness of "never having a home, frequent heart-wrenching farewells to friends, struggling to learn new languages, always the foreigner, the outsider wherever you were landed."[23]

One of Bruce's favorite stories recounted how he met her when she interviewed for a job in his Secret Intelligence branch in Washington. Most of the vacancies were filled, he told her, and besides the language requirements were incredibly stringent. To his chagrin, he had to tick off five or six languages before he got to one she did not know in part. Her own recollection was more prosaic. After that chance meeting with Donovan, she applied to OSS but could not remember later that one of her interrogators was in fact Major Bruce, only that he was an older man whose hair was beginning to turn gray.[24]

In February 1943 the new London station chief quickly learned to appreciate the assistant he inherited from Phillips. The earliest evidence in the record is an April 1943 postscript to a letter he sent back to his Virginia friend and OSS colleague Francis Miller: "This beautiful typing is done as usual by E. B., who is absolutely invaluable."[25] Typing was, however, the last thing on his mind, and a surprise visit by Donovan galvanized him into action. Out the blue, Donovan asked Bell if she might like to be reassigned to India. When she said the prospect intrigued her, she recalled, "I noticed that D[avid] turned pale, and ran after him to ask him if he was sick and whether I could get him some medication . . . 'I am NOT sick' he answered 'but I have just heard you give a ridiculous answer. If you will meet me for a drink tonight I will explain why you should not leave London.'"[26] She agreed, and over drinks at Claridges Bruce asked her to marry him.

She had a knack for organization and maintained a high level of efficiency in the boss's office. Hubert Will, then head of OSS/London counterintelligence (X-2), admired her competence and said that Bruce relied on her to keep things running smoothly in a constantly chaotic environment.[27]

She wore a second OSS hat. Her facility for languages, especially her idiomatic French, made her a valuable resource for the unit that fabricated identification papers. It was a demanding task, both technically and emotionally. It required skill to match stolen identification stamps with the fake papers and fictitious life stories that OSS concocted for the agents being sent to Occupied Europe. The stress of knowing that the quality of their work literally spelled the difference between life and death for the agents was as draining as the long hours. Like many of her colleagues, she got to France soon after the liberation, in her case hitching "a pillion ride on the back of an OSS motorbike for a tour of central Paris."[28]

Earlier, when she first arrived at the London office, Evangeline Bell created a sensation. People later described her as a luminous and stylish beauty, a cultivated woman of impeccable taste perennially on everyone's best-dressed list. Francis Miller called her "one of the most beautiful women of her generation."[29] During the war she was still a reticent young woman, not the sophisticate who elicited these later superlatives. Even so, her youthful beauty — "willowy" is a word that inevitably appears in most accounts — anticipated that future elegance and attracted the attention of her male OSS colleagues.

Historian Arthur M. Schlesinger Jr., who knew her as an undergraduate, would write long after, "I can still conjure up the young girl's wry grace, effortless style, shy and subtle intelligence and indestructible beauty."[30] And she was tall, for David liked tall women. "No pocket Venuses" for him, Evangeline recalled. Some of the women in the office had wondered if their new boss, with his languid accent and foppish affectation for silk handkerchiefs, would be interested in women at all. They were wrong. Years later one of her children asked if she had been sexually harassed as one of the few women in the London office. "Yes. By your father," she jokingly replied.[31]

The romance blossomed like thousands of others in wartime London, lovers brought together by chance, living for the moment. Little wonder that *Casablanca* was their favorite film of the war. On rare occasions they slipped out of town, sometimes to Ditchley Park, sometimes to the West Country to spend the weekend with Betty and Robert "Bobbety" Cecil, the future fifth marquess of Salisbury. The Salisbury family album for 1943 captures in faded black-and-white snapshots some of these fleeting escapes to the country, with David in his Brooks Brothers uniform, Evangeline stylishly dressed for the country house scene, and one of the inevitable springer spaniels that became their constant companions.[32]

Bruce kept his personal life strictly private, but word of the commanding officer's romance spread rapidly through the mushrooming empire of OSS London. Unlike earlier affairs, this one was serious, and it forced him to reassess his modus vivendi with his wife.

David and Ailsa's marriage was dead in all but name and had been for almost a decade. His earlier resolve to spare her the trauma of divorce, however, was not absolute. It was easy enough to maintain as long as nothing more than a fleeting infatuation appeared on the horizon. His attraction to Evangeline Bell put that resolve to a severe test. In December 1943 David asked Ailsa for a divorce.

In Washington during the early months of COI/OSS, he would tell Ailsa stories from the office, among them the one about the young woman he interviewed who knew so many languages. He must have told it with special flair. When he finally asked Ailsa for a divorce and said he wanted to marry an OSS employee, his wife asked, "Is it the girl with the languages?"[33]

Ailsa resisted. In the spring David returned to America on OSS business. He brought Audrey a copy of the Peter Rabbit books in French; to her mother he renewed his unwelcome demand for a divorce. Back in London he wrote again. "Ever since I left there I have thought constantly about the same problem and the answer is always the same. There is no aspect of it which I have not considered with the greatest care and the conclusion I reach invariably is that feeling as I do a divorce is the only possible solution. I love E very deeply and I want beyond everything to marry her. I know it is something that will not change under any circumstances and with my conviction that my happiness depends on such a marriage[,] life on other terms would be completely unsatisfactory. I say this with a full awareness of how drastic and fundamental divorce is and everything that it means in our particular case."[34]

She still resisted. His frustration gives an added dimension to his reckless actions during the liberation of Paris. As soon as he returned to London, five days after storming the Ritz with Hemingway, he sent a determined letter to Ailsa's lawyer demanding an end to the "unfair and unreasonable" delay in the inevitable. "I have been deeply in love for a long time, with an individual whom I want above everything to marry," he insisted. "There is no possibility whatever in this regard that my sentiments will undergo any change."[35] Knowing that this letter would become evidence in any divorce proceeding, he worded it carefully, omitting Evangeline Bell's name, yet it brimmed with frustration and barely concealed emotion like few other letters written by this intensely private, discreet, and controlled man. Finally, near the end of 1944, a year after he first asked her, his wife relented.

In the last spring of the war, it fell to Ailsa Bruce to reenact the painful ending of her parents' marriage. That central event of her childhood, which had shriveled her psyche, now bruised her once more as it resonated in her own divorce. Thankfully, the vicious custody fight and allegations that poisoned the earlier breakup were not repeated. It would be bad enough. She had known a break was coming and later recited a litany of what-might-have-beens if she had acted differently. "She deserved it, she was very spoiled," her best friend, cousin Peggy Hitchcock, admitted. Another friend said that afterward she kept saying "I wish I'd done this, I wish I'd done that" to prevent the inevitable. Because they knew how difficult, even imperious, Ailsa could be, the Mellon family "went out of their way" to let David know they bore him no ill will.[36]

Divorce then was not the casual transaction it has since become, not even for the rich. Once she had given in to her husband's request, in October 1944 Ailsa bought a house in Palm Beach to establish Florida residency in order to qualify for a divorce there. The bill of complaint she filed against him the following April alleged "great anguish and sorrow, resulted in loss of appetite and weight, and seriously and injuriously affected the health and peace of mind." His actions, her lawyers said, constituted "extreme cruelty" and "wilful, obstinate and continued . . . desertion."[37] With cold formality, the accusatory language of the law was invoked against him. In his formulaic response, Bruce went through the required motions. It meant treading the fine line between acknowledging that he had requested a divorce and denying that his actions caused his wife mental and emotional harm.

He readily conceded custody of Audrey and agreed that "I shall have only the right to visit her at such times and under such conditions as shall be agreeable to you."[38] Such a stipulation was no sacrifice. He felt no need to be close to his daughter; the occasional visit would be enough. If Audrey had been older, perhaps he would have reacted differently. Later, when she was a young adult, he enjoyed her company, but that spring she was only eleven. He was of a generation and a class that relegated small children to the out-of-sight province of nannies and private tutors. Despite his own happy memories of childhood, he agreed entirely with his caustic English novelist friend Nancy Mitford, who said, "I love children, especially when they cry, for then someone comes and takes them away."[39]

Some of Bruce's friends noticed the marked difference between his attitude toward children and adults. One explained it by describing a small dinner party at which she had included her niece, about Audrey's age at the time of her parents' divorce, to begin to introduce her to the social affairs of the adult world. When the guests had departed, the aunt, delighted with the success of her party and enchanted once more by Bruce, asked her niece if he was not the most fascinating man she had ever met. She was surprised when the girl vehemently disagreed because he had ignored her the whole evening.[40]

Ailsa attended the hearings before a magistrate called a "special master" appointed to consider her complaint at the county courthouse in West Palm Beach.[41] The OSS colonel was legally present in the person of his attorney. There were other witnesses. When asked when the couple last lived together "as husband and wife," Audrey's nurse tactfully said she could not answer. To the same question, Ailsa replied "prior to October 1943" and not much the year or two before that because he was abroad so much. Her friend Alice Harding Allen testified that because of David's repeated demands, Ailsa began to look tired, lost weight, became depressed, and stayed home all the time. "It was all I could do to make her go out to lunch," Allen declared. Ailsa called David's first letter "a great shock to me and it was an extremely humiliating experience and it had a rather bad effect on my health and on my nerves." She began taking more sleeping pills every night. Though her lawyers carefully coached everything she said, it is easy to see the pain that her husband's requests inflicted on her.

David's attorney offered no evidence for his client, though earlier he requested that the official record omit any reference to Evangeline Bell. In a statement that struck all those present for its irony, Ailsa Bruce, the richest woman in America, promised to make no claim on her husband for alimony or child support.

In the final week of the war in Europe, the special master found that the plaintiff was entitled to a decree "forever annulling and dissolving the bonds of matrimony" on grounds of desertion and mental cruelty. Three days later David and Evangeline were wed in Boston. The ceremony took place in the chapel of Emmanuel Church, at the edge of the

Public Garden, near the statue of Bruce's idol, George Washington.[42] Oddly, Evangeline's family objected to her marriage. To the Bells and their Old New York friends, the Mellons were nouveau riche, and here was Evangeline marrying one of their former in-laws. Her mother sniffed in agreement. Etelka had met the Mellons and was not impressed. Besides, her daughter deserved nothing less than real aristocracy: "Only a British title would have satisfied her."[43]

Despite the cold, official tone of the divorce proceedings, David and Ailsa — or Mrs. Mellon Bruce as she began to style herself — remained on friendly terms. When he passed through New York, he would often stop to see her. Their divorce became, like so many in the Mellon family, an ever-so-discreet, civilized affair, without rancor or recrimination — at least to the eyes of the outside world — in contrast to that first Mellon divorce.

Bruce resigned from the board of the National Gallery after the divorce. Ailsa became, after her father and brother, the museum's greatest patron. She made possible acquisition of the *Genevra de' Benci*, the only Leonardo in the Western Hemisphere. Her benefactions, together with Paul's, led even later to the gallery's East Wing, designed by I. M. Pei, a building that made as much a statement about its time as the original one did during the depression. And yet, she was never able to enjoy her hundreds of millions, as David had so effortlessly done. He continued to be a valued friend of the gallery by prodding her with ideas for donations. "I have fiddled around with deeds of trust," he noted some years later, "and now would like to start an art collections fund in honor of Mr. Mellon, hoping Ailsa will sweeten it up in a big way."[44] The gallery's director thanked him for his continuing help. After one particularly long talk with her, the director said to David, "I realized even more clearly than I had before how much the Gallery owes to you in these matters."[45]

Not long after the divorce, Ailsa said she would marry Lauder Greenway. Indecisive as ever, she brought the subject up repeatedly, only to drop it a few days later. Once, on the morning of the day they were to be married, she could not find the right shoes and so canceled the ceremony. Greenway's cousin, who called Ailsa the most private person she had ever met, thought what put her off was the possibility of having to deal with Lauder's large, close family. That prospect was too much for Ailsa to bear. She never remarried for another reason. Fond as she was of Lauder, in an old-fashioned way, she always thought she was still married to David. "She loved him to the grave," family friends said.[46]

She became even more reclusive. She rarely traveled, even to the houses she maintained in Palm Beach and Greenwich, but remained in her Manhattan apartment or at Syosset, surrounded by her expensive bibelots and lapdogs, a sad figure in the shadows. Her indecisiveness grew worse. Her inability to make up her mind drove art dealers to distraction, and those who lent her paintings on approval rued their foolish indulgence. The canvases stacked up in odd corners on the floor. "It used to concern me," a friend said, "that the dog might appear some afternoon and pee all over a masterpiece."[47]

Washington now became home for Bruce. He kept the house he had bought just before the war in Georgetown on 34th, between P and O streets. And Staunton Hill, of course. Without a government post, he spent more time at the mansion than ever before. For all the money and hope he had invested in Staunton Hill, he and Ailsa had never been happy there. But now he was happily married, and what was more, by fall 1945 Evangeline was pregnant. In May the first of three children was born to the Bruces, a daughter they named Alexandra and always called by the Russian diminutive, Sasha.

The dramatic changes in Bruce's personal affairs did not come without cost in his family. Louise and Cabell, strict Episcopalians who categorically opposed divorce on principle, were profoundly shocked. Evangeline Bruce was at a severe disadvantage even before she met her in-laws. Even more telling than their religious scruples, they were devoted to their darling granddaughter and were convinced David was making a terrible mistake. Out of fear that she would lose access to Audrey, Louise pushed Cabell to write David in London to warn him what a disastrous step the divorce would be for his daughter.

Louise's attitude first began to soften when Ailsa reassured her she could see Audrey as often as she wanted. With that fear allayed, David's mother could accept these dramatic changes with more equanimity. Her remaining apprehensions dissolved soon enough when she saw how happy her son was with his new wife. When David went back to Europe for OSS in summer 1945, Evangeline stayed with her in Maryland. She and her new daughter-in-law developed a fondness for one another, deepened by Louise's joy at learning that Evangeline was pregnant.[48]

Louise did not live to see the baby but died at age eighty in autumn 1945. David said, "I shall miss her terribly. In spite of various differences of opinion, I loved and admired her profoundly and she was a Rock of Gibraltar in many respects."[49]

Some relatives, who did not know how close Louise and Evangeline had become, thought the divorce hastened Louise's decline. As she lay dying, the family gathered around the deathbed of this woman now strangely bereft of the energy that had been a vital part of her personality. James and his wife, Ellen, were there throughout the last illness. Before David could arrive, as James sat by the bedside holding his mother's hand, Louise kept asking, "Where's David? Where's David?" It enraged Ellen. Her mother-in-law seemingly ignored James and kept calling for the absent son.[50]

Cabell, after a long decline, died at age eighty-six the following spring, unreconciled to his younger son's actions.[51] With his father's death, David Bruce experienced the chief milestones of middle age — all concentrated into only thirteen months. Divorce, remarriage, the birth of a child, and the death of both parents transformed his life as completely as the war had done.

Like all veterans, he was changed by the war. The contradictory elements of his young adult personality were subtly resolved. After World War I he had displayed a frivolous, dilettantish exuberance. After nearly two decades in his failed marriage to Ailsa, the sadder elements grew stronger, the inherited Bruce reserve and detachment more visible. The result of this blending was all to the good, for the winning personality of his later years now emerged more fully. His elegance of manner and worldly-wise knowledge of the creative and fine arts had something to do with it. What gave him such immense appeal, however, was not these qualities but that rarer ability to impress on each man or woman he talked to the feeling that he was sincerely, deeply interested in that person. He had the great gift of listening as well as talking.

Financially he was very wealthy. After his parents died, his share of their estate came to a quarter of a million, about $5 million in present value.[52] But this inheritance paled next to the fortune he had amassed on his own. He was no longer married to the nation's richest woman, but his own shrewd investments gave him his independence. Though in later life he became increasingly conservative in his investments, like many members of the *rentier* class, before the Crash he had not minded gambling on Wall Street. Sitting on all those corporate boards gave him plenty of insight, too, which he used to enhance the value of his portfolio. He hardly noticed the cost of transforming Staunton Hill into the grand country estate of his dreams.

In taking stock of himself, Bruce had every reason to be pleased. He was not. Not as dissatisfied as on the eve of the war, but he still felt unfulfilled. He had realized that goal, first articulated at Bordeaux University in 1919, of setting himself up at Staunton Hill as a Virginia country gentleman, with his books, his wine cellar, his independent means, and, indeed, a new wife and baby. It was not enough. The war marked a critical turning point in his life, and not just because he found love.

Wartime service gave him a taste of achievement and public service — the achievement of a contribution, made at personal risk, to a great cause. He found it was a rewarding experience to be close to the sources of power in the service of the republic. His ambition, his internationalist outlook, and the postwar revolution in American foreign policy ensured that rustication in the backwoods would not satisfy him. Neither would a return to the exclusive ghettos of the Upper East Side and Long Island. He looked on the 1930s as a personal lost decade. If World War II gave him a sense of purpose, it did not give him the opening he needed. For more than a year after, he became increasingly frustrated as no new opportunity appeared on the horizon.

He rejected politics. His prewar foray into the legislature gave some Virginians the idea that Charlotte County's most famous son might seek election again. One trial balloon came from his OSS friend Stacy Lloyd, a patrician publisher who was divorcing his own wife, Bunny, so that she could marry Bruce's former brother-in-law, Paul Mellon. Through an editorial in his Berryville, Virginia, newspaper in 1946, Lloyd proposed Bruce for the United States Senate. The state's senior senator, irascible Carter Glass, who had supported Bruce's forlorn effort for appointment in the early New Deal, had died that summer. A native of Lynchburg, the closest town of any size to Staunton Hill, Glass was an authentic character of an earlier time. An opponent once said that elevating him to the Senate was worse than Caligula making his horse Roman consul because the emperor at least had the good sense to appoint both ends of the horse. When no strong candidate emerged to take Glass's place, a group of Charlotte County worthies encouraged Bruce to run. He agreed to meet with them but told them outright in his slow Tidewater drawl that he did not stand "a goddamn chance."

Before Pearl Harbor the speaker of the Virginia House of Delegates had chastised him for saying "Civil War" instead of "War Between the States." Despite his love of southern history, that provincialism put him off. A society that embraced the past because it could not envision a different future was not for him. Despite the hopes he and Ben Robertson had expressed as they lay on their backs in the wildflowers of Shakespeare Cliff, looking up at the sky during lulls in the Battle of Britain, the voices speaking for the South were the same old constricted ones as before.

In 1946 he joined a lobbying campaign to undo President Truman's termination order and reconstitute OSS. This effort began at Bruce's Washington home, where he brought together Donovan, William Casey, and other OSS veterans to conspire around his dinner table.[53] (Unknown to them, literally just around the corner two Soviet spies, not yet unmasked, lived on P Street — Alger Hiss and Donald MacLean.) Truman eventually realized his mistake in killing OSS and created in its place a National Intelligence Authority, but it was a superficial entity — no director, no independent budget, and not much of anything else besides a name. The task Bruce and his OSS colleagues set for themselves was to give the NIA, or some other agency, the teeth to do the job they believed was crucial for national security.

Bruce wrote an article recounting the trials and accomplishments of OSS. On the eve of the war, he argued, the small military and naval intelligence offices cared little about world affairs: "The chiefs of these departments all too often regarded their tasks with distaste, incomprehension, and frustration." America's foreign service shared the insularity: "At the State Department a spirit of smug self-satisfaction prevailed. The relation of stirring events in China, Russia, Abyssinia, and Spain sometimes lost its dramatic value when presented to a Pennsylvania Avenue audience. While Mr. [Cordell] Hull breathed tranquilly over his Eden, primitive forces throughout the world had become unloosed, and were threatening the very foundations of our national existence."

As a result, said Bruce, employing Thomas Jefferson's metaphor for slavery, "the attack at Pearl Harbor startled us like some gigantic dissonant firebell in the night of our false security. We felt betrayed and indeed we were." Personal experience gave weight to his denunciation of OSS's foes in military intelligence, the FBI, and the State Department. The nation could not afford to live in the dangerous postwar world without a robust successor to OSS. "An efficient strategical intelligence agency," he concluded, "is the country's first line of defence."[54] These efforts bore fruit the following year, but they did not solve Bruce's immediate, personal problem.

The condition of the State Department was also a barrier. The department would need drastic overhauling, he thought. On board the *Tuscaloosa* waiting for D-Day, he said, "the resentment of all officers that one meets here against the bureaucratic methods, and lack of vision in the State Dept. is striking." Further, "unless it undergoes a radical internal reorganization, involving a drastic housecleaning of present personnel, and the attraction to it of new blood, it will prove incapable of coping with its vastly increased responsibilities, and make our country seem unfit to meet its obligations as the greatest world power."[55]

In the year after the war his future course was undecided, but he had accumulated the assets needed for making a shift from the indolent lifestyle that now seemed unfulfilling. More than money, he had accumulated experience. Bruce's role, providentially thrust upon him, gave him the experience to take the next step toward further service to the state.

All of these advantages were real, not least a new wife who supported him in ways Ailsa Mellon Bruce could not begin to fathom and who was capable of a partnership in public affairs that few spouses could provide. But in 1946 all was still maddeningly only potential. He could easily have slipped back into the familiar world of the cosseted rich, immured in their private clubs and country estates, doing good works (but not too strenuously) and clipping the bond coupons that they had inherited or married. He still enjoyed the good life to the hilt, but his notion of fulfillment went beyond working on his tan and amassing a world-class wine cellar.

He began to shed the idle friends of the 1930s and cultivate new ones he had acquired during the war. His frustration even tainted his enjoyment of private happiness. He had wanted a son, not a daughter, as he revealed a few years later when he said of a friend who had three, "I wish I had such a quiverfull of boys myself." A visitor to Staunton Hill in the summer of 1946 remarked on his disappointment at the gender of the new baby and the irritation he radiated because he had not found an outlet for his renewed sense of purpose.[56]

CHAPTER 10

Immediate and Resolute Action

After 1945 the United States did not move to assert world leadership accidentally or reluctantly. . . . It did so because a group of true believers . . . had crossed the desert of isolationism and survived. They had provided leadership in the great crisis of World War II. After it, their moment came, and they did not mean to let it slip.

— Geoffrey Hodgson, *The Colonel*

*I*N MARCH 1947 David and Evangeline Bruce settled into their cabin on board the crowded *Queen Elizabeth* in New York harbor and prepared to sail for England. Plowing through late winter storms, the liner reached Southampton overdue a week later. On the quay, mountains of food packages brought for friends and relatives dramatized the shortages in postwar Britain. Bruce observed people at the dock and on the train to London and thought them "weary and depressed," as though they and not the Germans had just lost the titanic struggle for mastery in Europe. "The old British politeness was worn pretty thin," he thought, "and a change in manners is everywhere noticeable and remarked upon." At Claridges the Bruces escaped the gastronomic pallor of a nation rarely cited for cuisine and still subject to wartime rationing. But they could not ignore the evidence of reduced living standards even in the homes of their well-to-do friends, where they found that electricity too was rationed and heating nonexistent.[1]

When they boarded the Golden Arrow at Victoria Station and crossed the Channel to visit Evangeline's sister, they found Virginia's flat in the exclusive 16th arrondissement "desperately damp and cold." The gloom began to lift when they attended Easter services at Chartres, bringing vividly to Bruce's mind the last time he saw the cathedral, under German fire. "It was interesting to me," he observed, "to motor along the road from Versailles to Chartres via Rambouillet, with which I was so familiar in 1944. The French have done an amazing job of repairing the badly bombed railroad tracks and buildings along it." The couple picnicked on Easter Monday among the daffodils in the forest of Compiègne. For a month they took trips to the Loire *châteaux* he first visited with Macgill James and also had entrée to diplomatic Paris, thanks in part to Virginia's husband, Ashley Clarke, number two to the British ambassador, Duff Cooper. Attending embassy dinners, the latest plays, and Jean Cocteau's film *La Belle et la Bête*, the Bruces renewed old acquaintances and made new ones.[2]

Even without the diplomatic connection, as a rich American, Bruce would have had little contact with the straitened circumstances of ordinary French citizens. That picnic in Compiègne — simple peasant fare washed down by a plain white Bordeaux and reminiscent of his scrounged wartime meals — was as close as he got. Instead, nightly forays to chic restaurants, recorded in loving detail in his diary, paint a surreal picture of Paris that spring. For those with the dollars — and it did not take many — haute cuisine and fabulous vintages were there for the asking. They went to the Tour d'Argent and, just as he and Macgill had done during that summer of discovery in 1920, dined "on the glass-enclosed roof which gives an incomparable view of Paris." His reputation as a gourmet was never in question, and his preoccupation with wine lists raises doubts about his sensitivity to deprivation in postwar France.

He proved, however, that it was possible to compare vintages of Saint-Emilion and Montrachet and at the same time keep an ear attuned to geopolitical realities. In both countries that he visited, he sought out old allies in the espionage trade. In London he dined with Sir Stewart Menzies, former head of MI-6, uneasy ally and sometimes antagonist of OSS. In Paris he saw André Dewarin, de Gaulle's former chief of intelligence. Although he was a genuine war hero, Dewarin could not shake the accusation, much as he tried, that he had been in the Cagoule, a prewar neofascist cabal.[3] Because Bruce kept up with

Frenchmen like Dewarin, he opened himself to criticism, but he valued loyalty in friends and gave it unstintingly himself.

He made these contacts with comrades-in-arms not just for the joy of reliving adventures over a good claret. From them and from others, he learned about the mood of the two nations, or more precisely of their ruling elites. His banker friends in the City of London gloomily questioned their country's ability to repay war loans and "think it doubtful that [the] UK can within the next decade balance her imports with exports."[4] Although he noted more finery in the shops of the Faubourg St. Honoré than in London's West End, he found confidence in short supply everywhere. After returning home, he favorably critiqued a memorandum from Allen Dulles promoting a centralized, strategic intelligence service. "In the last few months," he told Dulles, "I have seen instance after instance where such an organization, properly conducted, would have been of immense value to the State Department."[5]

Bruce took the trip not only to revisit scenes of his wartime exploits and introduce his new wife to old friends, but also to gather firsthand insights if he returned to government service abroad. It was not a far-fetched idea. His espionage friends were making progress toward creation of the CIA, political contacts were putting in a good word for him in high places, and his old patron Averell Harriman was newly appointed secretary of commerce. "This is a belated letter of congratulations," Bruce wrote him from Stanton Hill. "Even in this sparsely settled rural area the news of your appointment engendered a widespread feeling of confidence and enthusiasm. I am living here on my farm, and enjoying every moment of it. When we come up to Washington during the winter I hope to have the pleasure of seeing you."[6] Harriman had reason to doubt the bit about "every moment." Far from reveling in arcadian solitude, his friend itched to return to government service. In January the chairman of the Democratic National Committee recommended Bruce to Truman for an assistant secretaryship at the State Department, the same post he had sought in 1933 from FDR. Whether he knew the FBI ran a character check on him is unclear. Certainly his hope for appointment was justifiably high.[7]

As his letter to Dulles shows, the trip to Europe resonated, if more faintly, with the fact-finding mission that Bill Donovan undertook for

FDR during the Battle of Britain. For, as in summer 1940, in that second spring after the war an American president was collecting information about troubling conditions in Europe.[8]

When Bruce sailed from New York, Europe struggled to dispel the memory of a bad winter. It had been a season of bitter cold, with blizzards on a scale not seen in Britain since the turn of the century. The weather seemed to reinforce the pessimism that infected government and business leaders. An American expatriate in Paris explained their gloom: "Europe has been the victim of cannibalism, with one country trying to eat the other countries, trying to eat the grain, the meat, the oil, the steel, the liberties, the governments, and the men of all the others. The half-consumed corpses of ideologies and of the civilians who believed in them have rotted the soil of Europe."[9] To the east the Soviets carted off German machine tools, rolling stock, even whole factories, and set up peoples' democratic republics that were none of those things.

Europe's place on the international stage shrank too. When Bruce's OSS colleagues had nervously joked that they were fighting to "Save England's Asiatic Colonies," they worried unnecessarily. Victory doomed the colonial empires. Picking neurotically at the scab of 1940, the French were blinded to this unforeseen result. Indochina and Algeria as well as metropolitan France would pay a bitter price. OSS aided Ho Chi Minh in fighting the Japanese, but the French spurned him and so he prepared for the long haul. Twice in the next quarter-century his tenacious struggle in Southeast Asia would cross the path of the quondam head of OSS London.

Unlike Churchill, most Britons did not mind if they elected a king's first minister to preside over the dissolution of the empire. In 1947 the British quit India. They saved the subcontinent from Japan but not their faith in the white man's burden. At the same time they washed their hands of Palestine. A third retreat, at first glance unimportant compared to the end to three centuries of the Raj, was most critical. In February, the State Department received word that the flamboyant British ambassador, Lord Inverchapel, wished to deliver an aide-mémoire about Greece and Turkey. The British were so severely strapped that they meant to end aid to both nations immediately. This latest retreat would not have been so critical if there had not been more sinister threats that year.

When to mark the beginning of the Cold War is still debated. Bruce had thought FDR's "blithe" toleration of the Soviets "unrealistic."[10] Few such illusions remained in Harry Truman's White House. Opinion in the country, though, was divided. On the left, some feared to upset Stalin, others even defended him. On the right, isolationist Republicans earned the title of "The Stupid Party" for many reasons but most bizarrely for appearing to want to fight communism by pulling out of Europe.[11]

The previous year Churchill had given his Iron Curtain speech. By then the peoples' republics set up in the wake of the Red Army were showing their true colors. Containment of Soviet expansion as the basis of American foreign policy began to win broad acceptance among the policy elite. The shock produced by Inverchapel's note spurred Truman and his team to step into the breach. They did not hesitate, but it would take a herculean dose of backstage maneuvering, and crude simplification too, to win bipartisan support for this novel foreign commitment.

Truman spoke on March 12, 1947, to a joint session of Congress, perhaps the most important address of his presidency. Reading from an open notebook, he spoke slowly and forcefully. It was all over in eighteen minutes.[12] What began as an effort to replace the British presence on the southeastern fringe of Europe became the Truman Doctrine, a commitment of resources to the cause of democracy around the world, and a harbinger of what a later president would describe as his country's willingness to bear any burden, pay any price. Truman thought he needed to clothe his proposal in sweeping, idealistic terms to have any hope of winning approval. People with more leisure than he enjoyed have criticized him harshly. Yet it is difficult to see how he could otherwise have gained approval from a skeptical, parochial Congress. These dramatic events took place just before Bruce sailed to Europe.

Once it secured aid for Greece and Turkey, the administration groped toward a broader application of the Truman Doctrine. The first trial balloon came in a speech by Undersecretary of State Dean Acheson. His remarks did not create a national stir, but the right people read about them. Republican Senator Arthur Vandenberg demanded to know if the speech prefigured a vast increase in foreign aid. He had come to believe that America could not stick its head in the sand, but he did not intend to allow Congress to be ignored. To its credit, the administration heeded his words. Together the incongruous pair of Acheson and Vandenberg, who disliked one another personally, deserve much of the credit for making the Truman Doctrine the foundation of American foreign policy, especially through economic aid to Europe.[13]

Truman left the details to his subordinates but made one crucial contribution. One adviser suggested that they call the program for European recovery the Truman Plan. The president, knowing his unpopularity in the country, shrewdly offered instead the name of his secretary of state. George C. Marshall, architect of victory in the war and a latter-day embodiment of Roman civic virtue, in David Bruce's words, radiated "a sort of majesty about his selflessness." He was "a wonderful combination of strength, understanding, and almost gentleness. He always speaks to the purpose. Although he never thunders like a prophet, you find yourself clinging to every syllable he utters, afraid of missing any of it." He was not a man to be trifled with, "an impressive personality, soft spoken and charming, but not one with whom anybody would dare to take liberties. His moral character is almost physically apparent."[14] Besides, Truman said, the choice of Marshall would sell "a whole hell of a lot better in Congress."[15]

On June 5, 1947, Marshall spoke about his eponymous plan at Harvard. He cloaked it in high-minded phrases about fighting "hunger, poverty, desperation and chaos" and pointedly declared it was not directed "against any country or doctrine." Finally, he said the initiative must come from the Europeans themselves to decide how best to use this offer. His emphasis on concerted action carried an early hint of Washington's desire for European integration.

Acheson wanted to ensure that Europe grasped the meaning of his boss's speech. The day before, he lunched with three British journalists and filled them in. American papers gave scant coverage to Marshall's remarks, but one of Acheson's three reporters read the speech over BBC radio the next day. Listening in London, the Labor foreign secretary, Ernest Bevin, called the address "a lifeline to a sinking man. It seemed to bring hope where there was none." He rushed off to confer with his French counterpart.

The resulting all-European conference met in Paris. True to Marshall's promise, no nation was excluded. Such magnanimity carried a risk. Long before Congress voted on the plan, Stalin could have killed it. All he had to do was participate, and Truman's enemies in Congress would have seen to the rest. In refusing to allow the Soviet prison house of nations to participate, Stalin also blocked aid to his newest inmates in Eastern Europe.

The creators of the Marshall Plan devised it out of a sense of self-confidence about America's place in the world. They had fought isolationists before the war; victory proved them right. After the war they fended off those same isolationists on the right and idealists on the left who thought they could reason with the tsar of the Gulag. After decades of bipartisan support for American involvement abroad, their achievement is too easily taken for granted. They "wanted to restore Europe, not change it," according to one account, and "by seeking change in order to preserve, these men were, in their own way, revolutionaries in the cause of order."[16] In this instance, the Eurocentric foreign policy establishment that Bruce represented was more enlightened than the general public.

Thanks once more to Harriman, whom Truman had made Commerce secretary after firing the erratic Henry Wallace, Bruce returned to government service. Everything he had done since the Battle of Britain made him a fully paid-up member of the internationalist cause. When the FBI ran a background check in 1947, it found praise from many sources for his admirable qualities. One person Hoover's agents questioned, however, wondered whether Bruce had not been made "a little lazy" by his good fortune, never having a "strong incentive to direct and continue his efforts in productive work."[17] Bruce would not have dissented from that assessment of the 1930s, but he was determined the same would never be said of him again.

Not quite two years had passed since he left OSS. Staunton Hill once more became only a holiday retreat. During the war he had written about his Georgetown residence, "I definitely do not want to sell it on any terms — it will always be useful."[18] He was especially glad for that forethought, for the house on 34th Street now served as more than a pied-à-terre. He began as an assistant to Harriman with the understanding that he would be appointed to a higher post if Congress authorized it. With his usual modesty, he told Allen Dulles he was indifferent to titles: "Personally, I do not much care, since I am very interested in the work I am now doing."[19] The new post was eventually approved, and he became assistant secretary for foreign and domestic commerce.

As one of Harriman's team, he moved into Commerce's vast, neo-classical headquarters on the Ellipse. It was another edifice built by his late father-in-law, for long before the National Gallery, Mellon had set in motion a plan that swept away blocks of ramshackle buildings and transformed the face of Washington. The huge Federal Triangle gave the city a core of classical design and defined the open space of the Mall. Critics dismissed the style as "facadism," "brutal stone masses built in an eclectic style as boring as it was massive and unoriginal."[20] They were convinced Mellon had inflicted on Washington the architecture he had praised in Mussolini's Rome when he visited Ailsa and David there in 1926.

Harriman's assistant did not have time to contemplate these agreeable ironies. Commerce, according to veteran New Dealer Raymond Moley, had been falling apart ever since FDR took office.[21] Henry Wallace had scared the business community silly with his naive view of the Soviet Union. With Harriman at the helm, the nation's mostly Republican business leaders found a sympathetic advocate, even if he had been a staunch Roosevelt man.

Bruce spent his time granting export licenses to American firms and responding to complaints about foreign trade barriers. He also did his share of testifying before congressional committees, especially because his boss was a notoriously leaden speaker. In early 1948 Bruce appeared twenty-three times on the Hill, an unnecessary inoculation against the remote chance he might overcome his disdain for Congress. It irritated him to waste time waiting to testify, especially because he then had to spend most evenings at his office catching up. But he kept his counsel. When asked long afterward why he did not protest, he said drily, "You would find that one did not express such views at my level in Government."[22]

Sometimes he had to defend his chief. One morning when he testified before the House Interstate and Foreign Commerce Committee, the chairman, Democrat Richard Harless, denounced "deliberate attempts to sabotage the foreign policy of the United States by mismanagement of export license." Bruce replied heatedly that Harless had falsely impugned Harriman's integrity.[23] Annoying as these issues were, they were diversions from the larger work.

Testifying on Capitol Hill no more suited Bruce than writing letters to Senator Byrd about aid to Britain in 1940. The Commerce Department, though, was a necessary means to an end, for his sights, and the administration's, remained firmly fixed on passing the Marshall Plan. The chance to work in Europe once more to help administer this program — assuming it passed — was the reason Bruce accepted Harriman's offer in the first place.

From summer 1947, through the fall and winter and on into the spring, the administration concentrated on selling the plan. Acheson appointed a bipartisan committee to help sway wary legislators. Under Harriman's chairmanship, this group of largely Republican industrialists reviewed the plan and pronounced it good for business.

Bruce played a vital role in persuading the business community. In October at a national foreign trade convention in St. Louis, he told conferees bluntly that America's role in the world had changed irrevocably: "No longer can we Americans, protected by the oceans, hold ourselves aloof from the quarrels and concerns of other nations. Nor can we maintain even our economic security if hunger, greed, disease and despair stalk unchecked abroad." He appealed not just to the idealism of his audience but to their self-interest as well by reminding them that in spite of America's unparalleled production, such prosperity "cannot continue indefinitely in the absence of world recovery." The program, he said, promoted both American business and world peace: "It is true that the success of the Marshall proposal will promote our foreign trade. We are more interested in it, however, because it will aid in the economic recovery of Europe which is essential to the economic stability of the world. And we know that we shall not have peace, which is our first concern, until such stability is reached and the level of world prosperity, including our own, is higher."[24]

This was familiar work for a veteran of the Fight For Freedom Committee. He knew he would run up against the same Little America mentality of his isolationist foes in 1940–41, but he had an argument that he believed in even more fervently than before the war. The day after his St. Louis speech, he spoke in Nashville. "Are we to retreat within ourselves and reconcile ourselves to anarchy outside our hemisphere?" Such a supine course, he said, would lead only to World War III. Here was the lesson the internationalists learned from the war and that they applied, for good and ill, over and over again during the next generation. They denounced the evils of Munich and of isolationism. America should match its economic strength against the forces of disruption and darkness. Two great powers faced one another across a prostrate world, in Bruce's view, one insisting on the freedom of the individual, the other on the supremacy of the state.[25] Substituting Stalin for Hitler, this sounded a lot like the argument he had prepared for the Virginia legislature just before Pearl Harbor. With this change of adversary, his argument clearly expressed Washington's view of the world that had emerged from the turmoil of global war.

Bruce's experience in OSS prompted Secretary of Defense James Forrestal to seek his advice on countering Communist subversion in Europe. With the benefit of hindsight about Forrestal's suicide, Bruce would recall him as "talented, attractive, a dedicated public servant, but a queer duck, introspective and egocentric. He liked to be considered tough and hard boiled, but actually was sentimental and, to some, especially women, affectionate."[26]

Bruce carefully pointed out in his response that he was not proposing "acts of violence, such as the assassination of enemy leaders." Rather, he suggested that some of the propaganda perfected by OSS would be effective: "Such a naif belief that the truth alone will prevail and eventually will conquer does not seem justified in the light of human experience." Besides selling the Marshall Plan to Europeans, America should also plan "to engage the Communists on their own ground, in the field of propaganda, and to battle in the twilight zone where fact and falsehood are almost inextricably intermingled." He thought propaganda would be useful in France and Italy, "whose subjection to communist influence would constitute for us a crisis of the greatest gravity." He especially recommended an approach that became an extensive American campaign throughout the Cold War: "By subsidy of native papers, or by careful establishment of new organs of public opinion, there is no reason to doubt that American inventiveness in the field of journalism, if realistically applied, might counter the influence of Soviet dominated propaganda."[27]

For all the heavy firepower the administration threw into the battle, some legislators denounced the Marshall Plan as a "bold socialist blueprint" and an "International WPA." Although Harriman's committee of rock-solid Republican businessmen helped squelch such talk, the outcome hung for a long time in the balance.

Stalin, having spurned Marshall aid, redoubled his efforts to destabilize Western Europe. Especially in France and Italy, Communist parties and Communist-dominated unions agitated to bring down governments. They caused economic damage but at the cost of harming themselves in the public opinion battle. Anti-Communist European leaders exploited this agitation. Pierre Mendès-France, whose later decisions as French prime minister would dramatically affect Bruce's career, cynically admitted the Red menace served a useful purpose: "Because we have a 'Communist danger,' the Americans are making a tremendous effort to help us. We must keep up this indispensable Communist scare."[28]

In the end it did take a Red scare, a real one, to push through the plan. For all the lobbying on Capitol Hill, passage was still not assured as winter faded into spring. Czechoslovakia made the difference. The defeat of pro-Western politicians there by ciphers beholden to Moscow appeared as part of Stalin's plan to subvert the last free state in Central Europe. Unwilling to be found wanting in the face of aggression, like Britain and France at Munich, Congress finally passed the plan.

In recent years it has become fashionable to doubt that the Marshall Plan gave the essential catalyst for reviving a prostrate Europe. Some writers point out with the clarity of hindsight that Europe was beginning to pull out of the slump even before Marshall aid began. Further, American dollars supplied only a small part of the total invested in European capital formation. What the critics overlook, however, is the way the money was spent and the immense psychological boost it gave. The dollar amount — $14 billion in all over four years — was very large, and its appearance at a time of gloom and depleted foreign currency reserves provided just the tonic needed to revive confidence. With black markets the only growth industry, Communist-inspired strikes threatening to disrupt production and overthrow cabinets, and the menace of Stalinism hanging over the Continent, European governments greeted the Marshall Plan as a godsend.

That is not to say that America and its beneficiaries viewed the plan the same or to deny that Washington intended it to promote a greater degree of integration than the Europeans wanted. Some of those delegates to the Paris conference viewed the American offer like "lofty and demanding beggars approaching an apprehensive millionaire."[29] Intrusion into the domestic affairs of the nations receiving Marshall aid would be as unprecedented as the aid itself and bound to stir resentment.

Once passed, the Marshall Plan took concrete form as the Economic Cooperation Administration (ECA). Truman wanted to make his articulate, caustic undersecretary of state, Dean Acheson, the chief ECA administrator. Wiser heads persuaded him not to, because Acheson's disdain for Congress would prejudice ECA's chances from the outset. Truman decided instead to appoint Paul Hoffman, former president of Studebaker Corporation, to take charge of ECA/Washington and Harriman to run ECA/Europe from a base in Paris. Each participating country would also have its individual resident head of mission. A cheerful, energetic prototype of the can-do American executive, Hoffman gave superb bipartisan coloration to the plan. He was, he joked, "the least obnoxious of the Republicans." His zeal for increasing productivity — Bruce called him an "evangelist" on the subject — gave the plan its focus.[30]

To replace Harriman at Commerce, Truman chose Charles Sawyer, a vain, prickly Ohio politician and former ambassador to Belgium. Sawyer hoped to rely on Bruce, his Georgetown neighbor, to learn his way around the department. He would need the help: on his first visit Sawyer literally lost his way in the labyrinthine building. When he finally reached his office, his undersecretary, William Foster, came in to say he was leaving for Paris to work for Harriman. After he failed to dissuade Foster, Sawyer was dumbfounded later the same day when Bruce came to say he was resigning too — to be head of mission for ECA/France. Sawyer accepted, but he complained that he would be "seriously handicapped" by the loss of Bruce's services and charged — accurately — that this was a "decision made by you and Harriman some weeks ago." According to the New York Times, Commerce's "top level of officials has been stripped" by Harriman. Sawyer was furious and vowed to thwart anyone else who left for ECA and expected to return to Commerce once "the fun was over or when they had tired of it."[31]

He should have known better. It took monumental indifference to ignore Washington's absorption with the Marshall Plan. Sawyer only fooled himself by thinking Harriman's assistants were going to pass up this adventure, as they viewed it, to help Europe back on its feet. Their attitude gave the plan its impetus and its vitality. It also bore the seeds of problems, for what Americans saw as a helping hand, some proud Europeans viewed as interference in their internal affairs disguised as charity.

Fancying himself a hard-nosed pragmatist, yet admittedly idealistic about Europe, Bruce shared that perspective and its implication for relations with France. Harriman held him in high regard. He called his work at Commerce "a terrific job" and expected no less when Bruce went to Paris.[32] Both shared the internationalist view of the leading role they believed America must play. In the flush of optimism that greeted passage of the Marshall Plan in spring 1948, they looked forward to accomplishing great things.

Within days of Congress's approval, ships sailed with food for the malnourished and raw materials for idled factories. The first merchantman departed from Galveston carrying wheat. Another cleared Baltimore harbor with tractors and chemicals and others with their holds filled with farm machinery, oil, and cotton. Before long, more than 150 ships would be on the high seas at any one moment, bottoms filled with goods provided by Marshall Plan aid. The psychological effect as well as the boost to production was electric and immediate.[33]

CHAPTER 11

The Problems of French Recovery

He incarnated for me that finest of times during "Le Plan Marshall" when we all shared the great hope that we might participate in the creation of a new and better civilization, which would unite the best of Europe and the best of America.

— John L. Brown, on David Bruce

*I*N JUNE 1948 the newly appointed heads of Marshall Plan missions to France and Britain prepared to sail for Europe on the Holland-America liner *Nieuw Amsterdam.* Well-wishers thronging the pier at Hoboken to see them off created a massive traffic jam. In the crush at the departure gate, journalists crowded around to hear what these novel emissaries in American foreign affairs had to say. As expected, David Bruce and Thomas Finletter expressed pride in the plan's role in rebuilding war-scarred Europe.[1]

Bruce really did believe the confident predictions he made to the reporters. His appointment fulfilled his search for purpose since the war, and he was ecstatic. Now he had a chance to contribute at the highest levels to the nation's foreign affairs. What grander way to serve than to help revive the stagnated economy of France, that font of the arts he had admired since his youth, the nation, he wrote, that "has for so long nurtured the best hopes and aspirations of western culture"?[2]

"It would be an extremely valuable experience," he had said in 1919 while with the army in France, "to be attached to an embassy during the reconstruction period."[3] The chance finally came nearly thirty years later. If Truman lost the 1948 election as everyone expected, the top ECA people would soon be lame ducks. What mattered more, though, was the chance, however brief, to make a difference during an anxious period of European history. For Bruce, America's frontier in 1940 lay on the far side of the Atlantic; eight years later it had marched inland to the inter-German border that marked the westernmost limit of Stalin's writ.

Bruce had just passed his fiftieth birthday. He was a middle-aged man whose appealing personality and cosmopolitan background were already becoming a fixture of Georgetown lore — an authentic son of the genteel South, favored by Mellon riches, worldly-wise in his knowledge of European culture, and surrounded by the mystique of OSS. All of these elements gave him an aura that he quietly played to his advantage.

Years later he became used to being described as belonging to a former time. A "distinguished statesman out of another era" was how Henry Kissinger's biographer would portray him.[4] In fact, he displayed that persona from the outset of his new career, because in 1948 he had been styling himself an eighteenth-century gentleman for quite some time. Once maturity had buffed the brasher edges off his youthful exuberance, he exuded all of the refined courtliness that that image suggests. But for all his sophistication and reserved calm, some things could still revive the enthusiasm that intoxicated him in 1919. One was the idea of European unity.

It was more than simply a matter of economics. In the third spring after the war, political crises rivaled the Continent's daunting problems of reconstruction. The Czech coup unnerved politicians everywhere even as it gave Truman the momentum to push the Marshall Plan through Congress. As Bruce crossed the Atlantic, the Western Allies took the first step to create a German state out of the slice of the Reich they occupied. Before he had been in Paris a month, the Soviets responded with their blockade of western Berlin — then an enclave administered by the United States, Britain, and France deep inside the Russian occupation zone. The Allies sustained the city with a twenty-four-hour-a-day bridge of planes ferrying everything from coal to powdered milk. The Berlin blockade was one of many crises that could have triggered World War III. Bruce and his colleagues had cause to believe the Soviet threat gave their task great urgency.

He realized when he reached Paris that the French had made progress, and in an official ECA analysis he noted "tremendous improvements in physical plant and in services." These advances, however, were measured from a baseline of widespread destruction and hardship. "The Liberation restored liberty," he said, "but it could not bring the dead back to life, rebuild the half-million homes that had been totally destroyed, or repair the other million and a half that had been damaged."[5] In the first year after liberation, France was a nation "haunted by hunger and cold" whose chief inheritance from Vichy, a cynic observed, was "the mystique of the black market."[6] Any progress since then was cold comfort for the average family as long as basic commodities, even bread, were still rationed and most gasoline came from under the counter.[7] France's foreign currency reserves were exhausted, and despite the improvements Bruce noted, its transportation and industry were antiquated.

Most important, France suffered from lack of will. Its political elites were riven by faction, resentful of their diminished world role, and resigned in bitter pessimism to a bleak future. "The population too," Bruce concluded, "was, in part, as demoralized and disorganized in spirit as the physical plant was in substance."[8] The self-confident nation that he had witnessed in Paris on the day of liberation was sunk into the slough of despond.

De Gaulle, who said he had "picked the Republic out of the gutter," led the nation briefly after liberation.[9] He was a divisive figure, though. According to Paris graffiti, "de Gaulle has his head in the clouds and his feet in the shit."[10] He denied the Communists the influence they craved, and chafing under a flawed constitution, he resigned in 1946 to sulk at his country home. He later said in jest, "How can you govern a country which has 246 varieties of cheese?" Then it was no laughing matter.

"For the politicians, de Gaulle's departure was like the rolling away of a great stone, even though something resembling a political nest of maggots was exposed."[11] At first the Socialists adhered to the morally bankrupt maxim *pas d'ennemi à gauche*, no enemies on the left. With the Cold War, this sentiment crumbled, and the Communists were expelled from the cabinet, though not from parliament. Where instability had once come from their presence in the governing coalition, it would now come from their expulsion. The way was open for the Third Force, a mutating coalition among Socialists, Christian Democrats, and others, sandwiched between Communists on the left and Gaullists on the right.[12]

France stumbled along under a succession of weak coalitions, the "ballet of the parties," in de Gaulle's contemptuous phrase.[13] Bruce put it this way: The French, having had "unfortunate experiences with 'strong' government — are operating under a constitution which attaches virtually no penalty to the overthrow of a cabinet."[14]

Washington hoped its support would strengthen the middle parties. As much as the aid money they dispensed, it was that weakness at the center that gave American officials in France like Bruce such leverage. If Washington exerted influence, however, it rarely had its way completely. There was little the French could do to emancipate themselves from American tutelage in the early days of the plan because they needed the aid.[15] This dependence, however, boded ill for the future of Franco-American relations and for Bruce.

Harriman set up overall European headquarters for the Marshall Plan in Paris at the Hôtel de Talleyrand, an appropriate choice, named for that consummate diplomat-survivor of the French revolutionary generation.[16] Located just across the rue de Rivoli from the Tuileries Gardens and touching a corner of the Place de la Concorde, ECA/Europe looked out onto the political heart of France. Harriman picked a corner office full of antiques, decorated in rich greens and golds, with floor-to-ceiling windows that opened out onto the great public square. In the corridors of the Talleyrand, especially in the downstairs snack bar, journalists traded gossip and learned more about America's policy in France than at the embassy.[17]

As head of ECA/France, Bruce set up his own office in more modest quarters nearby, the annex connected by an overhead walkway to the imposing American embassy. Designed by Billy Delano, the architect who had remodeled Staunton Hill, the embassy, like the Talleyrand, enjoyed a diagonal view of the Place de la Concorde. Being so close to his boss in the Talleyrand and closer yet to the ambassador was a mixed blessing. The memory of being scrutinized by the top brass in wartime London was still fresh in his mind.

He started with a small staff in chaotic quarters, just like the early days of OSS. Ultimately the staff grew, though unlike his OSS empire, it never much exceeded fifty. But these few Americans, flush with money, power, and a sense of ascendancy, inhaled the narcotic of postwar Paris and remembered it for the rest of their lives, much like the young Baltimore doughboy wandering starry-eyed through the same cobbled streets at the end of the last war. Many of them went on to senior positions in foreign affairs. Their views on Europe and America's presence there would bear the stamp of their time in the Marshall Plan and of Bruce's leadership and enthusiasm for European unity.

Their boss had to maintain a delicate balancing act. The domineering head of ECA/Europe held court a minute's walk away, and Bruce's staffers joked to one another that the rue Royale separating their office from the Talleyrand was more dangerous to cross than the English Channel in a gale. Harriman was his benefactor three times over, but Bruce feared to be under the thumb of the gruff, insensitive financier, no matter how generous he had been. Bruce kept on good terms, but he constantly had to fend off attempts by Harriman's people in ECA/Europe to chip away at his authority. It helped that he stayed in regular contact with Hoffman. He had learned that lesson in the Red Cross when he kept in touch with Norman Davis during the Blitz. Thanks to Bruce's efforts, ECA/France escaped the micro-managing that both ECA/Washington and ECA/Europe inflicted on missions to other countries.[18]

Every morning Harriman briefly assembled the half dozen men who reported directly to him. As the only head of a country mission based in Paris, Bruce attended just to keep a finger on his boss's pulse. Two decades after Bruce worked for him on Wall Street, Harriman still showed little interest in day-to-day management, only in making the big deals. One Harriman staffer remembered that in that small group Bruce always projected an air of cool assurance, was never caught without an answer, always gave the appearance of being in complete control of his mission.[19]

Looking beyond his colleagues in ECA/Europe, who were keen to invade his turf, Bruce knew that his neighbors in the embassy fancied even less the new people horning in on their annex. He had faced that attitude before. OSS was nothing if not an upstart agency, and he had spent more of his time than he cared to recount thwarting interference by the American army and British intelligence. It really was not so odd that Bruce, a conservative, establishment figure, was drawn to ad hoc, *arriviste* organizations like OSS and the Marshall Plan. They provided the best way someone his age could make up for time lost before the war. Journalist Teddy White observed that through all of Bruce's various attributes "runs the thread of an unorthodoxy almost as extreme as the elegance which is its outer husk."[20]

OSS prepared Bruce well to deal with Jefferson Caffrey, the stiff, quirky, cold fish who was America's ambassador to France. Caffrey — a foreign service classmate of Evangeline Bruce's father — sniffed in contempt at the improvised, take-charge corporate culture of ECA. Caffrey's people viewed the Marshall Plan office as an impertinence and a slight. They thought they were perfectly capable of administering foreign aid, and they resented Bruce's contacts with top French officials. Their passive hostility was easier to overcome than OSS's combative enemies or even Bruce's colleagues in ECA/Europe. Rubbing salt into their wounds, Bruce found that his team could coopt the embassy's younger, less hidebound diplomats.[21] The subversion of his staff infuriated Caffrey. A punctilious career diplomat of some accomplishment, he failed to see that through Bruce he could have advanced his own interests too. His own biographer described him as "a relentless perfectionist, chary of praise and incapable of flattery," who depended on a few staff favorites to mitigate his abrasiveness.[22]

There really was nothing he could do about the Marshall Plan, though: it was the cornerstone of American policy. In 1948 it enjoyed a sex appeal that eluded traditional diplomacy. A later ambassador in Paris, James Dunn, found himself in the same awkward spot. How could he compete, he told a visitor, with an agency that held the power to dole out such large sums of money?[23]

With his own staff Bruce was correct, protective, loyal. Good at arranging his time efficiently, he learned which people he needed to deal with directly and which he did not. He kept a distance from most of the staff, a detachment that became a trademark of his style. Even for those far removed from him, though, he projected a reassuring presence. Extremely reserved, speaking with that languorous southern

accent, he imparted a sense of confidence and serenity during the
frequent crises that year. The calm, deliberate manner that worked in
OSS now inspired his Marshall Plan staff. To them, he was an enormously cultivated, urbane figure, with a background more fascinating
than any they had encountered before.

Among his most crucial decisions were his choices for key subordinates. Chief among these was William "Tommy" Tomlinson, his young
financial attaché, seconded from the Treasury Department. Though
"just a kid from Idaho," Tomlinson brilliantly mastered the technical
minutiae of the French economy and perfected a gift for dealing with
the stiffest *fonctionnaire* of the Paris bureaucracy. He was "a major
source of strength," so adept, in fact, that Ambassador George Ball
later said his friend David Bruce's greatest contribution as head of
ECA/France was in giving free rein to Tomlinson's talent.[24] That was
no backhanded compliment: Bruce was a gentleman amateur not a
professional technician. His achievement lay in acknowledging the
distinction between the roles, performing his own adroitly and trusting
people like Tomlinson to keep the Marshall Plan running smoothly.

Bruce's own skill was most apparent with the stream of powerful
politicians who passed through his office. Europe under the Marshall
Plan was the junket opportunity of a lifetime. The dollar was strong,
Paris was Paris, and with America embarked on a grand, altruistic
program, what legislator could resist making a "fact-finding" tour? He
conducted the briefings by himself rather than turn them over to staff.
He knew the value of cultivating the goodwill of important visitors,
but he also just liked giving a grand *tour d'horizon* that placed ECA in
the broadest context. It was a chance for him to convey his enthusiasm
for European unity. His performance served as an example too. One
subordinate, Arthur Hartman, later a highly successful ambassador to
France and the Soviet Union, said he consciously modeled his own style
on these virtuoso Bruce performances that so impressed him as a junior
ECA economist.[25]

The Marshall Plan made it possible for France to import food to sustain
its malnourished citizens and raw materials to feed its industry. France
received free much of the fuel, metals, and textiles that kept production
from falling at a time when the nation lacked the foreign currency
reserves to import basic goods. Thanks to ECA, France imported capital

goods to increase productivity: equipment for potash and coal mines, excavating machinery, rolling stock for railroads, even complete plants shipped from America, such as a strip steel mill, an aluminum foil plant, and a pharmaceutical plant.

In Bruce's enumeration, the plan's objectives were "to increase production, to restore confidence in the currency, to stem inflation, to balance the budget, to stabilize the cost of living, to relax the economic pressures making for political disunity, to repair many of the ravages of war, to increase exports." The most important goal, he said candidly, was "to strengthen the moderate and democratic forces of the nation in their fight against Communism."[26]

Supervising the distribution of goods did not constitute the most important influence of Bruce's mission. The real power lay in approving the use of "counterpart funds," francs that accumulated when the French government sold internally to private companies the goods it acquired free through the Marshall Plan. These francs could not be spent at will because the Americans worried the French would fritter them away and fuel inflation. A solution was at hand. France needed not just the goods provided by ECA for current production, it needed to invest in modernization. It was Bruce who recommended the disbursement of these counterpart francs as investment capital and who decided, in consultation with the French, which projects to fund. In 1948 most counterpart francs supported modernization in agriculture and industry, including power plants, rail lines, and coal mines.[27]

If Washington focused mainly on Berlin in 1948, from his vantage point Bruce saw an equal threat, no less insidious. He feared that Communist-inspired strikes would undermine France from within. Violence spread as Communists fought Gaullists in town halls across the country. France teetered on the brink of civil war. As in Italy — where the Christian Democrats countered Communist strength at the polls with the slogan "In the voting booth God can see you but Stalin can't" — it seemed as though Soviet victories would not stop in Central Europe. Remembering those months, beginning when Bruce arrived in France and stretching on through autumn 1948, Jacques Fauvet, historian of the Fourth Republic, called it a "terrible year."[28]

In his assessment at the end of the summer, Bruce expressed increasing alarm. "Financial situation in France heading for tragic climax unless immediate steps taken to cure present distemper. Prices still rising; uneasiness in rank [of] non-Communist labor has made hold-the-line attitudes of leaders nearly untenable in face of threatened strikes. . . . Unless checked soon, inflation will destroy gains painfully achieved during first six months 1948. Steady deterioration of confidence in currency constitutes menace not alone to French economy but to whole European recovery effort."[29]

The cramped syntax of diplomatic cables accentuated the urgency. Bruce and other American observers really feared the possibility of a total collapse of French society. He correctly saw that "political instability is root of failure to deal constructively with economic situation. Uneasy and almost unnatural party coalition commanding, even when united, a bare majority and dependent upon constitution unsuited to modern emergencies makes governmental authority object of derision and cynicism."[30]

In autumn the economic slide accelerated. Prime Minister Henri Queuille, "a country doctor famous for his lack of panache," who once said that "no problem is too intractable to resist an absence of decision," asked Bruce to advance the release of counterpart funds.[31] Bruce, alarmed about labor unrest and hyperinflation, supported the crafty Queuille's extraordinary request to prevent a financial collapse. "Prime Minister Queuille man of character and determination, skilled in political arts. Program suggested by him, in our opinion, is from fiscal viewpoint most courageous and satisfactory proposed to meet present difficulties."[32] Far from the scene, officials in Washington branded Bruce's telegram outright blackmail.[33] They would learn soon enough that the French in their weakness were not without power.

In October one faction in the State Department thought threats rather than aid would have a salutary effect. Harry Labouisse and Ben Moore feared that France, the recipient of more aid than any other country, jeopardized the whole European recovery program. In an internal draft paper called "The French Crisis," they proposed to withhold the full amount of aid already allocated until the French put their house in order. When news of the draft leaked, anger and outrage coursed through official Paris. Bruce, Harriman, and Caffrey joined forces to protest the proposal. They feared it would play into the hands of the Communists. The next weeks vindicated them as the Communists overreached their grasp and their coordinated wave of strikes failed.[34]

Nevertheless, Bruce and his colleagues did begin exerting unprecedented pressure on the French to adopt "responsible" fiscal measures. These were necessary, Bruce told Queuille, if ECA were to have a chance of convincing Congress to appropriate more money. He made his case in a letter to the prime minister that "despite its gentlemanly tone, had the hallmark of an ultimatum."[35] Here was a little blackmail in the opposite direction.

In December he took his argument public and attracted a thunderclap of protest. In this one instance was distilled the essence of all the ill will, misconceptions, and frustrations that beset postwar Franco-American relations: to French opponents of ECA, confirmation of the sinister intentions of their benefactors; to French supporters, sad evidence of American insensitivity; to American opponents, proof that foreign aid was a waste; to American supporters, another headache caused by French ingratitude.

The occasion for this outburst of bad feeling was Bruce's speech at a dinner given by business leaders in the northern industrial town of Lille.[36] It was a symbolic choice. Marshall Plan coal kept the local steel mill running, and the previous December saboteurs had derailed the Paris-Lille night express, killing twenty.[37] In his speech he summarized ECA's accomplishments during its first half-year. He reminded his audience literally where their bread was buttered. "Without these imports," he said, "French food rations would have been absolutely insufficient." He reminded them too that "Marshall aid has also made possible the importation of coal, petroleum, copper, zinc, textiles, wool and cotton," without which "many factories would have to discharge tens of thousands of workers." These words were enough to irritate journalists looking for an excuse to attack him. What he said next guaranteed an incendiary reaction.

"Despite the magnitude of American aid," he argued, "it is obvious that the greatest contribution to the rebirth of prosperity in your country must and can be made by the French people themselves. Many Frenchmen think that France's contribution, since the Marshall Plan came into effect, has not been completely satisfactory." He warned of the need for further "substantial sacrifices." France must adhere to the austerity measures the National Assembly was then drafting if it expected more American aid. "The Congress of the United States will convene in a few weeks, and shortly thereafter will begin consideration of the question of a continued contribution by American taxpayers to the recovery of the French economy. These are fateful days. The measures which the people of France now take in the interest of their own future and that of Western civilization may well be a decisive factor in preserving that civilization."

Blunt words. For once, Bruce's measured French, spoken with that quaint Tidewater inflection, failed to charm.

He would not have worried if he had been vilified by only *L'Humanité*, which ranted on cue against "the insolent Mr. Bruce." "The French government has cried on Mr. Bruce's shoulder in its attempt to obtain some more dollars," the Communist daily fulminated. "Now the Marshall Plan official kindly lets Mr. Queuille know what his answer is. No, no, Mr. Bruce, this country will never foot the bill for your war preparations." Other papers chided him for statements "contrary to the spirit of Marshall's speech at Harvard." "Mr. Bruce must not forget that he is not at home." Even the conservative *Le Figaro* regretted that he had not shown "a more subtle view" of France's economic woes and asked plaintively "is it not rather unjust to criticize France at this time when our country is serving as a testing ground for the maneuvers of the men of the Cominform?"[38]

Harriman, with whom Bruce had shared an advanced draft of his speech, leaped to his subordinate's defense. The *Washington Post* rejected complaints about a speech that was "a model for ECA diplomacy" and argued that Bruce would have been remiss if he had ignored the difficulties France faced.[39]

A week after Lille, the government introduced its celebrated *loi des maxima*, finally putting its finances on a sound footing for the next year. It is uncertain to what extent Bruce's admonition influenced this stern measure. What is clear is that Queuille's seriousness in dealing with the problem impressed Bruce, and he pushed Washington to increase aid. Franco-American relations seemed to be headed in a positive direction. It would not last.[40]

The enthusiasm of their American benefactors made the cold hand of charity all the more offensive to some French politicians. The self-confidence of ECA diplomats reinforced old stereotypes. One official who considered himself a francophile said his colleagues looked on the French as dishonest, filthy, lazy, mercenary, morally deficient malingerers seething with hostility toward Americans. In turn, he said, the French felt humiliated and resentful. American reports cited the supposed French inferiority complex that reinforced their view of Americans as materialist, predatory, hedonistic, and selfish.[41]

Bruce's deep affection for French culture led him to think he could speak more frankly than he ought. The French did seem eager to take offense and confirm a disagreeable Gallic stereotype. "The French," he had written just before the liberation of Paris, "although a most agreeable and attractive race, and in many respects an admirable one, are often, even to their friends, somewhat irritating; when they deliberately seek to annoy . . . they must be absolutely maddening."[42]

Continuing Franco-American disputes over the Marshall Plan illustrate the inability of each party to appreciate the other's point of view. In particular, this was apparent in disputes over how to use the counterpart funds and how to publicize the fruits of the plan.

Some in Washington wanted to use counterpart money to build a consumer society and provide housing, hospitals, and schools. They wanted to show that capitalism could provide for the proletariat better than communism. Housing, however, was not part of the French government's investment plan, and ECA was never able to dissuade the French from spending most counterpart funds on modernizing industry and transportation. The French won this argument with Washington, made from a position of weakness, in part because they had the confidence of Bruce and Tomlinson in their vision for modernizing the economy. Counterpart francs could not be released, Tomlinson snorted, "at the whim of well-meaning Americans for red, white, and blue drinking fountains in public squares."[43]

American insistence on publicizing the work of the Marshall Plan caused an ongoing headache. Most of the pressure came from Washington and put Bruce's mission in the middle. When headquarters insisted that every ECA-funded project be publicized, Bruce's staff sarcastically spoke of the "bronze plaque" policy. On this issue Bruce was more attuned to French sensibilities than Congress.

Harriman's people at the Talleyrand would not be outdone by Washington in the quest for obtuse publicity stunts. One called for Bruce's office to attach a helium balloon to the Eiffel Tower with a sign saying "Merci, Marshall Plan." Another called for outfitting a barge to tour the canals of France with a similar message. Bruce's people punctured that idea too by pointing out that if saboteurs sank the barge and blocked a major waterway, ECA would have more publicity than it could handle.[44]

Home for the Bruces was a *rez-de-chaussée* apartment on the rue de Lille, with a garden, three rooms listed as historic monuments, and an unpleasant past.[45] The flat had once belonged to the unfortunate Princesse de Lamballe, the friend of Marie Antoinette who was hacked to death during the Revolution to show "how the people avenge themselves on tyrants."[46] The tenants before the Bruces — a homosexual couple — had had a spectacular row that for reasons unknown led to the sale of all the furniture except a large Louis XIV bed.

Evangeline Bruce had not wanted to go to Europe but agreed it was an opportunity her husband could not decline. When he told her the Marshall Plan offered him either London or Paris and asked which she preferred, she told him there was no contest. It must be Paris: the English obsession about rabies meant they could not take their dogs to London. She was surprised to see how relieved he was. He had feared she would favor London. Until that moment, she had not realized how intense a francophile he was, and he must not have realized until then just how much she loved her dogs.[47]

In 1921 he had said, "It always seems to me that the sun shines more brightly here than elsewhere, that the people are more gracious and friendly."[48] Some things never changed with him. Paris in 1948 was exactly where he wanted to be. He was passionate about his work, convinced of its importance, and thrived on the long hours. During that year "David woke up happy every day," his wife recalled.[49]

Bruce made an even more important contribution than astutely employing Marshall Plan counterpart funds. Indeed, what allowed him to identify productive uses for counterpart funds in the first place was his relationship with the diminutive, self-promoting Frenchman who fathered the major postwar schemes for European integration.

Before World War I, Jean Monnet had hawked his family's cognac in western Canada. He promoted the American aircraft industry during the crucial months before World War II. He proposed a union of Britain and France after Dunkirk. After the war he became the chief economic adviser to the French government. "You talk of grandeur," he said to de Gaulle, "but today French people are pygmies. There will only be grandeur when French people are of the size which justifies grandeur. For that, they must modernise."[50]

After the war he proposed a coordinated plan to do just that. American officials who viewed economic planning in their own country as anathema embraced the Monnet Plan as a reliable guide out of the mire of France's postwar stagnation.[51] One of them ironically was Bruce, a tooth-and-claw foe of New Deal domestic programs. The appeal was more persuasive because Monnet did not create a bloated planning bureaucracy but, as one writer called it, a "rockhard little directorate of disciples working from cramped offices in the rue de Martignac."[52] Not all of his ideas worked. His *Plan de Modernisation et d'Equipement* met few of its targets, but it did make productivity and growth the nation's supreme priorities.

With single-minded skill, Monnet ferreted out the sources of power to sell his ideas. Once, after listening impatiently to a laborious explanation of a particular problem, he interjected, "*Exacte!* But *dites-moi*, on whose table should I pound to get the decision?"[53] He found his most influential disciples at ECA/France, where he did not need to pound on tables. It was, in fact, under Monnet's direction that Bruce applied the counterpart funds to rebuild France's obsolescent infrastructure. "There was in effect," Monnet's biographer has written, "a triangular alliance between Bruce and Tomlinson, Monnet, and a few key officials in the Finance Ministry . . . who saw to it that Marshall aid was used directly or indirectly to maintain basic investment."[54]

Bruce met weekly, sometimes daily, with this quiet, intense Frenchman, whose trademark black tie and somber, double-breasted suit clashed with his zeal for development. On a personal level, Bruce, who made a career of compartmentalizing public and personal life, greatly admired both "glorious" Sylvia Monnet and the "intense privacy" her husband gave to their own domestic affairs. Bruce most admired Monnet's grasp of Europe's needs and his vision for the future. He called him simply "the foremost political philosopher of the Twentieth Century."[55]

Monnet summed up that philosophy in a single sentence: "Nothing is possible without men: nothing is lasting without institutions."[56] Through his friendship with Monnet, Bruce became intimately involved with the men and the institutions conjured by the Frenchman. Their partnership illustrates the complexity of the Marshall Plan. It was not just imposed on an unwilling France but was an intricate collaboration between like-minded factions within the ruling elites of both countries who were opposed by powerful skeptics in America and in France. Through his leadership of ECA/France, Bruce imbued the bright technicians administering the plan with the gospel according to Monnet and nurtured a generation of American converts to the cause of European integration.

In 1948 Monnet's influence made ECA work. Bruce would later say, "It was Monnet who made the Marshall Plan productive in France."[57] Monnet reciprocated and became an early member of the large club of influential Europeans who admired Bruce. "I should describe him as essentially a civilized man," Monnet recalled, "because for me this general term has a very precise meaning. Bruce always takes account of others, and listens to them without trying to impose his point of view or insist that he is always right. He is always anxious to be fully convinced before attempting to convince others." If Bruce thought Monnet made the Marshall Plan work, Monnet gave him equal credit. Without Bruce's cooperation, Monnet flatly declared, "I should never have succeeded in persuading the US Administration to allow hundreds of billions of francs' worth of counterpart funds to be used by the French Government; and I should have found it hard to persuade the latter to allocate them to the [Monnet] Plan."[58] He was right. In 1949 fully 90 percent of resources invested by the Monnet Plan came from Marshall Plan counterpart funds.

French sensitivity may have been a daily problem that overshadowed the plans he and Monnet discussed, but what seemed like rank interference on one side of the Atlantic was branded gross timidity on the other. When Bruce returned to Washington to defend ECA, he heard reverberating through the halls of Congress the echo of Calvin Coolidge, who had said of earlier American largesse for Europe, "They hired the money, didn't they?" The stark difference between the arguments needed to mollify the French and appease Congress appealed to his sense of irony.

Not a technical expert, Bruce nevertheless prided himself on being conversant in broad terms with the minutiae of French electrification and steel production, of coal tonnage dug and textile yards woven. When he went to Washington in late 1948 to brief his political masters, he crammed into his suitcases so many memoranda, news clippings, press releases, and position analyses that he needed a fat index to keep them straight. While in the capital he gave a deft overview of ECA in an interview for the Voice of America. In February 1949 he told a congressional committee that "France lent its great prestige without any reservations to the success of this solemn enterprise and pledged to its fulfillment the energies of its people. It has reduced these high resolves to concrete economic goals."[59] He could be forgiven for smiling to himself if he recalled as he read this statement the fulminations of French papers against his speech at Lille.

He was proud of the plan's accomplishments. When he went to Paris in June 1948 the economy was in chaos, but the strikes that autumn that crippled France and seemed about to bring the country to its knees were only a bad memory by spring. Production was up, inflation under better control. In his report for the year, he laid out the ambitious schedule envisioned by ECA — to increase production by 40 percent by the time the plan was due to expire in 1952. "If you were living in France in the winter of 1947 or 1948," he told the *New York Times,* "you did not need an economist to tell you that things were not going well. Now, after twelve months [of ECA], France still cannot be called prosperous. But there has been a steady improvement month by month."[60]

Despite this upbeat comment, though, conditions were still uncertain, in his own words, "too many elements of chance, too many providential occurrences, too many unknown variables could weight the scales."[61] Virtually his last cable as head of ECA/France sounded depressingly like those of the previous summer, urging Washington to give more aid lest the French government flush itself down the toilet: "As long as Queuille administration is willing to tackle difficult problems, it deserves any assistance we can properly give. Refusal [of] counterpart would create government crisis."[62]

He was right to suspend judgment on the outcome of America's effort to stabilize France. The Fourth Republic was congenitally unable to exorcise the demons that tormented it. Perversely, most French intellectuals, and many politicians too, looked on America as an alien occupying force as bad as the Germans. In the cause of aiding America's oldest ally, David Bruce would have more headaches to endure, headaches as big as the Ritz.

CHAPTER 12

Making Europe

While his friends in Washington wanted European integration, David Bruce
was obsessed with it.

— John Taft, *American Power*

*I*N 1949 David Bruce's brother, then ambassador to Argentina,
bumped into a threat to his plans for promotion. Bluff, corpulent, and
stolid, James Bruce could not match the worldly appeal of his younger
brother. But he had made a name for himself in business, and more to
the point, in raising funds for the Democratic party, a talent that
emboldened him to think he could write his own ticket to the embassy
in London. Indeed, Truman promised him Britain as the reward for
going to Argentina first.[1] It was a shock, then, when James found the
way blocked by his own brother.

The trouble came from a scheme hatched by Acheson, Harriman,
and Hoffman to reshuffle ambassadors in Europe. Part of their plan
called for moving Jefferson Caffrey from Paris to another post (poor
Caffrey, it turned out to be Cairo) and installing David Bruce in his
place. James saw the danger at once: placing one Bruce in the Paris
embassy would make it awkward for the president to send another to
London at the same time.

Truman approved the shuffle but then balked. The plan incensed
Maryland Democrats. They thought David unworthy because he lacked
partisan zeal. They said he used abusive language when asked for a
donation during the 1948 campaign and even refused to give when

solicited by his brother.[2] David was the first to admit he was not a yellow-dog Democrat. How could he be when the memory of FDR's treatment of Mellon still rankled?

Maryland's U.S. Senator Millard Tydings phoned Acheson in a last-ditch effort to convince him James was the more deserving brother. It irritated Truman that objections arose so late in the game, and he responded by "pointing out the desirability," as one aide bluntly put it, "of stopping the David Bruce appointment."[3] But it was too late to reverse gears without a good deal of chagrin all around: State had already formally requested approval of David from the French. Truman allowed the nomination to go forward and, according to a self-serving memo to the file written by Acheson, "absolved the State Department from any criticism."[4] More credible was Acheson's remark on another occasion that "a memorandum is written not to inform the reader but to protect the writer."[5] The unsavory Bruce contretemps left a foul taste in Truman's mouth.

David's nomination received the Senate's unanimous blessing on May 9, 1949, and as he was already in Washington for consultation, he went to the White House to pay his respects. When he offered the obligatory platitudes about hoping to justify the confidence placed in him, the president said he was only trying to find the best people to represent the nation. With a sly little chuckle, he added, "If they were Democrats and loyal to him, it would be so much the better."[6]

Two weeks later, the brilliant but boorish journalist Joseph Alsop publicly attacked James as a corrupt man, unworthy of appointment. "The London Embassy," Alsop's column screamed, "will shortly be sold for cash on the barrelhead." Worse, the sentiment for James "almost prevented the appointment of his brother" to Paris. It was bad enough without Alsop's invidious comparison. James said it seemed like there was a contest "between the good Bruce and the bad Bruce." His brother urged him to say nothing. Objecting would only inflame matters, David said. "If he thinks he has gotten under our skins he'll be worse."[7]

Despite Truman's promises, James Bruce never got London. When he complained that the secretary of state was undermining him, the president lamely said, "It's true that Acheson doesn't want you to have anything to do with U.S. foreign policy. But the fact is, he doesn't want me to have anything to do with it either."[8] On the day Truman finally reneged on his pledge, he told a senator, "I have just broken my sacred word of honor to Jim Bruce."[9] James loyally claimed, without conviction, that time and his friendship with Truman healed the wound. Despite their denials, the episode hung forever after between the brothers.

David and Evangeline flew back to Paris on May 14, 1949. As light rain spattered the tarmac and Evangeline accepted a bouquet of lilies of the valley, they were greeted by an honor guard, the press, staff from the embassy and Marshall Plan, and Virginia and Ashley Clarke.

Flanked by motorcycle outriders, they raced through the boulevards in the embassy's aging Cadillac to the ambassador's residence at 2 avenue d'Iéna. On Monday morning Bruce stopped first at the annex to greet the Marshall Plan staff. "It was wonderful to see them all again," he said, as though he had been away more than a few weeks.[10] They knew that the tense, often sulphurous, relationship between ECA chief and ambassador was a thing of the past. Bruce's Marshall Plan successor was his friend Barry Bingham, publisher of the Louisville Courier-Journal. Bingham, the ambassador said, "seems to have every good gift of personality and character, and to be wholly unaware of his charm and popularity."[11] Bruce himself would ensure that the embassy's unhelpful attitude toward ECA departed Paris with the difficult Mr. Caffrey.

An ambassador's tenure formally begins when he presents his letter of credence to the host government. The American president's letter, couched in the baroque language of diplomacy that was as dear to David Bruce as it was foreign to plain Harry Truman, presented his new emissary to his "great and good friend" President Vincent Auriol "in the quality of Ambassador Extraordinary and Plenipotentiary."[12]

In the months to come, at social and ceremonial events Bruce regularly saw Auriol, a stout, thick-accented Toulouse lawyer and an anti-Communist Socialist of good humor. (A Communist politician called him "L'Intoxiqué de l'Elysée."[13]) Auriol disdained the incompetence of ambassadors at his annual diplomatic shoot on the presidential hunting estate near Rambouillet and was delighted to discover Bruce's skill with a shotgun — one weekend he bagged 115 pheasants of 490 shot.[14] The talent for slaughtering birds bred for that fate was still the mark of the compleat country squire and enhanced his reputation as a gentleman-diplomat.

The private reaction of Jacques Dumaine, chief of protocol at the Quai d'Orsay, the foreign ministry, reflected the attitude of many French officials. Caffrey, though well disposed toward France, had been, by turns, "diffident and masterful, pious and cynical, a fanatic in spite of his intelligence." Of the "sound and charming" Bruce, Dumaine wrote in his diary, "there is nothing shallow about him." Because he was "too obviously a devotee of our culture, of our history and of our way of life," the French diplomat cynically concluded, "the State Department will discount his views as being those of a francophile."[15]

Franco-American relations resembled an edgy friendship. Many in France feared the intrusion of American popular culture, an alien presence trundled into La Belle France in the Trojan horse of Marshall aid. A powerful Communist propaganda campaign, which all too often found enough scraps to give even its goofier claims plausibility, fed the resentment. Those rows of big, black American cars with diplomatic license plates parked every day on the Place de la Concorde lent credence to the alarmists.[16] Of all the nations aligned with America, France most strongly resented the subordinating consequences of World War II. In the words of long-time expatriate Janet Flanner, the nation "talks like a spoiled old beauty who still wants her hand kissed in admiration."[17] The more it relied on American aid, the more unhappy the relations.

His year with the Marshall Plan acquainted Bruce very well with these problems. Now he would be tested even more as he stepped into the shoes first worn by Benjamin Franklin. "Perhaps what Acheson and others saw in Bruce was a Platonic archetype of themselves," a modern commentator has said, "the sort of person that they at their best wanted to be. For its new diplomatic role, the United States apparently needed a very old diplomatic model."[18]

He routinely arrived at the embassy at 9:30 each morning. Unlike the punctilious Caffrey, who expected the marine guard to snap to attention and carry his briefcase up the grand staircase, the new ambassador took the elevator to his office without fanfare or escort. Bowing to French protest, he ended Caffrey's practice of posting sentries at the residence and outside his office door. To the marines' dismay, he also ordered them to exchange their bright blue uniforms for more somber dress.

In the early weeks he tried to meet each of the 650 people who worked for him, though not to encourage intimacy and certainly not to convey the image of the ambassador as a regular guy. That David Bruce never was. A shrewd manager of his time, he selected a few key staff to deal with directly. To the others, as in ECA, he was a respected and admired but remote presence. To those in his intimate circle and those who watched from a distance, he exuded an equanimity that made it easier to handle crises. "He was enormously persuasive. He did not raise his voice. He did not have to."[19] One of his staff said later at the end of his own distinguished career that the best ambassadors "shared with David Bruce the quality of equableness. There were never 'catastrophes' in their professional lives — there were difficulties, and when they encountered these difficulties they set about quietly to overcome them. Above all, they reserved their time and attention for essentials; and they knew how to use their staffs."[20]

Reporters, it is said, want to seduce their subjects so that they can betray them later. On balance it was Bruce who did the seducing. In their private chats in his office, he would lean back in his swivel chair, lift up a leg and rest it on an opened desk drawer, tamp some Virginia tobacco into his pipe, and proceed to beguile his guests with his broad, discursive commentary on the state of Europe, liberally sprinkled with historical allusions.[21] He knew trust was not a word one used with journalists, but as a diplomat he learned how to nurture a symbiotic relationship.

Vogue and *Harper's Bazaar* could not believe their luck in the material served up by the cosmopolitan ambassador and his stylish wife, the best copy imaginable for the tony, escapist gloss that they purveyed to a public hungry for vicarious elegance. More important, Bruce stayed on intimate terms with writers like Teddy White, David Schoenbrun, and Cyrus Sulzberger, whose articles in more serious journals were read by opinion makers back home. It did his reputation no harm when they cited him repeatedly as one of the most astute American observers stationed abroad. "Bruce, though a modern diplomat," White declared, "is one of the most skillful practitioners of the older diplomatic arts of quiet and secret conversations, of cultivation and persuasion of key personalities."[22] He became so chummy with reporters that when he left the embassy, four of them gave him a gold

Directoire toothpick case as a going-away present, hardly practical but a token of genuine affection all the same.[23]

"The French," Janet Flanner said, "are tired of being occupied, even if for their own welfare, and especially of being occupied by Americans who, in their own phrase, 'never had it so good.'"[24] The Coca-Cola company was an especially despised symbol stoking the fires of anti-Americanism. The firm's advertising campaign embodied for many French people an attempt to ram American popular culture down their throats — at the point of bayonets if the Communists were to be believed. Reactionary wine producers stood arm in arm with leftist parliamentarians in paranoid denunciation of the transatlantic menace. A bill was introduced to ban the drink and thwart the "Coca-Coloni-zation" of France. Even *Le Monde* admitted that opposition was less to "the drink itself than the civilization, the style of life of which it is a sign and in a certain sense a symbol."[25]

The company scandalized Parisians with plans to drape a mammoth sign from the Eiffel Tower, never mind that French advertisers had once hung a huge, blinking ad for Citroën there. The thought of a neon sign flashing its obnoxious American message across the night sky was enough to induce fits in Parisians. Bruce suspected as much. He scornfully noted that, after "regretfully" giving up the Eiffel Tower idea at his request, "the Coca Cola people are determined to go ahead and also to engage in their usual advertising displays, including . . . a blazing sign on a 142 foot tower."[26]

As ludicrous as it seems in hindsight, with the logos of international firms cluttering the skyline everywhere, the threat of economic retaliation was serious business. If France banned Coke, Bruce knew what would happen when time came for Congress to renew foreign aid. Compelled against his wishes to warn the French, he privately called the company's campaign "psychologically extremely stupid" and its personnel insensitive to local feelings.[27] In his calming way, he tried to lower the temperature of both sides. (It gave his argument a boost when a photograph turned up showing the French Communist party boss drinking a Coke.) He was both bemused and irritated that a brand of sugared water could put the whole Marshall Plan at risk.[28]

Advancing that plan was his most important task. For this alone he was an improvement on Caffrey. Meetings with Bingham and Tomlinson to determine each month's release of counterpart funds dominated his calendar. As before, they went toward development projects identified by Monnet, with whom the ambassador met as frequently as before.

By nature, an ambassador's duty demands perpetual ceremony. Protocol dictated that a new envoy greet formally not just officials of the host country but the emissary of every nation accredited there as well. "All of this would appear to require some sixty to seventy man hours of conversation," Bruce calculated, "and much epistolary exercise. Evangeline meanwhile must pursue a similar course with the wives. At the end of all this we will be considered purified."[29]

Despite the Cold War, his introductory call on the Soviet ambassador was entirely pleasant. Ambassador Vladimir Bogomolov, whom he described privately on another occasion as a "poisonous looking weasel," appeared as though he would "just as soon cut my throat as look at me."[30] And yet, at the Russian's house on the narrow rue de Grenelle, the two men sat in the garden on a hot summer day and chatted amiably, airily, and at great length in French about constitutional theory.

Claims of London and Rome aside, the diplomatic community of Paris was the most vibrant then. Among Bruce's favorites was its doyen, the papal nuncio. A stout figure, witty, and jovial, Monsignor Roncalli prided himself on the talents of his chef, for the nuncio was known as "a powerful fork."[31] With the empathy of a fellow gourmet, Bruce described the future Pope John XXIII as "benignant in his scarlet and black cassock. . . . huge in girth and a monument of good living."[32] He wished his friend Duff Cooper were still the British ambassador. At least the Coopers still kept a house at Chantilly where the Bruces were frequent guests at Lady Diana's flashy parties. He got along with Cooper's successor, Sir Oliver Harvey, and the two of them agreed with Alexandre Parodi, at the Quai d'Orsay, to have regular informal meetings to keep more closely in touch.

Now and then he dabbled in what the intelligence trade called private enterprise. Usually these forays came to nothing, as when he plotted Franco's retirement. This intrigue unrealistically envisioned a papal blessing and a dukedom to expedite the generalissimo's departure. He pressed the idea on Acheson but "the matter got into the hands of the Spanish desk of the State Department and strangled in red tape."[33]

On more familiar ground, he tried to entice Armenian oil baron Calouste Gulbenkian to give his art collection to Washington. Gulbenkian owned a palatial house on avenue d'Iéna, where, behind burglar alarms and guard dogs, "a large slice of the cultural heritage of mankind was jealously kept for the enjoyment of his private eye alone." The short, paranoid octagenarian, Bruce said, was "a determined and rather naughty character." When Gulbenkian finally visited his neighbor, his refusal to eat or drink anything out of fear that his enemies might poison him presaged the fate of Bruce's argument for moving the art to America.[34]

"The job is mostly seeing people," Bruce said.[35] As the president's personal representative, he was there to serve his compatriots as well as provide liaison with the French government. The variety of his days can be seen by viewing one of the many — neither slow nor hectic — taken up by an unconnected string of visitors rather than by staff meetings or diplomatic conferences.

The morning of January 16, 1951, began slowly enough.[36] After a visit from an American journalist, a bookseller brought by the volumes of Buffon's *Birds* that Bruce had sought, with their thousand fabulous plates. His old friend Raoul Boyer, the sommelier who had parlayed Bruce's 1920 loan into a lucrative wine trade, stopped by. Next Congressman John F. Kennedy came for lunch. "He is an intelligent man," Bruce said, "and wrote when he was young a book called 'While England Slept.' He is not at all in sympathy with his father's isolationist views."

After lunch Princess de Robeck brought him information on her family's chateau, which she thought might interest General Eisenhower, newly appointed Supreme Allied Commander Europe. Another journalist dropped in to quiz him on French rearmament. Then he listened to the woes of TWA's chairman. Warren Pierson, the ambassador drily noted, "expressed considerable bitterness regarding Pan American. The Pan American people had previously expressed considerable bitterness about TWA." Finally free of the airline executive, he left to confer with Prime Minister René Pleven. That evening he and his wife went out to a costume ball that lasted into the early morning hours. The job might well have been "mostly seeing people," but it was not all pro forma diplomatic *politesse* and nighttime frivolity.

On the last Friday in April 1950, the high wind and driving rains that had buffeted Paris for the past week continued without letup. In the morning Monnet called, as was his habit, to talk with Bruce about the state of Europe. Later in the day the ambassador read documents at Monnet's office giving more detail about the matters they discussed before noon. Here, more than a week before France announced it to a startled world, Monnet shared with his good friend a concept more radical than his earlier designs, more dramatic than the Marshall Plan itself.

Monnet later insisted he had not divulged the idea to any foreigner before revealing it informally to Bruce and visiting Secretary of State Acheson on the eve of the public announcement. Only a handful of French officials knew, not even all of the cabinet. Monnet's claim is disingenuous. He and Bruce were so close that he had long before divulged his thoughts about the need for Europeans to transcend their economic rivalries. It was irrelevant for him to say years later that the two men had "many talks on the 'philosophy' but none on the actual proposal."[37] That he shared the outline of his dramatic plan with the American who had done so much to support his work was only natural, for Bruce was a reliable sounding board for the Frenchman's protean schemes for European integration.

Bruce omitted the most sensitive details of their talks from his diary. But once the secret was out, he went back and added a few short notes that explained what they had discussed on that rainy Friday a week earlier and many other times — Monnet's "revolutionary matter," as the amended diary called it, for "a Franco-German economic union," which he "had previously informed me about."[38]

In May the world learned of France's proposal for the European Coal and Steel Community (ECSC), also known as the Schuman Plan for the foreign minister, Robert Schuman, who announced it. This design was the forerunner of the Common Market, later the European Community, today's European Union. Acheson greeted it coolly at first, but Bruce helped bring him around. In fact, he became the most articulate American advocate of European integration. Critics who considered him a superficial, social ambassador had to admit that for the big ideas he worked very hard indeed.

Despite its title, the Schuman Plan was wholly Monnet's. It was not in his nature to resent someone else's name being attached to his ideas. Washington recognized that the Schuman Plan could solve the problem posed by the industrial colossus of the Ruhr, control of which lay behind a century of discord. In the space of five years, American policy moved from the wartime Morgenthau Plan for turning Germany into a cowpasture to the Schuman Plan for unifying Europe economically around the revived muscle of the Ruhr. Reintegrating Germany into Europe would fulfill the goal of the Marshall Plan.[39]

The familiar postwar image of Russians dismantling German factories and carting them off wholesale is true enough. The Allies, however, were doing the same thing, an odd way to promote recovery, it seemed to some. The key to a more rational approach was finding a way to allay French fears of German resurgence, and this the ECSC proposed to do. At least since Marshall's speech at Harvard in 1947, American diplomats had advocated some form of European coordination.

Britain must play a vital role. That was axiomatic. At a conference in 1949, Bruce said "no integration of Western Europe was conceivable without full participation of the UK."[40] The British remained cool. Bruce recalled later the reaction of the bluff Labor foreign secretary to European integration: "'I don't like that Pandora's box,' said [Ernest] Bevin; 'if you open it a lot of Trojan horses are likely to tumble out.'"[41] To Bruce's regret, Britain did not join, and he and Monnet consoled themselves with the smaller version consisting of France, West Germany, Italy, and the Benelux countries — the Six.

The Schuman Plan proposed taming the Ruhr by pooling Europe's coal and steel resources under a supranational High Authority. In fact, it restored the Ruhr to power. Doing so produced its single, overriding accomplishment — the process of integration that it set in train became the bedrock of economic and political change for a generation.[42] Here were the first steps on the path that led the nations of Western Europe to find it harder and harder to contemplate another war among themselves.

Proposing the plan was only a start. It took more than a year of wrangling before the Six crafted the idea into concrete form. In order to persuade prospective members, Monnet knew American support was crucial. Bruce's enthusiasm for his ideas led the Frenchman to count on rapid American backing. Bruce's support in the months to come would be essential.

The day after Schuman's dramatic announcement, the ambassador accurately called it "the most constructive thing done by the French government since Liberation." He cabled Washington to urge its strongest support. "Audacious in nature, comprehensive in conception," the Schuman Plan "opened a new possibility of European integration and at least offered a prospect of moderating the century-old antagonism between France and Germany." His enthusiasm never waned, even when Monnet sometimes momentarily despaired. America's moral support, Bruce concluded, "is of cardinal importance."[43]

From the day of Schuman's announcement, the embassy became the vanguard of American support for European integration. George Ball, then a lawyer privately working for Monnet, recalled the ambassador as the chief American promoting the Schuman Plan: "A resourceful and loyal supporter of Monnet's efforts since his days as chief of the ECA Mission in France, Bruce was a major source of strength." "I had known Bruce earlier," Ball recalled, "now Tommy [Tomlinson] and I became such close co-conspirators that during periods of crisis I would sometimes move my operations to a small office in the embassy chancery adjacent to his." It all had Bruce's blessing. "Such a complete sharing of information and insights could arise only among individuals totally dedicated to a central idea," Ball wrote; "we all believed fervently in Monnet's goal of a united Europe, which, we thought, was quite as important to Americans as to Europeans."[44]

In the meantime, Bruce maintained the full agenda of social and ceremonial events that are the lot of ambassadors. Just as during his year with ECA, the stream of American visitors was unending, including those with the magic passport — a note written on White House letterhead. One such letter announced a visit by the president's daughter, and in June 1951 Margaret Truman arrived with her tiny retinue of three and a single Secret Service man. She returned home full of gratitude to the Bruces. They had entertained her elegantly, and when she asked to meet musicians, Evangeline Bruce organized a scintillating evening with the leading lights of Paris music.

There was one flaw. Hellé Bonnet, wife of the French ambassador to

Washington, took it upon herself to accompany the president's daughter and attempt to orchestrate her visit. The Bruces made the mistake of not including Bonnet in all of the events, and in payment she blackened their names all over Washington. As Bonnet told it, the musical evening brought together an unsavory mélange of bohemian decadents, unsuitable company for Miss Truman.

Bruce knew it was futile to defend himself. "What I regret is that Margaret's desire . . . not to see any French officials was so faithfully observed by us. I expect, in her dudgeon, Hellé will make trouble for us with the President and Madame Auriol, with whom we have always had such an unusually pleasant relationship. This would be unfortunate, for I can never explain Margaret's attitude either to the Auriols or the Bonnets. In trying to protect her, I unprotected ourselves. But *tant pis*."[45]

For the American colony in Paris, the annual Fourth of July party was a sacred tradition; for the ambassador, a traditional bother. According to custom, anyone with an American passport had a right to attend. Bruce's first Glorious Fourth took place in the garden of 41 rue du Faubourg St. Honoré and gave him a rude shock. Eight thousand guests made short work of the wine-Cointreau-cognac punch. The few teetotalers consoled themselves with Coca-Cola. The Bruces left in the early evening after the official reception, but the party continued and became increasingly rowdy. Marine guards summoned by the overwhelmed French gendarmes failed to restore order. Recalling this shambles years later, Bruce wrote, "Copulating couples refused to be dislodged from the shrubbery; incontinent individuals urinated or defecated on the front steps and the lawn."[46]

Although he made sure the party in following years was respectably sedate, he loathed it, and not just because he personally paid the caterer's bill. He tried unsuccessfully to persuade ambassadors to cancel the party throughout Europe. "There have been a good many complaints from individual American citizens," he argued, "that it is in bad taste, especially at the present time, to engage so publicly in what the natives of various countries sometimes regard as ostentation."[47] His diary took on the quality of a private *cahier de doléance*, as he recorded the lamentable record for sponging. "Thousands of our compatriots," he opined, "really seem to think that an American Ambassador is stationed abroad to run a non-stop entertainment (almost entirely at his or her expense) for visiting transients."[48]

For the next year's Independence Day reception, journalist David Schoenbrun decided to be the first and last guest in order to observe the Bruces' social skills in action. The ambassador and his wife stood in the receiving line for five hours without betraying boredom or fatigue. Their hands were swollen for a week. Schoenbrun concluded that a diplomat must be "a man with hands of steel, no bladder and an infinite capacity for saying, 'Yes, indeed,' when what he means is 'I never heard such nonsense in all my life.'"[49]

"Dining," Lord Palmerston once said, "is the Soul of Diplomacy." By that measure, Bruce ministered to the needs of American policy with the worldly aplomb of a Renaissance pope. The venue was the residence on avenue d'Iéna, one of the spokes that radiate out from the Arc de Triomphe into the chic 16th arrondissement. Built in 1885, the house had a small garden and ground-floor rooms ideally suited to large receptions. It took a company of servants, gardeners, kitchen help, and the effervescent head housekeeper, Odette de Wavrin, to run the house. With the staff in constant motion and the ubiquitous pack of floppy-eared springer spaniels padding about, it was never a quiet place.[50]

Bruce had accepted a job that enshrined hospitality, even apotheosized it. His urbanity and his stamina to endure the demands of *politesse* made him ideal for the work, but he complained that the constant giving and receiving of invitations was "a nuisance and a bore. It is social big business, and requires quite a few people and lots of time to cope with it. I rather envy the Russians who are neither asked nor asking. However, with E. everything has some element of fun or humor in it."[51] This sentiment was at odds with his reputation as the master of the art of social representation. The answer to the riddle lies in the last sentence of the quotation. Evangeline Bruce electrified Parisian society just as she had done when she first walked into the headquarters of OSS London in 1942. By the time they vacated avenue d'Iéna, she would be known, in the words of *Time* magazine, as "one of the most successful diplomatic hostesses in Europe."[52] It was a durable reputation. "Nearly fifty years later, veteran politicians of the period still sigh as they remember: 'Ah, *la charmante Madame Bruce!*'"[53]

The ambassador knew he had to augment State's meager entertainment allowance — the price of appointment to an important embassy. But she was the one who made sure the special dinners and the cocktail parties they held every week for never fewer than a hundred guests succeeded.

Letitia Baldrige, later arbiter of taste in Jacqueline Kennedy's White House, earned her spurs as social secretary to Evangeline Bruce. The job description, she recalled, required the incumbent to be an "expert in the Art of Bluff, have sturdy arches, a firm handshake, a superb memory, and an unceasing compassion for meddlesome old ladies."[54] Her boss was still new to the work of a diplomatic hostess, but her reputation was already formidable. It was not just her ethereal beauty and knack for staying on international best-dressed lists, both of which society writers invariably mentioned. Nor was it her talent for explicating the finer points of protocol, discussing menus with the chef, or mastering the indispensable art of writing original thank-you notes by the score. Rather, her success depended on an uncommon pairing of hard-headed planning with an instinctive sensitivity to her guests.

First came the right guest list. The usual crowd of parliamentarians, society luminaries, diplomats, and a few denizens of the American colony and of artistic and literary Paris was a start. The real leaven came from a judicious sprinkling of attractive young people — the more beautiful and the more unattached the better. Just as David's dashing good looks had given him entrée to the "gilded throng" at embassy parties in 1920s Washington, so now others were brought into the Bruce circle in Paris.

The hand-written invitations went out on cards with the United States seal engraved at the top, embossed in white or gold. Then came the tracking of acceptances and regrets on the "Plan de Table," a gold-embossed leather proxy for the dining room table with a slot for each guest's name. Seating could be tricky. Once the Bruces were appalled when everyone sat down and "the entire dining room was suddenly lulled into stillness." In her ignorance, Baldrige had placed a high official next to his wife's lover. Conversation quickly resumed — "the usual parrot-house noise of a French dinner party" was the snide description novelist Nancy Mitford used for such occasions — and the next day social Paris tittered about the American ambassador's daring new rationale for seating guests.[55]

A kaleidoscopic guest list and the finest wines, menu, and dinner service were still not enough. What really mattered was the hosts. Looking at their ease, even when they were not, they both worked hard to make each guest feel like the center of attention. When they spotted one who seemed to withdraw, they would go over and make him or her a special part of the evening. "No one was allowed to be a wallflower," Baldrige remembered. Evangeline Bruce's gift for transmitting warmth, through her soothing, well-modulated voice, sprinkled with soft, infectious laughter, became the shared memory of her guests.[56]

Not just formal dinners vied for the ambassador's time with the more important matter of promoting the Schuman Plan. Before Bruce's efforts in behalf of the plan shifted into high gear, events far from Paris distracted Americans from European integration and then led them all the more insistently to support it. In June 1950 Russian-made tanks of the North Korean army blasted the State Department out of its preoccupation with Europe. Eight and a half years before, Pearl Harbor had plunged the United States into war on two fronts. Korea threatened to do the same. Would Stalin use the distraction to strike across the inter-German border and complete his conquest of Europe? Korea made rearming Germany more desirable than ever to the Americans, an idea that rang alarm bells throughout the Continent, most loudly in Paris.[57]

Bruce learned about the attack early on a lazy Sunday morning. He immediately drove to the embassy to call his French counterparts and disrupt their weekend leisure. To his dismay, there was no instantaneous American response to the invasion. He and his staff glumly discussed the seeming failure of their government to realize that inaction in Asia would echo ominously in Europe.

As they ruminated in the ambassador's office, a cable arrived from Washington. It announced Truman's resolve — Bruce called it "the President's bold and wise decision" — to make the dramatic military response they hoped for. Energized by the news, he hurried to tell the foreign minister. "Thank God," Schuman said, his eyes filling with tears as he thought of Munich, "this will not be a repetition of the past." Bruce agreed. "Whenever we have shown determination and strength in the past," he noted privately, the Soviets "have halted their activities, and I believe will do so again."[58]

Up to this point, like most Americans he had discounted the threat of a Soviet invasion. They resigned themselves to the Continent's division. There was plenty of time to build up NATO, then still very much a paper force. Korea shattered that complacency. Panic swept through Western capitals. In Bonn a member of the Bundestag said that "there's not a gram of cyanide to be bought," because his colleagues had hysterically prepared to commmit suicide when the Communists invaded. The need to rebuild Western armies became the most urgent American goal. Creation of the post of Supreme Allied Commander Europe (SACEUR) headquartered at the Supreme Headquarters Allied Powers Europe (SHAPE) had its origins in Korea. In early 1951 Eisenhower arrived in France, and his immense prestige helped calm jittery nerves. "He is absolutely first rate," Bruce said, "determined, vigorous, sensible, apparently with great intuition regarding the problems of foreign nations, and tactful to an extraordinary degree."[59]

If NATO were to have a prayer of a forward defense east of the Rhine, it could not avoid rearming West Germany. That prospect made much of Europe uneasy; it terrified the French. The Americans were not to be deterred, however, and France responded with an alternative plan for a common European army that would minimize the Teutonic role. The idea had been kicking around for some time. Bruce had suggested a similar notion that July. "It will remain politically impossible to rearm German manpower or convert German industry to military production," he wrote, "as long as the European peoples see in such action the risk of a resurgence of German military might. A truly common effort is the only way out. If Germans are made soldiers in an Atlantic community army *or even a European army,* the question will then be viewed in a quite different light."[60]

The French plan included some German military contribution without permitting them a national army or revival of their hated General Staff. Named for the French premier and former Monnet assistant René Pleven, who proposed it in October 1950, the Pleven Plan proposed a European Defense Community (EDC). Nations would contribute medium-sized units from their own forces to serve in a common army under — and this was the key point — supranational European command. Like the Schuman Plan, the Pleven Plan was Monnet's idea and thoroughly embroiled his friend the American ambassador.

"Personally," Bruce wrote, "I am enthusiastic about this approach, which would do much toward bringing about a closer association

amongst the free nations of Europe." He realized that delicate negotiations lay ahead, and in his year-end summary he cautioned against
undue optimism, seeing little progress yet "toward the consolidation of
military strength, social equilibrium and political unity toward which
the majority of Frenchmen profess to strive."[61]

On a wintry evening in 1951, the American ambassador appeared at
the front door of a mansion on Place des Etats-Unis wearing a butler's
uniform. To conceal the poor fit of his black wig and fake whiskers, coal
soot covered his silver-gray hair. His wife, despite being eight months
pregnant, sported the high, flaming red wig and voluminous black dress
of a Toulouse-Lautrec cashier. They had come to one of the costume
balls that regularly amused high society. Christian Dior had visited
avenue d'Iéna earlier with a wig and makeup man to outfit the Bruces
and his own party of four, who together staged a sensational entry to
the ball.[62]

Thanks to Evangeline Bruce's contacts, the American couple often
saw the principals of haute couture. Marie Louise Bousquet, arbiter of
Paris fashion, was a frequent dinner companion, and Dior's creations
often had the benefit of *madame l'ambassadrice* as a model. Bousquet
brushed aside criticism of the lavish balls, which, even when given in
aid of a charity, seemed staged largely for the display of the rich. "Those
invited to the ball," she decreed, "say as an excuse that it makes work
for the dressmaking trade and those not invited say it is frivolous
merde."[63]

The Bruces' hostess that winter evening was Marie-Laure de
Noailles, a famous, eccentric *salonnière* descended from the Marquis de
Sade who "wanted to be both avant-garde and the Vicomtesse."[64] Bruce
said she "knows everybody in the artistic and musical world."[65] Despite her lavish patronage of the arts and the fact that her father was
Jewish, she kept up her parties during the Occupation. She continued
them after the war, as though the service of in-laws in the Resistance
excused her sin of entertaining Nazis.[66] Former Vichyites and veterans
of the Resistance nurtured their grudges, for they had yet not settled
enough scores. "I was facing the Gestapo," André Malraux, de Gaulle's
confidant once famously groused, "while Sartre, in Paris, let his plays
be produced with the authorization of the German censors."[67]

The gradations in wartime records encompassed more shades of gray than most people were willing to admit. The myth of self-liberation induced far more French citizens to pretend they were with the Resistance than was so. Many sought to forget or at least color the past. Pamela Churchill, Sir Winston's former daughter-in-law, future wife of Averell Harriman and future American ambassador to France herself, presented a cosmopolitan example of the scramble to forget. She was living in Paris then with Fiat heir Gianni Agnelli and preferred to accentuate his support of the Allies late in the war, not the profits that accrued to his family for making more than a few tanks for Herr Hitler.[68]

Bruce did not believe his private contempt for collaborators excused him from the demands of civility. One day he visited the legendary couturier Coco Chanel, who, with her German lover, had passed the war living at the Ritz. She was an "odd woman, rich as Croesus and mean with money AND unpopular with her workers."[69] A keen consumer of gossip, the ambassador delighted in hearing about her "long connection" with the second duke of Westminster — she did not mention the German — but saved his most telling comment for last. "She has an entirely unique personality," he concluded, "but I fear behaved badly during the war."[70]

The June after the de Noailles ball, the Bruces attended a party given by others who had behaved badly during the war. The duke and duchess of Windsor lived in luxurious, bored exile. Because they sometimes invited the Bruces to their dinners, the ambassador had a chance to observe his boyhood friend from Baltimore and her vapid royal husband. He thought them unhappy, "both rather pathetic, to my way of thinking."[71] At the Windsors' party, Evangeline Bruce stole the show when her dress caught fire from a candle. She recovered her composure, and she and her husband went on from there to a masquerade party given by that egregious, self-promoting hostess, toadlike Elsa Maxwell. They reached home at dawn.[72]

On most evenings David and Evangeline Bruce kept up a frantic pace. They moved in exclusive company indeed, an elite defined more by style and money than blood. The aristocrats they knew tended to be those who could afford to travel in the fast lane rather than haughty, impecunious descendants of the ancient nobility, who "crouch in their apartments discussing marriage settlements and degrees of consanguinity."[73] When he was invited to the wedding of the penniless heir to the Habsburg throne, Bruce looked around the church at the down-at-heel dispossessed princelings and noted wryly that "there were seventeen European princes, and heaven knows how many Archdukes, Dukes, Marquises, Counts, etc., — probably all the surviving Central European Almanach de Gothaites outside the Iron Curtain countries who had enough money to get there. I must say on the whole they were not an inspiring looking lot."[74]

The Bruces did not consort only with couturiers, lightweight cosmopolites, and titled Parisians. They kept attuned to artistic and literary France, for example, with the prolific Raymond Aron, whom Bruce called the "most sympathetic of all French writers."[75] Of course, Aron and his anti-Stalinist opinions were utterly out of fashion. Most intellectuals reviled America while they adored the Soviet Union. At first Communists criticized Jean-Paul Sartre's existentialism as decadent philosophy, but soon enough Sartre, and Simone de Beauvoir too, joined them spending their energies elegantly whoring after anti-Americanism.[76]

Bruce frequently bumped into old acquaintances. Ghosts from his indolent years turned up now and then, and OSS comrades were thick as tourists in August. Though his networks were denser in London, that an American ambassador in Paris could be so well connected stood the nation's interests in good stead. He even discovered a relative when he ventured among the intelligentsia of the Left Bank.

Natalie Barney was a distant cousin. He had never met her before, but they shared an early infatuation with French culture, imparted to both of them by the same woman, Bruce's francophile great-grandmother Louise Este, who was the sister of Barney's grandmother. Barney had been an exotic figure of the expatriate scene since before World War I, the most celebrated and promiscuous lesbian poet of Paris. Her literary salon on the rue Jacob was perhaps the most glittering of the 1920s, though after World War II it had become rather dowdy. It gave the ambassador one more sweet sensation of kinship with Paris to discover that this Left Bank icon — and such a notorious one — was a relative. He kept in touch and years later would say, "I do love Cousin

Natalie. At 85, she is much more amusing than most of my contemporaries."[77]

As intrigued as he was by French society, the ambassador never lost his focus. Indeed, his ability to surf without effort across a punishing schedule of frivolous sociability while keeping his eyes and energy focused on the crucial issues of American policy awed his subordinates and gratified his superiors. As a leading supporter of EDC, he took a keen interest in the months-long conference that convened in Paris in February 1951. In Bonn, the American high commissioner, John J. McCloy, shared Bruce's preference for EDC as the best means of integrating West Germany into the alliance. At first most officials in Washington, especially Acheson, viewed the EDC as an obstructionist French plan designed to delay the full rearming of Germany. They were right. Under it, Germany would not be an equal partner. For a time two parallel tracks of negotiations deliberated about Western defense. In the German town of Petersberg, negotiators worked on a fast track that envisioned quick integration of large-scale German units into NATO. The EDC talks represented the track preferred by the French. The Petersberg design was complete in spring 1951 and offered no concessions to the French. When they rejected it, the crisis was at hand.[78]

The State Department poured gasoline on the fire by ordering Bruce to obtain the impossible — French acceptance of German participation in NATO without the safeguards envisioned by the Pleven Plan. In response to this bombshell, on July 3, 1951, Bruce composed a lengthy cable spelling out the logic for the Pleven plan. Rather than confronting the EDC skeptics head-on, he pitched his argument to Washington's great desideratum: a rapid buildup of German military strength. By accepting the EDC, he reasoned, the United States would be in the best position to insist that France permit substantial equality to Germany. "In other words," he argued, the "French must recognize that German integration with European community through Schuman Plan and European Army must be their main safeguards."[79]

That leverage would evaporate if Washington spurned Pleven and precipitated a Franco-American split. "Such rift in Atlantic community," he warned, "would be most damaging and great opportunity would have been missed to create real situation of strength in Europe, perhaps for period far into future."[80] By offering Washington the ultimate goal of a strengthened alliance rather than arguing why the Petersberg solution was wrong-headed, Bruce convinced his political masters.

In a speech in London on the same day Bruce cabled Washington, Eisenhower endorsed the European Defense Community without mentioning it by name. He had been in France as SACEUR since early 1951, and under the influence of Monnet and Bruce in France and McCloy in Germany, he shed his soldierly skepticism of EDC and became "what the cynics call a 'hot gospel' European Union man."[81]

For Bruce and McCloy, and then for Eisenhower too, the European army offered the magic solution to the Continent's major problems — the traditional animosity between France and Germany and the newer threat from the East. Little more than a month after it asked Bruce to pressure the French, Washington reversed itself. The decision to back the EDC happened because American Europeanists, mainly Bruce, Eisenhower, and McCloy, saw a vision of long-term benefit in the military as well as the economic integration of Europe.[82] Bruce could not take sole credit, but his telegram and his crucial influence on Eisenhower gave him a prominent role in the fateful decision to support a common European army.

Acheson recalled being wary of the intricate negotiations even after being won over to support EDC. Of Bruce and Tomlinson he said, "Neither of them could impart understanding of the negotiations to the rest of us; indeed, Bruce would not try. The Europeans, he said, liked to do things in a way that seemed to us like beating up a soufflé of generalizations. It would come out all right, if we would leave it alone and worry about something else."[83] Bruce complained that in Paris and Washington many believed the problems were too complex. "I pay no attention to this," the normally serene ambassador wrote. "Of course it is a gamble, but it must be made to succeed; there is no satisfactory alternative."[84]

Whether he was in Paris spreading the gospel according to Monnet or in Washington reporting to his political bosses, Bruce lived and breathed the European Defense Community and European integration during 1951. The acronym EDC became as familiar to him as his own initials. In September he spoke on NBC television on the "revolutionary" transformations taking place in Europe. As in his radio broadcasts during the Blitz, he revealed his passion for Europe. He praised NATO as the "most daring conception in foreign policy to which we have ever subscribed" and the Schuman Plan and European Army as "magnificent" French initiatives. "It seems almost incredible," he concluded, "that only six years after the termination of the greatest war in history, the countries occupied and devastated by Germany are now working with her to construct a community in which narrow nationalism will have no place."[85]

Nancy Mitford, in her acerbic novel about the Paris diplomatic scene, *Don't Tell Alfred*, captured the way EDC insinuated itself into every discussion. She did it through a character modeled in part on Evangeline Bruce. "Your American colleague has a beautiful wife whom everyone wants to please," a French character tells the British ambassador. "No Frenchman can bear to see somebody so exquisite looking sad for a single moment. So wherever she goes, in Paris or the provinces, the deputies and mayors and ministers . . . say 'of course' to whatever she tells them. And she tells them, most beguilingly, that they are going to accept the European Army."[86]

Rough sledding lay ahead. At a high-level NATO meeting, Bruce found himself "almost its sole upholder" when the subject of EDC came up within the American delegation. He urged State to forget about alternatives and to pressure "participants to bring matter to conclusion as rapidly as possible." He called the NATO Council's ratification of EDC "the most significant political action (outside of war) taken in Europe for centuries." He knew the critical point would come later when individual parliaments voted on the plan, and he anguished over what he called Washington's insensitivity to French concerns and the Pentagon's pro-German attitudes.[87]

Though a private man, Bruce enjoyed being amused and surrounded by wit and sparkling conversation. His fascination with people may explain some of the appeal of his intense social life. But the narcotic of being the personal representative of the president, of executing the foreign policy of the republic, in fact, of helping fashion that policy and through the Schuman Plan and the EDC binding America to the goal of European integration — these were the real reasons he tolerated the sacrifices to private life.

His answer to a journalist's question about his children was most revealing: "'I almost never see them. They're usually in bed by the time I get home.' Then he adds, with a smile: 'Maybe it isn't good for children to see too much of their father.'"[88] With the arrival of Sasha's brother, David Surtees, in 1948, there were two. A third, Nicholas Cabell, who made that flamboyant prenatal entrance at the de Noailles ball, was born in 1951. Bruce's account of dealing with his children and the dog Brucie in a train station suggests more bemusement at his ineptitude for domestic affairs — and relief that they did not intrude more often — than affection for the children: "E. arrived by train from Le Havre about 9 P.M. complete with nurse and two children. We finally got them in a car, and I stayed with Sasha and Brucie to cope with the baggage. It wasn't a great success. The baby and the dog tugged at me, the porters disdained my appeals, and finally I threw the suitcases on the baby carriage and trundled it through the station with the baby and the dog tripping me and each other up."[89]

"What Heaven Paris would be if one had no definite occupation," he sighed one Sunday morning. "I long to lie late abed and then dawdle all day."[90] Unfortunately, that particular day he had to go to Orly to welcome a junketing cabinet secretary. He decided that leasing a house for weekend getaways would make the most of what free time he enjoyed. After looking for a year, he chose the Pavillon de La Lanterne, built in the time of Louis XVI for the governor of Versailles and now needing root-and-branch remodeling. It was ready during Christmas 1949 and gave him a retreat he jealously guarded.

When he had only a few hours of free time, often after spending Saturday afternoons catching up on cable traffic, he relaxed by prowling the antique shops. The house on avenue d'Iéna, and then La Lanterne too, began to fill up with his gilded magpie acquisitions. "I walked down into the quarter of the antique merchants," he said of a weekend foray to Bordeaux, "and emerged with the purchase of a Directoire bird cage, a bronze door-knocker with a dolphin motif, a wooden snuff box of Alexander I of Russia, another of Charles X of France, and three saucers suitable for ashtrays. In a moment of enthusiasm I let myself be driven ten miles into the country to look at two stone statues of Rousseau and Voltaire which did not appeal to me."[91]

If he had done nothing else in Paris, he would have endeared himself with his knowledge of French wine. With a bank account equal to the task, he stocked cellars on both sides of the Atlantic to tempt the jaded oenophile. One weekend he drove down to Philippe de Rothschild's château, where he imbibed some legendary vintages, not just prewar Montrachet and Margaux but a Mouton and a Lafite from before the turn of the century.[92] Once, in a speech to Burgundian wine tasters, he summed up his sentiments by saying, "J'ai fait le sacrifice de mon foie à la France" — "I have sacrificed my liver for France."[93]

It was difficult enough even for Bruce, with his legendary stamina, to juggle the public image of relentless sociability, all the while scheming behind the scenes with Monnet. But other matters intruded, too, and the most critical was Indochina. The conflict between France, attempting to reassert control over its colonies, and Ho Chi Minh, seeking independence, ratcheted upward in intensity. As the Cold War unfolded, the French saw advantage in recasting this conflict as a struggle against international communism. Here was a way to wean the Americans from their traditional anticolonial bent. The tactic paid off. Especially after Korea, Washington sent a torrent of aid, ultimately half the total cost of France's effort in Indochina. Ironically, this subsidy only bruised the wound of French dependency.[94]

In December 1949 — half a year before the first shipment of American military supplies reached Indochina — Bruce urged Washington to support the French. "We as a nation," he said in a cable, "have a vital interest in the establishment and maintenance in Indochina of a non-Communist Govt."[95] If France did not stop communism in Indochina, the cable declared in words that resonate down the decades, "Burma and Siam will fall like over-ripe apples." He concluded that the French were waiting for America to take the lead. "Any course of action we may decide upon involves some risks but the greatest risk and one certain to precipitate failure is that consequent upon continued inaction. A view that Ho-Chi-Minh will inevitably take over Indochina is dangerous and defeatist."

On colonialism in general he sympathized with Europeans out of fear of the chaos he believed would follow rapid decolonization. He thought Americans, "in their enthusiasm for any Nationalist movements," were too idealistic on this issue.[96] By the end of 1951, though, he could see that France was being consumed by the war, "the most difficult and disturbing affair" to trouble the nation that year. It made "a full military contribution by the French to NATO almost impossible without completely wrecking the French economy. It is a subject which constantly preoccupies us."[97] By then, too, he knew that a pullout from Indochina would produce a sigh of relief across France. French assertions that they were turning the military corner were, he realized, "whistling in the wind."[98]

Indochina, like the Schuman Plan and the EDC, pointed up Bruce's dilemma. The French often ignored his support of their position in Washington and complained about interference when he differed with them. Once he discussed the problem over lunch with his friend finance minister Maurice Petsche. "We tried to analyze the various sources of irritation now existing between the U.S. and the French Governments," he wrote with sadness. "Unfortunately they are numerous."[99] At the same time, State often thought he uncritically parroted the views of the French. By his own admission, in Washington his embassy was "considered to have been engaged in making Cassandra-like utterances" about the consequences of failing to support France in Indochina.[100]

Exasperated by European squabbling, Marshall Plan chief Paul Hoffman once grabbed French foreign minister Georges Bidault, a small, bibulous man (known among the diplomats as "In Bido Veritas"), almost lifted him off the ground, and shouted, "Integrate, damn you, integrate."[101] No one could imagine Bruce doing that. Nevertheless, as an urbane, confident man of the world, he represented the proconsul from the New World that many French could do without. Despite his love of all things French, Bruce the enthusiast for European integration represented an American policy no less offensive to some than Hoffman did.

Opponents of the Schuman Plan focused on Bruce's coziness with the French elites who supported it. De Gaulle, on the sideline, disdained the plan because it would limit French sovereignty. At the other end of the spectrum, the left railed against Schuman in strident, xenophobic, even antisemitic terms. A cartoon in the Communist daily L'Humanité showed "men of the American party" — including Jewish premier René Mayer — all with crooked noses. They looked on as Communists stoutly sang the "Marseillaise" and asked one another, "Do we know that tune?" "No, it must be one of those French songs."[102]

On January 17, 1952, a severe cold kept the ambassador in bed. When a messenger arrived with a telegram marked "personal and eyes only for the Ambassador from the Secretary," Bruce knew what it would say. He had discussed the matter with Acheson before.[103] The secretary of state now raised the stakes and secured Truman's approval for his plan to appoint Bruce his undersecretary. "As I have told you," Acheson wrote, "much as you are needed in France I believe there is even greater need for you here." Bruce had no alternative if he wanted to remain in public service. He made one last effort to change Acheson's mind — "must repeat, without reference to my own preference to remain here, that I personally believe in view of overall situation in NATO you are making mistake."[104] Political intrigue and the EDC debate seemed to him to make a change of ambassador ill advised. Helping create the European army was dearer to his heart than being number two to a vigorous secretary of state who was under political attack in Washington. To him the advancement was a poisoned chalice, not a well-earned promotion. The next day Acheson replied with finality that political considerations demanded that Bruce's name be sent immediately to the Senate for confirmation.

To Bruce's disappointment, the EDC negotiations still hung fire. In compensation, he at least had the pleasure of being asked formally by Monnet for something they had long planned. Monnet asked that American aid earmarked for European countries be diverted to the ECSC High Authority when that supranational agency came into being. With the ratification of the Schuman Plan by the French, Dutch, and German parliaments, the time had come.[105]

Looking back on Bruce's appointment, some people not surprisingly called him an inconsequential social ambassador. How seriously could one take a man who stayed out all hours of the night in the company of socialites and couturiers? And was there really any substance beneath the relentless charm that he radiated? The frippery of costume balls, and the foie gras and crème brûlée, and the Louis Seize bibelots, and the cases upon cases of spectacularly expensive claret seemed to some observers just a bit too much. Was he an ostentatious, rich American imbibing from a civilized culture he understood only superficially? Such a picture had elements of truth — that sybaritic streak of his youth had grown to luxuriant maturity — but was manifestly unfair.

As head of the Marshall Plan and as ambassador, he was obsessed with some very large ideas that he advocated with passion and consequence. This commitment brought him purpose, occasional frustration, and in a later instance, crushing failure. Most important, however, it enabled him to make a personal contribution to refashioning postwar Europe that resonates down to the present day.

His greatest contribution as ambassador lay in his unflagging support of Monnet's ideas: the application of counterpart funds under the Marshall Plan and then the European Coal and Steel Community and then the EDC. His support for the Schuman Plan during a difficult time earned him a place of honor alongside Monnet and others for nothing less than shaping postwar Western Europe. The ECSC made possible "fundamental changes in attitude" in both France and Germany, the former acceding to the economic dominance of the Continent by the latter, and Germany truly committing itself to European integration.[106] Schuman's 1950 announcement of Monnet's idea led to a revolution in European thinking and cooperation. Bruce had been a part of it, both the discussions with Monnet that led to the plan and then his efforts to ensure American support and European adoption of Monnet's revolutionary ideas.

When the Bruces prepared to leave the embassy, the wife of a minor diplomat there, better known later as Susan Mary Alsop, said, "All Paris reveres David and is in love with Evangeline."[107] That did not include the Communist party, would-be wreckers of the Marshall Plan. Neither could she have been thinking of those parliamentarians who blamed Bruce for the intrusion of popular American culture into France.

Her comment, however, was not entirely hyperbole. The diplomatic community held Bruce in high regard, as did much of the elite of the French capital, that portion of it, at least, that praised his efforts in favor of European integration. Near the end of his tenure, he was surprised on returning to the residence to find a gathering of some of his aristocratic friends. Dressed in their finery as knights of Malta, they inducted him on the spot into their order. President Auriol made flattering remarks at the farewell luncheon he gave in Bruce's honor.

Monnet was there, of course, as were five former prime ministers. Auriol presented the Bruces a set of white Biscuit de Sèvres table decorations. "The President said they wanted to give me some exalted rank in the Legion of Honor," Bruce noted appreciatively, "but understood I could not accept it as long as I was in Government service." The most touching gift came from Robert Schuman, who sent him a rare book on Versailles, a gift from one bibliophile to another.[108]

On February 6 the Senate confirmed him as undersecretary of state, the same day Buckingham Palace announced the death of George VI. In the midst of arranging his affairs and a daunting round of farewell dinners, not to mention dashing off to London for the state funeral, Bruce worked feverishly to promote the EDC, then at a critical point in the negotiations. The American Club postponed its traditional dinner on Washington's birthday to give it in Bruce's honor, bringing together the American colony and luminaries of the French establishment, men with whom Bruce had worked for nearly four years. The club gave him a silver gilt candelabra, but neither it nor the good wishes from his staff could assuage his unhappiness with leaving.

March 10 was his last day at the office. At lunch he uncorked his last bottle of 1906 Château Lafite. In the afternoon the staff gathered in the main hall to give Evangeline Bruce an armful of roses and the ambassador two silver cigar boxes. By evening the couple was on a TWA flight to America.

Over it all hung the gloom of the stalled European army talks. The big issues that Bruce faced when he was first appointed remained. The Schuman Plan had finally gained approval of the Six, but little practical work had been done. Its promise still lay in the future. The EDC negotiations seemed an endless quagmire, to Bruce's profound disappointment. Indochina weighed more heavily on the French. "This whole situation is critical," he lamented. "France is of all countries in NATO making, except for the United States, the largest effort in defense on a comparative basis. But the war in Indochina is bleeding her white. . . . Meanwhile, my personal view is that U.S. Government policy is too unsympathetic and unrealistic about France's plight, and too pro-German, especially in Pentagon circles. . . . I cannot help thinking how efficiently, practically, and brutally the Germans would have handled this affair, had they been victorious in the late war and were now faced with a Soviet threat."[109] The unstable French parliamentary system seemed immutable. For Bruce, there was much to look back on with a sense of accomplishment, but in all honesty there was much that remained unresolved. Washington, by contrast, might seem to offer fewer problems, but he knew better.

CHAPTER 13

Into the Cockpit

The paradox was this . . . in terms of willingness to commit funds, material, even men, to the new global policy of "containing" Soviet power, the Fair Deal Democrats of the Truman era easily outstripped their Republican critics.

— David Caute, *The Great Fear*

THE CAPITAL that Bruce returned to bore little resemblance to the carefree Washington of his youth. And only in its outward appearance was it like the place he knew from the exciting early days of OSS. It was instead a city obsessed by what one writer called a "pestilence of the mind."[1] The internationalists who had prevailed during the war and had created the Marshall Plan were under siege. Harry Truman, the man who had roused the West against Soviet aggression abroad, was now under attack for insufficient zeal in routing out domestic Reds. He denounced communism no less fervently than he did isolationism and punished disloyalty among government workers with vigor, even with excess. To no avail. The spirit that Joseph McCarthy stood for, though he did not invent it, was in the ascendant.

In retrospect it seems odd that McCarthy, a pugnacious bully addicted to innuendo and half-truth, could have cowed his powerful opponents for so long. A few years before, a press poll voted him the worst United States senator. But in 1950 this crude bumbler rocketed to national attention when he discovered the enormous appeal of attacking domestic communism, especially when it tarred the elite

Eastern establishment. For McCarthyism was about style as well as ideology. He — whom Bruce called a "cheap skate, and almost unbelievable cad" — depicted Ivy League internationalists as pretentious, lying, Anglophile traitors.[2] Acheson, with his clipped accent, British military moustache, and impatience with Congress, was an easy mark. The Marshall Plan, NATO, and all the State Department's efforts to bolster Europe against Stalin counted for nothing to McCarthy.

As a wealthy Democrat of cosmopolitan tastes and European sympathies, Bruce was equally suspect; that Tidewater accent was not proof against the hatred of the enemies of internationalism. The Wisconsin senator boasted that McCarthyism was Americanism with its sleeves rolled up, a neat metaphor that slyly impugned the ability of effete, chalk-striped foreign policy elitists like Bruce and Acheson to do the honest work of patriotism. Bruce learned that, despite his labors in Europe, the struggle against communism that counted had to do with fighting suspected traitors in the State Department, not resisting the real threat abroad.[3]

He had been forewarned before he left Paris. He knew that, two years before, the cultivated, conservative Democratic Senator Millard Tydings of Maryland, with "the aloof bearing of a European dignitary," had lost his bid for reelection because of McCarthy's smear tactics.[4] While he was abroad, Bruce himself had even had a brush with the overheated loyalty investigations.

One of the great spy scandals of the era, and one that ultimately hurtled Congressman Richard M. Nixon to national attention, began on a hot July morning in 1948 just after Bruce left for the Marshall Plan in Paris. The star witness, Elizabeth Bentley, instantly dubbed "the blond spy queen" by the press, appeared before the House Un-American Activities Committee to denounce alleged Communists in government. Her most sensational charge fingered an accomplished young Ivy League employee of the Commerce Department.[5] Bentley said William Remington was a Communist and had given her classified documents. The legislators wanted to know who kept Remington in a sensitive post, and that quest led them to Bruce.

As assistant secretary he had apparently taken lightly a report alerting him that Remington was under investigation for espionage. Asked for an explanation, Bruce sent a cable from France denying any recollection of the warning. A few months later he sent an affidavit vouching for Remington's character. Remington had always taken a tough line regarding exports to the Soviet Union, tougher even than Bruce thought appropriate. When the FBI reviewed this evidence twelve years later, it was impressed less with Remington's innocence than with what it misleadingly said was "how gullible Bruce was." His commendation could not prevent Commerce from suspending Remington. When found guiltless of the charges, he extracted an out-of-court settlement of his own for libel, but his tormenters would not let him rest. He was convicted of perjury in 1953. He began serving a three-year term at Lewisburg Penitentiary, where the prison roster also included the name of Alger Hiss. A few months later a fellow inmate beat Remington to death.[6]

Bruce had known about the possibility of returning to Washington since the previous December when Undersecretary of State James Webb said he would resign. Acheson mulled over the wisdom of moving Bruce to State. On one hand, the likelihood of Democratic defeat in the 1952 election — whether Truman ran or not — meant that neither Bruce nor his replacement could count on keeping his job for long. Despite Bruce's contribution in Paris, Acheson needed him more at home and said as much to the president. At the time, Truman had not made public his decision against running for reelection, but even when he did it did not alter Acheson's plans. (It is possible Bruce knew of Truman's decision earlier; the president privately told Harriman and a few others of his intentions several months before announcing them publicly.[7])

The public reasons given for Webb's resignation were not the important ones. It was not just that the undersecretary needed a rest or that he had completed his task of overseeing the postwar expansion at State. Acheson was increasingly irritated by Webb's insensitivity. A more sympathetic person at his side would make McCarthyite attacks a bit more endurable. He shared the hopes of historian Arthur Schlesinger, who said in congratulating Evangeline Bruce on her husband's promotion, "The effect of getting that sodden personality of Jim Webb off the neck of our foreign policy should be wonderful."[8]

By then Acheson himself was damaged goods. Since he injudiciously vowed in 1950 not to turn his back on Alger Hiss — an honorable defense of a guilty party that Bruce thought ill-advised to state in public — Acheson had come to personify urbane Democratic evil to the rabid right.[9] Blinded by their hatred of his hauteur, his elitist polish, and his contempt for small minds and provincial views as much as his supposed softness on communism, they would not admit that he had done more than anyone else to stiffen the West against Soviet threats. They would rather fulminate about malfeasance in the State Department, or, as Nixon called it, "Acheson's College of Cowardly Communist Containment."

Acheson knew Bruce would hate to quit Paris. He knew of his distaste for working in Washington and for testifying before Congress. He therefore tried to make the promotion more palatable by promising that he, Acheson, and others in the department would carry part of that load.[10] After making his case for staying in Paris, Bruce consented to the shuffle. He also knew the press of events would prevent Acheson from keeping his promise about limiting the disagreeable aspects of the job.

Three days before Bruce's first one at the office, Truman announced that he would not run for reelection. From the larger perspective, the rest of the lame-duck administration was anticlimax, with attention focused on the nominating conventions and election. From the perspective of the new undersecretary, though, it was no anticlimax at all. The last months of the Truman era were a harrowing time for Bruce, cast as he was into the center of Washington intrigue during an ugly election year.

During Bruce's first week on the job, Truman fired his attorney general over a mishandled corruption probe and precipitated a constitutional crisis by seizing America's steel mills to thwart a strike. Those problems were not Bruce's, luckily. As number two at State, he had enough to do monitoring the department's daily operations, an assignment that gave him a far different perspective than in Paris. From his first day in office, April Fool's, he dealt with every country the United States recognized. He no longer had the pleasure of writing his own cables but merely endorsed the words of others. The wider scope meant he spent more of his time being briefed, and the demands on his time increased. It did not surprise him one morning when he was literally hauled out of the dentist's chair in mid-filling for an urgent conference back at the office.

The soft-spoken undersecretary did not always carry out his duties with the aplomb that distinguished his Paris years. Once, at a ceremony on the occasion of Japan's joining the World Bank, Bruce momentarily forgot the full, formal name of the bank and floundered in befuddlement before the newsreel cameras. To accentuate the fiasco, a large kleig light crashed down, missing the Japanese ambassador by inches.[11] More typically, recalled Murat Williams, a junior foreign service officer, Bruce's style had a calming effect. In contrast to anxious, fretful John Foster Dulles, employed as State's token Republican consultant, Bruce radiated composure. "Mr. Dulles was always tense and in a hurry when I saw him," said Williams. "Mr. Bruce was relaxed, calm and obviously the master of what he was doing. . . . [his] dignity put him above the furor that has marked much of our policy-making."[12]

As the undersecretary feared, there were frequent trips to Capitol Hill to testify before congressional committees. When Acheson was out of town, he served as acting secretary. This was a common occurrence in 1952, and he attended cabinet meetings and went for regular briefings of the president more often than most undersecretaries.

Though he could not hope to be conversant with the operational details and policy issues of every American embassy, in August he spoke to the National War College on foreign policy writ large. It was a chance to put current policy in historical context and to plump for his favorite initiatives, the Schuman Plan and the European Defense Community. European integration, he argued, was the most promising initiative since the war and offered a solution to the German problem: "The attraction of Western Germany to the Atlantic community is the most important thing which has happened in the West."[13]

As undersecretary he dealt with personnel problems, only now it was at the level of ambassador, which meant dealing with egos on a grander scale than before. A particularly aggravating case was that of Perle Mesta, a political society hostess and Truman's envoy to Luxembourg. When Bruce refused her request to come home at government expense for consultation, a privilege she had abused before, "she circumvented me by getting the President's personal approval. Naturally, this was much resented in the Department. Thereafter, she crowed over me as to how she knew how to get her way." It gave him satisfaction later when Eisenhower spurned her groveling request to be reappointed to Luxembourg, for she was, Bruce said, "almost universally detested in the Department as a phoney, an ignoramus and a pretentious bore."[14]

Bruce was uneasy about Washington's obsession with vetting people, from federal employees to applicants for passports and visas. Having earned minor praise in 1940 as a Virginia legislator when he defended free speech, he now found himself the department's chief policeman. He had had an introduction to the business of vetting in Paris. It was repugnant to him to pass judgment on Pablo Picasso's request for a visa to visit America as part of a group called the World Congress of Partisans of Peace, identified by the State Department as a Communist front organization. He warned Washington of the potential negative fallout. "In view [of] his worldwide reputation, refusal of visa to Picasso would certainly cause unfavorable comment here, particularly in intellectual and 'liberal' circles. It would also tend to suggest that we have something to fear from Communist 'peace' propaganda."[15] Ever the pragmatist, he went on to say that if State did decide to refuse Picasso, it should do so quickly: the longer it delayed, the more unfavorable press the Communists could generate. Publicity arose also over the case of Maurice Chevalier, accused of being a "mild collaborator" during the war — he sang for the Paris radio run by the Germans — and a Communist after. Bruce called him "weak and opportunistic."[16]

He could brush these unpleasant incidents aside in Paris, but in Washington they intruded more frequently. Sometimes he won small victories over the system, as in November when he obtained visas for a French couple, Jean-Louis Barrault and Madeleine Renaud, who had previously belonged to a Communist front organization in France. Bruce considered them the most talented French actors of their day and went to New York to see them perform and savor his little personal triumph.[17]

He also personally became involved in the case of Linus Pauling, the Caltech chemist who later won the Nobel Peace Prize and whose English colleagues were livid that his previous links with Communist organizations kept him from speaking at Cambridge. On the same day the Republicans nominated Eisenhower for president, Bruce and his colleagues came to an unsatisfactory, Solomonic decision in the

Pauling case. They gave him a limited passport in return for his signing an affidavit denying membership in the Communist party. The next month Bruce wrestled with the problem of how to justify denying passports to people for political reasons other than Communist party membership. He found the whole proceeding distasteful because he believed it was impossible to describe such a category "without gravely impairing civil liberties."[18]

The case of Owen Lattimore, a Johns Hopkins University expert on China, illustrated Bruce's unhappy lot. In 1950 McCarthy had hounded Lattimore for the "loss of China," calling him a spy who somehow had conspired with both Kremlin and White House to sell out the Chinese people to Mao Zedong. Even though the Senate Foreign Relations Committee exonerated him from these charges, the professor suffered continuing harassment. The State Department became involved in May 1952 when it received a warning from the CIA that Lattimore was about to flee to Moscow. State knew that if he left, his flight would not just confirm his guilt; it would also give the McCarthyites evidence — accurate for a change — to crucify the administration.

Ruth Shipley, the dreaded head of the passport office, put out an alert to the Customs Service to detain Lattimore if he appeared at any port of exit.[19] "Ma" Shipley ran her office as a personal fiefdom and had caused OSS much grief over agent documentation during the war. In the meantime, Hoover's FBI discovered that Lattimore had not purchased an airline ticket abroad, indeed had not even applied for a passport. It was all a hoax. As federal agencies scrambled to avoid blame, McCarthy accused State of trying to help Lattimore flee. The department, it seemed, would be blamed whatever it did.[20]

Bruce was in the thick of the flap. When he learned that the FBI had determined the whole affair was bogus, he concluded with disgust, "State will no doubt have to eat crow." It appalled him that no one high up in the department had been consulted before the passport office issued the controversial stop order. It was Bruce's hapless task to discuss with Truman the best face to put on a deplorable business. The president told him State would have to issue an apology to Lattimore and in the future would need to rein in the overzealous Shipley.[21]

Denying passports to Americans and visas to foreigners was bad enough, but cases involving the department's own personnel were the most troubling to Bruce. In a vain attempt to deflect McCarthyite criticism, and in part because it believed the times required them, the administration set up loyalty boards to search for traitors within. Several hundred employees, mostly innocent, were dismissed by the end of Truman's term.[22] As Acheson's second in command, Bruce bore part of the burden, and the blame too, for the work of these tribunals. He and the secretary tried to defend their people, but the excesses of the loyalty boards were not shining moments in the annals of the department.

After State bowed to the loyalty board and suspended foreign service officer John Carter Vincent, Bruce could only note in his diary, "This has been a hideous day at the office." McCarthy, "a nasty piece of work," was destroying the department. It would have been small comfort for Bruce to know that it would get much worse under the Republicans. He shared the widespread feeling among foreign service officers that they were being persecuted by, as he put it, "an evil man drumming up for his own selfish ends . . . an animosity which could do nothing but harm the public employees."[23]

Sitting in the undersecretary's chair, Bruce put his imprint on American policy all over the globe. Most dramatically, he scotched a clandestine operation hatched by companies that feared Communist subversion on their Central American plantations. These firms, their CIA friends, and their political supporters (including Henry Cabot Lodge, "the Senator from United Fruit") concocted a scheme to use Guatemalan exiles and Nicaraguan ruler Anastasio Somoza García to overthrow Guatemala's leftist president. Truman had approved Operation Fortune, and Somoza promised the Americans he would "clean up Guatemala for you in no time." Bruce learned of the plan when crates of — what else? — "agricultural implements" for Somoza were already at sea on board a United Fruit vessel. The undersecretary convinced Acheson the operation was illegitimate and persuaded him to ask the president to cancel it.[24] Several years later the CIA would dust off the plan and execute it, to the disgust of the former head of OSS London.

His opinion on Indochina changed from when he was ambassador in France. By 1952 he was convinced it would best serve America's interest if France eventually left Southeast Asia. To counter the Communists, whom he still opposed, he argued for an early version of what a later president would call Vietnamization. Bruce wanted to increase aid to train the indigenous leadership in Indochina that would assume the responsibilities of the departing French. His idea was not adopted.[25]

Though he was removed from the negotiations on the European Defense Community once he left Paris, he kept in touch with this initiative, second in his affections only to the Schuman Plan. Probably the least unpleasant of his appearances before a Senate panel gave him the chance to brief the Foreign Relations Committee on this project so close to his heart.[26]

Bruce was an entirely sympathetic person to serve as Acheson's number two. There was little to distinguish the views of these two Ivy League internationalists on America's role in the world. They also shared a similar perspective at home. At the beginning of his administration, Roosevelt had fired Acheson as undersecretary of the Treasury, and Acheson, like Bruce, advocated FDR's defeat in 1936. Acheson later discreetly described his attitude toward Roosevelt as "one of admiration without affection."[27]

Bruce admired Acheson as a "superior" individual, witty, learned, and intellectually rigorous. "The persistent torrent of abuse so long levelled against him," Bruce wrote while still at the Paris embassy, "must have cruelly wounded his spirit, but even his most bitter enemies speak of his remarkable courage. I think his position is as painful as the history of American public life can record. He is the scapegoat for the failures of and frustration of his fellow-countrymen." Acheson reciprocated his regard by saying that not since Benjamin Franklin had any American ambassador been as understanding of the French as Bruce, and that included Jefferson.[28]

There was not a perfect fit between the two, though. Before Acheson was convinced of the merits of EDC, he complained about the "Bruce cult" in Paris pushing Washington hard to embrace the European army scheme. At other times Acheson showed his pique that Bruce claimed to know more about the EDC than anyone. In turn Bruce said that, though Acheson was excellent company, he could be severe against anyone he disliked or distrusted. "Intolerant of fools," "a man of absolute integrity," Acheson was in Bruce's opinion one of the greatest secretaries of state.[29]

Occasional strain between the two men showed when Bruce had to put up with the secretary's exacting guidelines to be followed in his frequent absences from town. According to Bruce, George Marshall had said that every three months or so, Acheson needed to "let fly against something" or he would explode from his tightly bottled up emotions.[30] Bruce was no less contemptuous than Acheson of congressional buffoonery but was more adept at concealing his feelings. Because of Bruce's emollient personality, the department often fared better in its relations with Capitol Hill the many times that year when he testified when Acheson was away. Acheson may have had that quality in mind, and been jealous of it a bit, in the backhanded compliment he paid to Bruce in his memoirs. He recalled that he brought the diplomat back from Paris because he was well regarded by Congress, "in part because of the charm that distance had lent during his years in Europe."[31]

Because Bruce served as acting secretary nearly half of the time, he had regular contact with the president. He had not met Truman until that interview in 1949 before leaving to take up his post as ambassador to France. Harry Truman was decidedly not the suave cosmopolitan, sharing the elite tastes and experiences that Bruce and Acheson did. Indeed, he exhibited the classic Midwestern scorn for elite Easterners and all his life denounced what he called "high hats."

Fourteen years older than Bruce, he had had a far more typical American youth as a product of rural and small-town Missouri. Like Bruce he had joined a National Guard artillery unit as soon as Congress declared war in 1917 and like him was forever changed by the conflict. But when he came home and married, it was not into one of the great fortunes of America. His haberdashery store in Kansas City was one of the many businesses that failed in the short postwar recession. As he locked the door of the shop for the last time and turned away, Truman cursed "Old Mellon" for engineering the slump.[32] What would he think of Mellon's erstwhile son-in-law as his acting secretary of state? If Bruce's appointment as ambassador against the wishes of Maryland Democrats left any residual wariness on Truman's part, the president did not show it, and Bruce repaid the chief executive's courtesy with loyalty and admiration.

On occasion the Bruces dined at the White House with the Trumans. Unlike glittering state dinners, these were usually quiet affairs. The massive remodeling of the mansion that Truman had undertaken some months before, in which the facade remained but the interior was entirely gutted, was completed the week Bruce became undersecretary.

To dine simply in that august setting impressed this student of the presidency with the weight of the office even more than his past proximity to high politics through his father and father-in-law.

Whenever Acheson was away, Bruce saw the president during the secretary's regularly scheduled Monday and Thursday morning meetings, and sometimes on a daily basis. Truman relied on Acheson more than any other member of his cabinet. Acheson was, as David McCullough has said, "the President's continuous contact with the world, his reporter and interpreter of world events."[33] Bruce could not fill those shoes, but he did hope to perform satisfactorily sitting at Truman's right in the Friday morning cabinet meetings and whenever else the president turned to him for advice.

He thought Truman a sympathetic figure, but he knew one did not waste his time. He knew the president was a great reader and remarked on his "searching manner" in questioning him on minute details of the department's work. He rated Truman very high on foreign affairs — especially when contrasted with what Bruce called FDR's "blithe," "unrealistic," attitude toward Stalin — but was noticably silent on his handling of domestic matters. His only criticism, made years later, was that Truman's impulsive partisanship, combined with an undue tolerance for the failings of his cronies, sometimes got the better of him. All in all, though, Bruce thought Truman an "uncommonly good" chief executive.[34]

While her husband did a quick study of State, Evangeline Bruce set about to replicate in their Georgetown home a bit of the éclat that illuminated the Paris embassy. Her reputation preceded her. Noting her husband's promotion early in 1952, the British embassy sent a cable to London quoting with approval the opinion of *Time* magazine that she was one of the most accomplished hostesses in Paris. The house on 34th Street near the western edge of the hothouse that was Georgetown was much smaller than the mansion on avenue d'Iéna. Nevertheless the small dinner parties that the Bruces held regularly came to be coveted invitations among the village's power brokers. Honing his skill as a raconteur on the most outrageous OSS tales — of which there were no lack in Bruce's retelling — he showed Washingtonians why he was known in Paris as a hardworking bon vivant.

There was less time than in Paris, however, for entertaining or any other diversions. The need to report to the secretary when Acheson was in town, to the president when he was not, and to the demands of Congress for testimony all made Bruce less his own man than he had been in France.

With Eisenhower carrying the flag for the Republicans in 1952 and the unpopularity of the Democrats at record levels, Bruce knew his tenure in office was nearing an end. Despite Truman's spectacular accomplishments in Europe, the electorate would punish the Democrats for failing to end the war in Korea. Though Eisenhower largely avoided demagoguery himself, he did not denounce McCarthy as he should have done, and the outrageous charge that Truman coddled Communists would not go away.

Bruce followed national politics more closely that summer than he had in many years. Despite his belief that conventions were a lot of "tomfoolery," he borrowed a television set to watch the Republican gathering from his house in Georgetown. Even when he escaped for two weeks to Staunton Hill for a hot summer holiday, he listened every evening to radio coverage of the Democratic convention in Chicago.[35]

Despite his disdain for party politics, as a senior administration official he could not escape being drawn into the fray. Just before election day he lashed out publicly at the "demogogic, vile and contemptible" allegations made against State. He did not mention McCarthy by name, but the press correctly identified the target of his outburst. "Like the old Arab proverb," Bruce had said, "'the dog barks but the caravan passes.'"[36]

The outcome was foreordained. There would be no repeat for Adlai Stevenson of the 1948 Truman miracle. Bruce stayed up to watch the election returns at a succession of Democratic households in Georgetown until nearly sunrise. It was a slow day for government workers, and most of the people Bruce saw had hangovers, "not altogether political."[37] For lame-duck officials the rest of the autumn was a morose time. Bruce did not have to worry as many of his colleagues did about the source of their daily bread after the inauguration, but their depression infected him as well. In fact the word "gloomy" pervaded his diary as he noted increasing French skittishness over EDC, further Republican sniping about alleged Communists in the American delegation to the United Nations, troubles in the Middle East, and "no note of gaiety" to be heard throughout the administration.[38]

It had been twenty years since the last change of party in the White House. After the slurs of the campaign, the Truman and Eisenhower camps eyed one another warily. Truman noted privately that "the President-elect has been coy about co-operating for the turnover. All that the present incumbent wants is an orderly transfer of authority. Ike and his advisors are afraid of some kind of trick. There are no tricks."[39] Someone had to handle the transition, and Bruce was a better choice than Acheson to explain the details of the State Department and foreign policy. Two weeks after the election, he began to meet with Henry Cabot Lodge, a Massachusetts Republican senator and George- town neighbor whom Eisenhower chose to head his transition team. During their long conversations, Lodge took copious notes of Bruce's advice. At their first meeting, Bruce dropped by Lodge's Georgetown house and left his own enumeration, written out longhand, of the most pressing matters in foreign affairs. High among these were the running sores of Korea, Indochina, and EDC.[40] Despite a few glitches, Bruce felt the transition went smoothly. Secretary of State Designate John Foster Dulles apparently agreed because he asked Bruce to stay on after the inauguration.[41] The undersecretary agreed to serve briefly as a consul- tant, but that did not stop him, as part of tidying up in the days before Christmas, from "destroying papers, and sorting out others from my files."[42]

Appointment as undersecretary at least let him keep in touch with his pet initiatives — the Schuman Plan and the EDC — and to advance them from the center in Washington. Being in charge of the day-to-day management of State and substituting for Acheson gave him a broader perspective on foreign policy. And, though he would have discounted the point, being in Georgetown for a year allowed him and his wife to create a Washington version of the glamorous social ambience that surrounded them in Paris.

These were small compensations in his eyes. Given his aversion to testifying on Capitol Hill and to administration in general, he would have been unhappy even without being on the receiving end of McCarthyite attacks. With disgust, he watched them continue under the new regime. "The shadow of McCarthy rests heavily over the State Department," he wrote the following spring. "His influence has been entirely destructive and he is really an evil man."[43]

One thing Bruce knew for certain, he did not want another appointment in the snake pit of Washington. "I found the atmosphere there depressing," he wrote a few months later, "mostly due to McCarthy's inquisitorial and terroristic witch-hunting activities that constitute a national disgrace and have markedly lowered our prestige as a nation at home and abroad."[44]

Early in the new year, right before Ike's inauguration, David and Evangeline Bruce took the train from Union Station to Baltimore. They stayed at the Stafford Hotel, just behind his childhood home under the outstretching hand of George Washington at Mount Vernon Place. Dining there with Macgill James and his wife (one of Bruce's cousins), and with other old Baltimore friends, he felt the tension of the past months begin to slip away. He relaxed. To anticipate exchanging government service for the quiet life of the private citizen was a luxury to savor. After four exhilarating years in Paris, and the less agreeable months in Washington, his diplomatic career seemed at an end. He had reached the rank of ambassador at arguably the most important embassy at the time. He took pride in his work for European unity even though the jury was still out. It had been a good run, but now it was time to settle down and watch the children grow up.

CHAPTER 14

Ambassador to a Dream

D'un côté, si on ne fait pas l'Europe, la France est perdue: de l'autre côté, si on fait l'Europe, la France est perdue.

> — Said in the French National Assembly, November 24, 1953

I am engaged in so many intrigues, even including newspaper leaks, that I am not clear in my own judgment as to how our cause is progressing. . . . Threats and cajolery, flattery and grandfatherly admonition are being employed to the best of our ability.

> — David Bruce to Livingston Merchant, March 1, 1954

*B*RUCE DID NOT LEAVE the public arena as he expected. Instead of dismissing him, the new administration gave him a challenge that eclipsed all others since the war. At Eisenhower's request, he returned to France to advocate as American policy his own most fervent hope — that Europe integrate into a unified whole, economically, militarily, and politically. More than the Marshall Plan, this mission gave him the power to fashion policy. But with exhilaration it also brought frustration, opprobrium, and defeat.

While Bruce temporarily enjoyed the quiet pleasures of private life, the new secretary of state flew to Europe to assess prospects for the European Defense Community. John Foster Dulles knew that without German manpower, Western defenses would remain anemic. He did not yet favor West Germany's direct entry into NATO because of the anxiety it would cause among the neighbors. Like Bruce, he embraced EDC and earnestly believed it was not yet dead, "only sleeping."[1] The knowledge, however, that none of the EDC signatories had pushed ratification through their parliaments since they signed the treaty in 1952 was disconcerting.

An intense, rigid, and blunt foe of communism, Dulles was described by Churchill as "the only bull who brings his own china shop with him."[2] Bruce once called him "an antique Cretan bull" and thought him arrogant and indiscreet.[3] Yet he later acknowledged the force of Dulles's personality: "By sheer pertinacity, mentality, and will, after a period of great unpopularity, foreign and domestic, he imposed his views on the Atlantic Alliance, and became its undisputed leader."[4] (Bruce was more generous than Acheson, who, on hearing of Dulles's death in 1959, silenced a dinner party with the words "Thank God Foster is underground."[5])

Bruce got along well enough with the brother of his old friend Allen Dulles, even though the incendiary rhetoric of the 1952 election made it seem impossible that bipartisanship in foreign affairs could survive. Acheson called Dulles's people "Cossacks quartered in a grand city hall, burning the paneling to cook with."[6] But Dulles, like Eisenhower, was an internationalist who shared many of Truman's attitudes about Europe. For Bruce it helped too that Dulles was yet another of Jean Monnet's many friends.

In 1953 Monnet, like Dulles, worried that in the absence of strong American backing, European hesitation would kill the EDC. He feared even more Dulles's hint that American aid might dry up if Europe rejected the common army scheme. Such a disaster would jeopardize all his efforts to promote integration.

Monnet was not one to fret in silence. On the day Dulles was to return home, Monnet suggested to him that the United States appoint a special envoy to promote European integration. The same idea had occurred to Alfred Gruenther, a friend of Monnet and Eisenhower's former chief of staff in Europe. Gruenther presented the idea to his old boss and recommended Bruce. Eisenhower liked the idea but balked at Bruce. Despite their friendship in Paris, Ike worried about the effect of hiring the number two man in the department that had been vilified during the election more than any other.

Dulles was even more skeptical but allowed himself, uncharacteristically, to be persuaded by Monnet about the post. Still, like Ike, he hesitated about sending Bruce. As soon as Dulles was airborne on his way home, Monnet rang Gruenther to orchestrate a campaign in Bruce's behalf. They need not have bothered. While Monnet was on the phone, on the plane Dulles was already warming to his suggestion. Two days later he called Bruce and offered him the job.[7]

When the offer came, the former undersecretary was in South Carolina shooting turkeys. He had his own reservations. He wanted to know one thing: Would EDC be the centerpiece of policy in Europe? When Eisenhower and Dulles assured him it would, he accepted.[8] Just a month before, he had told John McCloy he rejected the British assessment that EDC was "dead as mutton." If only the new administration would send an emissary "to infuse a spirit of optimism" in Europe, EDC could succeed.[9] The chance, unlooked for, to promote European unity transcended his desire to retreat from public life and suppressed any twinge of guilt at betraying his fellow Democrats. It was, after all, an internationalist policy he would be pursuing, one that he had helped persuade Eisenhower to endorse in 1950.

Less than ten days after Monnet first pressed the idea, Bruce became America's special envoy to the EDC talks, representative to the embryonic Coal and Steel Community, and observer of plans for European political union. At the White House, Eisenhower and Dulles "were, I think, relieved that I did not want to have the personal rank of Ambassador," though the position warranted it.[10] He was the highest-ranking Democrat on Ike's foreign policy team, and Dulles compared the role to his own as special Republican adviser in Truman's State Department. When opponents accused him of ignoring bipartisanship, Dulles trotted out Bruce's example.

It would not be an easy time for him. He would have done well to heed the chilling message he received shortly after arriving in France from an embittered Dean Acheson: "You & Jean [must] save us in Europe. There is no one here who can or who will do much to help you."[11]

Evangeline Bruce greeted the appointment philosophically. Though her husband admitted it was "disruptive of all our plans," she scrambled to shift her family back across the ocean.[12] There was little time: Bruce had to be in Paris a week after accepting the job. So, in high spirits, with their baggage and their springer spaniels, they arrived at Idlewild airport on February 25, 1953. In Paris they checked into an ornate suite at the Hôtel France et Choiseul. The next morning America's "emissary to Europe" briskly walked his dogs around the Place Vendôme, past the Ritz. He had come back, and not a moment too soon.

On the day the Bruces left New York, de Gaulle announced what everyone suspected — he opposed EDC, root and branch. He denied it would enhance French security and denounced "official and semi-official propaganda, money and foreign support" for the plan.[13] He called it "a Frankenstein," "an artificial monster," "a ghastly mess." In a barb directed at Bruce, he declared that "the Americans are using open and secret pressure to compel France to accept the EDC which can only condemn her to decay."[14]

In one respect he was right. The "present mood of extreme national depression" that he spoke of fairly described his country in 1953. Bruce thought the British ambassador in Paris, Sir Gladwyn Jebb, was a man of "colossal" vanity, but he agreed with Jebb that the French were "in a rather psychotic state of mind."[15] Ike's special envoy might not have pronounced himself "enchanted to be in Paris" if he had could have foreseen that, far more than during the Marshall Plan, he would become lightning rod, whipping boy, and scapegoat.[16]

Some observers hyperbolically likened the EDC debate to the Dreyfus Affair that rent France at the turn of the century. But if it was not on the lips of ordinary citizens, as Dreyfus had been, it did divide the senior civil service, the press, the army, and the political parties — those establishment elites with whom Bruce dealt.[17]

The political climate had changed since EDC was first proposed in panicky reaction to Korea. A week after Bruce arrived in Paris, one long-prayed-for death showed how quickly the climate could change. Stalin, having brutalized his own people for years and cowed Western Europe since the war, died on March 5. Opponents of EDC seized on hopes for an East-West thaw as a further excuse not to rearm Germany. No Stalin, they reasoned, no EDC.[18]

Bruce knew firsthand about the Fourth Republic's constitutional weakness. "The great underlying evil," he wrote, was "institutionalized instability."[19] Because it did not matter whether French governments fell or not, politicians had no interest in asserting authority. Bruce despaired about "the deep social malaise that afflicts this unhappy country." If only France would promote the EDC, it could revive its fortunes instead of "sinking into the quicksilver of foreign derision and criticism." France had proposed this bold idea nearly three years before. Why could it not live up to that dramatic promise?[20] Instead, "an irresolute government" preferred "as usual to procrastinate like Mr. Micawber for some outside power to save it from its own irresponsibility."[21]

Bruce's office was smaller than the ones in his previous posts as Washington's man in Paris, but its modesty, housed in the second-story wing of an old Rothschild mansion, belied the mission's importance. Though not formally an ambassador, he was the head of "an embassy to a dream," the dream of European integration.[22] With his small staff of about twenty working under the direction of Tommy Tomlinson, his energetic assistant from the Marshall Plan, Bruce set about to make a difference.[23]

In the meantime Evangeline Bruce set about to make a home for their family at 17 rue Alfred Dehodencq, in the posh 16th arrondissement, close to the Bois de Boulogne. Purchased by the U.S. government during the Marshall Plan, the house was one of those elegant dwellings that pass from one diplomatic family to another.[24] Bruce's fellow Princetonian Harry Labouisse was just leaving. Before him Barry Bingham lived there when he succeeded Bruce as head of ECA in France. The house came with a garden large enough for the dogs and the children, but Bruce was glad he had kept the lease on La Lanterne.

The Bruces resumed their active social life, made more pleasant because they no longer needed to entertain on the scale they did at 2 avenue d'Iéna. Even so, they retained a staff that included a cook, valet, butler, kitchen maid, lady's maid, house maid, nurse, chauffeur, and concierge. Bruce conceded that it was expensive: "Since I have been living for years beyond my income and eating up capital, I should not like to continue long at this rate."[25]

His private friendships helped now and then to divert him from the serious work of "making Europe." In April 1954, for example, Philippe de Rothschild and Pauline Potter decided to marry. She was one of Bruce's old Baltimore girl friends, and at the civil ceremony he served as one of her witnesses. Afterward the Bruces feted their friends at their Versailles house, complete with a Louis XVI–style wedding cake, topped by a pastry Eros. That last touch was an unhappy augury, for Pauline came to hate Philippe, and he later said he "gave her everything a man can give, except fidelity."[26] For the moment, though, all was happiness. "With so many Rothschilds present," Bruce prudently noted, "I thought it best to give them a red Bordeaux with which they were probably not particularly familiar."[27] Such pleasant diversions, however, became increasingly rare.

Shortly after he arrived in France, Bruce went to Luxembourg to address the High Authority of the European Coal and Steel Community. It was a symbolic moment he cherished, for Jean Monnet was president of the agency. In his remarks Bruce saluted "this daring and noble enterprise" and reveled in its promise for European integration and in his own good fortune at being America's representative.[28] Like old times, he and Monnet fell agreeably into their pattern of consultation, now redoubled in behalf of EDC.

After Bruce had talked to all six foreign ministers of the prospective EDC countries, he sent a report to Dulles. Not surprisingly, the foremost American champion of European integration declared himself "guardedly optimistic" that the parliaments would ratify EDC. France remained the "chief trouble spot," and its foreign minister, Georges Bidault, "is playing a deep game, is lone wolf operator and counsels with few."[29] Bruce advised Dulles how to handle Bidault when he visited Washington. The Frenchman, he said, quoting John Randolph, "rows to his objective with muffled oars." Dulles should threaten to withdraw from Europe if France continued to thwart the rearming of Germany under the safeguards of EDC.[30]

The "pro-Europeans" lionized Bruce. With unintended irony, an Italian cabinet minister called him the "godfather" of European integration.[31] Konrad Adenauer privately called him "the most adult American diplomat in Europe," a compliment to Bruce if not to his colleagues.[32] Less charitable observers dissented. One Frenchman who loathed EDC once tried to have him declared persona non grata.[33] Another called him "the biggest ignoramus the American Government ever sent to Europe."[34]

In June 1953 Bruce grumbled, "It is frustrating that we cannot get the prospective mother to the obstetrician."[35] He refused to accept that the abortionist had already been summoned by EDC's strident, irrational French opponents, and it only remained for the procedure to be performed, even though it took another year to accomplish.

It was easy enough from an American perspective to see why the French should endorse the EDC. It was not so simple for the French. True, France had originally proposed the idea, but it had been altered since then. The original discrimination against the Germans was gone; they would now get their national army back, the very thing the French originally proposed EDC to avoid. The supranational command structure of EDC was not enough to reassure them.

America was also seen to be forcing the idea down their proud throats. Not just Communists and Gaullists opposed the treaty. Even former president Vincent Auriol came out against it. If a sympathetic figure like Auriol could write privately that "the Americans are stupid, naive, and understand nothing," there was little hope that stiffer necks on either side would bend.[36] Some thoughtful French observers who supported greater European unity worried about having it orchestrated by what seemed to them an overbearing America. One of them ruefully told the National Assembly: "On one hand, if we don't 'make' Europe, France is lost; on the other hand, if we do, France is lost."[37]

Sometimes Bruce clashed with the American ambassador too. Douglas Dillon was less excited about the treaty. He called Tomlinson "a Euro-fanatic, under Monnet's thumb" and may have thought the same of Bruce.[38] The ambassador once objected to an analysis Bruce sent Washington at odds with a cable Dillon's people had just written. Bruce dismissed the spat and others like it as tempests in a teapot.

Though based in France, he had to deal with the five other prospective EDC nations, the most important being West Germany. He had lost none of the suspicion of Germans that he acquired honestly during the war. Yet he could only shake his head in wonder at their "tremendous vitality" compared to the apathy he saw in France.[39] French foot-dragging might push the Germans — "this formidable and dangerous people" — to insist on rearming entirely independent of EDC, a prospect he "bitterly opposed." He admired Adenauer, who shared his vision for European integration, and believed EDC and Adenauer were the keys to binding Germany to the West.

He proposed that America do "everything reasonable and possible" to assist Adenauer's reelection.[40] When that happened in September 1953, he urged Dulles to use this "magnificent victory" to press Paris anew.[41] But the boost that the German election gave pro-EDC forces quickly dissipated in ill-tempered Western disarray.

Churchill, prime minister once more, called for a summit among the United States, Britain, France, and the Soviet Union. In advance, the Western allies met at Bermuda to confer among themselves. Churchill gave lip service to EDC but kept Britain apart and privately called it a "sludgy amalgam."[42] New French demands destroyed any hope of Western unity. Shortly afterward a disgusted Dulles made his memorable threat that sent shock waves through the foreign ministries of Europe: he promised an "agonizing reappraisal" of American policy if France failed to ratify EDC. Once he was convinced the French would never face the issue without threats, he did not mince his words.

Bruce agreed. Before Bermuda he had urged Eisenhower to tell the French that "abandonment of the policy of European military integration might entail drastic changes in the present strategic plans of NATO."[43] When he heard Dulles threaten the French, he knew they would squeal about "brutal" American pressure. He was right. He described Dulles's words as shock treatment that put the French "on notice." Bruce himself would have made the point more delicately, but it was overly optimistic for him to say "quite a few" French politicians approved of Dulles's bluntness.[44]

He feared that by failing to pass EDC, the French risked losing their last chance "of holding the Germans in check."[45] He was too gloomy in his assessment of the Germans, but he was right about one point: whatever happened, the French would blame the United States. Nothing any French government had done in regard to EDC, he fumed, should lead anyone to take them at their word.

In March 1954 Bruce said, "We have tried reason, persuasion, generosity, understanding, sympathy, patience: All have failed and I see no alternative but to deal with French as cold bloodedly as they deal with us."[46] "For my own part," he wrote a friend, "I intend to continue to love these agreeable, attractive, and infinitely resourceful people, but love must be separated from gullibility over their political protestations!"[47] When, in a passing moment of discouragement, he told Monnet he was thinking of resigning, his friend persuaded him not to abandon the great schemes for integration the two men had labored for during the past five years.[48] He agreed to stay on, and his optimism returned, though by then it was too hopeful a sentiment. "We then plunged into the EDC morass and wallowed there," he said of a meeting.[49] On another occasion he asserted: "The French have no policy. We have. If we stick to it the positive should be stronger than the negative."[50]

Halfway around the globe, Ho Chi Minh's soldiers encircled the garrison at Dien Bien Phu. Bled white after years of fighting in Southeast Asia, France could neither win nor extricate itself despite the subsidy of hundreds of millions of dollars in American aid. In his inaugural speech to the National Assembly, a new prime minister resolved to settle affairs in Asia in a month or resign. Bruce called Pierre Mendès-France "a devious character at the best of times,"[51] but the premier was as good as his word. His success in ending the war enabled him to turn next to the running sore of EDC. Enemies whispered that in return for Soviet agreement at the Geneva accords ending the war, Mendès-France agreed to sabotage EDC. As much as he disliked the premier, Bruce did not believe the rumor, nor has any evidence turned up to confirm it.

With the war over, French dependence on American military aid declined, and with it the cost of offending the Americans. Mendès-France announced a new series of negotiating protocols that France's partners in EDC must accept before he would recommend ratification to the National Assembly. He made these demands with a cool effrontery that offended most participants in the negotiations.[52] Bruce cabled Washington that the protocols were "unacceptable beyond our worst expectations" and would eviscerate EDC.[53] He was especially angry with the anti-EDC faction at the Quay d'Orsay and in the cabinet, including the young leftist François Mitterand. Bruce believed the rumor that this future president of France opposed EDC because he hoped to replace Mendès-France.[54]

The negotiations, in their fourth year, headed toward some sort of resolution at an August meeting in Brussels to consider the French leader's demands. It was destined to be, as a recent chronicler of the Fourth Republic has written, a "spectacularly unsuccessful and bad-tempered conference."[55]

The other EDC countries greeted Mendès-France's protocols with the same outrage as Bruce. "The only thing missing," one German newspaper said, "is a provision that German soldiers must hand in their rifles every evening."[56] Washington believed the French premier meant to destroy the cornerstone of American policy in Europe.[57] Bruce described Mendès-France's demeanor at Brussels as petulant and arrogant, oblivious to the anger against his protocols in the other EDC nations.[58] The premier's biographer countered with the specious argument that Mendès-France was taken by surprise at the conference, when it was his bombshell that had made the meeting necessary: "It is possible that the French premier, wounded by the vindictive climate surrounding him and indignant at the American intrusion, was sometimes too abrupt. But it remains true that the Brussels conference was an ambush and that these fervent 'Europeans' served Europe badly."[59]

The press reported that Washington considered the French revisions "harmful, distasteful and destructive."[60] In Brussels, Mendès-France distorted a message from Dulles by telling the five other nations that America would accept any agreement they reached. Dulles was outraged. Bruce conveyed to the French leader the secretary's final threat — either support EDC or face the rearming of Germany outside the safeguards that the common European army provided.[61]

When Bruce saw Mendès-France in Brussels, the premier complained about the difficulties he faced governing his country and repeated that it was impossible to consider EDC unless the other five nations agreed to each of his protocols. Bruce "tried, with the best eloquence I could summon to the cause, to explain to him the store set by the American people generally on European integration projects, and how these appealed irresistibly to the idealism as well as the selfish security instincts of our people, acutely aware, from participation in two world wars, of the menace of German militarism. I might as well have been addressing myself to a stone." When Mendès disparaged Schuman's support for EDC, Bruce said he would stake his life on Schuman's backing. "My friend," Mendès replied, "evidently you hold your life of little account."[62]

Bruce witnessed the failure in Brussels with equanimity. He wearily cabled the State Department that he and his colleagues had "neither humor, force nor physical stamina" to continue talking in the face of French intransigence.[63] At the American embassy the code clerks, who transmitted and decrypted messages between Bruce and Washington, had had only snatches of sleep for seventy-two hours. His team was downcast. He did not let on at the time how dispirited he was himself and treated them all to lunch at the swankiest restaurant in Brussels in an effort to jolly them up. Tomlinson wanted to argue with Mendès-France some more, but Bruce calmed him over lunch by talking, as he did so well, about the long view.[64]

Bruce himself had not given up on EDC, though. On the eve of the debate in the National Assembly, the week after the Brussels talks collapsed, he was still planning. He believed that if the Americans and British formally backed the united stand of the five signatory nations who opposed Mendès-France, the French would relent. They would recognize that if they killed EDC, Germany would rearm in a fashion even less palatable to their interests. Asking the State Department to "hold your hat," Bruce tried without success to sell his plan in Washington and London.[65] Hopeful to the end, he implored Washington to give him the authority to call for a new conference among the EDC signatory nations.

When debate began in the French parliament, the public galleries were jammed. There was no room to move in the press box. The deputies' red benches filled to capacity. The most affecting speaker was the aging, crippled former premier Edouard Herriot, who rose to denounce the treaty, Germany, and America. "On the threshold of death," he melodramatically cried, "let me tell you that E.D.C. is the end of France."[66] After two days of caustic debate, the French killed the European Defense Community in a backhanded manner, with a vote on a procedural matter.[67] When the vote was announced — 319 to 264 against EDC — the chamber dissolved in pandemonium. Communist deputies sprang to their feet and sang the Marseillaise. Vanquished supporters of the treaty shouted at them, "Back to Moscow." EDC was, one of its enemies gloated, an idea "born in ambiguity, ripened in intrigue, lies and corruption." And now it was dead.[68]

As the final debate was about to begin, Bruce sketched an assessment in anticipation of defeat, calling it the greatest triumph of Soviet diplomacy since the war. He feared a resurgence of American isolationism, a retreat not just from supporting European integration but from any American presence in Europe.[69] For the next few days, he and Tomlinson were so despondent that they could do little but stare at the walls of their office. Monnet's assistant, Jacques Van Helmont, described them as utterly shattered by the defeat.[70] They were not alone. Adenauer was said to be so incensed that he could not speak for two days.[71]

Evangeline Bruce said the celebrations of the tenth anniversary of the liberation of Paris, held the week of the EDC vote, resembled a wake.[72] Her husband recorded his dismay on the evening Mendès-France spoke against the treaty in the National Assembly. "This evening might well be characterized, as was the famous night when Cortez's warriors battled their way out of Mexico City, as 'La Noche Triste,'" the night of sadness.[73]

In the postmortems, he came in for severe criticism. A venomous campaign in the French press denounced him for attempting to "browbeat" France into accepting America's policy for Europe.[74] Anti-American elements of the British press chimed in. The New Statesman and Nation accused him of participating in a smear campaign against Mitterand by allegedly sending Washington a list of Communist sympathizers in the Mendès-France government that included Mitterand's name. Bruce had to be content to deny the charges in private because he realized that a public debate would serve no purpose.[75]

Perversely, as soon as the French defeated EDC, they agreed to rearm Germany anyway. At a London conference the British promised to keep a stronger military presence on the Continent than before. Using this pledge as a figleaf, Mendès-France approved German entry directly into NATO, in effect allowing Germany to create the national army he had resisted all along. On the eve of this conference, Bruce wisely suggested that his colleagues lie low and avoid offering a solution with "made in America" written on it.[76] He approved of the conference because it achieved much of what EDC had sought, with one exception. The principle of supranational control, with its promise of true European integration, had been lost.

"The German Trojan horse," he mused, invoking half of Bevin's metaphor, "has been wheeled into the citadel."[77] His worries were unfounded. No new von Schlieffen or von Rundstedt arose to plot a vast new envelopment of France. The Germans, in fact, would adhere fastidiously to the limits their constitution imposed on military action.

Monnet did not pause to worry over the defeat. Bruce said, "He easily forgets yesterday, passes over today, and makes plans for tomorrow."[78] Tomlinson was not so lucky. The negotiations literally killed him. He had pushed himself mercilessly throughout the Marshall Plan, even more so as EDC's fortunes waned. Like Bruce, he burned the candle at both ends, partying late into the night after long hours of strategizing and cajoling. But Tomlinson had a bad heart and died from a coronary attack. Bruce and Monnet served as trustees of his children's educational fund, enlarged by generous contributions from the Bruces and, at Monnet's instigation, from the High Authority of the European Coal and Steel Community.[79]

For more than a year, as the fortunes of EDC waned, Bruce ruminated about returning home. He turned down the presidency of the American Red Cross and a generous offer from his friend Phil Graham to buy into ownership of the *Washington Post*.[80] By autumn of 1954 America's special envoy in Paris could at last make serious plans to go home.

Eisenhower and Dulles wanted to keep him on board in some capacity, but Bruce could not be tempted. During a break in the Four Power meeting in Paris in October, Dulles pulled him aside and offered him the embassy in Brazil or West Germany. Neither appealed to him, and he warned the secretary to send someone to Bonn who could speak German.[81] The next offer was the fuzzy one of ambassador-at-large. Bruce politely declined, and Eisenhower graciously wrote him, "I had so set my heart on impressing you into the service here."[82] The most the president could extract was an agreement to consult on European affairs, but for a few weeks only.[83]

Bruce remained adamant against charges he had exerted too much pressure in Brussels. He believed a firmer show of united opposition would have thwarted Mendès-France. It had been a grand display of diplomacy, he thought, in the best traditions of the profession. "I am glad I was at Brussels during the concluding sessions of the Foreign Ministers' meeting. The pro-Europeans went down with the flag of a great cause flying. Mendès, a clever but parochial man, would not, like Bidault before him, seize a great opportunity of historical importance, such as occurs seldom in the life of nations. The others realized how unique was the occasion — he was not blinded by the brilliance of the light, but shaded himself against it. He would have been singularly well fitted to bring this cause to fruition had he so desired. This is, I continue to think, the greatest lost opportunity in modern Western European history."[84]

He admitted that his mission — to rearm Germany within a supranational European organization — had failed.[85] Years later Maurice Couve de Murville, de Gaulle's polished foreign minister, and a Bruce intimate, offered an explanation. His friend, de Murville said, had gotten it wrong. Though he spoke "warmly of David Bruce and thought him very competent," he believed the diplomat "entirely misunderstood the French attitude" about EDC.[86] Bruce did not see that the French did not really want a common European army, even though they proposed it in the first place. That was a fair assessment, but de Murville conveniently neglected to say that France wanted only to shackle Germany and stubbornly failed to see that including rather than excluding the Germans, as Bruce proposed, was the best route to European peace.

Once the Americans adopted EDC as their own policy, French opposition increased. The more Bruce pushed the idea, the more repugnant it became. The outcome, however, would have been no different, even had he acted differently. Bruce admired that master of the diplomatic arts, Talleyrand, who "placed his trust in disguise rather than candor, civility rather than spontaneity, reflection rather than impulse, diplomacy rather than aggression, negotiation behind closed doors rather than orations to public meetings."[87] He liked to quote Talleyrand's maxim *Surtout, pas du zèle*, "Above all, no zeal," and followed it with consummate skill. In his obsession for the European Defense Community, however, even his affinity for Talleyrand's style was not enough.

Ironically, Bruce, who feared German rearmament outside a supranational structure, enhanced Germany's standing by giving Adenauer the chance, through the EDC talks, to prove his people were good Europeans. The European army that Bruce envisioned in the early 1950s was dead for the moment, and a NATO of sovereign states under American leadership took shape instead and stood against the Soviet threat for decades. Thirty-five years later, with the dissolution of the Warsaw Pact, the raison d'être of NATO would come into question. An idea for a supranational European army, not unlike the idea that Bruce supported years before, would flicker to life once more in the minds of French politicians. It was an irony he would have relished.

He could not know of the appointments that lay ahead, or indeed that any lay ahead. Circumstances certainly suggested his diplomatic career was at an end. He was fifty-seven. He was a Democrat. The assignment a popular Republican president had given him had ended in the defeat of American policy. He could not imagine that Eisenhower and four more presidents would call on him to serve again. It was just as well he could not see into the future, for with those assignments would come many frustrations and disappointments. To the public, the work of an ambassador was all glamour and drama. Bruce knew there were less agreeable aspects and would experience them again. And yet, through his prudent counsel, his appeal, and the reserved facade he showed to the world, he would many times over be the essential diplomat, the unsung hero who represented all the best of the Western Alliance and who helped guide it through the Cold War and toward, if not into, the unknown international climate beyond.

After a round of farewell dinners in Paris, David and Evangeline, their three children, two dogs, and nanny boarded a half-empty flight and headed for home five days before Christmas 1954. His retirement had come nearly two years later than planned. Away from the unwelcome glare of publicity, he spent the holidays at Staunton Hill. Instead of cajoling French politicians, he plunged into the mundane, agreeably concrete problems of farm management. Hanging pictures, playing with the children, hunting with his beloved dogs — "thought I was in an earthly Paradise."[88] In his rural arcadia, secluded from the world, he found the urge for self-pity irresistible. On New Year's Eve he sardonically told his diary he did not drink a toast to Mendès-France.[89] But the pain was never far away, and years later he often felt nervous phantom twinges from the amputated stump of EDC.

CHAPTER 15

Marking Time in Georgetown

Power is rather like how Oscar Wilde described society. Being in it is a bore.
Being out of it is a tragedy.

— Anonymous British cabinet minister

*A*FTER A THERAPEUTIC HOLIDAY at Staunton Hill, the
diplomat began the new year by reopening his Georgetown house. With
a host of workmen and cleaners, the Bruces turned off the burglar alarm
and swept into the house, which had been padlocked for a year. By
nightfall the furnace had broken down, the shipping crates were still
unpacked, and the owners were exhausted. By 1955 the Bruces had
shuttled between Washington and Paris enough for the foreign service
rule of thumb — "three moves equals one fire" — to catch up with
them. They were happy to sleep in their own home again, even if their
shivering dogs were not as they lay wrapped in Evangeline's best furs.[1]
The self-deprecating amusement with which he described this chaos
showed how quickly the former emissary to Europe shed the anxiety
of his last two years abroad.

For his private business affairs Bruce rented office space a short walk
down the hill on Wisconsin Avenue. The allure of being near the
center of things kept him from cutting himself off entirely from government. He again told Dulles he did not want any fixed appointment
but agreed to remain briefly as a consultant on European affairs.[2] With
the newspapers speculating about prospects for the administration's
highest-ranking Democratic appointee, Bruce called on Eisenhower.

The president bowed to his wish to return to private life, but he insisted on calling on him for counsel from time to time.[3] And it was time that would tell whether this was merely an expression of Eisenhower *politesse* or an honest wish to have the diplomat's advice.

The Bruces slipped easily into the intense social life that was their trademark. Georgetown was their metier. This cobblestoned WASP enclave boasted a greater aggregation of high-octane, well-connected residents than London SW3 or the 16th arrondissement in Paris. If not as exotic as the glittering salons of France, Georgetown parties nevertheless buzzed with the energy of insiders and would-be insiders. The village's self-regarding sophisticates could hold their own with Europe's haughtiest. They had something the Europeans did not: America was in the ascendant, an aphrodisiac to power junkies everywhere. Egged on by the hostess at one dinner, the brash young vice-president, Richard Nixon, made a fulsome speech praising Bruce. "He said the President had spoken in similar vein at today's National Security Council meeting," Bruce noted approvingly. "Anyhow, kind words break no bones."[4]

As one final bit of business, at a meeting of an interagency committee at State, he summarized the past two years: "I report the failure of a mission, not, to be grandiloquent, the death of a dream." He praised the postwar revolution in foreign affairs that ended American isolationism and extolled the movement for European integration. "History is a graveyard of bright spirits untimely interred, of philosophies derided, of generous impulses buried." He was unrepentant. "Over the horizon lies a hope. Harsh as it is to surrender, even in part, national homogeneity, to venture under supranational auspices, there is nothing in our past to make us proud of the achievements of nationalism. Our religions are universal; there is no reason why our political institutions, with necessary limitations, should function with less freedom than our individual beliefs."[5] He was very much a man of the world, for whom to be in Europe was not to be in a foreign land.

Just as Andrew Mellon had cited Ailsa's desire for broader horizons as a reason for moving to Washington in 1921, in Paris Bruce had talked of returning home to give his children an American education. Nice sentiments, but in neither case the prime reason for the move. Still, it did no harm for the younger Bruces to begin their schooling in their own country. It was none too soon; the youngest, Nicky, was known at first as "Frenchie" by his American schoolmates.[6]

Audrey, a student at Radcliffe, was touchingly ignorant of her financial worth as the only child of the richest woman in America. David advised Ailsa to broach the topic with their daughter. He approached the subject as the beneficiaries of old money often do, with the reticence of a prudish parent telling an adolescent about sex. He proposed delegating the task to a trusted family adviser. "It seems to me," he wrote his former wife, "it would be best, after she becomes twenty-one, for her to spend an afternoon with George White, who could explain in a matter-of-fact way what the situation will be. Later on, I'd be most happy to talk to her on the subject. I did somewhat this summer. The most important thing is to avoid as far as possible any public knowledge of her inheritance."[7]

True to her genes, Audrey was extremely introspective, living "completely in the shadows." Her Uncle Paul, hardly the back-slapping, gregarious type himself, called her "a true introvert," proof, indeed, of her descent from Mellon stock. "In her shy way," he said, "she loved all men and women, all children, all animals."[8] The divorce settlement in 1945 placed Audrey in her mother's custody. David knew Ailsa was hopeless as a parent, but the eye he kept on Audrey was a distant one. Though he did not care for children, he did for young adults. During his Paris years Audrey visited several times, and he delighted in showing her the glories of the city that captivated him when he was her age.

At college she found love. Bruce tried to dissuade her from marrying before she graduated but failed. She eloped with Stephen Currier, a New Yorker whose family hovered on the fringes of the wealthy set. "I think it had been difficult for her," Lauder Greenway recalled, "to find somebody she liked whom nobody else liked or was inclined to try and take away from her. Stephen came from a shattered family; he was thoroughly insecure. . . . He was unfortunate, he wanted to please, but he didn't have the ability to please."[9] Audrey's father could not undo the bonds tied by a justice of the peace. It fell to him to tell Ailsa. To her, a family friend confided, it was "a terrible blow."[10] And the *froideur* with which the family, both Bruces and Mellons, regarded their new son-in-law would never entirely thaw as long as Stephen Currier lived.

Elopement alone would have put Currier at odds with them. In addition, he was "a snotty sort of guy," according to Ailsa's personal physician, and he "disagreed . . . for the sake of disagreeing." Yet there was more to him than that. He and Audrey developed a program of benefactions that, to say the least, went in different directions from traditional Mellon philanthropy. And if their marriage was rocky for a time, in the end Stephen was a good influence on his timid wife.

As a man of means, Bruce began to accumulate the expected titular offices and badges of honor. He became a trustee of Johns Hopkins University, of the Lafayette Foundation, of the National Trust for Historic Preservation, of the Virginia Museum of Fine Arts. Eisenhower appointed him to the Woodrow Wilson centennial commission. And he sat on the Patrick Henry Memorial Foundation board, fittingly, as Henry's house, Red Hill, was the property adjoining Staunton Hill.

He was not interested in charity work, though, and took on only the honorific posts that entailed no more than signing a check or attending an occasional perfunctory board meeting. He was generous — objects presented to the Virginia Museum of Fine Arts, large donations to the restoration of Versailles, a special "Bruce fund" for scholarships for State Department children. But after his experience of war and diplomacy, good works exerted only a pallid attraction.

Gradually his depression over EDC faded to simple boredom. Although he never let himself be overcome by the bile that consumed Acheson in retirement, he did begin to mope around the house in Georgetown. Pamela Harriman remembered that he was "off kilter" and seemed to "need that rudder" that an appointment gave him.[11] Accustomed to dining with Rothschilds, conferring with presidents, and executing the nation's foreign policies, he reached the depth of self-pity on February 20, 1955. His diary read: "I cleaned up the back yard and painted the garbage and trash buckets."[12]

Wine, the psalmist said, maketh glad the heart of man. It certainly did for Bruce, who enjoyed it without apparent ill effect. In the 1930s he earned the nickname "Bordeaux Bruce" among his rummy friends in Manhattan café society.[13] He knew vintages like an idiot savant knows the multiplication tables and traded on that lore to good effect during his French appointments. In the mid-1950s, a tendency to overindulge crept up on him. Feeling "slightly torpid" one morning, he admitted that he and Macgill James may have overdone it the night before, citing as exhibits for the prosecution a bottle of Chevalier-

Montrachet 1947, one of L'Evangile 1943, and one of Clos des Goisses Campagne 1947.[14] Friends sometimes characterized him as "sybaritic" — the same word that Grandfather Charles Bruce elicited from his censorious half brother to describe his high-living style a century before.

In his boredom, he began to nurse a feeling that he had been ill used. By spring he had seen Dulles and Eisenhower only once. They obviously did not feel quite the burning need for his advice that they originally professed.[15] Bruce could not expect to have it both ways — be sought after for advice as a private citizen who refused any fixed assignment at State. When an editor from *Look* magazine asked him to write on European integration, he declined because it would be impossible to do the subject justice without offending many of the participants. It was apparent, though, that the request flattered him.[16]

Things began to look up in 1956 when Eisenhower appointed him to the President's Board of Consultants on Foreign Intelligence Activities, ironically to fill the vacancy left by the resignation of Joseph P. Kennedy.[17] The board deliberated in secret, and it sharply criticized some of the CIA's methods. In one bluntly worded report, Bruce denounced the agency's meddling in the affairs of other nations. The memory of thwarting the CIA's plot in Guatemala, only to have it revived later, was fresh in his mind. The CIA, he said with regret, was filled with "bright, highly graded young men who must be doing something all the time to justify their reason for being."[18]

Eisenhower set up the board partly to deflect scrutiny of the CIA.[19] It served that purpose, but Bruce and his colleagues refused to provide only window dressing. He was always bumping into former OSS colleagues and traded on the mystique more than many veterans. But he looked askance at the obsessions of the intelligence fraternity fighting a cold war that, in the metaphor of John le Carré, pitted half-angels against half-devils. He said after meeting one former OSS man that "the tendency to see a Communist in every corner and under every bed leads him into strange mental paths."[20]

Bruce's appointment was convenient for Ike. The press had begun criticizing him again for ignoring bipartisanship in foreign policy. As long as he held the EDC job, Bruce had made such complaints easy to refute, but that episode became instant ancient history the moment

France torpedoed EDC. Two years later Ike learned it did no harm to have Truman's former undersecretary of state sitting on the board of consultants in an election year.

The ambassador supported Adlai Stevenson in 1956 but knew that he stood no chance of winning. Bruce began to think that Eisenhower was becoming lazy — the conventional miscalculation made about this supremely controlled commander in chief and a judgment some people had made about Bruce, and just as much in error. In Paris Bruce had found the general "absolutely first class." Ike's support of EDC and European integration earned him high marks in the diplomat's assessment. Those earlier opinions in the end tipped the balance in Bruce's overall assessment of Ike. Even before Eisenhower appointed him to the intelligence board, he had come to believe that Ike had earned the status of president of all the people and not just of partisan Republicans.[21]

Soon after Eisenhower was reelected, he offered Bruce the embassy in West Germany. He declined at first, but Ike persisted. When Bruce received the blessing of prominent Democratic senators on the foreign relations committee, he accepted.[22] Confirmation came only after vocal moaning by Senate Republicans. They did not object to Bruce. On the contrary, they vied with the Democrats in singing his praises. But they chose to be highly offended that Ike handed a plum ambassadorship to a man who had given $1,000 to the president's Democratic opponent.[23] Bruce was very much the odd man out among Eisenhower's diplomats. A Senate probe found that nineteen ambassadors gave a total of $218,740 to Ike's campaign. Bruce was the only one who contributed substantially to Stevenson.[24]

Senate Majority Leader Lyndon Johnson chastised his Republican colleagues and branded their complaints about Bruce's nomination an "outrage" that insulted their own president.[25] In the end bipartisanship won out. Senator George Aiken of Vermont said he was "not going to raise any rumpus," but he concluded with poor grace that the appointment killed "any ardor we Senate Republicans might otherwise have to defend the administration from the attacks the Democrats are making on it."[26]

After a unanimous Senate vote, Bruce spent a month of meetings at the State Department, Pentagon, and White House. He knew how important good German-American relations were. One White House meeting in particular laid it out in dramatic fashion. Eisenhower wanted the Allies to rely on their own arms factories. In particular, he hoped West Germany would buy Britain's Centurion tank rather than America's M-48. During the meeting Defense Department bureaucrats made the mistake of revealing they had encouraged the Germans to choose the American tank. "The President almost went through the roof," Bruce said. "I thought he would levitate. His face became congested, his language profane."[27] Ike vowed he would not permit his will being thwarted again.

The diplomat met with the president one last time to take his leave and then flew with Evangeline to New York in Paul Mellon's plane before going abroad. The night before boarding a TWA flight to Europe, while the Bruces and the Mellons were dining out, the former Edward VIII of England and his wife turned up at the restaurant. The former king had often told Bruce how much he envied him for having known Wallis when she was a girl in Baltimore. In his awkward way, on this evening the duke reminded everyone of his dubious wartime loyalties and at the same time made Bruce uneasy about his deficiency in language: "The Windsors were there," the ambassador noted in his diary. "He addressed me in German, quite incomprehensible."[28]

CHAPTER 16

Proconsul on the Rhine

The Russians got the State Opera, the Royal Palace, the government buildings, and some of the worst slums; the Western Powers got the Zoo, the parks, the department stores, the nightclubs, and the villas of the rich in Grunewald. And spiked through both sectors, like a skewer through a shish kebab, there is the "East-West Axis."

— Len Deighton, *Berlin Game*

*D*URING THE NIGHT of June 23–24, 1948, two weeks after Bruce arrived in Paris for the Marshall Plan, Soviet patrols stopped rail and autobahn traffic into Berlin. Deep within Soviet territory and dependent on the outside for fuel and food, the non-Communist half of the city faced strangulation. At a stroke, Stalin undermined the Allies' tenuous hold on Berlin. They replied with a risky airborne relief effort that threw the challenge back at the Soviets, who could defeat it only by attacking the unarmed supply planes as they homed in on the jammed runways of Tempelhof field. Stalin declined to escalate to a shooting war and eventually backed down. Berlin forced the Allies to think hard about Germany's future. The Federal Republic that emerged rapidly thereafter would provide the setting for David Bruce's latest assignment abroad.

A decade after Hitler, western Germany's economic miracle, the *Wirtschaftswunder*, had transformed the land. Its immense power meant that once more the engine of European prosperity would bear a "Made in Germany" label. Internally the 1950s were tranquil. Chancellor Konrad Adenauer believed his country needed a long stretch of boredom *über alles*. An electoral system favoring the two big parties, Adenauer's Christian Democrats and the opposition Social Democrats, worked in his favor. Critics assailed him for a slavish pro-Western tilt and lack of imagination in dealing with the East. But it worked for the best.[1] Under the black, red, and gold tricolor of the nation's nineteenth-century democrats, he skillfully nurtured German fealty to the West. Paradoxically, it was the cranky, authoritarian Adenauer who sired modern democratic Germany.

Externally, things were less pacific. A divided Germany remained the central, unpredictable issue in Europe. In 1953 workers in the Communist German Democratic Republic in the east revolted and were put down brutally by Stalin's tanks. The Soviets branded West Germany a bastard, revanchist state run by crypto-Nazis who menaced all of Europe as they rearmed under the aegis of NATO. Whether the Soviets really feared the Bundeswehr, this line earned them points with Germany's wary neighbors. The Allies were not entirely pure either. They fervently called for reunion, secure in the conviction it would never happen.

Washington looked on West Germany as the linchpin in the defense against Soviet aggression. Bruce did not have to ask Eisenhower and Dulles the question he had posed when they wanted to send him to Paris in 1953, namely, whether they considered the job a top priority or window dressing. Germany was the hot seat of the Cold War. The objective he went to Bonn to uphold — keeping Germany tied firmly to the West — had been a constant of postwar American policy. Britain and France had vacillated in their nurture of Weimar, and Hitler showed how disastrously they miscalculated. America tried its hand once a democratic, truncated Germany sprouted from the rubble of war. This was the "German Problem" Bruce inherited and the one he and his generation bequeathed to those who followed.

At the Frankfurt airport on April 10, 1957, he met the first of the grand trappings of his office in the shape of the ambassador's personal train, a locomotive and three cars, which carried him in style the short distance to Bonn. Twelve years after the Allies had marched into the prostrate Reich — even after West Germany regained a measure of sovereignty — they still incongruously maintained a proconsular style more appropriate to occupiers than allies. The new ambassador knew how much Germany had changed since he toured the country for OSS in summer 1945, when cartons of Lucky Strikes and tins of Spam were the coins of the realm. Eight years later, during his visits for the prospective European Defense Community, he marveled at the "tremendous vitality" he saw in Germany, and it both amazed him and filled him with foreboding.[2]

Bonn was only temporarily the capital, which would move to Berlin after the unification that everyone gave lip service to but never quite believed would happen. Bruce expected this quiet university town, the birthplace of Beethoven, to have at best only a certain provincial allure. Bonn, wisecracks said, was twice the size of the Chicago cemetery and half as lively.[3] It was chosen over the more logical, larger cities, they said, when Adenauer realized that Rhondorf, his own village just across the river from Bonn, was too small.[4] For Bruce, wartime London, Marshall Plan Paris, and even Washington in Truman's troubled last year far outshone the dowdy village on the Rhine.

The ambassador's residence in suburban Bad Godesberg struck its new occupant on first sight as "architecturally ghastly." Behind the hideous yellow facade of the Victorian house on Rolandstrasse, though, were quite comfortable living quarters. The Bruces arrived just as the wisteria and pink horse chestnuts ushered in spring. At the back of the residence an enormous terraced garden sloped down to the Rhine, opposite the Drachenfels of the Siegfried legend and the rapids of Heinrich Heine's seductive Lorelei. A fifteen-minute walk along the bank took the ambassador to his office, with its own stunning view of the river.[5]

To be back in Europe, in harness once again, pleased him immensely. During the past two years at home he had kept the lease on La Lanterne, an extravagance even for him, but a way to retain a private European base. Now, given a chance to serve once more, he reluctantly decided to give up the Versailles retreat, "the happiest house I ever lived in."[6] Evangeline Bruce went to La Lanterne to ship their remaining belongings to Germany. She left a huge, cast-iron Diana they had planted in the garden, but her husband lovingly took possession in his

Bad Godesberg wine cellar of "some five-odd thousand bottles of nectar" from Versailles.[7]

His first order of business was to present his credentials and meet senior German officials. To start the process, he went not to the foreign ministry but to a spa run by Franciscans in the Black Forest. There he presented his letter of credence to the ailing president of the Federal Republic, Dr. Theodor Heuss. Heuss's doctoral thesis on wine gave the two men a common enthusiasm to talk about.[8]

Bruce had met Foreign Minister Heinrich von Brentano before — in his description, "polite and self-assured, a man of presence, neither handsome nor ugly, horn-rimmed as to glasses, a large, sometimes beaming face."[9] A chain-smoker like the American ambassador, the nervous, overweight minister preferred to conduct his rapid conversations in German, though he was perfectly fluent in English. Bruce was delighted to have as the state secretary of the foreign ministry his old friend from EDC days and fellow European unionist Walter Hallstein, a confidant to guide him through the nuances of German government and politics. When Hallstein's doctors forced him to take a month of complete rest, Bruce used the news to cable Washington about the "almost pathetic shortage [of] competent personnel" in the foreign office. Years of disarray caused by nazification, then war, then denazification had taken their toll.[10]

At the embassy he presided over a formidable establishment, almost five hundred Americans and twice as many German nationals. He was ambassador to an ally, no longer an occupied country, but as inheritor of the high commissioner's role, his domain was like no other in the foreign service. There was the usual superabundance of bureaucrats from other agencies whose loyalties sometimes conflicted with their nominal allegiance to the ambassador. They were part of all large missions. What set Bonn apart was the vast American military presence.

No other diplomat represented the president in a country that billeted so powerful an American army, several hundred thousand strong. With so many of his countrymen in West Germany, friction was inevitable. Bruce rated German-American relations good but had to cope with intermittent, arrogant complaints about too many German members of the embassy club and fights between German civilians and GIs.[11]

The huge CIA establishment also set Bonn apart. Fresh from serving on Ike's intelligence committee, he knew about the role of espionage when he became ambassador to the chief playground of Cold War spies. With more than a thousand Germans on the payroll, his embassy presented a fat target for agents from the East. Despite occasional flutters about spies underfoot agitating the staff, he intended to keep a tight rein on CIA activity and avoid embarrassment from the intelligence cowboys. He called in the CIA station chief, John Bross, and told him bluntly he did not want to hear the sound of a single CIA spade digging without his approval.[12]

That was not to say there was no digging. His Georgetown friend Frank Wisner, an OSS veteran, may have told him what to expect. Since the beginning of the decade, the wealthy, mercurial Wisner had manipulated the CIA's shadow warfare in Germany, spending hundreds of millions in unvouchered funds on what he called his "mighty Wurlitzer" of espionage schemes.[13] ("'Whenever we want to subvert any place,' he once allegedly confided about CIA operations world wide, 'we find the British own an island within easy reach.'"[14])

By the time Bruce arrived in Bonn, the futile, paramilitary operations against the East using émigré groups had diminished. Still, the CIA's appetite could not be sated for propaganda and for intelligence about life behind the iron curtain — not to mention the enormously expensive secret payments to politicians and labor leaders and subsidies of writers, arts festivals, and pro-Western but left-leaning journals and cultural activities, all in aid of the massive psychological campaign for hearts and minds in Central Europe. Bruce may not have been privy to all of these, but he was aware of their pervasive role on the front line of the Cold War.

On a less sinister level, he reserved great contempt for politicians who chided embassies to tighten their belts while their own hands were deep in the public till.[15] "David is furious about the scandalous use of American counterpart funds by congressional junkets," wrote a journalist friend. "They come abroad on missions, draw funds in local currency, and spend them on nightclubs, poker, presents. They don't have to account for this. The embassies are instructed to make money available and these 'missions' abroad are classified so nobody is able to check."[16]

Viewed from the angle of official entertaining, Bonn weighed less heavily than other capitals. Bruce even thought that a foreign service officer with little outside income might be able to afford the post.[17] He appreciated the less stressful ambience. "Compared with Paris," he said, "it is a long vacation from the cruel and unnatural punishment inflicted on the Ambassador and his associates there."[18]

Bruce had escaped the horrors of the trenches and returned home from World War I without hating the German people. The second war affected him differently. In 1943 he wrote, "I hope nothing like this [war] will ever be allowed to happen again. It means a vast and irretrievable waste of human effort and ingenuity aside from the loss of material things. And all due to the mad ambitions of one nation."[19] He would always remember the friends, especially Tommy Hitchcock, who died in Hitler's war, and he could never forget what the Gestapo had done to some of his OSS agents.

His mistrust of Germany endured long after the war and gave him another reason to support Monnet's goals for European unity. Finding himself ambassador to the source of so much grief, he wondered privately about the Germans: "How this seemingly docile, domestic, sentimental, animal and child-loving race can be turned into terrible warriors and cruel civilians, capable of . . . torturing a gallant foe, standing firm against insuperable military odds, and demonstrating such contradictions of character and behavior is beyond my comprehension."[20] The question had troubled thoughtful Germans ever since the kaiser's war. "I can imagine their beating the sword into a plough-share," Bruce observed, "but find it hard to envisage their attaining an undivided soul — Faust may be in most of them."[21] At the end of his tour, still skeptical, he reminded a friend of the old saw that Germans were either at your throat or at your feet.

Not surprisingly, in contrast to France, Bruce did not develop ties with a wide range of political and cultural figures. Because he never had an affinity for the Germans, many of them tended to "resent him as a snob or to underrate him as a hedonist," as one American journalist put it.[22] This shortcoming confirmed some of them in their belief that he was "more interested in his wine cellar than in German politics."[23] Though better-informed officials in Bonn dismissed these rebukes as complaints of the disgruntled, the impression was given and Bruce did little to dispel it.

His inability to speak the language did not help matters. Leafing through a German grammar during his EDC tour, he confessed, "I deplore my indifference to the attempts of the Fraulein, whom Mother engaged when we were children, to fix at least elementary German in my noodle."[24] His weekly German tutor in Bonn despaired, and his linguist spouse said she could not teach him to string together the simplest grammatical sentence *auf Deutsch*. Their frustration suggested more a lack of enthusiasm than of ability.

If he failed to develop contacts with a broad range of Germans, he knew very well how to cultivate good relations with the most important one. His success there more than compensated for any other failing, for he enjoyed the most frequent access and most intimate relationship with Adenauer of the whole diplomatic corps. He compared the chancellor's Germany to China during the last years of the dowager empress and attributed the lull in partisan discord to Adenauer's domination.[25]

At talks on the Schuman Plan when he was ambassador in Paris, Bruce had first observed the "granite-faced, hard and intelligent" Adenauer in action.[26] To his lasting credit, the chancellor resolved "to bring Germany into the family of western nations," Bruce said then, "but he talks too much and is tactless."[27] His opinion of Adenauer warmed when they were allies fighting for the EDC: "He is really a remarkable man, 77 years of age with great vitality, over six feet tall with an impassive face, rather flat features, almost mongolian in appearance. He is witty, and has great dignity."[28] In Bonn he spoke of Adenauer's magnetism and kindly appeal, traits that made him "paternal without patronization."[29]

As an exponent of Monnet's ideas, Adenauer shared the same vision for the Continent as Bruce. The ambassador looked on approvingly in 1957 as Adenauer signed the Treaty of Rome that enabled the Six — West Germany, France, Italy, and the Benelux countries — to form the European Economic Community. A Rhinelander mistrustful of Prussians, Adenauer was more a European federalist than a German anyway. Germans, he said, were "Belgians with megalomania."[30] Though he gave lip service to reunion, he was content to create a viable West Germany first. "I think patience is the sharpest weapon of the defeated," he said. "I can wait."[31]

Adenauer developed a personal relationship with Bruce despite differences in age and language. And personal habit. For the chancellor's loathing of tobacco drove the smokers in his inner circle to distraction and must have inhibited the ambassador's ability to relax in his presence. But they did share a love of art and wine that gave them agreeable topics to share beyond international politics. Speaking the language was not as important as personal chemistry; Adenauer disliked Bruce's predecessor, former Harvard president James Conant, despite Conant's flawless German.[32]

Adenauer valued Bruce's counsel and habitually asked him to come and chat informally, "as his friend Mr. Bruce and not as Ambassador." Bruce learned that whenever der Alte proposed a conversation on these terms he meant to express doubts about some aspect of American policy. He chose to look on these sessions as a way for Adenauer to "let off steam" and was careful about what he passed along through diplomatic channels because the chancellor also requested that his comments be considered private.[33] On the other hand, he found himself frequently cast as a go-between because Adenauer counted on him to relay his opinions to Eisenhower. Every meeting with the German leader, then, required Bruce to figure out exactly how much der Alte wanted him to tell Ike.

Now and then the press published bogus rumors of friction. In February 1959 the French paper *Le Monde* spread the story that the two had become so estranged that Dulles had to fly out to patch up German-American relations. When Bruce showed the article to Adenauer, der Alte "had a great cackle" over it.[34] He thought Adenauer showed a sound sense of his country's needs and obligations. Though many would not agree that the chancellor did enough to atone for German sins, Bruce believed he had done more than anyone thought possible in this regard in his relations with Israel.[35]

Bonn frankly bored Bruce. But he knew he had been sent there to be the chief contact with Adenauer, and that was exactly what he did.

Two weeks after arriving in Germany, his private train traveled east, through the Soviet zone to the former capital of the Reich, the anomaly that was Cold War Berlin. As ambassador, he wore the hat of high commissioner of the U.S. Occupation Power when in Berlin, hence the need for an early visit to show the flag. The city's typically leaden skies, beloved of spy novelists, derived in part from the pall of smoke that often covered the whole region, a product of the polluting brown coal burned in East German power plants. But on his first trip the weather did not lend its usual conspiratorial gloom. As the train clattered eastward through the German Democratic Republic, though the countryside looked pretty in the spring sunlight, it was ramshackle buildings and the rough, neglected roadbed rather than clouds that presaged the starker contrasts of Berlin itself.

Ever since the Berlin airlift, the city was fixed in Western minds as the flashpoint of the Cold War, the tripwire of Armageddon. The division of the city began to take shape before the airlift ended: the Soviets established a separate city council in their sector and cut off telephone service with the western half. Though the border reopened after the blockade, the axis dividing the city defined a contrast that grew sharper with each passing year.

The proconsular trappings that surrounded American officials in Germany persisted longest in Berlin. After stopping at the mission headquarters, Bruce received a nineteen-gun salute and reviewed the troops. A platoon of cavalry, the last in the whole American army, gave an archaic finish to the martial display honoring Eisenhower's personal representative in this outpost a hundred miles inside the Soviet empire.[36]

He met the mayor of West Berlin, the American, British, and French military commanders, and the Soviet ambassador to the Communist client state. Given Georgii Pushkin's reputation for ruthlessness, Bruce had not expected the short, well-mannered diplomat, with twinkling eyes and melodious voice, to be so witty and agreeable. After pleasantries over coffee, Armenian brandy, and Caucasian wine, however, when they set down to business, Bruce received his introduction to the sharp end of Cold War Berlin diplomacy.

Recent Soviet provocations demanded an official protest. Soviet control officers had prevented an American official, traveling under Bruce's orders on a diplomatic passport, from entering Berlin. It was the most recent in a string of cases infringing on clearly spelled-out rights of access. Pushkin, "unfailingly polite" throughout, disavowed any authority in the matter, saying his government had delegated control over checkpoints to the military. Bruce countered that he had no intention of dealing with the Red Army, only with Pushkin as his diplomatic equivalent. He concluded that these incidents were "unnecessary, time-consuming and extremely boring."[37] True, but all part of the game. Welcome to Berlin, Mr. Ambassador.

After he left the Soviet embassy, he gave a short speech at the Berlin Senat replete with the usual pledges of solidarity with the people of Germany and their desire for reunification. His hosts laid on a heavy Teutonic lunch interlarded with toasting and speechifying, an early example of what Bruce later called the Germans' "infinite capacity to absorb oratory in large doses."[38] He then answered questions from Senat members. The one that preoccupied them most was American intentions about the security of their city.[39]

Divided Berlin offered the stock symbol for Western propaganda during the Cold War. Bruce participated in the war of words by making periodic radio broadcasts that today sound stilted. They were hypocritical, as were all Allied statements on reunification, in denouncing "the tyrannical and illogical division" that most non-Germans secretly hoped would continue indefinitely. And yet, as stereotyped as they were, his speeches pointed to undeniable facts that no amount of special pleading by Western apologists of the Soviet system could controvert. "Nowhere," he said in a Fourth of July broadcast in 1957, "is the contrast better exemplified than in the city of Berlin. West of the Brandenburg Gate has arisen from ruins a vibrant, stimulating metropolis. The Soviet Sector of the same city presents a drab, monotonous, gloomy spectacle of a sullen population, arbitrarily deprived of the opportunity for rehabilitation, reconstruction or self-expression."[40]

On another trip to the city, he inspected the refugee camps for Germans leaving the East. Already as many as a quarter of a million people a year were streaming across the border. The ambassador admired the efficient system for processing the torrent of newcomers, who carried only a suitcase or two of belongings. They all received medical examinations, vetting by intelligence officers to weed out spies and pass on eligibility for asylum, and job interviews for employment in the West — all accomplished expeditiously so that no refugee remained in the facility for more than a few days.[41] But then the Germans had a certain talent for processing large numbers of people in camps.

Twelve years into his twenty-year sentence for war crimes, Albert Speer had reconciled himself to his drab routine within the electrified perimeter of Berlin's Spandau prison. A huge, dilapidated complex that once housed hundreds, Spandau in 1958 held only three Nazi war criminals. Speer, the official architect and war production wizard of the Third Reich, occupied his days writing and gardening. One morning as he crouched down to weed his small garden patch, under the not-so-watchful eyes of a bored personal guard, an unexpected visitor startled him. Before Speer realized what was happening, the visitor began pumping his hand vigorously, saying repeatedly in English, "You aren't forgotten."[42]

David Bruce had come to see Spandau for himself, last remnant of the wartime alliance between the West and the Soviets. With the connivance of American guards, who tricked their Russian counterparts, he was able to have a brief chat with Speer. He spoke of his effort, in accordance with American policy, to persuade the Soviets to release the Spandau inmates. Two months later, Speer gratefully noted that better lighting was installed in his cell. He had told Bruce that he gave up drawing because of the poor illumination and gave him credit for the new lights. Thanks to the ambassador's solicitude, Hitler's architect resumed his drawing and eventually his practice on his release eight years later.

The case of Speer stands out among the twisted biographies of the leading Nazis. Now it was the turn of the American ambassador, like others before him, to be charmed by the handsome, cultured architect. Many people shared Bruce's belief that the judgment at Nuremberg did Speer "a comparative misjustice" and jailed him "rather for his extraordinary ability than for proven crimes."[43] What Speer did with that ability, Bruce seems to have forgotten, had much to do with those Faustian qualities he had surmised were the most telling trait of the German people. Speer alone among the Nuremberg defendants acknowledged general responsibility for war crimes, but his denial of any knowledge of the death camps made his contrition specious. He was denying knowledge of a great evil that his brilliant labors as armaments minister greatly prolonged. Bruce, like many others, failed to see that the cultured, well-bred Speer was as guilty as the thugs who emptied the canisters of Zyklon B at Auschwitz.

An ambassador, as the mouthpiece of his country, must deal officially with people who in private life he would avoid. Bruce never flinched from treating in polite firmness with the most unsavory characters. He might privately call the Soviet ambassador "a poisonous weasel," as he did in Paris, yet in public he earned his reputation as the consummate practitioner of *politesse*. But it was allies more than enemies that required him to swallow hardest.

On Bastille Day 1958, he and his wife visited Alfried Krupp, heir to the notorious steel and munitions conglomerate. Krupp had been re- leased from prison seven years earlier and his vast properties returned to him in a controversial act of clemency by John McCloy, the American high commissioner. Apprehensive about the visit at first, Bruce found his host "about the last man one would casually think of as having been a war criminal."[44] Later he accepted Krupp's invitation to his private hunting preserve. Bruce did not reveal his thoughts about the irony of blasting away at Krupp's pheasants where, not so long before, Nazi bigwigs had been the honored guests.[45] His comments on Krupp's appeal, like his reaction to Speer, suggest that his emphasis on style had its limitations.

The ambassador's contact with Krupp, however, did advance the cause of justice in a small way. Bruce supplied the good offices of his embassy to help Jewish groups pressing Krupp to make financial res- titution to former slave laborers in his factories. Bruce was part of the soft approach. He arranged for Krupp to invite McCloy to lunch at his gargantuan, 300-room estate, Villa Hügel, during a visit in 1959. Be- cause of Krupp's personal debt to McCloy, perhaps the former high commissioner could nudge the industrialist in the right direction. In the end it took the hard approach — threats of lawsuits and confiscation of property — to force an agreement.

Bruce's office helped a little there as well. Finally, without admitting any legal liability, Krupp agreed to pay $2 million to former Jewish slave laborers, "to help heal the wounds suffered" during the war. The grudging spirit and the small sum each survivor received — less than $1,200 apiece — brought down widespread condemnation on the deal.

Still, small as the amounts were, if it had not been for the persistence of those demanding payment, Krupp would never have consented voluntarily.[46]

Shoring up Western defense topped the list of policies Bruce advocated in Bonn. He knew he must balance the need to urge an ally to maintain defense spending with the equal need to avoid the appearance of interfering in internal affairs. It especially irritated him to receive repeated demands from the Defense Department to badger the Germans about their military budget: "One of the greatest difficulties, it seems to me, in the successful formulation and execution of American foreign policy is due to the extent to which the Pentagon determines policy."[47] His distaste for the predominance of the military focused on its civilian head, Secretary Charles Wilson, "that meteor of Defense," no better, Bruce snidely thought, than Neanderthal man when it came to articulating American policy.[48]

His relations with the secretary of state were more complex. In June 1958 Adenauer had told him that the Soviet foreign minister complained "he would rather negotiate with the Devil than with Dulles."[49] Bruce did not dispute it. He knew how rigid Dulles could be and disliked his arrogance and inability to listen.[50]

Bruce, the consummate listener, saw that an intense command of argument often made for an inability to engage in real discussion. The secretary's forthright demeanor could serve the country well, and Bruce often remarked so. He marveled at Dulles's analytical power, his capacity to seize the salient point in a confusing problem and come to the heart of the matter.[51] But it more often than not caused irritation when a more emollient approach might succeed. It was left to Bruce, as the man on the spot, to soothe Adenauer's nerves when Dulles cavalierly misspoke in January 1959 about possible routes to reunification other than free, all-German elections. Bruce said, with more equanimity than he felt, "I wish Foster would stop dropping tinder into powder kegs by being over-frank in press conferences."[52]

Not long after arriving, Bruce anticipated trouble brewing for German-American relations. He feared that, after Adenauer, Bonn would see disarmament as the only route to unification.[53] If West Germany succumbed to the allure of neutrality, he believed, NATO would be dissolved and the way paved for an unpredictable, extremist regime in the united Germany.[54]

In 1957 his former colleague George Kennan brought the issue to the fore with a controversial lecture at Oxford. When questioned, Bruce admitted that Kennan was right about one thing: neutralization seemed the only likely way Germany could be united. Unlike Kennan, he thought that a disastrous outcome.[55] Because the New York Times garbled his interpretation, a State Department spokesman in Washington publicly slapped his wrists and dismissed his comments as "just a personal view."[56] The opposition Social Democrats magnified his chagrin when they circulated a memorandum implying he agreed with Kennan.[57]

In early 1958 Bruce's political specialists at the embassy thought they detected a growing receptiveness for the solution Kennan proposed. Despite Adenauer's reelection the previous autumn, "symptoms of malaise are unmistakable, and the Soviets have increased opportunity to influence and exploit this climate to suit their own purposes."[58] Adenauer resisted them, but the forces for accommodating the Soviets by disarming were growing in strength. In retrospect, this assessment was much too gloomy for the time, though it did anticipate German sentiment two decades later.

The German question troubled both East and West, but for the first part of Bruce's tenure in Bonn it only simmered. Then, in late 1958, Soviet leader Nikita Khrushchev touched off a crisis. He demanded that Berlin be demilitarized and made an "open city," leading to a peace treaty with both German states that would formally end the war. If the West refused, he threatened to turn over all Soviet rights in the former capital to the East Germans. The Western powers denied his right to abrogate the responsibilities that the Soviets shared with them in Berlin. Khrushchev's proposal outlined the policy he would follow for several years, with a free, united, and demilitarized Berlin as the ultimate solution. He further rattled the West by proposing the Soviet solution for Berlin as the model for the whole country.

The crisis convinced Bruce — incorrectly — that a divided Germany, with the added anomaly of Berlin, could not continue. Though he could not see his way out of the dilemma, he thought the West must try negotiating with the Soviets. America's position maintained that German disunity posed a great danger for Europe. He was not so sure. Still, he thought the United States should adhere to this line out of loyalty to Bonn. Perhaps in time, he thought, the hemorrhage of skilled East Germans and Soviet fears of a revived German military power might give America some leverage.[59]

During another visit to Berlin late in 1958, as was the custom whenever the ambassador came to town, he motored over to the Soviet sector to show the flag. As soon as his car passed the Brandenburg Gate and the grassy mound over the Führerbunker, the whole vista, not just the sky, turned gray. The Soviets had poured tremendous resources into their zone, just as the Allies had done to turn theirs into "a vitrine for Western prosperity within the Eastern bloc."[60] But the Soviets produced only drab monuments to their failure along Stalinallee, "dull as ditchwater," in Bruce's words. Piles of rubble and bomb-damaged buildings remained long after the western half of the city rebuilt. On his return to the Allied zone, Christmas decorations along the glowing Kurfürstendamm, gaudy though they were, greeted Bruce with yet another reaffirmation of the free West.[61] West Berlin's energetic young mayor, "generous, sympathetic and outgoing" Willi Brandt, struck Bruce as "just the man for a crisis."[62] But was the city really worth fighting for?

Back in Bonn he ruminated on the problem. In February he shared his thoughts in a cable to the secretary of state and the ambassadors in Paris, London, and Moscow. More than ever, he said, America must resist the chimera of German reunification on the basis of neutrality. Such a development would kill Adenauer's goal of linking Germany with Western Europe. Monnet's vision, embodied in the European Economic Community, remained at the forefront of Bruce's mind. By destroying the Federal Republic's allegiance to the West, neutrality would erode the "most promising development in Europe for centuries." The result would be "to accept the prospect of a vital people adrift in Central Europe, without anchor or moorings, repudiated by friends, wooed by enemies." Germany would become "a floating mine."[63]

Bruce's tenure in Bonn ended before Khrushchev gave both East and West a period of equilibrium with the twenty-eight-year Wall erected in 1961. Given the events of 1989–91, the fears Bruce expressed about German reunification and neutrality may yet prove prescient.

When he accepted the job, Bruce promised Eisenhower he would stay for two years. After only six months, Dulles heard a rumor that he was going to retire and nervously said he hoped the story was untrue. Bruce reassured him that he planned to remain *en poste* for at least the two years, as long as he retained Ike's confidence.

By the summer of 1959, press reports about his tenure passed the nuisance level.[64] What fueled the speculation was the fact that he did *not* leave after two years. The problems over Berlin, successive postponing of a foreign ministers' meeting and a possible summit, and German domestic political maneuvering all conspired to delay his departure. Adenauer jumped into the act by asking Bruce if he objected if he, the chancellor, request that the ambassador stay on until the planned visit of Eisenhower to Moscow.[65] When Ike visited Adenauer in the fall, the chancellor asked him if the diplomat could stay on permanently.[66] It was his way of complimenting Bruce and regretting the necessity of his leaving.

Bruce devised a graceful way to exit and avoid becoming hostage to the elusive summit schedule. He recommended that he return to Washington for consultation. His retirement would not be announced until Eisenhower had chosen a successor. Thus Adenauer would not feel left in the lurch. State agreed, and Bruce left at the end of October without the usual farewell pleasantries.[67] He learned later that Adenauer was not miffed and had even asked that Bruce be returned as ambassador to Bonn after his successor's tenure was up.

Bruce had been the most important American in the Federal Republic at a time when his country was Germany's most important ally. And yet the assignment never engaged him the way the Marshall Plan, the Paris embassy, and EDC had done. Neither did it call on him to function in time of great crisis. He missed Suez and the Hungarian revolution in 1956. He left nearly two years before the Berlin Wall. Nevertheless, he earned Eisenhower's respect as well as Adenauer's. Bruce, the president privately told a journalist, "was the best ambassador the United States had ever had."[68]

If Bonn did not excite him as much as directing the Marshall Plan in Paris or fighting for the doomed EDC, it did confer an important blessing. It kept him in play in the foreign policy game during the years of Democratic exile. He held an anomalous place in the American *nomenklatura:* he was not a career foreign service officer but neither was he a purely partisan appointee who might alternate diplomacy with elective office as Harriman did. But his wealth was a luxury that could work against him. If he had remained in private life, he would have lost his edge, his visibility, and his credibility as a leading member of the Democratic foreign policy elite. Bonn therefore usefully kept current his membership on the first team in case another, more desirable opportunity presented itself.

CHAPTER 17

An Honorary Englishman

English policy is to float lazily downstream, occasionally putting out a diplomatic boathook to avoid collisions.

— 3rd Marquess of Salisbury, 1877

Great Britain has lost an empire and has not yet found a role.

— Dean Acheson, 1962

ON A SUNNY, unseasonably warm March morning, David Bruce put on his top hat for the ride to Buckingham Palace. He was accompanied by the marshal of the diplomatic corps, whose predecessor had introduced him to George V at a levee nearly three decades before. Past a sparse group of staring tourists, he rode in a heavily gilded carriage drawn by two horses and outfitted with a footman in a long red coat. Though fading as a global power, Britain yielded place to no one in flaunting the appurtenances of imperial ceremony. After the carriage clattered into an inner palace courtyard, Bruce walked to the throne room to present his letters of credence to Queen Elizabeth II and introduce his wife. Protocol dictated that she, not being an official, arrive at a separate entrance by automobile — ironic, given the role she played in her husband's embassies.

The ceremony required no set speeches, though ritual dictated everything, down to the three bows made before a word was spoken. Monarch and diplomat enjoyed an animated chat, and the whole business was over in less than twenty minutes. When he returned to the residence in Regent's Park, the now-official American envoy ordered champagne for everyone and sugar for the horses.

In hindsight, the route from Bonn to London ran fairly straight, though at the time it did not seem so. After returning home from Germany in October 1959, Bruce was bemused and a little irritated at the reaction of his Georgetown friends. They regarded him, he testily noted, "as if I were already half dead" and seemed incapable of conceiving how he would pass his days cut off from the narcotic of affairs of state.[1] They should have known better. Even before he left Bonn, press reports anticipated his resignation as a move to position himself for appointment in the hoped-for new Democratic administration; some even named him as a potential secretary of state.

Georgetown, that ghetto of incumbents and aspirants to high office, was, *Town and Country* sniffed, a place "where 'the thinking rich' live — old-fashioned, upper-class liberals, Democrats who know how to dress yet devote themselves to government service."[2] Since their marriage, David and Evangeline Bruce had lived longer in Europe than at home. When they returned to the house on 34th Street in late 1959, though, they instantly ranked among the best-known and best-connected denizens of the nation's premier political village. For by then Evangeline Bruce had finely tuned the social antennas needed to remain at the center of things.

The state of the nation in 1960 combined anxiety and boredom. Worries over Sputnik and the bomb stoked fear of nuclear annihilation when people began to realize what the marriage of those two technologies meant. Civil defense became a watchword. When Bruce added a wing to his house and excavated beneath it for a wine cellar, the neighbors assumed he was digging a bomb shelter. America was also bored — bored with eight years of Eisenhower calm and ready for a change. Vice-President Nixon carried the baggage of incumbency but few of its advantages. Despite the legendary presidential debates, the mood for change more than Nixon's five o'clock shadow gave John F. Kennedy his brief shining moment in Washington.

Kennedy first had to win his party's nomination. That meant disposing of his rivals, the garrulous Senator Hubert Humphrey; Adlai Stevenson, the party's two-time albatross who dithered about running again; and Senate majority leader Lyndon B. Johnson. Kennedy money and influence enabled the brash, handsome senator from Massachusetts to forge ahead of the others.

Bruce knew from private chats that Stevenson lacked the temperament for political rough-and-tumble, in fact hated it. But the diplomat and his wife supported him out of solidarity with Marietta Tree, Stevenson's intimate friend and tireless promoter.[3] She had married Ronald Tree after he and Nancy, now Nancy Lancaster, divorced, and the Trees moved from England to Manhattan. After Macgill James, Ronnie Tree was Bruce's oldest friend. He remained an incorrigible Tory even as his new wife threw herself into liberal causes, laboring to transcend the stereotype of the beautiful grand dame. ("What do I have to do not to be called a socialite?" she once asked.[4]) She became used to having her husband burst into their apartment during her committee meetings demanding to know, in his plummy accent, "Who *are* all these rotters?"[5] And so for Marietta's sake, David and Evangeline loyally supported Adlai.

The Bruces went to the Democratic convention in Los Angeles with Kay and Phil Graham, although they backed different candidates. At the height of his powers as editor of his wife's *Washington Post*, brilliant, boorish Phil Graham was enjoying a last burst of manic energy before his final crack-up. He went to Los Angeles hellbent on playing the kingmaker, convinced he could deliver the nomination to Johnson.[6] As momentum built for Kennedy, Graham shifted allegiance just in time to back the winner. Despite this last-minute switch, he greatly influenced the nominee, even convinced him to break his promise to Missouri Senator Stuart Symington and offer second place on the ticket to Johnson.[7] Graham would later attempt to wield his power in Bruce's behalf.

After his nomination, Kennedy appointed Bruce to a team of national security experts to advise him. He wanted them divorced from the campaign so they could make broad, nonpartisan consultations. The goal, the senator said, was to have in place a plan to move swiftly during the transition in the pursuit of America's foreign interests.[8] The ambassador did not remain entirely above politics, though. Friends in Charlotte County urged him to speak out because they believed the Bruce endorsement still carried weight in Virginia. He obliged with a radio broadcast that denounced the "shameful" prejudice of many southern voters against Catholics. Virginia went for Nixon, but Bruce was proud he had opposed what he called the "clumsy, barbaric instrument" of religious bigotry, just as he had done in Maryland in the 1920s when he condemned the Klan.[9]

Kennedy squeaked past Nixon, thanks, the disgruntled said, to stuffed ballot boxes in Chicago and dead Texans doing their civic duty. Corruption and Republican sour grapes aside, however narrowly the people chose Kennedy, he put his stamp on the nation's mood. The Camelot image makers presented to an adoring public a sophisticated, stylish young leader who brought grace and energy to the White House. But the second son of Joseph P. Kennedy had inherited more than ambition from his ruthless father. The public idealism that Kennedy exuded concealed a cold, trimming pragmatism and his now-legendary adulteries.

For Bruce it was a sweeter transition than eight years before, not least because the newest parlor game in Washington — guessing who would become the new secretary of state — placed him at the center of speculation.[10] Senator Mike Mansfield of Montana had already announced on ABC television before the election that Bruce was "best qualified" for State.[11] Supreme Court Justice Felix Frankfurter counted himself part of a Georgetown cabal promoting the diplomat's chances. Dean Acheson privately urged JFK to appoint Bruce temporarily while grooming Paul Nitze, who was not senior enough to be appointed secretary outright. Even as he recommended his friend, Acheson knew he would loathe the job. "He certainly hated being undersecretary when I got him in there," Acheson recalled; "he hates going up on the Hill, he hates making speeches and all that sort of thing. But I thought he would do it and do it rather well for a short time."[12] He knew that Bruce would not disappoint Kennedy.

Phil Graham urged his new friend in the White House to give Bruce the State Department.[13] He had played an instrumental role in Ike's offer of the Bonn embassy to Bruce in 1957, and since the Democratic convention he had carried more weight with the new president than he ever had with Eisenhower.

Speculation narrowed to three names: Bruce, Senator J. William Fulbright of Arkansas, and former State Department official Dean Rusk. Stevenson, who wanted the post, never had a chance. Kennedy remembered past slights and also considered him too controversial. Discussing it over lunch with journalist Peter Lisagor, Bruce feigned surprise that the president-elect was weighing him so seriously for the job.[14] This may have been more than false modesty: Kennedy surely must have known without being reminded by Acheson how much Bruce despised working in Washington. Still, he did not deny an interest in State until after Kennedy made his choice. As Acheson argued, if offered the top post, it is hard to see how he could have turned it down. Even though he preferred an ambassador's independence abroad to a cabinet post, because his denials all came after the fact, they must be taken with a pinch of salt. When told years later that his colleague had disavowed any interest in State, George McGehee, who served as ambassador to Turkey and West Germany, dismissed Bruce's modesty out of hand. "We all wanted it," McGehee said, with the bittersweet tone of frustrated ambition.[15]

To the dismay of Washington insiders, JFK's younger brother took a hand in the decision making. Despite Bobby Kennedy's undeniable charm, which Bruce admired, the diplomat also called him impetuous and insensitive, "arrogant almost beyond belief."[16] According to Bobby, no one in the inner circle felt any special enthusiasm for Bruce, "a tired figure," and they rejected him for the unforgivable sin of age.[17] JFK himself suspected Bruce of lacking the de rigueur "fire in the belly," a fatal flaw in a regime obsessed with vigor and youth (and with concealing the president's own crippling case of Addison's disease). It did not hurt Bruce that he detested Joe Kennedy; few in Washington thought well of the old man's scheming to advance his son's career. What did harm his standing was a report that reached JFK's ears about the convention. Backers of other candidates for State sought to discredit Bruce by telling Kennedy that the diplomat's wife had burst into tears when he defeated her friend Marietta Tree's adored Adlai. What might that say about her husband's loyalty to the new president?[18]

Kennedy sought the advice of Robert Lovett, the nonpartisan, nominally Republican, pillar of the foreign policy establishment. Lovett's opinion in the end tipped the balance to solid, methodical Dean Rusk. Kennedy really did not want a secretary of state. He would be his own.

Whatever his private thoughts at being passed over for the top job, Bruce had no time to ruminate, for the president-elect next made him a different offer. How this happened reveals how much more casual, even sloppy, the transition of power was than the popular image suggested and indeed how selective were the memories of the players remembering those days. JFK asked Acheson what post Bruce should have if not secretary of state. Without hesitating, Acheson told him London was the ideal appointment and the only one Bruce really wanted. Kennedy demurred. He had heard that Bruce wanted Rome because his wife's sister lived there. Acheson could not dissuade the president-elect from his opinion.

When the former secretary of state saw Bruce a few days later, he found his friend pacing the floor, upset and agitated. JFK had just made him the unexpected, unwelcome offer of Rome. Kennedy had gotten his facts wrong. Evangeline's sister did live in Rome, where her husband was the British ambassador, but Virginia and Ashley Clarke were divorcing, and she planned to return to Britain. "Where in the world did he get this — this is the last place either Vangie or I would like to go," Bruce fumed in Acheson's account. A judicious call by Acheson sorted out the mess, and Kennedy then offered Bruce London.[19] In fact, Acheson was the one who had gotten his facts wrong. According to Bruce's wife, the diplomat was happy to go to Rome. Why Acheson would have remembered so incorrectly was never explained, nor was the reason JFK switched offers.

As the weeks passed after the inauguration, Bruce began to fidget, wondering why State delayed sending his nomination to the Senate. The culprit was the inept new undersecretary, Chester Bowles, "a pleasant idealistic fellow, naive and wordy," according to Bruce, but a terrible administrator.[20] Kennedy learned of the delay by chance when he saw Bruce at a dinner party and asked him why he was still in town. The normally unflappable diplomat was mortified. Kennedy gave the undersecretary a blazing reprimand, and in forty-eight hours Bruce appeared before Senator Fulbright's committee for its approval.

Like everyone else at State, Bruce was curious to know the names of Kennedy's other appointments. He thought highly of Dean Rusk, "deliberate, fair, forceful, knowledgeable," yet a bit too pliant when Kennedy foisted on him two incompetent high-level political assistants. In addition to the inefficient Bowles, G. Mennen "Soapy" Williams was, in Bruce's mind, a "ham" and equally bad for the department.[21] Bruce did not much care for John Kenneth Galbraith, the Harvard economist JFK sent to New Delhi. "Ken is certainly not easy to deal with," he said of the imperious, witty academic. "I only hope his judgment is as good as his repartee — I doubt it."[22]

He worried about the quality of personnel in the department. "Seldom," he lamented a few years later, "have so many incompetents wielded so much power."[23] He even had the temerity to urge President Johnson to consult more widely or run the risk of repeating the past, when "incompetents, status seekers, drunkards, and other undesirables" held the title of ambassador.[24] It was not just Americans, though. He liked to tell his friends that the "CD" on license plates in some European countries stood not for *corps diplomatique* but "crétins distingués."[25]

His opinion of his commander in chief was altogether positive. He had first met Kennedy in 1951 when the congressman paid a courtesy call at the Paris embassy. The most important thing in his favor, Bruce said, was his lack of sympathy for his father's isolationist views.[26] His good opinion of Kennedy as president rose every time he saw him. "His mind is acute, quick and comprehensive," Bruce reported. "He expresses his thoughts easily, and with polish. He is unusually courteous and hospitable. . . . There is no doubt of his masterful qualities. His leadership is at once apparent."[27] Of the president's darker side Bruce said nothing. As much as the Georgetown insider liked gossip, it is hard to imagine that none of Kennedy's philandering came to his attention when it was known and winked at all over Washington. Yet nowhere did he record anything to reflect adversely on JFK. Whether from loyalty or from being bowled over by the immense personal appeal of the president, Bruce would say nothing negative: "I find nothing in him unpraiseworthy."[28]

The ambassador and his wife arrived in London on March 8, 1961. American diplomacy and Grosvenor Square went back to the days when John Adams lived in the house that still stood at the corner of Brook and Duke streets. In 1960 a new chancery built of utilitarian reinforced concrete and glass filled the west end of the square. On first sight Bruce called it a "monstrosity."[29] Just as during the war, when hybrid outfits like his OSS branch occupied neighboring buildings, so in the 1960s offices of American agencies spilled out of the embassy and filled the neo-Georgian houses around the square. Many represented agencies other than the State Department, each tribe wanting its own people reporting directly back to Washington rather than through the embassy. With its thousand employees, the embassy dominated its corner of Mayfair, a well-known presence that later in the decade would attract unwelcome attention.

As in his other appointments, he worked hard during office hours, played long nearly every evening, and often stayed up late to compose his distinctive cables. If he did not arrive at the embassy at dawn the next morning, his nighttime labors more than compensated. He did not care for "public relations opportunities," cutting ribbons in the provinces, lunching with Rotarians, and addressing audiences that were "seemingly tolerant of endless flows of banal oratory."[30] In this he was less visible than the previous incumbent, his wealthy New York friend Jock Whitney, a gregarious sportsman who made it a point to show the flag around the country and not just in London. "I am ashamed of complaining, even to myself, about such things," Bruce grumbled in his diary, "for obviously if I considered them intolerable I could resign, and there would be numerous applicants for the succession. In an Embassy abroad, a Chief of Mission is subject only to a fraction of the servitudes imposed on key officers in the Department. Usually, I remember this with humility. The truth is I have become increasingly crotchety with age."[31]

Whitney had also been closer to the embassy staff than Bruce, who delegated more and maintained, as always, a reserved distance from the majority of the people who worked for him. This distance sometimes irritated junior officers, especially when he sent cables without vetting them with the appropriate specialist, as custom dictated, or brought in high-level guests without forewarning the staff.[32]

On the other hand, because he believed like a good practitioner of realpolitik that "we must deal in terms of power," his unsurpassed talent for keeping in touch with the establishment elite, not just cabinet ministers of the day, made him especially effective. If not in the public eye as much as Whitney, he stayed on intimate terms with the people who held power and those who were likely to do so in the future. He appeared aloof to some of his staff, but they all acknowledged their boss's diplomatic acumen. "The embassy's professional staff," recalled one of them, "particularly appreciated the subtle ways in which Bruce would use his unique political knowledge and diplomatic experience, and his sensitivity to presidential and prime ministerial behavior, to advance U.S. interest."[33]

His style of delegating gave his deputy chief of mission the maximum latitude. For the latter part of his London years, Philip Kaiser, an associate of Averell Harriman, held this position. Kaiser never complained about his boss looking over his shoulder. "Bruce dominated the embassy with an easy hand," the DCM recalled. "He gave his officers great leeway in carrying out their responsibilities, providing support whenever they needed it. There was never any doubt, however, about his ambassadorial authority."[34] Kaiser customarily approved all cable traffic sent from the embassy every day, and the next morning the ambassador would read through the pink carbon copies. He objected only once in five years to something Kaiser had written or approved. After years in the foreign service, Bruce knew the art of the diplomatic message. The first rule was to stifle the urge to write Washington about everything. The deputy chief of mission considered his boss a master at both composing and timing his own cables.

Bruce did not like meetings, and he gathered his senior staff no more than once a week. That was sufficient, for Kaiser convened them at least once a day in the interim. This distance by no means meant Bruce was indifferent to his work. He kept himself well informed but just did not interfere with Kaiser's duties. This division of labor allowed Bruce to be the most effective ambassador Kaiser had known at dealing with foreign leaders.[35]

Despite Bruce's distaste for making speeches, some were expected, a few obligatory. The Pilgrim Society dinner provided a familiar landmark on the map of Anglo-American relations. Shortly after arriving in town — and also just before retiring — American ambassadors were expected to address the Pilgrims. For his first speech, Bruce uttered the usual, safe remarks about the strength of the Special Relationship, though in fact Anglo-American ties had still not recovered from British bitterness over Suez, when Eisenhower in 1956 had undercut the Anglo-French-Israeli campaign against Nasser. Among the high holy days of the American civic calendar, Thanksgiving ranked after only the Glorious Fourth. As the chief resident American, the ambassador was required to read a Thanksgiving proclamation and offer the traditional toast "To the Day We Celebrate." He established his own tradition, to the amusement of his audience for these dinners, when he became so carried away with his informal remarks after reading the proclamation that he had to be reminded, five years running, to give the toast.[36]

The ritual of diplomacy was by then second nature. From signing the book of condolence at an embassy upon the death of a head of state to attending the queen's garden parties, Bruce moved through diplomatic London with the assurance of long practice. There were less familiar rituals too. Once he read the lesson at a mammoth Billy Graham rally at Wembley. The abstemious lifestyle the evangelist preached hardly appealed to Bruce, but he greatly admired Graham, "one of the most magnetic individuals I have ever met."[37]

The ambassador received hundreds of visits every year from legislators and hundreds of letters asking favors for their friends trooping through town. He still enjoyed giving his trademark foreign policy briefings to visiting dignitaries. On these occasions, Phil Kaiser said, "Bruce then put on an exceptional solo performance, leaving his senior colleagues gaping in silent admiration."[38]

His private reaction to these visits remained unchanged from previous encounters. One powerful congressman in particular, Wayne Hays of Ohio, brought out unkind thoughts in the ambassador. Uncouth, corrupt, and "despicable," Hays generated such ill will abroad that Bruce said he should be paid to stay home. The only time Kaiser ever heard his boss use scatological language occurred when Hays came to London. Frantic calls from the Paris embassy, where Hays visited first, implored Bruce, for the good of the service, to invite the congressman to the residence and jolly him up. The ambassador reluctantly agreed: "I'll do it. But you know, Phil, Hays is a real shit."[39]

He knew he would have to devote his time to trivialities, work he once characterized to Dean Rusk, in a rare fit of pique, as "liverish representational lunching and dining, attending meetings of Anglo-American good-will organizations, running a bar-room and restaurant for jet-borne countrymen."[40] Those tasks he accepted. But he did not have to like it when visiting Americans took advantage of the embassy, were rude to the staff, insulted the ambassador, and in general gave a poor representation of their nation to foreigners.

The more obnoxious they were, the more likely to trouble him personally. An early eminent offender, "charming and vain" Robert Frost, came to visit during Bruce's first month in London. Despite the luncheon given in his honor at the residence, the poet chose to be miffed that the queen did not ask to see him.[41]

A more familiar repellent stereotype arrived with a New Orleans dentist and his wife who thought letters of introduction from their senator would open all doors. Their odious progress across Europe gave London advance warning when the consul general in Amsterdam called to say that the wife was a particularly tiresome and demanding person. She insisted that Bruce arrange an appointment for her with the lord mayor of London and admittance to Buckingham Palace, verbally abused his secretary, and threatened to report his lack of attention to her powerful friends in Washington. Gritting his teeth, Bruce tried to accommodate the couple and even put an embassy car at their disposal.[42] A group of New York lawyers arrived on a chartered flight and asked to meet the royal family. When Bruce failed them, their leader denounced him as a model of the Ugly American diplomat.[43]

The ambassador could count on one constant in the flow of unexpected visitors and importuning Americans who crossed his path: there would be no lack of those who flaunted their connections with the White House. In April 1962 the president's sister Eunice Shriver let the embassy know she would be in town for a conference and wanted a "seven-passenger" car placed at her disposal for a side trip to Sheffield. "We have no seven-passenger car," Bruce fumed, "she is not here as an official, our chauffeurs are not on duty on weekends, so all in all we are rather put to it, and it will prove expensive to meet her request, with me probably paying for it."[44]

Dean Acheson mischievously proclaimed a year after Bruce's appointment that "Great Britain has lost an empire and has not yet found a role."[45] The British were still in the process of shedding colonies, and they invested great hope in the Commonwealth as the successor to empire. That tug of past connections kept them ambivalent about closer ties with Europe. Economically the country continued its long, gradual postwar atrophy, a decline masked by the welfare state and high employment. In a comment to de Gaulle, Adenauer aptly compared Britain to "a rich man who has lost all his property but does not know it."[46] This was the context of Bruce's appointment, and his assessments gave

Washington a perceptive analysis that mixed the sympathy and frankness of a friend. In his reading of the British scene he was much more knowledgeable than he had been in alien Germany.

Unusual for an American diplomat, he sympathized with Britain's colonial problems. Just as he had urged understanding for France's colonial woes a decade earlier, he argued against impatience with the speed of Britain's retreat from empire. Postcolonial regimes, in his view, were almost invariably inept except in corruption and brutality: "the competition between newly independent nations to excel each other in stupidity never seems to end."[47] Sympathy for the Third World remained a blind spot.

His sympathy for Britain waned too when he turned from its colonial problems to domestic ones. He was alarmed at economic trends, especially financial profligacy. "A vast majority of Britons are totally unconscious of the dangers to their finances and economy," he feared.[48] Worse, no one seemed willing to address the underlying problems. This theme resonated in his cables throughout his tenure in London.

As East-West tension grew over Berlin, he believed the British would reluctantly stick by America. The British, he sardonically observed, "regard themselves as the true herrenvolk" and distrust the Germans. Each advance of the West German economy galled them. "Joy through work is not a British ideal." In July 1961 he expressed a prescient worry. "Decline of influence is either unnoticed and unacknowledged, or, if publicly manifest, can embitter a proud people against those to whom the torch has passed."[49] In a private sentence, he anticipated the outraged British reaction to Acheson's remark about Britain not having a role.

He denied being a Macmillan intimate but developed excellent relations with the prime minister. Harold Macmillan affected an air of Edwardian lassitude much like that of the American ambassador. Of both men it could be said that, like Talleyrand, "he had long learned to cultivate a kind of studied languor that irritated the second-rate."[50] That similarity may explain why Bruce sized up Macmillan so well and also why he held him in high regard. He quoted Super Mac's opponents comparing him to Disraeli but said that, unlike the flamboyant Dizzy, his appearance was against him: he had the look of an English duke "accused of dressing in the cast-off garments of Irish beggars."

Appearance only added to the image. "At times," Bruce said, "he gives the impression of being shot through with Victorian languor. It would be a mistake to infer from this that he is lacking in force or decisiveness, as it would be to deduce from what is called his 'Balliol Shuffle' that he is not capable of swift action."[51] Bruce reckoned correctly that Macmillan, "a political animal, shrewd, subtle in maneuver," was the undisputed master of his cabinet.[52] It did not surprise him when the premier ruthlessly sacked cabinet ministers in 1962 to keep his administration afloat. Bruce said after it was over that "the tumbrils are no longer rattling around Whitehall. Cabinet members have ceased nervously to finger their necks."[53]

Bruce was a central figure for those who valued the Special Relationship between Britain and America. Like most of his peers, he did not look on the relationship as an equal partnership.[54] And he knew that Eisenhower's betrayal of the British, French, and Israelis over Suez in 1956 (which the ambassador deplored) still embittered Anglo-American relations. It had been Macmillan who ruminated during the war that as Britain receded on the global stage it might still play the Greek to the American Romans.[55] In his relations with the new president who had sent Bruce to London, Macmillan sought to develop that interpretation of the Special Relationship. The sympathetic chemistry of Kennedy and Macmillan arrested the decay in relations, but only for a few years.

In his first months on the job, Bruce worked overtime explaining American policy gaffes to the British. The Bay of Pigs debacle came only four weeks after he arrived, the Berlin Wall four months later. In between, Mennen Williams embarrassed the administration over Africa; Laos and the Congo turned ugly; and Kennedy could have done better at his first meeting with Khrushchev. The most startling events, however, came in October 1962.

In a more reckless move than in Berlin, the Soviet premier placed nuclear missiles in Cuba. On Sunday, October 21, Bruce suspected something was afoot when messages over three separate channels arrived at the embassy, all cryptically instructing him to meet a military jet arriving from Washington at midnight. That evening he and his CIA station chief drove out to the airfield at Greenham Common. To his astonishment, a presidential Boeing 707 landed and off stepped Acheson. Bruce had followed the department's bizarre order to bring a gun, though for what reason was a puzzle. He decided to take along a more useful item in his raincoat as well. When he greeted Acheson he mentioned the revolver but from the other pocket, with a magician's flourish, produced a bottle of Scotch and offered his former boss a drink.[56]

Acheson's orders took him on to Paris to see de Gaulle. In the meantime, Bruce was to take Chester Cooper, a CIA man and Acheson's fellow passenger, to see Macmillan the next morning. Acheson gave the ambassador a set of photographs taken by U-2 spy planes of the missile sites. He was to show them to the prime minister and tell him about Kennedy's forthcoming speech announcing a naval blockade of Cuba. At that point, for a few hours at least, Macmillan and de Gaulle would be the only non-Americans to know Kennedy's intentions. They knew they were being informed as a courtesy, not consulted for advice. Still, briefing them before JFK's public announcement was an important diplomatic gesture.

Macmillan expressed sympathy to Bruce and promised support, but he thought the British public might not be as trusting. Bruce understood his point later that week when thousands of demonstrators converged on Grosvenor Square to protest Kennedy's policy toward Cuba. They tried to break through the glass doors on the ground floor of the embassy, but the police held them off. The ambassador took the threat seriously and called Frankfurt to rush over a supply of tear gas canisters. At first he instructed his marine guards that under no circumstances should they use their guns, even if attacked. He then noted chillingly that, in the event the demonstrators overwhelmed the embassy, he wanted "to reconsider whether for the protection of the code room we should not, as a last resort, open fire."[57] He could not know it then, but far more violent demonstrations would become a matter of routine before his tenure in London ended. The embassy would never again have to send away to Germany for tear gas.

Macmillan urged him to release the damning but still classified photographs to the press. Bruce agreed. Acting on his own, without authorization from the White House, he gave the pictures to the BBC. It was a courageous decision, sticking his neck out as few other ambassadors would have done. The pictures' unexpected appearance on British television threw the White House into momentary turmoil. With American forces around the globe at Defcon-2, a notch away from war,

Evangeline Bruce, sketched here by René Bouché, became a star attraction in the fashion industry on both sides of the Atlantic. *(Evangeline Bruce)*

Through decades of foreign service, the Bruces were never without one or more generations of their dynasty of spaniels. *(Evangeline Bruce)*

As ambassador to Germany, Bruce had to perform some unsavory duties, such as going for a day's shoot with industrialist and war criminal Alfried Krupp (left). *(Evangeline Bruce)*

In the summer of 1960, the family enjoys Cape Cod while hoping that the coming election brings a Democratic team back to the State Department. David Surtees, Nicky, David, Evangeline, Sasha, dogs. *(Evangeline Bruce)*

In top hat and formal dress, Bruce rode in a gilded carriage to Buckingham Palace to present his letter of credence as ambassador to the queen. On returning to the ambasssadorial residence, he ordered champagne for everyone and sugar for the horses. *(Evangeline Bruce)*

There was no question which diplomat from the American embassy should meet the president's wife at the airport on her visit to London. *(Evangeline Bruce)*

Ambassador Bruce and
John F. Kennedy during the
president's 1961 visit to
London. *(Bettmann Archives)*

Ambassador and Mrs. Bruce
at Westminster Cathedral
on November 26, 1963, for
the memorial service for
President Kennedy.
(The Image Works, Inc.)

Vacationing in Venice with his friend from youth, Ronnie Tree. *(Evangeline Bruce)*

Soaking up the sun in the Caribbean during his first "retirement," 1969 – 1970. *(Evangeline Bruce)*

For his last three assignments—the Vietnam talks, China, and NATO—David Bruce worked closely with Richard Nixon's national security adviser, Henry Kissinger, shown here with the ambassador and his wife. *(Virginia Historical Society)*

The combination of declining health and vitriol from his opposite numbers across the table in Paris were likely the reason why Bruce usually looked so grim on the way to each Thursday's session *(UPI/Bettmann)*

Bruce was impressed by the wide-ranging conversation he and Kissinger had with the aging Mao. *(Evangeline Bruce)*

The shrewd Chinese foreign minister, Zhou Enlai, meets his match in diplomatic *politesse*. *(Evangeline Bruce)*

President Gerald Ford and Bruce, in increasingly frail health, review the troops on the occasion of Bruce's receipt of the Department of Defense's highest award for a civilian. The diplomat also received the Presidential Medal of Freedom from Ford. *(Virginia Historical Society)*

Evangeline Bruce, with two of her stepgrandchildren, Michael and Lavinia Currier, leaving the memorial service for her husband at Westminster Abbey, 1978. *(Evangeline Bruce)*

and no word yet on the Soviet response to Kennedy's quarantine, Washington's nerves screamed at the slightest abrasion. Defense Secretary Robert McNamara was taken aback when he informed reporters the administration was still weighing whether to release the photographs, only to be told that British television had already broadcast them. Fortunately for Bruce, the unfolding crisis quickly superseded the anger his independent action provoked in Washington. His decision did not affect the outcome of events in the Caribbean, but it did help steady Anglo-American relations in a time of crisis.[58]

When the threat in Cuba dissipated, all other problems paled in comparison. The euphoria that followed was one reason why a few weeks later a breakdown of communication between Washington and London nearly ruptured relations as badly as Suez.[59]

The rift came about because the British had become dependent on American technology to maintain their atomic deterrent. Before he left office, Eisenhower agreed to sell them the Skybolt missile then under development. Launched from the air, Skybolt would give a stand-off capability to manned bombers. Then, unexpectedly, Skybolt hit a snag. It failed in test after test. Whitehall showed no concern. The Americans had promised to develop the missile and share it. Surely they would overcome these technical setbacks. When McNamara cancelled Skybolt in autumn 1962, the British were dumbfounded. For itself, the United States had already developed the land-based Minuteman and the sea-launched Polaris missiles. With neither of these systems to fall back on, Britain without Skybolt would have no credible means of deploying its small atomic arsenal.

In December Kennedy and Macmillan went to the Bahamas for a summit meeting scheduled before the Skybolt flap but inevitably dominated by it. JFK offered the half-loaf of continued research on Skybolt, but Macmillan would have none of it. The lady, he said, had been violated in public. The resolution that saved the summit, and the alliance, was an American agreement to share Polaris. Even so, Nassau was no success for Kennedy. Because the uproar was months in the making and because both sides had ample opportunity to avert a crisis, the question of blame arose.

To analyze the affair, Kennedy appointed Richard Neustadt, whose book on the presidency he admired. There was plenty of blame, including some for the president, who preferred to deal only with a few individuals and unconvincingly complained that no one had kept him informed. Bruce might have anticipated the problem before it reached the boiling point, but he learned of the missile's cancellation too late. The irony is that with competent ambassadors in both London and Washington, such a problem should never have arisen. Neustadt absolved Bruce, but he compared Skybolt to another, grander, equally abortive program of military alliance politics, an idea long forgotten in 1962 by nearly everyone but David Bruce — the European Defense Community.[60]

In the aftermath of the Cuban crisis, but before Skybolt was resolved at Nassau, Anglo-American relations in London became testy. With "a degree of asperity" unknown since the mid-1950s, the embassy and Whitehall became embroiled in a dispute over whether the British government should have done more to encourage a less-critical tone in the newspapers toward America during the Cuban crisis.[61] Bruce did not consider the lack of press support especially worrisome. He blamed it on a passing combination of anti-Americanism stirred up by left-wing "Hands off Cuba" groups, resentment over loss of empire, and "a quite understandable desire" to remind the United States that it had undermined Britain at Suez.[62] On top of this unpleasantness, Acheson gave his provocative speech about Britain's not having found a post-imperial role to play, saying bluntly in public what Bruce privately agreed was so. The White House instantly distanced itself from Acheson and instructed Bruce to give emphatic background reassurances to major London papers.[63]

Bruce's own irritation showed in response to Britain's aversion to strong ties with the Continent. The United Kingdom had resisted Monnet's Coal and Steel Community and the European Defense Community, and had shunned the Common Market at its birth in 1957. More recently, it began to grope toward membership in the EEC. This looming decision over whether to press for entry into the Common Market seemed to Bruce, the devotee of a federated Europe, the most crucial choice facing the U.K.

During his early years in Britain, he frequently talked with Jean Monnet, both in London and on weekend jaunts to Paris, about the future of integration on the Continent. When Macmillan's government finally decided to seek entry, Bruce said, "I may yet live to see the U.S. and Canada linked with this great European complex in bonds so strong as to create lasting Western unity, with all that would connote for the preservation of Western civilization against aggression."[64]

Publicly, the ambassador's comments had been innocuous enough, but as debate over Britain's relations with the Community grew, they began to attract lightning bolts from opponents of British membership. In 1962 Bruce found himself in a contretemps over a speech he gave in Birmingham that resonated with that talk he had given long before in Lille about the Marshall Plan. Once again, the local press criticized him for interfering in a nation's domestic affairs.[65] America could push its allies only so much or they would recoil, sometimes with self-defeating illogic. Chastened by the Birmingham incident, he subsequently warned Washington to soft-pedal its support for Britain in Europe.[66] Anything Americans could say, he felt, "will only offend."[67] In fact, it was de Gaulle's long memory of past slights that prompted France to use the Anglo-American agreement on Skybolt as a pretext for denying British entry into the Common Market.[68] It was a very long memory, indeed. If the English had not burned Joan of Arc, one wit said, de Gaulle would have let them into the EEC.

Prickliness in Anglo-American relations spilled over into the so-called "Grand Design," Kennedy's plan to revitalize the Western Alliance. A key element was MLF, the Multilateral Force. MLF proposed a seaborne force of ships — manned by mixed crews chosen from all the NATO fleets — that would have nuclear missiles under joint NATO control. It was a logistical and technical nightmare. The British called it the "multilateral farce."[69] Macmillan sarcastically dismissed it: "Do you really expect our chaps to share their grog with the Turks?"[70] A misguided American effort to foster greater coordination within NATO, the MLF never materialized, under either Kennedy or his successor, who let it quietly die, unmourned.

Early in 1963, Kennedy brought Bruce back from London for three weeks and installed him in a White House office to conduct a review of policy toward Europe, including economic integration, MLF, the German problem, and American relations with Britain, France, and the Soviet Union. Following his old guiding principle, Bruce couched American interests in terms of European integration: "We should support, in every way we can, the movement toward European unity."[71] But was the goal of European unity feasible? Bruce's answer was never in doubt, and he concluded with a sweeping affirmation that integration was "an imperative of modern history."[72]

Even before he summoned Bruce back to work on European policy, Kennedy told journalist Arthur Krock that it had been "a mistake" to send him to London.[73] After reading Bruce's thoughtful cables for only several months, Kennedy realized that the ambassador's analytical talents were being wasted there because of America's easy relations with the British (this was before Skybolt). The situation was partly Kennedy's fault. When Macmillan had asked JFK to suggest candidates for ambassador to Washington, the president recommended his longtime friend, and Macmillan's in-law, David Ormsby-Gore. An upper-class bohemian from a family with "more than a streak of Welsh eccentricity," Ormsby-Gore seemed in his many enthusiasms never to have entirely grown up.[74] He was, however, like the American half of the "Two Davids" ambassadorial team, tough-minded in serving the interests of his country. His easy entree to JFK — the handwritten notes addressed "Dear Jack" were a tipoff that Ormsby-Gore did not need to go through the usual channels — caused more heartburn for Rusk in Washington than for Bruce in London.[75] But the reality was that as long as the president relied on Ormsby-Gore and also on the genuine friendship that he developed with Macmillan, he made Bruce almost superfluous in London.

In October 1961 he offered the ambassador the post of undersecretary of state. Bruce declined and asked Rusk to thank the president for the offer and to tell him he was ready to vacate the embassy whenever JFK wished it. But he could not be undersecretary again, being "temperamentally so opposed to assuming its duties and obligations that I would be ineffective."[76] Only when the Rabelaisian Texan inherited the White House did Bruce come into his own as ambassador to Britain.

CHAPTER 18

Ceremony, Salons, and Scandal

If, in the Sixties, the past was letting go of Britain, its grip was not to be prised loose without a struggle, and the Profumo affair can therefore be seen as the last struggle of the old, false standards (or, as some would have said and some would still say, the old, true standards) before a new attitude emerged.

— Bernard Levin, *The Pendulum Years*

*I*N HIS FIRST SUMMER at Grosvenor Square, Bruce set aside a morning to have his portrait drawn at the request of the *Illustrated London News*. The paper was running a series of sketches of eminent Londoners, and its editor hoped to entice the diplomat by praising the artist as a quick study who would be in and out in less than an hour. Cajolery proved unnecessary. After all, among the others who sat for the same series were members of the royal family.

The incident reflected Bruce's instant prominence in London. He did not disappoint expectations raised by his previous embassies. Socially, he and his wife set a tone and a pace that outshone even their Paris years. Being sketched by the artist from the *Illustrated London News* was thus a badge of Bruce's inclusion in the circles that counted. It was also an omen of unpleasantness to come.

Beginning with the presentation of his letters of credence to the queen, Bruce stepped into a job encrusted with ceremony, a position in which social events provided both gloss and substance. As one of the most important ambassadors in town, he led a life of ritual. Few diplomats were better equipped by experience, talent, or inclination to handle the work. But as much as this self-styled eighteenth-century gentleman reveled in the quaint rites of diplomacy, he also looked at them critically.

As his nation's representative, he witnessed Britain's great set-piece ceremonies. There was the splendiferous Trooping the Color. He was equally intrigued by the symbolism of the state opening of Parliament — lords decked out in their ermines and coronets, commoners symbolically asserting their independence, and all the glorious mumbo jumbo of tradition (even if some of it was of rather more recent origin than the British liked to admit). Equally ostentatious were state dinners at Buckingham Palace. One such occasion for King Hussein of Jordan pulled out all the stops because, Bruce surmised, it involved one monarch entertaining another. It was a command performance for all the lesser royals, whom the ambassador pitied for their tightly scripted, superficial roles, always with an aide or equerry guiding them by the elbow to yet another fleeting introduction. As well as the full orchestra playing out of sight and an army of footmen in Georgian livery and fake pigtails, the guests themselves, garbed in a rainbow of uniforms and costumes, lent a campy glamour to the occasion. The Knights of the Garter were out in force, dressed "in tight fitting breeches and silk stockings, with the great blue sash across their shirt fronts" and, Bruce impishly observed, "all sorts of jewelled stars stuck on their anatomies."[1]

Ten years earlier the original angry young playright, John Osborne, had called the royal family "the gold filling in a mouth full of decay." Bruce was too conservative to agree, but the repetition of lavish dinners at Buck House while the nation frittered away its resources gave him pause. A thoroughgoing Anglophile, with his own sense of aristocratic bearing, he rejected any suggestion that Britain would be well rid of both the House of Lords and the House of Windsor. Even so, it seemed to him that a deferential society based on arcane distinctions harking back to feudalism hardly encouraged the British to come to grips with the challenges of the mid-twentieth century.

He was also present for the grandest ceremony for a generation, the state funeral for the savior of the nation, whom the ambassador had known since those Ditchley weekends during the Blitz. He last saw Churchill in 1963, when he presented him a certificate of honorary

American citizenship. Visibly in decline, the great man uttered no classic bon mot, but he typically celebrated the occasion with champagne all around. Bruce reported to the president that Churchill "abandoned with reluctance the idea of sailing up the Potomac, and accepting the documents in person" and was "zestfully concocting plans for his funeral," an event that took place in accordance with the old man's blueprint less than two years later.[2]

Amid universal expressions of condolence, Churchill's remains lay in state in Westminster Hall, the first prime minister since Gladstone to receive that honor. Thousands passed before the catafalque. The Union Jack, topped with the insignia of the Garter, shrouded the coffin guarded by four officers and four tall yellow candles. The president ordered the Stars and Stripes flown at half-staff around the world, a tribute accorded no other foreigner since the founding of the republic.[3]

Bruce often professed ignorance of the stock market, but he was a shrewd custodian of his wealth. He calculated fairly closely before going to London what it would take of his own resources to make his embassy succeed. Kennedy knew Bruce understood the hidden costs of an ambassadorship and asked him before leaving Washington to talk about it to James Gavin, JFK's appointee to France. Bruce cautioned Gavin that the Paris embassy would require a minimum of $40,000 annually of his own money.[4] London, he knew, would take at least as much.

Much of that would be spent at the ambassador's residence in Regent's Park. Winfield House, given to the American government by Woolworth heir Barbara Hutton, dated only to 1937. Though it lacked stylistic distinction itself, its location was spectacular — set in magnificent grounds among the greenery of Regent's Park and surrounded by John Nash's gleaming white Regency terraces. Evangeline Bruce filled the downstairs reception rooms with the antiques that the couple had accumulated over the years. As in all of the houses she decorated, a profusion of large flowering plants towered over the guests. The ambassador's former brother-in-law, Paul Mellon, helpfully lent paintings from the National Gallery, not white elephants from deep storage but paintings of the first rank.

Running the household was like managing a small business. Evangeline took it all in stride and, as in Paris and Bonn, spared her husband much of the work.[5] But it was up to him to sort out servant problems. Winfield House required a staff of nearly thirty — chauffeurs, gardeners, maids, housekeepers, and kitchen help — many of them paid directly from the ambassador's purse. Once he had to dissuade the footman from quitting because the butler called him and his fellow Spaniards on the staff a bunch of "damned foreigners."[6] Speaking of his polyglot staff, he admitted that "this mixed crew does not make a happy ship," unconsciously articulating the flaw in the ill-fated Multilateral Force.[7]

His kindly Russian chef posed a special burden because he constantly tried to find jobs on the staff for his children. Bruce winked when he installed a daughter as a parlor maid and a son-in-law as footman. But then he brought back into the kitchen a son who had been expelled before for threatening the staff with a carving knife. The final straw came when the ambassador discovered yet another of the chef's errant sons at Winfield House, a former female impersonator in a Cairo nightclub. Bruce berated the chef, in French, and told him the residence was not a jobs program for his ne'er-do-well offspring.[8]

In 1962 Anthony Sampson published his influential study *Anatomy of Britain*, revised three years later as *Anatomy of Britain Today*. In it he said, "The old-style ambassadors, whatever their nationality, live grandly in surroundings which since the eighteenth century have become deep-frozen so that, like Oxford colleges, they and their families have become a temporary subsidised aristocracy, leading more ducal lives than most dukes, and popping in and out of the gossip-columns, as part of the fantasy-life of Britain."[9] It is not hard to imagine that this image was inspired in part by the patrician American at the mansion in Regent's Park.

In November 1966, Truman Capote organized a masked ball in Manhattan in honor of the *Washington Post*'s Katharine Graham. He touted it as the party of the decade, the defining moment for an emerging, more international East Coast social elite. His hand-picked 540 guests included the most glittering trend-setters — the famous, the gifted, the beautiful, as well as the merely rich. Vanderbilts and Fords and assorted titled folk from *Debrett's* held up the side for old money and blue blood, but the pizzazz came from the newer, brassier fortunes and their

fashionable literary pilot fish. (One wit, feigning horror at the ostentation, called them "an international list for the guillotine."[10]) Some
aggrieved socialites not on the list claimed they had to be out of town
the night of the party.[11]

Ambassador and Mrs. David Bruce did not go to the party — not
because they lacked one of the coveted invitations, for they were among
the 540 elect. Absorbed instead in their own dazzling social milieu in
London, they enjoyed the cachet of being among the pursued rather
than the pursuing.

The London salon had declined from Bruce's earliest residence during Mellon's ambassadorship, when Sybil Colefax and Emerald Cunard
dominated fashionable society. One of their leading successors after the
war was Lady Pamela Berry, whose family owned the *Daily Telegraph*.
Bruce had met her rival, Ann Fleming, in 1940, when she had been
"practically beyond the pale because of her recklessness and adventur-
ousness."[12] What he meant was that she was still married to Lord
O'Neill and seeing both Esmond Rothermere, soon to be her second
husband, and Ian Fleming, later number three. She used Rothermere's
money after the war to create a salon less partisan than Berry's.[13]

In this milieu the success of Winfield House under the Bruce regime
relied on more than the antiques-filled ambience or the magnificence
of the ambassador's wine cellar. "In a salon," Evangeline Bruce said,
"you can't be ponderous, egocentric. Anything other than a lucid,
witty, graceful style is simply not allowed."[14] Since the Paris embassy,
she had possessed a sixth sense about whom to invite. Her husband,
through visits stretching back four decades, had accumulated a broad
range of acquaintances, the expected assortment of diplomatic, political,
military, and clubland connections. Added to those were the aristocrats
into whose homes Bruce was a rare welcome American. These connections still amounted to a conventional, upper-crust mix. Evangeline
Bruce added the leaven that came from a familiarity with the artistic,
literary, and dramatic scene. Whether it was among the chattering
writers and artists of Hampstead or the coming young MPs of Westminster, she sensed who was important or, as one observer of her parties
put it, "Who Is and Who Will Be."[15]

She thought women better at running salons than men because they
were more likely to suppress their own egos and "take the time to be

sure that everyone shines." "The tone," she said, "has to be light, humorous, witty, and the more elusive the reference, the more prized."[16]

Sometimes this maxim could be taken to extremes, and some dinners at Winfield House owed their inspiration more to vaudeville farce than to bluestocking salon. The Bruces must have suspected as much the evening they planned a party for George Brown, the boisterous, often drunk, oftener offensive, but always entertaining Labor foreign secretary. (Anti–Harold Wilson politicians quipped "better George drunk than Harold sober."[17]) Some of those present were baffled by the antics of the guest of honor and another guest, Groucho Marx. Introduced to Lady Rothschild, Brown melodramatically dropped to one knee and, kissing her hand, said earnestly he always wanted to meet a female member of her illustrious family. A shy person, she was taken aback, both then and later when Groucho said to her, "Mrs. Rothschild, I suppose you are the richest woman in the world; and there is Mr. Astor opposite us, is he as rich as you?" From then on, Bruce noted, "It was sheer carnival," for Brown, "the soul of tactless jocularity," matched Marx outrage for outrage until he had to go off for a late-night vote at the House of Commons.[18]

On one occasion Evangeline Bruce's husband did not measure up to her high standard for conversation. It was an intimate dinner the couple shared with Ann and Ian Fleming. Complaining later to Evelyn Waugh that out of good manners she asked Bruce a simple question about politics and he droned on for nearly an hour in response, Ann Fleming wrote, "The boredom was acute and [to] Evangeline most of all, she did little to hide it — the same terrible tension as seen on Clarissa's face when Anthony [Eden] speaks."[19]

This was a rare lapse on Bruce's part, however, so unexpected that Fleming made a point of it. Most commonly, people who dined with him came away warmed by his personal concern. Because he was a sympathetic listener, he naturally encouraged people to unburden themselves to him. Roy Jenkins, a Labor cabinet minister and Bruce intimate, contrasted him favorably with Harriman, who, being intensely partisan, was often boring. Bruce, in his "allusive and elusive" style, could trip lightly — and without pretense — over a wide array of topics. He was a quiet ambassador, Jenkins told an interviewer, and gave the appearance of being wise. Whether he really was, was another matter. Jenkins, with a wink and a nod, would say only that his friend never said anything foolish and accomplished a lot with "an economy of intellectual effort."[20]

On their first weekend after arriving in 1961, the Bruces went for Sunday lunch at Hatfield House in the rolling plains of Hertfordshire. Bobbety Salisbury, the fifth marquess and Bruce's friend from before the war, had succeeded to his father's title. Though he had just resigned from his post in the Tory party, he was still one of the most important peers of the realm and a kinsman of the prime minister too. Bruce's friendship with him exemplified his intimate ties with the elite, whether hereditary nobles like Salisbury or members of the newer, untitled ruling class.

The Bruces' associations with literary, media, and stage luminaries were equally broad, exemplified in a small dinner that Fleur Meyer gave in their honor at her flat in Albany, just off Piccadilly. The guests included actress Leslie Caron and her friend Warren Beatty. Correspondent Charles Collingwood, on his way to assignment in Saigon, was also there. After dinner Mary Martin and her husband dropped in, as did Ingrid Bergman, "looking prettier off stage than on," Bruce thought.[21] At his small house in St. John's Wood, Sir Steven Runciman often arranged intimate luncheons for Bruce to meet the literary elite away from the glare of official duty.[22] One in May 1961 featured the historian C. V. Wedgwood and poet Stephen Spender and his wife, Natasha Litvin, the pianist.[23]

British writer Noel Annan described his friend the American ambassador as "worldly in the best sense of the word, casting a sagacious, penetrating but indulgent eye upon the frailties and follies of his friends."[24] Bruce described Yehudi Menuhin as "unknowing" about politics when the conductor periodically advocated bizarre solutions to strategic problems. Once the "gentle and pacific" Menuhin called Bruce to propose that the U.S. launch a preemptive strike against the Chinese before they could develop their nuclear missile capability.[25]

When his Georgetown friend Joe Alsop visited London, Bruce kept watch on the outrageous journalist's progress through West End drawing rooms and cabinet offices. "He seems to have been catholic about whose toes he treads on," the ambassador noted. "It is said that the Prime Minister, the Foreign Secretary, the Lord Privy Seal, Hugh

Gaitskell, and George Brown are numbered among those who will not receive him again."[26]

Entertaining on a large scale gave the Bruces' residence the character of a minor court. Invariably not all of the guests were what the hosts might have wished. At the 1966 Fourth of July party, a short, furtive-looking man was announced as the representative of the Swedish consulate. In the receiving line, Evangeline Bruce leaned over to her husband and whispered out of the corner of her mouth that the Swedish ambassador must have "scraped the bottom of a small barrel." They thought no more of it until, a short time later, the impostor was hauled out after proposing a toast "to all the dead and dying of Vietnam."[27] If that had been the only contretemps, they would have counted themselves lucky. But three years before the bogus Swede appeared, a great British scandal boiled over and almost scalded the American ambassador.

Today British political calumny revolves around sex and spies. It was not always so. In the early 1960s, Burgess and Maclean were fading memories, Philby had not yet decamped for Moscow, and Blunt was still puttering quietly about the queen's portrait collection, unmolested. As for sex scandals, they were not British. In 1963, however, the year of the death wish, as one wit described it, sex and spies came into their own as peculiarly British tools for bringing down the mighty. "Sexual intercourse began in 1963," the poet Philip Larkin cheekily wrote, "between the end of the Chatterley ban and the Beatles' first LP." What seemed like a trivial indiscretion mushroomed into a scandal that rocked Britain. What made it possible was the sea change in popular culture and mores, typified by the satirical television program *That Was The Week That Was*, which set the tone for the iconoclastic, swinging sixties by making risible "a stuffy Establishment, whose prudery was equated with libidinous hypocrisy."[28]

It all went back to that portraitist who had sketched Bruce for the *Illustrated London News* in 1961. He was no innocent, but Stephen Ward, soon to be vilified in screaming headlines around the world, the notorious society chiropractor and part-time artist who, the weekend after he sketched the ambassador, arranged the famous introduction at Cliveden of Defense Minister John Profumo and Christine Keeler. Two years in the making, the scandal that shook the establishment now pales beside more recent examples of squalor in high places. Yet the Profumo Affair tantalized and shocked Britain and America as nothing else in the innocent, early 1960s.

Keeler, looking older than her nineteen years, was one of the lithe young women whom Ward provided for the well-to-do lechers of London's West End. Unfortunately for Profumo, Keeler was at the same time sleeping with the Soviet naval attaché. Long after the defense minister ended the liaison, Keeler sold her story to the press. In the face of swirling rumors, Profumo's denial to the Commons in 1963 of any impropriety kept a lid on for a few months longer. That June the truth came out, and Profumo resigned in disgrace. His gravest transgression was not the adulterous episode itself but the unforgivable fact that he had lied to the House, "the sin against the Holy Ghost," in Bruce's wry phrase.[29] Bruce, who delighted in gossip, called the affair "one of the juiciest scandals in modern political history."[30] After a trip home for consultation, he wrote that "for days I have been questioned about Miss Christine Keeler and the Profumo imbroglio, as if I had lived under, if not in, her bed."[31]

On his return to London, even he was shocked by the rumors of depravity in high places that were making the rounds. "I've never witnessed such a mess," he said.[32] People really believed, according to journalist Bernard Levin, "that nine High Court Judges had been engaging in sexual orgies, that a member of the Cabinet had waited table in a rather daring form of *déshabillé,* and that yet another member of the Cabinet had been found under a bush in Richmond Park indulging in a somewhat unconventional form of sexual activity."[33]

The ambassador soon found his own name mentioned along with others in prominent positions. When a cable from the CIA asked Bruce to respond to this allegation, he indignantly denied ever having met Ward, whom he called "pimp, painter, bone cracker extraordinary."[34] After he sent his denial, however, a vague unease that he was overlooking something prompted him to consult his diaries. He discovered that the artist from the *Illustrated London News* who sketched him two summers before was in fact Ward. Bruce immediately sent an amending cable to explain this entirely innocent connection.[35] That was embarrassment enough; worse was to come.

A French magazine named Bruce among the frequenters of writer Lady Antonia Fraser's salon. This was true, but the article went on to suggest darkly that her "more enterprising guests resorted to the freer atmosphere" at Stephen Ward's flat in the nearby mews.[36] The ambassador shrugged off the innuendo as part of the price he had to pay for prominence. When he read in the papers that Ward had sketched nine members of the royal family, including Prince Philip, he wearily concluded, "So I am in goodly company."[37]

In answer to the CIA cable, Bruce told the truth but not all of it. He was aware of other information bearing on the scandal but concluded that there was no need to stir up trouble unnecessarily. Unfortunately for him, others did the stirring. His executive assistant, Alfred Wells, dutifully kept his boss apprised of his conversations with London political figures. Not surprisingly, among the bits of rumor that he passed along during early 1963 was information about the Profumo business, both before it became public knowledge and after. Back in the United States, J. Edgar Hoover learned of these circumstances when an American friend of Ward named Thomas Corbally went to the FBI with a startling tale. Corbally reported that he had informed the embassy of the scandal back in January, a month before Profumo lied to the Commons. The FBI garbled the information, although Corbally helped by giving a misleading spin of his own.[38]

Bruce had despised Hoover since the war, when the FBI chief tried to throttle the infant OSS. Since then Hoover had methodically compiled his files of compromising information on prominent Americans. Now the greatest blackmailer in Washington was about to embarrass Bruce personally. To the ambassador's chagrin, with malevolent glee Hoover passed along Corbally's testimony to Rusk. The secretary of state immediately asked the ambassador for an explanation. Bruce dutifully pieced together the chronology. Corbally had indeed shown up at the embassy on January 29 and, according to Wells's notes at the time, sketched out the relationship between Keeler and Profumo.

There was nothing sinister in the ambassador having that bit of gossip in January. Still, it embarrassed him because it was Hoover who informed the State Department. Wells sent copies of his memo of the meeting with Corbally to several officials at the embassy, including the CIA station chief. Had that kind of gossip belonged in a report back to State in Washington, it would have meant a deluge of chatty cables filled with nothing more than titillating rumor. It was Bruce's bad luck that Hoover learned the details directly from Corbally. The FBI chief then used Wells's justifiable omission of the State Department from the distribution list for his memo as a stick to beat Bruce.

Several writers have suggested a more sinister role for Bruce in the Profumo scandal. Two accounts have Corbally saying, many years after the fact, that it was Bruce who asked him to come to the embassy in the first place because his friend the prime minister had heard the gossip and wanted a very unofficial inquiry made. Corbally recalls, these authors allege, that "Ambassador Bruce asked me to find out what was going on and to let him know as quickly as possible," so he could inform Macmillan.[39] Bruce allegedly contacted Corbally because he knew he was a friend of Billy Hitchcock, the fast-living son of Bruce's deceased best friend, Tommy Hitchcock, and because the younger Hitchcock lived in London and knew Ward.

In fact, from the original FBI memo recording Corbally's testimony, it is clear that Corbally, not Bruce, initiated the contact. He did so when he heard that Keeler might go to America and sell her story to the press there, an unpleasant prospect for his friends Ward and Hitchcock. Later much was made of the fact that a full page is missing from the copy of Bruce's diary at the Virginia Historical Society for the day Corbally visited the embassy.[40] In fact, the original diary held by the State Department contains the missing page and its innocuous contents.

Bruce did meet with Macmillan on the last day of January, but it is unlikely that the premier would have asked him to investigate rumors about his own minister of defense. There is no question that Bruce and his associates knew about Profumo and Keeler weeks before the minister denied any impropriety in the House and months before he admitted the lie. Long before the scandal broke, suspicions had percolated through upper-class London. The Profumo-Keeler affair, at least among political circles, had become an open secret as early as the previous autumn. In November 1962 a cabinet minister, on hearing about the affair at a dinner party, replied, "So what? At least it's a girl. You too could have her for five pounds a go."[41]

By spreading Corbally's story around Washington, though, Hoover succeeded in causing the State Department and the CIA to launch their own investigations. They turned up nothing more. The intense interest shown in Washington about the affair, in fact, may have had little to do with British politics. At high levels of the administration there was a fear, some said, that the scandal would touch the man who allegedly met Christine Keeler when she visited New York in 1962 — John F. Kennedy.[42]

Once Profumo was publicly disgraced, the establishment closed ranks, protecting those of its members implicated and allowing the disgraced Profumo, and even more the outsider Ward, to bear the guilt. That others were involved was widely believed but never proven. Years later the prime minister's private secretary, Philip de Zulueta, admitted that the scandal would have been even more explosive had Air Minister Hugh Fraser, then the husband of Bruce's writer friend Lady Antonia Fraser, been implicated beyond the allegation made in the French press. In fact memoranda in the American embassy's files suggest that Fraser indeed knew Keeler.[43]

As one of those named in the fantastical, scurrilous press reports on the scandal, Bruce gave evidence to Lord Denning, who wrote the official — and opaque — report on the affair. In the meantime, the weight of the establishment came down on the wretched Ward.

Bruce began to calculate the damage to Macmillan. The government did not fall because of the scandal, but the prime minister never recovered politically. He was at fault for ignoring warning signs as the scandal unfolded, perhaps because the experience of being cuckolded by Lord Boothby for so many years kept him from prying into charges of adultery by his defense minister as soon as he should have done.[44] Bruce concluded that he "does appear to have displayed a remarkably credulous lack of sophistication" in ignoring the rumors for so long and would be punished for it.[45]

Official papers not declassified until 1994 reveal that Macmillan's office had been warned of the impending scandal at least by February 1 — three days after Corbally visited the American embassy — and fully a month before Profumo denied any wrongdoing in the Commons. It was not revealed at the time that the British security service, MI-5, was involved in the case from the start and had even used Ward as an agent.

Sir Isaiah Berlin once described David Bruce as a shrewd and honorable man who had a knack for avoiding disreputable people or circumstances that could lead to scandal or unpleasantness. In describing this quality, Berlin invoked a Russian proverb that says of such a man, "He emerged from the water dry." According to Berlin, Bruce never entered the water in the first place.[46] In the case of Ward, however, the august ambassador very nearly fell in over his head.

Ward's funeral, held at a crematorium, was attended by six people. A group of playwrights and drama critics, including Kenneth Tynan and John Osborne, sent a wreath of one hundred white carnations. The card said "To Stephen Ward/Victim of Hypocrisy."[47]

Though the fallout for the Conservative government came later, the symbolic denouement to the Profumo scandal occurred just before Ward committed suicide rather than face conviction for pimping. A week earlier a man quietly purchased from an art gallery the now-famous drawings Ward had sketched of the royal family. The purchaser was the Red Queen himself, Anthony Blunt, the haughty keeper of Elizabeth II's pictures and a faithful servant of the KGB.

CHAPTER 19

A Pall Over Our Spirits

'Enough of this bullshit' I heard Mr Johnson's voice exclaim on the booster, 'When are we going to get your boys in Vietnam? Hold your horses Lady Bird, I'll be right back.' . . . Then the voice became rather muffled, and the President remarked, 'It's [Harold] Wilson, baby. I know, but he's so dumb he can't find his ass with both hands.'

— "Mrs. Wilson's Diary," *Private Eye*, June 10, 1966

ONLY AFTER CAMELOT EXPIRED in a Texas hospital did Bruce come into his own as ambassador in London.[1] In temperament, in style, in most every way unlike the new president, Bruce nevertheless became important to a White House untutored in foreign affairs. But the overriding issue that dominated the rest of the decade tempered Bruce's enjoyment of his newfound importance to the Johnson administration.

The ambassador got along well enough with the new president, and not just because the ocean kept him agreeably at arm's length. Bruce described Johnson's crude, elemental energy as "an irresistible force of nature." He had met many national leaders and called LBJ the most "overwhelming personality" among them.[2] Johnson reminded him of "a great black leopard, magnificent, dangerous if cornered" and "a combination of Rodin's *Le Penseur*, a Texas Ranger, and Laurence Olivier."[3] "I'm not frightened of him," he told an interviewer, "but I must say that when he entered a room, particularly if you were going to be the only person in it, somehow the room seemed to contract —

this huge thing, it's almost like releasing a djinn from one of those Arabian Nights bottles. The personality sort of fills the room."[4]

He routinely submitted his resignation at the beginning of each year, but Johnson dismissed the courtesy as a waste of time and extracted his promise to remain in London indefinitely. Despite the chasm that separated the two men in style and finesse, Bruce retained a fondness for LBJ. Johnson reciprocated. "Every time I am with that David Bruce," he once told Senator Stuart Symington, "I learn something."[5] And when the president, in his typically dramatic fashion, took himself out of politics on national television, Bruce wrote a heartfelt note telling LBJ he was, like George Washington, "not only a Great Man but a Good Man."[6]

Within a year of Johnson's accession, the political landscape in Britain changed dramatically. Macmillan, in power since 1957, never recovered from the Profumo scandal. Critics mocked his campaign slogan, "You've Never Had It So Good," with the post-Profumo taunt, "You've Never Had It So Often." He passed the baton to Sir Alec Douglas-Home, whose quiet good sense never stood a chance of capturing the nation's affections. Macmillan and Home represented the tired Tory establishment, tweedy grandees easily satirized. The wily Labor leader, Harold Wilson, called them custodians of an effete, feudal Britain best swept into the dustbin of history. Forward-looking Socialists knew how to move the country ahead.

It was only a half-lie. The Tories of Macmillan's and Douglas-Home's stripe were in irreversible decline, devoid of a vision for the future. But Labor offered nothing more than continued government deficits in the misbegotten belief that prosperity grew out of Whitehall ukases and public sector spending. Britain's decline accelerated, now under the banner of trade union socialism rather than grouse moor conservatism. As Bernard Levin said of the two Harolds in his arch dissection of the decade, "Between them, then, Walrus and Carpenter, they divided up the Sixties."[7]

Bruce had been more comfortable socially with Tories than with the Labor opposition during the Macmillan years. But he was shrewd enough to keep in touch with members of the shadow cabinet and did not let his personal conservatism underestimate the prospects of Labor. He had found Wilson's predecessor as Labor shadow prime minister, Hugh Gaitskell, a sympathetic figure.[8] A moderate Oxbridge Socialist rather than cloth-cap Laborite, Gaitskell moved in the same London social circles as the ambassador. More stylish than their trade union colleagues, Gaitskell and his set looked down on plain Harold Wilson (who, they snobbishly alleged, hung china ducks on his sitting room wall).[9]

Bruce was especially close to another rising star of the Labor Party, Roy Jenkins, historian, intellectual, and soon-to-be cabinet minister. In Jenkins, Bruce found an empathetic, urbane friend who shared his views on Europe as well as his tastes in French wine, bespoke tailors, and sophisticated dinner conversation. Bruce said some in the Labor party doubted Jenkins was a "True Believer" in socialism and criticized him for "the amplitude of his social life." In the words of Wilson's biographer, Jenkins was "affected by the 'aristocratic embrace' of smart hostesses who liked to spice their social gatherings with witty socialist politicians."[10] Perhaps so, but as home secretary, Jenkins deserves credit for the most liberating deregulation of British society that was the Labor government's most lasting achievement. By the mid-1960s, he shared as little in common as Bruce with the backward-looking trade unions and increasingly strident, left-wing sentiments of Labor intellectuals. It took two more decades, but Jenkins eventually fulfilled Bruce's 1962 prediction that Labor would split and its right wing merge with the Liberals to form a middle way between a dirigiste, anti-Western Left and the resurgent Tories.[11]

Bruce's chief of mission in 1964, Philip Kaiser, provided another personal link with Labor because he had known many future Socialist politicians at Oxford before the war.[12] Bruce may not have moved in Labor circles himself, but through his and his team's contacts he was not, in Jenkins's metaphor, a beached whale, when Wilson won.[13]

His talents were not enough to keep Anglo-American relations on an even keel, for his boss in the White House had conceived, as Bruce put it, an "antipathy" for Harold Wilson.[14] Gone was the personal chemistry that helped Macmillan and Kennedy smooth over differences. After a particularly ribald presidential explosion, Bruce averted a serious rupture by persuading the prime minister to communicate with LBJ by teletype rather than telephone. Johnson habitually picked up the phone at odd hours when he wanted to put lesser mortals on the spot but resented anyone trying the same trick on him.[15]

When a Tory MP compared Wilson to an unpopular wartime commander whose men called him "Kipper" because he had two faces and no guts, Bruce thought it rude, but he understood why it struck a responsive chord.[16] He described the prime minister as "a cautious master of obfuscation," a highly talented political animal, a master of partisan infighting, "adept at making ambiguous public statements to serve his political aims."[17] "There is perhaps a touch of paranoia in Wilson," Bruce opined, "but he is undoubtedly one of the most adroit politicians in the world."[18]

He doubted Wilson's "freedom from prejudices" in economic and financial matters. He mistrusted Labor's faith in central planning and doubted the party's willingness to administer the fiscal castor oil necessary to save Britain from insolvency.[19] And he thought Labor too naive about the Soviet Union, too ready to believe utopian humbug about universal brotherhood and proletarian solidarity, too gullible for thinking that "if we are not nasty to the Soviets by being civil to the Germans, the dear old Russkies will give us pie in the sky."[20]

For all the popular press about Swinging London and Wilson's blather about harnessing the "white hot heat of technology," Britain in the mid-1960s entered a period of critical decline. The standard of living was far higher than in the austere years of rationing after the war, but it was a borrowed prosperity. Trade union defense of outmoded work rules, inept business management, unimaginative financial leadership in the City, and above all irresponsible government spending, all pointed toward disaster. Wilson did not sound the alarm and seemed increasingly indecisive. It would have been no better with a Tory cabinet. "No government could have worked wonders," as historian Walter Laqueur observed, "while the country failed to earn its way in the world."[21]

Bruce thought the British were overindulgent, living beyond their means. In a long cable to Washington written in July 1966, he denied that the country was going down the drain but warned that "every sluice gate is beginning to open."[22] It would take more than a decade of strikes, unemployment, near hyperinflation, and embarrassing subservience to the International Monetary Fund, before the British people elected a government intent on reversing the slide. That was for the future. During the rest of Bruce's time in London, the country lurched from one economic crisis to another.

With confidence in sterling plummeting, the ambassador despaired that even a currency crisis would wake up the British public. "A run on the pound," he grumpily concluded, "would be considered part of a nasty, ephemeral plot by dagos across the Channel."[23] He used the wrong generic British slur for Continentals: not "dagos" but "wogs" were said to begin at Calais, but his comment captured Britain's quirky brand of xenophobia and maddening resistance to change.

With the United Kingdom's economic decline came its diminution on the world stage, and with that retreat an increase in friction with America. Throughout the 1960s Britain hauled down the Union Jack around the globe, for the most part without violence. Wilson's intent to end Britain's military presence "East of Suez" prompted the greatest American outcry. Bruce denounced this policy privately as "calamitous, destructive, selfish, myopic, and threatening to world orderliness."[24] The decision, he exaggerated, was "the most deplorable resolve, except for Munich, that any British Government has taken during the last 150 years." He cited the pullout to justify his previous cables, dismissed at State as unduly pessimistic, about the decline of Britain on the world scene.[25]

He denounced his idealistic colleagues at State for their knee-jerk condemnation of the departing European colonial powers. In fact, it was America's traditional anti-imperialist stance — which Bruce emphatically did not share — that encouraged the British retreat from empire. Americans, like those members of OSS who derided Allied wartime policy for trying to "Save England's Asiatic Colonies," had no right to complain when Britain finally decided it was time to wind down the Raj, not just in India but everywhere.

Announcing the pullback from "East of Suez" unfortunately coincided with an official visit by Wilson to Washington. Following protocol, Bruce was on hand. The White House staff, worried about relations between Wilson and Johnson, consulted the diplomat on the wording of the toast LBJ would give at the state dinner. "The difficulty," he drily replied, "is how to couch the Presidential language so as to butter up the Prime Minister and Mrs. Wilson as guests, without being fulsome over his policies. One point is agreed — Wilson should not again be favorably compared with Winston Churchill."[26] The press poked fun at the marine band for selecting "On the Road to Mandalay" as part of their state dinner serenade, oblivious to the "East of Suez" connotation.[27] LBJ and Wilson talked alone for two hours, and the president confided to Bruce afterward that the session went well, "without rancor." It was as much as could be expected.

In 1954 French collapse at Dien Bien Phu doomed Bruce's beloved European Defense Community. A decade later, war ravaged Indochina again. The splenetic anti-Americanism that increasingly infected Britain found an easy target in Bruce and his chancery in Grosvenor Square. He was the ideal image of hate for people who conjured America as the Great Satan long before the idea occurred to bigots in Iran.

Just before he died, JFK approved the coup that toppled Ngo Dinh Diem, America's man in South Vietnam. A corrupt and ineffectual nationalist, Diem was not spared even though LBJ had once anointed him the "Winston Churchill of Asia." The little war grew very large in a hurry. By 1966 it obsessed Johnson and engulfed all considerations of policy, foreign and domestic. Bruce loyally supported Johnson even as his own doubts deepened. He defended LBJ whenever he could but often objected to the president's tactics for winning British support.

One especially unpleasant incident reinforced his unease about Johnson's penchant for playing the bully. He was appalled to read a cable from Washington in March 1965 that ordered him to dictate Wilson's words in a forthcoming Commons debate on the war. As long as the British embassy in Washington sought advice from the Americans on crafting a bland statement to suggest to the prime minister, Bruce saw no problem. But then the White House demanded that Wilson insert in his prepared text a sentence stating that "there must be an end to aggression from the North" before a ceasefire and negotiations could commence. The administration went so far as to say it would not welcome the foreign secretary's planned visit to Washington unless Wilson adopted the supplied script. (It compounded Bruce's annoyance that Washington had not informed him about this planned visit.) The ambassador cabled Dean Rusk to express his irritation about the lesser matter. On the larger point, presuming to instruct a foreign head of government what to say to his own parliament, he undertook his orders with great reluctance, calling it "a tasteless proceeding."

Bruce thought that under the circumstances Wilson made a masterly statement to the Commons.[28] Three days later, in a long conversation the prime minister explained what he, the ambassador, already knew: even Labor moderates were beginning to criticize the premier for being "a mere satellite" of America. Wilson explained in blunt terms the invidious position he found himself in, attacked for toadying to America on Vietnam and at the same time derided for being on bad terms with Johnson, "despite undignified efforts to curry favor with him." Wilson let Bruce know he resented the effort to influence his statement in the Commons. The ambassador tried his best to mitigate the hostility. He admired the president's tenacity and was amused when Johnson, explaining how he reacted to constant criticism, said, "Sometimes I just get all hunkered up like a jackass in a hailstorm."[29] But Bruce thought he should temper his anger at Wilson. "There is no room, in my opinion," he said, "for lack of conventional courtesies between chiefs of allied states."[30]

Even before Kennedy died, Bruce had questioned the wisdom of the war. In early 1962 journalist Robert Estabrook had a long lunch with him in London. The ambassador's conflicting feelings about Vietnam, as reflected in Estabrook's private notes, epitomized the predicament of so many American leaders: "Bruce is not sure that we should have made a commitment to either Laos or to South Viet-Nam in the first place. Getting bogged down with larger numbers of men but without confronting the real enemy is the way to suffer real attrition. But once we made the statement that we were concerned," we had to stick with it.[31] It was a pure statement of the way intentions, however noble, led down the road to perdition.

Two years later Bruce regretted that the war — he called it Johnson's "inherited scourge" — threatened to sabotage the president's ambitious domestic programs. In frustration, he told British press lord Cecil King that the Chinese and North Vietnamese were playing their cards ineptly. If they would just sit down at the conference table, Bruce said, they could take home all the marbles. He wished, only half in jest, that he was the political adviser to the Chinese, because "he would have the Americans out of Asia in no time."[32] If he and not LBJ were calling the shots, he would accept terms to end the war.

During a visit to Washington for consultation, he and Rusk ruminated about what might have happened if American policy had been different. Bruce, as ambassador in Paris more than a decade before, had urged his government to send military aid to Indochina. Rusk at the time had been State's chief expert on Southeast Asia. Both had had more to do with Vietnamese history than most of their peers in the foreign service. Bruce concluded that "one will never know how the dice would have turned up" if thrown differently. His own opinion at this stage, in 1965, was to continue military pressure but keep alert for "a diplomatic or military ploy" that could blunt the drive of the Vietnamese Communists without enlarging the war.[33]

Because Bruce was not an ideologue but a pragmatist who admired subtlety more than candor, Talleyrand more than Foster Dulles, he saw nothing dishonorable about continuing his support of LBJ in the face of his own growing doubts. He had always thought it was his duty to support his government's policy whatever his personal opinion and, if in good conscience he could not, to quit. As the war heated up, he remained a detached observer but took an interest in any effort to end the fighting. And he argued for taking more chances for a negotiated settlement than Washington seemed willing to do. In 1966, with speculation about peace talks in the air, he suggested to Harriman that the U.S. send former president Eisenhower as a private citizen to meet with Ho Chi Minh.[34] It was a hopeless idea but no more so than other abortive suggestions. In 1967 an opportunity arose to play a part in a more auspicious overture.

Among the many schemes LBJ's advisers toyed with for moving the dispute from battlefield to conference table was the so-called Phase A–Phase B plan. According to this formula, after the United States suspended bombing over the North, both American and North Vietnamese forces would gradually limit their actions in the South. In February 1967 Soviet Premier Aleksei Kosygin planned to visit London for a week. Wilson decided to enlist his help, using the A–B formula, to bring Hanoi to the bargaining table. By chance, Kosygin's visit coincided with the Vietnamese New Year holiday, Tet. The warring parties had already scheduled a ceasefire in the South and a pause in the aerial bombing of the North. The holiday truce thus seemed the ideal occasion to implement the A–B formula by prolonging the bombing halt.

Wilson believed the Soviets would welcome a settlement that made the North Vietnamese more beholden to them than to their Chinese rivals. Sino-Soviet relations had reached a nadir, with Beijing mobs burning Kosygin in effigy and attacking the Soviet embassy. Johnson resented Wilson's interference but allowed him to make the effort. Better that than more British complaints about America missing a chance for peace, however unlikely.[35]

Bruce leaped at the chance to be a part. He welcomed Chester Cooper, now with the State Department, back to London to help him monitor Wilson's discussions with Kosygin and provide the link with Washington. All week long they secretly conferred with the British about Wilson's conversations with Kosygin and engaged in incessant, frantic cabling and telephoning back and forth across the Atlantic. To avoid the suspicions of journalists about so many visits by the ambassador to Downing Street, the British surreptitiously led Bruce into Wilson's residence through a back entrance via the cabinet offices. He thought it all a bit too conspiratorial, and he was getting too old for skulking about like an aging spy. But he was glad enough to keep the press at bay.

If the North Vietnamese, replying through Kosygin, agreed to Wilson's proposal, Bruce and Cooper planned to press Washington to continue the bombing suspension. Early in the week Bruce cited real evidence for a breakthrough: the British had bugged Kosygin's suite at Claridges and took heart from his calls to Moscow.[36] What Johnson did not tell Bruce or Wilson was that he had just sent a letter to Ho Chi Minh that made the A–B plan obsolete. The Americans would not halt the bombing first. Ho must begin to wind down the fighting before LBJ would stop air strikes. Reconnaissance reports that came in during the holiday pause only reinforced Johnson's suspicions. One pilot reported that military traffic streaming down the Ho Chi Minh trail looked like "Sunday on the New Jersey Turnpike."[37]

Long hours of conferring late at night frayed everyone's nerves. Bruce and Cooper were frequently called to Downing Street after midnight for updates on the prime minister's latest conversation with Kosygin. Cooper was in constant touch with Washington and, being in London under wraps, could devote his entire time to the discussions. Bruce, who had to keep up his usual schedule to avoid attracting attention, was also becoming fatigued. The last night Kosygin was in town, he snatched a total of two hours of sleep between furtive meetings.

Just as the Soviet leader responded positively to Wilson's proposal, Bruce learned about LBJ's tough letter to Ho. Wilson was livid, "beside himself with fury and frustration."[38] Through his initiative, for the first time the Soviets had agreed to approach Hanoi about peace talks, and now Johnson was cutting the ground from beneath his feet. As the principal Americans on the spot, Bruce and Cooper were on the receiving end of Wilson's ire. "About ten o'clock tonight," the ambassador noted, "Chet and I went down to 10 Downing Street, where we had two and a half hours of rather rough handling. The Prime Minister was indignant over the changes made in what he had believed to be our firm negotiating posture."[39] Foreign Secretary George Brown, fatigued and, Bruce thought, probably drunk, raged incoherently. "The US had made a bloody mess of things." Brown and Wilson felt badly let down and even fell into bitter recriminations against one another in front of the embarrassed Americans. Cooper said he "sensed Anglo-American relations dissolving before my eyes." Some of the British muttered the word "betrayal." It smelled of Suez all over again.

The ambassador stepped in to find an alternative that would embrace Washington's sterner terms. As Cooper recalled, echoing so many other observers of the diplomat's style, "Bruce brought the discussion away from personalities and back to substance."[40] With the clock ticking on Kosygin's last hours in Britain, Bruce and Cooper proposed that the United States extend the Tet bombing pause if the North Vietnamese would refrain from moving south several units that were poised to do so. This was asking for less than the withdrawal demanded by LBJ's letter. At a minimum, Bruce thought it was necessary to refrain from restarting the bombing as long as Kosygin was in Britain. To resume would be a gross insult to Wilson.

Kosygin's final meeting with Wilson took place at the prime minister's official country house, Chequers. It was agreed to send Cooper there, out of sight, to keep open a direct link with Washington. His perch for this clandestine mission was a garret room with a window overlooking the courtyard. The administration had still not agreed to extend the bombing pause as Wilson and Kosygin wound up their discussions and the Soviet premier prepared to leave. In desperation, Cooper rang the White House and dangled the receiver out his attic window. Across three thousand miles of ocean, presidential adviser Walt Rostow could hear the police escort in the courtyard below rev their motorcycles in anticipation of leading the motorcade back to Kosygin's hotel.

That did the trick. By the time the Soviet premier reached Claridges, Washington had agreed to the extension. But the White House gave Kosygin only ten hours to relay the offer to the North Vietnamese and pass their response back to Wilson. The Russian agreed to try. Bruce called Rusk to oppose the deadline as ridiculous and to ask for several more days. As Cooper looked on, the ambassador implored Rusk to see the president and argue for more time. "I didn't hear Rusk's reply," Cooper recalled, "I didn't have to. I could read it in the Ambassador's face. The conversation ended with a brusque 'good night.' Rusk had told Bruce the British had been given all they were going to get, and Bruce was not to call him again on that subject."[41]

Bruce later said Washington acted "stupidly."[42] After angry talks with Walt Rostow, the principal White House hawk, who behaved "almost hysterically," the ambassador said others of the small White House group involved "are strung up to an exalted point of nervous tension."[43] Through it all, Bruce kept his own sense of humor. With Anglo-American friendship in tatters and Kosygin about to leave the country empty-handed, the ambassador wistfully remembered that it was his birthday, his sixty-ninth.

Nothing changed. The North Vietnamese did not respond. Kosygin left London. LBJ resumed the bombing. The war cranked up again. The Tet holiday a year later would not be as calm. Wilson fancied himself uniquely qualified to deal with the Soviets and believed he came close to pulling off a monumental coup, only to be thwarted by American deceit. Johnson just was not interested in a settlement. It was too soon for either side to concede what it would have taken to begin serious talks. "And so ended several months of initiatives, high expectations, and soul-destroying frustrations," Cooper wrote. "The peace efforts from November through mid-February ended in another pall of smoke over Hanoi."[44] David Bruce's moment to help end the war had passed — for the time being.

Early in 1965 the embassy received a crudely lettered warning: "An attempt to kill your ambassador and also the planting of a bomb in your embassy is about to take place." As though the writer feared the message was not clear enough, a marginal scrawl admonished, "Treat this like a joke and you make our task dead easy, bastards and pimps."[45]

A hoax on this occasion, threats against the embassy and the ambassador would became all too real soon enough.

In 1962 he had spoken to a student group at Oxford and fielded hostile questions about American policy on China, Cuba, race relations, and "our other fancied sins and mistakes." There were no threats of violence, however, and it was, he thought, "a stimulating evening."[46] A few years later such an exchange, adversarial but civilized, was no longer possible.

In October 1967 he dedicated a dormitory for American exchange students at the University of Warwick. In the background demonstrators chanted, "Hey, Hey, LBJ, How many kids did you kill today?"[47] A month later he unwisely agreed to speak on Anglo-American relations at Cambridge, where tomatoes, eggs, and taunts had greeted the prime minister two weeks before. The ambassador gamely spoke and submitted to interrogation for an hour and a half in a packed, hostile auditorium. A phalanx of police escorted him out of the hall, as protesters surrounded his car. A quick-thinking constable offered his own car to Bruce. Students rushed to the vehicle, jumped on the hood, and battered the windows with shouts of "bastard" and worse. The constable accelerated just enough to force his way through the mob, scattering cursing protesters to either side.[48]

Bruce credited the quick actions of the police for his escape without harm. Because of the experience, he revised his previous recommendation and strongly advised Washington not to allow Vice-President Hubert Humphrey to keep a planned speaking engagement in London. Given the size and violence of the demonstrations, a visit by the vice-president would be politically inadvisable — unless, he ended with a sardonic aside, the protesters injured Humphrey and made people feel sorry for him.[49]

The embassy in Grosvenor Square ("Genocide Square" to the demonstrators) became the focus of hatred in the late sixties. Opponents of American policy staged a massive rally there to coincide with the first big march on Washington in October 1967. The police arranged a path for the marchers and a place for them to assemble near the chancery, where their leaders would present a petition. Despite precautions, the event got completely out of hand. The police, on foot and on horseback, sustained injuries from stones thrown by the protesters, who tore up park benches, destroyed the hedge in the square, tried to overturn automobiles, and broke a dozen embassy windows.[50]

As a symbolic lightning rod for anti-American protests, the ambassador by 1967 found his freedom circumscribed. When the distinguished historian and philosopher Sir Isaiah Berlin invited him to attend the opening of Wolfson College, Oxford, Bruce reluctantly declined, fearing he would be "a source of embarrassment" to his friend and "an object of disorder." Berlin, perhaps the wisest and most civilized intellectual of his day, accepted Bruce's decision but felt deeply ashamed that it was no longer possible to invite an American diplomat to a public event in Oxford.[51]

Not even the Bruces' private gatherings were safe. One incident occurred at a birthday party they gave for their young friend Diana Phipps. There were the usual glittering names from London high society — the publisher George Weidenfeld, Lady Diana Cooper, assorted Pakenhams and other names from *Debrett's*. In their avant-garde attire, Phipps's own circle from the entertainment world outshone Evangeline Bruce's profusion of hothouse camelias. One of them repaid Phipps's and the Bruces' kindness in an odd fashion. Kathleen Tynan, a screenwriter newly married to playwright/theater critic Kenneth Tynan, pasted anti-American stickers in the rest room announcing an antiwar protest for the following month. She later explained her behavior with the sanctimony of the ideologue whose opinions supersede the obligations of civility toward her hosts.[52]

On the day Tynan's stickers advertised — Sunday, March 17, 1968 — the embassy again attracted demonstrators. The Vietnam Solidarity Campaign, a consortium of leftist groups, attracted 15,000 protesters to Trafalgar Square to hear speeches praising North Vietnam and denouncing Britain and America. Vanessa Redgrave read to the crowd the letter she had written to Bruce demanding American withdrawal from Vietnam. Wearing a white headband, the Vietnamese symbol of mourning, she presented her letter to an embassy spokesman when the surging mass of demonstrators reached Grosvenor Square. Her confreres were not content with such an unsatisfyingly nonviolent gesture and, with Viet Cong flags flying, threw rocks, blood bombs, smoke canisters, paint, and flour at the embassy. Hospitals admitted fifty wounded people, half of them police. Some of the mounted officers' horses had to be shot because of their injuries. Bruce was especially aggrieved by the large number of American students in the crowd.[53] He secretly hoped the rumor was true that they planned to pull down the statue of FDR in the square in the hope that such offensive behavior would finally galvanize British opinion against them.[54]

After it was over, a light rain began to fall. Trampled banners, posters, and assorted rubbish mingled with broken tree limbs, heavy with spring bud. "The lawn looked as though it had been plowed by some mad farmer," said one of Bruce's staffers. "I was sick at heart. As I returned to my flat, I thought, 'It's a good thing these people are pacifist. Think what it would have been like if they believed in war.'"[55]

The ambassador left for home for a visit a week later, "glad to get out of this country," which he found increasingly depressing.[56] Nineteen sixty-eight promised to be a febrile year on both sides of the Atlantic. Assassinations, riots, and violent demonstrations rocked the United States while anti-Americanism reached a crescendo in Britain. Across the Channel, student revolts nearly brought French society to a halt and shook de Gaulle's aging government. (The imperious old general had not lost his sense of humor, though. In response to the anarchistic desire of the students for change, he replied, "Reform yes, bedwetting no.")

October once again brought out demonstrations against the embassy. Bruce went to the chancery on the last Sunday of the month to be with his staff. After a rally drew thirty thousand protesters to Hyde Park, a splinter column converged on Grosvenor Square to attack the embassy. A thousand bobbies from the Metropolitan police kept the chanting mob from reaching the building. Threats made against the residence in Regent's Park never materialized. Watching from a chancery window, Bruce praised the conduct of the police, many of whom were beaten by demonstrators who taunted them and threw firecrackers.[57] When he left that evening, several hundred self-styled anarchists and Maoists were still milling about but were no match for the police. In the same week vandals dynamited the JFK memorial at Runnymede, splitting the seven-ton granite monument down the middle.[58]

While disagreement over Vietnam eroded civility at home and abroad, Bruce remained a firm, often ignored, voice for rational discourse. He was a founding member of the post–World War II internationalist establishment that confidently, at times overconfidently, guided America in its world role. Now like that establishment, his day was coming to an end, hastened by war in Indochina. But he refused to abandon tact and moderation, knowing from experience that those rare qualities ought not be discarded lightly. That was why the violent demonstrations pained him so much, and that was why he was keen to see that the representatives of authority did not succumb to the tactics and mentality of the stone throwers. After the Paris disturbances in May 1968 he commiserated with French diplomat Geoffroy de Courcel about the decline in civility. He was less troubled by the emotional excesses of students, he told his friend, than by the "intellectual nihilism of many of their elders."[59]

It upset him when he learned that the embassy's consular section had recommended against issuing a visa to Vanessa Redgrave for a trip to America. The decision called to mind the timorous behavior of Truman-era officials denying visas and passports to prominent figures like Picasso on the basis of unpopular political associations and out of fear of McCarthyite reaction. Bruce thought that stance unhelpful then and bad public policy now, no matter how much Redgrave had been a thorn in the embassy's side. His argument for granting her a visa harked back not just to his passport headaches as undersecretary of state. It called to mind his argument against the 1940 bill in the Virginia General Assembly that proposed a restriction on free speech that would, he said then with more prescience than he realized, merely dignify "talkative minorities."

Shortly after noon on June 5, 1968, President Johnson convened the 587th meeting of the National Security Council. The single item on the agenda was a discussion of issues affecting relations between the U.S. and the U.K. Secretary of the Treasury Henry Fowler and Secretary of Defense Clark Clifford worried mainly about prolonged financial weakness in London. Secretary of State Rusk summarized the current situation based on a cable he received from the ambassador the previous day, a classic Bruce dispatch.[60]

Bruce described the "disappointment, discouragement, and disillusion" that characterized British opinion, while at the same time he doubted that conditions favored the sort of dramatic social upheaval that had roiled Paris the previous month. Beyond weaknesses of the Labor government or the Tory opposition, he focused on the more fundamental problem: "Growing public criticism has been directed at

the political and social structures of the country, parliament's impo-
tence and inefficiency." Underlying these attitudes, he believed, were
serious problems. "The Brits — especially those old enough to remember WWII — have not repeat not yet fully come to terms with fundamental change in Britain's world role." Acheson was right. "Nor," Bruce
continued, "have they found the way to adapt national political and
social institutions, largely forged in a Victorian mold reflecting [a]
period of military and economic dominance, to current realities. This is
one serious source of misunderstanding with a younger generation
which was brought up on post-Suez realities, and to which empire and
even commonwealth are largely historical concepts. A leading role in a
uniting Europe could provide an alternative goal and focus of popular
energies — but this too remains frustrated." Further, he argued, de-
valuation of the pound and failure of economic plans had produced a
situation in which the public "remains in skeptical and self-flagellating
mood."[61]

Being ambassador was definitely not as rewarding as it been earlier.
The war, he wrote his brother, "casts a pall over our spirits."[62] But not
just the war and his own private doubts about American policy diminished Bruce's enjoyment of his post. When Johnson announced he
would not run for reelection, the ambassador had just turned seventy
and was beginning to feel his age. His unhappiness increased when the
voters chose Richard Nixon. The treatment his staff received during
the transition did nothing to persuade him to consider working for the
new administration.

The new president's desire to visit London gave Bruce his first taste
of the Nixon White House. He agreed to stay on a few weeks until his
successor, Philadelphia publisher Walter Annenberg, arrived. Once Annenberg's name went to the Senate for confirmation, Evangeline Bruce
invited the ambassador-designate's wife to visit Winfield House, a good
deed that did not long go unpunished. In the meantime, her husband
and his staff bit their tongues as they prepared for the president's
arrival. Bruce learned earlier than most Americans about the brash
Nixon team of crew-cut Teutonic gatekeepers and their surfeit of hu-
bris, which every change of party brings to the White House. Visits by
heads of state always generate protocol headaches. But the arrogance
of the new men, their obvious disdain for the State Department, their

ignorance of British punctilio, and their curt treatment of Bruce's staff soured the ambassador's last weeks in Grosvenor Square.

It appalled him that Nixon's men wanted to ask the queen to disinvite a guest from her palace dinner for the president. The object of their dislike was not an incidental figure but John Freeman, British ambassador-designate to Washington. Bruce could not believe the president himself had been consulted about such a spiteful request, just because Freeman, as a former journalist with the *New Statesman*, had written unkind words about Nixon before the election. Bruce quashed the idea when a White House underling suggested disinviting Freeman. He was pleased when Nixon graciously recognized Freeman during a toast at the dinner, welcoming him to America with the words, "I look forward to frequent meetings between the New Nixon and the New Statesman."[63] Bruce felt vindicated, but repeated slights of his staff by White House officials stuck in his throat. He promised himself to have a talk with William Rogers, the new secretary of state, to sort out this problem. Though he saw the fine hand of Nixon's national security adviser, Henry Kissinger, behind the London trip, he did not yet perceive that it was Kissinger and not the amiable, ineffective Rogers who called the shots.

Perhaps Kennedy was right to say he had made a mistake in sending Bruce to London. Clearly the Special Relationship was no more than a ghost of its former self. A transatlantic matrix of foreign relations experts, diplomats, and military officers still wielded influence in Washington and London, but much less so than before. America was mired in war, and Britain belatedly, tentatively had begun to eye closer ties with Europe. From another perspective, though, perhaps it was just the right time for Bruce to be Washington's man in London. Britain may have been less important to American foreign policy, but the fact that the United States could no longer count on its wartime ally was all the more reason to keep a living symbol of Anglo-American friendship installed at Grosvenor Square.

Throughout the farewell luncheons and dinners in his honor, few of the hosts failed to point out that Bruce was the longest-serving American envoy in London ever. After the last of the parties, David and Evangeline Bruce left London on the afternoon of March 19, 1969.

Chancellor of the Exchequer Roy Jenkins and his wife, Jennifer, were the last British friends to say goodbye.

Antiwar demonstrations targeting the embassy continued to grow. So too did the number of American students abroad whose participation so grieved the ambassador. London in the mid-1960s had became a refuge for American youth, a place of "'pot, easy lays and rock,' calm, stress-free, technologically backward, but a place of pilgrimage for a generation for whom unemployment and poverty were unimaginable."[64] Later Bruce exaggerated the turmoil, telling one interviewer, "I was besieged there practically every Sunday for about six months. I'm sorry to say that some of the most effective demonstrators, in the way of resorting to violence, were Americans."[65] Some of them, like William Jefferson Clinton, whose first London rally against the war was the last big one the Bruces had to endure, adhered to a strictly nonviolent approach.[66] But the ambassador was aging and tired and unwilling to give them the benefit of the doubt as he had done to those eager student opponents he had debated civilly at Cambridge years before.

On reaching the welcome sight of his Georgetown house, Bruce knew he was not yet entirely free from duty. A week or so of debriefing at the department remained. Shortly afterward, Secretary of State Rogers asked the Bruces to attend a little ceremony at the Thomas Jefferson Room, where they were presented with lifetime diplomatic passports. Rogers, Dean Acheson, Dean Rusk, and Averell Harriman all made comments. In his diary Bruce wrote, "Thus ended, as far as I can foresee, my diplomatic career."[67] The parenthetical expression revealed his hopes that it had not.

CHAPTER 20

Intermezzo

The secret of being miserable is to have leisure to bother about whether you are happy or not. The cure for it is occupation.

— G. B. Shaw, 1914

*I*N NANCY MITFORD'S SATIRICAL NOVEL *Don't Tell Alfred*, the new British ambassador in Paris is chagrined by the conduct of his predecessor's glamorous wife. It would have been hard enough for the diplomat, a sober Oxford don, to match the flair of Sir Louis and Lady Leone. Worse, Lady Leone feigned mortal illness rather than leave the residence and, instead of discreetly dying, requisitioned a room in the building and around her sickbed recreated her urbane salon under the noses of her hapless successors.

Mitford's readers knew she was parodying a famous real-life contretemps at the Paris embassy in 1948. Ambassador Alfred Duff Cooper and his wife, Lady Diana, like the fictitious Leones, discomfited their successors, the mild and owlish Sir Oliver Harvey and his wife, Lady Maud. The Coopers violated the unwritten rule to leave town until the new envoy had settled in. They continued their dazzling parties and encouraged the Paris diplomatic set to choose between them and the staid Harveys. In 1969 the Bruces committed something like the same sin as their English friends two decades before.

The ambassador and his wife looked for a suitable pied-à-terre after he retired. They chose the fabled Albany, just off Piccadilly, and rented two small apartments to be redone as one. They retained the design firm Colefax and Fowler, under the direction of Nancy Lancaster, who transformed the high-ceilinged rooms into a Louis XVI Parisian apartment that might have pleased the most famous of many celebrated earlier tenants, Lady Caroline Lamb.

In the meantime, Walter Annenberg worried about making a good impression. A successful publisher, he was driven by family shame. His father, Moses "Moe" Annenberg, had built his fortune in shady Chicago businesses and served time for income tax evasion. To be fair, the stylish Georgetown Democrats who moaned about this boorish tycoon being sent to London conveniently feigned amnesia about another one. "People began to speak," sneered one commentator, "as if Joseph Kennedy, the bootlegger and Nazi sympathizer, had never had the job."[1]

Before the Senate confirmed her husband, Lee Annenberg flew to London at Evangeline Bruce's invitation to see Winfield House. She tactlessly announced that she planned massive remodeling and brought two interior decorators with her. With clipboards at the ready, they took down the orders she barked out as they moved from room to room, criticizing as they went. On the plane home, she told her designers she needed to do her Christian Science meditation, otherwise, "I'll be a real bitch by the time we land."[2]

Once the Annenbergs moved in, there began what witnesses called a Restoration comedy. To the Bruces and their many friends, the new envoy was an entirely inadequate representative. The Annenbergs began to sense that society was snubbing them, and if the Bruces did not stay at Albany constantly, their frequent presence irritated the new ambassador. Annenberg, said his biographer, "was quick to find fault with the man whose shadow still fell so heavily upon him."[3]

Annenberg was an easy mark, a caricature of the obtuse American abroad, and with one spectacular gaucherie, he became the butt of jokes across the country. In a BBC film on the queen's daily routine, she was shown receiving the newly appointed Annenberg. When she asked about Winfield House, he harrumphed about "the discomfiture as a result of a need for, uh, elements of refurbishment and rehabilitation."[4] The queen, Gore Vidal wrote, looked as though an exploding cigar had just blown up in her face.[5] With one turgid phrase Annenberg became the laughingstock of England and gave the word "refurbishment" a comic resonance. Annenberg gradually overcame his disastrous start. The flap with the Bruces subsided. But the incident gave the denouement to their eight years at Winfield House a Mitfordesque flavor.

David Bruce had turned seventy in February 1968. He was alone in New York, having been called home from London for consultation. Celebrating quietly to himself, he "read a divine letter from E. written in French, full of love and whimsicalities."[6] It was an important milestone, a time for reflection. Though he was still ambassador to Britain, he was already looking ahead to retirement. When it came in 1969, it was exactly half a century after celebrating his majority with his fellow soldiers in a rough army billet in France.

He had lived abroad for sixteen of the twenty-four years since World War II. In *Don't Tell Alfred*, Nancy Mitford based her American characters partly on the Bruces, "the Henry James type of expatriates who live here because they can't stick it at home."[7] A snide exaggeration. Still, the London embassy was his longest continuous foreign posting, and during those eight years America had changed dramatically. Riots and assassinations were turning a prosperous decade into a fearful one. "Our racial problems," Bruce said, "are far more grave than anything that has happened in this country since the Civil War." His admiration for LBJ remained undimmed: "His predecessors paid lip service to equality; he has tried to bring it about."[8] And then the ascendancy of the old foreign policy establishment that Bruce exemplified was broken on the wheel of Vietnam. In the twilight of his life, just as at the beginning of his productive career in the months before Pearl Harbor, American opinion was horribly riven by a foreign war.

The national plague of disasters at the end of his career also coincided with personal tragedies and disappointments. The first came two years before he left London, and its residue magnified declining health and weariness as reasons for wanting to retire.

On January 18, 1967, in the midst of meetings leading up to the stillborn Wilson-Kosygin talks, a telephone call came from New York. The night before, a chartered Piper Apache had taken off from San Juan for the eighty-mile flight to St. Thomas in the Virgin Islands. The plane flew into a violent thunderstorm and after a single garbled radio contact was never heard from again. The plane carried a pilot and two passengers — Audrey and Stephen Currier. When LBJ heard the news, he put the Coast Guard and the U.S. Navy at the disposal of the search effort. At its height, more than eighty aircraft in addition to ships combed the Bermuda Triangle.

The ambassador and his wife flew to New York, but by then he had lost hope. "We still clutch at every straw," he said, "but it is impossible really to deceive oneself. The whole affair is utterly tragic."[9] The most poignant moment came when he visited Audrey's three children — his grandchildren — Andrea, the oldest at ten, Lavinia nine, and Michael five. "The two girls played the piano and sang for me," their grandfather said, "while Michael was as incessant in motion as a whirling dervish."[10] Despite the massive search, no wreckage was found. Civil rights leaders believed racists had planted a bomb to kill Currier because of his contributions to their cause. Some of them would never be persuaded to give up this theory even though no evidence surfaced to support it.

"Bushels of telegrams and letters of sympathy" greeted Bruce on his return to London. It had been, he concluded, "the most unhappy week of my life."[11]

From the outset of his marriage, Stephen Currier had never seen eye-to-eye with his father-in-law. If the personal chemistry had been different, the strain might have eased. As it was, both Audrey's father and Uncle Paul detested the younger man. "If they could have gotten away with it," a family friend remembered, "both Paul and David would have strung Currier up."[12] Currier's Mellon in-laws were especially upset at the way he arrogated to himself the decisions about how to spend the income on Audrey's vast fortune, some $250 million in the late 1950s. Worse, to their way of thinking, was the fact that the beneficiaries of his decisions were civil rights advocates, hardly the sort of people that people like the Mellons would normally bump into.

Currier was a classic rich white liberal, hardly a radical. In fact, some black leaders, notably Malcolm X, suspected him of conspiring with the Kennedy administration to divert their movement from mass, confrontational action to quieter efforts. Currier was indeed involved in transforming the 1963 March on Washington into a nonthreatening event palatable to the Kennedys. Black radicals were not entirely wrong: the purposes of the event had been subtly altered, though the intent was not as sinister as Malcolm X declared.[13] In the end, though, what is remembered is one of the great set pieces in the history of American oratory, Martin Luther King's "I Have a Dream" speech. Stephen Currier had reason to be proud. His work probably garnered more praise than the gifts of great art that were the Mellon trademark.[14] Perhaps that was another reason why the family disliked him so.

Bruce had seen in his youth how bigotry corroded southern society. In 1962, before even Kennedy was convinced to press hard against discrimination, he wrote that the president "has a chance to break the back of segregation; I am convinced he will take it."[15] If Bruce did not share the constricted perspective of his former in-laws, he did worry that Stephen dominated his timid daughter. Like so many self-appointed benefactors of the downtrodden, Currier found it exhilarating to love the masses but treated those closest to him like dirt. So it was with Audrey at the beginning. She was hardly one to protest. Early in her marriage she did volunteer work at a hospital, every day wearing the same shabby raincoat that was her signature garment from student days in Cambridge. The staff, not knowing who she was, passed the hat to buy her a new coat.[16]

Despite her shyness, she chafed at her husband's treatment. She once was so unhappy that she went to her father and asked for advice on divorce. Bruce responded eagerly, but the Curriers decided to try again to solve their problems. It did nothing for family relations when Audrey told her husband about the ambassador's enthusiasm for helping her arrange a divorce. And then, confounding all expectations, the marriage flourished. Even Ailsa's closest friend, cousin Peggy Hitchcock, agreed that Stephen was good for Audrey. "The fact was," Hitchcock said, "Stephen gave her great confidence. She was very happy, she bloomed like a flower. . . . They had three children and the parents read to them, they all said prayers together. They had a *wonderful* family life."[17]

The Bruces recrossed the ocean in February 1967 for the memorial service at St. James Episcopal Church in New York City, among the mourners Lady Bird Johnson, Governor Nelson Rockefeller, Senator Robert Kennedy, and Mayor John Lindsay. As the service took place, the Curriers' sailing yawl, which had joined in the fruitless search, strewed flowers on the surface of the Caribbean.[18] Fifty-nine years after his parents grieved over the death of a child, David Bruce experienced their sense of loss. "The consensus," he said at the end of the year, "was that it would be almost impossible for 1968 to be as unfortunate a period as 1967. For me, 1967 was the year of the most tragic experience I have ever had — the death of Audrey."[19]

In the years after her divorce, Ailsa Mellon Bruce had become increasingly reclusive, living an almost troglodytic existence, fussing over the repeated redecoration of her apartments and driving antiques dealers mad with her dithering. She filled her residences with ornate furniture and hundreds of antique *objets de luxe,* little bejeweled boxes and figurines that had kept artisans in the Parisian carriage trade busy and that now had no function other than to give a fleeting moment of pleasure to a sad old woman. Much of what she bought would be counted as expensive rubbish. Even the objects that had a function, in particular the sets upon sets of rare china to serve hundreds of people, only collected dust because she never admitted more than a handful of friends into her world. She still collected paintings — that seemed to be in the Mellon genes as much as shyness. With her fortune, she could make mistakes and still amass great art.

Ever since their divorce, Bruce dropped in occasionally to see her when he was passing through New York. He kept up the niceties of periodic letters, especially to suggest benefactions she might consider making. His cool, detached habit of sending birthday and holiday greetings by telegram rather than telephone is captured in the terse cable he sent from Germany in 1958, nicely timed to be transmitted at 11:35 P.M. on Christmas Eve: "Mrs. Mellon Bruce 2 East 67th Street NewYorkCity. Merry Christmas Love David."[20]

If he had never been close to Audrey, David nevertheless felt the pain when he learned of his daughter's disappearance. The news shattered Ailsa. He knew better than anyone about her withdrawn manner and excruciating indecision and was not surprised at the devastating effect their daughter's death had on Ailsa. He probably did not realize, though, how ill she had become. No one did. After all, her imaginary illnesses were legendary, and everyone attributed the minor respiratory problems and vague weaknesses to the self-centered hypochondria that had afflicted her since adolescence.

In 1969 it was not hypochondria. By then her body was riddled with cancer. Surgery was not possible because she put off treatment for so long. Even when she entered Roosevelt Hospital for the last time, the family thought it was only to treat recurrent hemorrhoids. Lauder Greenway moved into a room in the hospital to be with her at the end. Peggy Hitchcock, widow of David's polo-playing pal Tommy, said of her friend's end, "I never saw such a death."[21]

Ailsa left half a billion dollars to the Andrew W. Mellon Foundation, a hundred million each to Audrey's three children, and smaller bequests to servants, friends, Lauder Greenway, and David Bruce. "To my entire surprise," the diplomat said, "she left me a handsome legacy."[22] Years before, Paul Mellon had moved his father's remains from the crypt in Pittsburgh to the family plot on the farm in Virginia. He buried his sister there too.[23]

At her death about two hundred canvases, mostly Impressionist and Postimpressionist, cluttered her many residences, tucked away in odd corners and closets. The National Gallery got them all. "Especially rich in the works of French artists, her bequest included nine Bonnards, five Boudins, two Cassatts, a Cézanne, three Corots, a Daumier, a Degas, two Derains, three Dufys, another Fragonard, two Gauguins, four additional Manets, a Matisse, five Monets, four Morisots, five Pissarros, a Redon, twenty-two Renoirs, a Rouault, a Seurat, two Toulouse-Lautrecs, three Utrillos, ten Vuillards. Her legacy included drawings by Winslow Homer, the elder Breughel, Tintoretto, Rubens, Van Dyck, Gainsborough, Delacroix, and many other major works on paper."[24] Her other collections represented less discriminating taste. The silver and decorative items went to the Carnegie Institute, which deaccessioned masses of them at a Sotheby's auction. Many received no bid.[25]

By the end of the decade, Bruce's surviving children had passed through turbulent adolescent years. For them the normal crises of growing up were magnified by the need to come to terms with their father, a revered, living institution in the eyes of the State Department and in his children's eyes a famous and remote Olympian figure. After graduating from Radcliffe, Sasha poured intense but unfocused energy into a succession of activities. Only one had more than a fleeting half-life, a fascination with archaeology that led to an obsession for Orthodox icons and then to tragedy. Nicky, the youngest, had chronic academic problems. The middle child, David, got into worse trouble at school.

Harvard, like campuses across America, was in turmoil over Vietnam. Young David was caught up in the ferment and joined the protests against corporations that recruited on campus, the chief villain being Dow Chemical, manufacturer of napalm. For his role in obstructing Dow's recruiters, Bruce *fils* received an "admonition," a first-level disciplinary warning from the college. The elder David sent his own admonition, agreeing that students had every right to oppose the war but also an obligation not to obstruct the free speech of those they disliked, merchants of death included. Writing the letter just two weeks after screaming demonstrators had tried to prevent him from speaking at Cambridge heightened the anger he felt toward his son's actions.

Bruce *père* might have been more philosophical had he reflected on events at Princeton half a century before. Disrupting Dow recruiters was a far cry from the genteel rebellion against the eating clubs, yet the same spirit of revolt against parental authority lay behind both. Young David's air of detachment from the protests too, even as he participated in them, called to mind his father's youthful aloofness in 1917. In time he came to see the kinship of the extreme protesters with the mindlessness of Nazi students and Maoist Red Guards.[26] A sense of philosophical detachment and willingness to understand each other's position, however, were scarce commodities in both father and son in the late 1960s.

At their base in Washington, David and Evangeline Bruce continued the social life for which they were famous. Although the house was large by Georgetown standards, it was composed of many small rooms and narrow passageways. When they added the 1961 wing, they finally had the space to entertain on the scale they wanted. Their parties revolved around the large, salmon-apricot-colored garden room, which had no windows facing 34th Street but large ones, surrounded by voluminous lime-green curtains, that looked out to the enclosed garden behind the house. In or out of office, the diplomat could count on his wife and her parties to be "the epicenter of the world of the influential, the intellectual, and the wealthy of the nation's capital." "If Washington were the Sistine Chapel," the writer Sally Quinn said years later, "Evangeline would be *up* there on the ceiling."[27]

The flat at Albany provided the transatlantic pole for the schedule they expected to follow in retirement, alternating between Georgetown and London. High summer was an exception. For decades August meant soaking up the sun. Most often they chose Venice: the Gritti Hotel, tea at Florian's, nosing about the Piazza San Marco for bargains in the antiques shops, water-borne tours of Renaissance churches, bathing at the Lido, and promenading along the canals. Sometimes they chose a more rustic setting in Tuscany before the English arrived and turned it into Chiantishire.

There were holidays too at Paul Mellon's and Ronnie Tree's Caribbean retreats. A chance to let his hair down and swap the Savile Row suit for Panama hat and open-collared shirt was a change Bruce heartily embraced. Sitting under a pergola covered with the magenta flame of bougainvilleas, sipping rum and gossiping with his friends or lounging in a turquoise lagoon, he gradually revived and began to shuck the cares of diplomacy.

Just before he retired, Jacqueline Onassis had pressed him to head the Kennedy Center for the Performing Arts. He diplomatically thanked her but had no intention of taking on the job.[28] He wanted to be free of all such obligations. "Life with Albany as a base seemed to me absolutely glorious."[29] Once he had indulged himself for a few months, however, idleness became tinged with boredom. Despite his advancing age, and the infirmities that now would never entirely leave him, he began to itch again for some more purposeful occupation.

CHAPTER 21

Paris Again, By Way of Saigon

The American people are sick of the war in Indo-China, the atrocities that have accompanied it, and the lies of the Nixon Regime. We are also sick of old vultures like you who talk peace only to make more war.

— From an anonymous letter sent to Bruce

SEVEN MONTHS into Bruce's retirement, presidential counselor John Ehrlichman pored over the secret report he had requested from J. Edgar Hoover. Like all previous FBI files on Bruce, this one turned up "no pertinent derogatory information."[1] Was this an early spasm of Nixon White House paranoia, or was the diplomat being considered for an assignment? The answer is unclear, but what is indisputable is that eight months later Bruce accepted another post. Vietnam had soured his last years in London. Now it would deny him the repose most men of his age longed for. It was his own fault, though, because he was unwilling to decline a president's request, even if that president was the premier fiend in the capacious demonology of the Democratic party.

Nixon chose July 1, 1970, the day the last American soldiers returned from a dramatic raid into Cambodia, to announce his latest diplomatic move. He did it during an unusual, hour-long conversation with television reporters, held incongruously in the Hollywood studio of the game show *Let's Make a Deal*. He announced that he was sending David Bruce as his new chief negotiator to revive the peace talks in Paris that had begun the year before but that languished after months of fruitless posturing.[2]

Bruce, of course, knew about the conflict in Indochina long before most Americans — back when he had been ambassador to France and the name South Vietnam had not yet appeared on any map. Events now came full circle, linking his first embassy and the end of his career. In 1949 he had pushed Washington to aid the French army fighting Ho Chi Minh. Now, despite private doubts about a military solution, Bruce faced the consequences of his earlier opposition to the tenacious peasant guerrillas in black pajamas.

Two years had passed since the Viet Cong parlayed military defeat in the 1968 Tet offensive into psychological victory. That event convulsed American politics and paved the way for Nixon. Although he had no secret plan, as he claimed, the new president knew he must make an end of the war soon or suffer Johnson's fate. He tried open talks in Paris, secret ones with the North Vietnamese, clandestine bombing and outright invasion of Cambodia, and all the while withdrawing American soldiers from the fray. Gradual withdrawal was too slow to dampen unrest at home, however, and when Nixon launched his spectacular but futile raid into Cambodia in 1970, violent protest rocked the country. When Bruce went to Paris, discord at home and combat in Indochina seemed destined to drag on indefinitely. The war had become, as White House speechwriter William Safire feared, a "bone in the nation's throat."

By then Bruce had had a chance to observe the style of the new president and his national security adviser. There was plenty of evidence of their furtively circumventing the State Department.[3] Henry Kissinger's refusal to delegate made his office a bottleneck. "In the first year it was like a Moroccan whorehouse, with people queuing up outside his door for hours," one staffer recalled.[4] But there was also evidence of Kissinger's brilliance and of Nixon's willingness to chart new paths. And so on Independence Day 1970 at the San Clemente White House, Nixon introduced reporters to his new envoy to the talks. With soft-spoken, courtly humility, Bruce told them that the post "is foreign to my experience, but if I can make any contribution, no matter how slight, to bringing about a settlement of the difficulties in Southeast Asia, I will feel overjoyed."[5]

He knew that in choosing him, Nixon — like Ike years before — gained a bipartisan shield for his policy. As much was implied by Kissinger's double-edged comment later that any effort to which Bruce "was willing to commit himself had a strong presumption of being in the national interest."[6] Bruce knew about the secret talks that Kissinger had begun and that the public negotiations might be largely a facade for what went on behind the scenes. Bruce "embarked on a mission in which he knew that his opposite numbers had as their primary objective to wear him down. . . . There would be little glory for him in Paris; nor did he seek it." Still, it is important to keep in mind Kissinger's later comment that "in June 1970 we did not believe that matters were foreordained to end tragically."[7]

Bruce fancied himself an unsentimental realist and so could identify with Kissinger's European-style realpolitik. In his own personal equation the benefits still outweighed the negatives. Knowing these things — and that patience would be the chief skill required of him — he began his work expecting frustration but with the hope that he might have a chance to make a productive contribution.

The first American and North Vietnamese contact had taken place in 1968 when LBJ sent Averell Harriman to Paris. The four-sided talks (with South Vietnam and the Viet Cong, or Provisional Revolutionary Government, added to the original two) began the following February. The setting was not exactly auspicious: the old Hotel Majestic was best remembered as Gestapo headquarters during World War II. North Vietnam pursued a fighting-while-negotiating stance designed to win on the battlefield rather than at the conference table. For a while, the level of fighting declined, and it seemed the war might wind down through a process entirely separate from the talks. Hanoi used them as a vehicle for discrediting the South Vietnamese and promoting the Viet Cong as an alternative. Both sides, in fact, found the talks convenient for publicizing their policies.[8]

The New York Times, skeptical of Nixon and all his works, conceded the shrewdness of his choice. Bruce, the paper opined, "should be able to achieve a diplomatic breakthrough, if anybody can."[9] Anthony Lewis, whom Bruce considered a friend though he privately opposed the columnist's views on the war, agreed.[10] Was it possible, Lewis asked, that "Bruce could be seen as a facade, a way of projecting peaceful intentions without a real willingness" to make peace? He dismissed the thought because he believed the veteran diplomat would not knowingly accept a sham appointment. "If patience, good humor, self-confidence, wisdom and an ability to see the other man's viewpoint are essentials in a good negotiator," then Bruce was the ideal choice.[11]

To prepare himself, Bruce consulted the usual Washington mandarins. By coincidence, he had just been to Southeast Asia. In January the easternmost leg of a trip through South Asia reached into Cambodia. Of all the sites, the Khmer ruins at Angkor Wat intrigued him most. Bruce could not have known it then, but he was one of the last American tourists to see that ill-fated country before it descended into civil war and genocide.

In May his official tour of the war zone lasted all of three days. Under French rule, Saigon had blended acacia-lined streets, sidewalk cafés, and colonial villas set amid lush tropical gardens. The city teemed with a rich ethnic mix — Vietnamese women in their silken *ao dais*, merchants in the Chinese quarter, French colonial officials, Buddhist monks in saffron robes. Then the Americans came. They transformed the face of the city with construction projects and air-conditioned warehouses. A flood of consumer goods bloated the black markets. Prostitution, narcotics, and all the venerable forms of war profiteering gave a seamy cast to the once-idyllic setting. Now the Americans were going. When Bruce arrived, U.S. forces had declined sharply from a peak of more than half a million.[12]

In Saigon he called on ambassador Ellsworth Bunker and South Vietnamese president Nguyen Van Thieu. He had a cursory tour by helicopter outside the capital. At an artillery base in a clearing blasted out of the jungle, the red clay reminded him of Virginia, and he pitied the soldiers forced to call the place home. His VIP chopper returned him to Bunker's residence by way of the helipad on top of the chancery — in retrospect, a foreshadowing of those final, desperate scenes on the same roof five years later.

Flying unmolested above the green Mekong Delta, dining with bureaucrats, and dashing across Saigon in a motorcade of jeeps crammed with machinegun-toting guards gave him a poor facsimile of the real Vietnam. As the sophisticated giver of countless on-site briefings, he knew the genre's limitations. When he left, he wryly concluded,

"As far as forming any impression of the city, I might as well have been in the wilds of Alaska."[13]

A few days earlier, thirteen American soldiers died in a desperate nighttime ambush around Firebase Ripcord, a small outpost like the one he visited. The high command announced that the most recent week's casualties came to 66 Americans killed and 619 wounded.[14]

He reached France in August. The government provided him a suite at the Crillon, where he had first tasted Parisian luxury during talks at the end of another war. The large salon on the third floor offered an unrivaled view across the Place de la Concorde, symbol of so many turning points in Bruce's own life as well as French history. His office nearby occupied the same embassy annex he had used during the Marshall Plan. His staff of thirty-one was almost as large as it had been then, counting all the couriers, translators, and military liaison officers.

Security was more elaborate than when OSS first exposed him to such things. At the office his team used a plastic "tent room" for confidential discussions. He made a point to be even more tight-lipped than usual at the Crillon when he learned that the French, and possibly others, had bugged his suite. As hosts to the talks, the French took elaborate precautions. Four squads of three men each provided Bruce around-the-clock protection. It irked him that a guard followed him everywhere, even across the street to his office. Wherever he went by car, a French security vehicle followed.[15]

The delegation's routine was set before Bruce arrived. Every weekday morning at 9:30 he received a military briefing by a colonel seconded from Saigon. To give these reports a sense of immediacy (and to pad a lot of military résumés), a new colonel rotated in every few months. The military's vocabulary soon became familiar — technological jargon, Vietnamese place names, bomb tonnages dropped, acres defoliated, and always the antiseptic casualty reports. Plenary sessions took place every Thursday at the Majestic on avenue Kléber, near the Arc de Triomphe. The head of each of the four delegations gave a set statement and made a single rebuttal. Then the session adjourned, and each party spoke to the press. On returning to his office, Bruce customarily gave a television interview, whether there was anything to report or not.

Because the negotiations involved four parties, Bruce kept in touch with South Vietnamese ambassador Pham Dang Lam, a quiet, agreeable man more fluent in French than English. Madame Nguyen Thi Binh, the foreign minister of the Viet Cong's Provisional Revolutionary Government, proved the least pleasant of the parties across the table. "If possible," Bruce later wearily concluded, "she becomes more acidulous each week."[16] On the other hand, the North Vietnamese delegate, Xuan Thuy, another tough negotiator, at least showed occasional signs of civility and even a sense of humor that Bruce appreciated as a fellow professional.

Bruce's deputy, Philip Habib, had been acting chief negotiator before Bruce arrived. An outspoken deputy assistant secretary of state who rose from the ranks and was universally admired, Habib had attended LBJ's March 1968 meeting of the Wise Men, those fourteen senior officials whom the president asked for advice. Habib had bluntly told them that their South Vietnamese allies were incompetent. Bruce relied heavily on his assistant, for the chief of the American team freely admitted he knew little about the war. In turn, the younger diplomat said of Bruce, "I loved him as an older brother."[17]

America demanded that the North Vietnamese withdraw their troops from the South and opposed replacing the Thieu regime by any means other than elections. Hanoi demanded unilateral American withdrawal and the ouster of Thieu.[18] Despite these intransigent positions, in his opening remarks Bruce said he hoped "we can avoid propaganda and harsh language and settle down to businesslike discussion of the issues." When reporters asked him if the Communists were pleased to meet him, he admitted they were polite but sardonically observed, "I would not say they went into a state of ecstasy."[19]

They had, in fact, spurned his call for moderation, and letting him know his arrival made no difference, both Communist delegations repeated their incantation that Saigon was "corrupt, bellicose and dictatorial." Bruce privately described the next week's proceedings as "dreary," the other side interested only in "abusing" the Americans and South Vietnamese for "every kind of perfidy and brutality."[20]

Bruce's appointment did bring Xuan Thuy, chief North Vietnamese negotiator, back to Paris, but that was about the extent of his achievement that summer. He reacted sharply at one meeting to the comment that Nixon had "lied to the American people." The choice of words, he admonished Xuan Thuy, "with regard to President Nixon is shameful and completely inadmissible. At least one should be courteous if one cannot be quiet." Bruce had dealt with tough negotiators before but never such rude ones. In turn, the North Vietnamese spokesman said Bruce had "lost control of himself," a ludicrous description of this supremely disciplined diplomat.[21]

The death of Charles de Gaulle in November provided a backdrop for further diplomatic maneuver. In OSS Bruce had strongly backed the general's Free French forces, but later clashed with him over the European Defense Community. "Although I am always ready to denounce de Gaulle for his narrow Nationalism," he said, "I have never considered him to be animated by petty notions. When he errs, it is on the grand scale."[22] World leaders, including President Nixon, gathered in Paris to pay tribute to de Gaulle. The regular Thursday session at the Majestic was canceled. When he arrived at Notre-Dame for the memorial service, Bruce found he was assigned a seat only one removed from Madame Binh. Out of character, she surprised him by greeting him civilly. They bowed to one another, and when she extended her hand, Bruce shook it heartily.

He almost missed his prearranged meeting with Nixon. After the service the square outside the cathedral was jammed with people. In the crush, Bruce lost his car and the tag-along security vehicle and so set out on foot, by himself, in the pouring rain, plagued by bad circulation in his legs and little hope of finding a taxi among the throngs in the streets. He walked almost a mile before the crowds thinned and an empty cab came his way. He was half an hour late for his appointment, but Nixon still saw him.

Bruce endured the accusations made each week at the Majestic, but nothing brought home the tragedy of war and punctured his reserved demeanor more than the supplicant POW families who constantly came to him for some scrap of hope. Far from offering hope of release, the North Vietnamese refused even to accept a list of American servicemen missing in action. When Bruce decided to read off the names from the list, Madame Binh denounced him for trying to sabotage the talks. "I would like to ask the American delegate," she said with icy contempt, "if he came here to negotiate or to act as a public amuser?"[23]

In contrast to his earlier negotiating jobs in Paris two decades before, Bruce found that American journalists took a far more skeptical view of their government's actions. He believed press critics had got the wrong end of the stick. Bob Kleiman, an old acquaintance who worked for the *New York Times,* had written, Bruce thought, "exceptionally stupid editorials" on the war.[24] Despite his growing sense of futility about his work, though, he maintained the facade of genteel, cosmopolitan bonhomie with which he had always been able to beguile members of the Fourth Estate even while disagreeing with them.

More than antagonistic journalists, it was amateur supplicants, poseurs, and cranks who gave Bruce the most headaches. In December a distinguished French general asked his help in seeing Nixon. The old soldier wanted to press his scheme for broadcasting radioactive waste across the 17th Parallel dividing North and South Vietnam.[25] Two months later a wealthy New Yorker came to offer his large sailboat to either side for repatriating POWs.[26]

Well-meaning unofficial delegations constantly paraded through Paris. One group of American pacifists charged Bruce's team with "rigidity," by which they meant an unwillingness to accept unilateral withdrawal. Bruce met with a dozen of them for three hours of bitter, though orderly, argument that concluded with a Quaker woman praying for peace as her colleagues wept and Bruce stood in silence. The full delegation met later with members of his mission and ended with folk singer Judy Collins leading the group in singing "Give Peace a Chance."[27] Bruce considered the whole affair "distressing" because the pacifists, naively in his mind, endorsed the Communists' views entirely.[28] Two days later, at the next plenary session he gave the shortest speech on record — four sentences that concluded, "Apparently, you prefer propaganda maneuvers to serious discussion. I therefore have nothing further to say at this time."[29]

In the fall of 1970, Bruce played a substantive role in an initiative that he and the administration hoped would break the impasse. It was clear that the Communists would never agree to any proposal calling for mutual withdrawal of forces from South Vietnam. They had no intention of leaving. After the Cambodian raid in 1970, Nixon believed the South Vietnamese were better able to defend themselves alone. He therefore revived a stand-still ceasefire proposal that would not insist on withdrawal of North Vietnamese units already in the South. The concession horrified the South Vietnamese; most Americans involved in the talks agreed it might break the deadlock. Bruce and Habib strongly favored it. In early October they flew to Ireland to meet with Kissinger, Nixon, and Rogers. They agreed that Nixon would announce the plan in a televised speech the same day Bruce formally laid it on the table in Paris. At the end of the meeting, Bruce impressed Kissinger with a caution against impetuous action. Bruce, Kissinger wrote, "had seen too much lost through the impatience of negotiators, even more through their vanity. He was by nature not impatient, and now too old for vanity."[30]

The Nixon speech electrified opinion at home and abroad. His sharpest critics in the Senate endorsed it. Stopping all bombing throughout Indochina as well as dropping the withdrawal of North Vietnamese forces as a precondition to a settlement seemed a reasonable, even generous, concession. Thuy and Binh greeted Bruce's presentation of the plan with suspicion, agreed to study it, and the next week dismissed it out of hand. Disheartened, Bruce tried to keep the idea alive by refusing to accept rejection as their final word.[31]

On the face of it, Nixon had made a major concession. Despite some presidential waffling after the speech, in hindsight his offer represented the first, halting step toward abandoning mutual withdrawal as a goal.[32] The greater intransigence lay with the Communists, who renewed their demand that the South Vietnamese government be replaced. In fact, neither side was willing yet to grant what they both ultimately conceded.[33]

Ever since Bruce arrived in Paris, the administration's predictions about the talks had blown hot and cold. The press guessed they had to do with domestic politics. Once past the midterm elections, the White House seemed more willing to assess the talks realistically. By the end of 1970 Bruce uttered publicly the most pessimistic expectations for the talks of any senior U.S. official. "There have never been any true negotiations," he said in his press conference on the first of December.[34] The next month marked the one hundredth session, an anniversary of two years of failure and recrimination. Bruce observed the occasion by accusing the other side of distorting American policy "to justify your own recalcitrance at this table." Privately he called the words of his opponents "long statements as lifeless and repetitive as ever."[35]

With no progress at the table, action shifted back to the battlefield. Nixon and Kissinger believed they could thwart preparations for the next North Vietnamese offensive by cutting the Ho Chi Minh trail in Laos. American troops would not be involved on the ground; the thrust would show the progress of "Vietnamization" in preparing the South Vietnamese military to take care of itself. The operation proved a clumsy failure. The South Vietnamese barely reached their objective before having to make a disorderly retreat, mauled all the way back to their own border. Nixon claimed a victory; Bruce endured more abuse in Paris.[36]

In addition to providing a propaganda platform, the Paris talks served as a screen for secret discussions.[37] From the beginning the press speculated that if there was to be any progress in the negotiations it would come through secret talks and not the Thursday slanging matches on avenue Kléber. They also speculated that any secret talks would be between Bruce and Xuan Thuy.[38] In fact the two men had a few fruitless private conversations at a North Vietnamese safe house in Choisy-le-Roi.[39] Even without the complication of the South Vietnamese and Viet Cong delegations, though, the two negotiators remained as far apart in private as they were before the world's television cameras. The real secret talks, of course, gave Henry Kissinger the starring role.

Bruce was kept informed, and in summer 1971, when Kissinger and North Vietnamese Politburo member Le Duc Tho had six surreptitious conversations, he participated in the charade to keep the press in the dark. On July 11 Kissinger arrived in Paris and stayed at the residence of Arthur Watson, the American ambassador. The press staked out the house because Le Duc Tho, also in town, had publicly expressed an interest in meeting with Kissinger. Bruce arrived conspicuously at the residence and was greeted by Kissinger on the steps in full view of the waiting press. The two went inside, ostensibly to discuss the weekly negotiations. Unknown to the reporters, Kissinger then sneaked out the back door, hopped into his aide's car, slid down low in the seat, and sped off to meet Le Duc Tho. After three hours of discussion, both acrimonious and hopeful, Kissinger returned by the same subterfuge. He and Bruce, reversing their earlier charade, met the press at the front of the house to say they had completed their review. The reporters never discovered Kissinger in any of his secret discussions.[40]

Bruce's relationship with his superiors was complicated because the national security adviser rather than the secretary of state dominated foreign affairs. He first encountered Kissinger in his role as Nixon's Metternich in February 1969, when the new president visited London. The arrogance of Nixon's advance team put Bruce in an irritable frame of mind, especially when they asked him to arrange for top newspaper publishers and journalists to meet Kissinger, not Nixon. "I see no objection to this," he grumbled acidly, "except that Kissinger is not as well known in public circles here as is the President of the United States, a fact of which Kissinger . . . is not fully conscious."[41]

Bruce and Kissinger could hardly have been more unlike, but Bruce did admire Kissinger's tenacity. Perhaps the aging diplomat knew that Kissinger flattered representatives of the old foreign policy elite to their faces, men like himself, and disparaged them behind their backs. But — for a time — he was content with the bargain implicit in his appointment: he would provide the public facade of negotiations while the national security adviser conducted the real talks sub rosa.[42]

Despite the figurehead role, Bruce was better informed about the secret negotiations than even his nominal boss, Secretary of State Rogers.[43] But knowledge was not enough to alleviate the frustration. When he was encouraged to have private discussions with Xuan Thuy in autumn 1970, the White House micromanaged the affair, to Bruce's irritation. His eagerness to talk to Nixon at the time of de Gaulle's funeral — walking alone halfway across central Paris in the rain to make the appointment — stemmed from a desire to obtain greater latitude for meeting the other side informally. Although Nixon seemed to agree, nothing came of Bruce's request.[44] The longer Bruce stayed on in Paris, the more his displeasure with his role grew.

In May 1971 he flew to Washington for the annual dinner of Veterans of OSS to receive the William J. Donovan Award. More than a thousand veterans tried to buy tickets, but the hall at the Statler Hilton accommodated only half that number. Bruce was gratified to see so many old friends. Their praise reinforced the flattery he had received earlier in the day at the White House.

He had gone there to pay a courtesy call while he was in town, but he also wanted to repeat his decision to quit. He had told Kissinger and Rogers as early as December 1970 that he expected to remain no longer than the middle of the next year, and now it was time to go.[45] Rogers had forewarned him that Nixon wanted him to remain at least until the end of July, and Bruce succumbed to appeals to his patriotism. Nixon, in the happy times before his fall, was in high form and impressed the ambassador once more with his grasp of world affairs. Bruce said he "never had a pleasanter conversation with any President."[46] The prospect of prolonging his stay in Paris another month was softened because the secretary of state told him he need not be so religious in going to the office every day. No clearer signal could be given of the superficial character of Bruce's role.

The lack of achievement weighed on Bruce's mind, but he knew he had done his best. He had, Kissinger recalled, been "a steadying influence" within the counsels of the administration from the month of his appointment in 1970. Bruce provided a "calming effect" on Nixon, whose mood, Kissinger said, "oscillated wildly" in the weeks following the Cambodian raid. Bruce went into the job with low expectations. But it was one thing to anticipate a year of frustration, another to live through it. A year of it, especially at his age and with his health problems, was as much as any president could expect.

The administration announced his resignation in the middle of July and gave ill health as the reason. By 1970 a serious circulatory ailment was slowing him down. At the end of the year, he was having weekly medical treatments. Tests confirmed that he had suffered for years from heart fibrillation and constricted circulation in his legs.[47] Now an unpleasant routine of having his veins repeatedly punctured for blood samples joined the regular doses of Communist propaganda administered every Thursday.[48] In his case, retirement for reasons of health was true, but it was also a convenient mask for Bruce's unhappiness about rumors that the administration was dissatisfied with his performance.

In his diaries Bruce recorded his bitterness with the failure of the talks, repeating the disappointment of his last assignment in Paris nearly two decades before. Then at least the European Defense Community was a theoretical abstraction; in 1971 he dealt with a real war that produced real victims. The tenacity of the conflict and its corrosive effect on America, to say nothing of Vietnam, made this assignment the least enjoyable one he had ever undertaken. At least with EDC there was hope and, for a time, progress, toward a positive goal.

The domestic tragedy caused by Vietnam came home in spring 1971, when he phoned his wife, who was visiting Washington, and learned that an antiwar demonstration near Georgetown had turned ugly. No one at their house was hurt, but the wafts of tear gas drifting in from the sedate streets of their neighborhood filled the elegant rooms at 1405 34th Street with the astringent odor of civil unrest.[49]

As he wound up his work in Paris, he described the penultimate session in his diary with the words "these performances are utterly frustrating." Of the massive files of statements presented by the various parties, he said, "we have a complete record of them which I never expect to read."[50] Five months later he told an interviewer, "I'm glad I did it. I accomplished nothing. I'm sorry for it. [But] I'm glad I did it."[51]

His last appearance at the table, on July 29, was like his first — short statements by the parties talking past one another, full of hopeful words about a peaceful settlement that no one believed. He merely noted that he was leaving and hoped that future talks would produce "a just and lasting peace." There was no handshaking, no formal ceremony, no other forms of civility. Binh sneered that she was still waiting for Bruce to show "a serious attitude." Xuan Thuy, at least, wished him bon voyage.[52] The day after a farewell dinner at the Crillon with members of his staff and the South Vietnamese delegation, the Bruces set out for London and then Florence to spend some time with Ronnie and Marietta Tree at the Villa Capponi. It would not, however, be the veteran diplomat's final retirement.

In South Vietnam five soldiers from the Americal Division died when their armored personnel carrier ran over a mine near Danang. The United States command announced that the week's battlefield death toll was fourteen.[53]

"The Vietnam tragedy," said its chronicler Stanley Karnow, "is the story of squandered opportunities."[54] The war would drag on long after Bruce stepped down. When the diplomats finally signed an agreement in 1973, it was largely Nixon's stand-still ceasefire offer that the Communists had flung back into Bruce's face in 1970. It was designed to give the South Vietnamese a "decent interval" to prove they could defend themselves. "Peace with honor." Secretary of State Rogers sent Bruce one of the pens he used to sign the accord. For a time the South Vietnamese held on, but in spring 1975 they collapsed before the final Communist offensive. Decided at last on the battlefield after the diplomats had failed, the conflict was replaced by the quieter oppression of peacetime Leninism, which rated hardly a mention on the front pages of American newspapers.

CHAPTER 22

To the Middle Kingdom

I begin to think of myself as a Marco Polo about to embark on an uncharted adventure.

— From undated prologue to David Bruce's China diary

In our time. . . . only one of the great world powers has . . . worked itself into such a frenzy over power, policy, and personality as to cause loss of life in the hundreds of thousands, and years of diversion from rational purposes, out of a fixation on settling old scores — China.

— Ross Terrill, *The White-Boned Demon*

IN JULY 1971 Henry Kissinger flew to Paris, ostensibly to brief David Bruce but in fact to confer secretly again with Le Duc Tho. While there he told Bruce an even greater secret — he had just outwitted the reporters who dogged his trail and visited Beijing to talk with Chinese foreign minister Zhou Enlai. After Kissinger left, Bruce spoke to veteran journalist Don Cook, in very elliptical terms to be sure, about the good that might come from a diplomatic opening to China. He was so animated that Cook, well acquainted with the reserved Bruce manner, perked up his ears. When he cabled his next story to the *Los Angeles Times*, however, Cook did not elaborate on his suspicions but only alluded, ever so vaguely, to rumors that the administration might be talking secretly to the Chinese.[1] Three days later Nixon stunned the world by declaring an end to twenty-two years of pretending that the People's Republic of China did not exist. The old red baiter himself would visit Beijing. Cook knew then that Bruce had not been speaking only hypothetically.[2] Neither man yet knew what effect Nixon's bombshell would have on the diplomat's career.

For a century a pastiche of romantic fantasies molded America's image of China — tales of clipper ships on the Shanghai run and pious deeds of Victorian missionaries recounted to generations of Sunday School children. The notion that it was America's mission to civilize China seemed to some about to be realized in the 1930s through that good Methodist Chiang Kai-shek. The vision of Senator Kenneth Wherry of Nebraska captures the naïveté with pathetic economy: "With God's help, we will lift Shanghai up and up, ever up, until it is just like Kansas City."[3] The "China Lobby" in the United States was so strong that when Chiang's Nationalists finally collapsed in 1949, Americans quarreled over who had "lost" China, as though someone had misplaced an object that was his to mislay.

The fascination did not die, and it took only news of Kissinger's secret trip to revive it. From ping-pong diplomacy to Nixon's visit and the Shanghai Communiqué of 1972, Americans indulged in an orgy of Pearl Buck sentimentality, 1970s style. Entrepreneurs salivated over the prospect of cracking open a market of half a billion consumers.

Despite the euphoria, it was not possible to return relations to normal instantly after a generation of enmity that included a shooting war in Korea. It took more than getting used to saying People's Republic of China instead of Red China, Beijing instead of Peking. The largest obstacle was America's recognition of Taiwan, Chiang's rump republic, dedicated in theory to reconquering the mainland.

Early in the thaw, Washington made contact through the Chinese embassy in Paris or back channels to Beijing's delegation at the United Nations. The latter meetings took place in a CIA safe house, "a seedy apartment whose mirrored walls suggested less prosaic purposes."[4] Because of Taiwan, instead of full diplomatic relations, the two nations groped toward a compromise: "liaison missions" in Beijing and Washington that were embassies in all but name.[5]

Nixon had mentioned to Bruce in 1972 that if the situation with China ever opened up he wanted to send him to Beijing. A year of rest left the diplomat musing about yet another post despite his age and health. He had been rereading his diaries from the days of plotting

European unity with Jean Monnet, a pastime that helped revive the old itch and lull him into discounting the strain of his last post.

His first love was Europe, but China had always intrigued him. In 1955 he confessed to a friend that if the Democrats won the next election, he hoped they would recognize Communist China and send him as the first ambassador.[6] Despite his flawless Cold Warrior credentials, he was impatient for America to come to terms with China and had no sympathy for the defeated Nationalists in Taiwan. "Naturally, Chiang wishes a war, with us heavily engaged," he said. "Otherwise, he has no future. But I, for one, am totally unsympathetic to attempting to justify his past by launching another and terrible military gamble."[7]

Bruce had unknowingly figured into the sometimes bizarre relationship between Nixon and his national security adviser during the run-up to the first secret China trip. Resentful of Kissinger's reputation for flashy diplomacy, Nixon toyed with his adviser by feigning indecision over whom to send to Beijing. Kissinger wanted to be the one, but the president wanted to draw up a list of candidates. Kissinger suggested Bruce, perhaps because it would be easy to bump the aging diplomat from the list later: as long as Bruce was chief negotiator in Paris, the Chinese might not want him as their contact.[8]

In any event, it was Kissinger who went. Then, a month after the specious Vietnam treaty was signed in 1973, Zhou Enlai signaled China's readiness to establish the liaison missions. Nixon invited Bruce to the White House and offered him the job. He accepted with genuine enthusiasm. Once more the Democratic diplomat agreed to serve a Republican president. He had been two years old when the Boxer Rebellion cast his nation into common cause with the Europeans exploiting China; at seventy-five he would represent America before the Gate of Heaven.

Maddening delays at State reminded him that Beijing had no monopoly on the intrigues of palace mandarins. It seemed as though every American who wanted to visit China sought his help. He feared that "widespread euphoria" made Americans less realistic than the Chinese about the meaning and the value of the thaw. But he too had his own personal notions about what he might accomplish there. A television reporter interviewing him on the sidewalk outside his Georgetown house just before he left asked if the post, coming "so late in life," was especially exciting. Rather than taking offense at what could be construed as a patronizing remark, with a twinkle in his eye, Bruce chuckled and replied smoothly, "Anything that comes late in life is sometimes more satisfactory than what's happened previously."[9]

In 1844, when Washington sent its first envoy to China, the chief concern was whether he would be required to kowtow to the emperor.[10] One hundred and twenty-nine years later there was a different worry. During Bruce's farewell courtesy call at the White House, Nixon warned him about Chinese banquet diplomacy. Go easy with the *mao tai*, he said, referring to the fiery liquor poured liberally for the endless, obligatory toasts at state dinners, or you might not be able to raise a glass by the evening's end.[11]

After a television interview at National Airport, David and Evangeline Bruce said their good-byes and departed for the twenty-seven-hour trip to Hong Kong. Following a week of briefings in the British crown colony, on May 14, 1973, they boarded a train that took them through the intensively irrigated valleys of South China to Canton and then went by air to the capital. Beijing, ancient seat of dynasties, was the center of China under the red emperor too.

When he stood before the Gate of Heavenly Peace in 1949 to proclaim a new China, Mao Zedong ended years of fragmentation that followed the breakup of the last dynasty. But it was not an end to bloodshed. He incited violence in the countryside, just as Communists had broken the kulaks two decades before in the Soviet Union, when Andrew Mellon was buying pretty pictures from Stalin. For Western fellow travelers, China became the newest New Jerusalem. And just as chimerical. Mao's party burned with puritanical ardor and claimed to have ended beggary, prostitution, hunger, and corruption. It was a sham. As in Soviet Russia, the state became a Potemkin village on a vast scale.

A crude, wily strategist, Mao scourged China with repeated disasters. Like Hitler, a kindred utopian revolutionary, Mao sought to transform people by the sheer force of his will. He proved his ignorance of economics and indifference to suffering when he proclaimed the Great Leap Forward and made the peasants forsake their fields to tend so-called backyard steel mills that literally consumed even their farm implements. At a stroke he crippled industry and revived famine on a scale unknown before. Criticism was no longer possible within the ruling class, "nothing but adulation and lies," wrote Harrison Salisbury.

"Mao had turned his band of brothers into a claque, clapping hands and nodding heads like mechanical dolls."[12]

In 1965 Mao decreed the Great Proletarian Cultural Revolution, and China trembled. Red Guard students unleashed an orgy of vandalism on a colossal scale. The Great Helmsman set as their task the destruction of the Four Olds — old thought, old culture, old customs, and old habits. Looting museums and libraries, they destroyed millennia of China's cultural heritage. Aping the war of Hitler's brownshirts against learning, they attacked the "spectacle-wearers" of the intelligentsia in the greatest witch-hunt in history. In their fury, mobs of howling adolescents humiliated, beat, tortured, murdered, and even, in widespread acts of ritual cannibalism, ate the flesh of their victims.[13]

Under Mao, as before, power was displayed in the vast central square, Tiananmen. There in May 1919, while Second Lieutenant Bruce roamed the streets of Paris during the peace conference, students demonstrated against Chinese diplomats for signing away their nation's rights at Versailles, a protest movement that anticipated Mao's revolution. More recently, hordes of Red Guards pledged their lives to Mao there, waving copies of his little red book over their empty heads. When Bruce arrived in 1973, on one side of the square the Communists had built the giant Great Hall of the People, with an auditorium for each province and banquet seating for thousands. On the opposite side, the foreign legations, symbol of past subjugation, had given way to museums. Through the Gate of Heavenly Peace, on the third side, lay the entrance to the Forbidden City.[14]

Like their imperial predecessors, the PRC's leaders lived in the fabled compound of parks, lakes, and palaces that adjoined the Forbidden City. There Marco Polo had marveled at the splendor of China, and Kublai Khan built the lacquered palace that inspired Coleridge. High walls still obscured these sites from the gaze of ordinary people just as in the days of the emperors.

It was a time of dangerous drift. At the start of the decade, wrote Ross Terrill, "Mao entered a King Lear phase, Chinese politics became a cesspool of distrust, and authority in Peking began to fragment."[15] China struggled groggily to recover from the Red Guard madness. Deng Xiaoping, who eventually succeeded Mao, remained in disgrace until 1973. When he said he did not care if a cat was white or black as long as it caught mice, he blasphemed against Communist dogma and earned himself a cut-price sabbatical down on the collective farm. The Tenth Party Congress, convened during Bruce's first summer there, gave advantage to neither the leftist Gang of Four of Mao's wife, Jiang Qing, nor to Zhou Enlai's moderates. Mao brooded above it all.[16] This domestic turmoil, largely hidden from foreign view, would influence Bruce's mission throughout his time in China.

Speculation about the anomalous position of his mission preceded Bruce to Beijing. As his limousine sped down the airport road into the city for the first time, it stopped on the outskirts. An aide jumped out to unfasten the Stars and Stripes flying from the fender. The next day, when the car appeared again without the flag, journalists and diplomats concluded that Bruce was making a statement. The reason, in fact, was prosaic: the flag's supporting strap had broken on the way in from the airport. This incident underlined how keenly people watched the first official American presence in China since the revolution.[17]

Speculation focused too on Bruce's order of precedence at official banquets. Because his mission was analogous to that of the Palestine Liberation Organization, the prospect existed for the staid Bruce to be seated well below the salt and in the company of men he called PLO "zombies." Although some fully accredited embassies were already grumbling about alleged preferential treatment given to the Bruce mission, the Americans had more modest facilities than most foreigners. Bruce, with a string of embassies to his name no one else could match, however, carried his own specific gravity. Already his staff and some diplomats outside the American compound were giving him the courtesy title of ambassador.[18]

On his second day in town he called on the doyen of the diplomatic corps, the Nepalese ambassador, and set his mind at ease: his mission would take a low profile rather than use its anomalous position to see how many diplomatic privileges it could wring from the Chinese. Although accorded all the niceties, Bruce's mission was not officially on the diplomatic list. He therefore decided that the Americans would pay no formal calls on accredited embassies, nor attend National Day receptions or other such functions.[19] Similarly, only Americans and Chinese would be invited to the mission's proposed Fourth of July party.

After the grand houses on avenue d'Iéna and in Regent's Park, Beijing would be decidedly different. When the Bruces arrived, the Chinese had not completed either the liaison office or the adjoining residence, both within the same small walled compound in a district known as "Diplomats' Big Houses." For a month the Americans lived out of suitcases while construction crews worked around the clock. When completed, their modest residence consisted of a reception hall, living room, library, and four bedrooms. In the early days, the litter of packing cases reminded Bruce of the "dismantlement for reparations of a small German factory after the war."[20] When he first laid eyes on the State Department–issue furniture, he called it "hideous" stuff unfit for the meanest rural motel and regretted not being able to bring any of his own possessions.[21]

He could do nothing, though, about the environment. The lack of pollution controls on factory chimneys meant smog was everywhere. More irksome, the dust that relentlessly blew down from the Gobi Desert covered every room with grit.[22] Few of the seven million inhabitants of Beijing owned cars, but a sea of bicycles and buses created traffic jams even on the widest boulevards. The noise of construction and traffic surrounding the residence began before dawn every day, a clamorous wake-up call that put the clumsy trash collectors of Georgetown to shame.[23]

A short stroll along a covered concrete walkway took Bruce from the residence to his office on the second floor of the red-roofed liaison building. For a longer walk to fight his poor circulation, he went to a park across the road.[24] In contrast to the giant embassies in Paris, Bonn, and London, his complete staff in Peking barely topped thirty. Unlike other posts, where he was a remote figure to most of the staff, in Beijing he knew each of them very well. Knowing the interdepartmental rivalries that bedevil larger embassies, he won an important point before he left Washington: the White House agreed to limit staff positions to State Department officials only. No pilot fish from other agencies, no messy reporting lines confused by the presence of bureaucrats under his roof beholden to someone else. Despite howls of protest from Commerce, Agriculture, and others, he would not relent. Even the Pentagon was represented only by the six marine guards and the strong backs and engineering talent of a few Seabees needed to complete construction of the compound.[25] Bruce had to remain vigilant, though. Almost every week he fended off a different agency trying, as he put it, to stick "its camel nose under our Mission tent."[26]

Bruce's mission and the Chinese liaison office in Washington functioned as embassies in all but name. They each enjoyed diplomatic immunity, sent coded messages, issued visas, and handled issues of cultural and commercial exchange.[27] In the torrid Beijing summer — Bruce said it gave new meaning to the phrase "hot as the hinges of Hell" — the dress code kept pace with the climate. Everyone came to work in shirtsleeves, tieless.[28] Even the august, aging chief, famous for his elegantly tailored European suits, became a familiar sight shuffling between residence and office in his shirtsleeves and floppy old hat, clutching a little basket of secret papers under his arm.[29]

Bruce's minimalist style of reporting frustrated the State Department. Sometimes days passed without word from him, to the irritation of nervous colleagues at Foggy Bottom wanting microcommentary on every nuance the mission observed. He saw no need to send superfluous cables just to let the home office know his shop was still intact. The plain fact was that the mission was purely symbolic. Its importance was its existence.

Bruce's team contained a high concentration of China experts, the most talented group of foreign service officers, in his opinion, that he had ever led. Certainly the proportion of native speakers was higher than at any of his embassies in Europe, but their talents were often wasted, and they were little more adept than their boss at divining the minds of their hosts. He disregarded the tea-leaf reading of sinologists and trusted his own instincts. Given the formality of relations and the uncommunicative posture of their hosts, tea leaves and instinct were all there was to go on in deciphering the Chinese mind.

When he took the assignment, Bruce knew the importance of symbolism in the closed society of China. He knew that as the embodiment of the novel American presence in Beijing he would play a central role in whatever symbolic dramas the Chinese chose to stage in order to demonstrate their newfound relationship with America. The visit of the American basketball team a month after he arrived provided such an opportunity. As it turned out, the nuances were more fascinating than the Americans anticipated.

Given the importance of the sports exchange, Bruce expected a delegation from the foreign ministry to match the presence at the arena of his own small entourage. To his astonishment no less a person than Jiang Qing, the feared Madame Mao herself, presided over the occasion. Before the game she made a long speech on Sino-American friendship that was broadcast live on local television. During the game Bruce sat in the front row of seats next to her, with foreign service officer Nicholas Platt as interpreter. Seldom seen in public, Madame Mao on this occasion went into the crowd to shake hands and appeared to all as though she were an avid sports fan. When the American athletes presented her with souvenir emblem pins, she had nothing to reciprocate with. She rummaged in the pocket of her long gown (not a Mao jacket) and pulled out a handkerchief full of jasmine petals. She gave them to Bruce and told him to divide them among the teams to make jasmine tea.

She also invited the athletes as her guests to the opera, a gesture, Bruce's experts concluded, of "unprecedented" amity.[30] She laughingly told Bruce she would not invite him too because she did not handle foreign policy, and anyway it might make China's northern neighbors cross. She asked the American coaches to convey her greetings to the White House because "the American leaders had been brave enough to come and see for themselves that the Chinese were not 'freaks and monsters.'"[31]

The next day the Bruce mission cabled its assessment of this remarkable performance. Jiang Qing's endorsement, wrote the Americans more breathlessly than the occasion warranted, "transformed this international sports show into a major political event, with important domestic implications."[32] They erroneously interpreted the event as a demonstration to the Chinese people that the leftist faction supported friendship with America. "The leadership is at last united on what has long been a divisive subject," the cable concluded. "This, of course, is the message for us as well."[33] This sort of earnest, hopeful reaction was understandable in the mission's early days. Jiang Qing's appearance was of symbolic importance, but with the passage of time the Americans became jaded by gestures that never seemed to lead anywhere. Bruce next saw Jiang Qing in the autumn at a concert by the Philadelphia Symphony. Looking frailer than before, she still struck him as a forceful personality: "I should judge her a woman it would be wise not to offend; steel is evidently mixed with blandness in her."[34]

In contrast, he found Zhou Enlai a sympathetic figure, impressive, intelligent, and appealing without Madame Mao's sinister overtones. Zhou's bushy black eyebrows reminded Bruce of the American coal miners' leader, John L. Lewis. But the cultured Chinese premier was far more impressive, "his face impassive, except when joking, his elegant manners, courtesy, immaculate dress, comport with his fine appearance. He reminds me somewhat in physiognomy of Humphrey Bogart, but a much more aristocratic type." Zhou was born in the same year as Bruce and like him was in Paris in 1919 where he too discovered the great world. Bruce enjoyed his talks with Zhou and said of an early one, "Although it did not range from A to Z, it did go from cancer to the USSR."[35] He did not know then that Zhou was ill with the cancer that would eventually remove him from the scene in favor of much less sympathetic figures.

Nixon had told Bruce that through the art of giving state dinners the Chinese conducted much of their relations with the barbarians who came to pay homage at the court of the Middle Kingdom. After experiencing them for himself, Bruce told a friend, "China captures the Third World by banquets," vast entertainments for the least important visiting foreign leader.[36] This strategy for winning friends was superior to the "brutal, uncouth, begrudging" efforts of the Soviets. "Manners maketh man is not necessarily true," he concluded, "but they surely do lubricate the machinery of diplomacy."[37]

He knew that his age would be an asset in a society that respected elders. It was still a pleasant shock to be treated with such deference on account of age. "I am treated as if I were physically brittle," he noted. "My health is solicitously inquired about, and when I rise from a couch support is offered to my elbows, and I am cautioned to walk carefully on marble floors."[38] Like every American in the early days of the thaw, he was fascinated with the Chinese. "It is impossible to overstate the cordiality of these people," he observed. "The austerity of their personal lives gives place to lavishness in official entertainments."[39] Their cordiality, though, did not keep him from calling Chinese entertainment "intellectual crap but good propaganda" and describing his hosts as "zenophobic, homogeneous, and nationalistic, sensitive to any moves they might even wrongly construe as smacking of intervention."[40] In this assessment, he was more realistic than the many American officials who should have known better than to be swept up in China euphoria.

When construction of the liaison mission was complete, Bruce presided over a quietly emotional ceremony. In the dull early light of a July morning, before the summer sun began to bake the compound, he watched as the Stars and Stripes rose up the flagpole in Beijing for the first time since 1949. The small marine detachment, some wearing Vietnam campaign ribbons, stood rigidly at attention, watched in turn with intense curiosity by soldiers of the People's Liberation Army on duty at the mission gate. After Evangeline Bruce snapped a picture, her husband said, "Now we are in business" and turned away to walk slowly back to his office.[41] Those marine uniforms did not go unnoticed.

Once ensconced in their permanent quarters, the Bruces decided to hold a modest Independence Day celebration, the first in Beijing in twenty-four years. It was a novel challenge for Evangeline Bruce. With no furniture yet for the reception room, a borrowed table served as a bar. To hide the barrenness, she placed huge cabbage baskets around the room and topped them with fig trees, oleanders, and water lilies. One of her Chinese guests later asked if all American living rooms looked the same.[42] At the time, her decorations nearly went unappreciated because of unforeseen events.

On the morning of the party, three of Bruce's staff were summoned to the foreign ministry, expecting, as was the usual practice, a last-minute discussion about the composition of the Chinese delegation. "What a deception," Bruce said when they returned and told him the real reason — a reprimand for allowing the marines to wear their uniforms. Unless he corrected this abuse of protocol, no Chinese would attend his party. Calling it "bitter medicine," he swallowed his pride, gave the bad news to the marines, and with less good cheer than he had expected to show, toasted Chinese-American amity before the foreign ministry officials who eventually came to the party.[43]

The uniforms were not the real problem. In September Bruce was summoned to the foreign ministry and told the marines themselves must go. No other diplomatic mission had sent troops to guard its quarters in Beijing, nor did the Chinese insist on such precautions for their office in Washington. It did not help that the marines had set up a highly visible bar, the "Red Ass Saloon," that catered to the whole foreign community. The Chinese decided to use the questionable marine presence to remind Bruce where he was and who he was dealing with.[44]

He knew that, if enforced, the expulsion order would chill relations, much to the delight of the Soviets. It would embolden hostile regimes elsewhere to demand the withdrawal of marine embassy guards. He decided to temporize. The Chinese were masters at delay and would recognize his tactic, but it would put off a confrontation.[45] Dismantling the marines' bar but not telling them of the more serious threat created a morale problem. He took their sergeant into his confidence and told him of the Chinese order, which Bruce succeeded in delaying until Kissinger and Zhou met. The plaintive sergeant asked if he could have the American and marine corps flags crossed behind the cake table at their corps birthday party.[46] It seemed an innocent enough request but led to further shadow boxing over symbols.

Summoned by Lin P'ing, director of American and Oceanic Affairs at the foreign ministry, Bruce heard firsthand of Chinese displeasure with the marines' ominous birthday cake. They surmised correctly that a cake for 130 people meant that the marine party was for more than just the American contingent. Chinese confectioners refused to decorate the cake with the marine corps emblem. Knowing the effect it would have on morale, Bruce nevertheless canceled the party in order to avoid more drastic action that might prejudice Kissinger's forthcoming visit.[47] When the secretary of state came to Beijing, he won the right of the marines to remain.[48] But even his magic wore off six months later when the Chinese finally forced the Americans to replace the marines with civilian guards.[49]

The isolation of the American mission dampened any unrealistic expectations the staff may have had about relations with China. For a change, Bruce had a post with few official social obligations and no informal social contact with the host population at all.

It did not take many weeks to realize too that there was little of substance to do. They were there literally to symbolize the new relationship between the People's Republic and the United States. Nothing more was required. Others assigned to China had the same experience. Bruce reported that "many of the diplomats here are bored and discontented over their lack of substantive occupation."[50] He noted that they really had a good life in Beijing and ought not to complain because the Chinese provided them with every amenity. Life moved at a slower pace than in other capitals. Once he adjusted, he came to enjoy China. The lack of official social obligations became "a real joy" and gave him the chance to read he had never had before in diplomatic service. Even the longer time it took for mail to arrive from the outside world could be tolerated: "After a while, one adjusts to this situation, and cultivates one's own garden." He could understand the age-old Chinese attitude about the outer world: "If one did not hear the morning news on Voice of America, one might feel the world outside China had no importance."[51]

In the past he prowled the antiques shops of London and Paris as a release from tension on the job; in Beijing he did it to pass the time. That there was little to buy sharpened the challenge. He returned home once with an umbrella and a wicker wastepaper basket that seemed to him prizes beyond anything from Bond Street. A tailor shop became a favorite haunt because fabric was one item he could buy. On one occasion he took a great length of silk to be made into dressing gowns — one for Beijing, one for London, and one for Georgetown. A friend who went with him for the final fitting marveled at how the session relaxed Bruce, who preened unselfconsciously in front of the mirror as he modeled the voluminous, gaudy, dragon-figured gown, towering like a mandarin over the flock of wizened Chinese tailors fussing about the hem.[52]

Among the perks of the mission was the opportunity to see the sights of China hidden from Americans for decades. Bruce was bowled over by the Imperial City, whose fantastical architecture heightened the romantic allure of the emperor's entourage, those thousands of retainers, concubines, and eunuchs who, he said, "lived in opulence and intrigue" behind high palace walls.[53] And then there was picnicking among the giant marble statues at the Ming Tombs and, of course, visits to the Great Wall.[54]

He had been forewarned by all of those importunate phone calls and letters before he left Washington that all sorts of Americans would ask his help to finagle their way into China. Beijing in 1973 was the objective of every journalist and Washington official: a passport stamped by the PRC was the fashion statement of the season. It was just like Paris in 1919, where every diplomat tried to wangle an assignment at the peace talks, or like Paris again right after Liberation in 1944. Just as in those earlier defining moments, Bruce was where everyone wanted to be. Though the Chinese were agreeable about admitting the families of diplomats, he tried not to tax them with too many requests for visas for friends. Still, it was a rare week when he did not have at least one personal house guest staying at the cramped residence.

The liaison mission also coordinated the visits of exchange groups and delegations of scientists, doctors, and educators. Knowing the overheated fascination of his countrymen for all things Chinese, he suggested to one visiting group of academics — with little hope of being heeded — that they resolve not to pontificate about China when they returned home for at least a year, lest they emulate the other one-week wonders in the flourishing Sinology cottage industry.

Congressional delegations were more difficult. The worst was led by Senator Warren Magnuson, who arrived in a foul humor at not being met at the airport by, to use Bruce's dry phrase, "exalted Chinese officials."[55] Magnuson compounded his offense when he tried to make the foreign service officer attached to his delegation fetch a forbidden box of Havana cigars from the Cuban embassy. "It is a pity the Senator did not see the Cuban Embassy here," Bruce said. "On the outside wall is a glass faced cabinet in which is displayed a photograph of a skull with one eye socket covered by an American flag."[56] The legislators achieved their goal of meeting Zhou Enlai, and that was where the real trouble occurred. Magnuson stepped over the line by discussing the American bombing in Cambodia with Zhou. That damage could have been contained had the senator not talked indiscreetly to reporters. His meddling in the conduct of diplomacy irritated Bruce; it enraged Kissinger.[57] During another visit, Bruce regretted not warning Deng Xiaoping of "the dangers of Congressional garrulity." As a result, Deng's comments off the record about Zhou's illness were instantly communicated by Hubert Humphrey to the press.[58]

In November Bruce and Kissinger went for an extended talk with Zhou at the Great Hall of the People. Four hours into their conversation, a messenger brought word that Mao wished to see them. It took only ten minutes to drive there, speeding past smartly attentive PLA soldiers, through the ornate illuminated portal called the Gate of New China, and into the Imperial City compound and the residence of the absolute ruler of the Middle Kingdom.

The audience took place in Mao's library filled with thousands of books. The visitors sat in a semicircle formed by huge, garishly uphol-stered chairs and sofas and listened, in Kissinger's words, to "that incarnation of willpower who greeted us with his characteristic mock-ing, slightly demonic smile." Bruce was struck by the chairman's mas-sive, "majestic" forehead, balding in front but still sporting an abun-dance of black hair. Mao had lost weight; at least that was the impression given by the way his gray suit limply hung on his frame.[59] He laughingly apologized for his words being indistinct, saying he had just lost two teeth. It was a wonder he could even talk, for by then a bad heart, Parkinson's disease, periodic seizures, and a host of other maladies had ravaged his health. "Mao's body," said Harrison Salisbury, "was becoming a coven of miseries."[60]

The Great Helmsman set the Americans at ease by joking about Bruce's age, the youth of his assistant, Winston Lord, and his own advanced years. The meeting went on at great length, with Mao ranging discursively over political philosophy and world affairs. It lasted for nearly three hours, his longest interview with foreigners in years. He was eager to continue, but Zhou tactfully interjected that they were already late for the banquet in Kissinger's honor. When this astonishing performance ended, Bruce, who had met most world leaders of his time, said he had "witnessed the most extraordinary and disciplined presen-tation he had ever heard from a statesman."[61]

Not only were they late for the banquet, but they had also com-pletely missed the cocktail party that Bruce had planned for Kissinger and the whole diplomatic community.[62] The secretary of state thought that by standing up the diplomatic corps the Chinese ensured that all the ambassadors went back to their compounds and cabled home the news that the Americans had rated so highly with Mao. Kissinger thought a secondary reason was to remind Bruce that as only the head of a liaison office he overstepped his bounds by inviting accredited ambassadors to his cocktail party.[63] It is possible that the Chinese might wish to remind Bruce of his status but unlikely that the foreign ministry would have dared ask the revered Mao to contribute several hours of his time to make this point to Bruce.

The meeting with Mao was exciting tonic for the secretary of state and his mission chief. It capped the talks with Zhou and symbolized to Bruce and Kissinger the value of the new relationship between China and America. When they finally reached the banquet at the Great Hall of the People, that knowledge was as intoxicating as the repeated toasts of *mao tai*.

After the audience with Mao, though, Sino-American ties faltered. There were further cultural exchanges and an explosion of trips by hopeful entrepreneurs, but the momentum visibly slackened. Perhaps the novelty was wearing off for both parties. Only days after the marathon session with Mao, the chief diplomat at China's Washington office left for consultation at home. Observers took his prolonged absence to be a diplomatic signal. Then America appointed a new ambassador to Taiwan when people had speculated that the post would be left vacant after the incumbent retired. The Chinese seemed preoccupied with a growing antiforeign campaign. Even Zhou talked once more about Beijing's undying commitment to revolutionary struggles abroad. As 1973 drew to a close, the promise of the Shanghai Communiqué seemed more elusive than ever.[64]

Christmas in Beijing was subdued. Icy winds from Siberia ushered in winter, and the small holiday parties at Western embassies reinforced the sense of being far from home. The Sunday before Christmas Bruce sat in his deserted office catching up on correspondence, kept company only by a guard scanning incoming holiday packages for bombs with a detection meter that was irritatingly triggered by the smallest bit of tinsel.[65]

On Christmas Day the Bruces went to the British embassy for a service of lessons and carols. That night he ruminated gloomily over the state of world affairs. "Except during the two Great Wars of my time," he wrote, "the world has never appeared in this century to be in such disarray as now."[66] Worldwide recession exacerbated by the Arab oil embargo was part of the problem. More serious, he thought, was a lack of political will in the West. Kissinger's virtuoso performance remained the one bright spot, though Bruce noted that his enemies in the press were the same people "who ardently hope the North Vietnamese will ultimately overrun South Viet-Nam." They would get their wish. As a final thought, he concluded that "the cherished, illusory dream of Henry Luce that there would be an American Twentieth Century has been dissipated."[67]

As he prepared to leave Beijing for consultation at home in January 1974, he believed that there were few serious problems amenable to his intervention, only the usual nuts-and-bolts matters that embassies had to handle everywhere, and his staff was more than competent. There was nothing, then, to prevent him from taking a long leave, two months as it turned out. He left with the sad thought that he had not made a single Chinese friend in nine months. There was the equally sobering realization that American naïveté about bridging the psychological gap between East and West would cause what he called "acute disappointments" for some time to come.[68]

Bruce's absence from his post may not have been a subtle signal to the Chinese as some thought. Beijing was a miserable place in winter. The fine dust that constantly blew down from the northern desert and the bitter cold gave every Chinese upper-respiratory ailments. In the absence of tissues, seven million residents of Beijing blowing their noses on their fingers, made the capital a less than salubrious place for a frail, elderly foreign diplomat. If Bruce found a way to extend his stay in Washington, it was just as likely to be for reasons of personal health as byzantine signaling to the Chinese.

The bad circulation in his legs continually troubled him, but at his age it was flu that was the most serious threat. When he did take sick, his strategy was to retire to his bed and attack the infection gamely with whiskey and brandy from the stash of bottles he kept under the bed where he knew he could find them without relying on the servants, who left at six o'clock anyway. During one such spell two of his young friends, diplomatic spouse Maureen Molinari and house guest Lady Mary Manners, kept him company to jolly him up. To them he looked for all the world like an ancient mandarin himself, dressed in an elaborate nightshirt and a red cap, sitting up in bed and chatting as though holding court, and now and then reaching over to rummage under the bed for a different bottle.[69]

While he was at home that winter, Kissinger persuaded him to sit on a committee dealing with the worldwide energy crisis. It was pro forma work. More rewarding to the ambassador was the sight of forsythia and crocuses that gave a hint of spring to Georgetown. But other, less agreeable, omens obsessed the capital. "The generic term 'Watergate' is rarely heard anymore," wrote journalist Elizabeth Drew. "Gradually — almost imperceptibly — the word for what we are going through has become 'impeachment.'"[70] Not a bad time to leave Washington. Back in China, he concluded after his first day at the office that in his absence "nothing critical seems to have taken place."[71]

By his first anniversary in China, rumors circulated of his boredom and frustration. These sentiments were partly in the minds of journalists who had grander expectations about what he could accomplish in Beijing. He knew there was little for someone even of his stature to do that his subordinates could not handle. But he knew that someone of his stature was necessary for the sake of symbolism. He was not so much the senior American diplomat in Beijing, his special assistant Brunson McKinley recalled, as "the senior American hood ornament."[72] He was content to make that contribution. He had a rare capacity to enjoy himself whatever he was doing, even if it meant visiting, for the third time, the heroic Sino-Albanian Commune or some other Potemkin institution. And members of his staff agreed that he never communicated any sense of unhappiness to them or in any way undermined their morale.[73]

The tedium could not be denied. Kissinger warned George Bush, Bruce's eventual successor, that like the distinguished Virginia diplomat, he would "be bored out of his mind from the inactivity." And so the Bushes, like the Bruces, would spend more evenings at home reading and writing letters than was possible at any other ambassadorial post in the world.[74]

Bruce was feeling his age. It drove the point home that he knew his successor's father, Prescott Bush, with whom he worked at W. A. Harriman and Co. in the 1920s, better than George Bush.[75] When in the spring Kissinger proposed to send him as a roving ambassador to the European Economic Community, Bruce said archly that he did not know the present EEC leaders, "though I was on terms of friendship with the grandfathers of some of them."[76]

Press reports of his unhappiness irritated him, and he dismissed them as "pesky, malicious" gossip.[77] He did miss his friends in Europe and America, and he was getting on in years — he celebrated his seventy-sixth birthday in 1974. But he was content to lend his prestige as America's senior diplomat in China. The lighter schedule of duties actually suited him as his physical vigor declined, and he never tired of observing the "acute intelligence of the Chinese."[78] A visiting friend even thought he seemed "liberated" by the more spartan existence he led in Beijing.[79] So, content to enjoy his exotic setting, despite the tedium, Bruce planned to stay on a little longer.

When the time finally came to leave, on September 18, 1974, the Bruces gave a farewell reception for Chinese officials, members of the diplomatic corps, and journalists. Vice-foreign minister Ch'iao Kuan-hua, Bruce's favorite official, headed the Chinese delegation. The "companionable, sophisticated, gifted" Ch'iao had been a key player in the diplomacy that began the rapprochement and was a kindly and sympathetic contact. An ally of Zhou Enlai's moderate faction, he would be purged shortly after Bruce left China.[80]

The Chinese reciprocated the next evening with a banquet for Bruce presided over by Ch'iao at a symbolic location. Evangeline Bruce had asked several times, without success, for permission to visit the old American legation, where she lived when her father was assigned to Peking. The Chinese hesitated to display the former foreign quarter, scene of the siege during the Boxer Rebellion and symbol of a century of European exploitation. Thanks to the vice-premier, however, the banquet took place in that very same building.[81] It was a nostalgic moment and not just for Evangeline Bruce. During their tour, as she reminisced about her childhood there, one of the Chinese recalled his own memories of the legation: it had been he who in 1949 went there and notified the American consul general that the People's Republic had been established.

By the time Bruce left, China's internal politics were roiled anew as Jiang Qing's influence waxed once again. In disfavor for a time, she saw her chance as Mao cooled toward Zhou in early 1974. Bruce, like many China watchers, could not believe the rumors that Zhou had fallen from favor. It may have been because he identified with him as an urbane realist of his own generation, like Bruce a true courtier and so much more agreeable than the unsavory ideologues waiting in the wings. By the end of the year Jiang's xenophobic leftism would threaten to undo Zhou's works, among them the opening to America.

When Deng Xiaoping returned to Beijing just before Bruce first arrived, he jumped energetically into the task of undoing the Cultural

Revolution. But not until 1975 would Deng — described by Bruce as a squat, gnome-like figure with piercing eyes and a broad-shouldered physique to match his reputation for toughness — feel strong enough to confront Jiang Qing.[82] At last the White-Boned Demon, as the press began to call her, would stand defiantly in the dock. Condemned to death, she was given a suspended sentence. Though Deng began to lift the shackles of communism from China's economy, he like Mao became an ossified red emperor clutching the Mandate of Heaven. If Bruce imperfectly read the finer tea leaves of Chinese politics, he did understand the pressures that built up in a totalitarian state. "One would be rash," he wrote Jean Monnet shortly after arriving in China, "to guess at the ultimate outcome. On the surface, there is calm; if lava is boiling beneath, there are no signs of impending eruption."[83] Fifteen more years would pass before the massacre of Tiananmen.

For all its superficiality, the post in Beijing gave Bruce a chance to participate in the greatest démarche in American diplomacy since the Marshall Plan and NATO.[84] This revolution demolished the bipolar Cold War face-off between the two superpowers that had provided the context for his career. Now a new triangular dispensation opened the way for creative maneuvering, and he had played a part in making it all happen.

CHAPTER 23

Aeneas in Brussels

Distinguished old gentlemen in their dotage should abandon public affairs.

— From Bruce's diary, February 22, 1954

*A*T THE END of the century, with communism as dead as Marx and the Berlin Wall smashed into souvenirs for tourists, it takes an effort to recall the nightmare that for good reason addled the sleep of Western diplomats for so long. Ever since the Korean War, the West had lived with the fear of regiments of gray Russian battle tanks crashing through the German border and sweeping on to the Rhine. That incubus, which had obsessed the foreign policy elites during the noontime of Bruce's career, persisted into its twilight, even as the sclerotic Soviet empire stood, unbeknownst to anyone, on the brink of dissolution.

Richard Nixon too stood on a precipice in 1974. In August the threat of impeachment finally drove him from office in disgrace. ("Halleluja," Bruce wrote in his diary.) In the caretaker Ford administration the nation's senior ambassador found yet another assignment after China. A month after Nixon resigned, Kissinger, still dominating foreign policy, proposed to send Bruce to Switzerland. Communal strife in Cyprus threatened open conflict between NATO members Greece and Turkey. Kissinger attempted to bring the two to the conference table in Geneva, and he wanted Bruce there to guide them toward a compromise. He even took the liberty before cabling Bruce of mentioning his name to the Greek prime minister as an "earnest" of how seriously the U.S. took the Geneva talks.[1]

Bruce had expected to return to private life after Beijing, this time for good. The prospect of quiet evenings with London friends at the flat at Albany and of small dinner parties in Georgetown grew more appealing. More to the point, his next birthday would be his seventy-seventh, and he looked and felt every year of it. "Retirement had seemed within my grasp," he wrote, but then Kissinger's cable arrived and struck "a stunning pre-breakfast blow" on September 12, 1974.[2] He shifted gears quickly, however, and accepted the proposal. In agreeing, he cautioned Kissinger that he was completely ignorant of the Cyprus conflict and would need to advance the date of his departure from China to study it properly.[3] A week later, Washington's musical chairs offered up a more appealing prospect.

Ford decided that he wanted Donald Rumsfeld to be his White House chief of staff. That move left vacant Rumsfeld's post in Brussels of United States Permanent Representative on the Council of the North Atlantic Treaty Organization (or USPERMREP NATO, in the Alliance's shorthand). Kissinger recommended sending Bruce to Brussels instead of Geneva. Ford agreed and also tacked on the title of special representative to the European Community.[4] Here was something far more appealing than the Cyprus talks, yet another offer he could not refuse. In cabling to accept, he plainly, accurately summarized his whole career when he described NATO and the European Community as "the subjects in which I am most interested."[5]

The North Atlantic Treaty, signed in Washington in 1949, gave concrete form to the most dramatic peacetime commitment America ever made to other nations. At the time, Bruce headed the Marshall Plan in France, the economic parallel to the security alliance, and Gerald R. Ford was in his freshman term in the House of Representatives. A quarter century later, as president, he gave Bruce his charge when the aging diplomat arrived at the White House en route to Brussels. Ford told him he was beginning his new job "at a time when the Alliance is under strain as a result of the deteriorating world economic situation."[6] The severe 1974–75 recession put alliance members under strong pressure to cut defense spending. America's ambassador to NATO must stop the erosion and even urge increases. He would not have an easy time of it.

In addition to the brooding, minatory presence of Brezhnev's Soviet Union and domestic political pressures to reduce military spending, NATO suffered from other ailments. That dispute over Cyprus threatened war between two of its members. Then came the depressing denouement of the Vietnam tragedy. In spring 1975 Communist tanks raced not across the plains of Germany, but through the wide boulevards of Saigon and rang down the curtain with brutal finality on a disastrous era in Indochinese and American history.

Bruce seemed the ideal envoy to NATO at this particular moment. By virtue of his long experience, his interests, and his associations, he was the most European of America's diplomats, the most attuned to the sensibilities of his nation's allies. To Europeans with long memories, he was as well a living symbol of the most forward-thinking elements in America's foreign policy going back to the Marshall Plan and the high hopes he shared with Jean Monnet. In 1974, the cause of European integration, with the exception of Britain, was no longer the divisive issue it had been after the war. Among the governing elites it was the ruling orthodoxy. To have Bruce represent America in the councils of Europe was a positive step. Some Europeans of long memory may have had a less favorable opinion if they recalled that he also represented, according to their lights, a classic instance of American interference in their affairs. His previous advocacy of the European Defense Community did not generate favorable memories in some Paris circles, but the French in 1974 were no longer part of the NATO military command.

Serious disagreements still divided NATO. American demands that the allies pay more of the cost of billeting U.S. troops in Europe were the chief source of friction. Bruce's colleagues at NATO thought Washington unaware of the depth of that feeling. His old friend Andre de Staercke, dean of Belgian diplomats, feared isolationist tendencies on both sides of the Atlantic. The frustration of the smaller allies with American demands that they contribute more to the common defense would, de Staercke worried, drive them to despair and neutralism.[7] Indeed, Bruce had been given an impossible mission.

Brussels in 1974 was a small city with a future, the capital of a compact, prosperous state and the headquarters of both the European Community and NATO. Other cities had equal claim to be the capital of Europe — but few as good a symbolic claim to be the locus of the

Western military alliance, for Belgium had been the seat of war in Western Europe long before Wellington and Blücher met at Waterloo.

Evangeline Bruce looked forward to Brussels with mixed feelings. The State Department cable describing their official residence at 22 avenue du Vert Chasseur was enough, she thought, "to congeal the blood." But, in contrast to the temporary quarters that had greeted them in Beijing, she expected the house would at least be comfortable.[8] And there would be none of that damnable Gobi dust that choked everything in the Chinese capital. She knew too that the fast electric train between Brussels Midi and the Gare du Nord put Paris within striking distance as a day trip. And the flat at Albany was near at hand, only a one-hour hop from the Brussels airport to Heathrow.

The Bruces arrived in Brussels on the last day of November 1974. Although they did not know it, the coming winter would be milder than usual in Europe and even less taxing on the ambassador's health than the climate in northern China, if he had remained there.

On the other hand, he immediately faced a far more punishing schedule than Beijing, a routine in some ways more hemmed in by the conventions of ceremony and staff work than any previous embassy. He set his old routine of arriving at the office at 9:30 but had staff meetings every day, unlike the leisurely once-a-week routine of most of his embassies. Indeed, he had less control over his own schedule than during any appointment since the frantic months as Truman's undersecretary of state long before. Staff meetings, briefings, required calls on the other "Permreps," as his NATO colleagues were called, and nonstop visits by diplomatic and military officials from the Alliance members kept him at the office for a full day nearly every day. As America's representative to the North Atlantic Council, he could expect to meet every week with the Defense Planning Committee to coordinate the military side of the alliance.

Unlike Beijing, where there was not much to do in the evenings, official socializing matched the requirements even of the Paris embassy years before when he was younger and fitter. In contrast to London and Paris, there were fewer personal friends to socialize with in Brussels, but the number of official dinners, nearly all of them with invitations marked *cravate noire*, poured into the residence with alarming frequency. Beijing began to look better in retrospect. Given Bruce's increasingly frail health, making an early night of it more and more outweighed his lifelong penchant for sampling haute cuisine and wine and conversation into the wee hours.

His assignment also required him to tour the member countries, much as he had done two decades before for the abortive EDC. In January, for example, he flew with his NATO colleagues for a day trip to Lahr and Baden to visit Canadian forces in Europe.[9] In March he made a longer tour of U.S. Forces Headquarters. Flying first to Stuttgart on an air force plane, he changed to an army helicopter and was at the helipad of the United States European Command talking to the deputy commander by late morning. After briefings there until noon, he flew to Heidelberg for more of the same and then a black-tie dinner hosted by the general commanding. The next day took him, again by helicopter, to Ramstein to consult with the headquarters staff of the American air force.[10]

In June he visited NATO facilities in Naples, with the full range of briefings, dining at the officers' club, a helicopter visit to the aircraft carrier USS *Forrestal*, more briefings, and live-fire exercises.[11] One particularly hectic trip put him on an afternoon flight to Geneva. The next morning he breakfasted with Kissinger, flew to Paris for lunch with U.S. diplomats, met with Jean Monnet at Neuilly-sur-Seine, and caught the evening train from the Gare du Nord for Brussels by sundown.[12] It was too much for his old bones to take.

The chat with Monnet was the best part of the trip. These ancient conspirators in the cause of European unity did more than reminisce, though. They were up to their old tricks, for the future of the European Community was always on their minds. And in the depressing spring that witnessed the fall of Saigon, there was at least good news on one front — Britain voted in a plebiscite to join the Common Market.

At the end of May 1975 plans for the coming summit meeting of alliance leaders in Brussels absorbed the little diplomatic community of NATO. Bruce served as President Ford's host, meeting him at the airport, where King Baudouin formally greeted him and Mrs. Ford. For the next two days they were in the hands of the efficient staff organizers of the summit, with a full slate of public and restricted meetings. As much of the time was given over to ceremony, however, as to substantive discussion, from posing for a "family portrait" of the NATO heads of delegations and foreign ministers, to King Baudouin's black-tie stag dinner at the royal palace.[13]

The summit had its awkward moments, and not just because of the heightened friction among NATO members. Donald Rumsfeld, now the ambitious White House chief of staff, wanted the world to see that the president and not the high-flying secretary of state was in charge, "making sure that it did not seem as if Ford were merely lip-synching Kissinger's foreign policy."[14] Having Ford rather than Kissinger conduct the press briefings at the summit would make this point. Kissinger should have seen the value in having his president's stature enhanced but did not and in an evil temper denounced his enemies for trying to undermine him.

The following month Bruce flew home to attend a one-day symposium at the Naval Academy in Annapolis. Listening to papers on the legal future of seabed resources bored him. At least he had a chance to show his NATO colleagues the village where he entered political life as a member of the Maryland House of Delegates half a century before. The memory of his youthful enthusiasm then, in contrast to his flagging health in 1975, might have suggested to him that it was time to leave government service for good.

After nearly a year in Brussels, he implied to British journalist Kenneth Rose that long hours at the office and masses of paperwork made his work tedious. He rarely returned home before 7:30 in the evening. More than he told Rose, negotiations about standardization of NATO munitions and equipment bored him to distraction. The endless parties each time a NATO colleague rotated out of Brussels had become a tiresome duty. He even told Rose he preferred Beijing with its thinner schedule of official events and said the Chinese were much more interesting to observe.[15] Beijing had been all window dressing and no substance; NATO was both and too much of each. The customary farewell dinners and cocktail parties, now so familiar to the ambassador and his wife, began early in the new year. After saying good-byes to his staff and colleagues, Bruce left Brussels for home on January 30, 1976.

In his last three posts — the Vietnam talks, China, and NATO — all undertaken beyond the age of seventy, he had been given impossible tasks. The difference now was that Kissinger dominated foreign policy and circumvented the State Department even after he became its secretary. Nevertheless, Bruce was willing to serve. He had participated in yet another revolution in American foreign affairs as dramatic as the Marshall Plan. Nixon and Kissinger had finally, belatedly ended the Vietnam War and through the opening to China converted the bipolar Cold War into a three-cornered chessboard. The war need not have dragged on as long as it did. Perhaps the thaw with Beijing was inevitable, but Bruce's contribution to both efforts, however frustrating at times, gave him a sense of accomplishment that few diplomats of his age could point to. In his declining years he was again able to oppose the isolationist impulse that he had fought before Pearl Harbor and during the Marshall Plan. In the 1970s it was an isolationism of the left rather than of the right that defeat in Vietnam had fostered. From whichever end of the political spectrum, it was an inward-looking perspective that Bruce, with his eye on America's role in the world, would not countenance. He had kept his principles, regardless of personal cost.

In September 1975 he told Kissinger he planned to leave Brussels no later than his seventy-eighth birthday, the following February. *Newsweek* reported that the White House, aware of Bruce's intentions, had already offered the post at NATO to William Colby (recently fired as head of the CIA). The magazine said further that Bruce was incensed on learning this news and handed in his resignation on the spot. Privately angered by the report, he denied any irritation with the president and secretary of state.

When he did finally retire in January 1976, his farewell remarks summed up the Cold War orthodoxy his generation represented. "I see nothing in the policies of our most formidable potential enemy," he warned, "to justify belief that a millennium is about to arrive." Still smarting from the *Newsweek* flap, he took a swipe at the press for its reflexive "denigration and sensationalism." He denied the prevalent talk about "whether the West is not foundering into permanent decline." Some of the old self-mocking charm shone through as he exhorted "a renewal of confidence in our destiny," though admitting he had "only imperfectly fingered the fringes of the NATO tapestry."

He saved the driest of his allusive wit for the last. He realized he was leaving at a low point in the self-esteem of the American establishment — what was left of it — at a time of insecurity, drift, self-doubt, and irresolution throughout the Western Alliance. The Soviet Union seemed as menacing as ever, its final, mortal illness still not

apparent, its philosophy embraced by more and more dictatorial regimes in the Third World. Prolonged recession in the West masked the
superiority of free markets over the dead hand of socialism.

Because of this depressing climate, Bruce ended his remarks with a
Latin epigram, the only one he said he could recall, but one that again
showed his ability at the age of seventy-eight to take the long view
and also not take himself too seriously: *Et haec olim meminisse juvabit*.
It was a line from Virgil's *Aeneid* that he may have remembered from
Princeton. It certainly was not something a classically minded speechwriter cooked up for the occasion, for the ambassador had used it long
before, in 1919 when he wrote home to tell his parents about his
discovery of France. In 1976, with the Western Alliance beset by self-
doubt, the phrase was more appropriate and fit the occasion perfectly.
With Troy sacked and his wife killed, Aeneas leads the fugitive Trojans
in the remnants of their fleet to sail the Mediterranean in search of
another land to settle. They are rebuffed everywhere they drop anchor.
Then Juno, still angry at the Trojans, commands Aeolus, king of the
winds, to unloose a violent storm against the fleet. Most of the ships
are sunk; the rest run aground and are wrecked. The Trojans are
marooned on a shore that, for all they know, may be inhabited by
cannibals. Their food is spoiled and starvation threatens. Most of their
comrades have drowned. Aeneas, at this low point, looks around and
says to his fellows, *Et haec olim meminisse juvabit:* very loosely,
"Someday perhaps we'll look back on this and laugh."[16]

That his was a misguided modesty was clear to his colleagues in the
foreign service, and clearer still the following spring at a Pentagon
ceremony. On that occasion he received the Defense Department's
medal of distinguished public service, including a document that rightly
described his "imperfectly fingered" role as crucial to the founding and
preservation of the Atlantic Alliance. Just before the retirement ceremony in Brussels, Kissinger paid tribute to Bruce by threatening him
that this latest retirement could not take him beyond the reach of the
government: "We will press him into service for something or other
when we can catch him unaware."[17]

Gerald Ford did not attend Bruce's retirement ceremony in Washington as the State Department had hoped. He did, however, confer the
Presidential Medal of Freedom on the veteran diplomat "on behalf of
a grateful republic" at a simple ceremony in the White House cabinet

room on February 10, 1976, two days before Bruce's seventy-eighth birthday. Besides Evangeline Bruce and Ford, the gathering included Kissinger, Vice-President Nelson Rockefeller, NATO Secretary-General Joseph Luns, and a dozen or so friends, many of them former assistants of Bruce going back to the Marshall Plan days who had gone on to distinguished careers in the Foreign Service. In accepting the medal and his ambassadorial flag, Bruce stepped up to the microphone, stooping a little and needing a cane to support himself and yet still looking taller than his six feet just as he did as a second lieutenant in the Army Courier Service. He thanked Ford for the personal honor and for supporting that link tying America to Western Europe that had inspired his own life. "Again, Mr. President, I am deeply indebted to you for your own leadership and for the spirit in which you have animated, I think, so wisely American policies, and especially in respect to NATO, which to my mind should remain, as it has been, the keystone of American foreign policy."[18] In presenting the award to Bruce, Ford, who had made his mark in the House of Representatives, queried the ambassador about his experience as a legislator. "Was it the Maryland or the Virginia legislature?" the president asked. "Both," replied Bruce.

He was, as a fellow NATO emissary said, "an ambassador's ambassador," literally a living monument to the Western Alliance. But he was a monument in failing health. And he was weighted down by a great personal sorrow that even more than his frail constitution drained him of energy. For family tragedy denied him the well-earned right in his declining years to savor the accolades given him at the end of a distinguished, indeed, unique career.

CHAPTER 24

Shadows Lengthen

He raised his head without answering and gazed at the hearse. He turned
away with a sudden shock, for inside, in that tasseled, becurtained gloom, he
had caught a glimpse of the coffin, receptacle of all his love, which with panic
he realized must today disappear forever.

— William Styron, *Lie Down in Darkness*

WHEN HE WROTE in 1931 about the plantations of old Virginia, William Cabell Bruce boasted of Staunton Hill that "no grave
crime has ever been committed on it."[1] Forty-four years later a family
tragedy negated Cabell's assertion and hastened his youngest son's final
retirement.

Even for someone as wealthy as David Bruce, the ancestral house
was a financial drain. "When I am away from Staunton Hill," he
confessed during a visit one glorious Easter, "I often think it is madness
to bear the expense and trouble of it; when I am here, I cannot endure
the thought of leaving it."[2] It was a magical season. Every springtime
masses of flowering trees — Chinese and Japanese cherry, native dogwood and redbud — combined with drifts of daffodils and the purple
racemes cascading from an ancient wisteria to transform the grounds
into a botanical paradise. The overpowering scent of blossoms that
wafted over the lawn and into the open windows had a power even
after more than half a century to evoke those long-ago childhood idylls
at the mansion when he first imbibed the romance of southern history.
But by 1975 he had seen his last Easter springtime at Staunton Hill,

for the calamity that unfolded that autumn meant he would never return to the house as long as he lived.

Bruce was not a good father and never claimed he was. Indifferent to small children, he took an interest in them only when they reached an age to appreciate the things that fascinated him. But a shared enjoyment of eighteenth-century antiques and Chinese export porcelain, no matter how keen, was a cold substitute for sound emotional bonds between father and child. By the time such an appreciation was possible, the years of childhood had vanished forever, and with them the chance to cement an enduring relationship of warmth and strength.

For a time when the children were in their teens, there seemed to be no ill consequences. Throughout his London embassy all three children enlivened Winfield House during school holidays and summers. When Sasha brought a boyfriend to England from Harvard, the ambassador thought the young man must think the family barking mad because they never stopped teasing one another in uninhibited, high good humor.[3] When Nicky and Sasha visited Beijing in early 1974, their father felt invigorated by their exuberant spirits. "It is really a new generation, personified in their persons," he wrote. Their indifference to politics and "unquenchable intellectual curiosity" seemed to him all to the good.[4] He showed much more indulgence than Cabell Bruce ever did in dealing with the irritating enthusiasms of his youngest son. But those happy times and the ambassador's indulgence eventually came to an end.

The high standards of conduct and achievement that David Bruce represented in diplomacy posed a formidable obstacle to his children's desire to be close to him. To have a father held up by the world as the epitome of grace, culture, and diplomacy, a father who was also reserved and cool and detached, was a terrifying burden for his children, an impossible standard for them to emulate. And so they began to show their frustration with the normal rebellions of adolescents.

In young David's case it took the form of college protests against the Vietnam War. No surprise there. This was the fate of many, if not most, prominent families in American public life then. After Harvard David moved to Taiwan to study Chinese culture and get as far away from what he saw as the glare cast throughout America and Western Europe by the brilliant Ambassador and Mrs. Bruce. It was especially galling when, having moved halfway round the world, he learned that his father had been appointed America's top diplomat to Beijing. "I thought," he wrote in exasperation to a family friend, that in the Orient "I would be able to escape the shadow of my father's name."[5] His rebellion, however, was a normal phase that he grew out of. The same was not true of his unfortunate sister.

Sasha Bruce — she was never called Alexandra — became the proverbial apple of her father's eye. She had grown into a bright, shining, young woman, whose position in society was assured by the eminence and wealth of her parents. Sasha, the ambassador said with fatherly indulgence, "has so many fine qualities it seems impossible to fault her. Unselfish to a striking degree, she has an almost fierce attachment to her family and a deep sympathy for the unfortunate and dispossessed."[6] But early signs of trouble appeared during her years at boarding school. St. Timothy's, a strict Episcopalian academy outside Baltimore, prided itself on bringing up correctly the daughters of the social elite. Good manners and noblesse oblige rather than academics lighted the way to success at St. Tim's. During Lent the headmistress would read *Jane Eyre* to the girls while they knitted clothes for the poor.[7] It was a marvelously claustrophobic setting for stifling the rebellious fires of hotheaded youth.

No one would mistake Sasha for a Mellon descendant: the warning signs were not reticence and hypochondria but a restlessness that eventually led to a rejection of everything her family stood for. Like Peyton Loftis, the young woman in William Styron's *Lie Down in Darkness* who could not emotionally escape from her aristocratic southern parents, Sasha felt increasingly oppressed by her family. She railed against the burden of living in "a genealogical prison" fashioned, so she thought, by her parents' accomplishments and excessive expectations of her.[8] It was a jail of her own imagination. She felt as though the charm that surrounded her parents, like that of Evelyn Waugh's too-precious characters, blighted everything it touched. Unlike her father, who struggled fifty years earlier against the plans prescribed by his own accomplished parents, Sasha turned her energy inward in self-destructive rage.

The crisis held off until after she graduated from Radcliffe. But then she fell into disastrously bad company. It happened through a combination of her interest in art, specifically icons of the Orthodox Church, and her abysmal taste in men. According to friends, she showed an unerring talent for choosing cads. A shady Greek national with the unlikely name of Anton von Kassel used her money to advance his London antiques shop and draw her deeper into his questionable business affairs in the Middle East — smuggling icons and, the rumors had it, faking them. Sasha's louche friends and dubious business dealings in London during the early 1970s caused her parents intense private anguish.[9] But she was over twenty-one, had access to her trust fund, and seemed bent on doing herself the greatest harm. Financial independence in her case was an unmixed disaster. The trust income let her escape from messy relationships in London and attempt to find herself in the imagined arcadia of Staunton Hill. But she was too troubled to realize that dream, a bizarre version of her father's youthful wish to install himself among his books on the family estate.

For a time the locals watched in bemusement as this daughter of the county's most illustrious family tried to make a go of chicken farming. Sasha's problem was that she brought to Staunton Hill a Greek bounder from London. Not von Kassel, but another even more sinister figure. Marios Michaelides was not simply the wrong sort of man, as Sasha's father thought from the first he heard of him: he was spectacularly wrong.

The ambassador had turned over Staunton Hill to his children in 1973. "As you know," he told them at the time, "I have deep sentimental attachment to this place."[10] For a while it seemed as though his own fond dream of 1919 might come true: the old family home would be "certain to influence for the best anyone who lives on it." It never happened. Although Michaelides lacked von Kassel's gift for nefarious business deals, he excelled in the psychological hurt he caused Sasha. He demanded that she subordinate herself to him in all things, as a good traditional Greek wife should. He mesmerized her. She gradually allowed him to undermine her independence, and the good, effervescent bits of her personality faded. She became subdued. She obeyed his decree to banish her friends from Staunton Hill. David Bruce sized up Marios as no good from the beginning, but Evangeline was willing to be more charitable because her daughter, it seemed, had finally found love. Mother and daughter were on the phone incessantly, but the constant solicitude was not enough to save Sasha from her private demons. Sasha agreed to Marios's demand that she make him her sole heir, but only if he agreed to marry her. They were wed in summer 1975.

Three months later, on a foggy November afternoon it came to an end. Out beyond the mansion house, beyond the stone wall that encircled the south-facing lawn, under a gnarled, ancient cedar that had been there when her grandfather had looked up from his games and heard the guns at Appomattox a hundred and ten years before, Sasha Bruce Michaelides lay dying. They found her in a pool of her own blood, shot through the temple by a .22 caliber handgun. The paramedics raced her to the Lynchburg hospital forty miles away. By chance her father had just arrived in Washington from Brussels for consultation with President Ford. David Bruce rushed to Lynchburg and sat, stricken and numb, by his daughter's bedside until she died near dawn the next morning without ever regaining consciousness.

They dug her grave in the red clay of the family plot on the lawn at Staunton Hill. Overcome with grief, David Bruce never returned to the house of his ancestors again.

He would have left NATO soon anyway, but the blow of Sasha's death hastened his departure and his physical decline. One friend, who saw him in London shortly after, noticed that he had lost the magpie zest for shopping for antiques that had given him such diversion all his life.

Was the assumption of suicide correct? Could Marios have murdered his wife? A year after she died, Bruce hired a freelance detective. His findings did nothing to lessen the sleazy aura that hung about Marios's name. Rare books from the library at Staunton Hill continued to turn up for sale at New York and London auction houses, prize volumes collected by the ambassador's discerning eye over half a century and that Marios had persuaded Sasha to sell. Gone too were many of the silver heirlooms, silver that Charles Bruce had saved from marauding deserters in the Civil War by burying it on the grounds, silver that had then passed bright with promise to David and Ailsa at their marriage.

Marios's divorce from his first American wife, secured under dubious circumstances in Haiti, raised the possibility that his marriage to Sasha was invalid. An accumulation of circumstantial evidence led authorities in Charlotte County belatedly to issue a warrant for the arrest of Michaelides on a charge of murder. By then it was far too late. He had hung about the estate for some weeks after Sasha's death, professing to be distraught, but fled to Greece when suspicions fell on him. In the absence of an extradition treaty between the United States and Greece, he was safely beyond the reach of the Charlotte County sheriff. Rage over Marios's escape, constant rage and anger over the whole tragedy, ate at Bruce and accelerated his decline.

To this day the question of Sasha Bruce's death provokes debate in Charlotte County, with the weight of opinion inclined toward a verdict of murder. Sasha's troubled personality, her odd willingness to abase her free spirit to Marios's authority, and a previous, half-hearted attempt at suicide throw doubt on such an easy verdict. The purported criminal is safely out of the country, and the combination of his foreignness, his unsavory character, and his abusive treatment of Sasha make him an easy target for suspicion. There was little reason for him to strangle the goose that laid the golden egg, however. "Just because you're a bastard," he would later say, "doesn't mean you're a killer."[11] He knew that Sasha's wealth would allow him to live without financial worry. But if Marios did not himself pull the trigger, his mental torture of Sasha — and physical abuse as well — was enough to indict him morally in her death even if it was technically suicide. Shortly before she died, Sasha privately admitted, "He knew every way to inflict pain."[12]

For so long — ever since he began his diplomatic career after World War II, in fact — David Bruce projected an unchanging image. Tall, erect, gray-templed, distinguished in appearance, he was the model image of an ambassador. The stamina that allowed him to bear so lightly a grueling pace gave substance to the appearance of good health. By the end of his Grosvenor Square years, though, his age began to catch up with him.

He had rarely been sick. Occasional flu, ptomaine poisoning once from an embassy dinner in London, laryngitis now and then from heavy smoking — nothing serious afflicted him until the end of his time in England. By then his inherited susceptibility to cardiac and circulatory problems, his fondness for rich food and drink, and especially his nicotine habit began to tell.

Since the mid-1960s he had been taking medication for a heart irregularity. The doctors did not detect any organic disease but did caution him about the effects of age, smoking, and lack of exercise.[13]

By the Paris talks on Vietnam, he looked much older and frailer, and he moved slower. He recognized that his famous stamina was slipping away. The man who set a record of shooting birds at Rambouillet to the delight of the French president finally sold his 12-gauge Purdey guns in 1970.[14]

At the end of that year, when reporters were first speculating that his frustration with lack of progress in the Vietnam talks might prompt him to resign, he was having weekly medical treatment for heart fibrillation and constricted circulation in his legs.[15] The doctors prescribed an unpleasant course of blood tests every few days and an anticoagulant. Though the medication improved the circulation, he did not notice any improvement in the difficulty he had in walking.[16] His doctors told him he needed to walk more; his sedentary style of life was the problem.[17] The stated reason for leaving the Paris talks, declining health, was not entirely a fiction then, even though he had yet to serve in China and Brussels.

The doctor's admonition that he give up smoking, not unexpected, was nevertheless yet another unpalatable pronouncement. On a visit to London, he even stooped to see a hypnotist recommended by friends who swore the man cured them of the desire to smoke. The visit was a failure. Another doctor, who did not know his patient well, recommended that he give up alcohol. He was damned, Bruce told a friend, if he was going to trade one of his greatest pleasures for the uncertain promise of perhaps few more months of life lived in unaccustomed asceticism.

With the end of his China post, he finally stopped writing the diary that he had kept during every government appointment, excepting only the Marshall Plan, an omission he later regretted. Despite this accumulation of thousands of typed pages, he never contemplated writing his memoirs. Approached by a publisher, he politely declined with the fiction that no one would find his career of interest. Yet he thought enough of his daily jottings to offer them to the Virginia Historical Society, whose director responded with alacrity.

The passion for travel that first possessed Bruce during the summer of 1919, and that enticed him across the Atlantic at least twice a year ever since, stayed with him nearly to the end. He was not, as close friend "Kisty" Christian, Lady Hesketh, wryly recalled, exactly a mad, keen gardener willing to bury himself in the countryside for a last few years of pottering about the estate — even if Staunton Hill had not acquired its tragic aura. He loved *les affaires,* and for all his life-long cultivation of the image of rustic eighteenth-century gentility, he was a man of the city, in America, in France, or in Britain.[18]

Bruce's doctors had long grumbled over his too-sedentary lifestyle, and now that his infirmities were creeping up on him, they insisted he at least take daily walks. Neighbors in Georgetown became accustomed to seeing Evangeline gently accompany her reluctant husband out the front door of their house on 34th Street, but only for a slow, brief shuffle: by then "he could only walk holding on to an arm, with frequent stops along the block for aching legs."[19] Because he never stopped smoking, his poor circulation and heart problems made him increasingly frail. Though he could no longer ignore his health or the ravages of age, he resisted the mentality of aging. Almost until the end — certainly until Sasha's death — he retained the joy that came from having young people around him. And as a female friend recalled, until the day he died, "he was as dashing, as exquisitely groomed, as sought after by women of all ages as any man I've ever known."[20]

On Saturday afternoon, December 5, 1977, he went to visit his bedridden boyhood friend, Macgill James, who also lived in Washington. Fifty-seven years before, the two doughboys had taken their walking tour of Europe, sampling what the Continent's capital cities had to offer, flaunting gunmen in the Irish war, indulging the delights of Paris. They had reminisced many times since about that summer of discovery, and they may have done so again that evening. On returning home, just before his dinner guests arrived, Bruce felt chest pains. His wife called an ambulance that rushed him to intensive care at nearby Georgetown University Hospital. He had a small heart attack while the doctor was examining him. Evangeline stayed with him until midnight and promised to bring him the next morning all the things they had no time to bring in the ambulance. Just after 2 A.M., the doctor called her to say that her husband had had a second and fatal attack.[21]

Bruce had said he did not want to suffer a lingering, bedridden death and got his wish. He would have been eighty the following February. It was as though, a friend consoled herself and his widow, he had decided with his instinct for good manners, that it was time to go, "to walk out, his mind still unimpaired — quite simply, as he might out of a room."[22]

As the tributes poured in from both sides of the Atlantic, Evangeline Bruce set into motion plans her husband had made for his own funeral. The service took place the following Friday at St. John's Church, across Lafayette Square from the White House. He had said, with his usual self-deprecating humor, that he did not want his funeral in a big church because the lack of people attending would be painfully obvious. St. John's was packed. The order of service for funerals laid down in the Episcopal Prayer Book appealed to Bruce in its reassuring repetition of traditional and familiar passages, and he altered it little in plans for his own service. The opening rubric from the prayer book had been a special favorite of his, and it began the service now as he had wished: "I am the resurrection and the life, saith the Lord; he that believeth in me, though he were dead, yet shall he live." Of course he specified the rite using the King James Version.

But the bare-bones ritual, comforting though it was to the bereaved in its fixed order of service, could not do justice to the memory of so full a life. Each of the friends who gathered in the church had his or her own favorite anecdotes about this master raconteur whose career spanned the century. One of them was Lynda Johnson Robb, who, as the president's daughter visiting London in the 1960s, had been captivated by the Bruce appeal. As much as she loved the Episcopal service, she thought that in this case more than most, it slighted the memory of the deceased. How much better to make room in the service for the ambassador's friends to tell their own stories about him?[23] But he had left explicit instruction that there be no eulogies, and the service was over quickly. The stories had to be shared in private.

Even after his death, the investigation into Sasha's tragic end that Bruce belatedly set in motion ground on. Two weeks after the diplomat died, a Virginia pathologist performed an autopsy on Sasha's remains and upheld the original ruling of suicide.[24] The remains were cremated and reburied, not at Staunton Hill, but beside the grave of David Bruce at Oak Hill Cemetery in Maryland, beneath his tombstone carved from the same Tennessee marble that was used to build the National Gallery of Art, a stone that turns pink in the rain.

Epilogue

Everyone, without exception, so far as I can tell, in every country in which his name was known, respected [Bruce] deeply, and behaved better and thought better of themselves in his presence. Not since General Marshall, I think, was there such a consensus, public and private.

— Sir Isaiah Berlin

*J*UST BEFORE MIDDAY on February 23, 1978, the streets around Westminster Abbey became momentarily more congested than usual for a windy, midwinter Thursday. Black London taxis and chauffeur-driven Bentleys and Rolls-Royces dropped their passengers near the abbey in the thin morning light. They were greeted by the dean and chapter at the great west door — a three-minute walk from the house in Queen Anne's Gate where David Bruce had slept during the Blitz. At noon the clerics processed through the nave to begin a service in his memory as the choir sang the familiar words "I am the resurrection and the life, saith the Lord." A more elaborate rite than the one held at St. John's in Washington, the London memorial gave Britain's political and diplomatic establishment the opportunity to pay tribute to one of its greatest American friends of the century. Former prime ministers Macmillan and Home assisted in reading the lessons. Long after, people remembered Macmillan's melodramatic performance as a high point of the service. The passage from Philippians was fitting: "Let your moderation be known unto all men" was the crucial sentiment. Though Bruce often noted in his London diary that his special favorite was that most English of hymns, William Blake's haunting, revolutionary "Jerusalem," it was not sung. The recessional was Julia Ward

Howe's "Battle Hymn of the Republic," the same hymn that would be sung thirteen months later at the funeral of Jean Monnet. As the last chords faded away, the bells began to ring. Passersby who thought to look up could have seen the Stars and Stripes flying at half-mast over the abbey for the first time since the death of President Kennedy. The American ambassador, Kingman Brewster, had brought Evangeline Bruce and her sister Virginia to the service in his official car, but he left early and the two sisters, along with two of the Currier grandchildren, took a bus back to the flat at Albany where a small group of friends gathered to remember David Bruce.

At the National Gallery of Art in Washington the board of trustees, under their chairman, Chief Justice Warren Burger, and their president, Paul Mellon, passed a resolution in memory of Bruce. It expressed their "affection and esteem for him as a gentle, humane and cultured friend — the very epitome of the Greek Aristos."[1]

From the time he joined the colors on the day America declared war on the kaiser, David Bruce showed a knack for being present at the most dramatic turning points in his country's foreign affairs during the twentieth century. He first saw Paris during the Versailles spring when everything seemed possible and America seemed poised to invest itself in Europe's future. A lifelong friend of England, he shared London's defiance during the Battle of Britain and the Blitz. With "Wild Bill" Donovan, he saw and heard and felt the guns pounding Normandy on D-Day. With a jubilant crowd of civilians, he and Ernest Hemingway reveled in the liberation of Paris from Nazi rule. He was there again in charge of the Marshall Plan when the future of postwar Europe appeared in doubt. At what seemed the pinnacle of his diplomatic career, he enjoyed the London of the Swinging Sixties only to be at the epicenter of Europe's most virulent anti-American protests during the Vietnam War, a conflict that sundered not just American society but the foreign policy establishment that he exemplified. And, quite unexpectedly, it was given to him late in life to represent his country before the mysterious imperial Communist court of China during the twilit struggle for power to succeed Mao Zedong, a time of another seismic shift in America's foreign affairs.

Even when he was not present at great events, he lived closer than most Americans to the defining experiences of the mid-twentieth century. From basking in the hedonistic twenties to being among the vilified malefactors of great wealth during the depression, he represented, in the public eye, both the best and the worst of America's elite.

From an early age, though, the gilded facade that Bruce turned to the public gaze concealed disappointment. With his limited vision in the 1930s, he might have resigned himself to being nothing more than a Virginia country squire cum New York philanthropist, gradually consumed by the pastimes of the cosmopolitan voluptuary. But World War II saved him and gave him a hunger for the diplomatic career that followed.

After reading a summary of that career, his friend the British statesman Roy Jenkins said, "Is the picture too perfect? Do the reiterated statements that [Bruce] had no enemies, and was never ill spoken of, cause one to ask 'why not?' Was there insufficient conflict? I raise the question with temerity, and I answer it by saying that I suspect it went on within himself. He absorbed it all, probably not without pain, and gave wisdom and pleasure to the world."[2] Toward the end of his life, it seemed that for every honor and award showered on him, another private sadness was added, and ultimately a family tragedy that threw a shadow over his glittering public career. To his credit, he bore these burdens without public complaint and without withdrawing from public service until he was almost seventy-eight.

Most often characterized in his mature years as a courtly and generous man, he could also be reserved and icily correct. Whatever his mood and demeanor, he was tight-lipped even among friends. He kept his private affairs to himself and manipulated prying journalists by erecting a public persona into which he poured all of the wonderful, embellished set-piece accounts of his life — the army courier service, the Blitz, Donovan and D-Day, Paris and Hemingway. Behind this shield he remained a private man. Despite his public roles he was, if not shy, at least reticent. The oral history interviews he gave for the libraries of the presidents he had served are revealing in what they do not reveal.

In retirement Bruce began to wonder whether he had done as much as he should have with the talents given him. He began to have doubts. Long before, he had written of his hero George Washington that "no man ever better repaid an early gift of rank."[3] What had he done with his own life, so richly blessed by connection and wealth and repeated presidential appointment? He was too hard on himself. In the diplomatic world many would have quit when they reached the age he attained during his London embassy. But not for him the quiet life of a few last years of peace with his books, deep in the countryside.

He was the essential diplomat, the unsung hero who represented his nation with aplomb and firmness. Most who remember him recall the social panache of his embassies in London and Paris. But his greatest contributions were arguably in the posts of adversity, especially the doomed effort on behalf of the European Defense Community, the thankless service at the peace talks in Paris, and even the symbolic boredom of Beijing. Above all, for a generation he was one of a select band of brothers who kept the Atlantic Alliance alive.

To those who knew him, he was the ultimate embodiment of courtly reserve. He developed a talent for making everyone he talked to, no matter what their rank or importance, feel they were the center of his attention. His charm misled many people into thinking he was an intellectual lightweight. But they dismissed him unfairly, for he was a tough-minded man who valued realpolitik and scorned woolly-headed idealism.

He admired integrity and character in others and received their good opinion for the same qualities in his own personality. His private eulogy of Christian Herter on the death of Eisenhower's second and less well known secretary of state sums up Bruce himself: "Not brilliant, but he was a man of impregnable honor, which is much rarer and more important than brilliancy."[4] He disliked the brash "young hatchet boys" of Kennedy's White House and disdained the same arrogance he saw in Nixon's team.[5] But he got along with them all.

No iconoclast, he believed that if a diplomat felt he could no longer support his government's policy, he should resign — quietly. He embodied Talleyrand's dictum, *Surtout, pas du zèle.* "Diplomacy," he liked to say, "is the management of international relations by negotiation. It is not a system of moral philosophy, it is rather the application of intelligence and tact to the conduct of official relations between the governments of independent states."[6]

He could not know it in Paris in 1919, but he was destined to be a close observer and fashioner of America-in-Europe during the twentieth century. He was a shining example of the transnational elite that dominated American foreign policy in an age now long gone. Useful tools of membership were money and the connections it made possible. More important was a desire to serve the republic.

His life paralleled America's course through the century. Born in the nineteenth, temperamentally more at home in the eighteenth, he contributed to his nation's role on the world stage in the twentieth. And, not surprisingly, his imprint on the world influenced more the shape of Europe than that of his own country.

He valued ideas and had an instinct for recognizing the important ones. Those he learned from Jean Monnet especially fired his imagination. The prospect for European unity, and an end to the Continent's perpetual civil war, gave him a personal goal that resonated throughout his career in American-European relations.

An Anglophile from an early age, he adopted the pro-British sentiments of most wealthy Easterners in the early twentieth century. The Mellons' world reinforced and gave scope to his own inclinations. He earned a niche on the Olympus of Anglo-American friendship, that Special Relationship so fondly nourished by Churchill during the Second World War. That he risked his personal safety during the Battle of Britain both endeared him to the English and gave him a badge of honor that few other Americans earned in the dangerous months before Pearl Harbor united a divided country.

Fervid though he was in his friendship for Britain, he never let the Special Relationship stand in the way of preaching European unity to skeptical English friends. It was a measure of his intimacy with so many members of the British ruling class that he could frankly discuss with them this pivotal issue that Britain stubbornly avoided for a generation after the war. Through his role in the Marshall Plan, and his enthusiastic advocacy of European federation, Bruce exemplified the best that America had to offer. The liberal internationalists who dominated American foreign policy for the generation after World War II had no better exemplar.

Similarly, his last years trace the decline of the foreign policy establishment, broken apart by Vietnam. The frozen geopolitical landscape that he and his contemporaries took for granted has now passed away, but his legacy lives on in the record of steadfastness of the Western Alliance during the decades of the Soviet threat. We live in an era seemingly beyond the age of expansionist totalitarian empires. Once more it is a time when American foreign policy is adrift and at risk from grounding on those old pre-World War II shoals of isolationism, protectionism, America Firstism, and all the inward-looking, small-minded ideas that Bruce and the best of his generation rejected. That achievement alone merits a place of honor in his nation's foreign affairs. Even more, his legacy lies in the European Union of today.

Charles Bruce, surveying his kingdom from the heights of Staunton Hill, assumed the plantation world would continue forever. It was swept away. His son, Cabell, watching David say his wedding vows in the National Cathedral in 1926, assumed the WASP elite would always rule American society. Depression, war, and prosperity changed all that. His son, David, assumed that the geopolitical dispensation set by the Cold War would continue indefinitely. He did not live to see that world order pass away, but it has gone as assuredly as the assumptions of his father's and grandfather's worlds. Two decades after the ambassador died, his son David and his family make Staunton Hill their home. Once more the mansion built amid wooded hills and red clay tobacco fields on a remote bluff high above the Staunton River shelters another generation of Bruces.

It is a pity David Bruce did not live to see the triumph of the ideas he embraced most, Western victory in the Cold War and Monnet's dream for European federation. Ironically, dissolution of the Soviet Union has made integration more difficult as former Soviet Bloc nations clamor for admittance to a European Union unsure of its course. Without American leadership, NATO is adrift. And so, nearly two decades after his passing, the outcome of that dream of European integration that Bruce espoused so warmly is still in doubt.

Notes

Abbreviations Used in the Notes

AMB	Ailsa Mellon Bruce (first wife)
DB	David Kirkpatrick Este Bruce
DSB	David Surtees Bruce (son)
EBB	Evangeline Bell Bruce (second wife)
JCB	James Cabell Bruce (brother)
LB	Louise Este Fisher Bruce (mother)
WCB	William Cabell Bruce (father)
WJD	William J. Donovan
DDE Lib.	Dwight D. Eisenhower Presidential Library
FOIA	Freedom of Information Act
FRUS	*Foreign Relations of the United States*
LBJ Lib.	Lyndon B. Johnson Presidential Library
JFK Lib.	John F. Kennedy Presidential Library
LC	Library of Congress
NA	National Archives
NYH	*New York Herald* (European edition)
NYT	*New York Times*
TT	*Town Topics: The Journal of Society*
HST Lib.	Harry S Truman Presidential Library
VHS	Virginia Historical Society
VMHB	*Virginia Magazine of History and Biography*

Prologue

1. DB diary, August 24, 1944, VHS.
2. DB diary, August 25, 1944, VHS.
3. Ogden, *Life of the Party*, pp. 177–78.
4. DB diary, August 25, 1944.
5. Beevor and Cooper, *Paris after the Liberation*, p. 44.
6. Marshall, "How Papa Liberated Paris," p. 5.
7. DB diary, August 29, 1944, VHS.
8. Taft, *American Power*, p. 142.

9. Arthur M. Schlesinger Jr., quoted in Hersh, *Mellon Family*, p. 408.
10. Bruce, comp., *David K. E. Bruce*, p. 16.
11. All quotations in this paragraph from Bruce, comp., *David K. E. Bruce*, respectively, pp. 26, 30, 20, 13.

Chapter 1: Under the Shadow of Washington's Hand

1. James Coles Bruce to Charles Bruce, September 6, 1844, Bruce family papers, box 1, VHS.
2. Lewis, *More Taste Than Prudence*, pp. 77, 86, 149.
3. James Coles Bruce to Charles Bruce, April 13, 1863, in Bruce, *Bruce Family*, p. 105.
4. Simms, "Childhood at Staunton Hill," p. 26.
5. Perdue et al., eds., *Weevils*, p. 228.
6. WCB, *Recollections*, p. 33.
7. Ibid., p. 121.
8. Unsigned article, "Genealogy," *VMHB*, 12:1 (July 1904): 94.
9. Moore, "William Cabell Bruce, Henry Cabot Lodge," p. 355.
10. Crooks, *Politics and Progress*, p. 50.
11. WCB, *Recollections*, p. 127.
12. Emmanuel Episcopal Church, Baltimore, parish records, film M-501, Maryland State Archives.
13. JCB, *Memoirs*, p. 3.
14. Stockett, *Baltimore*, p. 18.
15. Mencken, *Happy Days*, p. 55.
16. Cooke, comp., *Vintage Mencken*, p. 10.
17. WCB, *Recollections*, p. 121.
18. DB diary, March 3, 1969, VHS.
19. Mencken, *Happy Days*, p. 263.
20. WCB, *Recollections*, p. 120.
21. Wickes, *Amazon*, pp. 17–18.
22. DB diary, March 3, 1969, VHS.
23. Secrest, *Between Me and Life*, p. 263.
24. WCB, *Below the James*, p. 130.
25. The comparison of Virginia genealogy and Shintoism oddly enough came from Richmond newspaperman and R. E. Lee biographer Douglas Southall Freeman.
26. WCB, *John Randolph of Roanoke*, 1:10.
27. DB diary, October 16, 1968, VHS.
28. WCB, "Plantation Retrospect," p. 546.
29. DB to LB, November 23, 1912, in LB, "Footprints," p. 129, DB papers, box 1 of 7, VHS.
30. Winston Churchill on his school days, quoted in Manchester, *Last Lion, Alone*, p. 377.
31. DB to LB, February 1906, in LB, "Footprints," p. 105, DB papers, box 1 of 7, VHS.
32. James Branch Cabell on Thomas Nelson Page, in Flusche, "Thomas Nelson Page," p. 464.

33. JCB, *Memoirs*, p. 13; DB made the reference to his brother James, but it applied equally to himself, DB diary, September 17, 1973, VHS.
34. DB diary, June 27, 1961, VHS.
35. LB, "Footprints," p. 114, DB papers, box 1 of 7, VHS.
36. Ibid., pp. 123, 128, DB papers, box 1 of 7, VHS.
37. DB to LB, summer 1914, in LB, "Footprints," pp. 164–65, DB papers, box 1 of 7, VHS.
38. Quoted by Simon Schama, in *History News* (November/December 1992), p. 11.
39. JCB, *Memoirs*, pp. 8–9.
40. DB to AMB, October 25, 1945, Paul Mellon papers.
41. WCB, "Plantation Retrospect," p. 548.
42. DB to Evelyn Mackall, February 10, 1920, LB papers, box 5, VHS.
43. Account written by LB in Staunton Hill guest book opposite entry for August 1915, DSB papers.
44. Special inquiry on DB, January 27, 1947, DB file, FBI FOIA.
45. *Daily Princetonian*, September 28, 1915, p. 2.
46. DB to LB, October 11, 1915, in LB, "Footprints," p. 171, DB papers, box 1 of 7, VHS.
47. DB diary, April 8, 1951, VHS.
48. Isaacson and Thomas, *Wise Men*, p. 77.
49. *Daily Princetonian*, October 13, 1916, p. 2.
50. Ibid., January 8, 1917, pp. 1, 3.
51. Samuel Muir Shoemaker to LB, January 8, 1917, LB papers, box 6, VHS.
52. Thomas H. Atherton Jr. to DB "and others," January 21, 1917, LB papers, box 14, VHS.
53. *Daily Princetonian*, January 6, 1917, p. 2; January 11, 1917, pp. 2, 3.
54. WCB to DB, February 26, 1917, DB papers, box 1 of 7, VHS.

Chapter 2: The Discovery of Europe

1. Cowley, *Second Flowering*, p. 4.
2. John J. McCloy, quoted in Bird, *Chairman*, p. 41.
3. DB to LB, July 6, 1915, in LB, "Footprints," p. 166, DB papers, box 1 of 7, VHS.
4. WCB to DB, July 12, 1915, DB papers, box 1 of 17, VHS.
5. Perry, *Plattsburg Movement*, pp. 37, 42, 52.
6. Newspaper clipping by DB, August 1915, in scrapbook, p. 308, LB papers, box 8, VHS.
7. Ibid.
8. Bird, *Chairman*, pp. 42–46.
9. Harbaugh, *Roosevelt*, p. 468; Heckscher, *Wilson*, p. 441.
10. Falls, *Great War*, pp. 199–201.
11. DB to LB, May 9, 1918, LB papers, box 5, VHS.
12. DB to LB, April 3, 1918, LB papers, box 5, VHS.
13. DB to LB, May 9, 1918, LB papers, box 5, VHS.
14. Diary entry for July 3, 1918 (typescript version), in DB to LB, November 10, 1918, DB papers, box 2 of 17, VHS.

15. Diary entry for July 4, 1918 (typescript version), in DB to LB, November 10, 1918, DB papers, box 2 of 17, VHS.

16. Printed postcard, DB to LB, received July 26, 1918, LB papers, box 5, VHS.

17. Diary entry for July 5, 1918 (typescript version), in DB to LB, November 10, 1918, DB papers, box 2 of 17, VHS.

18. Churchill, *Roving Commission*, p. 65.

19. DB to LB, July 22 [?], 1918, LB papers, box 5, VHS.

20. Tuchman, *Guns of August*, p. 275.

21. DB to LB and WCB, August 14, 1918, LB papers, box 5, VHS.

22. DB to family, September 29, 1918, LB papers, box 5, VHS.

23. Cowley, *Second Flowering*, p. 6.

24. DB to family, September 29, 1918, LB papers, box 5, VHS.

25. DB to family, September 11, 1918, LB papers, box 5, VHS.

26. DB to LB, September 29, 1918, LB papers, box 5, VHS.

27. DB to LB, April 5 [?], 1918, LB papers, box 5. VHS.

28. DB to family, September 29, 1918, LB papers, box 5, VHS.

29. DB to LB, October 25, 1918, LB papers, box 5, VHS.

30. Manchester, *Last Lion, Visions of Glory*, p. 651.

31. DB to family, November 11, 1918, LB papers, box 5, VHS.

32. DB to LB, October 25, 1918, LB papers, box 5, VHS.

33. DB to LB, November 26, 1918, LB papers, box 5, VHS.

34. WCB to DB, December 27, 1918, DB papers, box 1 of 17, VHS.

35. DB to family, February 9, 1918, LB papers, box 5, VHS.

36. DB to family, February 17, 1919, LB papers, box 5, VHS.

37. DB to family, February 13, 1919, LB papers, box 5, VHS.

38. DB to family, February 13, March 6, 1918, LB papers, box 5, VHS.

39. DB to LB, March 14, 1919, LB papers, box 5, VHS.

40. Ibid.

41. Heckscher, *Wilson*, p. 499.

42. DB to family, November 2, 1918, LB papers, box 5, VHS.

43. Angela Partington, ed., *Oxford Dictionary of Quotations*, 4th ed., p. 288.

44. Dos Passos, *Mr. Wilson's War*, p. 458.

45. Ward, *First-Class Temperament*, p. 423.

46. DB to LB and WCB, April 3, 1919, LB papers, box 5, VHS.

47. DB to LB, April 30, 1919, LB papers, box 5, VHS.

48. DB to family, April 11, 1919, LB papers, box 5, VHS.

49. DB to family, June 5, 1919, LB papers, box 5, VHS.

50. DB to family, April 11, 1919, LB papers, box 5, VHS.

51. DB to LB, May 13, 1919, LB papers, box 5, VHS.

52. DB to LB and WCB, May 1, 1919, LB papers, box 5, VHS.

53. DB to family, May 3, 1919, LB papers, box 5, VHS.

54. DB to family, June 5, 1919, LB papers, box 5, VHS.

55. DB to family, April 11, 1919, LB papers, box 5, VHS.

56. Dos Passos, *Best Times*, p. 46.

57. DB to LB and WCB, March 29, 1919, LB papers, box 5, VHS.

58. DB to family, April 11, 1919, LB papers, box 5, VHS.

59. DB to family, November 5, 1918, LB papers, box 5, VHS.

60. Hersh, *Old Boys*, p. 15.

61. DB diary, March 22, 1959, VHS.

62. Dos Passos, *Nineteen Nineteen*, p. 385.

63. DB to LB, April 23, 1919, LB papers, box 5, VHS.

64. Wiser, *Crazy Years*, p. 24.

65. DB to LB and WCB, March 29, 1919, LB papers, box 5, VHS.

66. DB to LB and WCB, June 1, 1919, LB papers, box 5, VHS.

67. DB to LB, May 10, 1919, LB papers, box 5, VHS.

68. DB to LB and WCB, June 1, 1919, LB papers, box 5, VHS.

69. Davies, *White Eagle, Red Star*, p. 21.

70. DB to LB and WCB, May 1, 1919, LB papers, box 5, VHS.

71. DB to family, July 4, June 20, 1919, LB papers, box 5, VHS.

72. DB to family, July 7, 1919, LB papers, box 5, VHS.

73. DB to family, April 8, 1919, LB papers, box 5, VHS.

74. DB to family, July 7, 1919, LB papers, box 5, VHS.

75. DB to LB, June 25 [?], 1919, LB papers, box 5, VHS.

76. DB to LB, May 10, 1919, LB papers, box 5, VHS.

77. DB to LB, December 25, 1918, in LB, "Footprints," p. 314, DB papers, box 1 of 7, VHS.

78. DB to LB and WCB, April 30, 1919, LB papers, box 5, VHS.

Chapter 3: On a Holiday Excursion

1. DB to LB, October 11, 1919, DB papers, box 2 of 17, VHS.

2. DB to LB, March 23, 1919, LB papers, box 5, VHS.

3. DB to LB, May 1, 1919, DB to LB and WCB, June 1, 1919, LB papers, box 5, VHS.

4. Interview of Virginius Dabney, January 17, 1990.

5. Meyers, *Poe*, p. 21.

6. LB, "Footprints," p. 443, DB papers, box 1 of 7, VHS.

7. WCB to DB, November 19, 1919, DB papers, box 1 of 17, VHS.

8. DB, "Tobacco," p. 784.

9. WCB to DB, February 22, 1918, DB papers, box 1 of 17, VHS.

10. DB diary, 1920, p. 1, DB papers, box 1 of 7, VHS.

11. Clipping of DB article in Baltimore *Sun*, June 20, 1920, LB papers, VHS.

12. DB to WCB, May 26, 1920, in LB, "Footprints," p. 446, DB papers, box 1 of 7, VHS.

13. Philip A. Bruce to LB, July 15, 1920, in LB, "Footprints," p. 447, DB papers, box 1 of 7, VHS.

14. DB diary, 1920, pp. 4–5, DB papers, box 1 of 7, VHS.

15. DB diary, 1920, p. 6, DB papers, box 1 of 7, VHS.

16. Putnam, *Paris Was Our Mistress*, pp. 51–52.

17. DB diary, 1920, pp. 9–10, DB papers, box 1 of 7, VHS.

18. DB diary, 1920, p. 13, DB papers, box 1 of 7, VHS.

19. Finlayson, *Tangier*, pp. 4, 58.

20. DB diary, 1920, pp. 15–16, DB papers, box 1 of 7, VHS.

21. DB to LB, July 26, 1920, in LB, "Footprints," p. 451, DB papers, box 1 of 7, VHS.

22. DB diary, 1920, p. 31, DB papers, box 1 of 7, VHS.

23. Tuchman, *Guns of August,* p. 22.
24. Clipping of article by DB in Baltimore *Sun,* July 1921, album, LB papers, box 9, VHS.
25. Ibid.
26. DB to LB, June 8, 22, 1921, DB papers, box 2 of 7, VHS.
27. Chesson, *Richmond after the War,* p. 210.
28. Emily Clark's paraphrase of DB, Emily Clark to Joseph Hergesheimer, February 1923, in Langford, ed., *Ingénue,* p. 120.
29. Hobson, *Serpent in Eden,* p. 11.
30. DB to family, November 2, 1918, LB papers, box 5, VHS.
31. Emily Clark to Joseph Hergesheimer, September 1923, in Langford, ed., *Ingénue,* p. 185.
32. Emily Clark's paraphrase of DB, Emily Clark to Joseph Hergesheimer, February 1923, in Langford, ed., *Ingénue,* p. 120.
33. DB, "Random Reflections of a Gourmet," draft typescript, Bruce papers, VHS. This passage was deleted from the published article of the same name in *The Reviewer* (May 1922): 462–67.
34. Emily Clark to Joseph Hergesheimer, August 13, 1922, and June 1923, in Langford, ed., *Ingénue,* pp. 83, 150.
35. DB, "Et Cetera and Wine Glasses," pp. 123–24. DB's editor misspelled "coulisses" as "conlisses."
36. DB, "Random Reflections of a Gourmet," p. 462.
37. Kellner, *Van Vechten,* p. 133.
38. *Dictionary of American Biography,* supplement 7, p. 754.
39. Rampersad, *Hughes,* 1:109.
40. Clark, *Innocence Abroad,* pp. 144–45.
41. WCB to Philip A. Bruce, November 9, 1918, in Rutman, "Philip Alexander Bruce," p. 402.
42. DB, "In the Ancestral Lair of Volstead Dry Law," June 12, 1921, clipping in album, LB papers, box 9, VHS.
43. DB, "Et Cetera and Wine Glasses," p. 123.
44. Clipping in album, LB papers, box 15, VHS.
45. Clippings in album, LB papers, box 9, VHS.
46. Untitled, privately printed pamphlet, rare book number F186 K3 o.s., VHS.
47. Philip A. Bruce to DB, May 1, 1921, LB papers, VHS.
48. Putnam, *Paris Was Our Mistress,* p. 218.
49. Joseph Kraft to Evangeline Bruce, in Bruce, comp., *David K. E. Bruce,* p. 18.
50. DB to LB, September 9, 1919, DB papers, box 2 of 17, VHS.
51. Clark, *Innocence Abroad,* pp. 78–79.
52. Emily Clark to Joseph Hergesheimer, August 13, 1922, in Langford, ed., *Ingénue,* p. 83.
53. See Wolff, *Black Sun.*
54. MacDonald, *Cabell,* pp. 215–16, 257, 267; Hunter Stagg to Carl Van Vechten, November 17, 1924, copy at James Branch Cabell Lib., Virginia Commonwealth Univ., original in Carl Van Vechten papers, Yale Univ.
55. Carl Van Vechten to Hunter Stagg, November 1, 1925, copy at James Branch Cabell Lib., Virginia Commonwealth Univ., original in Carl Van Vechten papers, Yale Univ.

56. Ink drawing on stationery from DB's 1921 Norway trip, album, LB papers, box 9, VHS.
57. Conversation with DSB, March 16, 1995.
58. F. Scott Fitzgerald, *This Side of Paradise*, pp. 1–2, 18, 48.
59. Clipping entitled "Mirrors of Maryland," by "Oswald," Baltimore *Evening Sun*, March 14, 1924, in album, LB papers, VHS.
60. Philip A. Bruce to LB, July 15, 1920, in LB, "Footprints," p. 447, DB papers, box 1 of 7, VHS.
61. Kellner, *Friends and Mentors*, p. 7.
62. Cowley, *Second Flowering*, p. 19.
63. DB to LB, May 19, 1919, LB papers, box 5, VHS.

Chapter 4: Ailsa

1. Woodrow Wilson to Cordell Hull, September 12, 1922, Link, ed., *Papers of Woodrow Wilson*, 68:134–35.
2. Jacob, *Capital Elites*, p. 197.
3. *TT*, January 8, 1925, p. 8, February 22, 1923, p. 9.
4. DB, "Vanitas Vanitatum," p. 384.
5. Bryan and Murphy, *Windsor Story*, p. 21.
6. LB, "Footprints," p. 444, DB papers, box 1 of 7, VHS.
7. Emily Clark to Joseph Hergesheimer, August 13, 1922, February 1923, and September 1923, in Langford, ed., *Ingénue*, pp. 83, 120–21, 184.
8. *NYT*, January 18, 1925, p. 29.
9. Ketchum, *Borrowed Years*, p. 18; Lucius Beebe quoted in Koskoff, *Mellons*, p. 67.
10. Koskoff, *Mellons*, p. 129.
11. Ibid., p. 32.
12. Ibid., pp. 45, 82.
13. Ibid., pp. 47, 147.
14. Ibid., p. 55.
15. Ibid., p. 60.
16. Ibid., p. 63.
17. Kopper, *Gallery*, p. 59; see also, Koskoff, *Mellons*, pp. 129–42.
18. Mellon, *Reflections*, p. 39.
19. Hersh, *Mellon Family*, pp. 192–93.
20. Koskoff, *Mellons*, pp. 182–85.
21. Ibid., p. 253.
22. Kopper, *Gallery*, p. 51.
23. Amory, *Who Killed Society?*, p. 363.
24. Kopper, *Gallery*, p. 63.
25. DB diary, August 13, 1964, April 13, 1965, VHS.
26. Kopper, *Gallery*, p. 259.
27. DB, "Vanitas Vanitatum," p. 387.
28. Kopper, *Gallery*, pp. 66–67.
29. *TT*, April 19, 1923, p. 9, May 3, 1923, p. 10, December 13, 1923, p. 8.
30. Baltimore *Sun*, May 25, 1926, pt. 2, sec. 1, p. 1; *TT*, June 19, 1924, p. 10.
31. Koskoff, *Mellons*, pp. 177–78.
32. DB diary, February 21, 1954, VHS.

33. *TT,* June 7, 1923, p. 9.
34. *TT,* March 1, 1923, p. 10.
35. *TT,* June 19, 1924, p. 10, January 8, 1925, p. 8.
36. Hersh, *Mellon Family,* pp. 266–67.
37. *TT,* January 8, 1925, p. 8.
38. *TT,* May 13, 1926, p. 9.
39. Fitzgerald, *Great Gatsby,* p. 120.
40. DB to Ellen Keyser, February 20, 1919, LB papers, box 14, VHS.
41. *TT,* June 3, 1926, p, 8.
42. Clipping, May 29, 1926, album, LB papers, box 11, VHS.
43. Kopper, *Gallery,* p. 72.
44. LB to Andrew W. Mellon, April 22, 1930, Finley papers, box 63, LC.
45. LB to Andrew W. Mellon, June 10, 1926, Finley papers, box 63, LC.
46. Clipping entitled D. K. Este Bruce, "Speaking of Armaments," Baltimore *Evening Sun,* December 6, 1921, LB papers, VHS.
47. Clipping, May 14, 1926, album, LB papers, box 11, VHS.
48. Isaacson and Thomas, *Wise Men,* p. 143.
49. WCB to James Farley, February 9, 1933, box 4, LB papers, VHS.
50. DeConde, *Half-Bitter,* p. 190.
51. Gallagher, *Enemies,* pp. 103, 108.
52. DeConde, *Half-Bitter,* pp. 178–205.
53. *NYT,* June 3, 1926, p. 14.
54. Chief, Div. of Foreign Service Administration to U.S. Dispatch Agent, New York City, June 15, 1926, Bruce 123 B836/4, RG 59, NA.
55. Cowley, *Second Flowering,* pp. 54–58.
56. DB diary, June 29, 1920, pp. 11–12, DB papers, box 1 of 7, VHS.
57. *NYH,* August 8, 1926, p. 1, August 9, 1926, p. 1, August 11, 1926, p. 1.
58. Leon Dominian, Consul in Charge, to Secretary of State, August 9 and 10, 1926, telegrams, Bruce 123 B836/7 and B836/9, RG 59, NA.
59. Andrew Mellon to Hon. Frank B. Kellogg, August 9, 1926, telegram, Bruce 123 B836/8, RG 59, NA.
60. Cover memorandum to telegram from Leon Dominian, Consul in Charge, to Secretary of State, August 9, 1926, Bruce 123 B836/7, RG 59, NA.
61. *NYH,* August 21, 1926, p. 7.
62. *NYH,* August 25, 1926, p. 9.
63. DB to Secretary of State, January 7, 1927, Bruce 123 B836/12, RG 59, NA.
64. Hersh, *Mellon Family,* p. 269.
65. DB diary, August 30, 1974, VHS. Bruce would also be at the embassy in London in 1932 to greet Amelia Earhart on her arrival as the first woman to fly the ocean solo (*NYH,* May 24, 1932, p. 1).
66. Mellon, *Reflections,* p. 97.
67. *NYH,* August 24, 1926, pp. 1, 4.
68. *TT,* March 10, 1927, p. 11, June 16, 1927, p. 9.
69. *TT,* September 15, 1927, p. 9.
70. Clipping from *Washington Post,* July 9, 1927, album, LB papers, box 9, VHS.
71. Leon Dominian, consul in charge, Rome, to secretary of state, August 12, 1927, 125.7714/104, RG 59, NA.
72. *NYT,* December 17, 1927, p. 20.

Chapter 5: The Mellon Embrace

1. Descriptions of Harriman from George Kennan, quoted in Isaacson and Thomas, *Wise Men*, p. 228, and Taft, *American Power*, p. 105.

2. Reporter's typescript article based on interview of DB, undated but probably 1927–28, DB file, Hearst newspaper morgue, Harry Ransom Humanities Research Center, University of Texas.

3. Abramson, *Spanning the Century*, pp. 192–93, 201.

4. Hersh, *Mellon Family*, p. 337.

5. DB to W. Averell Harriman, August 10, 1931, Harriman papers, box 23, LC.

6. Hersh, *Mellon Family*, p. 316. Another version of this story reversed the roles to make Hoover the butt of the joke.

7. *Time*, April 18, 1932, p. 7, April 25, 1932, pp. 20–21; *NYH*, April 15, 1932, p. 1.

8. C. L. Sulzberger, "Bursting at the Seams," *International Herald Tribune*, January 29, 1969, clipping in DB diary, January 29, 1969, VHS.

9. Clark, *Another Part of the Wood*, p. 212.

10. McLeod, *Passion for Friendship*, pp. 1, 76.

11. Ibid., p. 87.

12. *NYH*, April 19, 1932, p. 4; Stannard, *Waugh: Early Years*, pp. 286–98.

13. Macgill James to DB, postmarked August 13, 1932, LB papers, box 14, VHS; DB diary, April 15, 1962, VHS; *NYH*, June 2, 1932, p. 4.

14. DB to W. Averell Harriman, July 7, 1932, Harriman papers, box 23, LC.

15. Schlesinger, *Crisis of the Old Order*, p. 3.

16. Smith, *Shattered Dream*, pp. 62–63.

17. DB to AMB, March 7, 1933, Paul Mellon papers.

18. DB to AMB, February 18, 1933, Paul Mellon papers.

19. LB to Cary Grayson, February 10, 1933. Copy courtesy of Gordon Grayson.

20. DB to AMB, February 18, 26, March 12, 1933, and undated letter probably written in mid-February 1933, Paul Mellon papers.

21. Koskoff, *Mellons*, p. 254.

22. Warren, *Hoover*, p. 129.

23. Schlesinger, *Coming of the New Deal*, pp. 569, 570.

24. Koskoff, *Mellons*, p. 317.

25. Ibid., p. 254.

26. Hersh, *Mellon Family*, p. 349.

27. O'Connor, *Mellon's Millons*, p. 240.

28. Pearson and Allen, *Washington Merry-Go-Round*, p. 162.

29. Koskoff, *Mellons*, p. 270.

30. DB, "Parody on Argument of Government Counsel, re Privilege, April 29, 1935," DB papers, VHS.

31. Hersh, *Mellon Family*, pp. 280, 267; DB diary, June 7, 1967, VHS.

32. DB to AMB, August 2, 1935, Paul Mellon papers; interview of EBB, May 20, 1989.

33. Kopper, *Gallery*, p. 59.

34. Johnson, *Modern Times*, pp. 268–69; Kopper, *Gallery*, p. 88. See also, Tomkins, "Profiles: For the Nation," pp. 59–61; Van Dyne, "Art and Money," pp. 127–31; Finley, *Standard of Excellence*.

35. Kopper, *Gallery*, p. 106.
36. Behrman, *Duveen*, chapter 1.
37. Kopper, *Gallery*, p. 86.
38. Hersh, *Mellon Family*, p. 337.
39. Stokes, *Chip Off My Shoulder*, p. 75.
40. Hersh, *Mellon Family*, pp. 351–52.
41. Kopper, *Gallery*, pp. 139, 155, 168.
42. Mellon, *Reflections*, p. 153; Hersh, *Mellon Family*, p. 408.
43. Kopper, *Gallery*, pp. 258–59; Hersh, *Mellon Family*, p. 337.
44. *NYT*, June 30, 1991, sec. 2, p. 28.
45. Kopper, *Gallery*, p. 21.
46. Ibid., p. 147.
47. Philip A. Bruce to DB, May 1, 1921, LB papers, box 14, VHS.
48. DB diary, July 3, 1965, VHS.
49. Clipping from *Christian Science Monitor*, April 29, 1939, LB papers, box 15, VHS.
50. DB, *Revolution to Reconstruction*, pp. 284–85.
51. DB, *Seven Pillars*, pp. 36, 37.
52. Smith, *Dewey*, p. 131.
53. *NYT*, July 14, 1935, sec. 3, page 10; DB diary, December 26, 1951, VHS; Irey and Slocum, *Tax Dodgers*, p. 138.
54. DB to W. Averell Harriman, April 1, 1934, Harriman papers, box 23, LC.
55. Marie Gordon Pryor Rice to Mrs. Thomas B. Clarke, SH Historic Structure Report & Maintenance Survey, p. 32, VHS.
56. DB to LB and WCB, June 1, 1919, LB papers, box 5, VHS.
57. DB to Nancy Tree, November 3, [1933?], EBB papers.
58. DB to AMB, December 7, 1933, Paul Mellon papers.
59. Ibid.
60. William Adams Delano, "Reminiscences," p. 47, Yale University, ms. group 178, box 16, folder 341 (copy courtesy of Betsy Fahlman).
61. Quoted in Jane Stuart Conner, "David K. E. Bruce's Gift of County Libraries," p. 35.
62. DB to Nancy Tree, November 3, [1933?], EBB papers.
63. Reginald Pettus to author, August 27, 1992; DB to Mr. Titsworth, June 10, 1938 (courtesy of Reginald Pettus).
64. Key, *Southern Politics*, p. 19.
65. DB to editor of *Charlotte Gazette*, May 6, 1939, DB papers, box 14, VHS.
66. Clipping from Bristol (Va.) *Herald Courier*, July 26, 1939, album, LB papers, box 15, VHS.
67. Interview of Giles Robertson, September 16, 1992.
68. Harry F. Byrd Sr. to LB, March 29, 1939, DB papers, box 2 of 17, VHS.
69. Miller, *Man From the Valley*, p. 156.
70. Clippings, album, LB papers, box 15, VHS.
71. Fitzgerald, *Great Gatsby*, p. 39.
72. Robert Bruce Lockhart diary, June 11, 1942, in Lockhart, *Diaries*, p. 172.
73. Aldrich, "Upper Class," p. 66.
74. Interview of EBB, April 4, 1993.

Chapter 6: The Heat of Burning London

1. Stated as the theme of Churchill's *Gathering Storm*, vol. 1 of his *History of the Second World War*.
2. Cave Brown, "*C*," p. 123; DB diary, October 31, 1962, VHS.
3. DB to Ernest Swift, July 13, 1940, American Red Cross papers, RG 200, 941.08, NA.
4. *Irish Times*, July 8, 1940, p. 6.
5. Interview of Nancy, dowager countess of Dunraven, September 11, 1990.
6. DB diary, November 15, 1957, VHS.
7. Tree, *When the Moon Was High*, pp. 125–28.
8. Cooper, *Old Men Forget*, p. 260.
9. *Dictionary of American Biography*, supplement 3, pp. 218–19.
10. Transcript of telephone conversation between DB and Norman Davis, July 18, 1940, p. 5, American Red Cross papers, RG 200, 941.08, NA.
11. Ernest Swift to DB, August 2, 1940, American Red Cross papers, RG 200, 941.08, NA.
12. DB to Norman Davis, August 13, 1940, American Red Cross papers, RG 200, 941.08, NA.
13. DB to Norman Davis, August 24, 1940, American Red Cross papers, RG 200, 941.04, NA.
14. Robertson, *I Saw England*, p. 93.
15. Sheean, *Between the Thunder and the Sun*, pp. 204–5.
16. Robertson, *I Saw England*, p. 97.
17. DB to LB, July 29, 1940, LB papers, box 5, VHS.
18. DB to LB, August 22, 1940, LB papers, box 5, VHS.
19. Cave Brown, "*C*," p. 303; clipping from *PM* magazine, October 17, 1940, p. 5, album, LB papers, box 15, VHS.
20. Robertson, *I Saw England*, p. 200.
21. Clipping from *PM* magazine, October 17, 1940, p. 5, album, LB papers, box 15, VHS.
22. Ibid.
23. DB diary, July 16, 1957, VHS.
24. Robertson, *I Saw England*, p. 135.
25. DB broadcast from London, 1940, box 3, DB papers, VHS.
26. Bowen McCoy to Ernest Swift, February 14, 1941, American Red Cross papers, RG 200, 941.08, NA; Stella Reading to Norman Davis (copy), September 21, 1940, LB papers, VHS.
27. Jones, *Colefax and Fowler*, pp. 27–28.
28. Tree, *When the Moon Was High*, p. 194; Hitchens, *Blood, Class, and Nostalgia*, pp. 314–16.
29. DB diary, July 30, 1961, VHS.
30. Kennedy, *Business of War*, pp. 78–79.
31. DB diary, February 19, 1952, VHS.
32. DB to W. Averell Harriman, January 27, 1941, Harriman papers, box 23, LC.
33. Address by DB to ARC National Convention, April 1941, transcript, DB papers, box 2, VHS.

34. Chadwin, *Hawks of WWII*, p. 177.
35. Speech by DB, clipping from *Charlotte Gazette*, June 26, 1941, box 3, DB papers, VHS.
36. Stated as the theme of *Their Finest Hour*, vol. 2 in Churchill's *History of the Second World War*.
37. London *Times*, July 16, 1940.
38. Stevenson, *Man Called Intrepid*, p. 34.
39. Ranelagh, *Agency*, pp. 47–48.
40. Ibid., p. 51.
41. Persico interview of DB, February 19, 21, 1977.
42. Special inquiry, July 18, 1956, Bruce file, FBI FOIA.
43. DB diary, January 1, 1974, VHS.
44. Troy, ed., *Wartime Washington*, p. 9.
45. From a speech at the annual dinner of Veterans of OSS, May 26, 1971, DB papers, VHS.

Chapter 7: OSS at War

1. DB diary, June 1, 1944, VHS.
2. Ranelagh, *Agency*, p. 61 note; McDonald, "Office of Strategic Services," p. 9.
3. DB, "National Intelligence Authority," pp. 363, 360.
4. Smith, *Shadow Warriors*, p. 95.
5. Ibid., p. 107.
6. Investigation report on DB, April 3, 1942, Bruce file, CIA FOIA.
7. "Major Bruce's Residence," Interoffice memorandum, December 11, 1942, Bruce file, CIA FOIA.
8. From Drew Pearson's "Washington Merry Go-Round" column for December 3, 1941, quoted in Smith, *OSS*, p. 1.
9. Smith, *Shadow Warriors*, p. 127.
10. Ranelagh, *Agency*, p. 57.
11. Smith, *OSS*, p. 3.
12. DB to WJD, October 13, 1942, OSS interoffice memo, Bruce file, CIA FOIA.
13. Smith, *OSS*, p. 1.
14. DB diary, November 14, 1968, VHS; Costello, *Treachery*, pp. 351–52.
15. Quoted in Bryan and Murphy, *Windsor Story*, p. 75.
16. Robert Bruce Lockhart diary, June 11, 1942, in Lockhart, *Diaries*, p. 172.
17. DB diary, August 18, 1942, VHS.
18. DB diary, August 24, 1942, VHS.
19. Cave Brown, *Last Hero*, chapter 23.
20. Quoted in Smith, *OSS*, p. 123.
21. DB diary, August 27, 1942, VHS.
22. DB diary, August 25, 1942, VHS.
23. DB diary, September 4, 1942, VHS.
24. Cave Brown, "C," pp. 361, 395–96.
25. Arthur M. Schlesinger Jr., quoted in Hersh, *Mellon Family*, p. 408.
26. Francis Pickens Miller to DB, January 26, 1943, EBB papers.
27. Translation from article, datelined Lisbon, in the *Frankfurter Zeitung*, February 27, 1943, Bruce file, CIA FOIA.

28. Casey, *Secret War,* p. 22.

29. Cave Brown, "*C,*" p. 493.

30. DB to WJD, March 20, 1943, Bruce file, CIA FOIA.

31. Philby, *My Silent War,* p. 92.

32. Cave Brown, "*C,*" pp. 126–27; Schoenbrun, *Soldiers of the Night,* p. 295.

33. Muggeridge, "Book Review," p. 94.

34. Strategic Services Officer — London, war diary, OSS papers, RG 226/147/3, NA.

35. DB to WJD, March 27, 1943, Bruce file, CIA FOIA; Ranelagh, *Agency,* p. 83.

36. DB diary, March 9, 1950, VHS.

37. DB diary, June 12, 1944, VHS.

38. DB to WJD, February 13, 1943, Bruce file, CIA FOIA.

39. DB to WJD, February 27, 1943, Bruce file, CIA FOIA.

40. DB to Col. G. Edward "Ned" Buxton, September 18, 1943, Bruce file, CIA FOIA.

41. DB to WJD, January 7, 1943, Bruce file, CIA FOIA.

42. DB to WJD, May 29, 1943, Bruce file, CIA FOIA.

43. DB to Col. G. Edward "Ned" Buxton, June 27, 1943, Bruce file, CIA FOIA.

44. DB diary, July 14, 1943, VHS.

45. Stannard, *Waugh: Early Years,* p. 406.

46. DB diary, July 17, 19, 1943, VHS.

47. DB to Col. G. Edward "Ned" Buxton, September 18, 1943, Bruce file, CIA FOIA.

48. Winks, *Cloak and Gown,* pp. 264–65; interview of Judge Hubert Will, September 7, 1991.

49. McDonald, "Office of Strategic Services," pp. 9–13.

50. The Sussex and Jedburgh paragraphs below rely on Smith, *OSS,* pp. 172–85, and Cave Brown, "*C,*" pp. 544–50.

51. DB to WJD, March 8, 1943, Bruce file, CIA FOIA.

52. DB to WJD, March 20, 1943, Bruce file, CIA FOIA.

Chapter 8: The Liberation of Europe

1. This paragraph and the following two are based on Larrabee, *Commander in Chief,* pp. 452–54.

2. This paragraph and the following ones about Bruce's and Donovan's experiences of the invasion are taken from Bruce's diary entries for May 30–June 9, 1944, in Lankford, ed., *OSS,* pp. 47–69. The published version of the diary is cited because it includes, in addition to the VHS version, a fragment of Bruce's diary now in the William J. Donovan papers, U.S. Army Military History Institute, Carlisle Barracks, Carlisle, Pennsylvania.

3. DB to Whitney Shepardson, August 16, 1958, DB papers, VHS.

4. Ambrose, *Ike's Spies,* pp. 105–6.

5. Collier, *V-Weapons,* pp. 11, 76.

6. Terraine, *Time for Courage,* p. 541; Collier, *V-Weapons,* pp. 143–44.

7. DB diary, July 15, 1944, VHS.

8. DB diary, June 24, 1944, VHS.

9. DB diary, June 27, 1944, VHS.
10. DB diary, June 24, July 24, 1944, VHS.
11. DB diary, July 25, 1944, VHS.
12. DB diary, August 13, 1944, VHS.
13. Ibid.
14. DB diary, August 10, 1944, VHS.
15. DB diary, July 20, 1959, VHS.
16. Lacouture, *De Gaulle: The Ruler*, pp. 75–77.
17. Ernest Hemingway to DB, November 27, 1948, EBB papers.
18. Beevor and Cooper, *Paris after the Liberation*, p. 45.
19. DB diary, August 25, 1944, VHS.
20. Ibid., p. 174.
21. DB diary, August 26, 1944, VHS.
22. Astor, *Blood-Dimmed Tide*, p. 75.
23. DB diary, November 16, 1944, VHS.
24. Dispatch of May 21, 1945, Nicholas, ed., *Washington Despatches*, p. 566.
25. From Stewart Alsop and Thomas Braden, *Sub Rosa: The OSS and American Espionage*, quoted in Henry Fairlie, *The Kennedy Promise*, p. 192.

Chapter 9: A Few Changes

Epigraph: John Walker, director of the National Gallery of Art, speaking of Ailsa Mellon Bruce, in Walker, *Self-Portrait with Donors*, p. 195.
1. DB diary, July 31, 1944, VHS.
2. Clipping dated June 6, 1926, from *Philadelphia Enquirer*, box 11, LB papers, VHS.
3. Hersh, *Mellon Family*, p. 266.
4. Mellon, *Reflections*, p. 379.
5. Ibid., pp. 96–97.
6. *Life*, vol. 2, no. 1, January 1979, p. 18.
7. DB to AMB, [undated, February 1933], Paul Mellon papers.
8. DB to AMB, March 7, 12, 1933, Paul Mellon papers.
9. DB to AMB, March 12, 1933, Paul Mellon papers.
10. Hersh, *Mellon Family*, pp. 337, 408.
11. Ibid., p. 336.
12. DB diary, January 18, 1954, VHS.
13. Hersh, *Mellon Family*, pp. 409–10; interview of Anna Garner, May 30, 1990.
14. Adams, comp., *Uncommon Scold*, p. 104.
15. Alice Winn to author, April 19, 1988; Nancy Lancaster to author, April 27, 1988.
16. Interview of Helen Kirkpatrick Milbank, September 20, 1991; Robertson, *I Saw England*, p. 192, n. 1; March 27–29, 1941, Staunton Hill guest book, 1934–69, DSB papers.
17. Aldrich, *Hitchcock*, pp. 286–87.
18. EBB to author, September 26, 1994, and March 5, 1995.
19. Interview of EBB, May 20, 1989; Phillips, *Ventures in Diplomacy*, p. 329.
20. Muir, comp., *Oxford Book of Humorous Prose*, pp. 168–69; *Oxford Dictionary of Quotations*, p. 672; interview of EBB, June 1, 1993; DB diary, May 13, 1950, September 17, 1966.

21. EBB to author, September 26, 1994.
22. Ward, *Before the Trumpet*, p. 248.
23. Clipping from David F. Schoenbrun article, *Herald Tribune*, August 7, 1949, in JCB papers, University of Maryland.
24. Interview of EBB, May 20, 1989.
25. DB to Francis Pickens Miller, April 29, 1943, Bruce file, CIA FOIA.
26. Quotation in EBB to author, March 5, 1995; interview of EBB, May 20, 1989; Phillips, *Ventures in Diplomacy*, p. 329; interview of Jan Laverge, July 5, 1989.
27. Interview of Judge Hubert Will, September 7, 1991.
28. Beevor and Cooper, *Paris after the Liberation*, p. 75.
29. Interview of EBB, May 20, 1989; Miller, *Man from the Valley*, p. 105.
30. Schlesinger, "Evangeline Bruce in London," p. 165.
31. Interview of EBB, September 28, 1994.
32. Salisbury family photography album for 1943, Salisbury family archives, Hatfield House.
33. Interview of EBB, December 18, 1993.
34. DB to AMB, May 1944, divorce hearing, DB papers, VHS.
35. DB to Donald D. Shepard, August 30, 1944, divorce hearing, DB papers, VHS.
36. Hersh, *Mellon Family*, p. 408; Koskoff, *Mellons*, p. 363.
37. Bill of complaint, April 6, 1945, divorce hearing, DB papers, VHS.
38. Answer of DB to bill of complaint, April 11, 14, 1945, divorce hearing, DB papers, VHS.
39. Adams, comp., *Uncommon Scold*, p. 43.
40. Interview of Helen Kirkpatrick Milbank, September 20, 1991.
41. All the quotations in this paragraph are in the special master's report, April 14, 1945, divorce hearing, DB papers, VHS.
42. Divorce hearing, DB papers, VHS; *NYT*, April 21, 1945, p. 14; newspaper clipping, April 24, 1945, album, box 15, LB papers, VHS.
43. EBB to author, September 26, 1994.
44. DB diary, April 4, 1959, VHS.
45. John Walker to DB, December 5, 1966, EBB papers.
46. Hersh, *Mellon Family*, p. 446; interview of Anna Garner, May 30, 1990; Koskoff, *Mellons*, p. 367.
47. Hersh, *Mellon Family*, p. 412.
48. EBB to author, September 26, 1994.
49. DB to AMB, October 25, 1945, Paul Mellon papers.
50. Interview of Louise Bruce (DB's niece), August 10, 1992.
51. Death certificate for LB, died October 22, 1945, Baltimore County (film SR3180) and death certificate for WCB, died May 9, 1946, Baltimore County (film SR3183), Maryland State Archives.
52. Administration accounts of estates of LB and WCB, Baltimore County probate records, 1946–47, p. 468 (film CR9082), 1947–48, pp. 121, 161, 519 (film CR9082), 1948–49, p. 222 (film CR9083), Maryland State Archives.
53. Persico, *Casey*, p. 97.
54. DB, "National Intelligence Authority," pp. 355–69, quotations on pp. 359, 369.
55. DB diary, June 3, 1944. This passage does not appear in the version of Bruce's

diary at the VHS. It comes from another version of his diary for May 11 to June 9, 1944 located in the William J. Donovan papers at the U.S. Army Military History Institute, Carlisle Barracks, Carlisle, Pennsylvania.

56. DB diary, June 27, 1949, VHS; interview of Lucinda Leigh, November 29, 1989.

Chapter 10: Immediate and Resolute Action

1. DB, "Travel Notes," March 22, 29, 1947, DB papers, box 1, VHS.
2. DB, "Travel Notes," April 6, 7, 9, 1947, DB papers, box 1, VHS.
3. Cockett, Astor, p. 109; Beevor and Cooper, Paris after the Liberation, p. 14.
4. DB, "Travel Notes," April 1, 1947, DB papers, box 1, VHS.
5. DB to Allen W. Dulles, June 23, 1947, copy courtesy of James Srodes.
6. DB to W. Averell Harriman, September 9, 1946, Harriman papers, box 226, LC.
7. Robert E. Hannegan (chairman, Democratic National Committee) to Harry S Truman, January 16, 1947, and J. Edgar Hoover to George J. Schoeneman (special executive assistant to the president), January 31, 1947, HST Lib.
8. The genesis of the Marshall Plan presented in the following paragraphs is based in part on chapter 13 of Isaacson and Thomas, Wise Men.
9. Janet Flanner, quoted in Wineapple, Genêt, p. 186.
10. DB oral history interview, March 1, 1972, p. 36, HST Lib., DB's personal copy, VHS.
11. O'Neill, American High, p. 99.
12. McCullough, Truman, pp. 547–48.
13. Isaacson and Thomas, Wise Men, pp. 410, 467–68.
14. DB diary, October 17, 1959, January 30, 1951, October 11, 1950, VHS.
15. Isaacson and Thomas, Wise Men, p. 410.
16. Ibid., p. 407.
17. Special inquiry on DB, January 29, 1947, Bruce file, FBI FOIA.
18. DB to AMB, June 12, 1943, Paul Mellon papers.
19. DB to Allen W. Dulles, July 2, 1947, copy courtesy of James Srodes.
20. Kopper, Gallery, pp. 79–83.
21. Abramson, Spanning the Century, p. 411.
22. DB oral history interview, March 1, 1972, pp. 13–14, HST Lib., DB's personal copy, VHS.
23. NYT, March 2, 1948, p. 39.
24. Address by DB to Thirty-Fourth National Foreign Trade Convention, St. Louis, Missouri, October 20, 1947, DB papers, box 6, VHS.
25. Speech to civic clubs of Nashville, Tennessee, October 21, 1947, DB papers, box 3, VHS.
26. DB diary, January 17, 1964, VHS.
27. Typescript with heading in DB's hand "October 8, 1947 For Forrestal; Letter from DB at Sec'y Forrestal's request on Subversion," DB papers, VHS.
28. Isaacson and Thomas, Wise Men, p. 426.
29. Sir Isaiah Berlin, a member of the British delegation, quoted in Beevor and Cooper, Paris after the Liberation, p. 316.

30. Mee, *Marshall Plan*, pp. 247–48; DB oral history interview, March 1, 1972, p. 17, HST Lib., DB's personal copy, VHS.

31. Charles Sawyer to DB, May 6, 1948, Commerce Department papers, RG 40, file 105199, NA; *NYT*, April 30, 1948, p. 2; Sawyer, *Concerns*, p. 177.

32. W. Averell Harriman to JCB, March 11, 1948, Harriman papers, box 260, LC.

33. Mee, *Marshall Plan*, p. 246.

Chapter 11: The Problems of French Recovery

Epigraph: John L. Brown to Evangeline Bruce, in Bruce, comp., *David K. E. Bruce*, p. 14. Brown was Bruce's chief of the ECA/France information staff.

1. *NYT*, June 6, 1948, p. 75.

2. DB, "Problem of French Recovery," p. 23, printed ECA report, DB papers, VHS.

3. LB, "Footprints," p. 298, in DB papers, box 1, VHS.

4. Isaacson, *Kissinger*, p. 671.

5. DB, "Problem of French Recovery," p. 6, printed ECA report, DB papers, VHS.

6. Lacouture, *De Gaulle: The Ruler*, p. 66.

7. Giles, *Locust Years*, p. 94.

8. DB, "Problem of French Recovery," p. 6, printed ECA report, DB papers, VHS.

9. Johnson, *Modern Times*, p. 589.

10. Beevor and Cooper, *Paris after the Liberation*, p. 223.

11. Cook, *De Gaulle*, p. 301.

12. Giles, *Locust Years*, pp. 68–71.

13. Johnson, *Modern Times*, p. 590.

14. DB to Department of State, "The French political situation as of December 15, 1951," December 20, 1951, *FRUS, 1951*, 4:465.

15. Wall, *Making of Postwar France*, pp. 1–9.

16. See Schama, *Citizens*, pp. 10–12.

17. Abramson, *Spanning the Century*, p. 428; Mee, *Marshall Plan*, p. 250.

18. Interview of Helen Kirkpatrick Milbank, September 20, 1991; interview of Amb. Arthur Hartman, December 21, 1989.

19. Interview of Langbourne Williams, February 23, 1990.

20. *NYT*, January 17, 1954, sec. 6, p. 15.

21. Interview of Amb. Arthur Hartman, December 21, 1989.

22. Dur, *Caffery*, p. 50.

23. Sawyer, *Concerns*, p. 289.

24. Ball, *The Past Has Another Pattern*, p. 89.

25. Interview of Amb. Arthur Hartman, December 21, 1989.

26. DB, "Problem of French Recovery," p. 9, printed ECA report, DB papers, VHS.

27. Monnet, *Memoirs*, p. 269; transcript of DB interview for Voice of America, undated but late 1948, Marshall Plan papers, RG 256, box 122, NA.

28. Lacouture, *De Gaulle: The Ruler*, p. 144.

29. DB to Hoffman, September 14, 1948, *FRUS, 1948*, 3:649.

30. Ibid.

31. Beevor and Cooper, *Paris after the Liberation*, p. 359; Duchène, *Monnet*, p. 154.

32. Giles, *Locust Years*, p. 104; DB to Hoffman, September 14, 1948, *FRUS, 1948*, 3:649.

33. Wall, *Making of Postwar France*, p. 166.
34. Memorandum by the Coordinator of Foreign Aid and Assistance (Harry Labouisse) and the Assistant Chief of the Division of Commercial Policy (Ben Moore), October 16, 1948, *FRUS, 1948*, 3:668–70; Bullock, *Bevin*, p. 640.
35. Wall, *Making of Postwar France*, pp. 168–69.
36. All quotations in this paragraph and the following one are cited from "English text of Speech by Mr. David Bruce at a Dinner Given by the Central Wool Committee on December 6, 1948, at Lille, France," Marshall Plan papers, RG 256, box 122, NA.
37. Giles, *Locust Years*, p. 84.
38. DB to Secretary of State, December 10, 1948, Marshall Plan papers, RG 256, box 122, NA.
39. Clipping from *Washington Post*, December 21, 1948, Marshall Plan papers, RG 256, box 122, NA.
40. Wall, *Making of Postwar France*, pp. 169–72.
41. Ibid., pp. 37, 58.
42. DB diary, August 14, 1944, VHS.
43. Irwin M. Wall, "Jean Monnet, the United States and the French Economic Plan," p. 100, in Brinkley and Hackett, eds., *Jean Monnet*; Wall, *Making of Postwar France*, p. 179.
44. Interview of Helen Kirkpatrick Milbank, September 20, 1991.
45. Interview of EBB, April 4, 1993.
46. Schama, *Citizens*, p. 635.
47. Interview of EBB, April 4. 1993.
48. DB to LB, September 7, 1921, DB papers, VHS.
49. Interviews of EBB, April 4, December 18, 1993.
50. Giles, *Locust Years*, pp. 91–92.
51. Taft, *American Power*, p. 121.
52. Gillingham, *Coal, Steel*, pp. 137–38.
53. Schwartz, *America's Germany*, p. 100.
54. Duchène, *Monnet*, pp. 172–73.
55. DB diary, September 30, 1962, VHS.
56. Grosser, *Western Alliance*, p. 102.
57. DB diary, September 30, 1962, VHS.
58. Monnet, *Memoirs*, pp. 269–70.
59. *NYT*, February 11, 1949, p. 6.
60. *NYT*, April 3, 1949, p. 13.
61. DB, "Problem of French Recovery," pp. 21–23, printed ECA report, DB papers, VHS.
62. DB to Hoffman, April 4, 1949, *FRUS, 1949*, 4:638.

Chapter 12: Making Europe

1. JCB, *Memoirs*, p. 266.
2. Donald S. Dawson, memorandum for the president, April 11, 1949, Harry S Truman papers, Official File, HST Lib.
3. Ibid.

4. "Memorandum of conversation with the president, Item no. 4, Mr. David Bruce," April 11, 1949, Dean Acheson papers, HST Lib.

5. Partington, ed., *Oxford Dictionary of Quotations*, p. 1.

6. DB diary, May 12, 1949, VHS.

7. Joseph Alsop column, *Washington Post*, June 1, 1949, quoted in JCB, *Memoirs*, pp. 344–45; DB to JCB, undated, 1949, JCB papers, SI, box 1, DB folder, University of Maryland archives.

8. JCB, *Memoirs*, p. 352.

9. Ibid., p. 356. The senator was Stuart Symington of Missouri.

10. DB diary, May 16, 1949, VHS.

11. DB diary, August 3, 1950, VHS.

12. Harry S Truman to Vincent Auriol, May 10, 1949, Bruce 123 file, 1945–49, State Department papers, RG 59, NA.

13. Beevor and Cooper, *Paris after the Liberation*, p. 281.

14. DB diary, October 29, 1950, VHS.

15. Dumaine, *Quay d'Orsay*, pp. 209–10.

16. These points appeared in an analysis by the British ambassador in Paris of the image of Americans in France, an analysis that also reflects British unease about American influence in Europe. Oliver Harvey to Ernest Bevin, statement on Franco-American relations, February 22, 1950, FO 371–89108, Public Record Office, Kew.

17. Flanner, *Darlinghissima*, p. 150.

18. Taft, *American Power*, p. 142.

19. Herz, *David Bruce's "Long Telegram,"* p. 2.

20. Ibid.

21. Unpaginated clipping, *Richmond Times-Dispatch*, July 24, 1949, vertical file, Richmond Public Library.

22. *NYT*, January 17, 1954, sec. 6, p. 15.

23. DB diary, March 10, 1952, VHS.

24. Flanner, *Paris Journal*, November 5, 1952, p. 182.

25. Ibid., January 11, 1950, pp. 117–18.

26. DB diary, December 3, 1949, VHS.

27. Ibid., (there are two copies at the VHS with marginal notes in Bruce's hand, from which these quotations are taken and which date from much later than 1949, in one case at least from 1972, when Bruce went back over his journals); *NYT*, December 30, 1949, p. 30.

28. Louis and Yazijian, *Cola Wars*, p. 78; DB diary, February 23, 1950, VHS.

29. DB diary, May 18, 1949, VHS.

30. DB diary, June 14, July 11, 1949, VHS.

31. Elliott, *John*, pp. 180–82, quotation on p. 182.

32. DB diary, January 23, 1951, VHS.

33. Paraphrase of DB's words in Cyrus Sulzberger diary, July 3, 1961, in Sulzberger, *Giants*, p. 766.

34. Hewins, *Mr. Five Per Cent*, p. 194; DB diary, October 6, 1949, VHS. Quotation is in DB's handwritten notation from 1972 when he reread the diaries.

35. Unpaginated clipping, *Richmond Times-Dispatch*, July 24, 1949, vertical file, Richmond Public Library.

36. This paragraph and the following one are based on DB diary, January 16, 1951, VHS.

37. Monnet to DB, undated, in DB diary, April 28, 1958, VHS.

38. DB diary, April 28, 1950, VHS. Added to the entry for May 7, 1950, the phrase "that Monnet had previously informed me about" referred explicitly to the just-announced coal and steel community and was written in Bruce's hand in January 1973 when he reread his typed diaries for the Paris years.

39. Gillingham, *Coal, Steel*, pp. xi–xii, 50, 96–99.

40. Bullock, *Bevin*, p. 732.

41. DB diary, December 28, 1961, VHS.

42. Gillingham, *Coal, Steel*, pp. xi–xii, 299.

43. DB diary, May 10, 1950, VHS; DB to Washington, cable, June 3, 1950, in DB diary, June 3, 1950, VHS.

44. Gillingham, *Coal, Steel*, p. 235; George Ball, *The Past Has Another Pattern*, p. 90.

45. DB diary, August 9, 1951, VHS.

46. DB diary, July 4, 1949, VHS. The quotation was made in DB's hand much later than 1949 in one of the two copies of this year of his diary at the VHS.

47. DB diary, May 31, 1951, VHS.

48. DB diary, July 1, 1953, VHS.

49. *NYT*, April 16, 1961, sec. 6, p. 37.

50. Baldrige, *Of Diamonds and Diplomats*, p. 11; DB diary, May 14, 1949, VHS.

51. DB diary, June 27, 1949, VHS.

52. Quoted in report from B.A.B. Burrows, British Embassy, Washington, D.C. to American Department, Foreign Office, London, February 15, 1952, FO 371/97582, Public Record Office, Kew.

53. Beevor and Cooper, *Paris after the Liberation*, p. 393.

54. Baldrige, *Of Diamonds and Diplomats*, p. 5.

55. Ibid., p. 14; Mitford, *Don't Tell Alfred*, p. 102.

56. Baldrige, *Of Diamonds and Diplomats*, pp. 4–18; quotation on p. 18.

57. Taft, *American Power*, pp. 138–39; Gillingham, *Coal, Steel*, p. 251.

58. Bohlen, *Witness to History*, p. 292; DB diary, June 27, 1950.

59. Fursdon, *European Defense Community*, p. 67; Bird, *Chairman*, p. 339; DB diary, January 23, 1951, VHS.

60. DB to State Department, July 28, 1950, in Herz, *David Bruce's "Long Telegram,"* pp. 7–8 note.

61. DB diary, October 24, 1950, VHS; DB to the Secretary of State, December 13, 1950, *FRUS, 1950*, 3:1446.

62. DB diary, January 16, 1951, VHS; Alsop, *To Marietta from Paris*, pp. 163–64.

63. Baldrige, *Of Diamonds and Diplomats*, p. 19; Flanner, *Darlinghissima*, p. 143.

64. Beevor and Cooper, *Paris after the Liberation*, p. 205.

65. DB diary, January 16, 1951, VHS.

66. Bernier, *Fireworks at Dusk*, pp. 140, 320; Flanner, *Darlinghissima*, p. 446.

67. Johnson, *Modern Times*, p. 576.

68. Ogden, *Life of the Party*, pp. 211–13.

69. Beevor and Cooper, *Paris after the Liberation*, p. 139; quotation from Flanner, *Darlinghissima*, p. 454.

70. DB diary, December 24, 1953, VHS.
71. DB diary, August 28, 1950, VHS.
72. DB diary, June 11, 1951, VHS.
73. Beevor and Cooper, *Paris after the Liberation*, p. 198.
74. DB diary, May 10, 1951, VHS.
75. DB to secretary of state, January 10, 1951, *FRUS, 1951*, 4:293.
76. Judt, *Past Imperfect*, p. 4; Beevor and Cooper, *Paris after the Liberation*, p. 181.
77. Secrest, *Between Me and Life*; Wickes, *Amazon*; DB diary, July 3, 1951, September 24, 1962, VHS.
78. Gillingham, "Debacle," pp. 21–23.
79. Herz, *David Bruce's "Long Telegram*," p. 19.
80. Ibid.
81. White, *Fire in the Ashes*, p. 274.
82. Schwartz, *America's Germany*, pp. 222–34.
83. Acheson, *Creation*, p. 557.
84. DB diary, September 6, 1951, VHS.
85. DB diary, September 9, 1951, VHS.
86. Mitford, *Don't Tell Alfred*, p. 59.
87. DB diary, November 26, 1951, February 22, 25, 1952, VHS; DB to Department of State, January 3, 1952, *FRUS, 1952–1954*, 5:574.
88. Unpaginated clipping, *Richmond Times-Dispatch*, July 24, 1949, vertical file, Richmond Public Library.
89. DB diary, May 24, 1949, VHS.
90. DB diary, July 3, 1950, VHS.
91. DB diary, September 29, 1950, VHS.
92. DB diary, September 29, 30, 1950, VHS.
93. In a speech given January 7, 1950, according to Dumaine, *Quai d'Orsay, 1945–1951*, p. 447.
94. Harrison, *Reluctant Ally*, pp. 6–10, 37–40.
95. All quotations in this paragraph come from DB to Secretary of State, December 11, 1949, in DB diary, December 31, 1951, VHS.
96. DB diary, October 24, 1951, VHS.
97. DB diary, December 31, 1951, VHS.
98. DB to Secretary of State, December 26, 1951, in DB diary, December 26, 1951, VHS.
99. DB diary, December 2, 1950, VHS.
100. DB diary, November 8, 1951, VHS.
101. Beevor and Cooper, *Paris after the Liberation*, p. 116; Giles, *Sundry Times*, p. 82.
102. Johnson, *Modern Times*, p. 592.
103. The rumor that Bruce was slated to return to Washington as undersecretary appeared in public as early as the previous December (*NYT*, December 10, 1951, p. 1).
104. Excerpts from Acheson to DB, January 16, 1952, and from DB to Acheson, January 17, 1952, in DB diary, January 17, 1952, VHS.
105. Jean Monnet to DB, January 22, 1952, AMG 28/2/8, Fondation Jean Monnet Pour L'Europe.

106. Gillingham, *Coal, Steel*, p. xii.
107. Alsop, *To Marietta from Paris*, p. 194.
108. DB diary, March 6, 8, 1952, VHS.
109. DB diary, February 25, 1952, VHS.

Chapter 13: Into the Cockpit

1. Caute, *Great Fear*, p. 18.
2. DB diary, March 7, 1954, VHS.
3. Taft, *American Power*, pp. 150–51.
4. Keith, *For Hell and a Brown Mule*, p. 13.
5. Morris, *Nixon*, pp. 383–85; Caute, *Great Fear*, p. 287.
6. DB to Seth Richardson, chairman, Loyalty Review Board, affidavit, November 3, 1948, in FBI special inquiry on DB, June 6, 1956, Bruce file, FBI FOIA; Mr. Rosen to Mr. Parsons, FBI interdepartmental memo, December 23, 1960, in FBI special inquiry on DB, December 23, 1960, Bruce file, FBI FOIA; Caute, *Great Fear*, pp. 287–89.
7. Abramson, *Spanning the Century*, p. 487.
8. Arthur Schlesinger Jr. to EBB, February 10, 1952, EBB papers.
9. An example of Bruce's high praise for Acheson appears in DB diary, January 30, 1951, VHS.
10. Acheson, *Creation*, p. 588.
11. *NYT*, August 14, 1952, p. 6.
12. Murat W. Williams (special assistant to DB's deputy, H. Freeman Matthews, 1952–53) to author, October 25, 1989.
13. DB diary, August 25, 1952, VHS.
14. DB diary, October 20, 1952, March 3, 1953, VHS.
15. Quoted in *NYT*, November 11, 1990, sec. 2, p. 39.
16. Beevor and Cooper, *Paris after the Liberation*, p. 61; DB diary, May 1, 1951, VHS.
17. DB diary, November 20, 1952, VHS.
18. DB diary, July 10, 11, August 16, 1952, VHS.
19. Caute, *Great Fear*, p. 246.
20. Newman, *Lattimore*, pp. 389–94.
21. DB diary, June 22, 23, 27, 1952, VHS.
22. Isaacson and Thomas, *Wise Men*, p. 495.
23. DB diary, December 15, October 27, 1952, VHS; DB oral history interview, March 1, 1972, p. 44, HST Lib.
24. Hersh, *Old Boys*, p. 338; Ranelagh, *Agency*, p. 265 note.
25. Memorandum of conversation by the director of the policy planning staff (Nitze), May 12, 1952, *FRUS*, 1952–54, 13:141–42.
26. DB diary, April 25, 1952, VHS.
27. Acheson, *Creation*, p. 3.
28. DB's Truman oral history interview, pp. 28–29; DB diary, January 30, 1951; Acheson, *Creation*, p. 294.
29. DB diary, January 30, 1951, VHS.
30. Ibid.
31. Acheson, *Creation*, p. 588.

32. Koskoff, *Mellons*, p. 232.

33. McCullough, *Truman*, pp. 751–52.

34. DB's Truman oral history interview, pp. 31, 35–37, 43–47.

35. DB diary, July 9, 28, 1952, VHS.

36. *NYT*, November 1, 1952, p. 13.

37. DB diary, November 4, 5, 1952, VHS.

38. DB diary, December 10, 1952, VHS.

39. Truman diary for November 15, 1952, quoted in Ferrell, ed., *Off the Record*, p. 273.

40. Henry Cabot Lodge to DB, February 14, 1974, DB papers, VHS.

41. Memorandum for the president, by the secretary of state, January 12, 1953, *FRUS, 1952–1954*, 1:38; DB diary, November 30, 1952, VHS.

42. DB diary, December 22, 1952, VHS.

43. DB diary, May 3, 1953, VHS.

44. DB diary, June 4, 1953, VHS.

Chapter 14: Ambassador to a Dream

Epigraphs: Fursdon, *European Defense Community*, p. 225; text of letter from DB to Livingston Merchant included in DB diary, March 1, 1954, VHS.

1. Fursdon, *European Defense Community*, p. 210.

2. Manchester, *Last Lion, Visions of Glory*, p. 34.

3. DB diary, January 30, 1954, VHS.

4. DB diary, May 24, 1959, VHS.

5. Isaacson and Thomas, *Wise Men*, p. 581.

6. Brinkley, *Dean Acheson*, p. 17.

7. Pascaline Winand, "Eisenhower, Dulles, Monnet, and the Uniting of Europe," in Hackett, ed., *Monnet and the Americans*, pp. 118–19.

8. DB diary, February 16, 1953, VHS; Cyrus Sulzberger diary, March 24, 1953, in Sulzberger, *Candles*, p. 847.

9. DB diary, January 9, 1953, VHS.

10. DB diary, February 18, 1953, VHS.

11. Dean Acheson to DB and EBB, April 15, 1953, EBB papers.

12. DB diary, February 17, 1953, VHS.

13. Fursdon, *European Defense Community*, p. 211.

14. Giles, *Locust Years*, pp. 177, 182.

15. DB diary, July 29, 1954, VHS; Jebb, *Memoirs of Lord Gladwyn*, p. 272.

16. DB diary, February 25, 1953, VHS.

17. Giles, *Locust Years*, pp. 179–80.

18. Fursdon, *European Defense Community*, p. 217.

19. DB diary, August 22, 1953, VHS.

20. DB diary, August 12, 1953, VHS.

21. DB to Department of State, March 2, 1954, *FRUS, 1952–1954*, 5:883.

22. *NYT*, January 17, 1954, sec. 6, p. 15.

23. Gillingham, "Debacle," p. 36.

24. DB diary, October 5, 1967, VHS.

25. DB diary, April 27, 1953, VHS.

26. Littlewood, *Baron Philippe*, p. 326.

27. DB diary, April 8, 1954, VHS.
28. DB diary, March 3, 1953, VHS.
29. DB to State Department, March 12, 1953, *FRUS, 1952–1954,* 5:766–69.
30. DB diary, July 7, 1953, VHS.
31. DB diary, March 17, 1953, VHS.
32. *NYT,* January 17, 1954, sec. 6, p. 50.
33. DB diary, November 27, 1953, VHS.
34. DB diary, June 6, 1954, VHS.
35. DB diary, June 16, 1953, VHS.
36. Grosser, *Western Alliance,* p. 105.
37. Fursdon, *European Defense Community,* p. 225.
38. Giles, *Locust Years,* p. 173.
39. DB diary, June 21, 1953, VHS.
40. DB diary, July 9, 1953, VHS.
41. DB to Department of State, September 8, 1953, *FRUS, 1952–1954,* 5:800.
42. Giles, *Locust Years,* p. 174.
43. DB diary, December 1, 1953, VHS.
44. DB diary, December 15, 17, 1953, VHS.
45. Cyrus Sulzberger diary, January 25, 1954, in Sulzberger, *Candles,* p. 953.
46. DB to Department of State, March 21, 1954, *FRUS, 1952–1954,* 5:904.
47. DB to Livingston Merchant, March 30, 1954, in DB diary for March 1954, VHS.
48. DB diary, May 8, 1954, VHS.
49. DB diary, July 25, 1954, VHS.
50. DB diary, June 21, 1954, VHS.
51. Fursdon, *European Defense Community,* p. 267.
52. Gillingham, "Debacle," p. 46.
53. DB diary, August 15, 1954, VHS.
54. Ibid.
55. Giles, *Locust Years,* p. 222.
56. Weymar, *Adenauer,* p. 479.
57. Fursdon, *European Defense Community,* p. 285.
58. DB diary, September 8, 1954, VHS.
59. Lacouture, *Mendes France,* p. 276.
60. *NYT,* August 18, 1954, p. 4.
61. DB diary, August 20, 1954, VHS; interview of Amb. Arthur Hartman, December 21, 1989.
62. DB diary, August 21, 1954, VHS.
63. DB to State Department, August 21, 1954, *FRUS, 1952–1954,* 5:1063.
64. Interview of Amb. Arthur Hartman, December 21, 1989.
65. DB to Department of State, August 26, 1954, *FRUS, 1952–1954,* 5:1081, note 1.
66. Flanner, *Paris Journal,* September 1, 1954, p. 243.
67. Editorial note, *FRUS, 1952–1954,* 5:1088.
68. Giles, *Locust Years,* p. 229.
69. DB diary, August 27, 1954, VHS.
70. Jacques Van Helmont to author, April 23, 1990.
71. Prittie, *Adenauer,* p. 191.

72. EBB to Arthur M. Schlesinger Jr., September 11, [1954], Schlesinger papers, JFK Lib.

73. DB diary, August 29, 1954, VHS.

74. DB diary, September 20, 1954, VHS.

75. DB diary, October 10, 11, 1954, VHS.

76. Memorandum of conversation, September 23, 1954, *FRUS, 1952–1954*, 5:1256.

77. DB diary, October 13, 1954, VHS.

78. DB diary, October 15, 1954, VHS.

79. DB diary, June 6, 1955, VHS.

80. E. Roland Harriman to DB, July 15, 1953, and DB to E. Roland Harriman, July 21, 1953, in DB diary for July 1953, VHS; Phillip L. Graham to DB, August 10, 1954, DB to Phillip L. Graham, August 15, 1954, in DB diary for August 1954, VHS.

81. DB diary, October 21, 1954, VHS.

82. DB diary, November 22, 1954, VHS.

83. *NYT*, January 11, 1955, p. 18.

84. DB diary, December 20, 1954, VHS.

85. Cyrus Sulzberger diary, November 12, 1954, in Sulzberger, *Giants*, p. 109.

86. Cyrus Sulzberger diary, July 2, 1962, in Sulzberger, *Giants*, p. 894.

87. Schama, *Citizens*, p. 12.

88. DB diary, December 29, 1954, VHS.

89. DB diary, December 31, 1954, VHS.

Chapter 15: Marking Time in Georgetown

Epigraph: Sampson, *Anatomy of Britain Today*, p. 672.

1. DB diary, January 3, 1955, VHS.

2. DB diary, January 5, 1955, VHS.

3. DB diary, January 12, 1955, VHS.

4. DB diary, January 13, 1955, VHS.

5. DB, "Talk by DB to Interagency Committee at State Dept After Defeat of EDC," no date, DB papers, VHS.

6. DB diary, August 14, 1957, VHS.

7. DB to AMB, September 27, 1954, Paul Mellon papers.

8. Koskoff, *Mellons*, p. 534.

9. Hersh, *Mellon Family*, p. 415.

10. Koskoff, *Mellons*, p. 535.

11. Interview of Pamela Harriman, March 14, 1991.

12. DB diary, February 20, 1955, VHS.

13. DB diary, January 3, 1963, VHS.

14. DB diary, January 15, 1955, VHS.

15. Cyrus Sulzberger diary, April 14, 1955, in Sulzberger, *Giants*, p. 165.

16. DB diary, January 26, 1955, VHS.

17. *NYT*, August 8, 1956, p. 14.

18. Schlesinger, *Robert Kennedy and His Times*, p. 475.

19. Ranelagh, *Agency*, p. 279.

20. DB diary, November 22, 1966, VHS.

21. Cyrus Sulzberger diary, October 22, 1955, in Sulzberger, *Giants*, p. 208.

22. DB to W. Averell Harriman, January 24, 1957, Harriman papers, box 384, LC.
23. *NYT*, February 27, 1957, p. 55.
24. *NYT*, August 7, 1957, p. 12.
25. *NYT*, February 27, 1957, p. 55.
26. *NYT*, February 28, 1957, p. 20; *Richmond Times-Dispatch*, February 26, 1957, p. 4.
27. DB diary, April 2, 1957, VHS.
28. DB diary, April 9, 1957, VHS.

Chapter 16: Proconsul on the Rhine

Epigraph: Deighton, *Berlin Game*, p. 114.
1. Laqueur, *Europe in Our Time*, p. 375.
2. DB diary, June 21, 1953, VHS.
3. Norman Stone, "Rearing Its Ugly Head Again?" London *Sunday Times*, November 29, 1992, "The Culture" sec., p. 4.
4. Lewis, *Europe: Road to Unity*, p. 310.
5. DB diary, April 11, 1957, VHS; Lewis, *Europe: Road to Unity*, p. 311.
6. DB diary, April 28, 1957, VHS.
7. DB diary, April 26, 1957, VHS.
8. DB diary, April 17, 1957, VHS.
9. DB diary, April 12, 1957, VHS.
10. DB diary, June 24, 1957, VHS.
11. DB diary, July 2, 1957, VHS.
12. Ranelagh, *Agency*, p. 446.
13. Prados, *Presidents' Secret Wars*, pp. 34–35.
14. Hitchens, *Blood, Class, and Nostalgia*, p. 337.
15. DB diary, January 2, 1958, VHS.
16. Cyrus Sulzberger diary, April 29, 1958, in Sulzberger, *Giants*, p. 469.
17. DB diary, June 9, 1957, VHS.
18. DB diary, July 17, 1957, VHS.
19. DB to AMB, August 21, 1943, Paul Mellon papers.
20. DB diary, August 12, 1957, VHS.
21. Ibid.
22. *NYT*, April 16, 1961, sec. 6, p. 35.
23. Ibid.
24. DB diary, January 7, 1954, VHS.
25. DB diary, October 24, 1958, VHS.
26. DB diary, April 14, 1951, VHS.
27. DB diary, February 5, 1952, VHS.
28. DB diary, March 12, 1953, VHS.
29. DB diary, July 2, 1957, VHS.
30. Johnson, *Modern Times*, p. 580.
31. Quoted in Barnet, *Alliance*, p. 55.
32. Hershberg, *Conant*, pp. 702–3.
33. DB diary, September 30, 1959, VHS.
34. DB diary, February 3, 1959, VHS.
35. Cyrus Sulzberger diary, March 20, 1959, in Sulzberger, *Giants*, pp. 553–54.

36. DB diary, April 29, 1957, VHS.
37. Ibid.
38. DB diary, June 17, 1957, VHS.
39. DB diary, April 30, 1957, VHS.
40. DB diary, July 1, 1957, VHS.
41. DB diary, May 17, 1957, VHS.
42. Albert Speer diary, September 8, 1958, in Speer, *Spandau*, p. 327.
43. DB diary, September 8, 1958, VHS.
44. DB diary, July 14, 1958, VHS.
45. DB diary, October 28, 1958, VHS.
46. Ferencz, *Less Than Slaves*, pp. 80–89, 188–89.
47. DB diary, April 20, 1957, VHS.
48. DB diary, June 13, 1957, VHS.
49. DB diary, June 12, 1958, VHS.
50. Cyrus Sulzberger diary, October 22, 1955, in Sulzberger, *Giants*, p. 208.
51. DB diary, August 1, 1957, VHS.
52. DB diary, January 14, 1959, VHS.
53. DB diary, June 24, 1957, VHS.
54. DB diary, December 23, 1957, VHS.
55. DB diary, December 10, 1957, VHS.
56. *NYT*, December 11, 1957, p. 6.
57. DB diary, January 4, 1958, VHS.
58. DB to Secretary of State, February 4, 1958, in DB diary, February 5, 1958, VHS.
59. Cyrus Sulzberger diary, December 7, 1958, in Sulzberger, *Giants*, pp. 520–21.
60. *NYT Magazine*, February 5, 1995, p. 46.
61. DB diary, December 27, 1958, VHS.
62. DB diary, December 30, 1958, VHS.
63. DB to secretary of state and others, February 17, 1959, in DB diary, February 17, 1959, VHS.
64. DB diary, July 22, 1959, VHS.
65. DB diary, August 8, 1959, VHS.
66. DB diary, September 30, 1959, VHS.
67. Secretary of State to DB, October 23, 1959, and DB to Secretary of State, October 23, 1959, in DB diary, October 23, 1959, VHS.
68. *NYT*, December 7, 1977, p. 29.

Chapter 17: An Honorary Englishman

Epigraphs: Partington, ed., *Oxford Dictionary of Quotations*, p. 553; speech at West Point, December 5, 1962, in Partington, ed., *Oxford Dictionary of Quotations*, p. 1.
1. DB diary, November 5, 1959, VHS.
2. Sherrill, "Georgetown On My Mind," p. 80.
3. Brenner, "Marietta Tree," p. 213.
4. Ibid., p. 215.
5. Ibid., p. 218.
6. Felsenthal, *Power*, p. 174.

7. Reeves, *Question of Character*, p. 177.
8. *NYT*, August 31, 1960, p. 18.
9. H. B. Chermside Sr. to DB, September 27, 1960; typescript of speech labeled in DB's hand "J F Kennedy Campaign 1960. Radio Broadcast. DKE Bruce," DB papers, VHS.
10. *Wall Street Journal*, November 10, 1960, clipping, DB papers, VHS.
11. *Washington Post*, August 7, 1960, clipping, DB papers, VHS.
12. Dean Acheson oral history interview, 1964, p. 7, JFK Lib.
13. Felsenthal, *Power*, p. 184.
14. Peter Lisagor oral history interview, April 22, 1966, JFK Lib.
15. Interview of Amb. George McGehee, December 20, 1989.
16. DB diary, January 27, 1964, VHS.
17. Robert F. Kennedy oral history interview (eighth), February 27, 1965, p. 600, JFK Lib.
18. Halberstam, *Best and Brightest*, p. 31.
19. Dean Acheson oral history interview, 1964, JFK Lib.
20. DB diary, March 8, 28, 1961, VHS.
21. DB diary, March 28, July 20, 1961, VHS; Robert Estabrook memorandum of conversation with DB, November 2, 1961, JFK Lib.
22. DB diary, December 14, 1962, April 4, 1963, VHS.
23. DB diary, April 24, 1965, VHS.
24. DB to LBJ, December 14, 1964, in DB diary, December 14, 1964, VHS.
25. DB diary, August 6, 1953, VHS.
26. DB diary, January 16, 1951, VHS.
27. DB diary, December 19, 1962, VHS.
28. Ibid.
29. DB diary, March 9, 1961, VHS.
30. DB to secretary of state, in DB diary, January 31, 1964, VHS.
31. DB diary, May 25, 1966, VHS.
32. Interview of Frazier and Susan Meade, May 6, 1991.
33. Kaiser, *Journeying*, p. 220.
34. Ibid., p. 222.
35. Interview of Amb. Philip Kaiser, October 27, 1989.
36. DB diary, November 25, 1965, VHS.
37. DB diary, June 21, 1961, VHS.
38. Kaiser, *Journeying*, p. 222.
39. Interview of Amb. Philip Kaiser, October 27, 1989; DB diary, September 22, 1967.
40. DB diary, February 1, 1964, VHS.
41. DB diary, March 25, 1961, VHS.
42. DB diary, July 31, 1964, VHS.
43. DB diary, June 14, 1963, VHS.
44. DB diary, April 4, 1962, VHS.
45. Horne, *Macmillan*, 2:429.
46. Quoted in article in the *Economist*, April 20, 1991, based on Peter Hennessy's *Premiership*.
47. DB diary, October 31, 1966, VHS.
48. DB diary, July 2, 1965, VHS.

49. DB diary, July 16, 1961, VHS.
50. Schama, *Citizens*, p. 12.
51. Horne, *Macmillan*, 2:308.
52. London to Secretary of State, December 12, 1961, National Security Files, JFK Lib.
53. DB to secretary of state, July 17, 1962, National Security Files, box 170, JFK Lib.
54. Watt, *Succeeding John Bull*, pp. 136–37.
55. Horne, *Macmillan*, 2:282.
56. Dean Acheson oral history interview, 1964, p. 25, JFK Lib.; DB diary, October 21, 1962, VHS.
57. DB diary, October 24, 1962, VHS.
58. Chester L. Cooper oral history interview, May 16, 1966, pp. 23–29, JFK Lib.; Nunnerley, *President Kennedy and Britain*, pp. 45, 77; unidentified press clipping, JCB papers, Univ. of Maryland.
59. This analysis of Skybolt is based on Nunnerley, *President Kennedy and Britain*.
60. Neustadt, *Alliance Politics*, pp. 132, 142.
61. Clipping of Joseph C. Harsch article, *Christian Science Monitor*, December 1, 1962, National Security Files, box 170, JFK Lib.
62. Robert Estabrook memorandum of lunch meeting with DB, undated but in autumn 1962, Robert Estabrook memoranda, JFK Lib.
63. White House memorandum to State Department, December 7, 1962, National Security Files, box 170, JFK Lib.
64. DB diary, August 9, 1961, VHS.
65. DB diary, April 18, July 27, 1962, VHS.
66. DB diary, May 23, 1962, VHS.
67. DB to secretary of state, July 27, 1962, in DB diary, July 27, 1962, VHS.
68. Brinkley, *Dean Acheson*, p. 184.
69. DB diary, November 26, 1964, VHS.
70. Horne, *Macmillan*, 2:437.
71. DB, "Preliminary Report on European Policy," February 11, 1963, p. 6, in DB diary, February 11, 1963, VHS.
72. Ibid., p. 2.
73. Diary notes for October 11, 1961, Krock, *Memoirs*, p. 372.
74. *Dictionary of National Biography, 1981–1985*, pp. 305–6.
75. Horne, *Macmillan*, 2:306–7.
76. DB diary, October 29, 1961, VHS.

Chapter 18: Ceremony, Salons, and Scandal

Epigraph: Levin, *Pendulum Years*, p. 62.
1. DB diary, July 19, 1966, VHS.
2. DB to secretary of state, April 11, 1963, National Security Files, box 171, JFK Lib.
3. Levin, *Pendulum Years*, pp. 406–9.
4. DB diary, prologue to London diary, 1961, VHS.
5. DB diary, May 3, 1963, VHS.
6. DB diary, July 21, 1962, VHS.
7. DB diary, November 29, 1964, VHS.

8. DB diary, August 5, 1968, VHS.
9. Sampson, *Anatomy*, p. 324.
10. Felsenthal, *Power*, p. 254.
11. Curtis, *Rich and Other Atrocities*, pp. 87–93.
12. DB diary, March 10, 1969, VHS.
13. Amory, ed., *Letters of Ann Fleming*, p. 42.
14. Konolige, *Richest Women in the World*, p. 305.
15. Rothschild, "Amazing Bruces," p. 123.
16. Konolige, *Richest Women in the World*, p. 305.
17. Pimlott, *Wilson*, p. 330.
18. DB diary, March 31, 1965, VHS.
19. Ann Fleming to Evelyn Waugh, May 5, 1963, Amory, ed., *Letters of Ann Fleming*, p. 325.
20. Interview with Roy Jenkins, July 10, 1990.
21. DB diary, February 9, 1966, VHS.
22. Sir Steven Runciman to author, August 25, 1990.
23. DB diary, May 1, 1961, VHS.
24. Noel Annan to author, August 17, 1990.
25. DB diary, May 14, 1967, VHS.
26. DB diary, June 1, 1962, VHS.
27. DB diary, July 4, 1966, VHS.
28. Pimlott, *Wilson*, p. 269.
29. DB diary, June 20, 1963, VHS.
30. DB diary, June 10, 1963, VHS.
31. DB diary, June 13, 1963, VHS.
32. DB diary, June 20, 1963, VHS.
33. Levin, *Pendulum Years*, p. 58.
34. DB to president and secretary of state, cable, June 14, 1963, in DB diary, June 14, 1963, VHS.
35. DB diary, June 22, 1963, VHS.
36. DB diary, June 24, 1963, VHS.
37. DB diary, June 25, 1963, VHS.
38. "Christine Keeler; John Profumo" FBI memorandum, June 19, 1963, DB papers, VHS.
39. Knightley and Kennedy, *Affair of State*, p. 157.
40. Summers and Dorril, *Honeytrap*, pp. 168–69.
41. Knightley and Kennedy, *Affair of State*, p. 126.
42. Ibid., pp. 205–7; Roosevelt, *For Lust of Knowing*, p. 470.
43. Al Wells to DB, memoranda, June 18, 19, 1963, Bruce papers, VHS.
44. Horne, *Macmillan*, 2:495.
45. DB diary, June 9, 1963, VHS.
46. Interview of Sir Isaiah Berlin, July 13, 1990.
47. Knightley and Kennedy, *Affair of State*, p. 247.

Chapter 19: A Pall Over Our Spirits

1. Watt, *Succeeding John Bull*, p. 144.
2. DB diary, December 5, 1964, VHS.

3. DB diary, March 26, June 29, 1965, VHS.
4. DB oral history interview, December 9, 1971, tape 2, p. 13, LBJ Lib.
5. Stuart Symington to DB, January 12, 1966, EBB papers.
6. DB to LBJ, April 1, 1968, in DB diary, April 1, 1968, VHS.
7. Bernard Levin, *Pendulum Years*, quoted in *Oxford Dictionary of Quotations*.
8. "Background talk with David Bruce," Robert Estabrook memorandum, October 17, 1961, JFK Lib.
9. Review of Pimlott's *Wilson*, in *Guardian Weekly*, December 6, 1992, p. 28.
10. DB diary, November 30, 1967, VHS; Pimlott, *Wilson*, p. 488.
11. "Luncheon with American Ambassador David K. E. Bruce," Robert Estabrook memorandum, Nov./Dec.[?] 1962, p. 2, JFK Lib.
12. Interview of Amb. Philip Kaiser, October 27, 1989.
13. Interview of Lord Jenkins of Hillhead (Roy Jenkins), July 10, 1990.
14. DB diary, March 22, 1965, VHS.
15. Brandon, *Special Relationships*, p. 210.
16. DB diary, August 9, 1966, VHS.
17. DB to undersecretary of state, July 11, 1966, in DB diary, July 11, 1966, VHS.
18. DB diary, March 3, 1966, VHS.
19. DB to undersecretary of state, July 11, 1966, in DB diary, July 11, 1966, VHS.
20. DB diary, October 10, 1965, VHS.
21. Laqueur, *Europe In Our Time*, p. 366.
22. DB to undersecretary of state, July 11, 1966, in DB diary, July 11, 1966, VHS.
23. DB diary, July 2, 1965, VHS.
24. DB to William Bundy, January 15, 1968, in DB diary, January 15, 1968, VHS.
25. Ibid.
26. DB diary, February 6, 1968, VHS.
27. DB diary, February 8, 1968, VHS.
28. DB diary, March 7–9, 1965, VHS.
29. DB diary, March 23, 1965, VHS.
30. DB diary, March 22, 1965, VHS.
31. "Luncheon with Ambassador David Bruce," Robert Estabrook memorandum, February 23, 1962, JFK Lib.
32. Cecil King diary, April 6, 1966, in King, *Cecil King Diary*, p. 65.
33. DB diary, December 22, 1965, VHS.
34. DB diary, July 22, 1966, VHS.
35. This account of the Kosygin overture is based largely on: Karnow, *Vietnam;* Cooper, *Lost Crusade;* Goodman, *Lost Peace;* and DB diary, February 1967.
36. Kaiser, *Journeying*, p. 221.
37. Cooper, *Lost Crusade*, p. 357.
38. Pimlott, *Wilson*, p. 462.
39. DB diary, February 11, 1967, VHS.
40. Cooper, *Lost Crusade*, p. 363.
41. Ibid., pp. 366–67.
42. DB diary, June 7, 1971, VHS.
43. DB diary, February 11, 1967, August 1, 1968, VHS.
44. Cooper, *Lost Crusade*, p. 368.
45. Anonymous letter dated March 24, 1965, in DB diary, March 29, 1965, VHS.

46. DB diary, November 9, 1962, VHS.
47. *London Times*, October 5, 1967, p. 2.
48. DB diary, November 14, 1967, VHS.
49. DB to secretary of state, November 16, 1967, in DB diary, November 1967, VHS.
50. DB diary, October 22, 1967, VHS.
51. DB to Sir Isaiah Berlin, March 22, 1968, and Sir Isaiah Berlin to DB, March 28, 1968, in DB diary, March 31, 1968, VHS.
52. Clipping from *Daily Express*, February 27, 1968, in DB diary, February 28, 1968, VHS.
53. DB diary, March 17, 1968, VHS; *NYT*, March 18, 1968, p. 1.
54. DB diary, March 15, 1968, VHS.
55. Schmitt, "London Bloodshed," p. 36.
56. Cecil King diary, March 26, 1968, in King, *Cecil King Diary*, p. 186.
57. DB diary, October 27, 1968, VHS.
58. DB diary, October 28, 1968, VHS.
59. DB to Geoffroy de Courcel, June 9, 1968, in DB diary, June 9, 1968, VHS.
60. Summary Notes of 587th NSC Meeting, June 5, 1968, by Bromley Smith, NSF-NSC meeting file, box 2, vol. 5, tab 69, current US/UK, LBJ Lib. (copy courtesy of Douglas Little).
61. DB to secretary of state, June 4, 1968, following entry in DB diary, June 6, 1968, VHS.
62. DB to JCB, February 25, 1968, SI, box 1, DB folder, JCB papers, University of Maryland.
63. DB diary, February 25, 1969, VHS.
64. Watt, *Succeeding John Bull*, p. 149.
65. DB oral history interview, December 9, 1971, tape 2, p. 6, LBJ Lib.
66. *London Sunday Times*, October 25, 1992, sec. 2, p. 2.
67. DB diary, dated March 19, 1969, but written on March 28 or later, VHS.

Chapter 20: Intermezzo

1. Hitchens, *Blood, Class, and Nostalgia*, p. 57.
2. Cooney, *Annenbergs*, p. 323.
3. Ibid., pp. 342–43.
4. Fonzi, *Annenberg*, p. 218.
5. Hitchens, *Blood, Class, and Nostalgia*, p. 58.
6. DB diary, February 12, 1968, VHS.
7. Mitford, *Don't Tell Alfred*, p. 29.
8. DB diary, April 6, 1968, VHS.
9. DB diary, January 23, 1967, VHS.
10. DB diary, January 21, 1967, VHS.
11. DB diary, January 28, 1967, VHS.
12. Hersh, *Mellon Family*, p. 416.
13. Hodgson, *America in Our Time*, pp. 194–97.
14. Hersh, *Mellon Family*, pp. 418–20.
15. DB diary, September 30, 1962, VHS.
16. Hersh, *Mellon Family*, p. 420.

17. Ibid., p. 416.
18. *NYT*, February 16, 1967, p. 39.
19. DB diary, December 31, 1967, VHS.
20. DB to AMB, December 24, 1958, Paul Mellon papers.
21. Hersh, *Mellon Family*, p. 446.
22. DB to Sasha, David, and Nicholas, March 23, 1970, copy courtesy of Reginald Pettus.
23. Hersh, *Mellon Family*, p. 446.
24. Kopper, *Gallery*, p. 263.
25. Koskoff, *Mellons*, pp. 364–67.
26. Kelman, *Push Comes to Shove*.
27. Wells, "Last Empress," p. 102.
28. DB diary, January 22, 23, 1967, VHS.
29. DB diary, June 15, 1970, VHS.

Chapter 21: Paris Again, By Way of Saigon

Epigraph: Anonymous letter quoted in DB diary, April 13, 1971, VHS.
1. J. Edgar Hoover to John Ehrlichman, October 30, 1969, Bruce file, FBI FOIA.
2. *NYT*, July 5, 1970, sec. 4, p. 1; July 2, 1970, p. 1.
3. Isaacson, *Kissinger*, pp. 136–38.
4. Ibid., p. 189.
5. CBS evening news, July 4, 1970, courtesy of Vanderbilt Television News Archives.
6. Kissinger, *White House Years*, p. 521.
7. Ibid., pp. 520–21.
8. Goodman, *Lost Peace*, pp. 88–91.
9. *NYT*, July 3, 1970, p. 24.
10. DB diary, March 3, 1971, VHS.
11. *NYT*, July 5, 1970, sec. 4, p. 10.
12. This description comes from Karnow, *Vietnam*, pp. 435–45.
13. DB diary, July 21–26, 1970, VHS.
14. *NYT*, July 23, 1970, p. 1, July 24, 1970, p. 3.
15. DB diary, August 3–4, 1970, VHS.
16. DB diary, January 14, 1971, VHS.
17. Karnow, *Vietnam*, pp. 561–62; Habib to secretary of state, December 5, 1977, Department of State, FOIA.
18. Isaacson, *Kissinger*, p. 165.
19. *NYT*, August 7, 1970, p. 2.
20. Ibid.; DB diary, August 13, 1970, VHS.
21. *NYT*, November 6, 1970, p. 3; DB diary, November 5, 1970, VHS.
22. DB diary, July 16, 1968, VHS.
23. *NYT*, January 15, 1971, p. 5.
24. DB diary, June 16, 1971, VHS.
25. DB diary, December 8, 1970, VHS.
26. DB diary, February 12, 1971, VHS.
27. *NYT*, March 10, 1971, p. 5.
28. DB diary, March 8, 1971, VHS.

29. *NYT,* March 12, 1971, p. 2.
30. Kissinger, *White House Years,* p. 980.
31. *NYT,* October 16, 1970, p. 1.
32. Isaacson, *Kissinger,* p. 313.
33. Karnow, *Vietnam,* pp. 626–29.
34. *NYT,* December 6, 1970, sec. 4, p. 3.
35. DB diary, January 21, 1971, VHS; *NYT,* January 22, 1971, p. 8.
36. Karnow, *Vietnam,* pp. 629–31, 635.
37. Goodman, *Lost Peace,* p. 91.
38. *NYT,* October 9, 1970, p. 1.
39. DB diary, November 16, 1970, VHS.
40. Kissinger, *White House Years,* pp. 1026–29.
41. DB diary, February 22, 1969, VHS.
42. Interview of Amb. Brunson McKinley, September 25, 1992; Isaacson, *Kissinger,* p. 142.
43. Kissinger, *White House Years,* p. 448.
44. DB diary, November 12, 1970, VHS.
45. DB diary, May 20, 1971, VHS.
46. DB diary, May 26, 1971, VHS.
47. DB diary, December 11, 1970, VHS.
48. DB diary, January 8, 1971, VHS.
49. DB diary, May 5, 1971, VHS.
50. DB diary, July 22, 1971, VHS.
51. DB oral history interview, December 9, 1971, tape 2, p. 10, LBJ Lib.
52. *NYT,* July 30, 1971, p. 3; DB diary, July 29, 1971, VHS.
53. *NYT,* August 6, 1971, p. 5.
54. Karnow, *Vietnam,* p. 629.

Chapter 22: To the Middle Kingdom

Epigraph: Terrill, *White-Boned Demon,* p. 17.
1. *Los Angeles Times,* July 13, 1971, pp. 1, 11.
2. Interview of Don Cook, April 30, 1992.
3. Karnow, *Vietnam,* p. 14.
4. Kissinger, *Years of Upheaval,* p. 61.
5. Ibid., pp. 60–63.
6. Cyrus Sulzberger diary, October 22, 1955, in Sulzberger, *Seven Continents,* pp. 209–10.
7. DB diary, January 1, 1955, VHS.
8. Isaacson, *Kissinger,* pp. 339–40.
9. CBS evening news, March 15, 1973, courtesy of Vanderbilt Television News Archives.
10. *Washington Post,* May 16, 1973, p. A-19.
11. *NYT,* May 4, 1973, p. 43.
12. Salisbury, *New Emperors,* p. 183.
13. Johnson, *Modern Times,* pp. 556–57; Salisbury, *New Emperors,* p. 242; *Richmond Times-Dispatch,* January 7, 1993.
14. Salisbury, *New Emperors,* pp. 187–88.

15. Terrill, *White-Boned Demon*, p. 303.
16. Ibid., p. 333.
17. *NYT*, May 18, 1973, p. 5.
18. Ibid.
19. DB diary, May 16, 1973, VHS.
20. DB diary, June 19, 1973, VHS.
21. DB diary, June 7, 10, 19, 1973, VHS.
22. DB diary, June 11, 1973, VHS.
23. DB diary, June 29, 1973, VHS.
24. *NYT*, July 11, 1973, p. 10.
25. *NYT*, April 29, 1973, p. 3.
26. DB diary, August 5, 1973, VHS.
27. *NYT*, July 11, 1973, p. 10.
28. DB diary, August 4, 10, 1973, VHS.
29. Interview of Maureen O'Ryan (formerly Maureen Molinari), November 4, 1992.
30. DB diary, June 19, 1973, VHS.
31. DB diary, June 20, 1973, VHS.
32. Ibid.
33. Ibid.
34. DB diary, September 16, 1973, VHS.
35. DB diary, June 25, 1973, VHS.
36. Cyrus Sulzberger diary, October 22, 1973, in Sulzberger, *Postscript with a Chinese Accent*, p. 369.
37. DB diary, November 2, 1973, VHS.
38. DB diary, June 7, 1973, VHS.
39. DB diary, May 16, 1973, VHS.
40. DB diary, July 29, May 25, 1973, VHS.
41. *NYT*, July 11, 1973, p. 10; DB diary, June 26, 1973, VHS.
42. *NYT*, October 15, 1973, p. 54.
43. DB diary, July 4, 1973, VHS.
44. DB diary, September 26, 1973, VHS.
45. Ibid.
46. DB diary, October 18, 1973, VHS.
47. DB diary, October 31, 1973, VHS.
48. DB diary, November 13, 1973, VHS.
49. DB diary, May 31, 1974, VHS.
50. DB diary, August 13, 1973, VHS.
51. DB diary, July 5, 1973, VHS.
52. Interview of Maureen O'Ryan (formerly Maureen Molinari), November 4, 1992; DB diary, January 16, 1974, VHS.
53. DB diary, May 26, 1973, VHS.
54. DB diary, May 28, 1973, VHS.
55. DB diary, July 3, 1973, VHS.
56. DB diary, July 8, 1973, VHS.
57. DB diary, July 7, 1973, VHS.
58. DB diary, September 6, 1974, VHS.
59. Kissinger, *Years of Upheaval*, p. 689; DB diary, November 12, 1973, VHS.

60. Salisbury, *New Emperors,* p. 330.
61. Kissinger, *Years of Upheaval,* p. 695.
62. DB diary, November 12, 1973, VHS.
63. Kissinger, *Years of Upheaval,* p. 695.
64. *NYT,* March 31, 1974, sec. 4, p. 5.
65. DB diary, December 23, 1973, VHS.
66. DB diary, December 25, 1973, VHS.
67. Ibid.
68. DB diary, January 25, 1974, VHS.
69. Interview of Maureen O'Ryan (formerly Maureen Molinari), November 4, 1992.
70. Drew, *Washington Journal,* p. 217.
71. DB diary, March 23, 1974, VHS.
72. Interview of Amb. Brunson McKinley, August 19, 1992.
73. Ibid.
74. Green, *Bush,* p. 144.
75. DB diary, September 5, 1974, VHS.
76. DB diary, February 14, 1974, VHS.
77. Secretary of state to U.S. Liaison Office, Beijing, April 17, 1974, Department of State FOIA; DB diary, April 20, 1974, VHS.
78. Kenneth Rose diary, September 10, 1975, courtesy of Kenneth Rose.
79. Sulzberger, *Marina,* p. 467.
80. DB diary, September 19, 1974, VHS.
81. Ibid.
82. DB diary, July 4, 1974, VHS.
83. DB to Jean Monnet, June 8, 1973, in DB diary, June 7, 1973, VHS.
84. Isaacson, *Kissinger,* pp. 333–34.

Chapter 23: Aeneas in Brussels

1. Henry A. Kissinger to DB, September 11, 1974, in DB diary, 1974, VHS.
2. DB diary, September 12, 1974, VHS.
3. DB to Henry A. Kissinger, September 14, 1974, in DB diary, 1974, VHS.
4. Henry A. Kissinger to DB, September 21, 1974, in DB diary, 1974, VHS.
5. DB to Henry A. Kissinger, September 23, 1974, in DB diary, 1974, VHS.
6. From "Talking Points for use by the President in his meeting with Ambassador Bruce," November 8, 1974, State Department, FOIA.
7. Cyrus Sulzberger diary, June 7, 1973, Sulzberger, *Postscript with a Chinese Accent,* p. 246.
8. EBB to Joseph Alsop, October 1, 1974, Alsop papers, container 140, LC.
9. DB diary, January 17, 1975, VHS.
10. DB diary, March 13–14, 1975, VHS.
11. DB diary, June 28–July 3, 1975, VHS.
12. DB diary, July 10–11, 1975, VHS.
13. DB diary, May 28–31, 1975, VHS.
14. Isaacson, *Kissinger,* p. 605.
15. Kenneth Rose diary, September 10, 1975, courtesy of Kenneth Rose.

16. Sara B. Bearss kindly provided the translation and context for the Virgil quotation.
17. *Department of State Newsletter,* February 1976, p. 15.
18. Press release, Office of the White House Press Secretary, February 10, 1976, Ford Lib.

Chapter 24: Shadows Lengthen

Epigraph: Styron, *Lie Down in Darkness,* p. 42.
1. WCB, "A Plantation Retrospect," p. 557.
2. DB diary, April 18, 1965, VHS.
3. DB diary, August 16, 1968, VHS.
4. DB diary, January 8, 1974, VHS.
5. DSB to Joseph Alsop, March 29, 1973, Alsop papers, box 138, LC.
6. DB diary, August 24, 1968, VHS.
7. Mellen, *Privilege,* p. 44.
8. Ibid., p. 62.
9. Her father worried about her being "madly interested" in icons mainly because he feared her traveling to the unsettled Middle East. DB diary, September 19, 1970, VHS.
10. DB to Sasha, David, and Nicholas, March 23, 1970, copy courtesy of Reginald Pettus.
11. Mellen, *Privilege,* p. 287.
12. Ibid., p. 295.
13. DB diary, December 23, 1966, VHS.
14. DB diary, October 5, 1970, VHS.
15. DB diary, December 11, 1970, VHS.
16. DB diary, January 8, 1971, VHS.
17. DB diary, May 20, 1971, VHS.
18. Interview of Kisty Hesketh, September 23, 1990.
19. EBB to author, March 5, 1995.
20. Joan Braden, *Just Enough Rope,* p. 261.
21. EBB to author, March 5, 1995.
22. From a letter by the Countess Sternberg in Bruce, comp., *David K. E. Bruce,* p. 4.
23. Lynda Johnson Robb, conversation with author, January 29, 1993.
24. Mellen, *Privilege,* p. 260.

Epilogue

Epigraph: Quoted in Bruce, comp., *David K. E. Bruce,* p. 12.
1. "Resolution in Memoriam," adopted by the trustees of the National Gallery of Art, January 26, 1978.
2. Bruce, comp., *David K. E. Bruce,* p. 37.
3. DB, *Seven Pillars,* p. 7.
4. DB diary, January 6, 1967, VHS.
5. DB diary, October 1, 1961, VHS.
6. *NYT,* December 6, 1977, p. 42.

Bibliography

Interviews

Interviews that do not give a location after the date were conducted over the telephone.

Nancy Adare, dowager countess of Dunraven: September 11, 1990.

Susan Mary Alsop: September 8, 1990.

Sir Isaiah Berlin: July 13, 1990 (All Soul's College, Oxford).

David Surtees Bruce: August 18–19, 1989, April 28–29, 1995 (Staunton Hill).

Evangeline Bell Bruce: May 20, 1989 (Washington, D.C.); July 15, 1990 (London); May 22, 1992 (Washington, D.C.); April 4, 1993 (Washington, D.C.); June 1, 1993; December 18, 1993 (Washington, D.C.); September 28, 1994.

Louise Bruce: August 10, 1992.

Joseph Bryan III: January 18, 1991 (Richmond, Va.).

Don Cook: August 13, 1992.

Virginius Dabney: January 17, 1990.

Anna Garner: May 30, 1990 (Richmond, Va.).

Katharine Graham: April 13, 1990 (Washington, D.C.).

Kay Halle: October 27, 1989 (Washington, D.C.).

Amb. Pamela Harriman: March 14, 1991.

Amb. Arthur A. Hartman: December 21, 1989 (Washington, D.C.).

Christian, Lady Hesketh: September 23, 1990.

Roy Jenkins, Lord Jenkins of Hillhead: July 10, 1990 (London).

Philip Kaiser: June 1, 1989; October 19, 1989; October 27, 1989 (Washington, D.C.).

Jan Laverge: March 16, 1989 (Richmond, Va.).

Lucinda Leigh: November 29, 1989; December 21, 1989 (Washington, D.C.).

Amb. George McGehee: December 20, 1989.

Amb. Brunson McKinley: August 19, 1992; September 1, 1992; September 25, 1992.

Roger Makins, Lord Sherfield: September 4, 1991.

Frazier and Susan Meade: May 6, 1991 (Richmond, Va.).

Helen Kirkpatrick Milbank: September 20, 1991 (Williamsburg, Va.).

Helen Hill Miller, January 18, 1988 (Richmond, Va.).

Maureen O'Ryan (formerly Maureen Molinari): November 4, 1992 (Washington, D.C.).

John Mowinkel: May 2, 1991.

Reginald Pettus: August 22, 1989 (Richmond, Va.).

Diana Phipps: September 8, 1990.

Anthony Powell: February 26, 1991.

Virgil Randolph: May 30, 1989 (Richmond, Va.).

Giles Robertson: September 16, 1992.

Lord and Lady Salisbury: July 16, 1990 (Hatfield House, England).

John Wells: July 4, 1991.

Judge Hubert Will: September 7, 1991.

Langbourne Williams: February 23, 1990 (Rapidan, Va.).

Alice Winn: July 12, 1990 (London); July 6, 1993.

Woodrow Wyatt, Lord Wyatt: October 14, 1990.

Select Bibliography

Abramson, Rudy. *Spanning the Century: The Life of W. Averell Harriman, 1891–1986.* New York: William Morrow, 1992.

Acheson, Dean G. *Present at the Creation: My Years in the State Department.* New York: Norton, 1969.

Adams, Abby, comp. *An Uncommon Scold.* New York: Simon and Schuster, 1989.

Aldrich, Nelson W., Jr. *Tommy Hitchcock: An American Hero.* n.p.: Privately printed, 1984.

Aldrich, Nelson W. IV. "The Upper Class, Up for Grabs." *Wilson Quarterly,* vol. 17, no. 3 (Summer 1993).

Alsop, Joseph W., with Adam Platt. *"I've Seen the Best of It": Memoirs.* New York: Norton, 1992.

Alsop, Susan Mary. *To Marietta from Paris, 1945–1960.* Garden City, N.Y.: Doubleday, 1975.

Ambrose, Stephen E., with Richard H. Immerman. *Ike's Spies: Eisenhower and the Espionage Establishment.* Garden City, N.Y.: Doubleday, 1981.

Amory, Cleveland. *Who Killed Society?* New York: Harper and Brothers, 1960.

Amory, Mark, ed. *The Letters of Ann Fleming.* London: Collins Harvill, 1985.

Astor, Gerald. *A Blood-Dimmed Tide: The Battle of the Bulge by the Men Who Fought It.* New York: Donald I. Fine, 1992.

Baldrige, Letitia. *Of Diamonds and Diplomats.* Boston: Houghton Mifflin, 1968.

Ball, George W. *The Past Has Another Pattern: Memoirs.* New York: Norton, 1982.

Barnet, Richard J. *The Alliance: America, Europe, Japan: Makers of the Postwar World.* New York: Simon and Schuster, 1983.

Beaton, Cecil. *The Wandering Years: Diaries, 1922–1939.* Boston: Little, Brown, 1961.

Beevor, Antony, and Artemis Cooper. *Paris after the Liberation: 1944–1949*. New York: Doubleday, 1994.

Behrman, S. N. *Duveen*. Boston: Little, Brown, 1972.

Bernier, Olivier. *Fireworks at Dusk: Paris in the Thirties*. Boston: Little, Brown, 1993.

Bird, Kai. *The Chairman: John J. McCloy: The Making of the American Establishment*. New York: Simon and Schuster, 1992.

Bohlen, Charles E. *Witness to History, 1929–1969*. New York: Norton, 1973.

Braden, Joan. *Just Enough Rope: An Intimate Memoir*. New York: Villard Books, 1989.

Brandon, Henry. *Special Relationships: A Foreign Correspondent's Memoirs From Roosevelt to Reagan*. New York: Atheneum, 1988.

Brenner, Marie. "Marietta Tree: Serious Money." *Vanity Fair* (December 1991).

Brinkley, Douglas. *Dean Acheson: The Cold War Years, 1953–71*. New Haven: Yale University Press, 1992.

———and Clifford Hackett, eds., *Jean Monnet and the Path to European Unity*. New York: St. Martin's Press, 1991.

Bromberger, Merry, and Serge Bromberger. *Jean Monnet and the United States of Europe*. New York: Coward McCann, 1969.

Bruce, David K. E. "Et Cetera and Wine Glasses." *The Reviewer* (January 1924).

———. "The National Intelligence Authority." *Virginia Quarterly Review*, vol. 22, no. 3 (Summer 1946).

———. *Revolution to Reconstruction*. New York: Doubleday, Doran and Company, 1939.

———. *Seven Pillars of the Republic*. Garden City, N.Y.: privately printed [Country Life Press], 1936.

———. "Tobacco." *The Reviewer* (January 1923).

———. "Random Reflections of a Gourmet." *The Reviewer* (May 1922).

———. "Vanitas Vanitatum." *The Reviewer* (October 1924).

———. "The Wearing of the Cane." *The Reviewer* (October 1923).

Bruce, Evangeline, compiler. *David K. E. Bruce* (n.p., 1980).

Bruce, James Cabell. *Memoirs*. Baltimore: Gateway Press, Inc., 1975.

Bruce, John Goodall. *The Bruce Family: Descending from George Bruce (1650–1715)*. Parsons, W.Va.: McClain, 1977.

Bruce, Louise Este Fisher. "Footprints" (see list of manuscript sources).

Bruce, William Cabell. *Below the James: A Plantation Sketch*. Boston: Houghton Mifflin, 1927.

———. *John Randolph of Roanoke: A Biography Based Largely on New Material*. New York: G. P. Putnam's Sons, 1922.

———. "A Plantation Retrospect." *Virginia Quarterly Review*, vol. 7, no. 4 (October 1931).

———. *Recollections*. Baltimore: King, 1936.

Bryan, Joseph, III, and Charles J. V. Murphy. *The Windsor Story*. New York: William Morrow, 1979.

Bull, Hedley, and William Roger Louis, eds., *The "Special Relationship": Anglo-American Relations since 1945*. Oxford: Clarendon, 1986.

Bullock, Alan. *Ernest Bevin: Foreign Secretary, 1945–1951*. New York: Norton, 1983.

Casey, William. *The Secret War Against Hitler*. Washington, D.C.: Regnery Gateway, 1988.

Caute, David. *The Great Fear: The Anti-Communist Purge Under Truman and Eisenhower*. New York: Simon and Schuster, 1978.

Cave Brown, Anthony. *"C": The Secret Life of Sir Stewart Graham Menzies: Spymaster to Winston Churchill*. New York: Macmillan, 1987.

———. *The Last Hero: Wild Bill Donovan . . .* New York: Times Books, 1982.

———, ed. *The Secret War Report of the OSS*. New York: Berkeley, 1976.

Chadwin, Mark Lincoln. *The Hawks of World War II*. Chapel Hill: University of North Carolina Press, 1968.

Chesson, Michael B. *Richmond after the War, 1865–1890*. Richmond: Virginia State Library, 1981.

Churchill, Winston S. *History of the Second World War*. Vol. 1: *The Gathering Storm*. Vol. 2: *Their Finest Hour*. Boston: Houghton Mifflin, 1948.

———. *A Roving Commission: My Early Life*. New York: Scribner's, 1930.

Clark, Emily. *Innocence Abroad*. New York and London: Knopf, 1931.

Clark, Kenneth. *Another Part of the Wood: A Self-Portrait*. London: John Murray, 1974.

Clifford, John Garry. *The Citizen Soldiers: The Plattsburg Training Camp Movement, 1913–1920*. Lexington: University of Kentucky Press, 1972.

Cockett, Richard. *David Astor and The Observer*. London: André Deutsch, 1991.

Collier, Basil. *The Battle of the V-Weapons, 1944–45*. New York: William Morrow, 1965.

Collier, Peter, and David Horowitz. *The Kennedys: An American Drama*. New York: Summit Books, 1984.

Conner, Jane Stuart. "David K. E. Bruce's Gift of County Libraries to Rural Virginia" (M.S. thesis, University of North Carolina, Chapel Hill, 1984).

Cook, Don. *Charles De Gaulle*. New York: Perigee, 1983.

Cooke, Alistair, comp. *The Vintage Mencken*. New York: Vintage Books, 1990.

Cooney, John. *The Annenbergs*. New York: Simon and Schuster, 1982.

Cooper, Alfred Duff. *Old Men Forget: The Autobiography of Duff Cooper (Viscount Norwich)*. New York: Dutton, 1954.

Cooper, Chester L. *The Lost Crusade: America in Vietnam*. New York: Dodd, Mead, 1970.

Costello, John. *Mask of Treachery*. New York: William Morrow, 1988.

Cowley, Malcolm. *A Second Flowering: Works and Days of the Lost Generation*. New York: Viking Press, 1973.

Crooks, James B. *Politics and Progress: The Rise of Urban Progressivism in Baltimore, 1895 to 1911*. Baton Rouge: Louisiana State University Press, 1968.

Curtis, Charlotte. *The Rich and Other Atrocities*. New York: Harper and Row, 1976.

Davies, Norman. *White Eagle, Red Star: The Polish-Soviet War, 1919–20*. London: Macdonald, 1972.

Dean Acheson: The State Department Years.

DeConde, Alexander. *Half-Bitter, Half-Sweet: An Excursion into Italian-American History*. New York: Scribner's, 1971.

Deighton, Len. *Berlin Game*. New York: Ballantine Books, 1985.

———. *Fighter: The True Story of the Battle of Britain*. With an introduction by A.J.P. Taylor. New York: Knopf, 1978.

Dictionary of American Biography.

Dictionary of National Biography.

Dos Passos, John. *The Best Times: An Informal Memoir*. New York: New American Library, 1966.

———. *Mr. Wilson's War*. London: Hamish Hamilton, 1963.

———. *Nineteen Nineteen*. New York: Grosset and Dunlap, 1932.

Drew, Elizabeth. *Washington Journal: The Events of 1973–1974*. New York: Random House, 1975.

Duchène, François. *Jean Monnet: The First Statesman of Interdependence*. New York: Norton, 1994.

Dumaine, Jacques. *Quai d'Orsay, 1945–1951*. Paris: Julliard, 1955; London: Chapman and Hall, 1958.

Dur, Philip F. *Jefferson Caffery of Louisiana: Ambassador of Revolutions, An Outline of His Career*. Lafayette, La.: University of Southwestern Louisiana Libraries, 1982.

Elliott, Lawrence. *I Will Be Called John: A Biography of Pope John XXIII*. New York: Reader's Digest Press/E. P. Dutton, 1973.

Fairlie, Henry. *The Kennedy Promise: The Politics of Expectation*. Garden City, N.Y.: Doubleday, 1973.

Falls, Cyril. *The Great War*. New York: Capricorn Books, 1961.

Felsenthal, Carol. *Power, Privilege, and the Post: The Katharine Graham Story*. New York: G. P. Putnam's Sons, 1993.

Ferencz, Benjamin B. *Less Than Slaves: Jewish Forced Labor and the Quest for Compensation*. Cambridge: Harvard University Press, 1979.

Ferrell, Robert H., ed. *Off The Record: The Private Papers of Harry S. Truman*. New York: Penguin Books, 1980.

Finlayson, Iain. *Tangier: City of the Dream*. London: HarperCollins, 1992.

Finley, David Edward. *A Standard of Excellence: Andrew W. Mellon Founds the National Gallery of Art at Washington*. Washington, D.C.: Smithsonian Institution Press, 1973.

Fitzgerald, F. Scott. *The Great Gatsby*. New York: Scribner's, 1925.

———. *This Side of Paradise*. New York: Scribner's, 1920.

Flanner, Janet. *Darlinghissima: Letters to a Friend*, edited and with commentary by Natalia Danesi Murray. New York: Random House, 1985.

———. *Paris Journal, 1944–1965*, ed. by William Shawn. New York: Atheneum, 1965.

Flusche, Michael. "Thomas Nelson Page: The Quandary of a Literary Gentleman." *Virginia Magazine of History and Biography,* vol. 84 (October 1976).

Fonzi, Gaeton. *Annenberg: A Biography of Power.* New York: Weybright and Talley, 1970.

Foreign Relations of the United States.

Fursdon, Edward. *The European Defense Community: A History.* New York: St. Martin's Press, 1980.

Gallagher, Dorothy. *All the Right Enemies: The Life and Murder of Carlo Tresca.* New York: Penguin Books, 1988.

Giles, Frank. *The Locust Years: The Story of the Fourth French Republic, 1946–1958.* London: Secker and Warburg, 1991.

————. *Sundry Times.* London: John Murray, 1986.

Gillingham, John. *Coal, Steel, and the Rebirth of Europe, 1945–1955: The Germans and French from Ruhr Conflict to Economic Community.* Cambridge: Cambridge University Press, 1991.

Goodman, Allan E. *The Lost Peace: America's Search for a Negotiated Settlement of the Vietnam War.* Stanford: Hoover Institute Press, 1978.

Green, Fitzhugh. *George Bush: An Intimate Portrait.* New York: Hippocrene Books, 1989.

Grosser, Alfred, trans. by Michael Shaw, with a foreword by Stanley Hoffmann. *The Western Alliance: European-American Relations Since 1945.* New York: Continuum, 1980.

Hackett, Clifford, ed. *Monnet and the Americans.* Washington, D.C.: Jean Monnet Council, 1995.

Halberstam, David. *The Best and the Brightest.* New York: Random House, 1969.

Harbaugh, William Henry. *The Life and Times of Theodore Roosevelt.* New York: Collier, 1961.

Harrison, Michael M. *The Reluctant Ally: France and Atlantic Security.* Baltimore: Johns Hopkins University Press, 1981.

Heckscher, August. *Woodrow Wilson.* New York: Scribner's, 1991.

Hersh, Burton. *The Mellon Family: A Fortune in History.* New York: William Morrow, 1978.

————. *The Old Boys: The American Elite and the Origins of the CIA.* New York: Scribner's, 1992.

Hersh, Seymour M. *The Price of Power: Kissinger in the Nixon White House.* New York: Summit, 1983.

Hershberg, James G., and James B. Conant. *Harvard to Hiroshima and the Making of the Nuclear Age.* New York: Knopf, 1993.

Herz, Martin F. *David Bruce's "Long Telegram" of July 3, 1951.* Washington, D.C.: Institute for the Study of Diplomacy, Georgetown University, 1978.

Hewins, Ralph. *Mr. Five Per Cent: The Story of Calouste Gulbenkian.* New York: Rinehart, 1957.

Hitchens, Christopher. *Blood, Class, and Nostalgia: Anglo-American Ironies.* New York: Farrar, Straus and Giroux, 1990.

Hobson, Fred C., Jr. *Serpent in Eden: H. L. Mencken and the South.* Chapel Hill: University of North Carolina Press, 1974.

Hodgson, Godfrey. *America in Our Time.* Garden City, New York: Doubleday, 1976.

———. *The Colonel: The Life and Wars of Henry Stimson, 1867–1950.* New York: Knopf, 1990.

Hoopes, Townsend. *The Devil and John Foster Dulles.* Boston: Little, Brown, 1973.

Horne, Alistair. *Harold Macmillan,* vol. 2, *1957–1986.* New York: Viking, 1989.

Irey, Elmer L., and William J. Slocum. *The Tax Dodgers: The Inside Story of the T-Men's War with America's Political and Underworld Hoodlums.* New York: Greenberg, 1948.

Isaacson, Walter. *Kissinger: A Biography.* New York: Simon and Schuster, 1992.

——— and Evan Thomas. *The Wise Men: Six Friends and the World They Made: Acheson, Bohlen, Harriman, Kennan, Lovett, McCloy.* New York: Simon and Schuster, 1986.

Jacob, Kathryn Allamong. *Capital Elites: High Society in Washington, D.C., after the Civil War.* Washington: Smithsonian Institution Press, 1995.

Jebb, Gladwyn. *The Memoirs of Lord Gladwyn.* New York: Weybright and Talley, 1972.

Jenkins, Roy [Lord Jenkins of Hillhead]. *A Life at the Center: Memoirs of a Radical Reformer.* New York: Random House, 1991.

Johnson, Paul. *Modern Times: The World from the Twenties to the Eighties.* New York: Harper and Row, 1983.

Jones, Chester. *Colefax and Fowler: The Best in English Interior Decoration.* Boston: Little, Brown, 1989.

Judt, Tony. *Past Imperfect: French Intellectuals, 1944–1956.* Berkeley: University of California Press, 1992.

Kaiser, Philip M. *Journeying Far and Wide: A Political and Diplomatic Memoir.* New York: Scribner's, 1992.

Kalb, Marvin, and Bernard Kalb. *Kissinger.* Boston: Little, Brown, 1974.

Karnow, Stanley. *Vietnam: A History.* New York: Viking Press, 1983.

Keith, Caroline H. *For Hell and a Brown Mule: The Biography of Senator Millard E. Tydings.* Lanham, Md.: Madison Books, 1991.

Kellner, Bruce. *Carl Van Vechten and the Irreverent Decades.* Norman: University of Oklahoma Press, 1968.

———. *Friends and Mentors: Richmond's Carl Van Vechten and Mark Lutz.* Richmond: Friends of the Boatwright Memorial Library, 1979.

Kelman, Steven. *Push Comes to Shove: The Escalation of Student Protest.* Boston: Houghton Mifflin, 1970.

Kennedy, Sir John. *The Business of War: The War Narrative of Major-General Sir John Kennedy, G.C.M.G., K.C.V.O., K.B.E., C.B., M.C.* London: Hutchinson, 1957.

Ketchum, Richard M. *The Borrowed Years, 1938–1941: America on the Way to War.* New York: Random House, 1989.

Key, V. O., Jr. *Southern Politics in State and Nation.* New York: Knopf, 1949.

King, Cecil. *The Cecil King Diary, 1965–1970.* London: Jonathan Cape, 1972.

Kirkpatrick, Lyman B. *The Real CIA.* New York: Macmillan, 1968.

Kissinger, Henry A. *White House Years.* Boston: Little, Brown, 1979.

———. *Years of Upheaval.* Boston: Little, Brown, 1982.

Knightley, Phillip, and Caroline Kennedy. *An Affair of State: The Profumo Case and the Framing of Stephen Ward.* New York: Atheneum, 1987.

Konolige, Kit. *The Richest Women in the World.* London: Collier Macmillan, 1985.

Kopper, Philip. *America's National Gallery of Art: A Gift to the Nation.* New York: Harry N. Abrams, 1991.

Koskoff, David E. *The Mellons: The Chronicle of America's Richest Family.* New York: Crowell, 1976.

Krock, Arthur. *Memoirs: Sixty Years on the Firing Line.* New York: Funk and Wagnalls, 1968.

Lacouture, Jean. *De Gaulle: The Ruler, 1945–1970.* New York: Norton, 1992.

Lacouture, Jean. *Pierre Mendes France.* New York: Holmes and Meier, 1984.

Langford, Gerald, ed. *Ingénue Among the Lions: The Letters of Emily Clark to Joseph Hergesheimer.* Austin: University of Texas Press, 1965.

Lankford, Nelson D., ed. *OSS Against the Reich: The World War II Diaries of Colonel David K. E. Bruce.* Kent, Ohio and London: Kent State University Press, 1991.

Laqueur, Walter. *Europe in Our Time: A History, 1945–1992.* New York: Viking, 1992.

Larrabee, Eric. *Commander in Chief: Franklin Delano Roosevelt, His Lieutenants, and Their War.* New York: Harper and Row, 1987.

Lears, T. J. Jackson. "Ambivalent Victorian: H. L. Mencken." *Wilson Quarterly,* vol. 13, no. 2 (Spring 1989).

Lerner, Daniel, and Raymond Aron. *France Defeats the EDC.* New York: Frederick A. Praeger, 1957.

Levin, Bernard. *The Pendulum Years: Britain and the Sixties.* London: Jonathan Cape, 1970.

Lewis, Flora. *Europe: Road to Unity.* New York: Simon and Schuster, 1992.

Lewis, Henry. *More Taste than Prudence: A Study of John Evans Johnson (1815–1870), an Amateur with Patrons.* Chapel Hill, N.C.: Borderer Press, 1983.

Link, Arthur S., ed. *The Papers of Woodrow Wilson,* vol. 68, *April 8, 1922–February 6, 1924.* Princeton: Princeton University Press, 1993.

Littlewood, Joan. *Baron Philippe: The Very Candid Autobiography of Baron Philippe de Rothschild.* New York: Crown, 1984.

Lockhart, Robert Bruce. *The Diaries of Sir Robert Bruce Lockhart,* vol. 2, *1939–1965,* ed. by Kenneth Young. London: Macmillan, 1980.

Louis, J. C., and Harvey Z. Yazijian. *The Cola Wars.* New York: Everest House, 1980.

Lovell, Stanley P. *Of Spies and Stratagems.* Englewood Cliffs, N.J.: Prentice-Hall, 1963.

McLellan, David S. *Dean Acheson: The State Department Years.* New York: Dodd, Mead, 1976.

McCullough, David. *Truman.* New York: Simon and Schuster, 1992.

MacDonald, Edgar. *James Branch Cabell and Richmond-in-Virginia.* Jackson: University of Mississippi Press, 1993.

McDonald, Lawrence H. "The Office of Strategic Services: America's First National Intelligence Agency." *Prologue,* vol. 23, no. 1 (Spring 1991).

McGehee, George Crews. *Envoy to the Middle World: Adventures in Diplomacy.* New York: Harper and Row, 1983.

McLeod, Kirsty. *A Passion for Friendship: Sibyl Colefax and Her Circle.* London: Michael Joseph, 1991.

Manchester, William. *The Last Lion: Winston Spencer Churchill, Visions of Glory, 1874–1932.* New York: Dell, 1983.

———. *The Last Lion: Winston Spencer Churchill, Alone, 1932–1940.* Boston and London: Little, Brown, 1988.

Marshall, S. L. A. "How Papa Liberated Paris." *American Heritage* (April 1962).

Massie, Robert K. *Dreadnought: Britain, Germany, and the Coming of the Great War.* New York: Random House, 1991.

Mayer, Marvin. *The Diplomats.* Garden City, N.Y.: Doubleday, 1983.

Mee, Charles L., Jr. *The Marshall Plan: The Launching of the Pax Americana.* New York: Simon and Schuster, 1984.

Mellen, Joan. *Privilege: The Enigma of Sasha Bruce.* New York: Dial, 1982.

Mellon, Paul, with John Baskett. *Reflections in a Silver Spoon: A Memoir.* New York: William Morrow, 1992.

Mencken, H. L. *Happy Days, 1880–1892.* New York: Knopf, 1940.

———. *Heathen Days, 1890–1936.* New York: Knopf, 1963.

Meyers, Jeffrey. *Edgar Allan Poe: His Life and Legacy.* New York: Scribner's, 1992.

Miller, Francis Pickens. *Man from the Valley: Memoirs of a 20th-Century Virginian.* Chapel Hill: University of North Carolina Press, 1971.

Miller, Hope Ridings. *Embassy Row: The Life and Times of Diplomatic Washington.* New York: Holt, Rinehart and Winston, 1969.

Milward, Alan S. *The Reconstruction of Western Europe, 1945–1951.* London: Routledge, 1992.

Mitford, Nancy. *Don't Tell Alfred.* New York: Popular Library, 1962.

Monnet, Jean. *Memoirs.* Introduction by George W. Ball. Translated by Richard Mayne. Garden City, N.Y.: Doubleday, 1978.

Moore, John Hammond. "William Cabell Bruce, Henry Cabot Lodge, and the Distribution of Ability in the United States." *Virginia Magazine of History and Biography,* vol. 86 (July 1978).

Morris, Roger. *Richard Milhous Nixon: The Rise of an American Politician.* New York: Holt, 1990.

Mosley, Leonard. *Dulles: A Biography of Eleanor, Allen, and John Foster Dulles and Their Family Network.* New York: Dial Press/James Wade, 1978.

Muggeridge, Malcolm. "Book Review of a Very Limited Edition." *Esquire* (May 1966), p. 94.

Muir, Frank, comp. *The Oxford Book of Humorous Prose: From William Caxton to P. G. Wodehouse*. New York: Oxford University Press, 1990.

Neustadt, Richard E. *Alliance Politics*. New York and London: Columbia University Press, 1970.

Newman, Robert P. *Owen Lattimore and the "Loss" of China*. Berkeley: University of California Press, 1992.

Newhouse, John. *War and Peace in the Nuclear Age*. New York: Knopf, 1989.

Nicholas, H. G., ed., with an introduction by Isaiah Berlin. *Washington Despatches, 1941–1945: Weekly Political Reports from the British Embassy*. Chicago: University of Chicago Press, 1981.

Nolan, Alan T. *Lee Considered: General Robert E. Lee and Civil War History*. Chapel Hill and London: University of North Carolina Press, 1991.

Nunnerley, David. *President Kennedy and Britain*. New York: St. Martin's Press, 1972.

O'Connor, Harvey. *Mellon's Millions: The Biography of a Fortune: The Life and Times of Andrew W. Mellon*. New York: John Day Company, 1933.

Ogden, Christopher. *Life of the Party: The Biography of Pamela Digby Churchill Hayward Harriman*. New York: Little, Brown, 1994.

O'Neill, William L. *American High: The Years of Confidence, 1945–1960*. New York: Free Press, 1986.

Partington, Angela, ed. *The Oxford Dictionary of Quotations*, 4th ed. New York: Oxford University Press, 1992.

Pearson, Drew, and Robert S. Allen. *Washington Merry-Go-Round*. New York: Liveright, 1931.

Perdue, Charles, Jr., et al., eds. *Weevils in the Wheat: Interviews with Virginia Ex-Slaves*. Bloomington: Indiana University Press, 1980.

Perry, Ralph Barton. *The Plattsburg Movement: A Chapter of America's Participation in the World War*. New York: Dutton, 1921.

Persico, Joseph E. *Casey: From the OSS to the CIA*. New York: Viking, 1990.

———. *Edward R. Murrow: An American Original*. New York: McGraw-Hill, 1988.

Philby, Kim. *My Silent War: The Soviet Master Spy's Own Story*. New York: Grove Press, 1968.

Phillips, William. *Ventures in Diplomacy*. n.p.: privately printed, 1952.

Pimlott, Ben. *Harold Wilson*. London: HarperCollins, 1992.

Prados, John. *Presidents' Secret Wars: CIA and Pentagon Covert Operations Since World War II*. New York: Morrow, 1986.

Prittie, Terence. *Konrad Adenauer, 1876–1967*. Chicago: Cowles, 1971.

Putnam, Samuel. *Paris Was Our Mistress: Memoirs of a Lost and Found Generation*. New York: Viking, 1947.

Rampersad, Arnold. *The Life of Langston Hughes*. Vol. 1: *1902–1941, I, Too, Sing America*. New York: Oxford University Press, 1986.

Ranelagh, John. *The Agency: The Rise and Decline of the CIA*. New York: Simon and Schuster, 1987.

Reeves, Thomas C. *A Question of Character: A Life of John F. Kennedy.* New York: Free Press, 1991.

Robertson, Ben. *I Saw England.* New York: Knopf, 1941.

Roosevelt, Archibald. *For Lust of Knowing: Memoirs of an Intelligence Officer.* Boston: Little, Brown, 1988.

Rothschild, Baronne Philippe de. "The Amazing Bruces: The Life in London of the American Ambassador and Mrs. David K. E. Bruce at Winfield House." *Vogue* (September 15, 1964).

Rutman, Darrett B. "Philip Alexander Bruce: A Divided Mind of the South." *Virginia Magazine of History and Biography,* vol. 68 (October 1960).

Salisbury, Harrison E. *The New Emperors: China in the Era of Mao and Deng.* New York: Little, Brown, 1992.

Sampson, Anthony. *Anatomy of Britain Today.* New York: Harper and Row, 1965.

Sawyer, Charles. *Concerns of a Conservative Democrat.* Carbondale: Southern Illinois University Press, 1968.

Sapp, Steven P. *The United States, France, and the Cold War: Jefferson Caffrey and American-French Relations, 1944–1949* (Ph.D. diss., Kent State University, 1978).

Schama, Simon. *Citizens: A Chronicle of the French Revolution.* New York: Knopf, 1989.

———. "Clio Has a Problem." *History News,* vol. 47, no. 6 (November/December 1992).

Schlesinger, Arthur M., Jr. *Robert Kennedy and His Times.* Boston: Houghton Mifflin, 1978.

———. *The Age of Roosevelt.* Vol. 1, *The Crisis of the Old Order, 1919–1933.* Vol. 2, *The Coming of the New Deal.* Boston: Houghton Mifflin, 1956, 1958.

———. "Evangeline Bruce in London: Reflections on a Life of Diplomatic Service in Historic Albany." *Architectural Digest* (March 1991).

Schmitt, George. "London Bloodshed." *American Heritage* (May/June 1991).

Schoenbrun, David. *Soldiers of the Night: The Story of the French Resistance.* New York: Dutton, 1980.

Schwartz, Thomas Alan. *America's Germany: John J. McCloy and the Federal Republic of Germany.* Cambridge, Mass.: Harvard University Press, 1991.

Secrest, Meryle. *Between Me and Life: A Biography of Romaine Brooks.* Garden City, N.Y.: Doubleday, 1974.

Sheean, Vincent. *Between the Thunder and the Sun.* New York: Random House, 1943.

Sherrill, Martha. "Georgetown On My Mind." *Town and Country,* vol. 146 (May 1992).

Simms, L. Moody, Jr. "A Childhood at Staunton Hill." *Virginia Cavalcade,* vol. 16, no. 2 (Autumn 1966).

Smith, Bradley F. *The Shadow Warriors: O.S.S. and the Origins of the C.I.A.* New York: Basic Books, 1983.

Smith, Gene. *The Shattered Dream: Herbert Hoover and the Great Depression.* New York: William Morrow, 1970.

Smith, R. Harris. *OSS: The Secret History of America's First Central Intelligence Agency.* Berkeley: University of California Press, 1972.

Smith, Richard Norton. *Thomas E. Dewey and His Times.* New York: Simon and Schuster, 1982.

Speer, Albert. *Spandau: The Secret Diaries.* New York: Macmillan, 1976.

Stannard, Martin. *Evelyn Waugh: The Early Years, 1903–1939.* New York: Norton, 1987.

Stevenson, William. *A Man Called Intrepid: The Secret War.* New York: Ballantine Books, 1976.

Stockett, Letitia. *Baltimore: A Not Too Serious History.* Baltimore: G. G. Norman, 1936.

Stokes, Thomas L. *Chip Off My Shoulder.* Princeton: Princeton University Press, 1940.

Styron, William. *Lie Down in Darkness: A Novel.* Indianapolis: Bobbs-Merrill, 1951.

Sulzberger, Cyrus L. *The Last of the Giants.* New York: Macmillan, 1970.

———. *A Long Row of Candles: Memoirs and Diaries, 1934–1954.* New York: Macmillan, 1969.

———. *Postscript with a Chinese Accent: Memoirs and Diaries, 1972–1973.* New York: Macmillan, 1974.

———. *Seven Continents and Forty Years: A Concentration of Memoirs.* New York: Quadrangle/New York Times Book Co., 1977.

Sulzberger, Marina. *Marina: Letters and Diaries of Marina Sulzberger,* ed. by Cyrus L. Sulzberger. New York: Crown, 1978.

Summers, Anthony, and Stephen Dorril. *Honeytrap: The Secret World of Stephen Ward.* London: Weidenfeld and Nicolson, 1982.

Taft, John. *American Power: The Rise and Decline of U.S. Globalism, 1918–1988.* New York: Harper and Row, 1989.

Terraine, John. *A Time for Courage: The Royal Air Force in the European War, 1939–1945.* New York: Macmillan, 1985.

Terrill, Ross. *The White-Boned Demon: A Biography of Madame Mao Zedong.* New York: William Morrow, 1984.

Tifft, Susan E., and Alex S. Jones. *The Patriarch: The Rise and Fall of the Bingham Family.* New York: Summit Books, 1991.

Tomkins, Calvin. "Profiles: For the Nation." *New Yorker* (September 3, 1990).

Tree, Ronald. *When the Moon Was High: Memoirs of Peace and War, 1897–1942.* London: Macmillan, 1975.

Troy, Thomas F., ed. *Wartime Washington: The Secret OSS Journal of James Grafton Rogers, 1942–1943.* Frederick, Md.: University Publications of America, 1987.

Tuchman, Barbara W. *The Guns of August.* New York: Dell, 1962.

Van Dyne, Larry. "Art and Money." *The Washingtonian* (April 1988).

Van Vechten, Carl. *Fragments from an Unwritten Autobiography.* New Haven: Yale University Library, 1955.

Walker, John. *Self-Portrait with Donors: Confessions of an Art Collector.* Boston: Little, Brown, 1974.

Wall, Irwin M. *The United States and the Making of Postwar France, 1945–1954*. New York: Cambridge University Press, 1991.

Ward, Geoffrey C. *A First-Class Temperament: The Emergence of Franklin Roosevelt*. New York: Harper and Row, 1989.

———. *Before the Trumpet: Young Franklin Roosevelt, 1882–1905*. New York: Harper and Row, 1985.

Warren, Harris Gaylord. *Herbert Hoover and the Great Depression*. New York: Norton, 1959.

Watkins, Thomas H. *Righteous Pilgrim: The Life and Times of Harold L. Ickes, 1874–1952*. New York: Holt, 1990.

Watt, D. Cameron. *Succeeding John Bull: America in Britain's Place, 1900–1975*. New York: Cambridge University Press, 1984.

Watters, Susan. "Paul Mellon: Above the Crowd." *W* magazine, March 16–23, 1992.

Wells, Gully. "The Last Empress." *Vanity Fair*, February 1995.

Wexler, Imanuel. *The Marshall Plan Revisited: The European Recovery Program in Economic Perspective*. Westport, Conn.: Greenwood Press, 1983.

Weymar, Paul. *Adenauer: His Authorized Biography*. New York: Dutton, 1957.

White, Theodore. *Fire in the Ashes: Europe at Mid-Century*. New York: Sloane, 1953.

White, William Allen. *Autobiography*. New York: Macmillan, 1946.

Wickes, George. *The Amazon of Letters: The Life and Loves of Natalie Barney*. London: W. H. Allen, 1977.

Wineapple, Brenda. *Genêt: A Biography of Janet Flanner*. New York: Ticknor and Fields, 1989.

Winks, W. Robin. *Cloak and Gown, 1939–1961: Scholars in the Secret War*. New York: William Morrow, 1987.

Wiser, William. *The Crazy Years: Paris in the Twenties*. New York: Atheneum, 1983.

Wolff, Geoffrey. *Black Sun: The Brief Transit and Violent Eclipse of Harry Crosby*. New York: Random House, 1985.

Periodicals

Christian Science Monitor

Daily Princetonian

Department of State Newsletter

International Herald Tribune

London *Sunday Times*

London *Times*

Maryland Historical Magazine

New York Herald (European edition)

New York Times

The Reviewer

Richmond News Leader

Richmond Times-Dispatch
Time
Town Topics: The Journal of Society
Virginia Cavalcade
Virginia Magazine of History and Biography
Wall Street Journal

Manuscript Sources

David Surtees Bruce (DSB) papers (private), Staunton Hill plantation, Charlotte County, Virginia
plantation guest book
David K. E. Bruce, "My books." Record of his library

Evangeline Bell Bruce (EBB) papers (private), Georgetown, Washington, D.C.
scrapbooks
photograph books

Louise Este Fisher Bruce (LB), "Footprints on the Sands of Time," unpublished typescript, DB papers, box 1, VHS

Central Intelligence Agency, Langley, Virginia
David K. E. Bruce FOIA request file

Federal Bureau of Investigation, Washington, D.C.
David K. E. Bruce FOIA request file

Fondation Jean Monnet Pour L'Europe, Lausanne, Switzerland
Correspondence of Jean Monnet and David K. E. Bruce

Gerald R. Ford Presidential Library

John Gillingham. "David K. E. Bruce and the European Defense Community Debacle." Unpublished manuscript. Dated September 23, 1990. Courtesy of John Gillingham.

Hoover Institute on War, Revolution, and Peace, Stanford, California.
Joseph E. Persico interview of David Bruce, February 19, 21, 1977. Tape 5. Joseph E. Persico collection.

Library of Congress, Manuscripts Division, Washington, D.C.
Joseph Alsop papers
David Finley papers
W. Averell Harriman papers

Lyndon B. Johnson Presidential Library, Austin, Texas
Oral history interviews

John F. Kennedy Presidential Library, Boston, Massachusetts
National Security Files
Oral history interviews
Robert Estabrook memoranda
Arthur M. Schlesinger Jr. papers

University of Maryland library, College Park, Maryland
James Cabell Bruce papers

Paul Mellon Papers (private), Upperville, Virginia
    Letters of David K. E. Bruce to Ailsa Mellon Bruce
National Archives, Washington, D.C.
    American Red Cross papers (RG 200)
    Marshall Plan (ECA) papers (RG 256)
    OSS papers (RG 226)
    Commerce Department papers (RG 40)
    State Department papers (RG 59)
Maryland State Archives, Annapolis, Maryland
    Death certificates
    Administration accounts of estates
Public Record Office, Kew, England
    Foreign Office papers
Richmond Public Library, Richmond, Virginia
    Clippings file
Marquess of Salisbury archives (private), Hatfield House, Hatfield, England
    Salisbury family photograph albums
Harry Ransom Humanities Research Center, University of Texas, Austin, Texas
    Hearst newspaper morgue
Harry S Truman Presidential Library, Independence, Missouri
U.S. Military History Institute, Carlisle Barracks, Pennsylvania
    William J. Donovan papers
Vanderbilt University, Nashville, Tennessee
    Vanderbilt Television News Archive
Virginia Commonwealth University, Richmond, Virginia. James Branch Cabell Library,
    Special Collections
    Hunter Stagg papers
    Carl Van Vechten papers (copies of originals at Yale)
Virginia Historical Society, Richmond, Virginia
    David K. E. Bruce papers
    Louise Este Fisher papers
    Bruce family papers
Yale University, New Haven, Connecticut
    William Adams Delano papers
    Carl Van Vechten papers

Index